D0103322

Architecture, Power, and National Identity

Second edition

Lawrence J. Vale

Routledge
Taylor & Francis Group
LONDON AND NEW YORK

NA
4195
.V35
2008
279
9-9-08

First published 1992
by Yale University Press

This edition published 2008
by Routledge
2 Park Square, Milton Park, Abingdon, Oxon, OX14 4RN

Simultaneously published in the USA and Canada
by Routledge
270 Madison Ave, New York, NY 10016

Routledge is an imprint of the Taylor & Francis Group, *an informa business*

© 2008 Lawrence J. Vale

Typeset in Gill Sans by The Running Head Limited, Cambridge,
www.therunninghead.com

Printed and bound in Great Britain by
Cromwell Press Ltd, Trowbridge, Wiltshire

All rights reserved. No part of this book may be reprinted or reproduced or utilized in any form or by any electronic, mechanical, or other means, now known or hereafter invented, including photocopying and recording, or in any information storage or retrieval system, without permission in writing from the publishers.

British Library Cataloguing in Publication Data
A catalogue record for this book is available from the British Library

Library of Congress Cataloging in Publication Data
Vale, Lawrence J., 1959–
Architecture, power, and national identity / Lawrence J. Vale. — 2nd ed.
p. cm.
Includes bibliographical references and index.
ISBN-13: 978-0-415-95514-0 (hbk: alk. paper)
ISBN-13: 978-0-415-95515-7 (pbk: alk. paper) 1. Capitols.
2. Architecture—Political aspects. 3. Architecture and society. I. Title.
NA4195.V35 2008
725'.11—dc22
2007032656

ISBN 10: 0-415-95514-9 (hbk)
ISBN 10: 0-415-95515-7 (pbk)
ISBN 13: 978-0-415-95514-0 (hbk)
ISBN 13: 978-0-415-95515-7 (pbk)

Contents

Preface to the second edition

Fifteen years after the publication of the first edition of *Architecture, Power, and National Identity* it is a privilege to be able to return to its themes and revisit its conclusions. In the intervening decade-and-a-half, capital cities have continued to grow and have even proliferated with the emergence of new nation-states, especially following the break-up of the Soviet Union and the former Yugoslavia. In parallel, there has been a growth of scholarship on capital cities new and old, and it no longer seems unusual to pair detailed criticism of design issues with similarly close analysis of political history. This willingness among other scholars to embrace the centrality of "design politics" in the interpretation of the built environment seems to me both welcome and necessary.

It is also astonishing to see how much a fifteen-year gap has altered the range of research methods and processes available to assess cities. I could not have imagined that I would be monitoring capital city development, from Tanzania to Palau, via Google Earth satellite photos viewed on a laptop. It did not occur to me that there would now be an entire academic journal devoted to *Place Branding and Public Diplomacy* ("A quarterly review of branding and marketing for national, regional and civic development"). Nor did I expect to find myself downloading election results from Kuwait, dissecting the reliability of official government websites, or touring the emerging capital of Kazakhstan through the eyes of countless video contributions on YouTube. The burgeoning flows of information exchange and image production have already irretrievably altered the meanings of each term in this book's title.

Although this is a book principally focused on the urban design and architecture of capital cities, it is not intended as a broad overview of capital city planning. Since 1992, several other books, including *Planning Europe's Capital Cities*, *Planning Twentieth Century Capital Cities*, *Planning Latin America's Capital Cities*, *Representing the State: Capital City Planning in the Early Twentieth Century*, and *Capital Cities—Les Capitales* have each provided some large-scale comparative perspective. These have been accompanied by numerous single-city monographs on capital cities, ranging from London to Abuja. My task here, as in the first edition, remains quite different from these other quests. Rather than describe the overall evolution of particular cities, my challenge is to explicate how the designs of particular parts of these places—the places of national government—help to clarify the structure of power in that society. *Design*, in this view, is not some value-neutral aesthetic applied to efforts at urban development but is, instead, an integral part of the motives driving that development. Though many urban designers and architects often seem to regard good design as somehow independent from social and political factors affecting its production and use, design efforts are influenced by politics in at least two important ways. First, architectural and urban design proposals may be subject to challenge by a variety of groups during the planning process. Second, political values, whether tacit or explicit, are encoded in the resultant designs.

In most places, however, my book stops short of analyzing the complex reception of government districts by diverse publics. Although I do discuss the ways capitol complexes have evolved in relation to changing political circumstances, I rarely go into much detail about what James Holston has usefully termed the "spaces of insurgent citizenship." The ways that subsequent citizen action alters the meanings of officially sanctioned and designed places is of great interest to me, but this is a subject that deserves far more detailed ethnographic treatment than a book surveying cities across the globe can possibly contain. I describe such acts of contestation in only a few places, notably Canberra and Brasília, but the processes of insurgent protest and re-valuation occur in every city, subject only to the degree of limitation enforced by the state.

The last century has seen an explosion of new nation-states, triggered by the dissolution of empires, buffeted by a Great Depression and two world wars, and tempered by the emergence of new federal systems and the growing importance of supranational groupings. All of this has found expression in architecture and urban design. If one looked at a list of world capitals in 1900 and did so again in 2000, there would be remarkably little overlap. Fully three-quarters of the cities that currently serve as national capitals were not capitals of independent states when the twentieth century began. This global transformation in political identity has entailed prodigious acts of invention and imagination, and much of this has been articulated through the built environment.

This book investigates the nature of the relations between built form and political purposes through close examination of a global array of design commissions in capital cities (especially government districts and major buildings within them). These avowedly "national" structures have been clearly motivated by political pressures. At some level, those buildings express the political balance of power in the society that produces them. In this sense, the architecture and urban design of government districts can become a diagnostic tool for understanding political relationships. Architecture helps to reveal who matters in a complex and plural society. It is the setting through which we express ideals like democracy, or freedom, or other kinds of national values, and this colors the way the citizen sees and perceives the government. For better or worse, our buildings serve as stand-ins for those that govern us. Most of us even in small places do not have the luxury of direct interaction with those who rule the places where we live. We meet them through the media, usually on television or on-line, with a backdrop of some sort that may reinforce their presence and power. We see them through the facade of their workplace, beyond the gates, behind the security barriers. Government buildings provide a kind of protective layer around the direct human interaction that we could claim if we were in a small town or lived a much less media-saturated existence. It becomes possible to diagnose wider social and cultural phenomena by looking closely at these most politically charged buildings.

It is important to do so with caution, however. The relationship between the social and the spatial is never a direct one. There are strong limits to it, occasioned in part by the value of abstraction in architectural design that permits the same place to have multiple meanings and prevents any single interpretation of a building from becoming definitive. It is also common for buildings to be used by a regime to convey to the world a level of democracy or openness that may well exceed its actual practice. Conversely, at a time of high security, building design may make the government seem more fearful and isolated than its leadership actually wishes it to appear. We cannot know that what gets built represents the intended will of a particular government to show its physical manifestation of democracy, and we cannot know whether the vision of the design team that produced it is completely synchronized with the visions of the client that commissioned the building. Moreover, buildings exist over time in cities, so a building that may well have expressed the political relationships at the time it was built may come to be seen as outmoded and provocative in ways we never anticipated at the time the building was finished. Clearly, architecture, power, and national identity are each a moving target.

ACKNOWLEDGMENTS

In two editions of this book, I have accumulated indebtedness on every continent save Antarctica. For this revised version, I owe a special thanks to Nnamdi Elleh for sharing his book manuscript on the evolution of Abuja, Nigeria. Similarly, I benefited greatly from the fieldwork in Abuja conducted by my former student Ifeoma Ebo for her master's thesis. She also provided additional research assistance for the second edition of this book, as did Shilpa Mehta and Annis Whitlow. I am particularly grateful to Nihal Perera and Anoma Pieris for keeping me abreast on developments in Sri Lanka, and to Saif Haq and Fuad Mallick for their assistance in updating the chapter on Bangladesh. I also appreciate the advice and assistance from Çağatay Özkul on Astana, Basak Demires on Ankara, Francisca Rojas on Santiago, Ross King on Putrajaya, Christopher Vernon on Pretoria and Canberra, and James Weirick and Kim Dovey on Canberra.

David Headon proved a congenial host in Canberra and, together with his other colleagues at the National Capital Authority, enabled me to expand and update my assessments of that city. I am similarly grateful for the hospitality shown to me by Arun Rewal and Raj Rewal in New Delhi, and greatly appreciate the assistance provided to me in Ottawa from John Taylor, Caroline Andrew, David Gordon, and the urban design staff of the National Capital Commission. Anoma Pieris and Julie Willis organized a memorable conference in Melbourne during 2006 that brought together many senior and junior scholars to discuss the theme of "Nation, City, Place: Rethinking Nationalism." This proved enormously helpful to me as a way to gauge emerging scholarship on the set of relationships that preoccupies this book.

More broadly, David Gordon's edited book project on twentieth-century capital city planning provided several years of fruitful interaction with leading scholars at the conferences of the International Planning History Society. The challenge of preparing a cross-cutting chapter for that volume focusing on urban design issues connected me to current thinking about many capitals, and helped inspire me to move forward on the new edition of my own book.

At MIT, students in my "Urban Design Politics" seminar continue to provide a basis for lively discussion and productively expand the boundaries of my world. I am also particularly grateful for the contributions of my colleague Diane Davis, who jointly taught with me in 2004 and took the lead in organizing our colloquium on "Cities Against Nationalism," which included provocative presentations by David Harvey, Leslie Sklair, Neil Brenner, Richard Sennett, and Peter Marcuse. At MIT, I also appreciate the assistance of Lisa Sweeney, Head of GIS Services for the MIT Libraries, who sorted through satellite imagery on multiple continents, and Janice "Radar" O'Brien, who cheerfully took on many logistical details related to this manuscript.

This all would have meant little without the enthusiasm of former Routledge editor Dave McBride, who showed immediate interest in this project, as well as the subsequent support of Caroline Mallinder in seeing it through. I am also indebted to David Williams from The Running Head who has edited my prose with commendable care and turned my manuscript into a thoughtfully designed book.

I thank Virginia Vale for asking me every week, without fail, whether my various administrative duties ever allowed me to make any progress on writing this book. Apparently, the answer to that question is "Yes, eventually."

A final significant difference for me in the second edition of *Architecture, Power, and National Identity* is that I can share it with Mira, Aaron, Jeremy, and Jonathan—all born during the 1990s when my scholarly pursuits thankfully focused on places that required less travel. They, like their mother Julie Dobrow, put up with my renewed sojourns to distant capitals, with my living room laptop, and with my excessive arrays of pre-book, post-book, and inter-book piles of papers. My five companions at home are constant reminders that the most important form of power remains rooted in domestic identity.

Lincoln, Massachusetts
June 2007

Preface to the first edition

Though I did not realize it at the time, work on this book began in December 1984, on a totally deserted highway in the Ciskei, one of South Africa's so-called independent tribal homelands. Having stopped my car to photograph a gleaming new sign proclaiming that "To Date There Have Been Nil Accidents On This Road," out of the corner of my eye I saw a pair of uniformed officials step out into the roadway about two hundred yards from where I was standing. They were pointing automatic weapons in my direction. Their concern, as three hours of questioning from successively higher levels of Republic of Ciskei Security Forces would reveal, was that I had entered Bisho, Ciskei's capital city, without the permit necessary for photography. While I thought I had been photographing a road sign, they believed me to be photographing Ciskei's massive new Parliament House, the soaring symbol of independence that they had been trained to guard. Eventually, their questions about my presence eased up and, once I agreed to promise that I would "never say anything bad to anyone about the Security Forces of the Republic of Ciskei," I was free to move on. With the cessation of their questions, my own questioning of this situation soon began, questions which would ultimately lead to this book.

Why were they so concerned about my photography near this parliament building when, as I would notice later that same day, the building appeared in full color on the cover of the Ciskei telephone book?

What was the purpose of this kind of architectural symbolism, which seemed so willfully advertised yet so carefully guarded? What prompts a government to sponsor the design of such a place? Where else have regimes tried to design capital cities and smaller parliamentary enclaves? What assumptions are made in the design of a capital city, and how is the presence of government within it expressed? Can the structure and appearance of such government-sponsored zones tell us anything about the balance of power in the society that produces them?

The book that has emerged from these initial questions investigates the nature of the relations between the built environment and political purposes. It does so through close examination of a wide variety of situations in which political leaders have asked architects and urban designers to give form to the central institutions of national government. Rather than producing an in-depth monograph on a single capital city, as has been done with some success by many others, I have chosen to identify a pair of themes—power and national identity—and to observe their variations in diverse capital city settings. I seek to explore the ways that a variety of national regimes have used architecture and urban design to express political power and control and to investigate how designers have manipulated the urban built environment to promote a version of identity that would support and help legitimize this rule.

No society is without its contradictions, and no building wants to celebrate them—least of all a government building. The sponsors and designers of such public facilities may wish to downplay or transcend these contradictions, or to highlight them in a way that reinforces their rule. The residue of conflict is present in every case, sometimes in spite of the efforts of designers and politicians, sometimes because of such efforts. By viewing architecture and urban design in the light of political history and cultural production, I hope to expand the agenda for criticism.

To do this, I have needed to draw upon insights from a wide range of disciplines and methodologies. In addition to using the work of architectural and urban historians, I have adapted theoretical frameworks from the political scientists Murray Edelman and Ernest Gellner, the interpretative anthropologist Clifford Geertz, the historian E. J. Hobsbawm, and the constructivist philosopher Nelson Goodman. My graduate work in architecture and urban design, combined with a doctorate in international relations, has provided the basis for the kind of connections I wish to advance.

Because there is almost always only one national parliament building in any given country, any attempt to seek generalizations about such capitol complexes necessarily entails work that is international and comparative. Moreover, given the prevalence of imported design consultants and the increasingly global interconnection of economic forces, even a single case study of this kind must itself be international and comparative. Nonetheless, it is not my goal to provide anything resembling a globally comprehensive treatment of the questions I raise. The examples I provide are intended as windows on a problem rather than exhaustive accounts. Recognizing that resources on each place are not necessarily comparable, I have resisted the temptation to squeeze material to fit a rigid format and have tried to use the variety of examples to make complementary points rather than strictly parallel observations. In focusing my attention upon the urban phenomenon that I call a capitol complex, I do not attempt to address in any detail many of the larger issues affecting the planning and economic development of capital cities. Most important, by focusing on the activities of governments and designers, I do not comment upon the multitude of ways capital cities (like all other cities) are built and transformed by less official means, through the labor of their citizens. So, too, the immense challenges of rapid urbanization are dealt with only tangentially. While a different book could take these issues as its centerpiece, this investigation into the role of capitol complex design reveals ways that the urban poor are, literally as well as figuratively, treated as a peripheral concern. Because it is directed and edited by politicians, there seems little room in the capitol designer's script for nonofficial actors on the political stage.

Part 1 of this book is a broad historical and conceptual overview of several capital cities. It is intended to identify the distinctive aspects of those capital cities which have been designed, and it focuses on the factors affecting the urban design of capitol complexes within such cities. Part 2 contains a series of four case studies of parliamentary complexes completed in the 1980s: those in Papua New Guinea, Sri Lanka, Kuwait, and Bangladesh. These extended essays provide opportunities to concentrate on architecture as well as on urban design. Perhaps the most obvious limitation of a comparative format of this length is my inability to explore the nature and significance of the cultural diversity of any of these places in depth. It is my intent that these be no more than preliminary studies of the interplay among architecture, culture, and politics. The four examples were selected chiefly because they feature intriguing buildings and because their diversity provides a useful framework for discussion. They are diverse not only in terms of their architecture but also in terms of their geographical location, their political and cultural contexts, their patronage, their architect's personal design priorities, their treatment of indigenous architectural traditions, and their spatial relationship to their capital. I have not touched on all of these aspects equally in each case, but have chosen to highlight one theme in each chapter. In the discussion of Papua New Guinea, I focus on the art and architectural allusions to vernacular forms in the new Parliament House; in the Sri Lanka chapter the emphasis is on the meaning of the capital's urban design setting; the discussion of Kuwait centers on the complexity of ties between a building and its political context; and the account of Bangladesh stresses the design priorities of the architectural designer. As an overarching means of organization, the four chapters are arranged to exemplify increasing degrees of abstraction in the use of architecture to delineate political power and pursue national identity.

The book is structured to present examples with increasing degrees of specificity and detail. Whereas Chapter 1 briefly considers seven European capitals, subsequent chapters consider fewer examples, leading to the chapter-length case studies of Part 2. The last chapter, by way of conclusion, attempts to draw together the strands of the argument and to outline the dilemmas facing designers who undertake such politically charged commissions.

Each place I discuss could be the subject of an entire book. In the case of those places mentioned in Part 1, many books have already been written. Without them, I would not have dared begin the task of synthesis. Though my first debt of thanks goes to the authors of such groundbreaking monographs, any author who draws material from all over the world develops a litany of global gratitude that could fill a monograph of its own.

It would seem almost inevitable that some aspects of a book which seeks to engage political issues in diverse war-torn parts of the world will be outdated even before it is published. While I cannot control such matters, I can accept responsibility for other errors that remain. Those who are not responsible for errors include the following:

At MIT's School of Architecture and Planning, I feel especially fortunate to have received much encouragement and assistance from Ronald Lewcock and Julian Beinart, as well as from several other past and present members of faculty and academic staff, including Edward Robbins, Akhtar Badshah, Masood Khan, Peter Droege, Lois Craig, William Porter, Ralph Gakenheimer, and Gary Hack. In addition, I am thankful for financial support from the MIT Dean's Professional Development Fund and the Edward H. and Joyce Linde Professorship Fund.

Pamela Rosi shared with me some of her dissertation materials about the Parliament House in Papua New Guinea and provided cogent criticism of my interpretations. I am grateful for the careful commentary of many others as well, notably that of Suhair al-Mosully, Ra'ad al-Mumayiz, Nihal Perera, Sikander Khan, Kazi Khaleed Ashraf, Martha Schteingart, and Saif-ul Haq, and for special encouragement from Julia Robinson and detailed critiques solicited by my editor at Yale University Press, Judy Metro.

In addition, my work has significantly benefited from conversations with Anthony King, Rifat Chadirji, Fuad Mulla Hussein, Ghazi al-Rayes, Abul Basher, Bashir-ul Haq, Mazhurul Islam, Shah Alam Zahiruddin, Abu Imamuddin, Fuad Mallick, Nurur-Rahman Khan, B. K. S. Inan, Faruqul Islam, Selina Afroz, Baykan Günay, Eleftherios Pavlides, Dimitri Phillipides, Glen Mills, Bill Hillier, Randolph Langenbach, Peter Serenyi, Raj Rewal, Balwant Saini, Florindo Fusaro, and Kim Dovey, and from materials supplied by C. Angelendran, James Rossant, Ron Burgess, Stanford Anderson, Peter Droege, and Anuradha Joshi. I am particularly grateful for the kindness shown to me by Roshanally Hirji, Hasan Ali, and many other members of the Aga Khan Foundation in Dhaka, and for the hospitality of Suhair al-Mosully and Ra'ad al-Mumayiz in Kuwait.

One of the great pleasures of working on this book has been the ongoing series of seminars entitled "Architecture and Politics" and "Urban Design Politics," for which I thank chiefly the student participants and my teaching assistants, Conrad Margoles, Kayed Lakhia, and Greg Havens. Kevin Low and Saif-ul Haq provided wonderful assistance with many of the illustrations, and Marsha Orent helped out in more ways than I could possibly itemize.

Most of all, my gratitude goes to my family, especially to Julie, who edited the manuscript, tolerated my absences in far-flung locales, and made coming home ever more wonderful.

Lincoln, Massachusetts
November 1990

Part 1

The locus of political power

CHAPTER 1

Capital and capitol: an introduction

Political power takes many forms. In addition to the power evinced by a charismatic leader, an indomitable military presence, an entrenched bureaucracy, or an imposing network of laws and statutes, many political regimes make especially powerful symbolic use of the physical environment. Throughout history and across the globe, architecture and urban design have been manipulated in the service of politics. Government buildings are, I would argue, an attempt to build governments and to support specific regimes. More than mere homes for government leaders, they serve as symbols of the state. We can, therefore, learn much about a political regime by observing closely what it builds. Moreover, the close examination of government buildings can reveal a great deal about what Clifford Geertz has termed the "cultural balance of power"[1] within a pluralist society.

Much recent writing on architecture and urban design rightly stresses that all buildings are products of social and cultural conditions. This book carries that argument a step further by exploring the complicated questions about power and identity embedded in the design of national parliament buildings and the districts that surround them in various capital cities around the world. It is based upon a simple premise: grand symbolic state buildings need to be understood in terms of the political and cultural contexts that helped to bring them into being. The postcolonial parliamentary complex provides an excellent vehicle for exploring these issues, since it is an act of design in which expressions of power and identity seem explicit and inevitable, both for the government client and for the designer.

HOW DO GOVERNMENT BUILDINGS MEAN?

In his essay "How Buildings Mean," the philosopher Nelson Goodman argues that we must consider the question of *how* a particular work of architecture conveys meaning before we are able to address the issue of *what* the

1.1 Meanings of the Lincoln Memorial: Lincoln's words speak directly.

building may mean. In so doing, Goodman aims to identify the categories of meaning that the built environment may convey as well as to elucidate the mechanisms by which these meanings are transmitted. This sort of analysis is crucial for understanding the nature of the relationship between the design of a parliamentary complex and its political history. As Goodman notes, "A building may mean in ways unrelated to being an architectural work—may become through association a symbol for sanctuary, or for a reign of terror, or for graft."[2] Such symbolism need not be so architecturally arbitrary, however. Buildings may also mean in ways very much tied to choices made by architects and urban designers.

Goodman identifies four such ways—denotation, exemplification, metaphorical expression, and mediated reference—each of which would seem to enhance the possibilities for multidimensional interpretation of government buildings. Some part of a building's meaning may often be read literally or otherwise directly denoted. In the case of the Lincoln Memorial in Washington, D.C., for example, meanings are denoted by the extracts from Lincoln's speeches carved into its walls and by the presence of the large statue of Lincoln himself (1.1). In this most direct of ways, the memorial communicates messages; these messages are, of course, open to multiple interpretations.

The Lincoln Memorial conveys meaning in a second way by drawing attention to certain of its properties to the exclusion of others. In this view, it is not only a self-contained building but also a dramatic urban design gesture, a terminus that gathers in the linear force of the Washington Mall (1.2). The solid-void-solid rhythm of the memorial's east facade draws the eye toward its center and the statue, even from a great distance. This mechanism for conveying meaning seems quintessentially architectural.

A third way that such a building may mean is through the expression of metaphor. This method is used quite powerfully in the case of the memorial, architecturally treated as a kind of analogous temple, with Lincoln taking the place of the classical deity (1.3). In case the metaphor is missed, however, the

1.2 Meanings of the Lincoln Memorial: exemplifying some architectonic properties more than others.

1.3 Meanings of the Lincoln Memorial: temple as metaphor.

message is reiterated quite literally, carved into the wall above the statue: IN THIS TEMPLE AS IN THE HEARTS OF THE PEOPLE FOR WHOM HE SAVED THE UNION THE MEMORY OF ABRAHAM LINCOLN IS ENSHRINED FOREVER.

Building on this predilection for metaphor, the Lincoln Memorial demonstrates a fourth way of meaning, that of mediated reference. There is a chain of reasoning that leads from the deification of Lincoln as a savior to broader consideration of the values of national unity and racial equality promoted by Lincoln's presidential acts. From this, in turn, the memorial becomes associated with the process of advancement of civil rights. It is not by coincidence that many of Washington's civil rights rallies are held in front of the Lincoln Memorial (1.4).

Such mediated references may lead the construction of meaning far afield from the detailed physical particularities of the architectural object itself. As Goodman puts it, "Even when a building does mean, that may have nothing to do with its architecture. A building of any design may come to stand for some of its causes or effects, or for some historical event that occurred in it or on its site, or for its designated use; any abattoir may symbolize slaughter, and any mausoleum, death; and a costly county courthouse may symbolize extravagance. To mean in such a way is not thereby to function as an architectural work."[3]

1.4 Meanings of the Lincoln Memorial: mediated references carry forward broad conceptual associations, from Civil War to civil rights.

Goodman's distinction is useful for identifying the mechanisms of "how buildings mean," but it is much less helpful as an analytical tool for understanding the subsequent question of *what* buildings may mean, since these sorts of nonarchitectural associations seem central to the way that most people think about buildings. What value is there, then, in privileging only those kinds of meanings that are termed architectural? It may be that because these other associative sorts of meanings are so powerful and often so predominant they threaten many architects and others whose professional self-esteem is dependent on their buildings' being able to communicate effectively their designer's intentions, whether aesthetic or social. How can a designer defend an exquisite formal gesture if it becomes publicly overshadowed or undermined by the indefensible acts of the building's institutional inhabitants or by some other historical relationship in which that building may stand?

To focus our concern only on the architectural portions of a building's meaning takes too limited a view of what is involved in the design of a building. If a goal of this book is to explore the complex meanings of government buildings, then one must treat the political designs of government officials as equal in importance, and often intimately related, to the physical designs of architects. So, too, if an overriding issue is the meaning that these places may hold for diverse segments of the public, one must try not to let interpretation of these buildings be too dependent on specialized knowledge of comparative architectural history and formal precedents. It is here that the mechanisms of metaphor and mediated reference become valuable analytical tools. Even if the average American citizen knows little about the details of classical systems of proportion and cannot comprehend the richness of meanings encoded into an ancient temple's entablature, that citizen will sense the metaphor of Lincoln as an enthroned deity and will know something of his deeds.

Government buildings would appear to serve several symbolic purposes simultaneously. Some of these meanings may be traceable to a designer's—or a politician's—intentions, even if the interplay of ideas within such designer–client partnerships cannot usually be clearly charted or differentiated. Other meanings are not introduced by an individual's formative act but arise as unintended and unacknowledged products of a widely shared acculturation. In the United States, citizens are socialized to regard the most prominent neoclassical edifices of Washington as the reassuring symbols of such concepts as "equal justice under the law" and government "of the people, by the people, and for the people." The buildings housing principal public institutions are unconsciously perceived as metonymous reinforcement for an idealized and stable democratic government, worthy of our tacit trust.[4] The political scientist Murray Edelman, author of a seminal book on the subject of political symbolism, has argued that such buildings "catalyze the common search for clarity, order and predictability in a threatening world."[5]

At the same time, however, the buildings themselves can appear to be part of that threat. "The scale of the structures reminds the mass of political spectators that they enter the precincts of power as clients or as supplicants, susceptible to arbitrary rebuffs and favors, and that they are subject to remote authorities they only dimly know or understand."[6] Moreover, this monumentality may reciprocally reinforce the self-perceptions of those government officials and bureaucrats who identify this exalted territory as their own. In this way, existing hierarchies can be legitimized at all levels, and extremes of power and impotence intensified.

The manipulation of civic space thus tends both to sanction the leadership's exercise of power and to promote the continued quiescence of those who are excluded. Reassuring civic messages and discomforting authoritarian ones engage in a kind of cognitive coexistence. As Edelman contends, "Everyone recognizes both of them, and at different cognitive levels believes both. . . . Logical inconsistency is no bar to psychological compatibility because the symbolic meanings both soothe the conscience of the elites and help nonelites to adapt readily to conditions they have no power to reject or to change."[7]

Design manipulation that promotes this dual sense of alienation and empowerment occurs at all scales of a country's civic space, ranging from the layout of a parliamentary debating chamber to the layout of a new capital city. The design of a government building's interiors holds many clues about the nature of the bureaucracy that works therein. The privileged location of a high official's office and the gauntlet of doors and security checkpoints one must traverse to reach it help clarify the structure of authority. Or, conversely, the deliberate locating of a leader's office or principal debating chamber so that it is open to public view (if not public access) may be an attempt to convey a sense of governmental approachability, either genuine or illusory.

Charles Goodsell's comparative analysis of the layouts of American city council chambers demonstrates how the distribution of political power can be observed even in a single room. Relying on close examination of the relative positions of speaker's podium, council members' seating, and public galleries in the design of seventy-five chambers constructed during the last 125 years, Goodsell identifies two basic and interconnected long-term trends in democratic governance: a trend away from "personalistic rule" expressed by "the shift in central focus away from the rostrum's presiding officer to the council's corporate existence" and a trend toward the "downgrading of geographic representation" as evidenced by a move from separated aldermanic desks to a common dais table. Equally indicative of evolving attitudes is the treatment of the public. The more illuminating architectural shifts include the reorientation of the council's seating in such ways that members communicate with the public instead of with each other, the downgrading or removal of barriers between government and public, the addition of increasingly greater amounts of public seating, and the provision of increasingly more prominent public lecterns. Taken together, Goodsell concludes, these and other changes "generally convey concepts of promoting popular sovereignty and democratic rule, of viewing the people as individuals rather than an undifferentiated mass, and of establishing the moral equality of the rulers and the ruled." To his credit, Goodsell takes his analysis one step further to question whether this seemingly positive visual trend toward increased democracy is, in practice, little more than an insidious deception, an "empty, hypocritical ritualism that only masks the powerlessness of the ordinary citizen."[8]

Thus, even in those contemporary council chambers in which government and citizens are spatially conjoined by seating arrangements, it surely seems possible that the dual sense of alienation and empowerment could be reinforced. Moreover, at the level of national government symbolism—the locus of this book's principal concern—the layout of parliamentary chambers, even contemporary ones, consistently treats the public as detached spectators of government rather than potential participants. Here, given the large number of elected representatives that must be seated in most national parliamentary chambers, it is the representatives themselves who tend to become the participatory audience for debate, with the public relegated to the periphery. In many places, even the seating of the parliamentarians is carefully choreographed to correspond with long-standing traditions and ongoing partisan divisions. The arrangement of the seating in a postcolonial parliamentary chamber frequently identifies much about the political traditions of the colonial regime that ruled before independence, with oppositional layouts reminiscent of the British House of Commons and curved, concave rows suggestive of the French Chamber of Deputies. The expression of meaningful hierarchies may well be centered in debating chambers where public access and participation are indirect at best, yet the symbolic expression of central government also reaches far outside the walls of parliament.

Not limited to matters of interior configuration and architectural expression, decisions about urban design may also foster mutually reinforcive alienation and empowerment by magnifying hierarchies in the outdoor public realm. The source of potential meanings for a government building extends far outward from its facades. A government building's spatial relation to other important structures sends additional complex messages about how the leadership wishes others to regard the institution it houses. Its apparent dominance or subservience depends on the scale of the building and the architectural manipulation of its proportions and materials, but also may be influenced by its relative degree of isolation and its accessibility to the public. To view government buildings as acts of urban design as well as instances of architecture is to be able to judge how the larger design carefully delimits the zones for public gathering and defines areas of increasingly exclusive privacy.

The influence of urban design on the structure of a government building's meaning is especially clear during times of high pageantry involving processions. All forms of procession—military review, presidential motorcade, celebratory parade, civilian protest—consist of power moving through space. All parts of the setting—the point of origin, the route, and the destination—may be symbol-laden and can become part of the meaning of the event.

The perceived need to make architecture and urban design serve politics is most salient in those countries where the form of politics is new and the forms of architecture are old, though the phenomenon has a long and global pedigree. In the emerging postcolonial world of the middle and late twentieth century, the leadership of newly independent states frequently attempted to use architecture not only to house a new form of government (parliamentary democracy), but also to proclaim the worthiness of the new regime and advance its status. The professed goal of such government buildings is to forge something most often termed national identity or national unity; yet, as I will argue, the design of these buildings remains closely tied to political forces that reinforce existing patterns of dominance and submission.

THE LOCUS OF POSTCOLONIAL POWER

Dozens of new states have gained their independence in the years since the Second World War. Not all of these, however, have had the appropriate combination of political and financial resources necessary to mark this independence with the design and construction of a new capital city or a new parliament building. On one hand, the commission of a new capital city—or even of the construction of a new parliamentary district within or adjacent to an existing capital—is too costly for many leaders to contemplate seriously. On the other hand, there is the temptation to expropriate and reuse the opulent edifices of the colonial ancien regime. To be sure, these two pressures have been frequently conjoined. In some instances, however, the government leaders of newly independent states have spent lavishly on new facilities despite the overall poverty of their country or the availability of transformable colonial structures. The decision to build a new place for government is always a significant one; the decisions about *where* and *how* to house it are more telling still.

Designing the place for national government in the postcolonial city involves far more than architecture. Parliament buildings are located not only in relation to neighboring buildings but also in relation to a city and to the country as a whole. These larger questions of siting are hardly matters left to architects alone, since many architects tend to regard the site as consisting merely of a building's immediate, visible surroundings. Beyond such relatively narrow concerns, the location of parliament buildings is a product of social and cultural forces. The placement of parliament buildings is an exercise in political power, a spatial declaration of political control.

In postcolonial states that have planned new parliamentary complexes in the twentieth century, the buildings are located in one of two ways. In places such as Australia, Turkey, Brazil, Pakistan, Belize, Mauritania, Nigeria, Tanzania, Malawi, Ivory Coast, Malaysia, and Kazakhstan the government has sponsored the construction of an entirely new capital city, whereas in places such as Israel, Bangladesh, Papua New Guinea, Sri Lanka, and Kuwait the new parliamentary complexes have been created within or adjacent to the existing capital.

Several examples of new capital cities are discussed in the first part of this book, while the latter category—capitol complexes—constitutes the major focus of the second . In this latter group, the construction of a new capital has, in effect, been distilled to its programmatic and symbolic essence. The capitol complex, by which I mean not only the capitol building itself but also the relation of that building to the assemblage of structures around it, is designed to house the means of government and to communicate this government visually to the governed. Not all capitol complexes contain exactly the same set of institutional elements or arrange them in the same hierarchy. Some juxtapose the parliamentary function with judicial and executive functions; some relate the legislature to the presence of other nearby national institutions such as museums and libraries; others isolate the capitol from everything else. Ironically, many of the more imposing capitol complexes deliberately exclude the strongest government powers. As architecture and as urban design, these places are necessarily infused with symbolism and are revealing cultural products. Examination of these parliamentary complexes offers an opportunity to assess certain architectural and urban design devices that seem markedly prominent in central areas of capital cities. This is not to suggest that any city (even ones established by executive decree) is solely formed by the actions of the state building for itself. It is merely an acknowledgment that a book that seeks to be both comparative and brief cannot hope to address the full range of pressing issues affecting contemporary urbanization. Though I do not focus on the multitude of social, economic, political, and cultural factors that affect the development of the postcolonial capital city as a whole, I do believe that close examination of their symbolic centers carries meaning for their peripheries as well as their cores. With this somewhat more bounded objective in mind, I seek to define and discuss the relationship between a designed capital city and its symbolic center, the capitol.

WHAT IS A CAPITOL?

Capitol is an odd word, even to those living in the fifty-one United States cities that have buildings bearing this name. Commonly confused with *capital*—meaning a city housing the administration of state or national government—*capitol* with an *o* usually refers to the building that houses that government's lawmakers. It is an old word, centuries more ancient than the domed edifices of Boston or Washington. And, as is true of many words that have a long evolution, the early meanings retain a core of relevance.

Capitol originally connoted a citadel on a hill. Rome's Capitoline Hill, site of the ancient Temple of Jupiter, within which the Roman Senate sometimes convened, provides a clue to both the political and topographical origins of the word. Moreover, the notion of citadel suggests roots that extend even deeper in the past. The word *citadel*, derived from the Italian *cittadella*, "little city," is an imperfect translation of the Greek word *akropolis*, "upper city." The ancient citadel, as an architecturally dominant minicity within a city, combines both of these notions.[9] It is, to be sure, a long way from the Athenian massif to a hillock above the Potomac, but one must not dismiss the connections.

Though the gap between an ancient citadel and a modern capital city may seem immense, important continuities remain. A capital city, more than most other cities, is expected to be a symbolic center. As such, it is not so distant from the primal motivations that inspired the first cities. According to Lewis Mumford, who drew rather generously upon the work of archaeologists, the "first germ of the city . . . is in the ceremonial meeting place that serves as a goal for pilgrimage." This city, he continues, is

> a site to which family or clan groups are drawn back, at seasonable intervals, because it concentrates, in addition to any natural advantages it may have, certain "spiritual" or supernatural powers, powers of higher potency and greater duration, of wider cosmic significance, than the ordinary processes of life. And though the human performances may be occasional and temporary, the structure that supports it, whether a paleolithic grotto or a Mayan ceremonial center with its lofty pyramid, will be endowed with a more lasting cosmic image.[10]

Even though the goal of pilgrimage has not infrequently been supplanted by the quest for patronage or the diffuse pleasures of tourism, some cities (many of them capitals) have not fully forsaken their claim to wider significance.

Capital cities have become almost unrecognizably large and complex, and autocratic political power has often been transformed to include varying degrees of democratic participation, yet certain cities retain their symbolic centrality and importance. According to the anthropologist Clifford Geertz, "At the political center of any complexly organized society . . . there is both a governing elite and a set of symbolic forms expressing the fact that it is in truth governing."[11] While these symbolic forms have changed in the intervening millennia, the need to signal the presence of the ruler to the ruled has not diminished. Geertz continues,

> No matter how democratically the members of the elite are chosen (usually not very) or how deeply divided among themselves they may be (usually much more than outsiders imagine), they justify their existence and order their actions in terms of a collection of stories, ceremonies, insignia, formalities, and appurtenances that they have either inherited or, in more revolutionary situations, invented. It is these—crowns and coronations, limousines and conferences—that mark the center as center and give what goes on there its aura of being not merely important but in some odd fashion connected with the way the world is built. The gravity of high politics and the solemnity of high worship spring from liker impulses than might first appear.[12]

If the activity of the center features a variety of rituals, nothing more directly "mark[s] the center as center" or legitimizes a regime that claims to be democratically supported than the architecture and planning of the seat of government—the capitol.

To the ancient Romans, the capitol was the *caput mundi*, literally, the head of the world.[13] This direct connection between the symbolic center of a city and the rest of the universe is, of course, hardly a claim made by Romans alone; cosmic conjunction is explicit in Chinese geomancy and in Indian mandala plans, and is implicit in less well understood ceremonial centers across all continents.[14] Some modern capital cities—Athens, Cairo, Jerusalem, and Moscow, for example—have grown up around ancient centers of power (though of these four, only the last city still attempts to use its Kremlin as the locus of a national government presence). In most other cities that have developed over many centuries, any surviving notion of a *caput mundi* functions much less overtly or dramatically. Still, though the urban umbilicals to the heavens have been weakened or cut in the centuries since capitals first unknowingly vied for cosmic centrality, earthbound articulations of power have remained robust.

The first city, according to Mumford, began with the coming together of shrine and stronghold in a single place.[15] As the centuries passed, this joining of spiritual and temporal power took on the characteristic form of the citadel, a precinct of power and privilege spatially dominant over the larger city:

> In the citadel the new mark of the city is obvious: a change of scale, deliberately meant to awe and overpower the beholder. Though the mass of inhabitants might be poorly fed and overworked, no expense was spared to create temples and palaces whose sheer bulk and upward thrust would dominate the rest of the city. The heavy walls of hard-baked clay or solid stone would give to the ephemeral offices of state the assurance of stability and security, of unrelenting power and unshakeable authority. What we now call "monumental architecture" is first of all the expression of power, and that power exhibits itself in the assemblage of costly building materials and of all the resources of art, as well as in a command of all manner of sacred adjuncts, great lions and bulls and eagles, with whose mighty virtues the head of state identifies his own frailer abilities. The purpose of this art was to produce respectful terror.[16]

The capitols of today continue to crown many a frail regime and still tend to delineate the head of the city. Whether, in so doing, they induce terror (respectful or otherwise) or merely enhance the cause of irony is another question, one to which I will return. For now, I wish only to suggest that the designers of modern capitols have repeatedly sought to regain or retain vestiges of the earlier notions of acropolis and citadel.

For centuries, it was conceivable for a capitol in its various nascent forms to exist almost independently of its surrounding city. In its walled precinct, the capitol appeared spatially separate, a ruler's refuge. As long as it was a sacred center as well as an administrative and a military one, access was strictly limited to the priests and the privileged. In palaces and courts, temples and shrines, the concept of a Forbidden City extended far afield from China. In this view, capitol precedes capital, or—as Mumford puts it—"the magnet comes before the container."[17] Magnetized by the presence of a monarch or a religious institution, the capital container grew around this capitol center, designed for ritual and devoted to ceremony.

WHAT IS A CAPITAL?

Capital cities may be categorized in many ways, but no single criterion for identification does justice to the complexity of forces that make cities. It is tempting to follow the lead of many geographers and historians and posit a clear distinction between cities that are *natural* capitals and those whose status as capital is *artificial*. There does seem to be some value in seeking criteria to distinguish a capital such as London from one such as Washington, D.C., yet these labels do not seem adequate to this task. Some capitals that may appear natural—such as Rome, Athens, or Moscow—have been redesignated as capitals only in the relatively recent past. Even modern capitals that appear to have a continuous history of administrative and symbolic centrality are not necessarily a natural choice. What tends to be termed natural is often merely that which has had its origins obscured by the passage of time and the accretion of complex layers of development.

The motives for designating a city as a capital are not easily separated. There are, however, identifiable and instructive characteristics. Capitals do not merely exist; they are the various products of human will and historical circumstance. The existence of a particular form of capital in a particular location at a particular time is dependent upon a delicate and shifting balance among many kinds of contending forces. A capital may be located for reasons of climate, which could push it into the interior or toward an area of great natural beauty. Its site might also be a function of geopolitical strategy, which could dictate that it be near or away from a sensitive border. A capital may be located at some central point for purposes of convenient access to and from all parts of the territory under its administrative control, or its placement may be deliberately eccentric to allow easy access to international trade routes. In addition, it may be chosen for its impact on regional development, which could require great distance between it and other existing cities. Alternatively, it may be envisioned as purely an administrative enclave that could parasitically rely on the nearby presence of established economic, social, and cultural networks. Capital placement may result from the idiosyncrasy of an indigenous leader's autocratic decree or may be externally imposed to service the needs of an overseas power. A capital may be established as a kind of binding center to mediate among rival regional or ethnic factions, or it may be sited explicitly to favor the claims of one group over others. So, too, the designation of a capital may be part of an attempt to revive some period of past glory or to disassociate a place from more recent historical events. And, finally, a capital may be selected to maximize international visibility, or it may be chosen for more purely domestic and regional reasons. The choice of a capital city is nearly always the product of compromise among these competing motives, frequently ones that seem most mutually contradictory. Every capital city's history reveals a different set of motives for its founding.

London, for example, has existed at least since Roman times and was the Romans' largest outpost on the island. Recent archaeological evidence of large buildings containing courts of justice and municipal offices as well as a governor's palace suggests that Roman Londinium was the imperially designated capital of Britain as early as the first century A.D.[18] The site of Londinium was selected because it constituted the first point at which the Thames was both navigable and bridgeable and because it featured a hill for the construction of a citadel.[19] Eventually, the geopolitical logic of this location led Norman rulers to take up residence in London in the eleventh century, more than 650 years after its Roman heyday. Still, London did not displace Canterbury as the ecclesiastical capital of Britain for many centuries, if it ever has. In short, it is difficult to say when and how London became a capital city rather than simply an intermittently large and influential one. Perhaps it was not truly a capital until it became the symbolic center of a United Kingdom, a union that has never remained entirely free of dispute.

Of course, no L'Enfant was hired to plan the whole of London in a single flourish, but the growth of London is not wholly attributable to natural forces either. As human creations, all cities are natural in one sense, but this human nature is always tempered and directed by the force of reasoned decisions. Cities are not the result of a biological inevitability; they arise out of choices. Even when the state has sponsored initial construction of a new city or district, it is up to a wide range of individuals and groups to sustain and extend urban development. As the product of a multiplicity of choices, cities are intellectual constructs as well as physical artifacts and social networks, and all three are closely related.

Geographer and urbanist Peter Hall has argued that there are seven types of capital city. His useful typology distinguishes such cities chiefly according to the functions they perform in the national and global economy, and in terms of the period and reasons for their ascendancy. In terms of economic influence, Hall discriminates between *political capitals*—those that were created chiefly to serve as a seat of government, such as The Hague—and those that serve more broadly as *multi-function capitals*, such as London or Stockholm. He also separates out *global capitals* for their transnational role in the global economy, and identifies *super capitals*—cities that house international organizations, but are not necessarily national capitals. Then, acknowledging that circumstances change, Hall distinguishes among various kinds of *former capitals*, depending on whether they were *ex-imperial capitals* or merely important cities, and on whether they retain important status as *provincial capitals* in federal nation-states.[20] Many capitals may fall into more than one category, and a chief advantage of this schema is that it acknowledges the historical dynamism that buffets and shifts capital city status. For better or worse, Hall's typology also permits a more inclusivist compass to the canon of capitals, since it admits cities such as New York based on its economic might ("global capital") or role in hosting the United Nations ("super capital"), and elevates Brussels less because of its role in Belgium and more due to its EU position as an alleged "capital of Europe."[21] Perhaps most importantly, Hall's framework also reminds us that the planning and design of national capitals cannot be detached from the political, economic, and social forces that sited them and shaped their development.

Of the many ways geographers have distinguished among capital cities, two distinctions—closely related to each other—seem useful. One is between cities that have evolved into capitals and cities that have been expressly designed to serve this function. The evolved/designed distinction, while more accurately descriptive than the natural/artificial schism, fails to do justice to the fact that any decision to designate a city as a capital is also an intentional move, an evolutionary break. If some cities appear to have always been capitals, they have been so only through our ignorance of their history. Whether gradual or abrupt, the capitalization of a city is guided by underlying physical, social, economic, and political motives. Nonetheless, there does seem some value in distinguishing between those capitals that have evolved to a point where they have been designated capitals and those cities where designation as capital has necessitated an entirely new overall design, premised upon the city's role as a capital. To posit the importance of this distinction between evolved and designed capitals is not, however, to deny that some capital cities are both evolved and designed at different stages in their growth. This changing nature of capital cities over time suggests the need for a second kind of measure.

Over the centuries, as cities have grown and forms of government have diversified, the nature of what it means to be a capital city has changed. Though we may call them both capitals, Roman Londinium and contemporary London, for example, bear little resemblance to one another in overall form, size, socioeconomic structure, or political sphere of influence. Moreover, cities that serve as capitals for long periods may evolve almost unrecognizably even without a gap in their status as capitals. Ancient Rome itself underwent many changes during its five-hundred-year tenure as a capital, clinging to its capital status long after it had ceased to be an appropriate demographic, commercial, industrial, or cultural center for the Mediterranean world.[22] Even over the course of a relatively short period, the role and jurisdiction of a capital may waver. The answer to the question Capital of what? or, more precisely, Capital of whom? is rarely resolved. Many distinctions could be made in discussing the evolution of the capital city as an idea. The most pressing need here is to differentiate between the premodern and the modern capital.

THE SYMBOLIC ROLE OF MODERN CAPITALS

In the modern age, by which I mean the two hundred years or so since the birth of the modern nation-state, the capital has taken on important new aspects. Even more so than in the past, the modern capital is expected to be, above all else, the seat of government and the focus of its symbolic presence. Programmatically, the modern capital is expected to be both the practical and the symbolic focus of national administration; furthermore, especially in states emerging from control by an external power, it is also required to serve as the focus of efforts to promote a sense of national identity. In these ways, modern capitals may differ from other cities.

As Arnold Toynbee notes, the cities that have been created expressly to serve as national capitals in the last 220 years are rarely as populous as commercial and industrial cities that have emerged in the same period, whereas capitals prior to the Industrial Revolution were commonly the largest concentrations of population.[23] What the modern capital lacks in size and diversity of economic base, it is asked to make up for in sheer density of symbolism. In this regard, the modern capital, far from being a departure, is heir to the practice of ancient empires by which a capital's splendor served to legitimize the power of the ruling individual or group. In most places, perhaps, the capital still acts as a drain on the resources of the peripheral areas under its administrative control; in this sense, too, its imperialism may operate domestically as well as internationally.

Although all capitals, beginning with the earliest citadel, have had symbolic roles that fortified and magnified the presence of government, nothing seems quite comparable to the manifold pressures of modern nationalism. In the modern capital, symbolic tasks seem both enhanced and increasingly complex. To the apologists of modern nationalism the capital itself is to be the grandest symbol of the cause. Many modern capitals must act as the mediator among a collection of peoples who, one way or another, have come to be recognized as a single sovereign state. In more distant times, selection of a capital was usually motivated by the presence of a shrine, a defensible fortress, or a trade route; in the modern age, new capitals are most often sited to favor political factions. Such rivalries may be rooted in ethnic or religious schisms or may result from competition among alternative poles of urban economic growth. Like the ancient citadel, constructed to combat enemies both from within and without, the modern capital is likely to be more a center of controversy than consensus.

The modern capital is more than the seat of government in another way as well. With the rise of parliamentary democracy has come an increase in the number of persons involved with government at every level. Though the notion of a government office building has existed at least since the time of the ancient Romans, the rapid burgeoning of the bureaucracy of government is a phenomenon of the last hundred years. While palaces had always been maintained as nearly self-sufficient minicities, the concept of designing a city to showcase the organs of government administration is a modern idea. In earlier eras, when the apparatus of domestic rule depended more explicitly upon a large military presence, an extended civil administration was unnecessary. In the present age, in which nearly every regime professes to be the bearer of democracy, an entire capital city can be dominated by the purposes of national administration, purposes that include the management of ceremony as well as the performance of more mundane tasks. A modern capital city of a large country is not only a source of pageantry but also the workplace for tens of thousands of bureaucrats who staff executive ministries and departments, serve the needs of legislative representatives, high court justices, and resident diplomats, run national libraries, archives, and museums, and toil away at an ever-burgeoning array of lobbying efforts, media coverage, and support services. In many places, the business of government has burst the bounds of the capitol to fill the capital as well.[24] With this transformation of the scale and structure of government, and often coincident with a resurgence of nationalism, comes the development of the modern capital city.

THREE KINDS OF MODERN CAPITAL

What follows, then, is an overview of examples of three types of modern capital cities, emphasizing two things: the reasons the capital was founded and the spatial relation between the capitol and the capital. The first two varieties, *evolved capitals* and *evolved capitals renewed*, are discussed in this chapter, while the third, *designed capitals*, is introduced here but becomes the subject of Chapters 3, 4, and 5. Cities in all three categories feature periods of large-scale urban design intervention in governmental sectors; no urban evolution proceeds at a uniformly even pace. To differentiate among the categories is therefore to identify a continuum and to recognize that each city is being observed from the perspective of its present-day development.

Evolved capitals: London, Paris, Vienna, and Berlin

For capital cities with long, complex histories, no simple model of spatial organization is likely to be usefully descriptive. In all cases it is possible to trace the architectural locus of government, but in no case is it an easy matter to comment upon the relation of this place to the larger city or to interpret meaning from this juxtaposition. Most European capital cities do not have a single, readily identifiable architectural center. They are polycentric, with a great multiformity of nodes, both sacred and secular (1.5, 1.6).

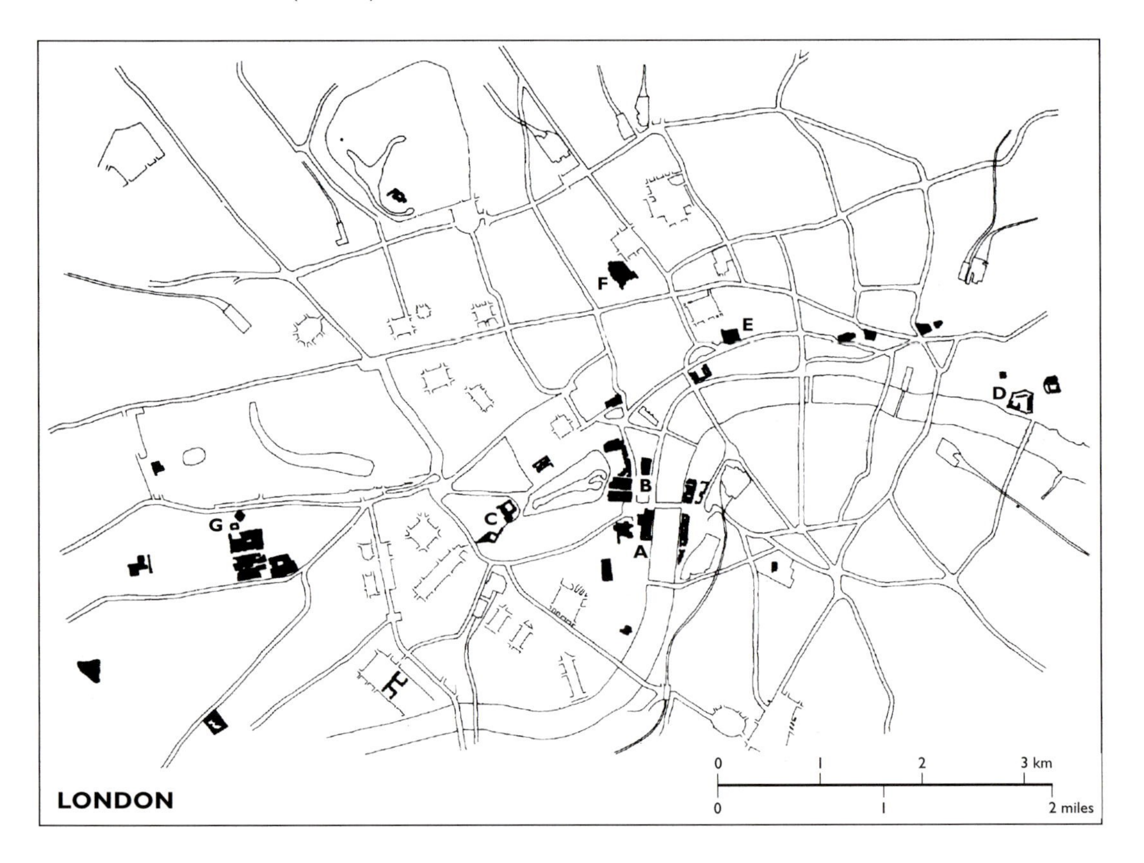

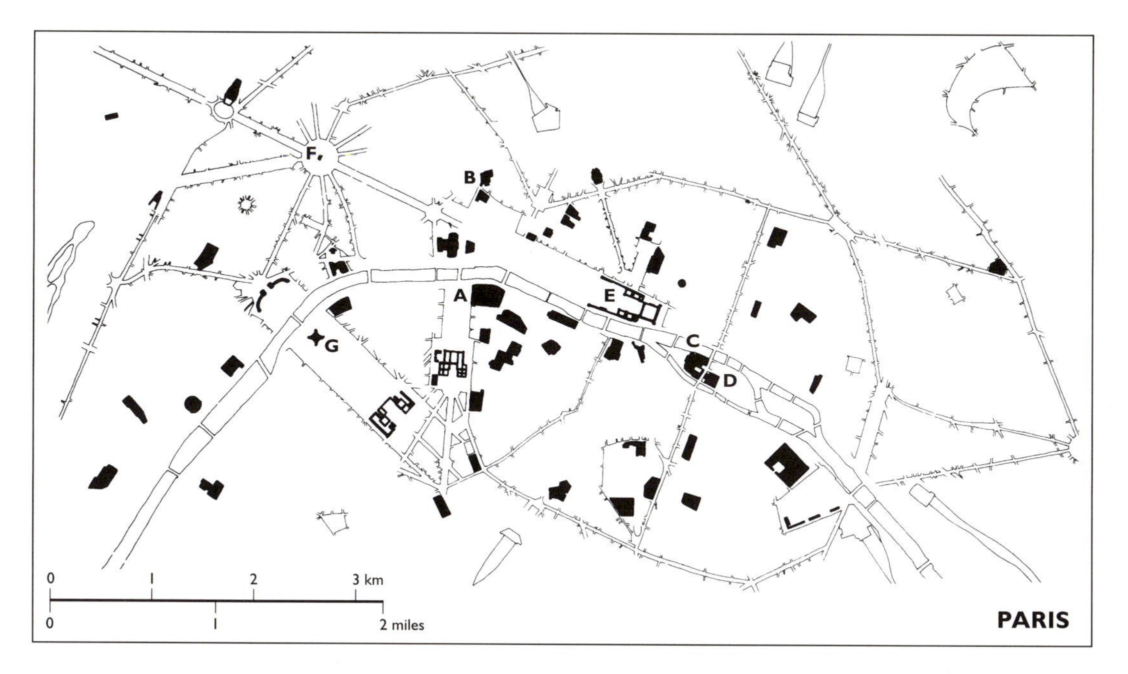

1.5, 1.6 London and Paris: dispersion of major government/civic institutions and monuments.

A Houses of Parliament
B Whitehall
C Buckingham Palace
D Tower of London
E Royal Courts of Justice
F British Museum
G Museums and colleges

A Palais Bourbon (French Parliament)
B Palais de l'Elysée (president's residence)
C Palais de Justice
D Notre Dame
E Louvre
F Arc de Triomphe
G Tour Eiffel

London

In London, the nineteenth-century Houses of Parliament together with the rest of the Palace of Westminster and Whitehall may constitute one such node, but parliament must share prominence with Buckingham Palace, St. Paul's Cathedral, and the capital's true citadel, the Tower of London, built in the eleventh century on the exact site of the Roman citadel that preceded it by a millennium.[25] This architectural power sharing is not surprising, given that political power in Britain in the last thousand years has shifted dramatically among crown, church, and parliament, and each of these forces retains its architectural presence in the London cityscape. What is missing, however, among these grand edifices is a monumental treatment of the contemporary center of British political power: the prime minister's abode is modestly located at 10 Downing Street and is known by that name only. In recent years, Downing Street having been fenced off, the residence is not even a visible part of the London streetscape (1.7).

David Cannadine argues that the British government's conscious physical

1.7 No. 10 Downing Street: no longer a street.

transformation of London into a capital city is of relatively recent origin, as is the profusion of ceremony associated with British royalty: "It was not until the closing decades of the nineteenth century, when national prestige was seen to be threatened, that action was taken, converting the squalid fog-bound city of Dickens into an Imperial capital." Aided by the creation in 1888 of the capital's first single administrative authority, the London County Council, architectural embellishment and urban design coordination soon became evident with the construction of County Hall, the War Office in Whitehall, and the Government Buildings at the corner of Parliament Square. This was matched, between 1906 and 1913, by the construction of London's first and only "triumphal way," achieved through the widening of the Mall, the building of the Admiralty Arch, the refronting of Buckingham Palace, and the construction of the Victoria Monument. With the addition of buildings to serve as headquarters in London for the various outposts of empire, the city—while still polycentric in its nodes of power—became somewhat more like imperial capitals elsewhere.[26]

In London, the relationship between government and architecture came under scrutiny in the 1980s in a different way, owing to provocation from an unlikely source, the Prince of Wales. A critique that initially centered on a single public building (the "monstrous carbuncle" proposed as an extension to the National Gallery) soon escalated into speeches, an exhibition, and a television program that lambasted postwar Britain's modern architecture and urban design. Carried to its logical conclusions in the social and economic policies that so deeply affected what was built, the prince's aesthetic archconservatism seemed, at least to some, to imply a social radicalism he presumably did not intend. In any case, the royal involvement sparked discussion not only about architecture but about the relationship between government power and design decisions. One extreme reaction, published in the *Architectural Review*, compared Prince Charles's interventions to Nazi propaganda. More recently, however, London has lost much of its centrality in the discourse about political architecture in the United Kingdom, with greater attention devolved onto the dramatic new presences granted to parliamentary autonomy in Scotland and Wales.[27]

Paris

The urban development of Paris since the 1970s has also raised controversial questions about government patronage and the distribution of public facilities across the city. Although the architectural iconography of modern Paris retains a medieval core on the Île de la Cité, the Parisian spatial hierarchy is also quintessentially polycentric, with grand squares to commemorate military triumph and boulevards designed for imperial procession and imperious promenade. The world-renowned royal axis, extended from the Louvre over a period of eight hundred years, has undergone a parallel set of alterations in its meaning (1.8). Until the end of the nineteenth century, as Wolfgang Braunfels has observed, "every stage in this development was conditioned by the attitude of the king and, later, the emperor toward Paris and their conception of the monarchy itself."[28] The end of the monarchy did not preclude further changes of meaning to the monarchically inspired traces that remained. This central axis underwent another shift of symbolism in the Second World War when, during four years of humiliating occupation of the city, the Nazis ritually repeated their triumphal march along the Champs Élysées every day at noon, passing in review at the Place del l'Étoile.

1.8 Paris's "royal axis" now conjoins high culture and high capitalism.

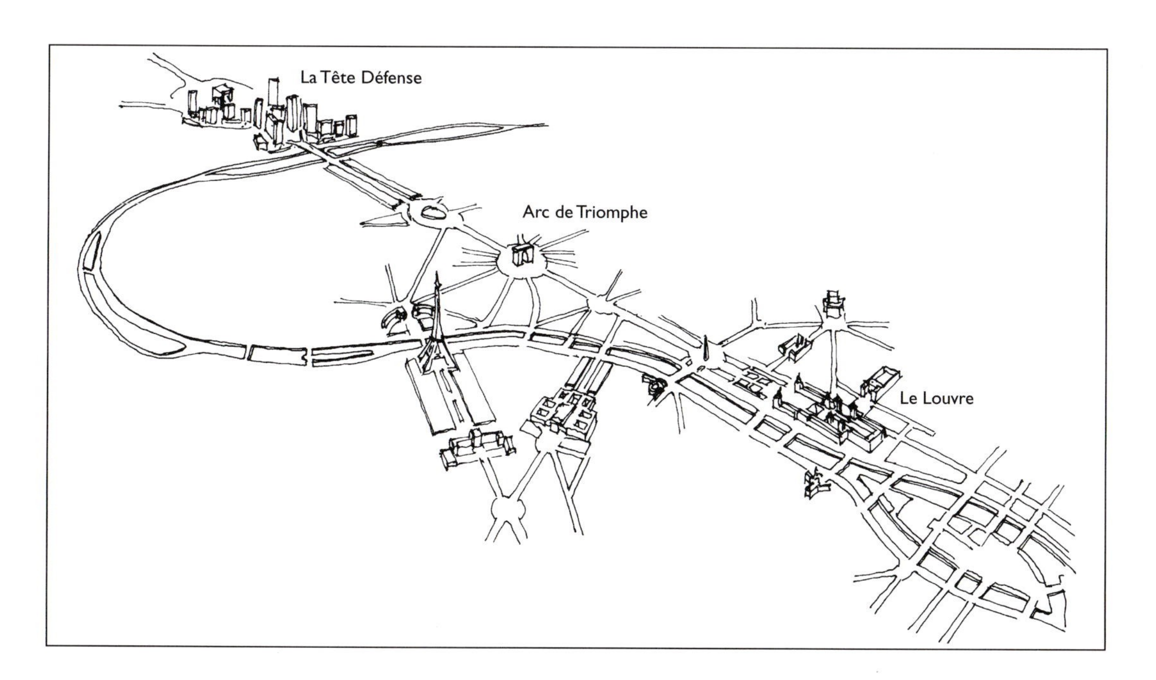

"Although the physical fabric of the city remained intact, major monuments received an appliqué of swastikas and German victory slogans, streets carried signposts in German to direct military traffic, and about two hundred bronze statues were removed by the Germans and melted down for their metal"; only procrastination by the German commander saved the city from Hitler's orders for an eleventh-hour destruction as Nazi power collapsed.[29]

In the late twentieth century, the symbolism underwent other profound shifts. With the redevelopment of the Louvre under I. M. Pei's glass pyramids and the extension of the axis through the high-rise business district of La Défense, culminating in Spreckelsen's Grand Arch, what once was a ceremonial way for kings now conjoins high culture and high capitalism. From the stone walls of the medieval fortress that have been excavated and revealed beneath the Louvre's new entrance court to La Tête Défense, the new Parisian axis of power reveals its military origins in name if not in function. And future extensions of the axis beyond La Défense will alter and expand its meanings yet again.

As successive French presidents try to consolidate central Paris as a district of museums and other cultural facilities, the presence of government, ironically perhaps, becomes less prominent. In its complex arrangement of urban axes and controlled building heights, Paris's most visible buildings are not ones that house government officials. As in most capitals that have evolved over many centuries and have gradually accommodated themselves to changes in the nature of government, the urban design of Paris provides no overwhelmingly privileged place for the trappings of contemporary parliamentary democracy.

Vienna

Vienna, of Neolithic origin and for seven centuries the seat of the Hapsburg empire, became a modern capital only in the late nineteenth century: the creation of the Ringstrasse epitomizes the transformation of a premodern into a modern capital. A half-circular boulevard fronted by civic institutions and parks, it was built on land freed after the dismantling of the city's defensive walls and glacis in 1857 (1.9). In Vienna, the citadel of the Hapsburgs was literally broken open to include a larger capitol complex, one that afforded greater public participation. Though initiated by a near-autocratic regime in the late 1850s, the buildings along the Ringstrasse were built in accordance with the wishes of a new, ascendant, liberal middle class that gained political power in subsequent decades. As Carl Schorske puts it, "Not palaces, garrisons, and churches, but centers of constitutional government and higher culture dominated the Ring. The art of building, used in the old city to express aristocratic grandeur and ecclesiastical pomp, now became the communal property of the citizenry, expressing the various aspects of the bourgeois cultural ideal in a series of so-called *Prachtbauten* (buildings of splendor)."[30] Its last building completed in 1913, just in time for the war that would bring an end to the imperial power that inspired its creation, the Ring became home not only to separate facilities for the three primary branches of liberal government (executive, legislative, and judicial)

1.9 Vienna: before and after Ringstrasse institutions.

***(above)* Remains of the defensive system around the old city are still visible prior to 1857.**

A Hofburg Palace
B St. Stephen's Cathedral

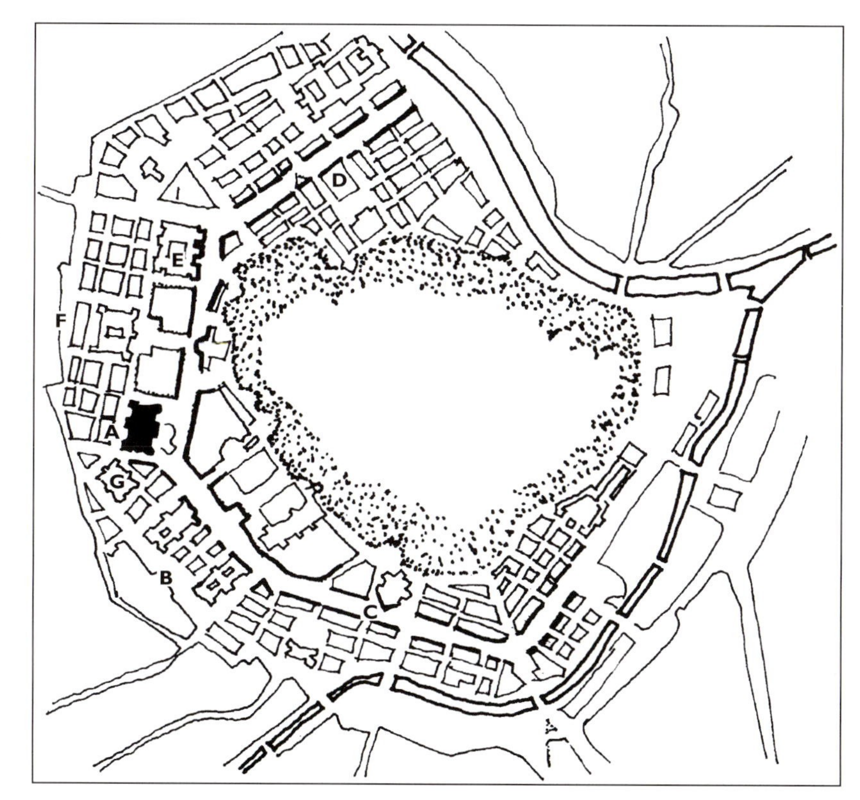

***(below)* New institutions built along the Ringstrasse include many features thought necessary for a modern liberal capital.**

A Parliament
B Museums
C State Opera
D Bourse
E University
F New town hall
G Palace of Justice

but also to a great assortment of cultural institutions. Not only was there a new portion added to the Hofburg Palace, a new Parliament building, and a new Justice Palace, there was also, among other buildings, a new university, theater, city hall, opera house, a pair of sizable museums, and many palatial apartment complexes for the new elite. Though fin de siècle Vienna was hardly a harbinger of democracy, the large-scale construction of buildings for civic and cultural institutions provides an index of those buildings thought necessary for a modern liberal capital.

Although Vienna's Ring renders it formally atypical of other capitals, it does exemplify the political changes that underlie the development of the modern liberal capital. It suggests that the institutions of democratic government have common origins with other bourgeois institutions and that it is possible to construct a new capitol sector within the boundaries of an existing capital. In Vienna, as in London and Paris, the political institutions of the capitol are set out as coequal with public institutions housing nongovernmental functions. In contrast to most modern capitals that came after it, in Vienna the institutions marking democratic government receive no special emphasis in the larger urban design. The new institutions are architecturally treated more or less equally, each subordinate to the horizontal movement of the boulevard itself—and all still less prominent than the mass of the Hofburg Palace or the spire of St. Stephen's. Vienna may serve as a reminder that the conversion of capital cities into centers of national culture and politics depends upon the existence of a growing middle class to staff and frequent the new institutions. All too often in new capitals the visibility of the architecture precedes the viability of the institutions it houses.

Berlin

An especially complex set of historical and political issues has influenced the urban form and symbolism of Berlin, raising questions that require a bit more elaboration than I have given for London, Paris, and Vienna. Even before serving as the capital of the Kingdom of Prussia, Berlin had existed for five hundred years. After 1871, it was successively the capital of the Second Reich, of the Weimar Republic, of Hitler's Third Reich, and, after World War Two, of East Germany. At the beginning of the 1990s, the status of Berlin shifted yet again, this time toward renewal as the capital of a reunited Germany. At each stage of Berlin's development, the ruling regime has imprinted signs of its power on the architecture and urban design of the city, though the most megalomaniacal dreams of Hitler and Speer for a monumental new Berlin were never constructed.

The growth of the twin towns of Berlin and Kölln (united as Berlin in 1709) began in the thirteenth century on an island in the River Spree, a strategic site for east–west trade. By the middle of the fifteenth century, this island site was marked by a well-fortified castle, and its significance as a center of rule continued to increase. That centrality was progressively reinforced by the construction of axial roads focused on the Palace, most notably Unter den Linden, the grand tree-lined way that was begun in the mid-seventeenth century. Intended as a military parade route, this ceremonial way demonstrated the power of the ruling soldier princes and the rise of the state.[31] With the extension of this major royal axis, its functions began to expand as well. Gradually in the nineteenth century, the avenue became lined with buildings that served a growing middle-class culture: an opera house, a university, the State Library, the Academy of Fine Arts, and on the island itself, the famous Altes Museum, designed by Karl Friedrich von Schinkel, Friedrich Wilhelm III's state architect. In this way, as with Vienna's Ringstrasse, the later nineteenth-century developments along Unter den Linden and other commercial and residential avenues helped Berlin surpass its status as a royal seat and strive toward that of a full-service capital.[32]

The tempestuous saga of united Germany's rises and falls between 1871 and 1945 changed the urban fabric of Berlin at every turn. I have chosen to look only at the beginning and the end of this period, ignoring the six decades in the middle that brought about both the continued rise of a capitalist bourgeoisie and the ascension to government of authoritarian and imperialist leaders that led to two world wars.

Bismarck, in making Prussian Berlin the capital of the imperial union of German states, could simply add his government's own mark as an extension to the existing city. The result was a new node of government buildings around the Königsplatz at the edge of the old city at the west end of the historic royal axis of Unter den Linden. The Reichstag, as the new National Parliament, was given ornate headquarters but far less elaborate powers; it was the most visible result of a constitution that served to "create the institutions for a national state . . . without, however, sacrificing, or even limiting, the aristocratic-monarchical order of the pre-national period."[33]

Hitler's grandiose plans for a new monumental Berlin envisioned a reshaping of the capital's center almost as dramatic as that caused by the destruction of the war, though in exactly the opposite extreme (1.10, 1.11). Albert Speer's Berlin Plan, which provided a massive cross-axial ensemble of enormous buildings (some of which were sketched by Hitler himself), attempted not only to outdo the urban axes of power of earlier German rulers but to outscale every effort at architecture and urban design that the world had ever known. Speer termed its north–south axis "a Berlin Champs Élysées two and a half times the length of the original." This was to culminate in a Great Hall capable of accommodating a standing audience of 150,000 to 180,000 to listen to Hitler. Speer described it as "essentially a place of worship" and wished that "over the course of centuries, by traditions and venerability, it would acquire an importance similar to that St. Peter's in Rome has for Catholic Christendom"; he noted elsewhere that the volume of St. Peter's would fit inside his own grand dome sixteen times over. On one side of the square fronting the Great Hall, Speer sited Hitler's multimillion-square-foot palace in which diplomats would have to hike half a mile in order to meet with the Führer. The proposed palace was no less than 150 times as large as the chancellor's residence in Bismarck's day. This monstrous display of power was also intended to overwhelm the dimensions of the Chancellery Speer had built for Hitler in 1937, which itself required visitors to Hitler's

1.10 ***(left)*** **Hitler's Berlin: model of the north–south axis.**

1.11 ***(right)*** **Hitler's Berlin: model of capitol complex.**

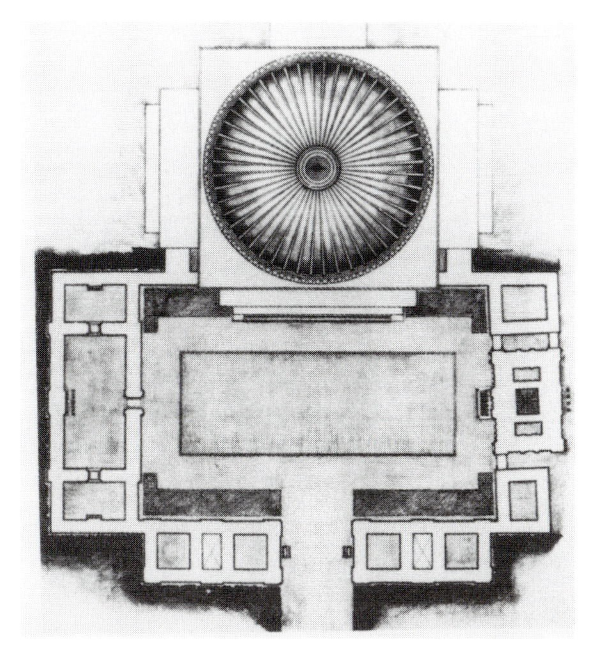

office to traverse a gallery "twice as long as the Hall of Mirrors at Versailles." Curiously, the building opposite Hitler's palace in this gargantuan capitol complex was to be the old Reichstag, though Speer assures us that it was included by "mere chance" and "in no way signified that Hitler meant the German parliament to play an important part in the exercise of power."[34]

The official and semiofficial German press viewed these schemes as another aspect of the party's revival of past German greatness. Masking substantial changes in national policy with rhetorical emphasis on stability and continuity, these documents "describe Hitler as building on the accomplishments of the Prussian monarchs, even fulfilling their greatest dreams for Berlin."[35] In the end, however, the Nazi plans for Berlin envisaged nothing short of a preposterous shrine to power and nationalism, "a second, self-absorbed city which made nonsense of prevailing traffic patterns, severing vital links and imposing new demands largely left unmet. Speer's design is little more than a display piece, a massive political stage set."[36] Fortunately, little of the plan was ever realized, and only a small portion of the east–west axis has survived.

When Berlin was divided into zones of Allied occupation following World War Two, the eastern part became designated as the capital of socialist East Germany, while the rest was developed as an urban island of the West. With West Germany's national government housed in Bonn, the status of West Berlin as a city suffered from the loss of national administration, as its role shifted from capital to merely capitalist. Divergent patterns of development on the two sides of the Berlin Wall during the next four decades highlighted different economic priorities by giving them architectural form, as West Berlin developed a typical capitalist central business district, while East Berlin's planners gave urban dominance to noncommercial facilities.[37] Unlike their eastern counterparts, West Berlin's planners consistently worked on

1.12 View past the Federal Chancellery toward the new domed Reichstag, 2005.

the assumption of eventual political and urban reunification, attempting to site major developments in ways which would be viable following a merger of the two urban centers.

Of the few government buildings of Berlin that had survived the war (and outlasted subsequent destruction aimed at exorcising reminders of the Nazi past), most were located in the eastern sector, which held the historic heart of the capital. The western sectors did gain the Reichstag building, isolated next to the wall between 1961 and 1990. Prior to German unification, the building was expensively restored in the hope that it could be used for periodic sessions of West Germany's Parliament, but when this intention proved too controversial the Reichstag became a museum of German political history. Following reunification, however, the Reichstag, dramatically reconfigured by Norman Foster, again plays an important part in this history, after decades of spatial and institutional marginalization. With the glass-topped Reichstag now joined by a "Federal Ribbon" of buildings including the Federal Chancellery (located on the Spreebogen site once designated for Hitler's gigantic Great Hall), twenty-first-century Berlin boasts a new capitol complex for a renewed pan-German democracy (1.12, 1.13).

In the former East Berlin, by contrast, urban design continues to be contested. In 1976, the East Germans erected the Palast der Republik to house the Volkskammer (people's chamber) on the site of the Berlin Palace and Lustgarten, the center of rule since the mid-fifteenth century (1.14). Located on a newly created government square known as Marx-Engels-Platz, the building included not only a parliament chamber but also an entertainment center. Although some experts felt that the venerable

1.13 Norman Foster's glass cupola allows visitors to ascend above the German parliament.

1.14 Berlin's center: from the Royal Palace to the Communist Parliament to . . .?

Some of the most important public buildings of postwar East Germany occupied the island in the Spree which used to be dominated by the Berlin Palace.

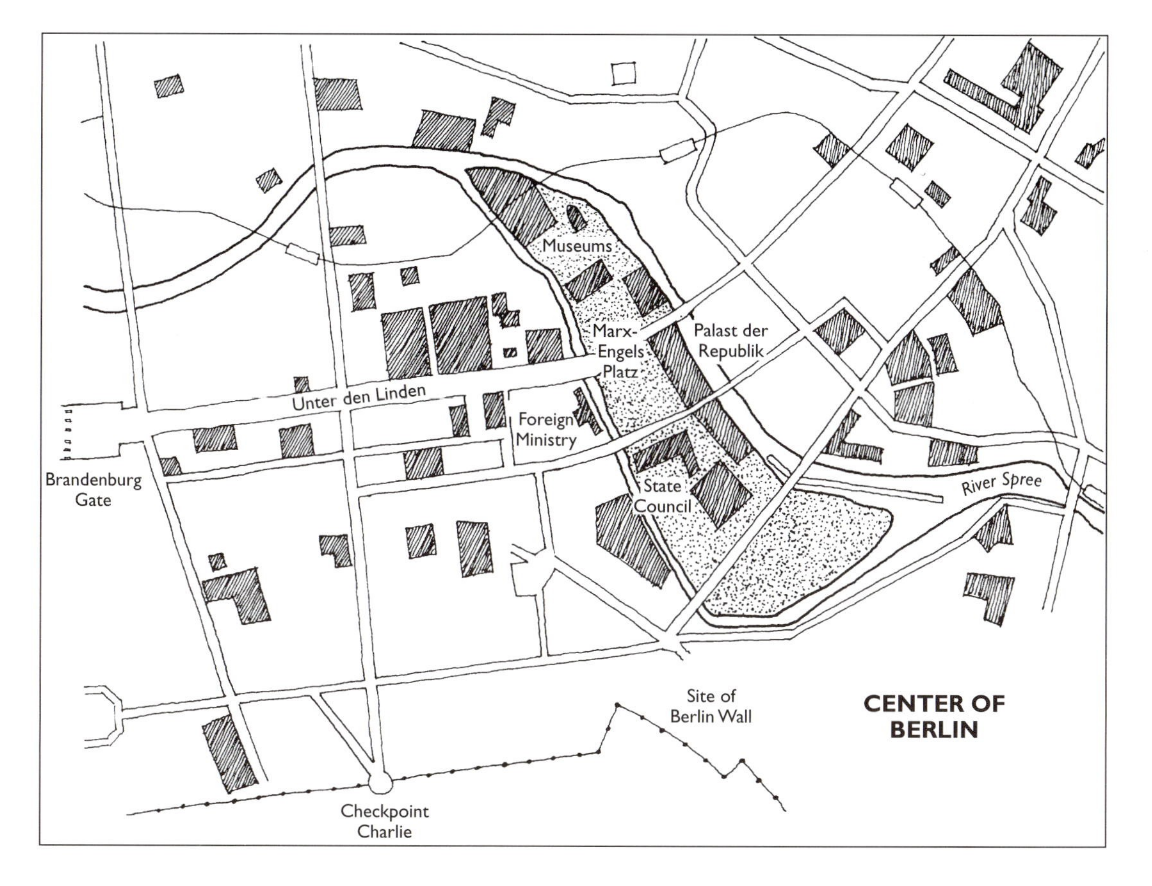

1.15 The waning days of the Palast der Republik, 2005.

"Zweifel" (doubt) seems appropriate commentary on the future of the decaying structure that once housed the East German parliament. The foreground shows archaeological investigation of past palatial glories.

Berlin Palace could have been restored, its destruction in favor of a modernist alternative seems to have been motivated partly by the East German regime's wish to demonstrate a departure from past symbols of oppression and partly by a need to expedite creation of the vast Marx-Engels-Platz for mass demonstrations. Whatever the logic behind this rather extreme capitol intervention, little has turned out as initially intended: the Marx-Engels-Platz soon became devoted to party parking lots rather than party rallies. Moreover, East Germany's parliament was hardly the most significant political institution of its regime. At the time the new home of the Volkskammer was constructed, real power emanated from party buildings located both nearby and in Moscow, a reminder that spatial centrality may connote the trappings of power but does not always mark its wellspring. Then, following reunification, the East German capitol slipped from calculated charade into irritating irrelevance. An abandoned Palast der Republik fell into severe disrepair amidst calls to replace it with a version of the old Palace (1.15).[38] As before, Berlin's planning and symbolism continue to evolve in turbulent and polemical ways.

Evolved capitals renewed: Rome, Moscow, and Athens

Some cities have actually been founded as capitals more than once, at different periods in their growth—Rome, Moscow, and Athens are good examples. Most capitals that have undergone centuries of evolution have, like Berlin, also served as headquarters for a variety of disparate regimes. Often, as in Beijing, new regimes have brought about significant transformations in city form and meaning. Following the People's Revolution of 1949, Mao demonstrated his consolidated power by turning the south-facing wall of the Forbidden City into a city-scaled gallery housing a single portrait—the iconic image of himself, scaled even larger than the massive archway beneath it. Mao also dramatically reconfigured Tiananmen Square itself, turning what had long been a more modest T-shaped palace approach into a vast masonry expanse intended to be able to assemble one million Party faithful.[39]

In an extreme case of an evolved capital renewed, such as Jerusalem, the heritage of successive capitals may stretch back thousands of years. There, as elsewhere, the controversies surrounding a capital's contemporary political status remain tied to interpretations of its earlier history. Some instances of momentous political change have been accompanied by dramatic acts of urban design and development. Architecture and urban planning can play a pivotal role in a city's symbolic renewal, sometimes by the consolidation of an image, sometimes by the polarization of debate. The symbolic recall of earlier golden ages, whether through works of architecture that make use of highly charged precedents or through the reclaiming of hallowed or strategic sites as capitals, has occurred throughout history and remains powerful.

Rome

Rome, designated as the capital of a united Italy only since 1870, is a capital that has undergone extreme variations of stature and influence. The Rome that was a capital of an ancient empire, the Rome that served as the seat of Renaissance papal power, and the Rome that is capital of a modern Italian state share a lineage that is common but hardly continuous.

Rome's selection in the nineteenth century as a national capital achieved many purposes simultaneously. Intended as a direct recall of earlier glories, the choice was also an attempt to find a compromise site acceptable to factions from both the north and south. As Toynbee comments, "It would have been difficult for the Italians to make a choice among this host of possible claimants to serve as the capital of a united Italy if one of them had not possessed a prestige that incontestably outshone the prestige of all the rest. The choice was bound to fall on Rome; yet, on every count except prestige, Rome was a still less suitable choice for the capital of modern Italy than Turin would have been."[40] In addition to the issue of prestige, however, the selection of Rome served directly as a form of national secular occupation of the papal center at a time when victory over the papacy was of preeminent concern.

Whatever its causes, the choice of Rome as national capital precipitated many changes in the city. The influx of persons needed to staff the government constituted only a small part of those attracted by the promise of employment opportunities in the new capital. In its first thirty years as Italy's capital, Rome's population doubled, reaching a half million. This increase brought new housing facilities, new institutional buildings, and a new infrastructure of roads and public services. Beyond all this, there was the need to build and develop a national image, what the architectural historian Spiro Kostof has termed "the iconography of unity."[41] Symbols of the Third Rome abound, many of them making conscious reference, whether literal or metaphorical, to the iconography of earlier Roman glories, even as some of those same glories were destroyed to make way for the new structures.

Rome's multiplicity of historical roles retains many prominent urban

1.16 Rome's Via della Conciliazione: urban rapprochement of church and state.

traces, both physical and symbolic. To many visitors, contemporary Rome still looks more like the capital of Catholicism than the capital of a modern secular state. It is the dome of St. Peter's and its carefully wrought centrality within the larger composition of Vatican structures that mark this place, even more than the citadels of the ancients, as the model for subsequent attempts to design a capitol complex. The Via della Conciliazione, carved out to commemorate the rapprochement of church and state following the Lateran Treaty of 1929, provides an axial approach to St. Peter's that extends the urban design presence of the Vatican complex toward other prominent parts of the city (1.16). In other ways, however, the shifting spatial relationship between the church and state may be better characterized by replacement than by rapprochement; the former papal summer residence in the Palazzo del Quirinale served as the royal palace from 1870 to 1947 and subsequently has been designated the official residence of the Italian president. By contrast, the central institutions of contemporary Italian government are housed much less pretentiously in urban palazzi marked by flags and guards, but otherwise urbanistically indistinguishable from other institutions in downtown Rome.

The ancient Capitoline Hill, redeveloped as the symbolic center of Roman government following the sixteenth-century design of Michelangelo's Campidoglio, constitutes yet another node of power in this most polycentric of cities. This place has undergone a succession of transformations of appearance and meaning. The hill that once featured a temple towering over the Roman forum and reached by flights of recently reconstructed steps has for the last eight centuries had its buildings oriented in the opposite direction, facing away from their ancient context. Michelangelo's re-planning of the Capitol accepted this basic orientation for the Senate building as the communal center for Christian Rome but also recalled the sacred meaning of the place as the *caput mundi*. In more recent decades, even as it has retained its central role in communal government, the Campidoglio's civic presence has been sorely undermined by the King Victor Emmanuel II Monument, a looming pile of nationalism that cuts harshly into Capitoline Hill's northern flanks. Though this placement may have been intended to signify an alternative authority to papal rule and even, through symbolic fusion, a kind of alliance with the periodic populist rule associated with the Capitoline's communal government, the juxtaposition was not wholly auspicious. Braunfels has commented that the commission and siting of this gigantic national monument served to "conceal the limitations of the state" and to make clear "the limitations and the utopian, fatalistic nature of this sacred hill. The two together are documents which, with the greatest precision, illustrate and interpret political situations and weigh their power."[42] As if competition from the Vittoriano monument were not insult enough, the insensate swath of a Mussolini-era boulevard at the base of the hill soon rendered the Campidoglio even more of an urbanistic orphan. Afflicted with a carbuncle more monstrous than anything threatening princely London, the urban context of the *caput mundi* has been almost unrecognizably defaced by the symbols of political megalomania and the perceived demands of modern traffic circulation (1.17, 1.18).

Even before the rise of Mussolini, then, there were attempts to fashion a national Italian identity through the glorification of the statesmen and soldiers of the Risorgimento. Yet these served as merely a preamble to the full range of Fascist symbol-mongering. Mussolini's heavy hand is visible in many of the Third Rome's urban design projects, which aimed not only to advance Italian nationalism but to do so by associating Fascist rule with the imperial triumphs of the past. In a speech made in 1925, Il Duce made his views clear: "In five years Rome must appear marvelous to all the people

1.17 The rear of the Campidoglio overlooks the Forum, as the Victor Emmanuel Monument looms behind.

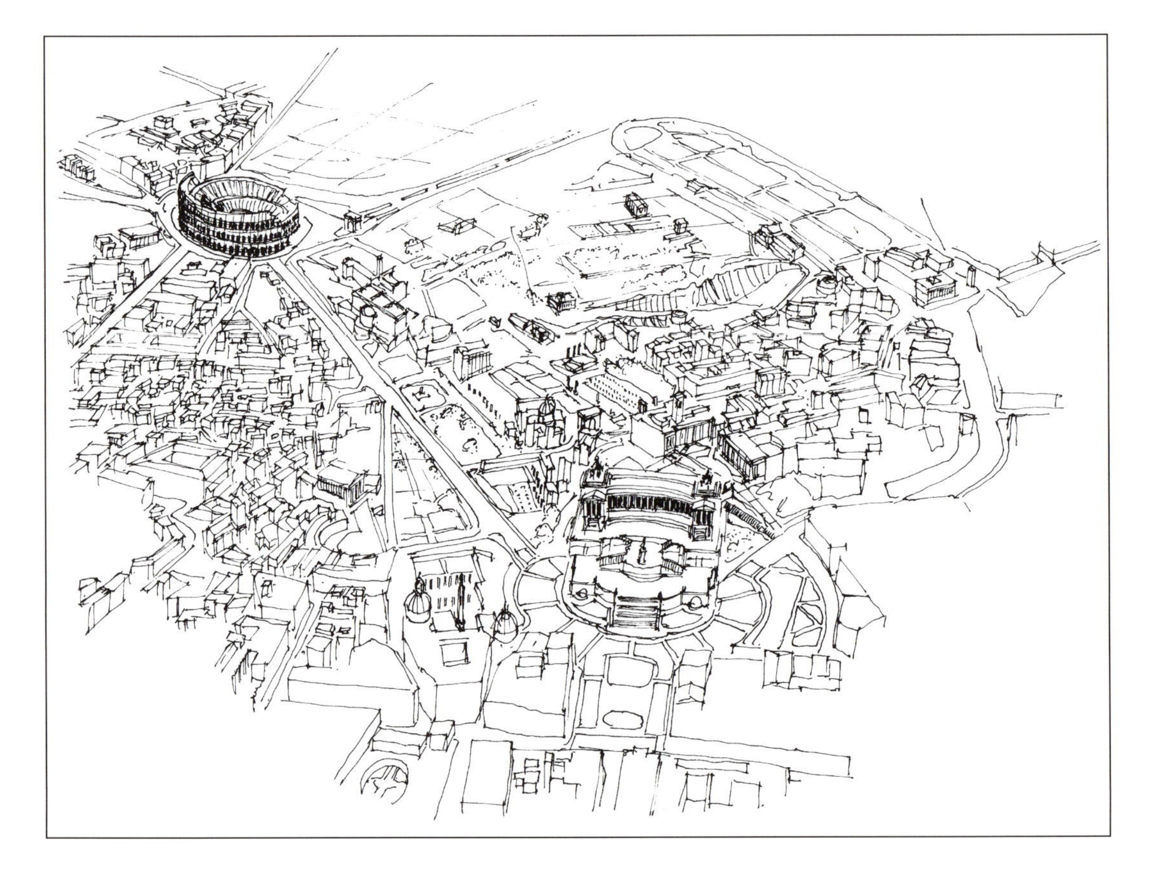

1.18 The Victor Emmanuel Monument overwhelming the Campidoglio.

of the world: vast, ordered, powerful as it was in the time of the first emperor Augustus."[43] In a succession of Haussmannesque interventions, Mussolini's planners and designers cut through a series of straight-line avenues linking favored monuments. Perhaps the most invasive of these was the Via dell'Impero, which destroyed 5,500 units of housing to expose the ruins of the imperial fora (a good portion of which were then buried under the roadway). Designed as a traffic link between two monumental urban presences, the ancient Colosseum and the Piazza Venezia, site of Mussolini's office and of the Victor Emmanuel Monument, the avenue was supposed to signify a continuum of power culminating in Fascism (1.19). Like Hitler, Mussolini wanted to outdo his imperial predecessors on their own terms. In 1934, he sponsored a design competition for a new and imposing twelve-hundred-room national Fascist party headquarters, to be located at the midpoint of this avenue, directly opposite the ruins of the Basilica of Maxentius. Like his old office in the fifteenth-century Palazzo di Venezia, this new central symbol of Fascist rule would need to have a high balcony from which the leader could address the assembled faithful, a conscious emulation of the pope's balcony outside St. Peter's. Though the plan for the new national party headquarters was not executed, the proposal is indicative of Mussolini's obsession that architecture and urbanism be under his political tutelage.

Mussolini's most overtly Augustan ambition came to pass in the mid-1930s with the construction of Piazzale Augusto Imperatore around the excavated remains of that Roman emperor's mausoleum, in bimillennial commemoration of his birth. While the idea of using a hall in the mausoleum's center for Fascist rallies was not carried out, the square surrounding the "liberated" structure was flanked on two sides by new buildings for the National Fascist Institute of Social Insurance, which featured friezes showing explicit iconographic comparisons between the powers of ancient and Fascist Rome.

1.19 Via dell'Impero: an avenue to link empires. Mussolini's avenue connects the Piazza Venezia (in front of the Victor Emmanuel Monument) with the Colosseum, cutting through the Imperial Fora.

The last major gesture of Mussolini's urbanism took the form of plans for something much like a new capitol complex, initially planned as the site of a forum to be held in 1942 to celebrate the achievements of Fascism. The event was known as the Esposizione Universale di Roma (EUR). Mussolini's architectural ambitions here were no less grandiose than the ideas that prompted them. Under the guise of a universal exposition, he sought a way to demonstrate that twenty-seven centuries of Roman and Italian culture had made superior contributions to human knowledge. Timing the exposition to coincide with the twentieth year of Fascist rule, Mussolini desired a global theater with a monumental stage from which to extol his regime's accomplishments. Like the rest of his urban interventions, this one aimed to emulate and surpass the physical achievements of his ancient predecessors. As he put it, EUR was "above all an act of faith in the destiny and constructive capacity of the Italian Nation, a solemn affirmation of its will to act."[44] Part of that destiny was to include the onward march of Rome to the sea, with EUR as a midpoint on a new Via Imperiale linking the ritual center of Piazza Venezia with the ancient port of Ostia.

Though the exposition was never held, the grand cross-axial scheme

1.20 EUR: the Square Colosseum.

for this alternative urban core did experience considerable growth after the Second World War. With its wide, tree-lined avenues and substantial buildings housing government ministries, a congress hall, numerous museums, and corporations, EUR is yet another symbolic node of political power in the Italian capital. Planned with clear reference to the imperial fora by Marcello Piacentini, Mussolini's favorite architect, the austere marble of much of the architecture, such as the arched cube of the Palazzo della Civiltà Italiana (later called the Palace of Labor and popularly known as the square Colosseum), was also intended to evoke earlier Roman buildings (1.20). Since 1960, by contrast, the main axis of EUR has culminated in the famous Palazzo dello Sport, designed by Pier Luigi Nervi and the ubiquitous Piacentini for the Olympics. And so, the complex layers of Roman architectural symbolism continue their accretion. EUR, with its urban references to the history of Roman civilization, to the ambitions of Fascist rule, and to the pageantry of international athletic competition, is, like the rest of the Italian capital, undergoing perpetual symbolic renewal and transformation.

Moscow

The tale of the glory and decline of Moscow is not quite so well rooted in ancient history as that of Rome but is at least as tumultuous, featuring more than eight centuries of sieges, invasions, and cataclysmic fires.[45] The development of its capitol complex, the Kremlin, was influenced not only by tsarist patronage but also by tsarist rejection and tsarist overthrow. Peter the Great's angry exodus from Moscow, commencing in 1712, to found

St. Petersburg on the swampy northwestern frontier of his empire was the move of a monarch and his court. Two hundred years later, when the capital was shifted back to Moscow, the move was of an entirely different order: it was that of a revolutionary government and its attendant bureaucracy to reclaim the historical heartland, at a time when Petrograd (as it was then known) was thought vulnerable to attack.[46] Pre-eighteenth-century Moscow was the undisputed capital of Russia and the center of the Russian Orthodox church; postrevolutionary Moscow was expected to be the capital of the USSR. The return to the Kremlin (the term is derived from *kreml*, meaning "citadel" or "high town")[47] afforded architectural proof of political authority, useful initially for consolidating Bolshevik control and subsequently as a symbol of Communist party rule over the distant and disparate array of non-Russian Soviet republics.

Designed concentrically around the Kremlin, Moscow epitomizes the power of a capitol to dominate a capital (1.21). Significantly, the evolving urban plan of St. Petersburg, Moscow's chief rival for capital status, had also featured a politically centralized design. Even in the new city of rational planning, "a city of science and exactitude rather than the medieval jumble of leaning buildings, narrow lanes, dirt and ignorance that was Moscow," the ancient need to draw special spatial attention to a secure center could not be denied. Thus, St. Petersburg's three major radial avenues converged upon the Admiralty Complex, opposite the Peter and Paul fortress and adjacent

1.21 Plan of Moscow in the seventeenth century, showing concentric growth out from the Kremlin.

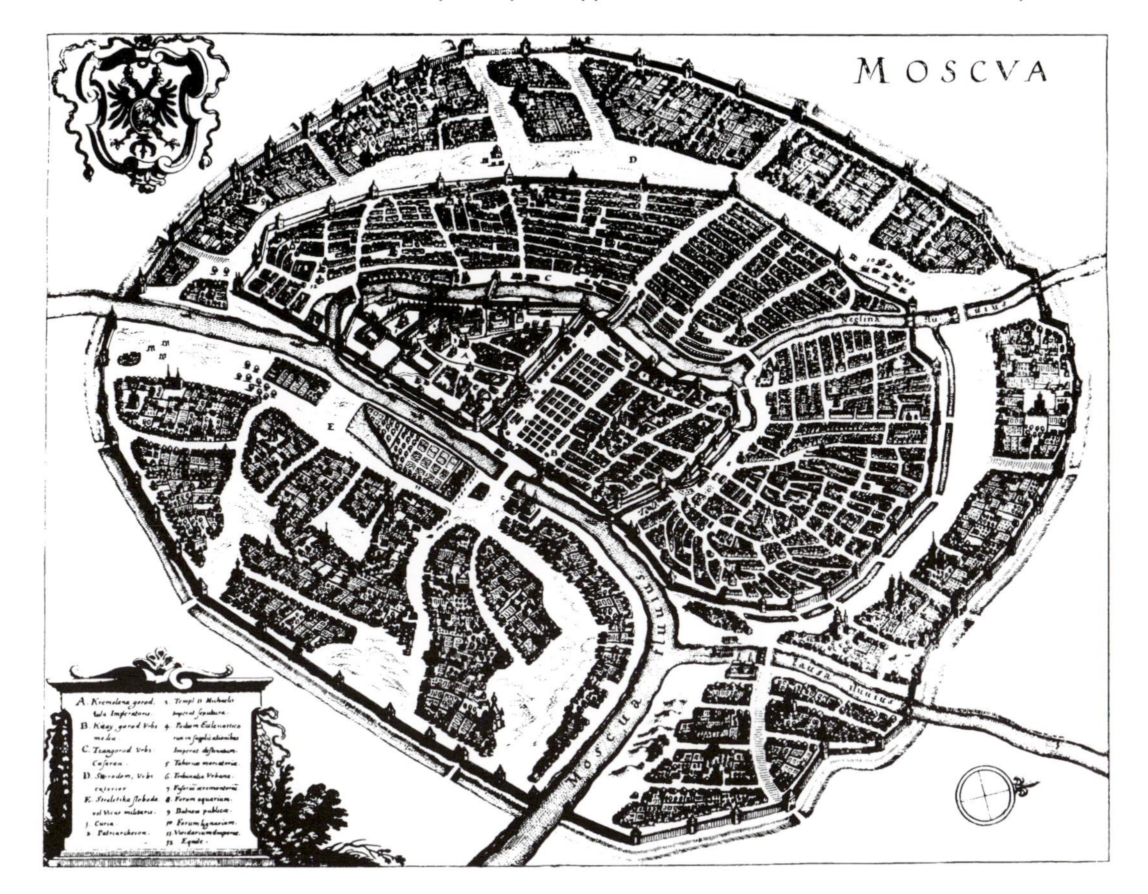

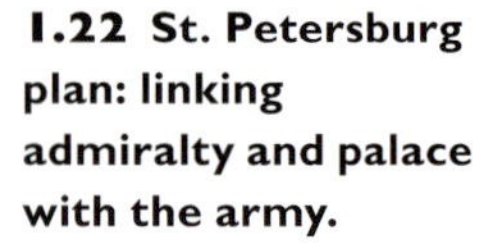

1.22 St. Petersburg plan: linking admiralty and palace with the army.

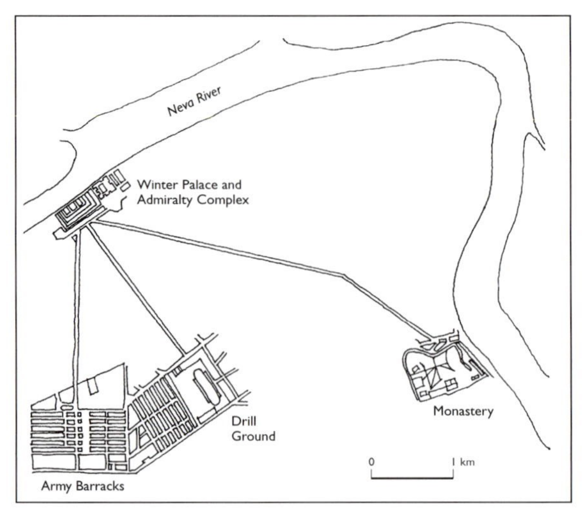

to the Winter Palace, seat of the autocracy. These same three radials led outward to the army barracks, the drill ground, and the Aleksandro-Nevskiy Monastery, thereby connecting the center of power with the means of its enforcement and its spiritual roots (1.22).[48]

Following the return to Moscow in March 1918, the Bolshevik leadership gained an even more reassuring spatial hierarchy (1.23). Though Leon Trotsky maintained that there was "great, almost universal" opposition to this move, it took place rapidly. Trotsky criticized the choice of the Kremlin with its forest of cathedral spires as a "paradoxical place to establish a stronghold of the revolutionary dictatorship" and found the "close daily contact between the two historic poles" in the Kremlin to be both "astonishing and amusing."[49] Nonetheless, with the bells in the Saviour's Tower adjusted to play the first

1.23 After the October Revolution: cathedrals and Communists within the Kremlin walls. The drawing shows the political institutions as of 1990, before the breakup of the USSR.

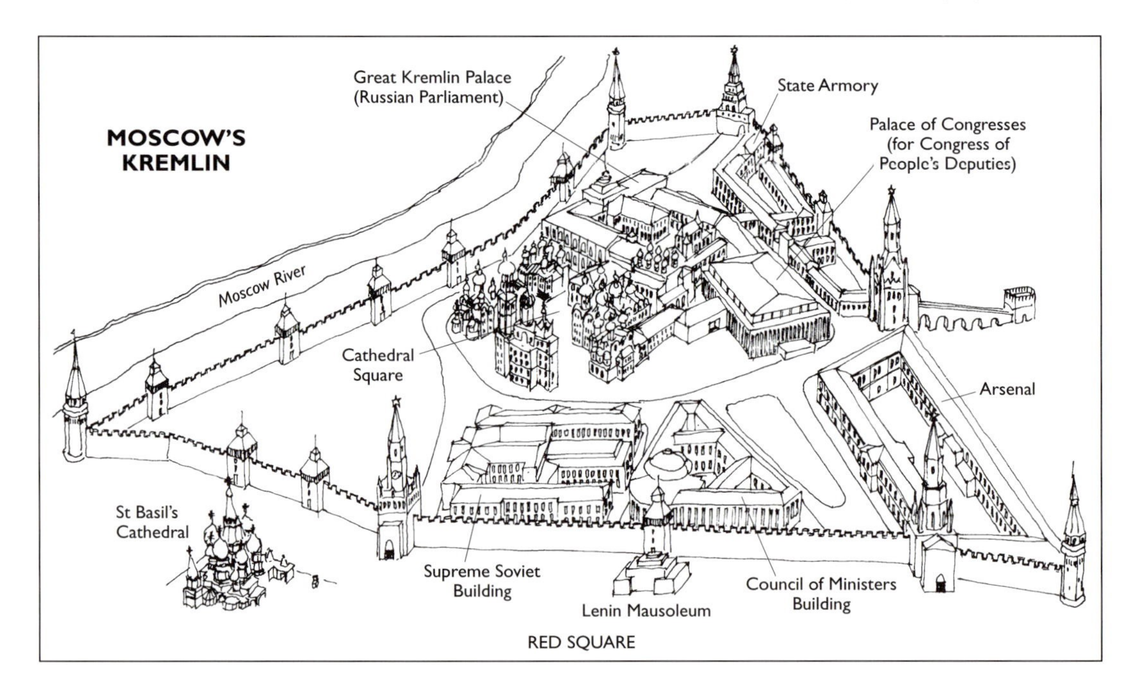

bars of the "Internationale" instead of "God Preserve the Tsar," Communist party occupation of the Kremlin continued. The immediate consequence of the Bolshevik occupation was that the whole Kremlin complex, which before the revolution had been a free museum, was closed to the general public in 1918, not to be reopened until 1955.[50] Its monasteries and cathedrals ceased to function as religious institutions, the red banner of the revolution flew over the buildings, and Lenin announced his Plan of Monumental Propaganda. By the 1930s, red stars were fixed atop the spires of the Kremlin's gatetowers, and Red Square (which was initially created in the fifteenth century as a firebreak in front of the Kremlin's walls and, after centuries of encroachments and redesigns, served as the location of nineteenth-century Moscow's main market)[51] became the site of massive military parades. It was reported that Stalin even planned to tear down the celebrated St. Basil's Cathedral because its placement at one side of the square disrupted the flow of troops. He was deterred, the story goes, only when a famous architect threatened to slit his throat on the cathedral's steps.[52]

As in Hitler's Berlin, the Stalin era's most grandiose proposals for urban transformation were not executed. Designs for the Palace of Industry and the Palace of the Soviets promised enormous buildings which would flank the Kremlin and challenge it for symbolic dominance. Intended for erection just downriver from the Kremlin on a 110,000-square-meter site cleared of two churches, the projected Palace of the Soviets was to be nothing less than the largest building in the world. In the design's final version of 1937, following the gradual intrusion of Soviet officialdom into a protracted design competition, two immense halls (with enough space to seat 20,000 and 8,000 persons), offices, and restaurants were contained in a massive stepped pedestal surmounted by a 75-meter-high statue of Lenin, his arm raised in a gesture curiously reminiscent of the Statue of Liberty (1.24). The height

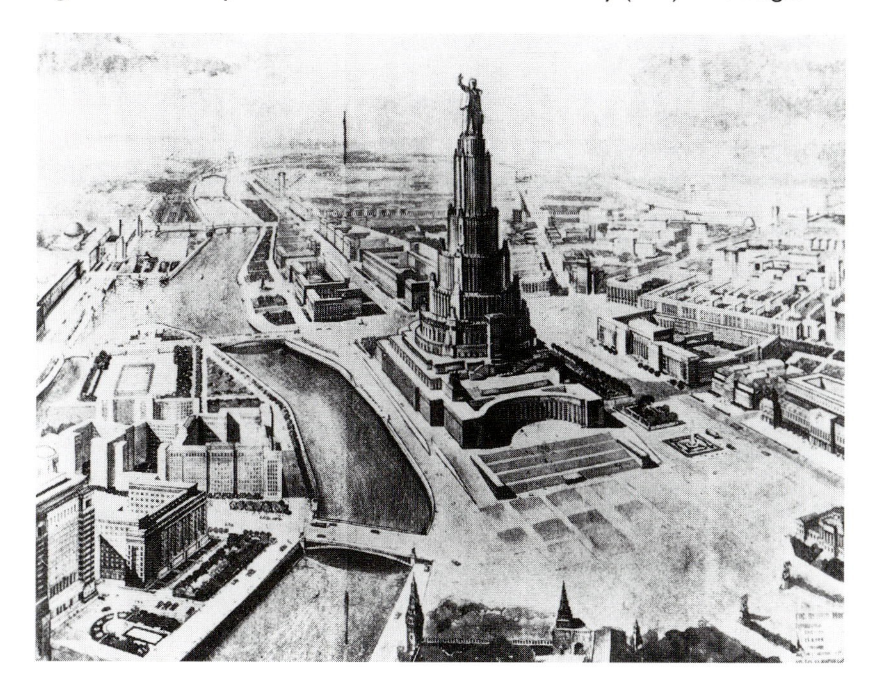

1.24 Proposed Palace of the Soviets: designed to outflank the Kremlin, shown at bottom of drawing.

of this tower of government managed to outstrip even capitalism's recent best effort, the Empire State Building, with which it was proudly compared. In any event, neither this structure nor the Palace of Industry, which was intended to sprawl from Red Square to the Moscow River, was ever finished. The poor soils of the riverbank site for the Palace of the Soviets threatened the foundations, and the huge steel superstructure was dismantled during the 1940s for use in the war effort. Eventually, in 1960, the foundations were reused for a massive municipal swimming pool, and a less immense Palace of Congresses was completed within the Kremlin complex itself.[53]

With the government's vital centers of decision making gathered within the walls, this fortress remained both the symbol and the synonym for Soviet authority. Apparently not even this satisfied Stalin. Beginning in the 1930s, he authorized construction of deep tunnels under the Kremlin, including a secret passage leading to a private station of the Moscow Metro, theoretically enabling the entire Politburo to evacuate Moscow secretly in fifteen minutes.[54] Such was the concentration of both power and paranoia. Even though the buildings for ministries and other government departments were scattered throughout the inner city, the Kremlin's metonymous image of totally centralized command long remained dominant. While many parts of the Kremlin are, at the time of this writing, open to visitation by the public at most times of the year, ceremonial public gatherings are kept outside and beneath the citadel's walls. For many decades, the Lenin Mausoleum in Red Square was probably the only Moscow government building readily identifiable to foreigners, who marveled at its long lines of pilgrims and its goose-stepping guards. In this snapshot view of Soviet political space, the Kremlin appeared as an insurmountable barrier of crenellated brick and distant spires, a generic expression of power lacking any evidence of human presence (1.25). Slowly, the combination of late-1980s glasnost and television

1.25 Lenin Mausoleum and Kremlin, as seen from Red Square in the 1980s.

began to yield more penetrating views of government activities within the Kremlin's buildings and elsewhere in Moscow.

Nearly three-quarters of a century after the government's return to the seeming impregnability of Moscow's Kremlin, however, the symbolism of this capitol complex shifted yet again. In 1991, as USSR leaders lost control over diverse and disaffected constituent republics, public open spaces in Moscow became transformed from rallygrounds for the party faithful into places of protest and Russian nationalist fervor. At the center of resistance to the failed coup of August 1991, the Russian Federation's Parliament building (known as the White House), located on the newly dubbed Square of Free Russia, challenged the Kremlin and Red Square for symbolic supremacy. In the symbolic landscape of post-Soviet Russia, the White House now houses the Russian government, the Parliament (Duma) is located in another nearby building, and the residence of the Russian president remains within the Kremlin itself. Once again in Moscow, architecture, power, and national identity have been conjoined in new ways.

Athens

No less intermittent in its glories than Moscow and the Eternal City is Athens, which, although resplendent in the age of Pericles, subsequently suffered through two millennia of repeated acts of warfare, invasion, and occupation. Like Rome and Moscow, Athens is the capital of a modern nation-state as a result of a relatively recent act of will inspired by the presence of the past. When Greece gained independence from the Ottoman Turks, establishing Athens as the new capital of its kingdom in 1833, there was almost no Athens left to so designate. In 1827, the Greek population of the city, who constituted 90 percent of the city's denizens, had to take sanctuary on the nearby island of Salamis; in 1831, the physical inventory of Athens consisted of "150 destroyed houses . . . 125 churches and very few public buildings." As an observer reported in 1835, "Athens, which before the War of Independence had three thousand houses, now has not even three hundred. The rest turned into shapeless piles of building materials. Most of them still remain like this."[55]

Under such conditions the choice of Athens as a capital was hardly inevitable. During the preceding fifty years the city had lost whatever regional role it had held in the Ottoman Empire and had experienced a decrease in population and the removal of administrative and educational institutions. As its roads declined, its isolation increased. From the beginning of the Greek Revolution in 1821, all major meetings and provisional governments were held elsewhere, and modern Greece's first capital was established at Nafplion in the Peloponnese, one of the few cities which had escaped wartime destruction and which featured buildings suitable for the temporary housing of a monarch, his court, and his army. Nafplion, however, had been a hotbed of internecine discord during the revolution and remained as such after independence. Leaders from many parts of Greece soon pressed for alternative capital sites. Peloponnesians, who had led the independence struggle, favored nearby Argos, Trípoli, home of the revolutionary leader Kolokotrónis, or Corinth, fortified and at the center of the new state. Others lobbied for Mégara in Attica and for the Aegean island of Syros, at the time a major commercial port. Still others argued that the only appropriate capital for Greece could be Constantinople, and that any new capital should be seen as temporary. Athens does not seem to have been among the sites initially considered.[56] In the end, the selection of Athens is perhaps best explained as an outcome of the romantic, neoclassical dreams of King Ludwig I of Bavaria and his son Otto, independent Greece's first monarch.

King Otto, like many of the world's rulers before him and since, treated the selection of a new capital as an executive decision, taken in collaboration with his viceroyalty. Sensitive to the internal rivalries that would inevitably plague the new state, the king and his advisers regarded the proposed new capital alternatives as tainted by "barren localist" considerations. As Eleni Bastéa observes in *The Creation of Modern Athens*, "The unified Greek nation, with one language, one culture, one religion, and a common historical consciousness was created after the War of Independence by the first governments . . .. It was primarily the Greek state, after 1833, that 'made the Greeks.'" One of King Otto's many complex cultural tasks was to help modern Greece "build a coherent national culture that was shared by its citizens." Moreover, as a monarch imported from Bavaria in an age when European royalty were "supplied from an interrelated set of families whose personal nationality (if they felt themselves to have one) was entirely irrelevant to their function as heads of state,"[57] the new king was interested not solely in issues of contemporary Greek protonationalism but, like his Germanic compatriots, in a broader revival of ancient classical civilization. One aspect of this interest was an international Greek Revival in architecture, spurred by a spate of archaeological expeditions and publications. Judging by the account that Ludwig von Maurer, a member of the viceroyalty, gave in 1835, Otto was willing to consider Corinth not because of its commercial, military, and strategic advantages, but because of its ancient ruins and historic vistas. Only if these last features are taken as the primary criteria for selection of a new capital does the ultimate choice of Athens become obvious. Extolling the Athenian litany of "memories" relating to classical civilization, von Maurer concluded with a rhetorical question: "Which king could choose another place for the headquarters of its government? At the moment, he had in his hands the intellectual spring of the world."[58]

Otto may well have also had in his hands a completed master plan for the development of Athens as the new capital of Greece, based on an unsolicited document prepared in 1832, when this notion carried little official support. In an explanatory memorandum sent to the royal headquarters in Nafplion, the master plan's architects, Stamatios Kleanthes and Eduard Schaubert, both educated in Berlin under Schinkel, confidently articulated the logic of their proposal: "Love for the cradle of the arts and sciences, Athens, and the absence of a good plan for it, which is noticeable to all visitors, prompted us . . . to make an exact map of the city and the nearby suburbs." Kleanthes and Schaubert expected that "the learned world of Europe would take an interest in this work," and also "believed that the government might later use our survey as a useful preliminary plan for the reconstruction of Athens out of its ruins, whether or not this city should be designated as the future capital of Greece." Then, casting aside doubt about the future status of the city, the architects concluded that "we had better foundations following public opinion in Greece and the collective expectation of the Hellenes; thus in our work we imagined Athens to be the future capital of Hellas and the seat of the king."[59] As it turned out, whatever the state of public opinion, the architects did indeed manage to anticipate the opinion of the state. In May of 1832, the provisional Greek government commissioned the youthful architects to design a new Athens, intended to be "equal with the ancient fame and glory of the city and worthy of the century in which we live."[60] When Athens was proclaimed the capital in 1833, King Otto and his regents approved the master plan as part of the same decree.

The neoclassical plan for Athens was as redolent of northern Europe as its client: a system of formal geometries, featuring a grid crosscut with radial streets, focused on freestanding public buildings and open squares. This plan (1.26), which bears formal relation not only to various European royal seats but also to such capitals as Washington, New Delhi, and Canberra, is premised on the exalted centrality of the King's Palace, sited to afford an unobstructed view southward to the Acropolis. The two great symbols of authority, those of ancient culture and modern politics, were in this way to be placed in a deliberate visual dialogue, with all else subordinate. The existing streets of the town were to be eliminated, reconfigured, or regularized to conform with the plan, and ancient names were assigned to them.[61] The plan as a whole revealed a mind-set common to many designers of major urban interventions: that which was new and modern should be treated not as a continuation of the old and indigenous, but as a substitute for it. Only the deep past of ancient Athens interested these architects; a vast zone for archaeological excavation was to be left free of all development. On the other hand, however, Eleni Bastéa astutely points out that Kleanthes and Schaubert also incorporated buildings for a Senate and a House of Representatives as well as several ministries, "even though Greece did not have a parliamentary system at the time." "While the formal design of New Athens may communicate a static vision of a city centered on the king," she concludes, "the diverse program . . . does acknowledge the needs and the sites of a commercial, political, and cultural center. Taken together, the plan and the memorandum for New Athens describe a capital that sits at the cusp of a transition from the monarchical to the bourgeois state."[62]

When a variety of disputes involving land expropriation caused this plan to be revoked after only eight months, a revised version was prepared by the famed Bavarian architect Leo von Klenze. Von Klenze was sent to Athens by King Ludwig, who remained the prime mover behind the plans for the new capital. Von Klenze's more compact plan retained the basic triangulated geometry of the earlier scheme but accepted more of the existing settlement and thereby offended fewer landowners. This scheme allocated the palace a less imperious site in the triangle's west node instead of at the central apex, and proposed to use that northern node to accommodate a

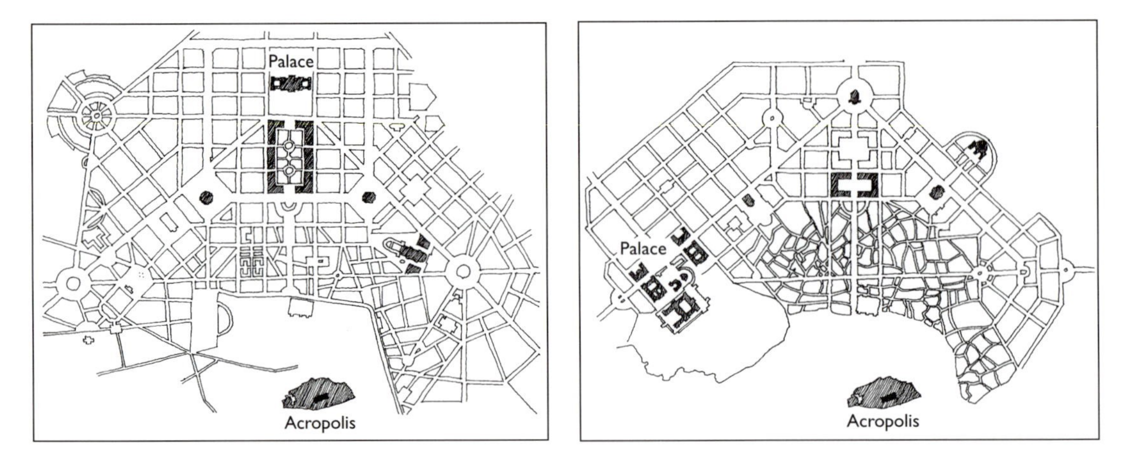

1.26 The Kleanthes and Schaubert plan for Athens. Centered on the palace, all of the urban fabric except the Acropolis is regularized.

1.27 The Von Klenze revision of the plan for Athens. Here, the king is shifted to one side, and there is less disruption of the existing urban fabric.

tall church (1.27). As an alternative to this plan, Schinkel himself proposed an even more extreme articulation of royal power: a design that dared to impose a sprawling new palace across the top of the Acropolis. This plan met with much objection on both practical and symbolic grounds. Following further compromises and alterations by the architect Friedrich von Gärtner, in which, at Ludwig's insistence, the palace was shifted to the east corner node (thought to be a healthier location and, not coincidentally, the point furthest from the existing public bazaar), a version of the original master plan was approved, though never substantially implemented.[63]

As Bastéa's account of the nineteenth-century development of Athens makes clear, big plans for capital cities face many local obstacles, even as royal political power offered "specific and prescriptive" decrees. "Nation-building presupposes the codification and showcasing of the *past*," Bastéa observes. Yet, as the growth of Athens progressed, "it was the unglamourous and needy *present* that primarily concerned everybody and with which the state had to contend. It is the ongoing anxiety about the present, bracketed in a politically and economically unstable framework, that made residents approach the grand designs alternately with awe and irrelevance, desire and irony. While the timeless shadows of Pericles, Pheidias, and the heroes of 1821 continued to be revered and recalled, the cynical press commentary captures the ever-changing, ephemeral nature of the city." Political space, Bastéa shows, is not merely the space of government but also the repository of meaning for residents. As early as 1834, it was clear that the plan for New Athens faced contentions between the nationalist goals of a new Greece and the local demands of established Athenians. "The former required a design that would facilitate settlement and showcase the capital of the new kingdom; the latter concerned the interests of the autochthon and heterochthon Greeks who had bought property in Athens and were going to be affected by any changes in the street pattern." Ultimately, the development of planned Athens proceeded less coercively than Haussmann's Paris, though the lax enforcement of regulations (seen as "negotiable propositions") may have resulted more from bureaucratic weakness than from commendable enlightenment.[64]

The subsequent turbulent history of Athens has been inextricably tied to the fate of the Greek state. Greece has had to overcome protracted conflict between Liberals and Royalists (who favored the Bavarian monarchy and supported the Germans in World War One), wars fought over the Balkans, a massive influx of refugees in the aftermath of Ottoman imperial collapse, destruction and occupation during World War Two, and a Civil War in 1946–1949, all accompanied by dozens of changes of government, which certainly worked against efforts at long-term planning. Only gradually did nineteenth-century Athens become more than an isolated outpost of administrative facilities and educational institutions, and only with difficulty did the Greeks manage to outlast the attempts of foreigners (as well as Greeks in the diaspora) to control their land and culture for the purposes of tourism, economic exploitation, and dewy-eyed aestheticism: colonialist planning influences linger long after independence movements seem to have been consolidated.

In spite of the subsequent century-and-a-half of near-constant political turmoil, basic traces of the early planning ideas seem to have influenced the placement and concentration of national government institutions in Athens. It is not only the government's administrative functions that are still highly centralized; most other national institutions seem to have followed the palace to the eastern side of the city center. The University of Athens, the Greek Academy, the National Library, the National Bank of Greece, the National Historical-Ethnological Museum, and even the National Tourist Office are grouped in an area not much larger than the Acropolis itself and are all within a ten-minute walk of the site allocated in the master plan for the palace (1.28). One Greek commentator, writing in 1960, described this central zone as being enclosed by virtual walls within which "all of Greece

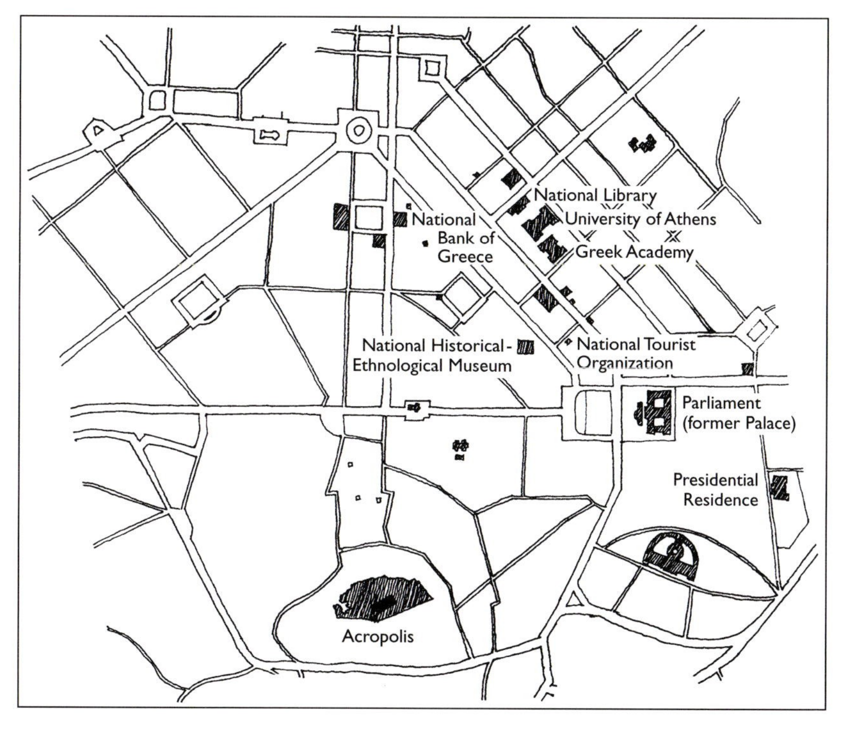

1.28 Contemporary Athens. The palace is transformed into a parliament building, and other significant national institutions are clustered nearby.

is judged and directed. The walls, at first view, are not closed to anybody. People are coming and going from their entries all day. Nevertheless, under the surface, the walls are entirely closed, the gates are impassable, as with the museum doors when the time comes. The 'inside' people live a life of their own, where nobody from 'outside' can penetrate."[65]

However daunting these institutional presences may remain, at least one symbolic shift did occur in the course of the tortuous rise of parliamentary democracy in Greece: the palace was transformed into the headquarters of the Parliament. This act symbolized that transfer of power in the most highly charged location, Síntagma Square, site of long-standing prodemocracy rallies. Though periods of military rule and one-party control suggest that the practice of Greek politics has lagged behind the idealism of its symbols, adaptive reuse of the palace, including the extensive National Gardens behind it, indicates yet again the need for a new regime to express its presence urbanistically. As Bastéa puts it, "In a newly-founded state, where even the notions of 'government,' 'kingdom,' and 'parliament' were novel and continuously redefined, architecture helped anchor them spatially and physically and allowed the Athenian public to begin forming a concrete image of its governing institutions."[66]

Evolutionary breaks: designing a new capital

The example of Athens represents an extreme case of an evolved capital's renewal. Here, the scale of design intervention is so large that nineteenth-century Athens could almost be considered an entirely new city. Yet the centrality of the Acropolis with all of its associations inextricably roots the new city in the old; Athens's existence as a new capital is predicated on its continuity with the past, however disjointed. In other large design interventions, however, the urge to create a new capital has been more pronounced than the urge to recall the glories of the past, though modernity is not always viewed as antithetical to a return to roots.

Any time capitals are designed as well as designated, political will is underscored by a physical plan, designed according to the priorities of those who hold power. This is true whether the design intervention is piecemeal or total. It is true at the level of the building, the square, the precinct, or the city. Most "evolved" capitals have sizable sectors that have been "designed," and it is the largest of these design interventions that reveal most about social–spatial fit and misfit. When a new capital city is designed as a whole, the designers necessarily confront a broader array of spatial and social relationships. Though much of capital city design may involve residential areas that seem to have little connection to government functions, the social and spatial hierarchies of the city must be seen as a totality. Privileged sectors for work and privileged places for residence are often intimately and complexly intertwined. Capital city design involves not only a new center of government, but also a new container in which to locate this center. The spatial resolution of this capitol–capital relationship can be immensely revealing of the political relationship between the governors and the governed.

The idea of a designed city, at least in the West, probably has its origins in the colonial outposts of ancient Greece and Rome. Here, cities were planned according to established principles and were intended as architectural statements about the superior civilization at the center of an empire. Like the subsequent Spanish colonization of Central and South America according to the Laws of the Indies, however, planned colonial cities cannot fully be considered national capitals. As long as a city is an imposed presence, an administrative outpost of an alien government, it cannot take on the symbolic attributes of an indigenously created center. From Miletus to British Imperial Delhi, the limitation is the same. Over time, however, such symbolic attributes will change, as when Imperial Delhi became rapidly transmuted into the capital of independent India. Here, as elsewhere, the colonial origins of *capital city* as a concept may retain relevance. Grafting and crafting the qualities of an indigenously created center onto a place which had its origins premised upon a different socioeconomic system is never an easy task.

Though the designed capital city is descended from colonially imposed cities of the past, its lineage may be traced to another important typology—the palace and its gardens. For centuries, most large-scale attempts at urban design were sponsored by the wealth of the court or the church and were intended as extensions of the royal or priestly realm into the public domain. From the Rome of Pope Sixtus V to the Versailles of Louis XIV, political power was extended horizontally across the landscape. No longer confined by the walls of a citadel, power went public. By the sixteenth century, in Europe the palace had begun to extend across the city and out into the countryside. As Mumford puts it, "Baroque city building, in the formal sense, was an embodiment of the prevalent drama and ritual that shaped itself in the court: in effect, a collective embellishment of the ways and gestures of the palace."[67] Even after the age of royal residence cities, like the suburban capital at Versailles, had passed, remnants of palatial baroque order continued to be set into the fabric of European capitals. In Paris, Madrid, Vienna, and Berlin, in Wren's unexecuted plan for London after the great fire, and, most audaciously, in St. Petersburg, grand processional axes, long, imposing facades, enormous squares, and converging diagonals provided a common design repertoire for the European capital city. When, in the inspired work of Major Pierre L'Enfant, these tools of baroque order were combined with the primal symbolism of the capitol and applied in the service of democracy, the world gained its first postcolonial designed capital.

As the world's first capital to be designed in the aftermath of a revolutionary change of government, Washington, D.C., was heir to more than the long history of European urban design that had so opulently served the powers of church and state. Washington's founders—designers as well as American politicians and other influential citizens—also needed to confront the perennial challenges of symbolizing a new country and demonstrating the legitimacy of its government. In the more than two hundred years since the founding of Washington, the leadership of new regimes across the globe has repeatedly exploited the potential of new capitals and capitols in support of these same goals. At their heart, these daunting tasks involve attempts to construct a sense of national identity.

CHAPTER 2

National identity and the capitol complex

Not all designed capitals have been constructed in the aftermath of an independence movement, though the symbolics of city building and nation building often do seem to be synchronized. In some cases, especially in Latin America, the decision to design a new capital city has been taken well after the cessation of colonial rule, motivated more by dreams of economic development of the country's hinterland than by regional and ethnic rivalries. In most places, however, the bold venture of capital city construction has been connected to the ruling elite's attempts to consolidate national unity and cultivate national identity in the face of multiple contending groups located in rival urban centers. If the United States was the first new country to respond to the factionalism of federalism with the design and construction of a new capital, it has certainly not been the last. Many successful movements of national liberation that have proliferated in the decades since World War Two have tried to use architecture, urban design, and planning to advance their status following independence. Whether through the design of an entire new capital city or, more modestly, through the design of a capitol complex, government leaders have attempted to define a sense of national identity by careful manipulation of the built environment. Before moving on to discuss in detail specific examples of postcolonial capital cities and their associated capitol complexes, I want to clarify this concept of *national identity*.

The process of decolonization involves far more than a political change of government; it entails a far-reaching alteration of social and cultural consciousness, one not easily or fully achieved. What gets termed *postcolonial* implies a clear break, but closer examination always shows surprising continuities, co-existences, and hybridities. The rulers may change, but rules about power, hierarchy, and spatial separation often persist. Moreover, as Clifford Geertz has observed, the battle against colonial rule is not at all equivalent to the "definition, creation, and solidification of a viable collective identity."[1] The nationalism that supported the drive for independence in the name of freedom and self-determination is not the same as the nationalism needed after the revolution to define the self that has been freed. In their relation to the institutions of the state, the two stages of nationalism may well be diametrically opposed. There is a *nationalism of aspiration*—embraced by those who do not yet control a nation-state but think that they should—as well as a *nationalism of consolidation*—championed by those who *do* control a nation-state but are struggling to make sure that the aspiring nations within its borders do not succeed in undermining the state's sovereign legitimacy. Crawford Young notes that the state which, before independence, had been "the foil against which unity was forged" is, after independence, "itself the main vehicle in the hands of the nationalist elite for the fulfillment of the mission."[2] For most political leaders, directing this postindependence nationalism remains a daunting task. Geertz comments: "Most Tamils, Karens, Brahmins, Malays, Sikhs, Ibos, Muslims, Chinese, Nilotes, Bengalis or Ashantis found it a good deal easier to grasp the idea that they were not Englishmen than that they were Indians, Burmese, Malayans, Ghanaians, Pakistanis, Nigerians, or Sudanese."[3] After the "easy populism" of the independence movement, Geertz continues, the leadership of a new state must face the difficult challenge of consolidating the identity of the "collective subject to whom the actions of the state can be internally connected."[4] In other words, national identity must be fostered internally—within each individual and among the constituent groups of the new state—rather than oppositionally.

WHAT IS NATIONAL IDENTITY?

National identity as a concept is logically inseparable from concepts such as nation and nationalism, which are even more difficult to define. Ernest Gellner, in *Nations and Nationalism*, defines nationalism as a "theory of political legitimacy" which holds that "the political and the national unit should be congruent."[5] In practice, most historians and theorists agree, it has been nationalism that has brought about the existence of nations, and not vice versa. As a speaker at the first session of parliament in newly unified Italy phrased it, "We have made Italy, now we have to make Italians"—not a trivial task, given that at the time only 2.5 percent of the population regularly spoke Italian.[6] National identity, in this view, is not a natural attribute that precedes statehood but a process that must be cultivated for a long time after a regime has gained political power.

Historically, the idea of nationalism is a modern creation, its origins tied to the development of industrial capitalism, and the term *nationalism* itself is a late eighteenth-century coinage that was not used frequently until well into the 1800s.[7] The development of modern nationalism is understandable only in the context of rapid urban population growth and the penetration of isolated communities both by an increasingly global economy and the administrative organs of an increasingly centralized but participatory polity. Moreover, as Benedict Anderson argues, nationalism descends from earlier cultural systems; it could become a powerful rallying force only after thoroughgoing challenges to earlier conceptions of social organization rooted in cosmological divine rule, the privileged role of a single transcontinental sacred language (e.g., Latin), and the temporal inseparability of cosmology and history.[8]

During the course of the nineteenth century in Europe, links between individuals and the state multiplied. By the end of the century, following shifts toward secular rule and electoral representation, a wide cross-section of citizens gained direct contact with those in power, and those in power increasingly had to nurture citizens' affections in the face of rival movements. As E. J. Hobsbawm has observed, this had direct consequences for the development of nationalism: "The democratization of politics, i.e. on the one hand the growing extension of the (male) franchise, on the other the creation of the modern administrative, citizen-mobilizing and citizen-influencing state, both placed the question of the 'nation', and the citizen's feelings towards whatever he regarded as his 'nation,' 'nationality,' or other centre of loyalty, at the top of the political agenda."[9]

National movements in mid-nineteenth-century Europe had stressed issues of linguistic and cultural continuity and, as in Italy and the German Empire, aimed at forming states out of acts of unification. The "principle of nationality" changed the map of Europe between 1830 and 1878 without yet relying upon mass political movements. The selection of Athens as the capital of modern Greece, as I have suggested, was motivated by the romantic notions of classically educated philhellenes in the diaspora while, as Hobsbawm has noted,

> The real Greeks who took up arms for what turned out to be the formation of a new independent nation-state, did not talk ancient Greek any more than Italians talk Latin. They talked and wrote Demotic. Pericles, Aeschylus, Euripides and the glories of ancient Sparta and Athens meant little if anything to them, and insofar as they had heard of them, they did not think of them as relevant. Paradoxically, they stood for Rome rather than Greece (*romaiosyne*), that is to say they saw themselves as heirs of the Christianized Roman Empire (i.e. Byzantium). They fought as Christians against Muslim unbelievers, as Romans against the Turkish dogs.[10]

By the end of the century, a great number of populist alliances, rooted in language and ethnicity, began to develop, expanding the domain of national questions from the realm of culture into the realm of politics. The earlier liberal movements toward a few unified nation-states (which assumed that each such entity possessed a certain threshold of size and economic viability as well as deep historical associations, a well-established cultural elite, and the demonstrated capacity to defend or extend its borders) gave way to the Wilsonian principle of self-determination, which advocated a multiplication of potential sovereign states through internal subdivision.[11] Increasing contacts between citizens and the state allowed nationalist movements, in competition with other appeals to the middle classes such as international socialism, to gain a broad-based political foothold. In some places, this meant that the concept of nationalism became associated with chauvinist, imperialist, and xenophobic movements of the radical right, precursors of twentieth-century Italian Fascism and German National Socialism. On the whole, though, national movements before 1914 were directed against states and empires seen as unjustly multinational.

After the First World War and the breakup of the Hapsburg and Ottoman empires, Europe was reconstructed more wholly according to principles of nationality, and many nationalist movements had their aims fulfilled. Such liberation, it may be noted, anticipated the situation of many African and Asian countries that gained political independence following World War Two and were subsequently faced with the challenge of creating a corresponding identity in terms of national culture. After the First World War, then, nationalist movements tended to advocate separatism from existing national states rather than alternative forms of union. Following the Versailles settlement and the official commitment of the victors to Wilsonian national self-determination, political leaders in the non-European world called increasing attention to their national liberation movements, efforts that stressed the need for liberation from continued European colonial domination rather than evidence for an autochthonous alternative basis for national status. Hobsbawm writes:

> The real and growing force of liberation consisted in the resentment against conquerors, rulers and exploiters, who happened to be recognizable as foreigners by colour, costume and habits, or against those who were seen as acting for them. It was anti-imperial. Insofar as there were proto-national identifications, ethnic, religious or otherwise, among the common people, they were, as yet, obstacles rather than contributions to national consciousness, and readily mobilized against nationalists by imperial masters; hence the constant attacks on the imperialist policies of 'Divide and Rule', against the imperial encouragement of tribalism, communalism, or whatever else divided peoples who should be, but were not, united as a single nation.[12]

Attempts to articulate nationhood could wait until after the revolution. Afterward, however, it usually became apparent that the leadership of the newly emancipated states asserted a national homogeneity that did not exist. Other nationalisms then arose to protest against the ethnic or cultural unacceptability of the territories into which the imperial era had partitioned the dependent world.[13] By the early 1990s, multiethnic nation-states such as Yugoslavia and the USSR also faced break-up, as provincial parliaments there and elsewhere staked claim to new or renewed national status. Whether nationalism enters politics as an imitative outgrowth of European ideologies of self-determination or as part of an antifascist, anticolonial, or antipostcolonial backlash, the perceived need to pursue development of a national identity persists long after statehood has been achieved.

DIMENSIONS OF NATIONAL IDENTITY IN ARCHITECTURE AND URBAN DESIGN

Public statements of collective identity take many forms and make use of many different kinds of symbols for support. These symbols, whether in the guise of a constitution, a military parade, or a capitol complex, help to give value and significance to the activities of the state. As Geertz puts it, "The images, metaphors, and rhetorical turns from which national ideologies are built are essentially devices, cultural devices designed to render one or another aspect of the broad process of collective self-redefinition explicit, to cast essentialist pride or epochalist hope into specific symbolic forms, where more than dimly felt, they can be described, developed, celebrated and used."[14] Objects and events, monuments and ceremonies, all contribute meaningful symbols to the production and consolidation of the "we."

The visible symbols of national identity take many forms. Flags come to mind first, along with icons of those leaders responsible for creation of the state. These, in turn, are often associated with party emblems and other accepted logos and slogans of national government. Such are the images on coins and bills, often in combination with depictions of indigenous flora and fauna. Similarly, such images of national identity predominate on those postage stamps that collectors curiously term noncommemoratives, presumably on the grounds that they do not commemorate a particular historical event.

Works of architecture and acts of urban design assume a peculiar place in this assemblage of national symbols. A few decades after the Lincoln Memorial was built its image displaced the words ONE CENT from the center of the tails side of the American penny. Likewise, on the nickel the head of Jefferson is backed by the image of his home at Monticello. These two buildings and a few others in and around Washington, D.C., not only are associated with individual statesmen but also have become infused with the symbolism of American democratic government. Although there may be few clues in their neoclassical architectural language to reveal the inevitability of their association with a specifically American national identity, such symbolic associations do remain powerful.

Capital cities and the parliament buildings constructed within them would seem to be ready purveyors of national identity, since they are ostensibly built to serve and symbolize a nation-state as a whole. Frequently, however, since their siting and appearance are chosen by the leadership rather than by the populace, the resultant place hardly resembles a truly national identity. Architecture and planning are often used as tools for promoting something called national identity, but many dimensions of this phenomenon remain unarticulated.

When one reflects upon the design of a new capital city or the architecture of a national assembly building within it, it seems appropriate to consider exactly what is being assembled. Postcolonial capitals and capitols, intended as visual evidence of the rightful existence of a new state, are designed with multiple simultaneous frames of reference. Yet, to the extent that these places are discussed at all, assessments are too frequently couched solely in formal terms. Or if there is some attempt to interpret the form, the place is reduced to a cultural symbol, detached from the social and economic forces that helped to produce it. Increasingly since the 1970s, though, as Neil Brenner shows in *New State Spaces*, "city-regions have become key institutional sites in which a major rescaling on national state power has been unfolding." Although some of this decentering and decentralizing has arguably impacted economically vibrant *non*-capital cities more deeply than administrative capitals, the overall effect has been to intensify the place-specific socioeconomic and symbolic assets of certain globally linked cities.[15] Thus, to begin to assess the role of a parliament building or a new capital in its culture and in the broader culture of globalization, many forces must be considered; national identity does not come about easily and is always molded from what has come before.

Conscious efforts by government leaders and their architects at expressing national identity in a parliament building (or, more dramatically, through the construction of a new capital city) take place within at least three frames of reference, each with its own implications for architectural form and cultural production. In addition to the set of issues regarding the spatial relationship between the capitol complex and the rest of the city, the symbolism of capitols is a product of (1) the subnational group allegiances and preferences of the sponsoring regime, (2) the priorities of the architect's long-term design agenda, and (3) the government's interest in pursuing international identity through modern architecture and planning, which may be tied to issues of economic development. In other words, what is passed off as a quest for national identity is in reality a product of the search for subnational, personal, and supranational identity.

National vs. subnational identity

It is simplistic to regard national assembly buildings as an architectural manifestation of national distinctiveness. Although some parliamentary architecture may be meant to demonstrate a visibly unique aspect of the newly constituted state, something that will differentiate it from neighboring states (important, perhaps, if there are regional conflicts), nationhood is not easily represented. Government leaders may view the design of a parliament building as an affirmation of the wisdom or necessity of statehood, as visual documentation of a distinct culture deserving of status in the international system of states, but this distinct culture is almost never coterminous with the country as a whole.

New states are rarely, if ever, culturally homogeneous, and national identity is rarely directed at the liberation of a single, clearly bounded cultural group to which all citizens claim membership. Rather, much of twentieth-century (and early twenty-first-century) statemaking involves mediation among factions; many potential nations may be forced to coexist, peacefully or otherwise, within the bounds of a single state. The borders of many postcolonial states are vestiges of an era when a colonial administration was in control, with varying degrees of brutality and effectiveness, over a multitude of groups having divergent interests and multifarious alliances. With the cessation of colonial administration and external political control, many of these regional and internecine hostilities were unleashed. Geertz writes of the "nationalism within nationalisms" and notes that virtually every state emerging from colonial rule has suffered from provincial or separatist strains, a direct and sometimes "immediate threat to the new-wrought national identity in whose name the revolution was made." Thus, Geertz concludes, "In apparent paradox (though, in fact, it has been a nearly universal occurrence in the new states) the move toward national unity intensified group tensions within the society by raising settled cultural forms out of their particular contexts, expanding them into general allegiances, and politicizing them."[16] To the leaders of such groups, the notion of a unitary state is either anathema or an irrelevance. Governments of postcolonial countries are often recognized by the United Nations long before they are accepted by factions within the country.

Another factor limiting the perception of national identity among a newly independent population is even more basic. Not only are most ex-colonial states divided into mutually opposed groups, they also tend to be overwhelmingly rural places in which the only community commanding active membership and loyalty is local rather than national or regional. Identity, according to Crawford Young, is "a subjective self-concept or social role," and, as such, it is "often variable, overlapping, and situational."[17] To make his point, he describes a hypothetical tenant farmer in rural India, whose identity is composed of many such parts: he is a cultivator, a tenant, a member of a family, and a member of a particular subcaste and caste; alternatively, he may identify himself as a speaker of a particular language, a follower of a religion, a resident of a region, or a supporter of a political faction. Only at the levels farthest removed from his daily life will he need to think of himself as a rural person or, ultimately, as an Indian.[18] Especially since most supralocal identities were not well developed before colonial rule, their cultivation by postcolonial national leadership remains a difficult task. Under these circumstances, national identity, whether taken in architectural or any other terms, becomes increasingly artificial and subject to the dictates of those in power.

The national identity communicated through the production of a parliament building usually highlights the identity of a dominant group within a plural society. The search for national identity in parliamentary architecture is, therefore, closely related to the political structure of the state. Although there may be some well-intentioned search for a unifying national symbol, normally the choice of symbol, if examined, reveals other structural, social, and economic tensions.

In his essay "The Integrative Revolution: Primordial Sentiments and Civil Politics in the New States," Geertz identifies six kinds of ties that bind groups together:

Assumed blood ties—ties based on untraceable quasi-kinship thought to be real, as among desert nomads

Race—ties based on phenotypical features such as skin color, facial form, stature, or hair type

Language—ties based on the primary means of linguistic communication

Region—ties based on topographical features, such as islands or intervening mountain ranges

Religion—ties based on systems of belief

Custom—ties based on patterns of behavior, especially important where one group believes itself to be the bearer of civilization.[19]

In highly plural postcolonial states, however, these six kinds of ties have come undone or else have never fit neatly within designated state boundaries: they are more notable for their divisiveness than for their bonding.

The symbols of national identity, whether architectural or otherwise, are derived from these six kinds of divisions. Some schisms are, of course, deeper in some places than in others, though a highly plural state such as India features a complex and interwoven pattern of allegiances that involves all six categories. Government leaders necessarily make choices among contending groups, and whether consciously chosen or not, symbolic structures such as parliament buildings are products of these preferences. The rhetoric may be about unity, but the symbols chosen to represent it are products of an elite with its own set of group preferences. As such, they are charged with highly divisive associations that reinforce, or seek to redirect, the cultural balance of power within a pluralist state.

Geertz's schema of multiple group ties is made still more complex since most of these allegiances do not fit comfortably within the boundaries of a single state. In many states, for example, a central division within the population is along lines of religion. Here, the issue is complicated by the fact that many religions operate transglobally. Thus, while the design of a parliament building may adopt some of the iconography of the religious majority in that state, this may do little to assist the consolidation of a specifically national identity, as in Catholic South America or a pan-Arabic context, for instance. Even without the international component, the relationship between national religion (official or otherwise) and national government is almost always problematical, especially where there are varying degrees and interpretations of orthodoxy. In places like Bangladesh, where religious facilities of the majority group are included as integral parts of a capitol building, religion can prove controversial at the level of architectural program and imagery. At a larger scale, religion can become an issue even in the siting of a new capital city. This happens where religious groups are relatively segregated by region, as in Nigeria with its predominantly Islamic north.

Other attempts by the leadership to manipulate group-based ties—or, more accurately, to reformulate them in ways that best serve the interests of those in power—are equally crucial. Closely related to Geertz's notion of assumed blood ties is the tendency of the national political leadership to want to assert architectural ties to some favored period of the past. Architecture and urban design may be used as an iconographical bridge between preferred epochs, joining the misty palisades of some golden age to the hazy shores of some future promise by neatly spanning all troubled colonial waters. Mussolini's architectural and urban treatment of the Third Rome would indicate that reliance on historical associations can arise without colonialism, while the reclamation of Athens as a capital suggests that this tendency applies to sacred sites as well as to favored styles. Any new parliament building should therefore be viewed in the context of that which preceded it, especially in relation to past capitol buildings and past capital cities. Though national identity may be promoted through attempts to demonstrate architectural evidence of cultural uniqueness, such identity may be forged oppositionally as well. In the most obvious instances, the new building (and, in some cases, the new capital city) is seen as the alternative to the old quarters of the colonial guardian. Stylistic differentiation—whether at the level of city form or architectural language—may itself become a virtue. If, however, the old quarters cannot be surpassed in scale and grandeur, they are sometimes, as in postindependence Delhi, appropriated.

The notion of appropriation suggests that the construction of parliament buildings and new capitals is, above all, a demonstration of power and a search for legitimacy. Most often, in the postcolonial period, this power has been invested not in a political system but in a single regime. The decision to proceed with the design and construction of a new capital city or a new parliament building—a decision that often implies the budget-straining commitment of a poor country to pay for it—is made by a regime, not by a nation. The classic example is, of course, Kubitschek's Brasília, but there are all too many others. In the case of capitol complexes, where the smaller scale of construction usually permits a faster realization than is possible for a capital, the identification between a particular ruler and a building is often very close. The project, whether seen as a success or a debacle, becomes associated with that regime politically and perhaps iconographically. If large financial resources are available, the occasion of a new capital or capitol complex may become a means through which a contemporary regime seeks to recall the imagery and monumental presence of some distant yet historically related precolonial empire. In so doing, leaders manipulate Geertz's six so-called primordial ties in the service of distinctly nonprimordial ends.

An evocation of the past can be effectively used as a call for a new future, yet the misguided yearning for some lost golden age yields architecture as stultified as it is sentimental, as in the overscaled neoclassicism of the Vittoriano or the proposed Palace of the Soviets. When political leaders possess such a mentality, the execution of a parliament building is an inherently conservative act. There is a curious—even bewildering—disjuncture between the monumentality of most new national assembly complexes or new capitals and the fledgling democracies they ostensibly signify. Such capitals and capitols may reveal far more about the fledgling nature of the regime than about any sincere notion of democracy. To a large degree, many postcolonial capitol complexes are, like ancient citadels, a refuge for rulers rather than a vehicle for the sharing of political power. In this way, a parliament complex may promote no national identity at all—

its purpose is to advance the power and independence of government as an institution. When faced with a monumental parliament building, one cannot help thinking that the line between national pride and governmental insecurity is a fine one indeed.

National vs. Personal Identity

A second influence on the design of new capitols and capitals is personal predilection, both that of the designer and that of the sponsoring politicians. These preferences may be colored by group affiliations, though it seems important to reiterate that design decisions are often made by individuals whose own sense of identity is projected onto that of the nation they seek to build. The designer's professional identity is consequential, especially since government leaders frequently import designers from far afield. Understanding this component of identity entails examination of architectural culture, the ways that a building is a product of the education, office practice, and aspirations of its designers. To date, most internationally prominent architects in the developing world have been educated in the West or have received a Western-influenced architectural education closer to home. Moreover, in an age of increased electronic communication and rapid dissemination of glossy periodicals, an architect designing a large public building in a developing country can scarcely avoid being aware of Western trends and preferences, especially since these may be his or her own as well. Such global architectural consciousness, fed by international competitions and prizes, makes a purely local design solution unlikely. When the scale of design is that of a city, designers are apt to be strongly influenced both by whatever was considered to be state-of-the-art at the time of their commission and by celebrated precedents, however far afield and however culturally inappropriate.

Another key aspect of international architectural culture is that the demands of large-scale capitol complexes in developing nations commonly exceed the capabilities of indigenous firms to implement them. Thus, even if a local architect is found, additional architectural, engineering, and managerial expertise must be imported. The need for multinational cooperation, entailing the use of building techniques unfamiliar to the architect or the construction team, may affect the kind of design decisions that can be made.

The chance to design a parliament building or a new city may be treated by the architect chiefly as an opportunity to reiterate the ongoing formal preoccupations of a highly personal oeuvre, to such an extent that the public issues of symbolism are not rigorously explored. If the architect is unfamiliar with the social, political, and cultural climate of the client's country, such personal and internal preoccupations can promote design solutions that seem to be alien intrusions. In an age of autographed buildings, a national assembly building can even become subject to the international personality cult of its architect. In these instances, the work is judged, at least by architecture critics, chiefly as the artistic expression of a revered master, as if the capital were a museum acquiring a major building by a major artist.

That the building may be a product of and for a developing country seeking more than a museum piece is ignored.

Yet the issue is complicated by the fact that the government leadership may well *want* a building that is a revered museum piece and an alien intrusion, as long as it can be promoted as a sign of progress. This seems especially true of designed capital cities such as Brasília, in which the established living patterns of the population were treated as the basis for critique rather than as a point of departure. The global architecture of parliament buildings still turns along a single major axis that runs between two poles: the economic pull of multinationalism and the magnetic attraction of personalism.

For those in power, these poles may exert simultaneous pressure, yielding symbols that seem rooted in some favored aspect of a component culture and that strive toward global homogeneity. As Gellner has observed, "If the nationalism prospers it eliminates the alien high culture, but it does not then replace it by the old local low culture; it revives, invents, a local high (literate, specialist-transmitted) culture of its own, though admittedly one which will have some links with the earlier local folk styles and dialects." This process, which reinterprets folk references in the context of participation in a global capitalist economy, is a reminder that "the nationalist state is not the protector only of a culture, but also of a new and often initially fragile economy."[20] The architecture and urban design of capitol complexes, like other large-scale public works intended as symbols of nationhood, can thus exhibit personal preferences with ties to both the local and the global economy.

National vs. supranational identity

A third frame of reference for the design of postcolonial parliament buildings and new capitals is the government's interest in treating architecture as a visible symbol of economic development. As such, these highly visible public works are supposed to promote national pride by bringing international recognition. Parliament buildings and new capital cities are intended as a demonstration of a developing country's ability to equal the West on its own terms. At the same time, efforts to consolidate a national identity have also had to engage a diaspora that is itself both increasingly westernized yet profoundly connected to the homeland, itself now irreversibly modernized. As Arjun Appadurai and Carol Breckenridge put it in 1995, "Modernity is now everywhere, it is simultaneously everywhere, and it is interactively everywhere." As communication possibilities have burgeoned, even a transglobal act of immigration is transformed by connective possibilities of cell phones and computers. Electronically transmitted remittances unite dispersed co-ethnics in powerful socioeconomic ways. The result is but the most recent incarnation of what Anderson famously termed "imagined communities." Anderson defines the nation as an "imagined political community" because it conceptually unites dispersed and diverse individuals who do not and cannot possibly know one another as individuals, "yet in the minds of each lives the image of their communion."[21] Both internally within the nation-state and internationally, this imagined national community seeks both national distinctiveness and global compatibility.

As Geertz describes it, the challenge for developing countries ("new states" which—in many cases—are now no longer so new) is to find a balance between cultural self-determination and international modernity:

> The peoples of the new states are simultaneously animated by two powerful, thoroughly independent, yet distinct and often actually opposed motives—the desire to be recognized as responsible agents whose wishes, acts, hopes and opinions "matter," and the desire to build an efficient, dynamic modern state. The one aim is to be noticed: it is a search for an identity, and a demand that the identity be publicly acknowledged as having import, a social assertion of the self as "being somebody in the world." The other aim is practical: it is a demand for progress, for a rising standard of living, more effective political order, greater social justice, and beyond that of "playing a part in the larger arena of world politics," of exercising influence among the nations.[22]

In short, as Edward Shils phrases it, "'Modern' means being Western without depending on the West."[23]

In many states in the developing world, formal political independence has been accompanied by sporadic and uneasy development; sporadic because of insufficient funds and factional infighting, and uneasy because of increasing dislocation from traditional ways of life. In extreme cases, whole cities have fallen victim to what James C. Scott calls "the imperialism of high-modernist planned social order," a "hegemonic planning mentality that excludes the necessary role of local knowledge and know-how." For Scott, large city-building ventures such as Brasília and Chandigarh (both of which are discussed in Chapter 4) epitomize the dangers that can occur when an authoritarian and self-interested state bureaucracy acts upon an uncritical ideological faith in science and technology, a process made especially dangerous when a "prostrate civil society . . . lacks the capacity to resist these plans." Like other failed efforts at social engineering (such as China's Great Leap Forward or various forms of forced collectivization), Scott sees high-modernist city building as a misdirected effort to make a society more legible to its rulers and therefore more controllable:

> The aspiration to such uniformity and order alerts us to the fact that modern statecraft is largely a product of internal colonization, often glossed, as it is in imperial rhetoric, as a "civilizing mission." The builders of the modern nation-state do not merely describe, observe, and map; they strive to shape a people and landscape that will fit their techniques of observation.[24]

Modernization, as a prominent component of supranational identity building, takes many cultural forms.

In its architectural manifestations ("modern architecture"), modernization has led to the gradual globalization of cheapened and diluted versions of the so-called international style. If anything, postcolonial urban architecture has been far less attuned to the specifics of place than were its hybrid predecessors designed under colonial regimes. Concrete-box parliaments have indistinguishably joined concrete-box offices and housing blocks, creating an international style far more ubiquitous than anything out of Hitchcock and Johnson.

In this context, national identity is not the overriding issue; the goal is identity in the eyes of an international audience. Consequently, part of the national identity of some developing countries has come to be defined according to the dictates and tastes of Western consumers. Parliament buildings, like many hotels, are designed to be in keeping with the preexisting international image of the country; the building must confirm—and thus perpetuate—a stereotype. The danger is that the cultural richness negated by international modernism will reappear in cartoon form. The box with the flag in front of it is replaced by a building that is a flag itself. One form of design denies the possibility of an architectural contribution to national identity; the other reduces architecture to a three-dimensional, government-sanctioned billboard advertising selected aspects of indigenous culture.

In his essay "Universal Civilization and National Cultures," Paul Ricoeur identifies a central paradox inherent in all efforts at forging a postcolonial national identity: "It is a fact: every culture cannot sustain and absorb the shock of modern civilization. There is the paradox: how to become modern and to return to sources; how to revive an old dormant civilization and take part in universal civilization."[25] The elements of the paradox, however, are more complex than Ricoeur's formulation would allow. Implicit in his essay is the notion of one national culture rooted in "an old dormant civilization." Yet, even in the most monolithic state, the residues of old civilizations are not one but many. Alternatively, the old civilizations are seen not as dormant but as being either co-opted by a neighboring state or an active threat to the pursuit of modernity. In a globally interconnected world of capitals where middle classes and elites now participate in a shared modernity, the very nature of an "old dormant civilization" has been revalued. Even so, national leaders retain a powerful political and symbolic need to find refuge in some form of deep historical legitimacy. Solutions, whether political or architectural, can never come easily as long as there is no peaceful correlation between officially recognized states and the multitude of competing would-be nations and affiliations that exist within them.

Moreover, the pursuit of national identity by the leadership involves not some neutral revival of the past but its careful recasting to serve political ends. As Gellner comments, "Nationalism is *not* the awakening of an old, latent, dormant force, though that is how it does indeed present itself. It is in reality the consequence of a new form of social organization, based on deeply internalized education-dependent high cultures each protected by its own state."[26] The preferences of those in power may yield choices of symbolism that either overblow or seek to circumvent the state's history, as in modern Turkey's selection of the ancient Hittites as the focus of its carefully edited past. Like the semiartificial promotion of Italian or Greek as national languages in the nineteenth century, the criteria for advancement of a national architecture may be far less closely tied to primordial cultural foundations than nationalist mythology would suggest. As Hobsbawm writes, while modern nations generally claim to be "rooted in the remotest antiquity" and be "human communities so 'natural' as to require no justification other than self-assertion," in reality they are both "novel" and "constructed," forged through what he terms "the invention of tradition." Akin to Anderson's notion of "imagined communities" and to Appadurai's "community of sentiment," invented traditions are one mechanism for active construction of nationalist feeling. Steven Kemper adds the important point that "Nationalist visions of the past are frequently unreliable as historiography, but they do not begin from scratch, for nationalists find many of their materials already at hand. Some nationalist practices are genuinely ancient; others are not." Whatever the dose of invention in the invocation of traditions, Hobsbawm astutely observes that "Modern nations rest on exercises in social engineering which are often deliberate and always innovative."[27] National architecture and the institutional rituals with which it becomes associated regularly play large roles in such invented traditions. In the attempt to revive the past through architectural design, then, pluralism is not well served either by denial or pastiche.

Rulers in every capital city express power and promote national identity through the design and construction of government buildings and capitol districts. Many cities that have maintained their status as capitals over the course of many centuries, I have argued, have assimilated such buildings into diverse quarters of their urban fabrics. Where democracy has been long established, there is less need to symbolize it in a single prominent place. Instead, over time, the institutions of democratic government and the buildings housing aspects of national culture become dispersed across the city. Newly designed capitals are pressed to accelerate the display of national institutions, since this is precisely the function any respectable capital is expected to serve. If a new capital is designed for a new state, the pressures on capital symbolism are tripled. Not only must the leadership push for rapid proliferation of national cultural institutions, it must also cope with the problem of defining what the national culture can be, while seeking assurance that this definition will serve those in power. In designed capitals created under conditions of colonialism, the architectural and urban practices of the core metropolis are transplanted to the dependent periphery; even in capitals created after independence, some of these old patterns of power relations tend to persist.[28]

Even when a capital city is designed as if by a single hand, the infusion of national symbolism into capital cities and capitol districts occurs over a long period of time. While there may be significant symbolic content suggested by the institutional juxtapositions called for in some grand master plan, this symbolism will inevitably undergo marked alteration during the long course of the city's growth and development. The fabrication of national meanings and the symbolic consolidation of political power occur in a great variety of ways, at variable rates, and are always subject to the vicissitudes of public opinion. Sometimes the manipulation of symbols occurs at the level of architectural form making, in which buildings may be designed to denote, express, or metaphorically recall favored past associations or current group ties. In urban design terms, powerful groups may claim key intersections or privileged high ground in the city to display their prestige. They may build elaborate processional routes that serve as settings in both space and time, binding individuals and groups with events considered vital to the state. At the largest scale, decisions about where to locate capital cities may indicate both conflict and compromise among rival groups. Both as places for pro-government rallies and as dramatic targets for political protest, capital cities and the capitols within them gain meanings that their sponsors could not possibly have anticipated. In consequence, the diversity of personal and group reactions to government-sponsored acts ensures that all national symbolism is in a state of continual transformation. From the early plans for Washington, D.C., to the most recent designs for capitol complexes in disparate corners of the postcolonial developing world, highly charged cityscapes provide a commonality of challenges for designers and for those who wish to interpret the disposition of power and the construction of national identity.

CHAPTER 3

Early designed capitals: for union, for imperialism, for independence

Any chronology of modern designed capitals must be somewhat arbitrary, since it is premised on the dates capital cities were founded in accordance with urban design plans. In reality, of course, all cities develop continually (as do the meanings of their component parts), and plans, even when implemented, are not one but many. Nonetheless, since the proponents of these master plans do seem to respond to the ideas of their planning predecessors and contemporaries to so great an extent that these designs form a kind of hermetic dialogue, there is good reason for exhibiting them in order of historical appearance. I make no pretense of this as a complete discussion of all designed capitals: what follows in the next three chapters is an overview. Still, the examples of Washington, D.C., Canberra, New Delhi, Ankara, Chandigarh, Brasília, Abuja, and Dodoma, together with more-brief mention of several others, do raise a broad spectrum of issues about power and identity and serve as a useful prelude to the more in-depth discussion of four designed capitol complexes in Part 2. Through an examination of the plans of these cities and the forces that helped produce them, I emphasize the reasons each was founded and analyze the urban and architectural presence of its capitol complex. By assessing decisions made with regard to architecture and planning, I want to elucidate the larger aims and biases that underlie these momentous partnerships among government leaders, local people, and designers.

Capitals, as I suggested, are selected by the leadership for a broad assortment of reasons. When they are not only designated but also designed according to some master plan, the siting and design of the capital are almost inevitably outcomes of major political change: unification, independence, or the accession of a new regime. Though physical change may lag behind the pace of political developments (the Arc de Triomphe, for example, was completed long after the fall of Napoléon I), political transformation does affect capital choices. In nineteenth-century Rome, the leadership was able to adapt an existing city to serve its purposes following unification, but for other leaders the arduous task of consolidating multiple constituencies into a single nation-state has suggested construction of a new compromise capital. Such compromise seems almost a necessity wherever factions are well organized and some modicum of democracy prevails. Washington, D.C., and Canberra are the most notable early examples of this phenomenon and, as such, constitute the focus of the first part of this chapter. They are representative of the early kind of nationalism, that which expressed itself through acts of unification and preceded any clear consideration of national identity. As Hobsbawm observes,

> Nations are more often the consequence of setting up a state than they are its foundation. The USA and Australia are obvious examples of nation-states all of whose specific national characteristics and criteria of nationhood have been established since the late eighteenth century, and indeed could not have existed before the foundation of the respective state and country. However, we need hardly remind ourselves that the mere setting up of a state is not sufficient in itself to create a nation.[1]

At their founding, then, Washington and Canberra were part of fledgling efforts at nation building, and the subsequent growth and disposition of government facilities in each place have continued to cultivate images for the nation.

WASHINGTON, D.C.: THE FIRST MODERN DESIGNED CAPITAL

Planned in the aftermath of the attainment of U.S. independence and the ratification of a federal constitution, Washington is the first postcolonial designed capital. Given the massive political task of changing from control by the colonial deputies of a European monarchy to a grand experiment in constitutional democracy, the physical design of the new city is less than revolutionary. As Mumford comments,

> Despite L'Enfant's firm republican convictions, the design he set forth for the new capital was in every respect what the architects and servants of despotism had originally conceived. He could only carry over into the new age the static image that had been dictated by centralized coercion and control. The sole feature that was lacking was the original sixteenth century fortifications, since there was no apparent need for military defence. As it happened, this was an embarrassing oversight, for such works alone might have saved the new public buildings in Washington from their destruction by British raiders in the War of 1812. Apart from that, the plan was an exemplary adaptation of the standard baroque principles to a new situation.[2]

Though there is great continuity in Major Pierre Charles L'Enfant's application of "standard baroque principles" (not surprising, perhaps, from a man who had grown up visiting Versailles while his father was decorating the Ministry of War), Mumford neglects to point out the most important ways the "new situation" brought altered meaning to such principles. The diagonals and axes may be redolent of the cities and gardens of imperial Europe, but Washington is a more democratically engendered product. In the choice of its site, in the intended accessibility of public space, and in the nature and juxtaposition of its monumental buildings, Washington marks a first partial attempt to free capital design from its association with autocratic control. As Scott Berg puts it, "The National Mall was designed to be a great civic meeting place, the greensward of Versailles turned on its political head, the Champs Élysées reincarnated and renovated in the cause of democracy, a horizon held in trust for the American people" (3.1, 3.2).[3]

Like St. Petersburg, Washington was located in a swampy wilderness, well away from any existing center of power. Unlike its Russian precursor, however, its site is the product of compromise rather than the direct outcome of a ruler's decree. Yet this compromise did not occur easily or quickly. Washington is not the first capital of the United States but, in fact, the ninth home of a peripatetic legislature that had met in cities in New York, Pennsylvania, Maryland, and New Jersey.[4] A New York newspaper editorial commented on the indecision in 1791: "Where will Congress find a resting place?—they have led a kind of vagrant life ever since 1774, when they first met to oppose Great-Britain. Every place they have taken to reside in has been made too hot to hold them; either the enemy would not let them stay, or people made a clamour because they were too far north or too far south, and oblige them to remove. . . . We pity the poor congress-men, thus kicked and cuffed about from post to pillar—where can they find a home?"[5] Though the eventual choice of home was no more than a morning's ride from George Washington's Virginia estate, Mount Vernon,[6] the first president was only

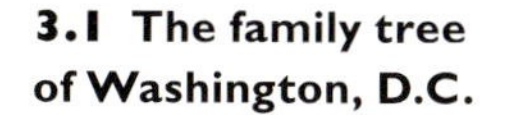
3.1 The family tree of Washington, D.C.

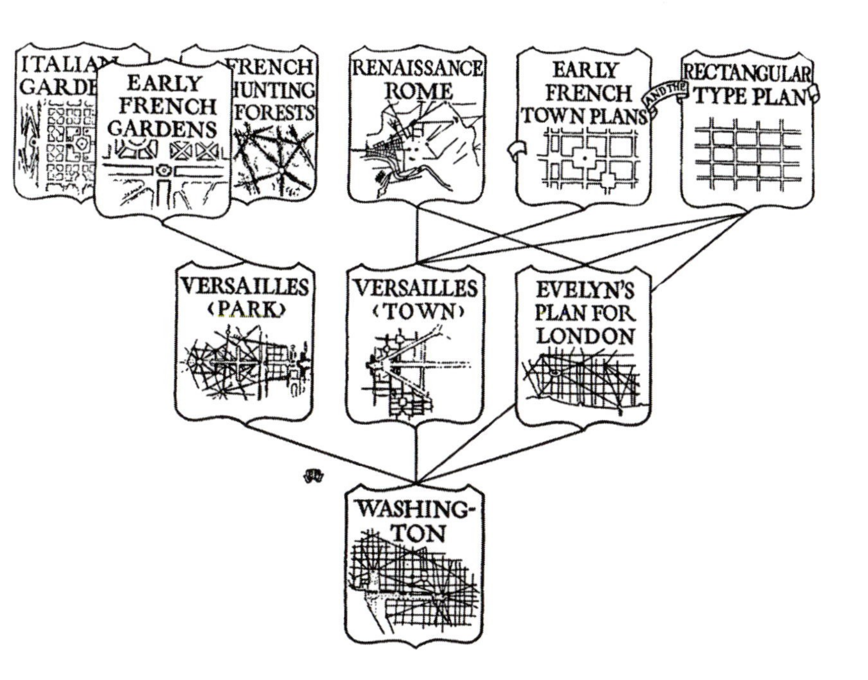

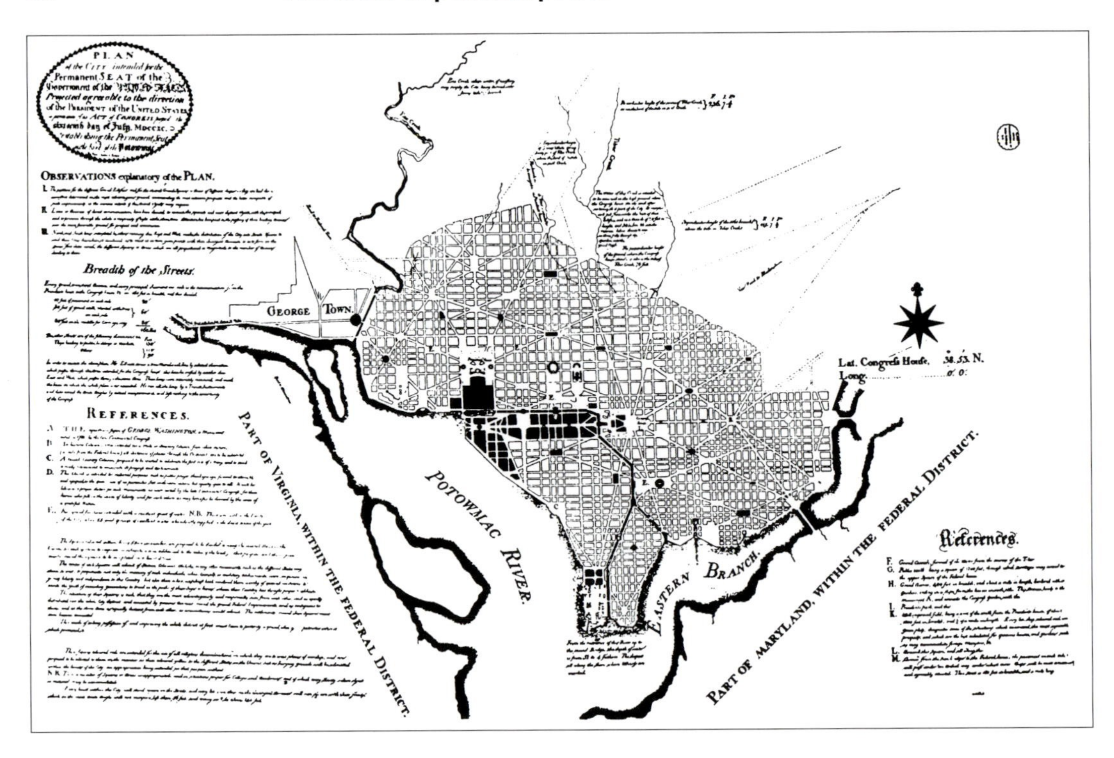

3.2 L'Enfant plan of 1791: imperial baroque adapted for democracy.

one of many politicians involved in the deal making that yielded the selection of site and pervaded the subsequent planning of the new city.

In the fall of 1783 the Congress approved tandem capitals, one to be located at the falls of the Delaware River north of Trenton, New Jersey, the other in Virginia along the Potomac.[7] The act prompted a wry proposal for a wheelable statue of George Washington to accompany the legislators' commute. The twin capital arrangement was repealed the following year, but the underlying problem was not so readily dismissed. The proposition of a double capital, with one location favored by leaders from the north and the other championed by southerners, illustrated the difficulties facing the new country and the seeming inevitablity of a federal solution for the disposition of its government. The United States was but the first of many newly independent countries to choose eventually to build an entirely new city as its capital rather than force a choice among existing urban rivals, each having its own powerful constituencies. The wrangle over the capital is just one manifestation of the inherent difficulty of forging a single nation-state out of the diverse and fragmented legacy of a colonial empire, to which the economies of American port cities had already begun to become globally connected. In the end, the choice of a southern site for the new capital, promulgated with the Residence Act of 1790, was part of a political trade-off brokered over dinner by Alexander Hamilton (as secretary of the treasury) and Thomas Jefferson (as secretary of state): northern support for a Potomac capital was exchanged for the acquiescence of two Virginians and one Marylander in Hamilton's proposal for funding the national debt (which had been generated by the war against England).[8]

As Carl Abbott cogently points out, however, "a national capital below the falls of the Potomac was not a sudden creative idea that came to Hamilton and Jefferson with a second bottle of wine. A Potomac location was a strong candidate from the start, with specific implications about the larger process of nation making and its many acts of politics, war, diplomacy, and cultural chauvinism." Specifically, Abbott argues, the Potomac site for the capital was less a mediation between North and South than a mechanism for advancing the westward aims of ambitious Virginia and Pennsylvania elites. Because Washington's location could be developed as a key river node linking the Atlantic to both the Ohio River and the Great Lakes, Virginians conceptualized the "Potomac corridor" site for Washington as "the essential link" in an "imperial vision" of a "national domain in the West" that could "promote national unity and confirm national interest in securing the Mississippi Valley against Britain and Spain." As Abbott concludes, Jefferson's deal with Hamilton "made sure that Virginia would be Pennsylvania's senior partner in the articulation of the American empire . . . Centrality did not mean splitting the difference between North and South by locating in an ambiguous borderland." Washington, in this sense, "was conceived as a city that would link Tidewater and Piedmont, coast and interior. It was expected to anchor and create a center of gravity that would draw Virginia, Maryland, and their Ohio Valley offspring into the dominant core region of the new nation." Ultimately, however, this regional dominance never happened. Other canals, railroads, and roadways—anchored to cities well north and east of the capital—forged stronger linkages to the western territories. Potomac Washington increasingly found itself to be the faultline of North–South sectional discord, rather than the path to national unity.[9] As an act of urban design, though, early Washington expressed the grandest possible national ambitions.

Major L'Enfant was eager for just such a large commission. He had already known General Washington since 1778, owing to his service as both soldier and illustrator. Further, he had been chosen in 1788–1789 to remodel the New York City Hall to serve as the first U.S. capitol and the site of Washington's inauguration as president. Like Washington, L'Enfant was ready to move onward. On 11 September 1789 (nearly a year before passage of the Residence Act), he wrote his friend the president to "sollicit the favor of being Employed" in designing "the Capital of this vast Empire." "No nation," he noted,

> perhaps had ever before the opportunity offer[e]d them of deliberately deciding on the spot where their Capital city should be fixed, or of combining every necessary consideration in the choice of situation—and altho' the means now within the power of the country are not such as to pursue the design to any great extant it will be obvious that the plan should be drawn on such a scale as to leave room for that aggrandizement & embellishment which the increase of the wealth of the Nation will permit it to pursue at any period however remote.

A year-and-a-half later Washington selected L'Enfant. The overwhelmingly ambitious scale of his subsequent plan—far larger than the then-occupied portions of New York, Philadelphia, or Boston, and comparable in footprint only to Paris or London—did indeed anticipate a city that has taken two centuries to fill out his framework of streets. L'Enfant told Washington that the metropolis would eventually house more than a million people, covering an area larger than any city in the world.[10]

In his "Observations explanatory of the Plan," engraved into the upper left corner of the plan, L'Enfant outlined his method for conceptualizing the city. He began with the identification of the site's most prominent topographical features and viewpoints; only after these were established as the nodes upon which the "Grand Edifices" and "Grand Squares" should be constructed did he develop the cardinally oriented gridded plaid and the famous diagonal "avenues of direct communication" that were intended to "connect the separate and most distant objects with the principal" and "preserve through the whole a reciprocity of sight." In this method, it is the "Congress House" which, appropriately, attains preeminent position on a hill L'Enfant described as "a pedestal waiting for a superstructure," noting that no other location "could bear a competition with this."[11] Only slightly less prominent was the site for the "President's House," placed on high ground to the west with a view down the Potomac and grandly indicated on the plan with what appears to be an eight-hundred-foot-long front facade, comparable in scale and footprint to Britain's Castle Howard.[12] If L'Enfant was still tempted by thoughts of past palaces, he was sensitive enough to the structure of the U.S. Constitution to have suggested the grouping of various executive departments around the presidential manse, far from the legislature's hilltop precinct.

Still, though much has been made of L'Enfant's spatial corollary to the Constitution's provision for a "separation of powers," L'Enfant made no recorded mention of this as a design determinant, and instead preferred to talk about the relationship of each building site to the Potomac. In any case, the notion of "separation of powers," taken as an ideogram, is neither wholly innovative nor accurate. A similar juxtaposition of separated executive and legislative functions was, for instance, evident in the eighteenth-century layout of colonial Williamsburg (3.3). Here, however, it indicated not separation between equal branches of government regulated by a system of checks and balances, but a system in which, despite the presence of a legislature that met in a prominently situated capitol, ultimate authority remained with the Crown-appointed governor. The comparison is yet another reminder that city plans, in themselves, are not simple reflections of government power. Rather, they are products of power and thus subject to wishful thinking or deliberate visual deception. Above all, they are products of a single moment of history, whereas the structure of government as well as the structure of cities is subject to continual evolution.

L'Enfant's design for Washington did not fully acknowledge the importance of an independent judiciary in the American political system. Though it is not labeled in his plan of 1791, an earlier memorandum to the president refers to a "Judiciary Court," which may have been projected to occupy the square on a rise located just north of the segmented avenue connecting the President's House and Capitol. This place, known as Judiciary

3.3 The plan of Williamsburg, Virginia, also reveals the separation between executive (governor) and legislature (capitol).

Square since the 1790s, now houses lower court facilities, though it has never been the site of the Supreme Court. Perhaps L'Enfant's missing judiciary was not an oversight, intentional or otherwise. In the engraving of Andrew Ellicott's revised plan (1792), this site again indicates an unlabeled structure located on a square that is given approximately equal prominence to squares believed to have been intended for other institutions such as the national bank, playhouse, market, exchange, and national church (3.4). In any case, the Supreme Court was not given this Judiciary Square site but was relegated to rooms inside the Capitol building. It did not gain its own quarters (and symbolic separation) until the 1930s, when it was given an imposing structure facing the east front of the Capitol.

In retrospect, it is understandable why the Supreme Court, as a new institution possessing neither a distinguished history nor a large bureaucracy to legitimate a need for architectural largesse, did not gain a position of

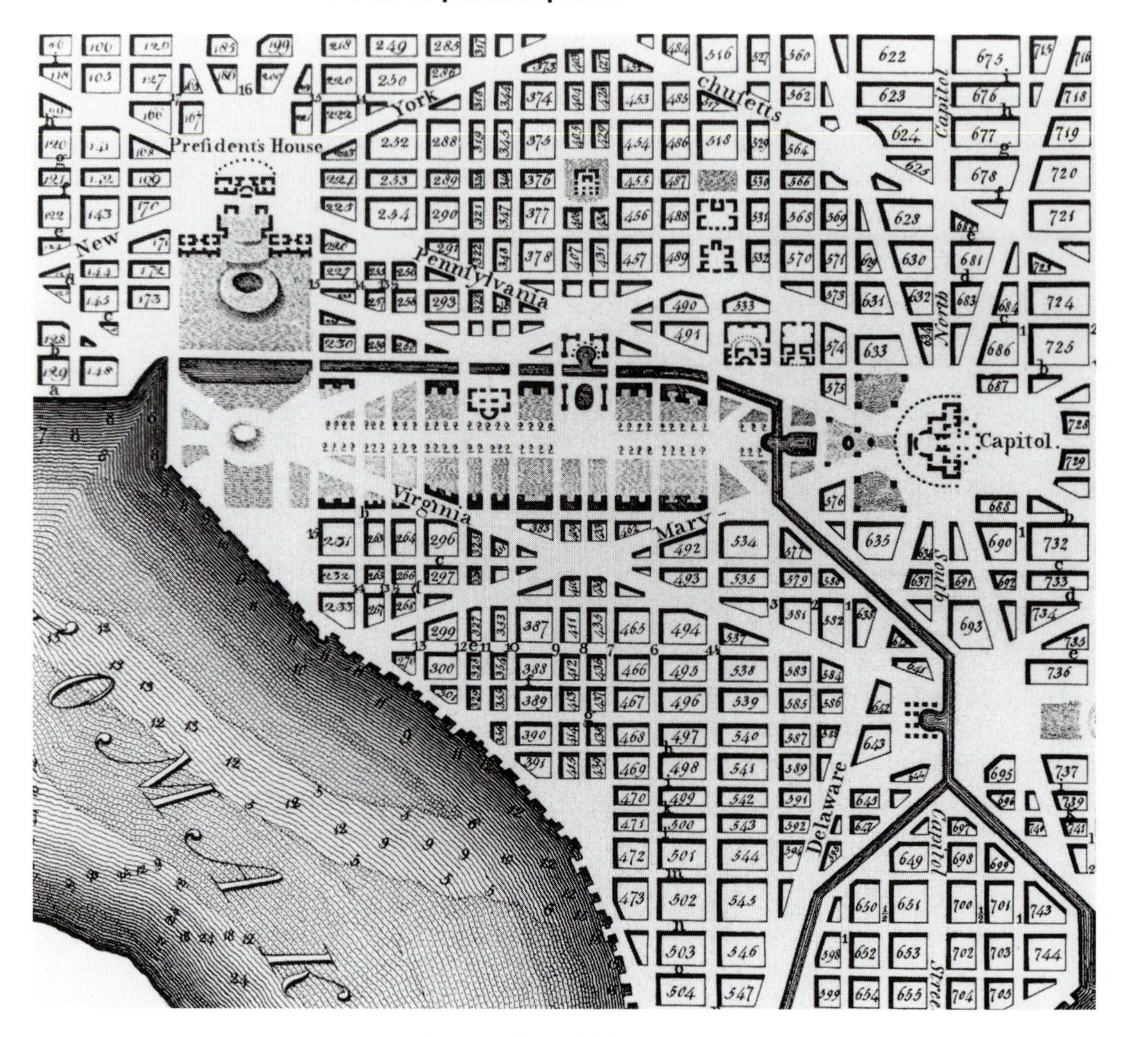

3.4 Capitol and President's Home (portion of Ellicott engraving of 1792).

immediate urban privilege. All the same, ever since the controversial decision in *Marbury vs. Madison* (1803) established the principle of judicial review by declaring an act of Congress unconstitutional, the United States Supreme Court has periodically played a more powerful role in constitutional government than even its contemporary urban (as opposed to architectural) presence would suggest. Two hundred years after L'Enfant's plan seemed to snub it, the National Capital Planning Commission revived serious debate about moving the Supreme Court to a more prominent location, though an actual relocation still seems unlikely. In some quarters, however, there is lingering resentment that the Lincoln and Jefferson memorials have usurped the most symbolically appropriate spots.[13] While triangulated urban placement of the third branch of government might better have indicated separation of powers, the more sophisticated constitutional system of checks and balances remains difficult to symbolize.

The rise in the institutional and architectural importance of the Supreme Court is but one indication of the ways the symbolism of monumental Washington has changed since L'Enfant. Today's tourist Washington is largely a twentieth-century product. The Mall, envisioned by L'Enfant as a "Grand Avenue, 400 feet in breadth," lined with spacious houses for foreign ministers and the like, has undergone numerous transformations. In 1851, following current practice, it was planted as a romantic park, utterly at odds with L'Enfant's tree-lined visions of France; soon afterward, it faced the incursion of a railway line and station at the foot of Capitol Hill. Only with the L'Enfantian revival ushered in by the report of the McMillan Commission in 1902,[14] which included plans for continuing the Mall axis past the Washington Monument to the site of a future Lincoln Memorial and for extending the cross-axis from the White House south to what would become the site of the Jefferson Memorial, did the center of Washington begin to gain something of its present appearance—a green swath of grass framed by trees and flanked by a panoply of museums. After all the changes, the position of the Capitol as the central focus of the whole urban composition has only been enhanced.

In two centuries of growth as the symbolic center of the United States and the repository of national life, Washington's promoters have faced many challenges. Though its very coming into existence marked one critical stage in the protracted postrevolutionary battle to define a usable symbolic center for the newly united collection of disparate ex-colonies, it was some time before Washington's position was consolidated, given its secondary importance to the national economy. When the country doubled in size after the Louisiana Purchase in 1803, the new center became eccentric almost immediately (though this extension merely confirmed the westward ambitions that underpinned the city's initial Potomac placement). More to the point, however, with sporadic development carried out in disparate corners of the so-called city, Washington's slow urban emergence must have seemed to many nineteenth-century observers not only eccentric, but sheer folly. Fifty years after L'Enfant's plan, a visiting Charles Dickens could still decry "spacious avenues, that begin in nothing, and lead nowhere; streets, mile-long, that only want houses, roads and inhabitants; public buildings that need but a public to be complete; and ornaments of great thoroughfares, which only lack great thoroughfares to ornament." With the resolute expansion of the country westward, Washington's detractors until as late as 1870 periodically advanced serious proposals to move the capital inland. But the only true challenge to Washington's centrality (other than the British attack of 1814) came with the Civil War, in which Washington stood at the brink of the sectional division.[15]

It is a commonplace that the Civil War was a turning point in American history; what is noteworthy for these purposes is the symbolic role played by the Capitol itself in the reunification of the country. The saga of the Capitol building design involved prominent architects of the day for nearly seventy years. Built in stages—first the two wings and only afterward the domed center—even the construction sequence bespoke its role as the central symbol of the United States. As George Washington told the commissioners in charge of the design competition, "It may be relied on, it is the progress of that building that is to inspire or depress the public confidence."[16] With work on the building interrupted by the War of 1812, Jefferson wrote to the architect Benjamin Latrobe, "I shall live in hope that the day will come when

3.5 Unfinished Capitol dome at Lincoln's inauguration, 4 March 1861.

3.6 *Lincoln Ordering the Building of the Dome to Continue*, 1863. Painting located inside House of Representatives wing.

an opportunity will be given you of finishing the middle building in a style worthy of the two wings, and worthy of the first temple dedicated to the sovereignty of the people, embellishing with Athenian taste the course of a nation looking far beyond the range of Athenian destinies."[17] Fifty years later, however, the shrine to democracy was still not complete.

When the Civil War broke out, Thomas Ustick Walter's enlargement of Latrobe's central dome remained unfinished, an unintentional but powerful commentary on the situation of the country it was to symbolize (3.5). In the words of Henry Adams, remembering his visit to the capital, "As in 1800 and 1850, so in 1860, the same rude colony was camped in the same forest, with the same unfinished Greek temples for workrooms, and sloughs for roads. The Government had an air of social instability and incompleteness that went far to support the right of secession in theory as in fact; but right or wrong, secession was likely to be easy where there was so little to secede from."[18] President Lincoln, extending his penchant for architectural metaphor made famous in his House Divided speech, saw great potential in the progress of the dome. "When the people see the dome rising," he commented, "it will be a sign that we intend the union to go on" (3.6).[19]

On 2 December 1863, amid ceremonial fanfare marked by a thirty-five-gun salute, the lantern of Walter's imposing dome was topped out by the placement of Thomas Crawford's statue of Freedom. Intended to boost the morale of Northern troops, the pomp and symbolism of Freedom was not without its ironic side, given that Crawford's plaster model was cast in bronze by slave labor. I have found no evidence that this inconsistency was a matter of concern at the time, but the symbolism of the Capitol statue's initial design was controversial in another way: "Senator Jefferson Davis of Mississippi noted that the figure wore a liberty cap of the kind worn by ancient Roman slaves who had been freed. He called this a provocation to the South. The harassed sculptor substituted a feathered eagle for the cap, and from the ground today Freedom on her high perch looks rather like an Indian with a disheveled war bonnet."[20] Such concern over the minutiae of symbolism seems unusual; the overall symbolism of the Capitol's design rested on much more loosely interpreted resonances.

Though his models were more often found in Republican Rome than in Periclean Athens, Jefferson, as the most informed and outspoken architectural advocate among America's founders, consistently looked to classical precedent for architectural and urbanistic inspiration. "Each age," Mumford has commented, "tends to flatter the part of the past that sends back its own image."[21] Washington's earliest architects and planners saw that reflected image undergo a dramatic transformation. Although no building in Washington was as literal in its recall of classical antiquity as the Virginia State Capitol (1780), Jefferson's endeavor to render the Roman Maison Carrée suitable for government offices, all forms of classical allusion faced two risks. Either the architecture would be transferred so generally that its intended recall of classical democracy would be indistinguishably diffused into reminders of classical empire and Renaissance courtly splendor, or it would be transferred so archaeologically that it would lack the capacity to meet the functional needs of modern government. In a letter to Jefferson in 1807, even the Grecophile Latrobe seemed aware of such dangers:

> My principles of good taste are rigid in Grecian architecture. I am a bigoted Greek in the condemnation of the Roman architecture of Baalbec, Palmyra, and Spalato. . . . Wherever, therefore the Grecian style can be copied without impropriety I love to be a mere, I would say a slavish copyist, but the forms & the distribution of the Roman & Greek buildings which remain, are in general, inapplicable to the objects & uses of our public buildings. Our religion requires a church wholly different from their temples; our legislative assemblies and our courts of justice, buildings of entirely different principles from their basilicas; and our amusements could not possibly be performed in their theatres & amphitheatres.[22]

Jefferson, for his part, seemed less concerned with such "improprieties." He viewed this broad symbolic scheme for housing the work of a democratic republic in the forms of its ancient precursors as a novel way of staking the new country's presence and proclaiming its new freedoms to the entire world. "Its object," he wrote, "is to improve the taste of my countrymen, to increase their reputation, to reconcile them to the rest of the world, and procure them its praise."[23] National identity, in this view, was something to be cultivated internationally through successful emulation. Unfortunately, as the architectural preferences of subsequent rulers—from Napoléon to Hitler—would reveal, the language of classicism may be manipulated for very different political ends.

In L'Enfant's plan, only the names and the functions of the buildings changed; the most basic planning principles remained constant. This was still a language premised on the exaltation of social hierarchy. No new method for conveying the new circumstances of "government of the people, by the people, and for the people" was attempted or sought after. Moreover, despite efforts to create "avenues of direct communication" with "reciprocity of sight," the most prominent street in Washington provides no such amenity. Looking northwest up Pennsylvania Avenue, one cannot even glimpse the White House. Even where visual contact is not lost, L'Enfant's design technique served to enhance distant views of government buildings rather than to facilitate access to them; it linked images and emphasized distances without connecting entrances or inviting closer contact between citizens and government.

John Reps comments, "It was a supreme irony that the plan forms originally conceived to magnify the glories of despotic kings and emperors came to be applied as a national symbol of a country whose philosophical basis was so firmly rooted in democratic equality."[24] Yet, while Reps is surely correct to emphasize the curious persistence of an anachronistic plan type, he overstates the new government's commitment to equality. The U.S. Constitution of 1787, from its infamous three-fifths clause defining the status of slaves to the institution of the electoral college as a check upon the power of the popular vote, was premised upon many principles that are neither egalitarian nor fully democratic. Though Jefferson and his supporters sought to use architecture to invoke Greco-Roman democracy, L'Enfant and the architects of the Capitol alluded more to the Roman Vatican than to the Roman forum. Thus, the experiment in democracy initially spawned no parallel experiment in planning or in architecture. Yet in placing the

3.7 Extending the Legacy Plan, National Capital Planning Commission, 1997.

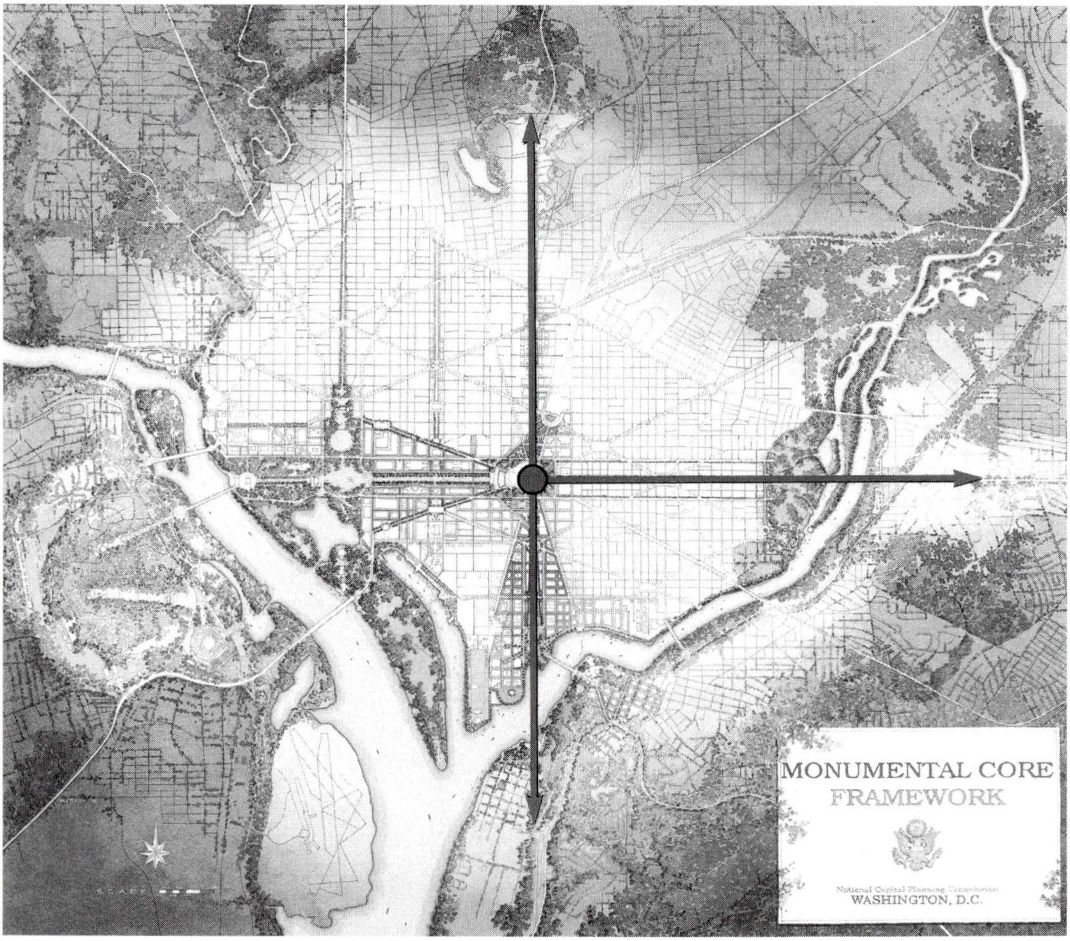

Capitol at the focal point of an entire urban composition, the designers of Washington established a precedent for all future capital cities.

In actuality, though, the centrality of the Capitol that appeared so clear in L'Enfant's original conception gradually gave way to a "Monumental Core" of museums and government facilities that focused tourist, commercial, and media attention almost exclusively on the northwestern quadrant of the city, relegating the Capitol precinct to the eastern edge. Similarly, Washington's planners clustered parkland development along the Potomac, while ignoring the Anacostia River in the city's impoverished east. Responding to this, the National Capital Planning Commission promulgated the "Extending the Legacy" Plan in 1997. The plan, purely advisory in nature, explicitly seeks to recenter Washington on the Capitol and extend development to the four quadrants of the city: "At the heart of *Extending the Legacy* is a new definition of the Monumental Core that includes not only the Mall and the traditional ceremonial spaces, but also North Capitol and South Capitol streets, the Anacostia River and adjacent areas. The Capitol once again becomes the symbolic center of the city, as L'Enfant intended, with its power radiating outward in all directions" (3.7).[25] As the twenty-first century begins, L'Enfant's legacy is uneasily conjoined with the legacy of the 9/11 attacks, leaving the designed capital of Washington to struggle over ways to balance the openness of democratic governance with the closure demanded by security concerns. In its dual preoccupation with both display and isolation, Washington's iconographic struggle typifies the challenges facing designed capitals worldwide.

COLONIALISM AND EARLY DESIGNED CAPITALS

As a designed capital for an independent country, Washington was at least a century ahead of most countries seeking new capitals, since many places remained governed by colonial regimes until well into the twentieth century. Some of these face various forms of dependency even today. In contrast to capitals created in the aftermath of an independence movement, the siting and development of colonial capitals served the interests of an overseas empire. The spatial politics of the modern colonial city is an enormous subject, with each colonizing power exhibiting idiosyncrasies, and is far too unwieldy to claim much space here. If we are to understand the politics and symbolism of the location of capitals and capitols in postcolonial situations, however, some discussion of the colonial capital experience is undoubtedly necessary.

In *Urbanism, Colonialism and the World-Economy*, Anthony King provides useful groundwork for a typology of European-imposed colonial cities, one which recognizes the diversity of factors affecting such settlements. Colonial urban development patterns, he suggests, may vary in relation to

the previously existing levels of urbanization in the colonized society (highly developed, as in India; limited or long-since destroyed, as in the Americas; or nonexistent, as in Australia);

the motives behind colonization (for example, economic exploitation, religious conversion, political strategy); and

the nature of coercion employed (for example, none—if uninhabited; some—through manipulation of contracts and treaties; large-scale enslavement; systematic genocide).

Moreover, these factors may change and develop over time, depending on such factors as the value of the colony's resources to the home country, the relative size and permanency of the colonizing population, the state of economic development of the indigenous people, and the nature and degree of resistance to continued colonial rule.

Not surprisingly, the circumstances of each act of colonial intervention affect the form of cities that are produced to serve it. King identifies a range of approaches to city making that have been employed by colonizing powers in various parts of the world. Where no precolonial settlement exists, colonizers may opt to build settlements solely for themselves by discouraging or prohibiting settlement by indigenous inhabitants and other non-colonial groups. Alternatively, they may build chiefly for themselves but include separate living areas for noncolonists. Less commonly, they may plan for an intermixture of all or most of the various groups.

In places where a previously existing indigenous settlement is found, there is a similar range of social altitudes implicit (or explicit) in the various options for transforming urban space. The colonizing power may choose to (1) occupy what is already there, (2) modify or extend what is already there, (3) tear down the existing settlement and build anew, (4) incorporate the existing system into a larger planned development, (5) build a new settlement adjacent to the old but separate from it, or (6) build a new settlement at considerable distance from the old.[26]

Though it is not an aim of this book to delve into the nature of residential segregation in the cities under study, there is, perhaps, an important parallel phenomenon at work in the social/spatial relations implied by the privileged placement of central government facilities in designed capital cities. In capital cities initiated by acts of large-scale, government-sponsored design, an extreme degree of separation seems to be the rule rather than the exception. Architecture and urban design are used both to highlight the locus of power and, except in the most open, stable, and democratic of societies, to remove that power from public access. Whether expressed through the separate location of a new capital distant (or equidistant) from other contending centers of power, or through the tendency to have the capitol dominate the capital, the designers of government-sponsored cities seem to regard their creations as defensive gestures. Such architecture and urbanism attempts to place the government, often quite literally, above challenge.

For colonial rulers, these challenges ordinarily assume the form of nationalist movements, which may take decades or even centuries to develop to the point of political realignment. Capital cities have been built or designated at all stages of this colonization and decolonization process.

While this book concentrates on examples of postcolonial capital and capitol creation, many contemporary states have reused precisely those capital cities, such as Imperial Delhi, that were designed to forestall formal political independence. Other capitals have been designed after formal political independence, yet have nonetheless been subject to heterogeneous neocolonial influences.

British-influenced capitals such as Ottawa and Canberra epitomize this middle ground between colonial status and full legal independence. Like Washington, these centers grew out of colonial settings in which the European colonizers, through immigration, segregation, and extermination, had become a majority. In most other places, such as India and South Africa, the colonizers remained a minority, ruling by superior force rather than by superior numbers, and the urban imprint of colonialism was even more marked. Each place had constraints that narrowed the range of desirable and viable options for capital city location and design.

South Africa's Pretoria, for instance, was founded as a compromise between rival settlements of Voortrekkers who had migrated to the Transvaal from the British-dominated Cape Colony. Though Pretoria successively became the capital of the Transvaal in 1860, of the Union of South Africa in 1910, and of the Republic of South Africa in 1961—and is still the administrative capital—South Africa's national political structure remains spatially divided, the legislature meeting in Cape Town and the Supreme Court in Bloemfontein. Moreover, in postapartheid South Africa, the name Pretoria (originally selected to honor the Boer leader Andries Pretorius) became predictably contentious. In 2000, the larger metropolitan region encompassing Pretoria was renamed the City of Tshwane and, in 2005, local African National Congress leaders launched complicated and controversial efforts to formally use Tshwane as the name for nearly all of Pretoria itself.[27]

Such divisions, rooted in ethnic and racial histories and carried out in spatial terms, also have many ramifications at the level of capitol architecture and urban design. Herbert Baker's Union Buildings in Pretoria were designed in anticipation of the Union in 1910 rather than in its aftermath and were not only to house the administration of the new Union but to exemplify it as well (3.8). Baker later claimed that his design symbolized the reconciliation of the two races of South Africa on equal terms, by which he meant, of course, not whites and blacks but Boer and Briton.

Though exemplifying a symmetry that could signify an egalitarian balance, the buildings are open to other interpretations. Surely, the strong influence of Sir Christopher Wren in the design left little doubt, at least among the architecturally initiated, about Baker's own cultural affiliations. Similarly, the siting of this capitol complex on the same level plateau as Government House, the Baker-designed British governor-general's residence, was a reminder that even political union, which rendered the governor-general an adviser, did not yet imply a break from the British Empire. In other ways, too, political resolution remained tentative. Baker's acropolitan idea of a hilltop Temple of Peace and a central domed Capitol (meant to be "a greater symbol of final union" and initially conceived to house the "future Parliament" that remained in Cape Town) was never carried out.[28] Lacking

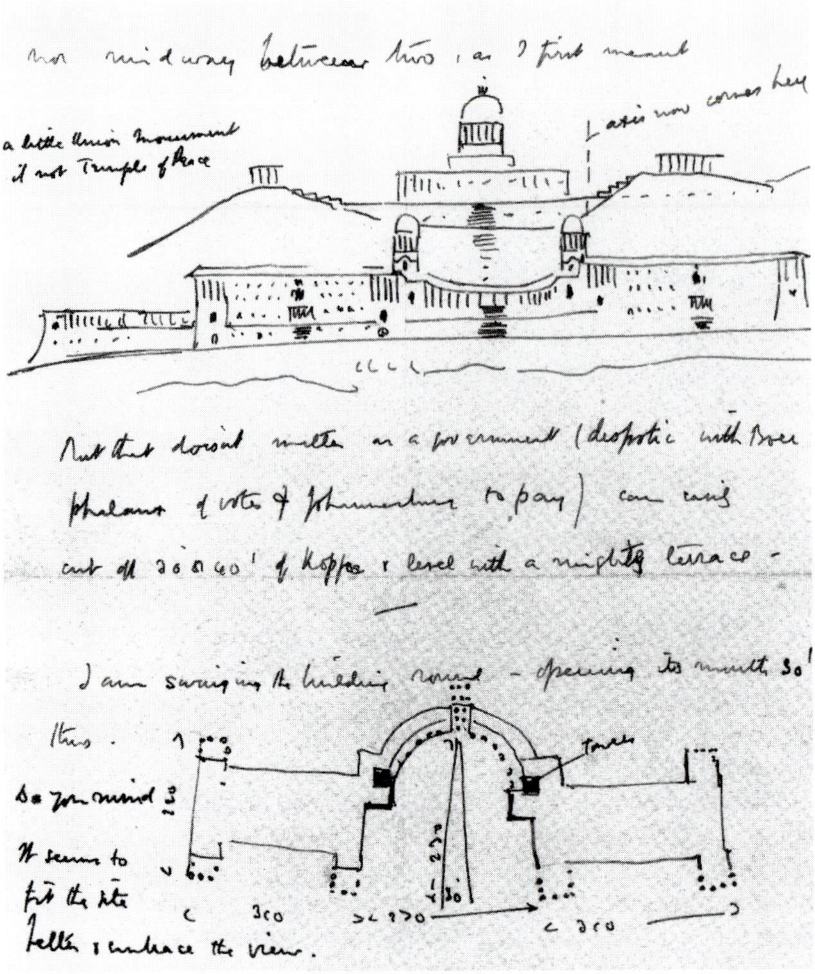

3.8 Baker's sketch of Pretoria's Union Buildings: exemplifying the joining of Boer and Briton.

this crowning centerpiece, even the bottom of Baker's sketch of the plan (1909) resembles a pair of battling rams (3.8).

South Africa's nonwhite population figured only peripherally in Baker's imperial vision, typified by an unexecuted design for a "small partly open Council Place for Native Indabas [meetings], where, without coming into the Building, Natives may feel the majesty of Government."[29] Three-quarters of a century later, much of this same attitude prevailed in actualized urban design plans for places like Mmabatho and Bisho, sponsored during the waning years of the apartheid regime. In their hollow grandeur, such places were no less condescending than Baker's ideas. The design of such new capitals, boasting imposing capitol complexes for each of the so-called independent homelands, was little more than a South African-subsidized urban charade intended to promote separate national identities for each of several black groups denied South African citizenship and other rights. With the collapse of apartheid, however, such sham cities finally gained some initial legitimacy, repurposed as provincial capitals in a "new" South Africa.[30] Given the polarities, both interracial and intraracial, expressed by a long history of fragmented capitals and capitols, it is hardly surprising that the capital politics of postapartheid South Africa have remained controversial and charged with symbolism.

Contemporary Canada's politics have been less turbulent than South Africa's, yet Ottawa too has colonial roots, and its promoters and planners have had to grapple with factional discord and cultural diversity. Only the name *Ottawa* bespeaks any interest in connection or compromise with native inhabitants; its existence as a capital is an outcome of the contending claims of its French and British settlers. Its designation as a capital was not a postindependence decision of a united Canadian government, but a ruling made in 1867 by Queen Victoria, who was asked to settle a dispute over which city—Montreal, Québec City, Toronto, and Kingston were the other contenders—should administer the Province of Canada. Ottawa, then, was a royally brokered federal compromise ten years before Canadian Confederation. Located, diplomatically enough, on the border between Upper and Lower Canada (equivalent to the contemporary border between Québec and Ontario), it was midway between Toronto and Québec City and housed both English and French linguistic and cultural groups. It also featured ample publicly owned land on a beautiful riverfront suitable for dramatic placement of government buildings; in addition, lying seventy-five miles from the U.S. border, it was also preferred for reasons of military security.[31]

Not shaped by formal, large-scale urban design plans until the twentieth century—and even then these official plans have had minor influence on the city's development compared to other capitals—Ottawa's slow initial growth encouraged skepticism. Derided as a "sub-arctic lumber village" at the time of its selection as capital, its detractors complained about "Westminster in the wilderness" even after completion of its magisterial clifftop Parliament Buildings later in the century in a suitably neo-British, neo-gothic style (3.9).

3.9 Approaching the Parliament Buildings, Ottawa.

In many ways, Ottawa has remained true to its picturesque roots, resisting much of the relentless axiality that has characterized other heavily planned capitals. To this day, Ottawa's neo-gothic parliamentary spires are designed to be best approached along the diagonal, enabling these imposing edifices to convey maximum surprise and visual appeal.[32]

Subsequent planning, beginning with Edward Bennett's elaborate City Beautiful scheme produced for Canada's Federal Plan Commission in 1915, envisaged more than a consolidation of impressive national government facilities. The planners sought in addition to promote a sense of a national capital region that encompassed not only Ottawa (on the Ontario side of the Ottawa River), but also Hull, in Québec. Bennett's politically astute gesture was not implemented, but similar efforts to unify the two sides continued throughout the twentieth century. As francophone separatist pressures increased, the symbolism of the capital district itself seemed to reach out toward Canada's disaffected French minority.[33] While such schisms will never be resolved through acts of urban design, the unusual nature of the circular Official Ceremonial Route deserves some comment (3.10). This processional way—now known as Confederation Boulevard—not only conjoins Parliament Hill with Government House (the residence of the governor-general, not of the prime minister), but also links, at least in theory, Ottawa

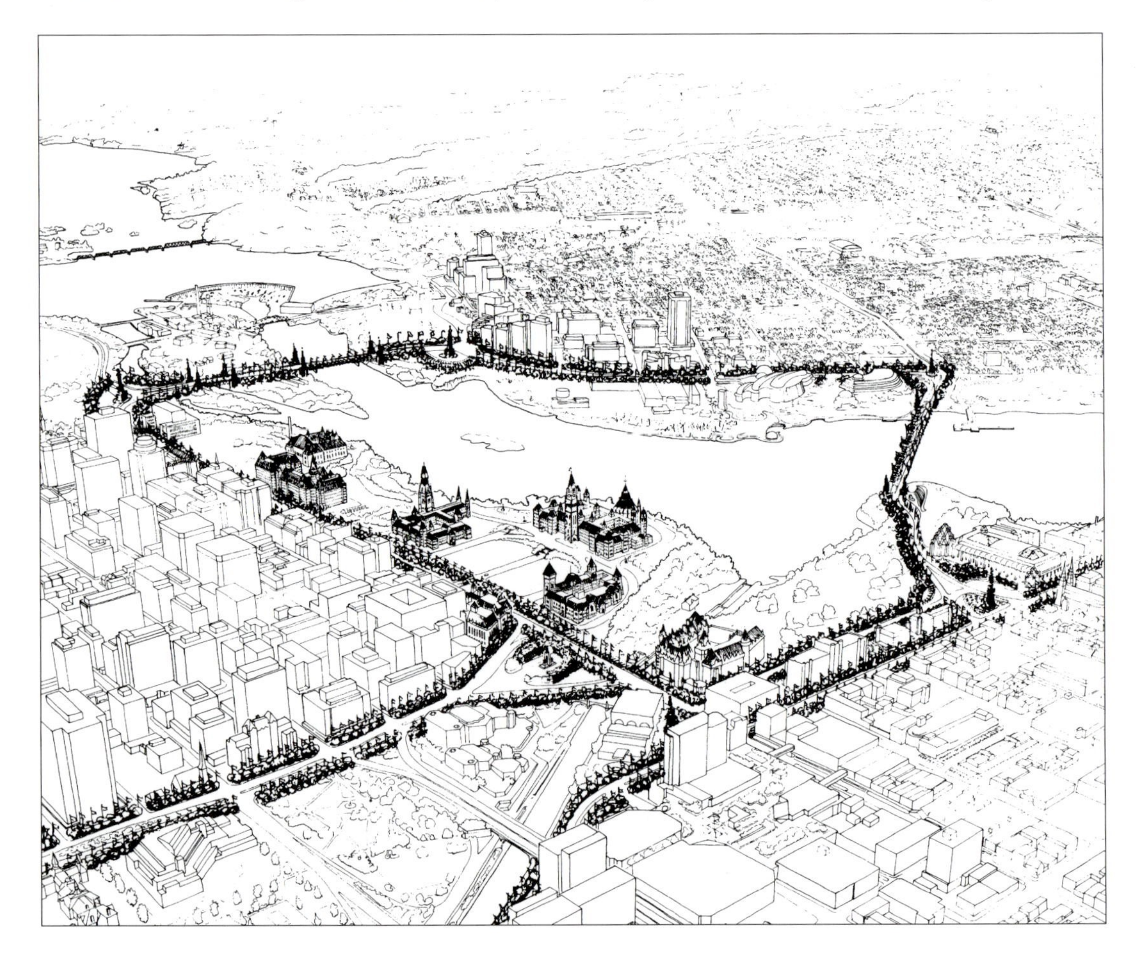

3.10 Boulevard Canada: a ceremonial route linking Ottawa and Hull/Gatineau. Ottawa is in the foreground, with the Parliament Buildings on a promontory overlooking the Ottawa River.

and Hull (renamed Gatineau in 2002, to sound more French). By extension, of course, it links Ontario and Québec. By distributing various national museums and other cultural and government facilities along this loop on both sides of the river and on Victoria Island in midstream, the Canadian planners seem to desire nothing less than some sort of nouveau-Ringstrasse. Although this Boulevard Canada linking liberal institutions will not replace actual walls, as in Vienna, the Canadians too have barriers to overcome. Some in the capital, however, feel that the walls are going up instead of coming down: "Parliament Hill will be the largest jewel on the necklace that will wind via the proposed ceremonial route (in one scheme using red asphalt paving) past the showcase buildings on both sides of the Ottawa River. The two cultures will be symbolically linked, the chief government buildings will look in on themselves, their backs to the two vernacular cities of Ottawa and Hull. A Citadel will have emerged as if by serendipity. The cause will certainly not have been planning."[34] Whatever the limitations, from its compromise site to its planners' culturally inclusive symbolic attempts at forging a more nationally representative urbanism, Ottawa has played a role in the symbolic development of a Canadian national identity.

CANBERRA: A CAPITAL DESIGNED FOR DEMOCRACY

Canberra, designed to house the national government of a newly federated Australia, emerged in a situation of relative social homogeneity and political continuity, yet it is hardly a place without tensions. With a dwindling Aboriginal population pushed aside, the issues of contention among the settlers centered on economic and political matters rather than racial and ethnic strife. Australia's Imperial/Commonwealth status even after federation implied divided loyalties and yielded a more tempered nationalism: Canberra's choice as federal capital required not only the approval of the Australian parliament, but also royal assent from overseas.

Understood by its promoters and its detractors alike to be the "Australian Washington," Canberra mimicked its American precursor in many ways. The choice of site, poised between the two major population centers of Sydney and Melbourne, comes as no surprise, though in fact it was the result of more than a decade of parliamentary false starts and compromises.[35] Though the capital site was selected after all the states of the Australian mainland plus Tasmania had agreed to federation, a more continentally central location was not seriously contemplated (3.11, 3.12). Because each state's infrastructure was still oriented toward its own old colonial capital, interstate competition remained acute. Still, the main concern of all but the Sydney parliamentarians was simply to keep the capital away from Sydney, Australia's Mother City. Section 125 of the Commonwealth of Australia Constitution Act of 1899 resolved this question for good but provided little guidance on site selection: "The seat of government of the Commonwealth shall be determined by the Parliament, and shall be within territory which shall have been granted to or acquired by the Commonwealth, and shall be vested in and belong to

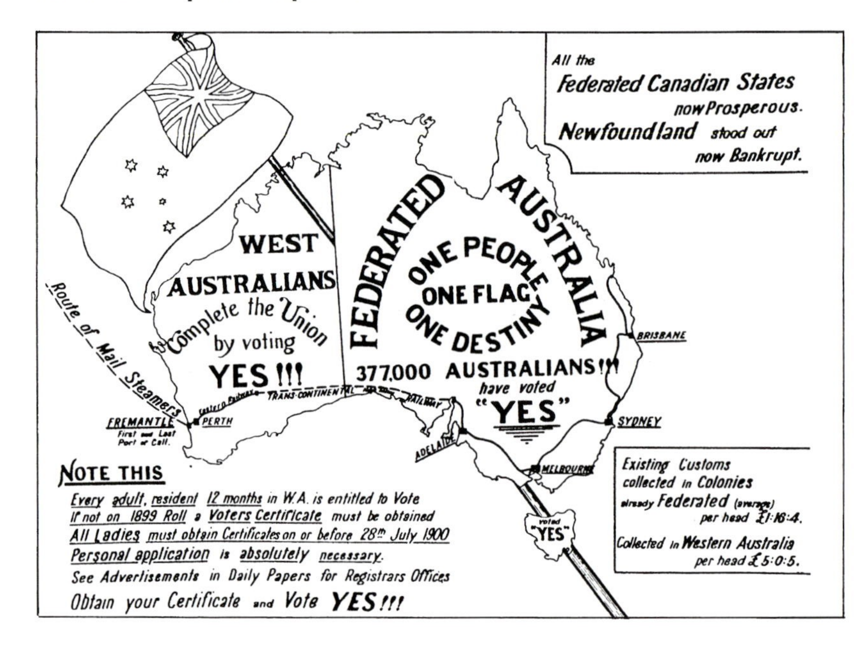

3.11 "One People, One Flag, One Destiny": Australia in 1900.

3.12 "This Building Is Being Erected for Australian Unity Coy. Ld. From Designgs by Nobuddy in Particular."

3.13 Canberra: the Bush Capital.

the Commonwealth, and shall be in the State of New South Wales, and be distant not less than one hundred miles from Sydney."[36] As one historian of Canberra puts it, "It was part of the romantic make believe of the time to pretend that it was the spontaneous conception of aspiring national idealism. But the legend was a plaything of a tiny minority. The great majority of Australians knew well enough that the national capital had been conceived, not in generous national enthusiasm, but in the haggling of provincialisms."[37] Known from the beginning as the Bush Capital, it was clear that its position within that bush would never stray very far from Australia's southeast corner. Even so, it was located in an area so remote that, when selected, the capital district's horses, cattle, and sheep each outnumbered its humans (3.13). Some of the site's appeal also seems rooted in a desire for a capital with a "cold climate," a preference rooted not just in a wish to escape the harshest aspects of an Australian summer but also in a racialized sense that Australia's Anglo-Saxon roots might best be deployed to full advantage in cool conditions.[38]

Even after a site was chosen, the name for the capital remained an open

3.14 A version of Griffin's plan for Canberra (1913). At the heart of the plan are the Government Center, the Municipal Center, and the Market Center, with a large Manufacturing Section to the north and a Suburban and Semi-Agricultural section to the southeast.

question. The public was invited to submit suggestions, and these provide a telling inventory of Australian feelings about the capital site and the process by which it came to be selected:

> Those who had lived through the battle of the sites must have given a wry smile at the suggestion of Sydmelbane, and there were a number of similar confections, the most euphonious of which was probably Sydmelperadbrisho. Wheatwoolgold, Kangaremu and Eucalypta headed a list of Australian animals, vegetables and minerals. Public reaction to fiscal policy produced Economy, Revenuelia, Gonebroke and Swindle Ville, and politics inspired Caucus City, Liberalism, Malleyking, Fisherburra and Cookaburra. Titanic and Great Scott referred to recent tragedies in the Atlantic and Antarctic, but might also have had something to say about Commonwealth–State relations. Anglophiles and classical scholars had put up Cromwell, Gladstone, Disraeli, Maxurba and Victoria Deferenda Defender.[39]

On 12 March 1913, Lady Denman, wife of the governor-general, announced the winner: "I name the capital of Australia, Canberra—the accent is on the Can." Canberra, "the mystic word that would be known all over the Empire a couple of hours later," was said by some to be an Aboriginal word for "woman's breasts" while others defined it as "meeting place."[40] In any case, it provided an Aboriginal name for a district whose last native Australian had died sixteen years before.

Canberra, so heavily contested by a fledgling commonwealth, carried enormous symbolic freight. Frequent commentator George Taylor, editor of *Building*, articulated the stakes in 1913 in an editorial called "Canberra Saved": "Canberra is the token of our nationality; and if it is to rise to the status of a national capital, big Australianism must assert itself; petty parochialism must be dismissed, and the people divided by artificial state boundaries must remember that they are Australians first of all, with their aspirations symbolised on that 'common ground', Canberra."[41] To get started, however, big Australianism needed help from a pair of smaller Americans.

The master plan for the new capital, designed chiefly by Walter Burley Griffin and rendered by his wife and business partner, Marion Mahony Griffin, was selected after an international competition that pre-dated the naming of the city. In spite of various compromises and delays, significant parts of it have been implemented (3.14).[42] The Griffin plan sought to make maximum use of the rolling topography of what many believed to have once been the most beautiful sheep station in Australia. As Christopher Vernon observes, the cross-axial plan responded with sensitivity to the site's physical features, and "fused geometric reason with picturesque naturalism." Griffin sited the main ceremonial axis of the city to align visually with distant mountain peaks (one of which, Mount Bimberi, actually turned out not to be visible) and envisioned a cross-axis formed by water. The most important government buildings, intended to symbolize the center of the nation, were to be built symmetrically about the land axis and contained in a triangle set

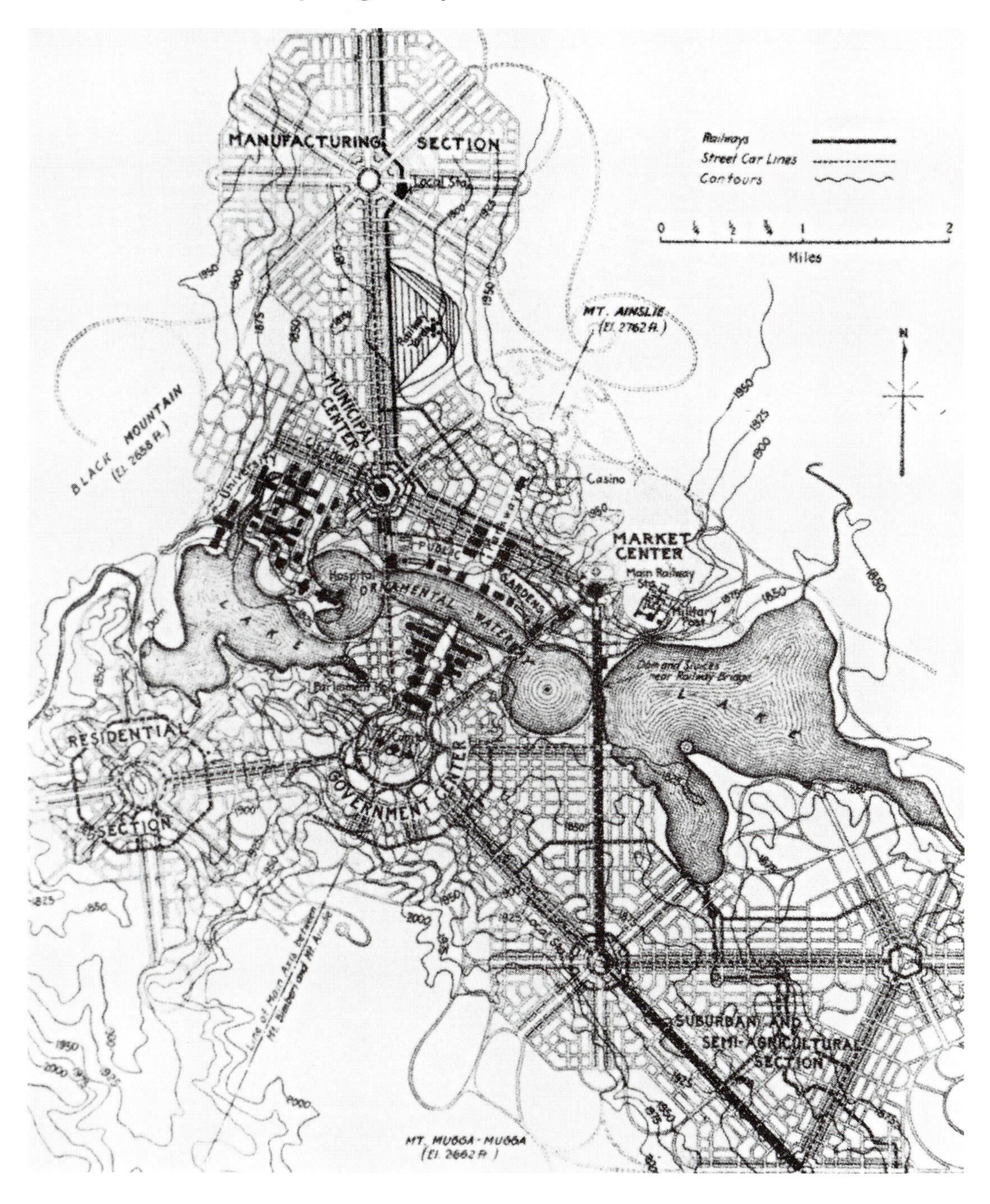

off by the water axis and the two grand, converging diagonal avenues that bridge it. This, Griffin felt, would enable the activities of government to take place in an "accessible but still quiet area."[43] As a reminder of Australia's imperial loyalties, the grand diagonal roads that ensure this access would soon be named Commonwealth and Kings, though the more democratically minded Griffin preferred to call the latter Federal.

At its heart, the major avenues of Griffin's official plan (1913) demarcated not just the presence of government but a grand triangle of functions, with three nodes—Government Center (centered on the Capitol), Market Center (centered on the main railway station), and Municipal Center (centered on a City Hall), with a Manufacturing Section located a safe distance to the northwest, in proper Garden City spirit. North of the water axis he proposed public gardens and a variety of civic institutions. Adjacent to these was Constitution Avenue, the boulevard linking the avenues named Commonwealth and Kings. Griffin initially referred to this street as Capital Terrace, suggesting his belief in the primacy of the view up the land axis to the place that became known as Capital Hill. Residential areas were proposed for several places in the plan, though resultant development differed fundamentally from Griffin's conception. Griffin stressed the need for both a public transit system ("borne as a public expense") and a diversity of house sizes and prices within each residential community in order to avoid social segregation, yet subsequent planners abandoned these goals.[44] After his departure in 1920, whatever remained of Griffin's proposal for a predominantly urban pattern of residential perimeter block row houses became gradually transmuted into suburban pockets of Australian bungalows. As Vernon puts it, "the Chicago-like urbanity envisaged by the Griffins" was "insidiously transformed into a disparate collection of garden suburbs." Moreover, K. F. Fischer notes that assignment to these residential areas was allocated to public servants according to salary and status, a practice that had profound consequences for the character of the future city:

> What was at the back of the planners' minds was a suburban middle-class ideal community with residential areas neatly graded according to salary and public service rank. Their approach was in fact a process of site planning carried out in a Victorian frame of mind that translated the anticipated social hierarchies into spatial hierarchies. Whether the planners were aware of it or not, when they arranged residential subdivisions and government housing in strict accordance with the occupational hierarchies in the public service, they were repeating the tradition in which the British used to design their administrative capitals in the colonies.[45]

Given this legacy, Fischer contends, "Canberrans can pinpoint the social status of every street of the capital with almost ludicrous precision."[46] Though the practice of segregation by income and job was criticized in Parliament as early as 1927, it would continue for a long time not only in Canberra, but also in planned cities in other so-called democratic countries.

In institutional aspects of urban hierarchy, Griffin's ideas also underwent transformation, most prominently in the treatment of Capital Hill, the plan's central focus. The apex of the triangle, the point where the diagonals and the central land axis come together, may have been called Capital Hill, but was not meant by Griffin to be the site of the Parliament building. Though Capital Hill is the highest of the many hills that lie within the center of the city, and though Griffin, echoing L'Enfant, envisioned these hills as the "elevated foundations for . . . buildings of dominating importance," he reserved the prime symbolic location for a public park and ceremonial meeting area. He confused matters somewhat by labeling this point the Capitol Building (to be flanked by pavilions for the governor-general and the prime minister). Yet Griffin's Capitol was purely for administrative offices and public gathering, what he termed "A National Shrine representing the sentimental and spiritual head, if not the actual working mechanism of the Government of the Federation." As Wolfgang Sonne comments, Griffin's unusual proposal "successfully solved the problem of representation of a democracy; separating the Capitol and the Parliament was a stroke of genius: the parliamentary building could serve exclusively for the assembly of the elected representatives of the people, without the nuisance of public access and without having to symbolize openness. These tasks were instead assumed by the Capitol, a public building in the true sense, which would have been open to the entire people and would have been able to symbolize the civic entity of the democracy above and beyond the triad of state powers."[47]

The Parliament House was to be placed on axis in front of Capital Hill and eighty feet below its summit, atop the lesser eminence known as Camp Hill.[48] Griffin's depictions of his idea for the Capitol contain something of a contradiction: what looks in the plan to be a relatively small trio of pavilions, when seen in elevation and in Marion Mahony Griffin's perspective rendering appears as a massive structure dominating the center of the city (3.15). Part of the seeming discontinuity stems from the enormous scale of Griffin's proposal—something that seems to be a traffic circle around the Capitol

3.15 Marion Mahony Griffin's rendering of Capital Hill area.

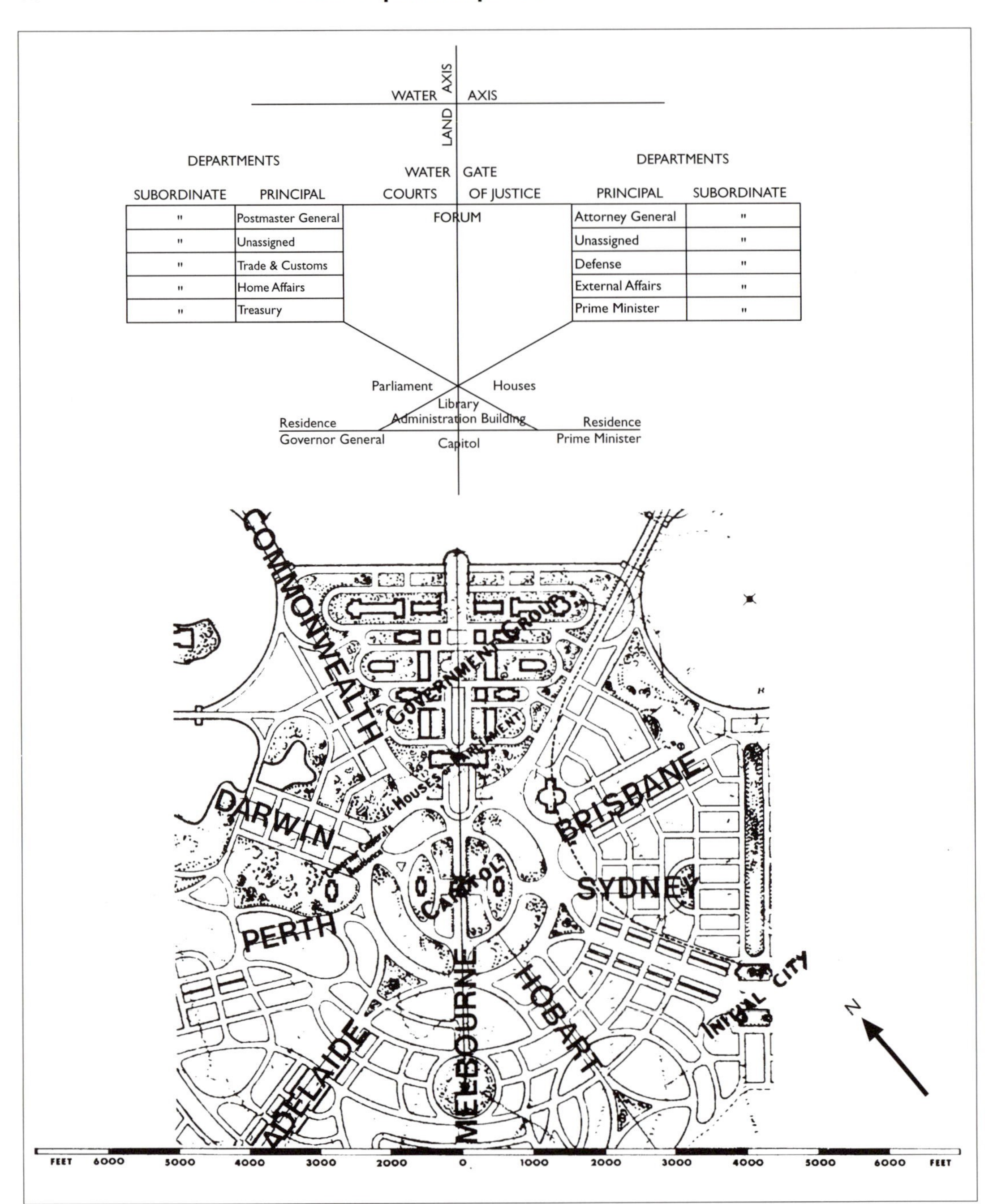

3.16 Detail of the Capitol area. Roads fan out in the directions of Australian state capitals, leaving the capitol on an island in the center.

and linking the radial avenues is in fact about a half-mile in diameter (3.16). In such an expansive setting, questions of both architectural dominance and urban design isolation would plague the designers working in this central area for decades.

As in Washington, many factors conspired to delay the completion of Canberra's central legislative building; what took sixty-five years in the United States took seventy-five in Australia. Griffin made no detailed architectural proposals for the Parliament House, treating it as visually subsidiary to the more prominent—but functionally subservient—hilltop Capitol building. He wrote of a "stepped pinnacle treatment in lieu of the inevitable dome," noting that such a form had been "the last word" in a number of ancient civilizations,[49] but the drawings show that this description applied to the Capitol, not to the Parliament House. The First World War and austerity measures delayed a design competition for the Parliament House, and instead of a permanent building the Australian government elected to commission a provisional structure, on Griffin's land axis, but below both Camp Hill and Capital Hill. This building, formally opened in 1927, signaled the transfer of Parliament to Canberra from Melbourne,[50] though many government departments would remain in Melbourne until well after World War Two.

The question of a permanent Parliament House did not go away, however, as the space requirements of a modern bureaucracy rapidly outgrew the provisional quarters. The issue was more than a matter of functional efficiency: it raised fundamental questions about the symbolism of Griffin's plan and, more generally, about the proper symbolism for a democracy. If Capital Hill were to be reserved for an administration building, for instance, central Canberra could face a situation similar to the unfortunate juxtaposition of facilities at the United Nations headquarters in New York, where the presence of the bureaucracy in its sleek skyscraper Secretariat dominates the more significant but less conspicuously housed Assembly and committee functions.[51] For decades, Australian parliamentary committees debated where in the capital the permanent Parliament House should be sited; the debate brought forth clashes not only between political parties but also between the Senate and House of Representatives and between Parliament and the National Capital Development Commission (NCDC).[52] In the 1950s, following the recommendation of the British architect/planner William Holford, it was decided to site the building in front of the existing provisional building, nearer to the edge of the water. Holford, believing hilltop parliamentary placement could appear domineering and therefore inappropriate for a democracy, apparently recognized no irony in his further conclusion that the highest point "should therefore be reserved for Her Majesty the Queen, who is also the Queen of Australia."[53] The report of a parliamentary committee reopened the question in the 1960s, and in 1968 the Senate voted for Capital Hill while the House of Representatives opted for Camp Hill. In 1969, the prime minister decided on Camp Hill, but that was quickly followed by passage of a dissenting motion in the Senate. Yet, four years later, the issue was thrown open again, and, as an editorial in the *Canberra Times* suggests, issues of symbolism remained at the fore:

> The intellectual heirs of the age of armorial bearings and escutcheons find it intolerable that the national parliament should be built on any but the most physically dominant site within the hallowed Parliamentary Triangle conceived by Burley Griffin. Hence the almost pathological fear that a Parliament House built on the lesser Camp Hill could one day find itself looking up to a mere administrative building erected on the more prominent Capital Hill, and the imperative necessity to "grab" the site

> now and "stick our building on it while we can". Apart from anything else, there is in this conception of what is fitting an element of pettifoggery as narrow as the proposal to limit to Australians only the competition for a design for the House. Pursuing this rich intellectual lode opened up by man's universal addiction to the use of symbols, some supporters of the Camp Hill site can be just as persuasive. Instead of isolating the Parliament in lonely splendor on Capital Hill, they advocate, with all the power this word conjures, the integration of the supreme law-making authority of the nation with the daily and multifarious concerns of the citizens. Parliament is concerned with people, not with separate pressure groups or abstractions.[54]

In 1974, perhaps indicative of their assessment of suitable symbolism, both houses concurred on the selection of Capital Hill for the Capitol. A further decision transferred authority for the development of the entire "Parliamentary zone"—defined as the triangle from Capital Hill to the Lake—from the NCDC to Parliament: any new building would henceforth need approval from both houses.

The following year, the internal political turmoil that had marked the period of Parliament House site selection and design became even more intense. The most dramatic event was the highly controversial dissolution of both houses of parliament in 1975, which caused thousands to rally in protest outside the Provisional Parliament House and ushered in a long period of cynicism and bitterness about the course of democratic governance in Australia. Moreover, the size of the rally, together with an incident in 1982 in which a large group of disaffected unemployed workers stormed into the Provisional Parliament and penetrated all the way to the prime minister's office, probably made Canberra's leadership even more security conscious than they were already. The new Parliament House competition, finally launched in 1977 on the fiftieth anniversary of the Provisional Parliament House's opening, was spearheaded by the Conservative government of Malcolm Fraser, which had gained power in 1975, and seemed intended to provide physical and programatic evidence of the renewed legitimacy of Canberra's ruling elite. The eventual selection of the design proposed by Mitchell/Giurgola & Thorp yielded the irony of an American-dominated international team of designers reworking an American-designed city plan as part of the attempt to restore faith in Australian democracy in time for the celebration of Australia's bicentennial in 1988.[55]

Intended to appear as if it were carved into the hillside, the resultant building is in fact a hill-shaped simulation of the real hill, which was bulldozed away. Still, with its most important functions located below the original profile of the ground, it is an extraordinary departure from the usual iconography of a capitol (3.17). At once modest and monumental, its roof is partially covered in grass, intended to allow for direct public access from the green swath of the Mall below it. As Paul Reid puts it, this ingenious solution meant that "the public got their hill and the politicians got their monument." Interestingly, this idea was prefigured in a report the NCDC made in 1974 to parliamentarians during the debate over the advisability of using the Capital

3.17 View of Land Axis toward Capital Hill, showing inscribed parliament (2006).

Hill site. In a section called "Public Access to the Summit," the NCDC noted "It would be possible to design a building on Capital Hill in such a way that members of the public could have free access to a roof viewing platform. This would be one way Griffin's desire to allow the People access to the highest point could be realized and at the same time allay fears that Parliament had retreated to a remote and dominant position. The complex of Parliamentary and other functions could be grouped below this viewing platform."[56] While it is not clear that Giurgola's firm used this report as a point of departure, it would not have been the first time that an architect had won a competition by delivering what the client wanted. In the resultant building, Griffin's original idea of Capital Hill as a parkland meeting place for the public may indeed be partly fulfilled, despite the fact that the parkland was replaced by an enormous building that cost more than Au$ 1 billion. Still, the idea of allowing the public to climb above its legislators seems a rather crude, if powerful, metaphor for popular sovereignty.

The validity of this sort of mediated reference (which jumps from topography to political theory) may, however, be challenged by pointing out the disingenuous nature of any attempt to charge the hill metaphor with great operational political significance. Natural hills may well have a parallel in bureaucratic hierarchies, yet Canberra's security-conscious lawmakers took care to ensure that such hierarchies would remain unchallenged by any form of mere proletarian ascent of Capital Hill. Issued to coincide with the opening of the Parliament House, the "Guidelines for the Conduct of

Public Demonstrations in the Parliamentary Precincts" outlined exceedingly stringent limitations on public gathering. They prohibited demonstrations, which referred to activity by one or more persons, in, on, or near the new Parliament House; even the distribution of petitions is prohibited. Much of what professed to be free and open in terms of urban design is constrained, if not denied, by legal and political reality. As one Australian critic comments, "The reconstituted hilltop would never be a democratic space, the ramps would never be accessible for any type of statement, protest or political demonstration. Australians standing above Parliament would never change anything because they would never be allowed to say or do anything while they were there: apart from being able to look at the landscape, mere tourists privileged to be somewhere near the centre of power."[57] Moreover, in the aftermath of the 9/11 attacks in the United States and enhanced concerns about terrorism worldwide, the Australians installed a double barrier of lightweight fences near the top of each grassy slope. As of 2006, it was possible to walk up part of the building from the bottom and also possible to ascend to the roof once inside it, but casual cross-perambulation of the structure by citizens and their dog-walking MPs had been sadly sacrificed in the name of security (3.18).

In spite of the ostensible openness and inclusiveness of this building's design, actual and symbolic forms of exclusion and distancing operate in many ways. The authors of the official Australian government-sponsored booklet *Australia's Parliament House: The Meeting Place of Our Nation*, perhaps sensitive to the ongoing influence of imported designers, stress that "90 per cent of the materials and products in the building are Australian" and that the building is "built by and for Australians" using the skills of individuals "from every State and Territory" in a manner which reflects the "ethnic diversity of the country."[58] Yet the place of the Australian Aborigines in all this diversity remains rather limited. Though the elaborately crafted

3.18 Capital Hill. Democratic access meets security concerns (2006).

3.19 Aboriginal entrance court.

entrance sequence into the building begins with a forecourt of desert-red gravel centered on a large mosaic derived from an Aboriginal painting, the symbolic Aboriginal presence in this capitol complex stops there (3.19, 3.20). The theme of the mosaic has to do with the "gathering of large groups of tribes . . . to enact ceremonial obligations," yet this spot is located *outside* the building intended to be the "Meeting Place of Our Nation."[59] And, given the restrictions on public protest, Aboriginal Land Rights demonstrations that marked the opening day of the new Parliament House were conducted still farther away from the center of decision making, safely beyond the ring road that circles the complex. To enter the building, visitors tread across the Aboriginal Forecourt and then pass through the detached trabeated portico, which signals "the advent of European civilization."[60] According to a book sponsored by the Royal Australian Institute of Architects, this rite of passage is part of the calculated symbolic spatial sequence of the building; how many visitors will notice this progression is hard to say.[61]

The basic organization of Mitchell/Giurgola's building takes its Beaux Arts cues from the axes of Griffin's plan and from the curves of the roadways flanking his proposed Capitol building (see 3.16). This symmetry, in turn, has exacerbated the daunting problems of symbolism in a building which needed

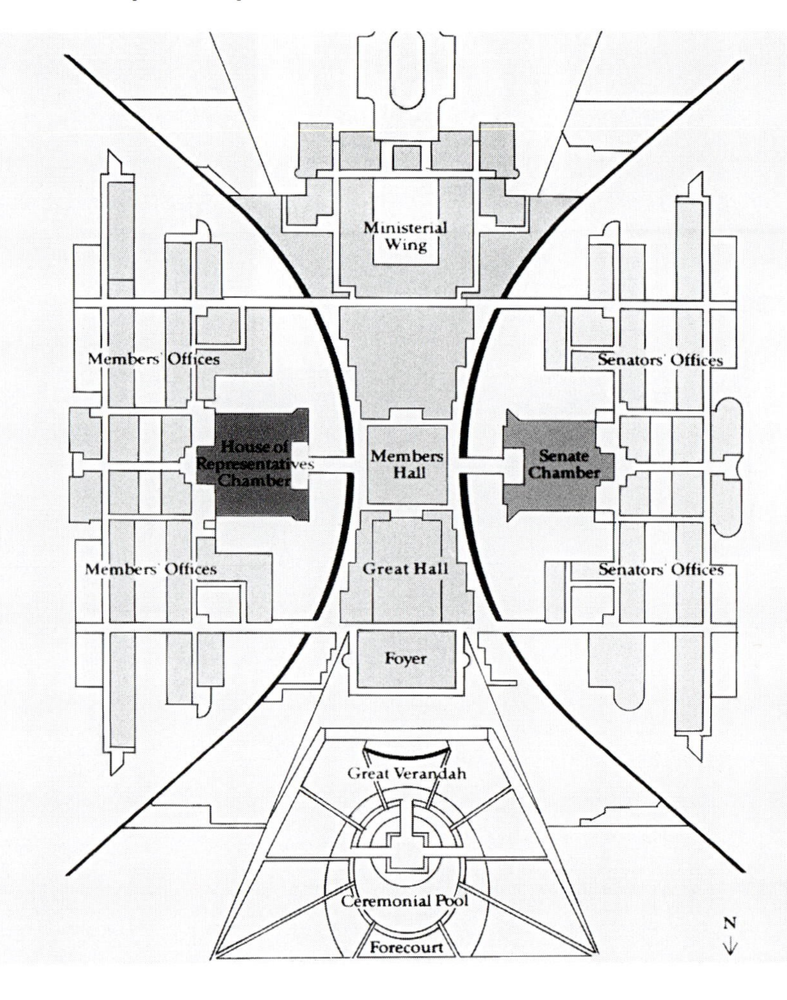

3.20 Diagram of Parliament House ground floor, showing facilities for bicameral legislature and for ministers.

to house not only a bicameral legislature but also an array of executive functions (see 3.20).[62] In Canberra there is nothing to correspond to Washington's clear, separate articulation between the legislative functions housed in and around the Capitol and the executive functions centered in and around the White House. Under the Australian parliamentary system the various ministers lead the executive branch of the government, yet in Canberra (unlike even London, for instance) they receive no separate home. In the Provisional Parliament House, the facilities for ministers had been thoroughly integrated with the legislative functions, and the exterior of the building did not give separate architectural expression to the executive presence within it. This integration, which also fostered close contact between parliamentarians and members of the press, was apparently a feature of the provisional structure that Canberra's leading politicians did not care to see repeated.

Giurgola's entry for the first stage of the Parliament House competition tried to resolve this programmatic and iconographic problem by resorting to a kind of central campanile marking the ministerial presence; but this gesture in turn cast doubt upon the supremacy of the elected legislature. In the final scheme, the Parliament House reaches a kind of compromise between executive supremacy and executive anonymity which gives the ministers a place of axial importance yet separates them from legislative activities and from any need to have face-to-face contact with the press or public. A separate automobile entrance enables them to bypass inquisitive reporters. The contrast with the intimacy of the Provisional Parliament House could hardly be stronger.

One result of the compromise on the role of the executive is that the center of the building is charged with architectural importance yet functionally empty and without much potential for use. At the sky-lit center of this vast complex, directly beneath the legs of the enormous flagpole which identifies the site of the Parliament House from any point in the city, is the Members' Hall, a room expected to serve as an informal meeting place for parliamentarians from both houses. The Capitol rotunda in Washington is also an open and functionless space between the two wings of a bicameral legislature, but it is open to the public and, until recently, was the starting point for public tours of the building. In Canberra, however, the system of public circulation through the building is lifted to a separate floor level, emphasizing distance not only from the places of parliamentary operations but also from the building's symbolic center. As James Weirick complains,

> The Mitchell/Giurgola team has committed us to the proposition that the rare commingling of Members and Senators in the center of the building is the most important event in Australia. So important that no members of the general public should intrude upon it. The Australian people are only allowed to watch. The citizens of this country are only permitted to look down on this space, obliquely, from first floor balconies. This is what they do. And for years on end there is nothing to see. Nothing at all, apart from the thrill of a highly polished floor, occasional reflections of each other in the high gloss surfaces, the bottom rails of gilt framed portraits hung just out of sight around the lower level walls and an *axis mundi* in the form of a water-sheathed black granite slab, into which many Australians feel compelled to throw more of their money.

This empty center, Weirick contends, compares unfavorably to Kings Hall at the heart of the Provisional Parliament building, a place which was "openly accessible, perfectly scaled [and] politically charged" and "where everyone was at the same level, in the Australian way."[63]

Above Parliament House's empty center there is what would seem to be yet another empty gesture. The building does manage to avoid the "inevitable dome," but what replaces it is yet another symbol that long ago attained the status of cliché: the flag. At first reading, this would seem to be the most neutral architectural solution imaginable, a sort of least common denominator of Australian culture. True, perhaps, but in Giurgola's skillful hand, what a remarkable way to fly a flag! The lower part of the colossal flag mast, which rises hundreds of feet in stainless steel, cleverly traces the pyramidal outline of the unbuilt Griffin Capitol. The hill-building's mast-crown provides a clear focus for the entire composition (and indeed for the entire city). Viewed on a sunny day while moving atop the hill, it is not the flag that dominates, but rather the gleaming elegance of its soaring support

3.21 **Giurgola's stainless steel flag mast.**

3.22 ***(above far right)*** **Diagram of Griffin's intended symbolism.**

3.23 ***(below far right)*** **Status of Griffin plan, 1956.**

legs. Seen close-up, the predictable symmetries and limitations simply evaporate and the structure swoops and soars (3.21). At such moments, it truly seems capable of becoming a galvanizing symbol. Marking the center of a huge building on a site that is both the most prominent and the most isolated in the city, it constitutes a last and rather desperate try at linking the capitol to the capital—and it actually succeeds.[64]

The saga of Parliament House is but one example of how the iconographical hierarchy of Canberra has evolved in ways sharply divergent from Griffin's intent. Although some aspects of the City Beautiful/Beaux Arts emphasis on long, axial avenue vistas have been developed despite economic pressures and a certain Australian resistance to concepts of urban design monumentality seen as outdated and inappropriate, much of the central government apex remained unbuilt into the 1980s. Even the creation of the lake and the basic central triangulation of avenues were not completed until the 1960s, and then only in altered form. In the course of nearly a century of development, the triangulated urban design plan that was supposed to direct visual attention to a Government Center, a Market Center, and a Municipal Center has retained some of its generating geometry but little of its generating symbolism. The market functions were removed from Griffin's Market Center in the 1920s, and the railway was never extended to reach it. Construction of the Australian-American Memorial in 1954 foreshortened Kings Avenue before it could meet with Constitution Avenue, thereby altering the position of the node itself (3.22–3.24). Beyond the memorial, expanding from the old Military Post mentioned in Griffin's plans, the Australians developed further defense-related facilities in the 1950s and Secret Service facilities starting in the 1980s. Thus, the current configuration of Canberra's symbolic center visually links not Government, Municipal, and Market functions but, instead, highlights the position of National Government, Central Business District, and National Defense/Secret

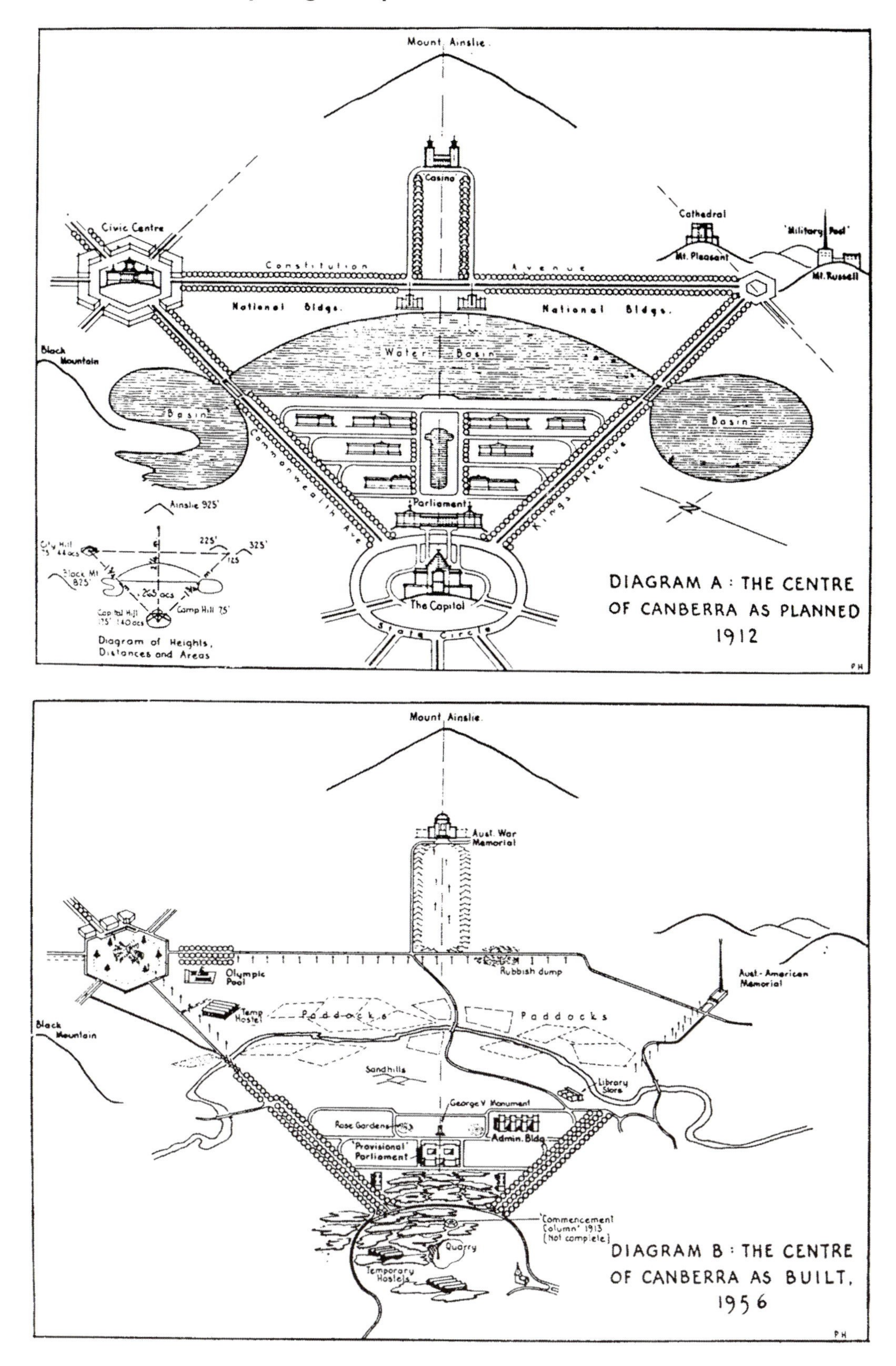
Mount Ainslie.
'Casino'
Civic Centre
Cathedral
Mt. Pleasant
'Military Post'
Mt. Russell
Constitution Avenue
National Bldgs.
National Bldgs.
Black Mountain
Water Basin
Basin
Basin
Commonwealth Ave
Kings Avenue
Parliament
The Capital
State Circle
Ainslie 925'
Diagram of Heights, Distances and Areas
DIAGRAM A: THE CENTRE OF CANBERRA AS PLANNED 1912
PH
Mount Ainslie.
Aust. War Memorial
Olympic Pool
Rubbish dump
Aust.-American Memorial
Temp Hostel
Paddocks
Paddocks
Black Mountain
Sandhills
Library Store
George V Monument
Rose Gardens
Admin. Bldg
'Provisional' Parliament
'Commencement Column' 1913 (Not complete)
Quarry
Temporary Hostels
DIAGRAM B: THE CENTRE OF CANBERRA AS BUILT, 1956
PH

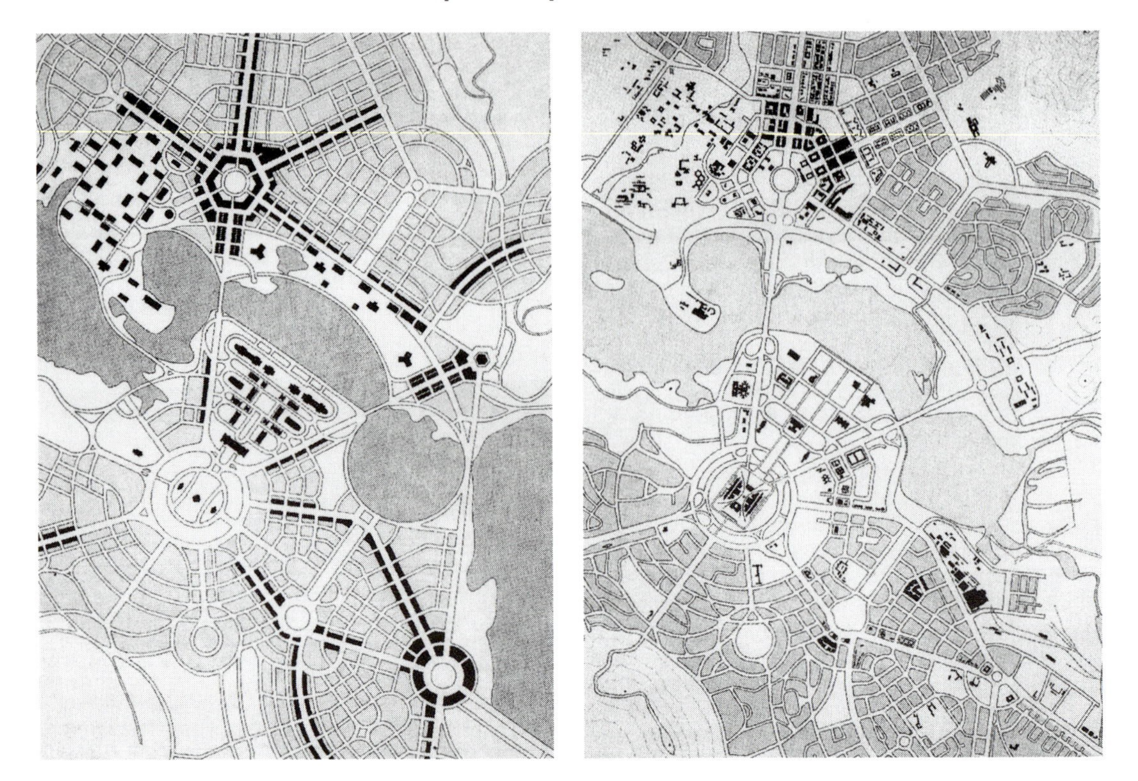

3.24 Status of Griffin plan, 1990. Three-quarters of a century after Griffin's proposal *(left)*, much of Canberra lacks the intended density *(right)*, especially along both sides of the lake.

Service.[65] This may arguably be a more honest expression of government priorities than that implied by Washington's placement of the Pentagon and CIA headquarters across the Potomac, but it is a striking departure from the emphasis on civic qualities that one usually associates with the center of Griffin's original plan.

The inclusion of defense functions into the functional and perceptual hierarchy of Canberra's center occurred in other ways as well. At the opposite end of the land axis from Capital Hill, the government erected an Australian War Memorial in lieu of Griffin's proposed entertainment casino, surely an ironic juxtaposition. In Wolfgang Sonne's interpretation, the result is not just irony but "radical semantic revaluation":

> Griffin's vision described a city harmoniously nestled within its shimmering natural environment with a meaningful vista from Mt. Ainslie onto a well-ordered government district; today, the principal vista has been reversed from the parliament hill to Mt. Ainslie, which has been redefined into an oversized burial mound by virtue of the war memorial placed in front of it. Unintentionally, Canberra has thus become a monument to the victims of war instead of a monument to serene peace and vital democracy.[66]

Griffin's Parkway, which formed the north end of the land axis, has been rendered as a ceremonial Parade Way leading to the War Memorial, leading another commentator to describe the whole of the north side of the lake as "a military cult zone with additional visual functions."[67] This reprogramming of the city superseded Griffin's idea of allocating public facilities on both sides of the lake. North of the lake, almost nothing of what he envisioned as a multiuse complex of sporting activities, civic institutions, and shopping has been implemented. That said, more recent urban design and planning efforts by the National Capital Authority (NCA), crystallized in the *Griffin Legacy* plan, have encouragingly invoked Griffin's original ideas for a higher density city. The call for renewed focus on pedestrian life through enhancements of the "City Hill" node, the lakefront, and Constitution Avenue could greatly enhance the liveliness of the central city (3.25).[68]

3.25 The Griffin Legacy Plan attempts to instill Griffin's intended densities.

Meanwhile, during the rest of the twentieth century (and beyond), the NCA, like its predecessor agencies, fitfully but inexorably inserted many of the paramount national civic institutions into the Parliamentary Zone side of the lake. Unfortunately, as one NCA publication admitted in 2000, "With the possible exception of the High Court of Australia and the National Gallery of Australia, the only discernible logic in the siting of the existing buildings in the Parliamentary Zone is to keep them well separated by their attendant landscape." The result has "exacerbated the perception of the Zone as being empty and more monumental than welcoming." Canberra's central civic axis exudes a Washingtonian vastness but lacks the latter's compensatory tourist throngs. The various institutions erected since the 1960s all adhere to one or the other side of a tree-studded green swath marking the larger passage of Griffin's land axis through the ensemble. Yet the buildings do so only as isolated pavilions, lacking anything like the continuous streetwall of government and cultural edifices that, over time, have filled in and defined the flanks of Washington's Mall. Despite incessant attention to enhancing the symbolic resonances of the larger parliamentary zone, the NCA's wish to make it "The Place of the People" has not yet been fulfilled.[69]

Moreover, some of "the People" have chosen to express their presence in ways that defy the official planning process. Starting on 26 January 1972 (an annual holiday known as Australia Day or Invasion Day, depending on one's politics) four Aboriginal activists began what has become a long-term encampment on Canberra's central axis, located just below the Provisional Parliament House (now known as the Old Parliament House). As Canberra cultural historian David Headon comments, the spatial appropriation began as a protest against the government's refusal to recognize Aboriginal land rights:

> Feeling themselves to be aliens in their own land, the protesters soon erected tents on which they placed an 'Aboriginal Embassy' sign—to resemble the foreign embassies of all the other 'alien' nations in Canberra . . . In the following years, amidst extraordinary media interest, sit-ins, police action, dismantlement, re-erection, parliamentary motions for and against, ACT Supreme Court judgements, the flying of the new Aboriginal flag designed by Harold Thomas, anniversary gatherings and the emergence of Aboriginal activist and writer Kevin Gilbert's *Draft Treaty*, the Aboriginal Tent Embassy established itself not just as a physical presence in Canberra but as a troubling psychological presence in the consciousness of Australia.[70]

In 1992, sixty protesters reestablished the Aboriginal Tent Embassy in its original position. As an evolving array of tents and brush shelters, together with a constantly tended ceremonial bonfire, it asserts a prior and alternative claim to "sacred land" at the symbolic heart of the capital (3.26, 3.27).

Remnants of the Tent Embassy remain in place at the time of this writing, but the NCA has also negotiated a less oppositional evocation of Aboriginal rights, now expressed on another prominent site inscribed partway between Lake Burley Griffin and the Old Parliament. Known as Reconciliation Place, this latest Canberran quest for infused meaning features a set of sculptural

3.26 Canberra's Aboriginal Tent Embassy on "Sacred Land," 2006 view.

3.27 Aboriginal Tent Embassy, 2006.

"slivers" narrating key turning points in the history of Australian government relations with its indigenous peoples. These pylons with text and images are set next to a series of large stone monoliths containing petroglyphs, evoking an era before European settlement. Reconcilation Place began as a more prosaic proposal by the NCA to commission an "East–West Promenade," intended to introduce a pedestrian friendly cross-axis between the National Library and National Gallery, a walkway that could also lead visitors to the entrance to the High Court building. Beyond this formal urban design role, however, Reconciliation Place (built following a competition in 2001) provides official sanction for an indigenous presence. As Christopher Vernon comments, "The controversial decision to locate Reconciliation Place at some distance from the long-established Aboriginal Tent Embassy led some to speculate that the aim of the new project actually was to relocate indigenous presence to a less confrontational position and to eliminate the embassy itself." As of early 2007, however, both presences remain. As a symbolically charged landscape intervention, the pathway of Reconciliation Place distributes its collection of markers on either side of the land axis, but also inhabits the center of the axis in the form of a low grassy mound, with notches for a bench and a speaker's podium (3.28, 3.29).[71]

3.28 Reconciliation Place mound and podium, Canberra, 2006.

3.29 Aboriginal slivers at Reconciliation Place, 2006.

Another recent addition to the urban design of the land axis is Commonwealth Place, a grassy amphitheater with a restaurant and exhibition area, located at the key point where Griffin's land axis meets the south side of his namesake lake. The sculpted terrace of Commonwealth Place culminates in a stone-lined passageway tracing the land axis in the direction of the parliament. For better or worse, however, the change of slope introduced by the low green mound at the center of Reconciliation Place serves to eclipse the framed view of the parliamentary facilities, both old and new (3.30, 3.31).[72] Clearly, not all is yet reconciled.

3.30 Commonwealth Place (with High Court at rear), Canberra.

3.31 Commonwealth Place, with view of parliament obscured by the mound of Reconciliation Place.

The numerous changes and slow pace of implementation have not sapped Griffin's plan for Canberra of its animating power, a power not without contradictions. As Fischer notes, "While it was intended to spell out democracy, Griffin's plan still spoke an aristocratic and imperial design language."[73] Given the divided political loyalties of an Australian population that was allied with Britain and its empire until the late 1940s, the tension exhibited in much early twentieth-century urban design had a social counterpart as well. It is a mark of the malleability of spatial and political ideograms that a design language similar to that employed by Griffin in service of an emerging democracy could be utilized by Edwin Lutyens a year later in an attempt to consolidate imperial British rule over India.

NEW DELHI: A CAPITAL DESIGNED FOR EMPIRE

When King-Emperor George V designated Imperial Delhi as the capital of British India in 1911, the possibility of Indian independence seemed distant. With colonial and native populations socially and formally apart, the capital was meant to be a clear reminder of British hegemony, an architectural affirmation of the superiority of Western civilization. Government buildings might adapt Indian motifs but the city remained an unmistakable outpost of empire.

The choice of the area around Delhi for the new capital can, however, be seen as a noteworthy bid to appease a colonized population. In choosing an alternative to Calcutta as the administrative capital of British India, the British were moving away from a port city with easy access for international trade to a place with deep historical resonances for the local population. The selection of Delhi was not without its own practical appeal, as it was centrally located in the rail network and equidistant from several of the major port cities of British India. Moreover, the proximity of the hill station at Simla offered the British convenient respite from summer heat.

Of at least equal importance to these factors, the decision to build a new capital adjacent to Delhi was a complex political move, directly tied to tensions in Bengal. Bengal had been divided in 1905, with Dhaka designated as the capital for its predominantly Muslim eastern part. Six years later, the announcement of the move of the imperial administration to Delhi was timed to coincide with the reunification of Bengal, an act which again placed a large Muslim Bengali population uncomfortably under provincial political rule from Calcutta. In leaving Calcutta, then, the British administrators were leaving an area of Hindu–Muslim unrest. Though Calcutta afforded the colonial governors economic advantages, there was an even greater political advantage to be had in a move to Delhi. This move, contemplated for a long time, was to an area that had been the political and ceremonial center of many empires over the centuries, from the ancient Indraprastha to the Mughal Shahjahanabad (3.32). The British viceroy, Lord Hardinge, declared that the move to Delhi should appeal to both Hindu and Muslim segments of the Indian population, but, as Robert Irving points out, its Hindu heritage was rather more remote than its prominent role as an Islamic capital from the

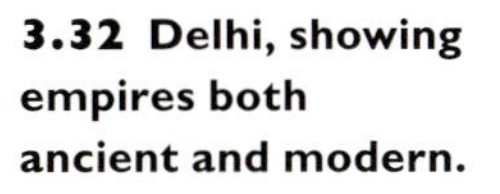

3.32 Delhi, showing empires both ancient and modern.

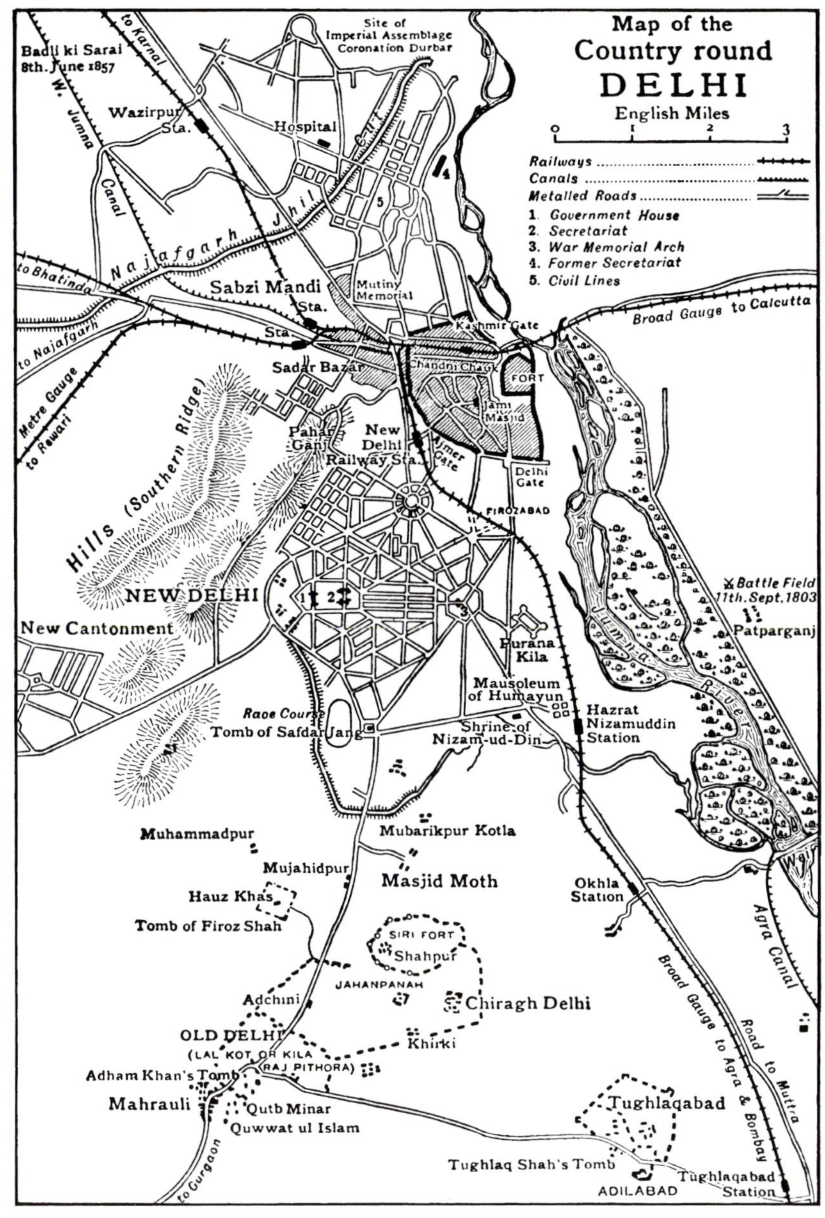

thirteenth to the nineteenth centuries: "Its revived importance, therefore, appealed chiefly to Muslim sentiment and was intended to play an essential role in placating disgruntled East Bengal Muslims, now part of a reunited province dominated by a rich and well-educated Hindu elite in Calcutta."[74] The siting of a new capital for British India, in contrast to that for the United States and Australia, entailed not only sectional economic interests but an active and conscious decision to mediate among the claims of rival ethnic groups. In this sense, it foreshadows the complex issues that underlie the siting of new capitals and capitols in factionalized postcolonial settings.

In 1911, however, the British viewed the selection of Delhi as not only an act of appeasement but also a reminder of domination. The sheer capacity to move the seat of British India by royal decree would be taken as evidence of the empire's continued vitality. Moreover, since the move was so closely identified with the personal wish of George V, no amount of unexpected costs or delays would be allowed to prevent the new capital's transfer at the intended scale. In planning the layout of the capital, which was known as Imperial Delhi until 1926, when it officially took on the more neutral sounding New Delhi, the king's private secretary, Lord Stamfordham, communicated George V's view that the building to house the British viceroy must be "conspicuous and commanding," not dominated by the structures of past empires or by features of the natural landscape: "We must now let [the Indian] see for the first time," he declared, "the power of Western science, art, and civilization."[75] The British Raj would take its place among many empires whose architectural legacy was visible in Delhi and, according to Delhi Town Planning Committee chairman George Swinton, it must "quietly dominate them all."[76] As the committee's final report concluded, the placement of the government buildings would do more than form the heart of a new city: Government House and its flanking Secretariats would constitute "the keystone of the rule over the Empire of India" (3.33, 3.34).[77]

Raisina Hill was selected as the focal point for a design of "quiet domination," and both Edwin Lutyens and Herbert Baker, who served as the

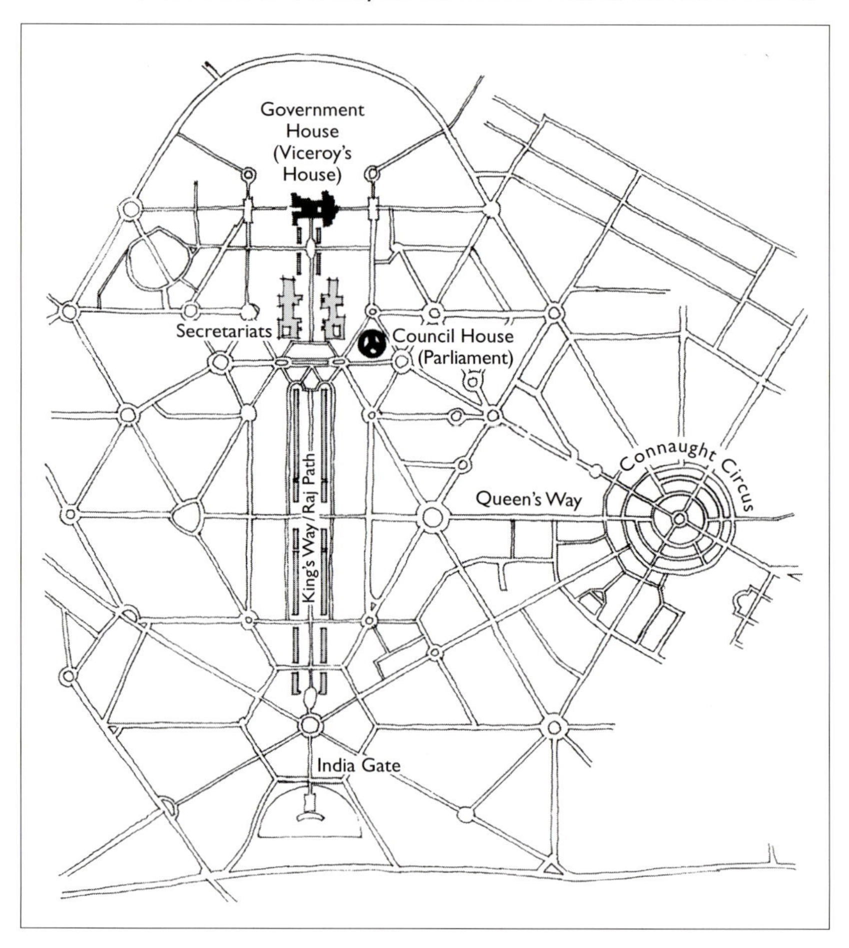

3.33 Government House and flanking Secretariats mark the culmination of Imperial Delhi's grand Central Vista.

3.34 The view up the Central Vista, New Delhi. Designed to reinforce imperial claims, it now serves as the setting for celebrations of Indian independence.

designers of the most prominent buildings, cited the Athenian Acropolis and the Roman Capitol as inspirations, each having paid a visit to these ancient outcrops only weeks before embarking for India. Baker, who designed the Secretariats, insisted that these buildings share the acropolitan heights with the Lutyens-designed Viceroy's House, finding further precedent in the "stupendous platform" of Darius the Great at Persepolis. As Irving comments, "Baker envisaged his Secretariats as a worthy propyleum to Lutyens's Parthenon." The official visitor would approach the raised trio of government buildings along the Queen's Way cross-axis leading south from a new railway station in the direction of the Anglican cathedral. At the junction of the Queen's Way and the King's Way, to be marked by four large edifices containing the Oriental Institute, National Museum, National Library, and Imperial Record Office, the visitor would turn to the west and proceed along the Central Vista of the King's Way, ascend past the plaza known as the Great Place, pass between the massive Secretariats, and, finally, reach the wide steps, portico, and dome of Government House—a 200,000-square-foot palace larger than the one at Versailles. To the architects, this spatial progression was deliberately symbolic: "The imagination is led from the machinery to the prime moving power itself." Unfortunately, the spatial progression up the steep rise of the Raisina acropolis is severely weakened by the gradual disappearance of Government House from view, a fact that an angry Lutyens was to learn only after it proved too late to alter the gradient. "It is bad design," he complained, "to terminate an architectural vista and Avenue with a disappearing Target."[78] Though designed at a time when it could still be said that the British Empire was a place where the sun never set, the eclipse of this dome as it dipped toward the western horizon did not augur well for the imperial future (3.35).

3.35 The "disappearing" Viceroy's House, New Delhi.

Other parts of the plan for Imperial Delhi, a design attributed chiefly to Lutyens, sought to foster symbolic continuity and juxtapositions between old and new, yet also became seriously altered in the execution. The principal King's Way axis (now called the Raj Path) runs between the Raisina acropolis to the All-India War Memorial Arch and continues east toward Indrapat, site of the oldest Delhi of all, Indraprastha. Little remains of these oldest ruins, however, and whatever might have been gained by orienting the urban design of the central part of the city toward this location was in any case undermined by the more recent construction of a stadium as the eastern terminus of the east–west axis. Branching off from the King's Way in a complex pattern of triangles and hexagons reminiscent of both Washington and the contemporaneous Canberra[79] are diagonals linking selected monuments from the past that Lutyens regarded as important. The Lutyens plan provided an aesthetic strategy to mirror Lord Hardinge's two-pronged political strategy: "acceding to Indian sensibilities in order to maintain British rule." As Sonne puts it, on the one hand, the viceroy "wanted to win the approval of the people of India by incorporating Indian motifs in the buildings, and on the other, he was determined to express British supremacy through the elevated location of the British government palace and the scale of the entire ensemble designed in the Western tradition."[80] In this way, the whole imperial history of Delhi was, symbolically, both conjoined and subjugated to the power of the British Raj. Yet here, as in Washington and Canberra, the grand linkages of institutions that can appear clear and powerful in two-dimensional plans are less convincing in three-dimensional reality. Still, as an index of the attitudes of architects and others in positions of control, the intentions behind such juxtapositions are revealing. As Irving notes,

> The capital's imperial flavor—emphasized by processional avenues, imposing plazas, and impressive facades—moved one critic to remark that the city suggested "a setting for a perpetual Durbar." Certainly the inclusion of King's Way and Queen's Way, triumphal avenues where a resplendent army could troop with awesome effect on the native spectator, was an inevitable part of the planning of the new city. Symbolically, these boulevards asserted the fact of British rule; practically, such wide avenues helped make authority without affectionate consent possible, expediting control in the event of disorder or uprising.[81]

The Imperial Delhi of Lutyens and his associates was, in this regard, not an entirely new departure; the concern for matters of hierarchy, segregation, and security had a long history in British colonial intervention in India. Until the middle of the nineteenth century, some of the British in Delhi did live outside of their military cantonment in relative peace and coexistence with the natives, but following the Indian Mutiny of 1857 (alternatively known as the First War of Indian Independence) the British rulers took increasing care to distance themselves from the colonized population.[82] The creation of Imperial Delhi was the most dramatic response to such perceived threats.

In Delhi, as elsewhere in India, a double system of stratification came into existence: a hierarchical British colonial organization imposed itself

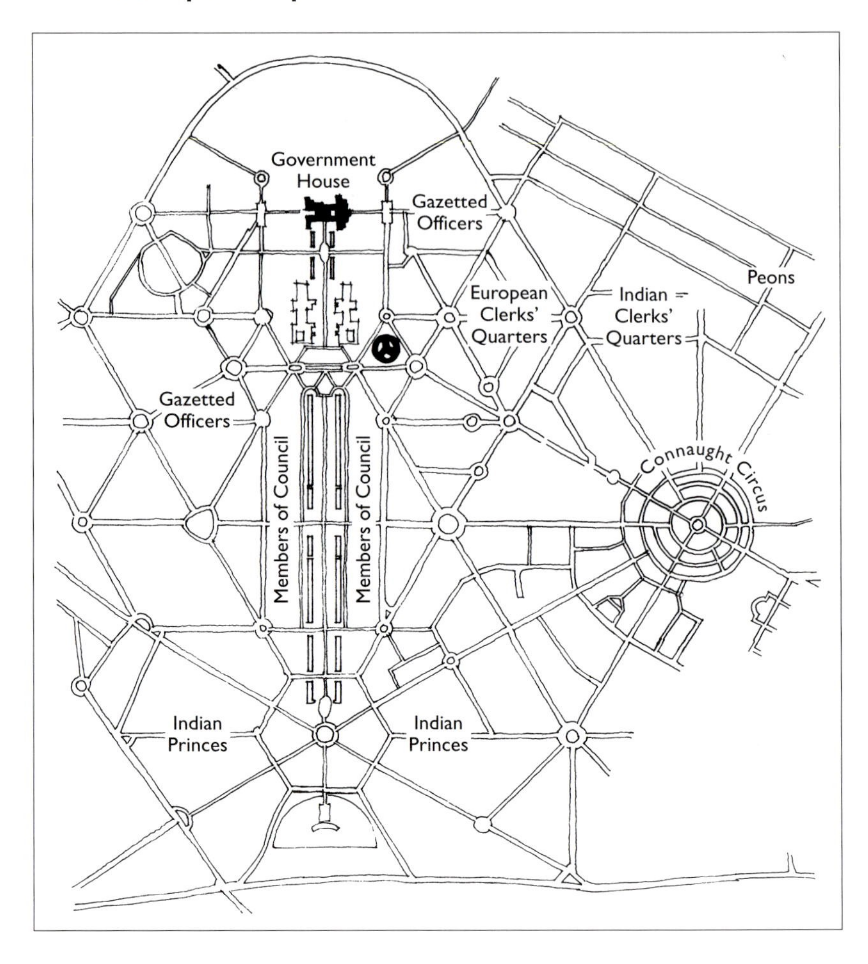

3.36 Imperial Delhi: a confluence of social and spatial status.

on indigenous societies characterized by strictly layered orders of status and caste. In his analysis of colonial urban development, Anthony King demonstrates how a system of land allocation based on criteria of race, occupational rank, and socioeconomic status put forth in the plan for Imperial Delhi gave "manifest physical and spatial expression" to these underlying forms of social distinction, which had until then been more tacitly understood. Within the plan's hexagons, five basic types of areas were created: "One for 'gazetted officers', mainly though not entirely European, the second for European 'clerks'; a third was set aside for indigenous 'clerks' and lower-ranking officials, and a fourth, for members of the indigenous elite, the nobility of the 'native states'. The fifth area was 'non-official' space, occupied by those with insufficient rank or status to qualify for a place within the Imperial City." Significantly, these groups were not merely segregated from one another but systematically removed from the center of political power in accordance with the same closely knit criteria of race, occupational rank, and socio-economic status (3.36).[83] Indicative of the extreme contrast between this new Delhi and the old, in 1940 the residential requirements of 640 families on multi-acre mini-estates occupied an area twice the size of the entire old city, which housed 250,000 persons.[84] This spatial distribution of groups had a vertical as well as a horizontal dimension. The ancient acropolitan association of height with power was reaffirmed in British-ruled Delhi, just as it was in the treatment of the topography of Washington and Canberra by L'Enfant and Griffin.

Whatever the degree of confidence in 1911, by the time the capital was completed twenty years later, British hegemony would be widely challenged. Was it coincidence that Lutyens's bedtime reading, as he designed for the Raj, was Gibbon's *The Decline and Fall of the Roman Empire*?[85] As the architect noted in 1920, postwar architecture on the subcontinent was the British swan song. As such, he wished that it might be "a good tune, well sung," a tribute to the dignity of both Britain and India.[86]

This is not the place to assess Lutyens's talents at architectural synthesis between East and West, but his effort is well worth noting. To an extent far greater than that of the early designers practicing in Washington and Canberra, Lutyens and Baker recognized the necessity of accommodating architectural design to the wishes of a diverse constituency. Baker stressed the primacy of empire, commenting that the design of Imperial Delhi's edifices should "give the Indian sentiment where it does not conflict with grand principles, as the Government should do." Lutyens's architectural inclusivity involved more complex transformations. In spite of his frequently voiced condescension toward both Hindu and Muslim architecture and a thorough dislike for the British Indo-Saracenic contributions to Indian cityscapes, Lutyens did seek to develop for India "some new sense of architectural construction adapted to her crafts" and to initiate "what may become a new and inspiring period in the history of her art."[87] In translating their hybrid visions, both Baker and Lutyens were drawn to the simpler forms of the oldest Buddhist monuments, imagery that was as nonpartisan as it was irrelevant. What mattered at this time were not the particulars of the indigenous references, but the fact that local architectural traditions were considered at all. As Irving observes, "The question was not simply one of taste, but also of high politics. The Viceroy was quite clear on this point: he felt it would be a 'grave political blunder' to place a purely Western town on the Delhi plain. The public in India, he claimed, was very emphatic that the capital's principal buildings should have an Indian motif. He could not disregard this opinion, lest Indians justly complain he had ignored their tastes while asking them to underwrite the cost."[88]

For some among the British leadership, the new capital was to be not merely a site for British rule, but the place where Indians would learn, in time, to rule themselves. New Delhi—unlike Calcutta—was designed on the assumption of eventual Anglo-Indian joint administration. Yet the chief architectural provision for this eventuality was not made until well after construction of the city was under way. In consequence, the Council House, as the present parliament house was then known, was not included in the initial concept of the capitol complex and, when finally accommodated, was given a site off to the side of the main axis of government. The area of the site was approximately the same as that provided for the principal European club, a sign of the Council House's existence as an appendage to the original plan and of its role as a secondary component of government. On this site, Baker designed a tricameral, cylindrical building in which all three chambers made use of amphitheater-style seating rather than the oppositional rows of Westminster, ostensibly to lessen the chance of two-party government split along religious lines.[89] In spite of Baker's elaborate architectural treatment, the larger urban design context of the legislature remained a spatial reminder of Indian political subservience to the viceregal acropolis of power.

Given its extreme levels of carefully contrived segregation, especially the wide buffer zone created between the new city and the walls of the old city of Shahjahanabad, it seems sensible to place Imperial Delhi in the same category of city-designing venture as Washington and Canberra. Yet, in spite of the endeavors of its designers to regard it as wholly separate and apart from all that preceded it, the city planned by Lutyens also fits logically in the category of what I have called evolved capitals renewed. Like Rome, Athens, and Moscow, Delhi's return to capital status in modern times hardly marks the beginning of its urban glories. Even so, in scale and in spirit this is a designed capital and a place premised on the primacy of government administration, albeit one that migrated to Simla for five months of the year. Imperial Delhi would also seem to be the first capital city to be designed on the assumption of automobile ownership, an index of the narrow range of persons who were intended to benefit from its extremely low densities. In contrast to L'Enfant's plan for Washington and Griffin's plan for Canberra, which envisioned streets lined with buildings, the planners of Imperial Delhi evinced little concern for increasing building densities in the future or for including a greater range of metropolitan functions.

With the advent of independent India in 1947, New Delhi became the capital of a very different place. Independence brought not only new symbolic status and a variety of new national institutions, but also a flood of refugees caused by the partition of India and Pakistan, a rapid increase of government bureaucracy (both Indian civil servants and foreign diplomats), and increasing commercial activity.[90] Yet, as the population of postindependence Delhi increased tenfold and twentyfold around it, much of the center of New Delhi with its broad avenues, elaborate greenery, and sparse building still appears as a kind of overgrown capitol complex, resolutely detached from the rest of the fabric of the city.

Its legislative functions architecturally and topographically subservient to the massive executive presence at the political and ceremonial center of its plan, the Indian capital reveals its colonial origins. Though Mahatma Gandhi, alert to the symbolism of capitols, characteristically talked about turning the Viceroy's House into a hospital after independence, his successors preferred to appropriate the buildings of the Raj for themselves (3.37). Government House, known as the Viceroy's House after 1929, became the residence of India's president, a largely ceremonial post; the Council House accommodated the Indian Parliament, and the Secretariats remained home to an omnipresent bureaucracy. If, over time, the architectural associations of these buildings with the British Raj have dissipated, the juxtaposition of buildings retains the British colonialist's view of the relationship between executive and parliamentary might. Though the government professes democracy, the city plan of its elite central area reinforces the long legacy of Delhi as an administrative center of empires.[91]

3.37 Republic Day festivities on the Raj Path. The British-inspired parades continue, but the canopy no longer shields a statue of King George V.

The adaptive reuse of Delhi as the capital of independent India was made more likely by the fact that Delhi, unlike Simla or Calcutta, for example, had a glorious history that long pre-dated the arrival of the British. Lutyens's Delhi constituted only one part of the metropolis, and this part was a comfortable and enticing one. The leaders of other newly independent countries, faced with overcoming a long legacy of urban occupation by nonindigenous forces, have made different choices. The earliest example of a designed capital that was a direct outgrowth of an independence struggle may well be Ankara.

ANKARA: A CAPITAL DESIGNED FOR INDEPENDENCE

In 1923, Turkey's leader, General Mustafa Kemal (later known as Atatürk) designated Ankara—and not Constantinople—as the capital of the newly founded republic, a decision that sought to reconfigure the distribution of political, cultural, and economic power in the new state. Closely tied to these power shifts, the move represented a search for an appropriate setting to nurture the development of a Turkish national identity for a new nation-state that had abolished both the Ottoman sultanate and the Islamic caliphate.

Ankara's advantages as a capital were many. Though Constantinople, known as Istanbul after 1926, had served as the capital of the region for fifteen hundred years, much militated against its selection as the capital for an independent Turkey. Geopolitically, it was at the far northwest corner of the new republic's territory, whereas Ankara was both securely inland and nearly centered on the large, rectangular expanse of Turkish Anatolia. Forty years before the more famous city-building venture of Brasília, Ankara's supporters recognized the potential for the strategic placement of a national capital to serve as a new pole for economic development of a region and the extension of a national commercial and transportation network. At the sociopolitical level, a move to Ankara could be seen as a decisive break from the more Europeanized and cosmopolitan ties of Constantinople to a place which could become somehow more independently Turkish while reducing the political influence of the semicolonial major port cities. Atatürk regarded the move of the political leadership to a new place as a kind of cleansing action from the corrupting effects of vested economic ties in the major metropolis, a viewpoint certainly shared by founders of new capitals both before him and since. As the center of Turkish resistance against European occupation of Anatolia following the collapse of the Ottoman empire, Ankara had already demonstrated the value of its strategic location and established itself as a focus of national sentiment.[92]

At a symbolic level, the choice of Ankara was a move away from many aspects of Ottoman rule and was also intended to demonstrate both the power of the new republic's leaders and their determination to generate a modern nation-state. In Toynbee's analysis, Atatürk deliberately chose a site for the capital of the Empire's Anatolian Turkish successor-state that was far removed from the original nucleus of Ottoman rule "in order to signify that the new Turkey was the common national patrimony of the whole of its now predominantly Turkish population." This central Anatolian base was essential, he claims, since the great majority of the present Turkish population of Anatolia are not descendants of the original Ottoman rulers. They are instead descendants of the Turkish populations of other Anatolian Turkish principalities that the Ottomans conquered in the fourteenth and fifteenth centuries; as such, these non-Osmanli Anatolian Turks, like the Greeks and Bulgars and Serbs, had been subjects of the Osmanli Turks for almost five hundred years. In this view, the transfer of the capital from Constantinople to Ankara was a "striking symbolic act" because it was "a signal to the Anatolian Turks that they had ceased to be Ottoman subjects and had become citizens of a Turkish national state."[93]

Sibel Bozdoğan's writings on the architecture and urbanism of Kemalist Turkey make clear the complex relations between architectural modernism and political modernization. In highlighting the sociopolitical program of early modernism before it descended into a merely stylistic canon, Bozdoğan and other commentators on the architectural legacy of Ankara lament the loss of modernism's "initial critical force, democratic potential, and liberating premises." This earliest notion of modernism, subtle and powerful, soon gave way to the "universalistic claims and totalizing discourse" that postmodernist critics decry. In this context, the Kemalism of the 1930s paralleled the course of modern architecture and urbanism in other parts of the non-West: it became "primarily a form of 'visible politics' or 'civilizing mission' that accompanied official programs of modernization, imposed from above and implemented by the bureaucratic and professional elites of paternalistic nation-states." Within this, Bozdoğan argues, Turkish architectural culture sought to meet Atatürk's aspiration "to be Western in spite of the West," yet struggled to deal with this paradox. The Kemalist design ethos "adopted the formal and scientific precepts of Western modernism and yet posited itself as an anti-imperialist, anti-Orientalist, and anticolonialist expression of independence, identity, and subjecthood by a nation hitherto represented only by the Orientalist cultural paradigms of the West." The result, notes Bozdoğan, is that "the entire architectural culture of the early republic was one big effort to reconcile the 'modern' with the 'national.'"[94]

When the decision to designate Ankara as the capital of a modern nation-state was taken in the 1920s, it represented the reinvigoration of a small town that had been inhabited continuously since the twentieth century B.C. It is frequently claimed in Ankara that the first settlers of the place may have been Hittites, a people who had transmuted the Middle Bronze Age into a kind of early Anatolian Golden Age. Whether or not this people actually made their home in the place that eventually became Ankara, there has been a strong attempt to advocate assumed blood ties to this group, thereby giving contemporary Turkish citizens in the capital a suitably non-Hellenic ancestor rooted deep in the past.

Though the site of Ankara is believed to have had a population of as many as 100,000 persons during Roman times and subsequently served as a military center under the Seljuks and Ottomans, at the time of the Turkish War of Independence it was little more than a provincial town of 20,000 with an imposing citadel.[95] The first parliament building for modern Turkey was built near the base of this citadel. Almost immediately, however, planners proposed to turn Ankara into a city more suitable for the capital of an ambitious if impoverished nation-state. Though many of the early republic's official buildings were designed in the nostalgic neo-Ottoman and neo-Seljuk First National Style, by the late 1920s, modern European architectural currents had reached Ankara.[96] For larger questions of urban design, Atatürk and his followers also looked toward Europe for guidance. In a competition held in 1927, three designers were invited to submit plans for the development of Ankara on a large tract of undeveloped land to the south of the old town. The master plan by Hermann Jansen of Berlin was selected, and most of the major government buildings in Ankara were subsequently designed by the Austrian Clemens Holzmeister.[97] Less rigidly geometrical and monumental than its alternatives, Jansen's plan emphasized the creation of Garden City kinds of neighborhoods and was not premised simply on the exalted depiction of government. Yet a capitol complex was given a high-priority placement in a triangulated sector of baroque symmetry pointing toward the heights of the ancient citadel.

The central organizing feature of Jansen's plan is a north–south boulevard named after Atatürk. It begins in the oldest part of the town beneath the citadel at the site of the first parliament building, crosses over the railway line, and continues south toward the capitol complex (3.38, 3.39). In so doing, the spine of the Atatürk Boulevard reveals a certain urbanistic scoliosis. Rather than a crippling deformity, this is in keeping with the more

3.38 Jansen's plan for Ankara.

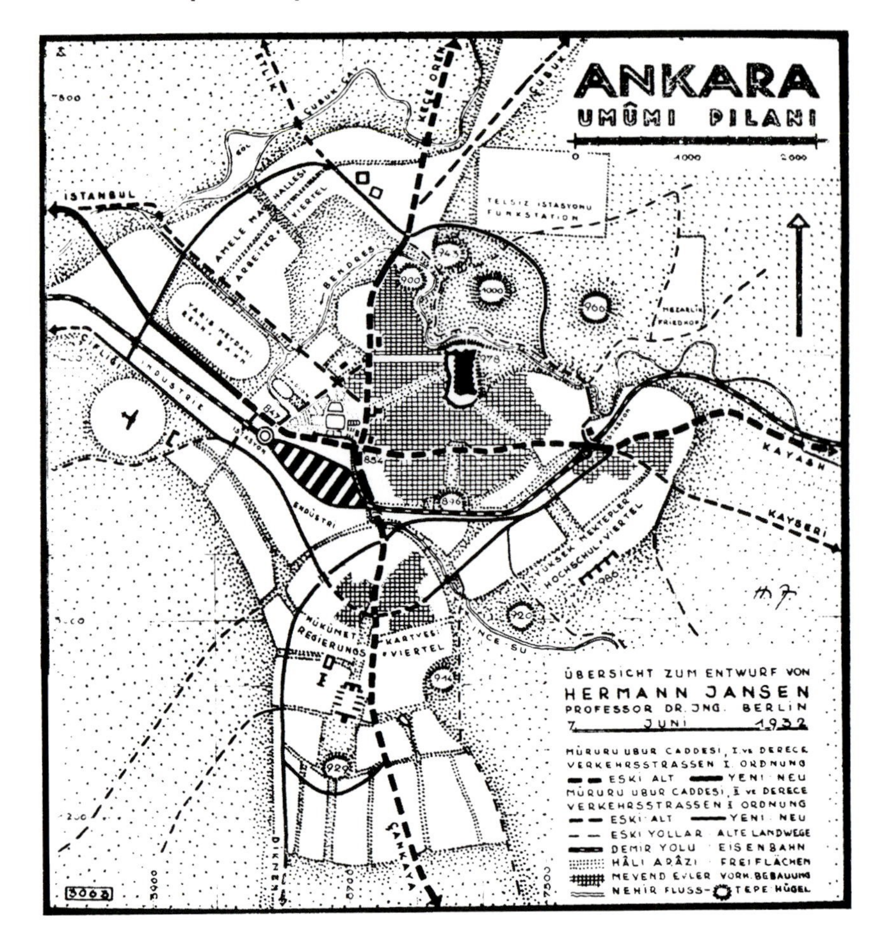

informal posture of the whole scheme. As is often the case, however, what goes on immediately beyond the boundaries of the plan is among its most significant aspects. The Atatürk Boulevard does not terminate with the capitol complex but skirts on past it for another two miles, culminating in the Presidential Palace. The choice of this location for Atatürk's headquarters, built to the design of Holzmeister in 1930–1932, served to encourage elite development all along the boulevard, yet the creation of a palace in a walled compound adjacent to a large military complex has certainly altered the symbolism of Jansen's plan.[98]

Holzmeister's design for the Grand National Assembly (1938) was not finished until the end of the 1950s, and, while certainly monumental, it does not quite occupy the pride of place given to the most prominent government buildings in Washington, Ottawa, Pretoria, Canberra, or New Delhi. Located at the intersection of the city's two major avenues, where the north–south Atatürk Boulevard meets the east–west Inönü Boulevard—named after Atatürk's presidential successor, this street was a later addition—the Turkish capitol has arguably been given the most prominent location possible. Yet its presence has been undercut, quite literally, by the swath of the Inönü Boulevard, which dips in front of the capitol and isolates its vast site from the rest of the government ministries in the capitol complex across

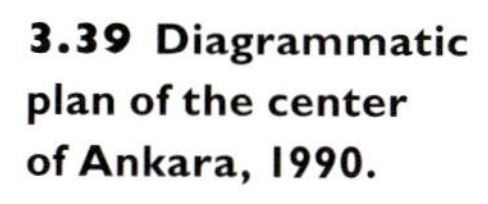

3.39 Diagrammatic plan of the center of Ankara, 1990.

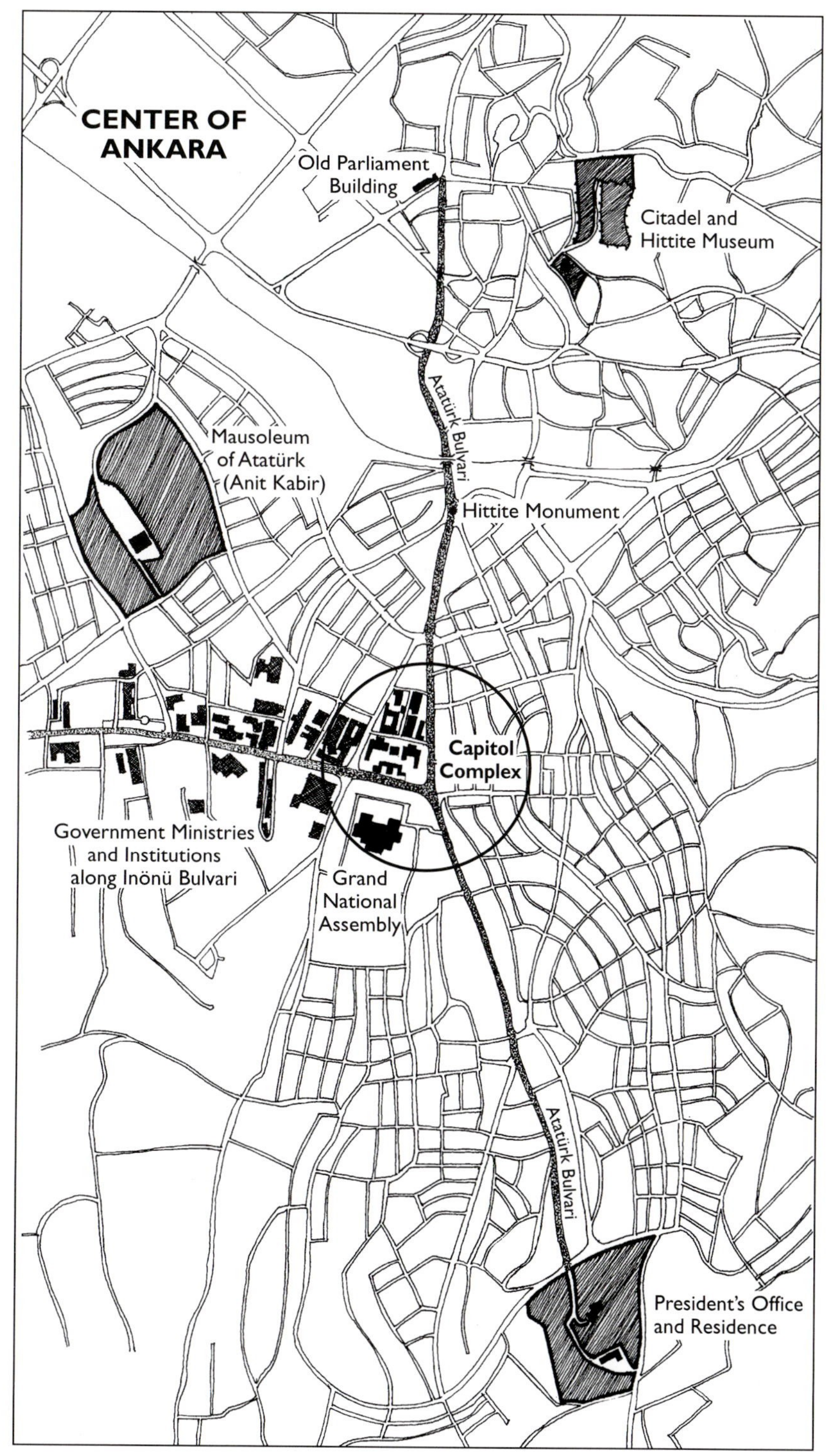

3.40 Ankara's Grand National Assembly, viewed from across the barrier of Inönü Boulevard.

the road. What is left is a curious contradiction, a confluence of mixed urban messages. The symmetrical building on luxuriantly landscaped high ground serves as a kind of visual terminus to the government complex, yet the stairs ascending toward it rise from across a multilane roadway. Other environmental cues act as an even greater deterrent. Pedestrian access to the wide flights of steps leading from the boulevard toward the capitol is effectively curtailed by armed guards, told to blow whistles at the first sign of a camera-toting visitor (3.40). Like the ancient citadel, the capitol zone is a place of power and privilege; unlike the earlier acropolitan destination, however, current public access to the capitol complex is thoroughly discouraged.

In Ankara, however, neither of these two citadels is the most conspicuous symbolic focus of the city. This status is reserved for the Atatürk Mausoleum (Anit-Kabir), a thoroughly Speerian acropolitan memorial that is visible from all over the city, both during the day and, grandly floodlit, at night (3.41). Like the Capitoline Hill in Rome, this hilltop with its neoclassical temple is a place that combines associations with both shrine and political rule. As Sibel Bozdoğan puts it, "From its conception, Anit-Kabir, located on top of Rasattepe Hill, was the ultimate monument to the casting of the nation as secular religion, the nationalist substitute for a space of ritual, prayer, and spirituality." Like ancient Egypt's Luxor temple, which must be approached along the Avenue of the Sphinxes, the Atatürk Mausoleum is reached by traversing a long, axial way lined by pseudo-Hittite lions. This symbol of the struggle for modern Turkey is, architecturally and urbanistically, treated as the culmination of past imperial glories. As such, it is the crown of a city that has undergone more than a 200-fold increase in population since the founding of the republic.[99]

The connection between the deep Hittite past and the aims of modern Turkish national identity is given urban design form again on the Atatürk

3.41 Atatürk Mausoleum.

3.42 Atatürk Boulevard with Hittite monument.

Boulevard, where a small Hittite bronze sculpture from the museum has been transformed into a huge monument at the center of a major traffic circle, facing north in the direction of the ancient citadel (3.42). When erected in the 1970s, the sculpture proved controversial because of its seeming glorification of a pre-Islamic past, but it is nevertheless indicative of the many ways the designed capital of Ankara has been charged with promoting both power and national identity.[100] Ankara's founders, seeking a divorce from the Ottoman past, embraced instead the essences of pre-Islamic Anatolia and the vernacular traditions of the contemporary Anatolian heartland, thereby both inventing and imagining a national community.

Within the larger history of designed capitals and the social, economic, and political circumstances that inspire them, the architecture and urban design of Ankara represent a turning point in the development of a postcolonial capital consciousness. Although modern Turkey did not emerge from a prototypical colonial context (since it was never officially colonized by Western powers), the symbolism that undergirded the selection and design of its capital prefigures the kind of sentiment that has animated many latter-day leaders of successful independence movements. The outcome of World War Two accelerated a broad commitment to the political independence of the remaining parts of the colonized world. In addition to the destruction wrought by the war itself, postwar urban designers were forced to come to terms with the aftermath of the ill-fated domestic urban adventures of Mussolini and Hitler in the 1930s and 1940s. In the new era, the earlier ambitions of city designers based on monumental reference to empires of the past would be called into question, as the designs of Griffin and Jansen had begun to do already. With the advent of modern architecture and urbanism, designers had a new set of tools with which to approach the perennial problems of power and identity.

CHAPTER 4

Designed capitals after World War Two: Chandigarh and Brasília

All philosophy, it has been said, may be construed as a footnote to Plato and Aristotle. To many architects and planners, Chandigarh and Brasília have this seminal status with regard to designed capital cities, though both places might delight chiefly the Platonist. In any case, as I have already argued, the genesis of the contemporary designed capital lies in a much earlier era—as early, in fact, as the days of those momentous Greeks. In both Chandigarh and Brasília the acropolitan origins of the capitol complex reemerge. The design of Chandigarh, though only a provincial Indian capital, was a noteworthy attempt to use modern architecture and urbanism to create a capital that symbolized progress and conveyed national identity in a postcolonial context. Brasília, equally notable, constitutes the first time that the abstraction and the social agenda of modernism were applied to the national capital of a major country.

CHANDIGARH: THE FIRST MODERNIST DESIGNED CAPITAL

Though Chandigarh was ostensibly intended to be a state capital for the Indian Punjab, its importance to India as a whole was inevitable from the beginning (4.1). If Imperial Delhi was to have been the capstone of British colonial rule, then Chandigarh was to be a symbol of independent India. In the aftermath of the partition that created Pakistan, the Punjab was itself divided, and Lahore, its governmental, commercial, and spiritual capital, no longer remained within India. Chandigarh, then, was proffered as compensation from the Indian government to Indian Punjabis for the loss of ancient Lahore. The homeless Punjabi government was temporarily forced to use the old colonial summer capital of Simla, wholly unsuitable for year-round occupation owing to its inaccessibility and harsh winter climate, not to mention its potentially awkward symbolism.

4.1 India.

Chandigarh's site was selected not only for its natural beauty and its access to transportation routes, but also for its strategic distance from the border with hostile Pakistan. The planning of the new capital went forward against a background of political turmoil not unlike that facing all India at the time. Not only were there millions of homeless Hindu refugees from Muslim Pakistan to contend with, there was also the perpetual tension between Hindu and Sikh, a schism that would eventually lead to a further partition of the bilingual Indian Punjab into two monolingual states, Punjab and Haryana, in 1966. As of 2007, the principal government buildings of Chandigarh's capitol complex are still subdivided to serve two different provincial governments—a reminder that partition continues to plague India even in the most literal of ways. In short, though Pandit Nehru could consider Chandigarh to be, like the new hydroelectric power plants, a "temple of the New India,"[1] there remained enormous disunity among the worshipers.

In such circumstances, it was likely no coincidence that Nehru favored a place named for Chandi, the Hindu goddess of power (the energy force behind all forms of important transformation) as an auspicious site for a new capital. After his first visit, he praised the site as "free from the existing encumbrances of old towns and old traditions" and extolled its potential to be "the first large expression of our creative genius flowering on our newly earned freedom."[2] He might also have added that this place was also free, at least temporarily, from the enormous influx of refugees that had doubled the size of many Punjabi towns—although building the city did displace dozens of villages housing thousands of residents. With the constitutional machinery of the Punjabi state government in a shambles, the national government stepped in, passing necessary legislation and providing substantial financial subsidy for the capital; subsequent federal status granted to the capital only added to the sense of Chandigarh as a "national" venture.[3] With the site selected, Nehru sought out the designers for his grand urban temple.

For Nehru, Chandigarh marked an important opportunity and forward-moving symbol after the violence of partition. As Vikram Prakash puts it,

"Nehru was convinced that by focusing on modernity he could sidestep the pitfalls of ancient identities. As Kemal Ataturk had done in Turkey, and as other postcolonial nations like Brazil and Nigeria had aspired to do, Nehru hoped that the newly independent Indian population would sufficiently identify itself with the idea of modernity, re-invent itself, and thereby avoid the continued specter of ethnic violence. If modernism was his new religion, then newness and change were its gospel." Prakash also rightly observes that this view of modernism carried forward strong aspects of an earlier colonialism that had also viewed itself as a triumph of an enlightened elite over a retrograde and static provincialism. "When Nehru proclaimed that Chandigarh must be a modern city, his claim was not different in substance from that made earlier by the colonist. But since it was made by Nehru in the name of an independent nation state, it was fundamentally different in form, and thereby, in legitimacy." Nehru, Prakash concludes, saw modernism as "a strategic catalyst of growth and change—the West on tap rather than on top." Nehru himself actually resisted the need to import Western architects, but the Anglo-orientation of senior Indian bureaucrats prevailed.[4]

The saga of Chandigarh's design—from the initial plans of Albert Mayer through the proposals of the tragically short-lived Matthew Nowicki to the domineering reign of Le Corbusier—is well told elsewhere and need not be repeated here. Prakash aptly comments that the production of the city was a "complex field of negotiated practices" among strong willed designers, a powerful Indian bureaucracy led by A. L. Fletcher, P. L. Verma, and P. N. Thapar (who themselves held contrasting views), and an ambitious national client. In a similar revisionist interpretation of the Chandigarh saga, Nihal Perera also argues that the plan was "negotiated between multiple agencies and is not the creation of a single author," however common it may be to associate everything with Le Corbusier. Instead, the effort to plan the city should be seen as an outcome of "contested modernities," and as "much more chaotic, hybrid, liminal, disorderly and diverse than its architect-centred discourse suggests." It is wrong, Perera argues, to treat Indian political leaders, Punjabi officials, Chandigarh citizens, and other architects as no more than background characters, minor players in a "politically passive context in which Le Corbusier can be considered as Chandigarh's grand creator."[5]

Each of the principal architects, engineers, and bureaucrats saw Chandigarh as an unrivaled opportunity to implement contemporary thinking about city planning, but they frequently differed on which aspects of city planning mattered most. They differed over how much deference to give to English or American Garden City precedents, and differed on what sorts of accommodations needed to be made to fit earlier models to the needs of India. And they differed over basic meanings of modernity itself. All, however, stressed the importance of Chandigarh as a symbol. Mayer (the American who got the initial commission largely because of his previous experience working in India) put it most bluntly: "We are seeking symbols, to restore or to create pride and confidence in [the Indian] himself and in his country."[6] In a letter to his patron dated April 1950, Mayer expressed the breadth of his design agenda:

> I feel in all solemnity that this [Chandigarh] will be a source of great stimulation to city building and re-planning in India. But I also feel that it will be the most complete synthesis and integration in the world to date of all that has been learned and talked of in planning over the last thirty years, but which no one has yet had the great luck to be allowed actually to create. Yet I feel we have been able to make it strongly Indian in feeling and function as well as modern.[7]

While the degree of Indianness of the resultant city is a subject for much debate, I wish here to raise this question only with regard to the position of its capitol.

If the design of Chandigarh's capitol complex has any resonance with India, it is with the India of New Delhi's Raisina acropolis. What in the hands of Lutyens and Baker was merely raised above the rest of the city, in Chandigarh becomes completely detached from it. Though reminiscent of certain ancient Chinese cities, this detachment is in marked contrast to the layout of traditional Indian cities, where the most important government functions were located in the heart of activity. In the plan of Chandigarh, the *caput mundi* takes on an especially anthropomorphic cast. As Jane Drew, who was responsible for the design of some of the housing sectors, put it, "The plan is almost biological in form. Its commanding head the capitol group, its heart the city commercial center, its hand the industrial area, its brain and intellectual centre in the parkland where are the museums, university, library, etc."[8] Yet, in *Chandigarh: In Search of an Identity*, Ravi Kalia finds the plan to have notable historical resonance: "By placing the 'thinking' function of the city analogous to that of the head in relationship to the body, Mayer was reaffirming the allegorical reference to the Indian caste structure in the story of Purusha (the Cosmic Man), in which his head represents the Brahamin (the priest-thinker), his arms represent the Kashtriya (the soldier), his thighs represent the Vaishya (commoner), and his feet represent the Sudra (slave)."[9] Whether any part of the allegory ever occurred to Mayer or how it could be construed as an appropriate city form for an emerging democracy, Kalia does not make clear. But obviously the plan of Chandigarh must be seen as an unambiguous articulation of hierarchy and segregation (4.2).

Le Corbusier's rhetoric in explaining the final version of Chandigarh's plan was filled with references to freedom, democracy, emancipation, and progress for all Indian citizens, yet the spatial allocation of residential areas remained part of the legacy of the British Civil Service and was based, as it had been in colonial capitals, on the structure of existing socioeconomic inequalities. As Prakash comments,

> Chandigarh looks and feels the way it does with its neatly hierarchical sectors and plans, not because Le Corbusier and Nehru forced the reluctant inhabitants to conform, but because the officiating bureaucrats, first Fletcher and then Verma and Thapar, who conceived and cast the basic mold of Chandigarh, selected a particular image for the city. The hierarchies in the housing, the densities of the sectors, the general spread

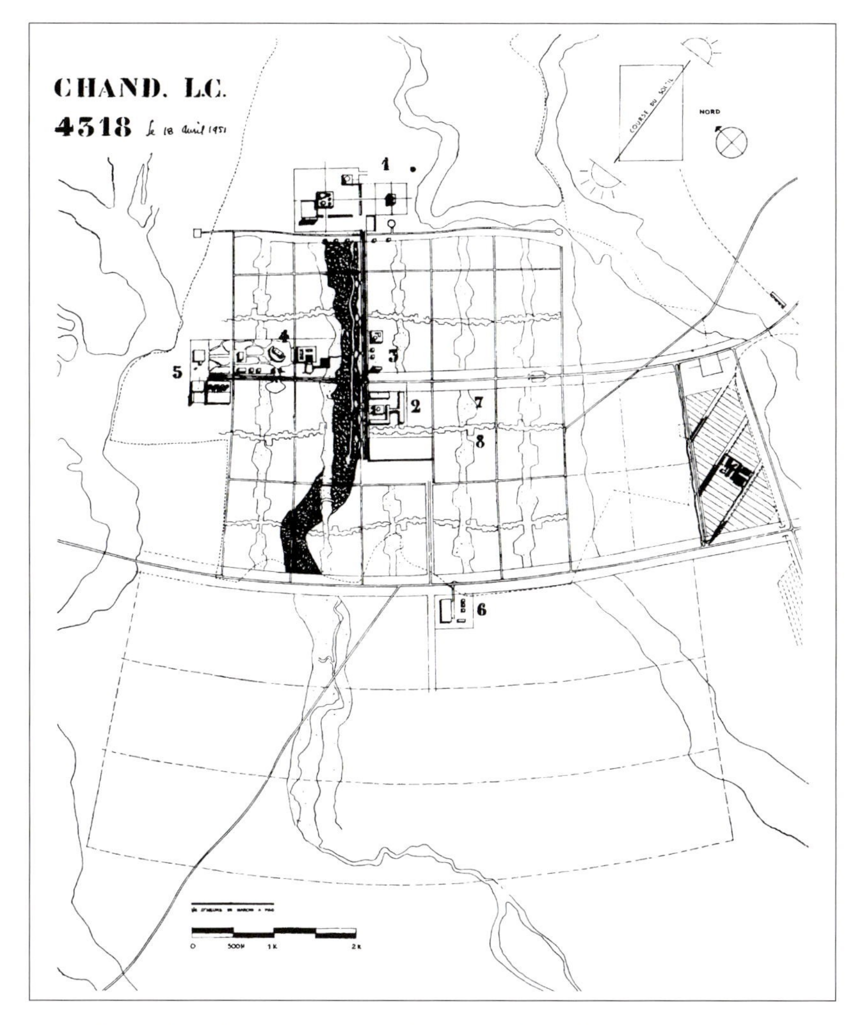

4.2 Chandigarh plan, as adapted by Le Corbusier.

Note how the capitol complex (no. 1 at the top) is separated from the rest of the city.

and sprawl of the city, the need for a special, symbolic administrative 'head,' etc., were all laid out and enforced by these officers. In the end, therefore, the fundamental character of Chandigarh's residential architecture derives from Indian bureaucratic interpretation of the English New Towns Act, derived in turn from the Garden City movement.

Socioeconomically, however, the city form also owed much to earlier colonial impulses. Madhu Sarin's analysis of Chandigarh's planning and development identifies a clear "hierarchic disposition from the rich to the poor downwards from the capitol"; she observes that "the highest paid government officials, with the largest houses, were provided for in low-density sectors in the north near the capitol complex," whereas the majority of government employees, belonging to the lowest income groups, were assigned housing much farther away from their workplace. Most other major employment centers in the plan were equally distant from low-income residential areas. As Sarin concludes, "The criteria used in determining the location of the capitol complex had little to do with the convenience of the majority of citizens. It was more a question of creating imposing and powerful images of the institutions of authority of the new State. In this respect, Chandigarh differed little from the logic behind Lutyens' plan for the Imperial capital of New Delhi." Moreover, Perera adds, "While a broad range of government servants were provided with housing, many others, including those who actually built Chandigarh, were excluded from the city."[10]

Mayer's plan underwent many transformations, but the position of the capitol as its head remained unchallenged. Believing that the government functions should be "spiritually" detached, Mayer vetoed ideas to put it near other centers of employment and sited the Capitol Complex (as it is termed by most commentators) on a "dramatic" ridge to the north of the city, set off against the backdrop of hills. He further isolated the complex by placing it between two branches of the seasonally dry Sukhna Cho River, proposing to keep the river flowing through a system of dams and thereby create "a sort of glittering necklace encircling the group."[11] Within the capitol complex, Mayer also emphasized the need for appropriate symbolism. Though he recognized that the spatial requirements of the bureaucracy far exceeded those of the legislature, he felt strongly that in a democracy "spiritually and morally the hall of the people's representatives should dominate." He was acutely conscious of two instances in which such symbolism had been distorted, one recent and nearby, the other still under construction in New York. He faulted both New Delhi, "where the two Secretariat buildings dominate in size . . . because of their elevated location," and the United Nations headquarters, "where the Secretariat of forty stories . . . dwarfs the Assembly building," and urged that Chandigarh have no tall buildings for bureaucracy.[12]

Matthew Nowicki, hired as Mayer's architectural assistant, proposed a novel way to let the profile of the Assembly predominate, while recognizing the greater spatial needs of the secretariat functions. Why not, he suggested, place "the legislative hall physically on top of the Secretariat structure, as a crowning shape above it." Mayer, however, rejected the idea, calling it "too much of a tour de force."[13] After Nowicki's death in a plane crash, Thapar and Verma, representing the Indian government, took this tragedy as an opportunity to seek new design advice from Europe. They appointed Maxwell Fry, Jane Drew, Le Corbusier, and Pierre Jeanneret to take over the architectural implementation of Mayer's plan. With Le Corbusier in charge of the Capitol design and exercising his usual influence over everything else, Mayer's role was almost immediately subordinated. Fry found Nowicki's sketches for the capitol buildings to be "rather romantically based on Indian idioms" and thought Mayer's site for the complex ill-chosen: "I studied the Mayer plan and found by projecting sections along major road lines that the Capitol buildings which he saw enlaced with water were rather like Lutyens' Viceregal Palace at New Delhi, largely eclipsed by the profile of the approach road."[14]

Le Corbusier altered the position of the capitol complex to make certain of maximum visibility for his buildings, retaining the idea of what he consistently referred to as "la tête," but placing it at an elevated level slightly to the northeast of the city.[15] He abandoned the idea of the water necklace as impractical and eliminated all housing from the vicinity of the government center as well. What resulted was a 220-acre enclave, "an

4.3 Hiding the city from the capitol complex.

acropolis of monuments" separated from the nearest housing by a canal and a boulevard and reached by way of a wide approach road that allowed the capitol complex to radiate its dominance for miles.[16] Trees, pools, sunken roadways, and an artificial horizon of man-made hills combine to block the view of lesser structures and activities, affirming the imperious presence of the Corbusian government citadel. In a sketchbook notation of November 1952, Le Corbusier emphasized the privileged position of the capitol in no uncertain terms: "Caution! [On the] city side, the capitol must be enclosed by a continuous glacis [consisting] of a horizontal embankment. (Hide all construction of the city.)" (4.3).[17]

For the north side of the capitol, facing the Shivalik Hills rather than the city, Le Corbusier adopted a completely different attitude. In a sketchbook entry from February 1954 in which he described the buildings to the south as "l'ennemi," he also noted that "the artificial hills must close off the *south*, and not the north.[18] "On the Himalayan side," he insisted, "it is admirable [to] let the cultures and the flocks run right up against a parapet," though he worried that "goats will come gobble up everything."[19] For Le Corbusier, the Chandigarh capitol was to be, in the words of the editor of his sketchbooks, the "last outpost of civilization before the Himalayas." In contrast to his earliest sketches, Le Corbusier's eventual design decisions for Chandigarh stressed the separation of capitol and capital, perhaps reflective of his own growing antagonism with the city and its other architects. Prakash's more psychoanalytical account also plausibly proposes that "Le Corbusier wanted to hide behind the walls and build his own compensatory universe, as if the brief space of idealization was sufficient to overcome the city of regrets."[20]

Though the design of the individual buildings bears little resemblance to the work of Lutyens and Baker on the Raisina acropolis, it seems clear, as Stanislaus von Moos argues, that Le Corbusier intended his effort to be "the Indian answer to the New Delhi Capitol."[21] In his preference for the axial vista leading to a privileged high place, Le Corbusier followed not only Lutyens but also L'Enfant, Haussmann, and Griffin. In emphasizing the view beyond the privileged high place, however, he parts company with these earlier planners. Le Corbusier does far more than lead the eye of the visitor *to* the capitol: his architecture leads the eye *through* it to the dramatic landscape of the Indian Punjab. The capitol is both the home of government and the place from which the rural parts of the territory that is governed may be surveyed.

In the layout of the buildings within the capitol, Le Corbusier's work exhibits remarkable continuity with the work of Lutyens as well as notable departures. Although much of Le Corbusier's Capitol plan was prefigured in his own work, especially in his designs for the League of Nations headquarters and the Mundaneum, it is also striking that he, like Lutyens, placed the Governor's Palace—and not the Assembly—in the premiere position. As von Moos comments, "Through all the stages of its development . . . the complex remained visually dominated by the Governor's Palace. This building, drastically overscaled in the initial stages of its planning, was designed to 'crown the Capitol' similarly to the way Lutyens's Viceroy's House crowned the city of New Delhi." In the Corbusian view of political power, the executive still reigned supreme (4.4). Ironically, through the exercise of this very power the Capitol came to take on a less imperial form. At the urging of Nehru, who was sensitive to this decidedly undemocratic bit of architectural juxtaposition, the Governor's Palace was never built. For Indian politicians, though not for Le Corbusier, the spatial centrality and prominence afforded the viceroy in Lutyens's scheme, in which parliamentary placement was an afterthought, could have no obvious parallel in a postcolonial capital. To coincide with the fiftieth anniversary of Chandigarh

4.4 Early sketch showing Le Corbusier's axial approach to the Governor's Palace.

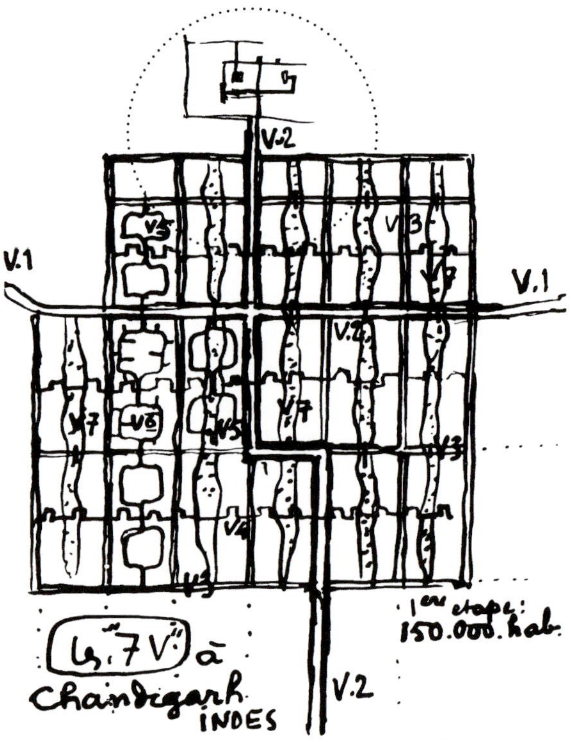

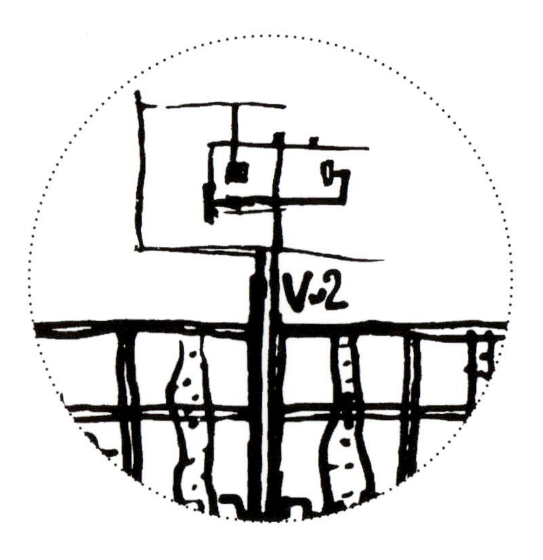

in January 1999, proponents erected a temporary version of the Governor's Palace out of bamboo and cloth, but this was not to last.[22]

Commentators on the Chandigarh capitol have stressed the primacy of the Governor's Palace over the other buildings, yet possibly this was not Le Corbusier's intention. While it is true that the Governor's Palace presented both the highest and most active silhouette of Le Corbusier's government quartet, the architect simultaneously used a variety of architectural devices to diminish its apparent centrality. In his detailed analysis of the Governor's Palace, Alexander Gorlin concurs with von Moos, describing this building as "the apex of the capital city" and noting that the "crown of the capital" appellation is Le Corbusier's own indication of the building's importance.[23] Seen alone in Le Corbusier's one-point perspective sketch, in which the roofline of the building eclipses even the mountain range beyond, the palace appears both central and decidedly crownlike (4.5). In the model and site plan, however, it appears far less prominently enthroned (4.6). For one thing, it would have been partially hidden by the artificial mounds that block out the city; for another, it is the building placed furthest back, reached on foot only after traversing a complex, nonaxial approach. By car, it could be reached only from the side. The nondirect approach, according to Gorlin, replaced the "deep space" of the Beaux Arts processional axis with a device intended to decrease the perceptual distance to the building and tie it more closely into the plaza that links the Assembly and High Court. Far from deliberately subordinating the rest of the design to the centrality of the Governor's Palace, Le Corbusier feared that it would be "lost in the background" and, revising his initial axial sketches, took steps to mitigate

4.5 Le Corbusier sketch of approach to the Chandigarh capitol's crown.

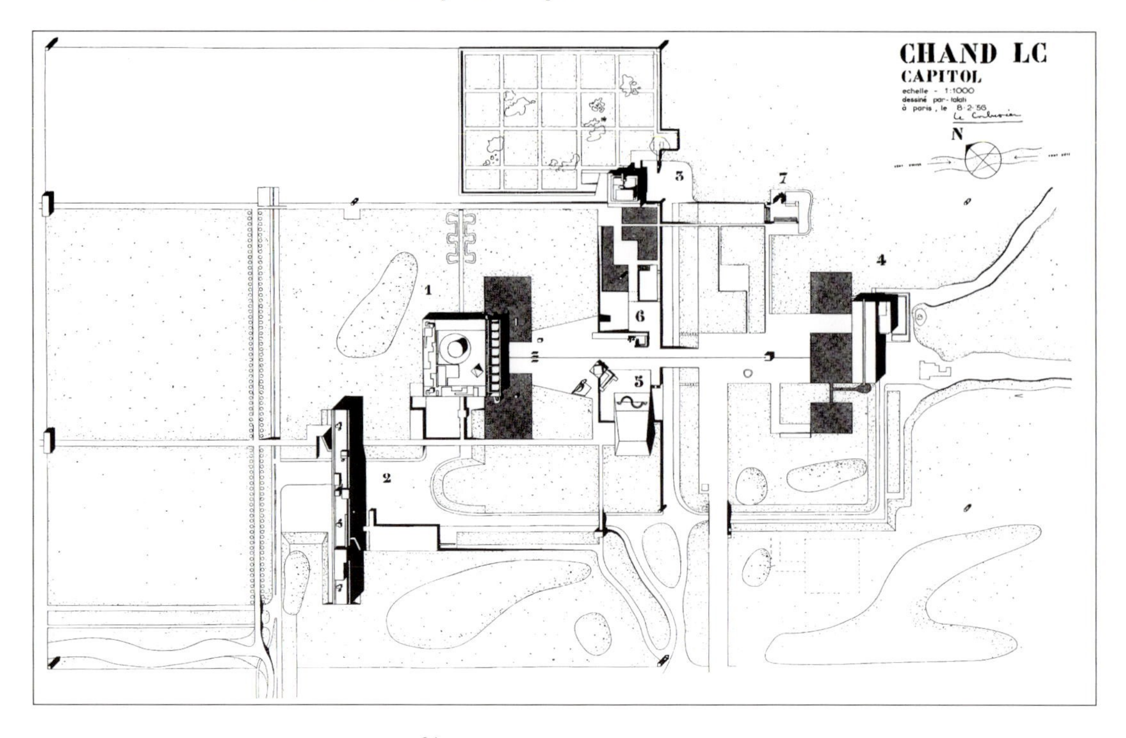

4.6 Plan of capitol complex, Chandigarh.

1 Assembly Building
2 Secretariat
3 Site of proposed Governor's Palace
4 High Court
5 and 6 Plaza
7 Open Hand monument

the problem.[24] Whereas Lutyens designed the Viceroy's House as the single focus of a long perspective (and even managed, however unintentionally, to build it at the vanishing point), Le Corbusier's Governor's Palace was to be one building among many, a participant in a complex system of plazas and framed views. Even when the palace was dropped from the scheme, the designer's need for a pavilion in that particular place did not disappear: Le Corbusier sought to replace the palace with a Museum of Knowledge. The placement of the Governor's Palace was more than a symbol of political relationships. To Le Corbusier it was also an indispensable formal element in a rich composition, one that transcended programmatic function.

Some aspects of the composition do manage to convey an appropriate hierarchy for democratic government, yet the capitol complex as a whole remains a disturbing political ideogram. In part because the Assembly Building and High Court lack a Governor's Palace to fit behind and between them, they currently face each other across a pedestrian-resistant expanse of plaza (4.7). The resultant place is not only compositionally incomplete, but also functionally purposeless. The theory of a people's plaza, an open zone at the very center of political institutional power that is available to all citizens and visitors, has an undeniable democratic appeal in both its implications of egalitarianism and its evidence of freedom; however, there is no good use for the plaza except as a place of transit for the carless or a place of photography for Le Corbusier aficionados. Why would a worker in one branch of government ever need to walk (much less want to walk) to the facilities of another cross-plaza branch? And, indeed, even the grand, plaza-facing entrance gestures of both buildings are only for ceremonial effect. The grand opening in the facade of the High Court belies the fact that direct exterior access to courtrooms is found elsewhere. On the Assembly

4.7 Pedestrian-resistant plaza.

Building across the plaza there is a massive, pivoting enameled door intended for ceremonial use by the governor following a processional route from the Governor's Palace for the formal opening of parliament. Without the palace, however, there can be no such procession. Lacking not only the Governor's Palace/Museum of Knowledge but also some of the self-reflexive sentinels to Le Corbusier's own design ideas, the plaza between the Assembly Building and High Court is even more barren than the photos suggest, despite the later erection of such features as the Open Hand and Solar monuments. In the end, the vast openness of this plaza creates a kind of ironic closure. Too far detached from the rest of the city, remote even from the parking lot of the Secretariat, this seemingly auspicious civic symbolism remains, literally, an empty gesture, to all appearances tempting chiefly those informed visitors possessing motorized transport. The other chief users of the plaza, Prakash observes, are villagers from Kansal (located to the north of the capitol complex) who use it as a shortcut, and cricketers who have found that the flat ground in front of the Open Hand monument makes for a fine pitch.[25]

Whatever its faults, Le Corbusier's scheme, as built, at least denied pre-eminent position to the bureaucracy. He lodged the elongated slab of the Secretariat farther off-center than the Assembly Building or the High Court, thereby acknowledging and accepting its secondary symbolic status. Moreover, by placing it parallel to the north–south approach road, he minimized its bulk, at least when viewed from a distance. Even these decisions, however, were not in accord with Le Corbusier's initial wishes; his first sketches showed a high-rise slab for the Secretariat that would have dominated the ensemble. Fortunately, this idea was roundly rejected by the city bureaucrats.[26]

To the extent to which one is willing to disregard the larger failures of his urban design and planning, each of Le Corbusier's buildings may be seen as an extraordinary formal achievement, both in relation to the architect's earlier work and as an attempt to devise a new symbolism for government buildings that aims to be both modern and evocative of Indian climate and traditions. Though it may be that no subsequent architect designing in a new capital has marshaled an equivalent richness of imagery, many have imitated his idea of a detached capitol complex in a segregated city. It is this idea, born in antiquity and revived whenever new capital cities have been designed, that received its first modernist urban design treatment at Chandigarh.

BRASÍLIA: INTEGRATING A NATION-STATE, SEGREGATING A GOVERNMENT

If the creation of a new capital for the Indian Punjab was demanded by immediate political conditions resulting from partition, the creation of Brasília was the outcome of just the opposite situation—a perennial longing for Brazilian geopolitical integration. Though Brazil has been legally independent from Portugal since 1822, Brasília is still in a sense a postcolonial capital. Colonial urban patterns persisted long after independence. Brazil comprises the fifth largest land area in the world, yet 80 percent of the Brazilian population lives within two hundred miles of the coast, a legacy of the colonial days when cities were located to serve as ports for the export of raw materials to Europe.[27] The capital, located in Salvador from the sixteenth through the eighteenth centuries and in Rio de Janeiro thereafter, had always remained tied to the Atlantic. By contrast, the vast interior was largely unknown. When visited at all, it was explored chiefly by Jesuit missionaries in search of converts, by cattlemen in search of pasture, and by *bandeirantes* (the Brazilian counterpart of *conquistadores*) in search of Indian slaves, gold, and precious stones.[28] The advent of Brasília instituted this centripetal pattern of migration more permanently (4.8).

4.8 Frontier capital: Brasília.

Though construction of the inland capital did not begin until the late 1950s, the transfer was said to be an issue as early as 1761 and was mentioned in a newspaper editorial in 1813: "This location, quite central, where the capital of the Empire ought to be located, seems to us to be indicated as the very elevated region of her territory, whence would descend the orders [of the government], just as there descends the waters which go to the Tocantins River to the north, the Plate to the south, and the São Francisco to the east."[29] With remarkable precision, this passage describes the area—with streams leading to three great river systems—that would be chosen for the Federal District 150 years later. The new capital would represent a watershed for Brazilian development, literally as well as figuratively.

For a long time, however, the inland capital remained a dream. In 1823, José Bonifácio de Andrada e Silva, known as the Patriarch of Independence, submitted a document to the Constituent Assembly proposing an interior capital to be called Brasília (or, alternatively, Petrópole, after independent Brazil's first emperor, Pedro I). Fearing the military vulnerability of Rio, he sought a safer alternative. Yet, also at the heart of the desire to transfer the capital was a deeply felt need to assert control over the sprawling new empire, by moving to claim its geographic—if not demographic—center. Nothing happened to give effect to this idea during the nineteenth century, but, following the establishment of the Brazilian Republic in 1889, a provision in the constitution of 1891 raised the question anew. An expedition in 1892 demarcated a district for the proposed city, and in 1922, to commemorate the independence centennial, a foundation stone was laid. Though the constitutional provision was reiterated in the new constitutions of 1934 and 1946, and exploration and site selection took place between 1948 and 1955, there was still little evidence that the new capital would progress beyond its single stone.[30] Then, in 1955, Juscelino Kubitschek, campaigning for president on a law and order platform that called for strict compliance with the constitution, pledged to build Brasília.

In the course of well over a century of unsuccessful advocacy, supporters of an interior capital had managed to advance a variety of reasons to justify such a move; under the determined rule of Kubitschek, all of these factors were marshaled. Some had favored the move chiefly as a means for signaling the symbolic end of rule from cities associated with Portuguese domination, while others had stressed the need to forge a unified Brazil out of an assemblage of distant and disconnected enclaves. Some had emphasized the increased military security that an inland capital would bring, while others saw the capital as a means for providing state services more efficiently. Increasingly, the opportunity had been phrased in terms of its potential for regional and national economic development leading to increased self-sufficiency. And when the building of the new capital finally began, its advent was treated by the government as a device for promoting and instilling a concept of national identity.[31] According to one commentator, "The foundation of Brasília signified nothing less than the re-foundation of Brazil itself at a national rather than a colonial stage of development."[32]

Presiding over a country in which public officials are closely identified with the public works they commission, Kubitschek—who was elected with only about one-third of the total vote—saw an opportunity for immortalizing his reputation. Living in a land where presidents were permitted a single five-year term, he knew that immortality would have to be developed very quickly. As Alex Shoumatoff puts it, "Juscelino was determined that his name should go down in history as the founder of the new capital; and to defeat the resistance that would inevitably arise, it would be necessary to make the move irreversible by the time his five-year term in office was complete."[33] Finding Rio overcrowded, European-oriented, prone to political ferment, and saddled with an indolent bureaucracy, Kubitschek, like so many other advocates of new capitals, hoped that a physical move could engender a change in mentality as well. He may well have seen himself as the spiritual heir to Peter the Great, but, whereas his Russian precursor had sought to build a "window on the West," the Brazilian fenestration would face Brazil's own interior.[34] In his memoir, *Why I Built Brasília*, Kubitschek wrote, "During our entire history, from the Discovery to my regime, we lived, to use the observation of our first historian, Friar Vincent of Salvador, 'scratching the sand of the beach, like crabs.'"[35] In moving the crustaceans of government inland, the president—dubbed by the press the Brazilian Pharaoh[36]—saw Brasília as part of a larger push for rapid development, consolidating "fifty years in five."[37] As Brasília's planner, Lúcio Costa, puts it, "Brasília was really Kubitschek's creation. To modernize the country he launched a series of measures; he opened new iron mines, built up the Navy, attracted foreign industry, especially automotive. He constructed an arch of which Brasília was the keystone, keeping all the others in place."[38] "With what now seems shrewd political insight," Norma Evenson comments, "Kubitschek seems to have sensed that the Brazilian people were ready for an adventure, and that popular imagination would respond to such a grand gesture more readily than to pedestrian and 'practical' enterprises."[39] And, indeed, one look at the automobile-inspired expanses of Costa's city confirms that Brasília is anything but pedestrian.[40]

Costa's *Plano Piloto* for the city, selected in 1957 after a national competition, took up the Kubitschek challenge to initiate accelerated development. As a diagram (and Costa's proposal was really no more than this), the city plan conveyed multiple images of flight. Whether one saw it as a bird, an airplane, or a dragonfly, it instilled a sense of rapid forward motion in keeping with the slogans of the ambitious president. Lest the metaphor of his *pilot* plan be lost on anyone, Costa added an extra hint, labeling the two sides of the Residential Axis North Wing and South Wing (4.9).

Calling Brasília "not the result of regional planning, but the cause," Costa described its foundation as "a deliberate act of conquest, a gesture of pioneers acting in the spirit of their colonial traditions."[41] Given that Brazilian "colonial traditions" included such diverse endeavors as mass extermination and enslavement of the indigenous population and the exploitation of natural resources for the benefit of foreigners, Costa's words may have more than their intended resonance. The colonial phenomenon that his drawings invoke, however, is the conquest of the missionary. The plan, he wrote, "was born of that initial gesture which anyone would make when pointing to a given place, or taking possession of it: the drawing of two axes crossing

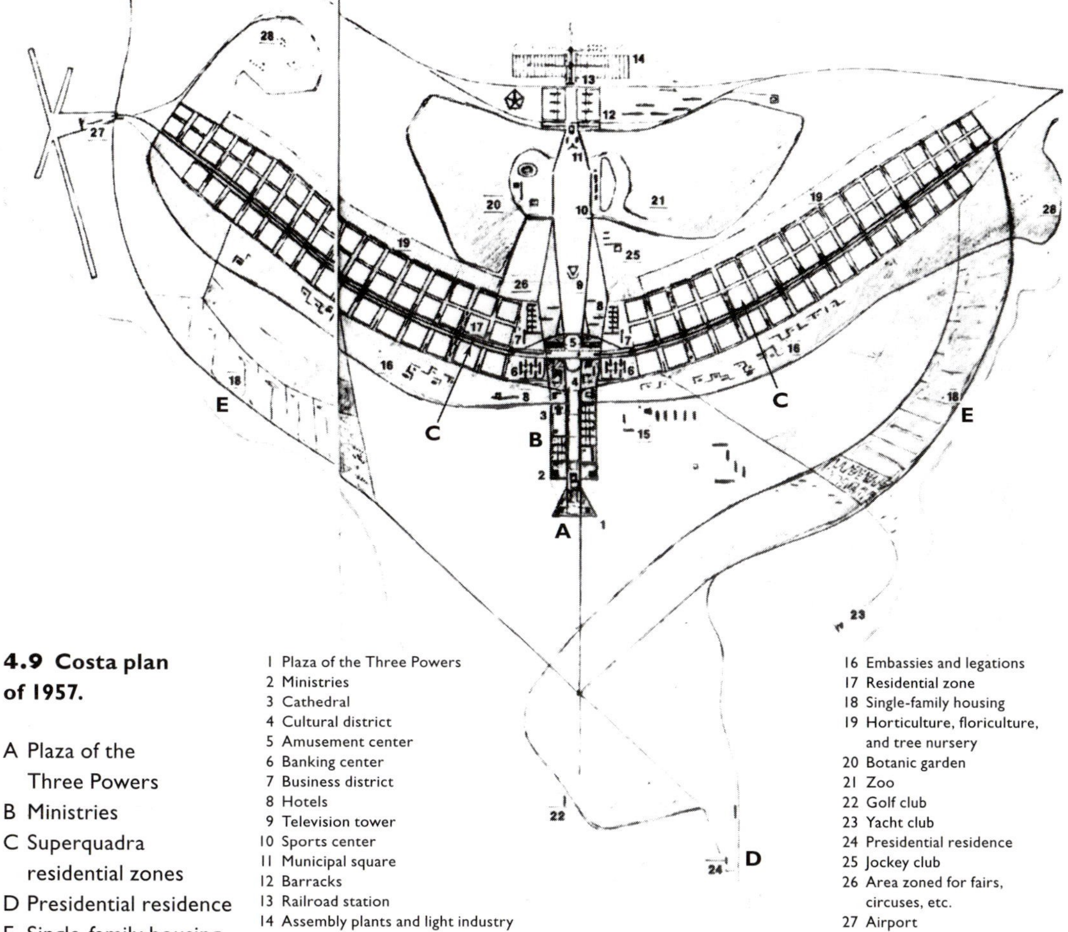

4.9 Costa plan of 1957.

A Plaza of the Three Powers
B Ministries
C Superquadra residential zones
D Presidential residence
E Single-family housing

each other at right angles, in the sign of the Cross" (4.10).[42] In Brazil, home to the world's largest population of Roman Catholics, such a gesture surely connotes more than the secularity of the *cardo* and *decumanus*, the major cross-streets that marked the center of the ancient Roman town. One commentator has developed a more extended interpretation of the Costa plan's Christian symbolism.[43] He relates this choice to the prophetic dreams of Father (later Saint) Giuseppe Bosco, who while in Italy in 1883 described his visions of the inland South American city and its lake, an "inconceivable richness" that "will happen in the third generation."[44] The first masonry structure that went up in Brasília was his shrine. However tempting it may be to search for deeper Catholic overtones in Costa's plan, the distinction

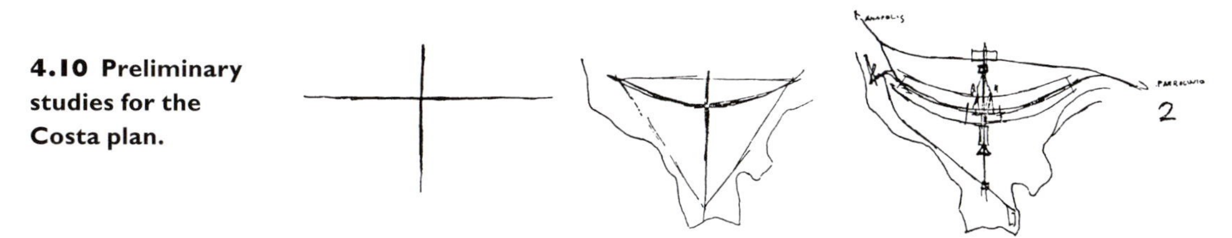

4.10 Preliminary studies for the Costa plan.

between a crossing and a Cross probably means nothing in terms of the way Brasília is now perceived, though the imagery may conceivably have contributed to the direct appeal of the drawing as a competition entry.[45] In Costa's plan, the sign of the Cross marks neither church nor capitol; his Monumental Axis and his Residential Axis come together at a massive traffic interchange. Raised on the Athens Charter, the new Jesuits spread the gospel of modern autos and modern architecture.

In his critique of Brasília, James Holston argues that Costa's invocation of primordial origins for the city ("born of that initial gesture") was an attempt to hide the more radical aspects of his proposal. By couching a high-modernist critique of existing Brazilian society in the dehistoricizing language of a foundation myth, Costa diverted attention from the social agenda of the modern movement; in providing "a mythological pedigree" for Brasília he disguised its historical one "by eliminating the history of Brazil and of modern architecture from the stated idea of the plan."[46] Brasília, in appearance as well as in social intent, was expected to be different; rather than being a solution that grappled with the problems and patterns of existing Brazilian cities, the new capital was designed as a de novo alternative.

In actuality, however, the construction, settlement, and organization of the new capital revealed ways Brasília was fundamentally tied to the rest of Brazil. Holston contends that "the government intended to unveil the built city as if it were without a history of construction and occupation. On inauguration day, it planned to reveal a miracle: a gleaming city, empty and ready to receive its intended occupants. This presentation of an inhabitable idea denied the Brazil that the city had already acquired: its population of builders." In the effort to create a pure city of government administration, the planners of Brasília had welcomed a mass immigration of "pioneers" to build the capital but insisted that they leave once the city was inaugurated. The Brazilian popular press referred to migrant construction workers of the late 1950s as latter-day *bandeirantes*, and "the term *bandeirante* came to mean not a frontier marauder but rather the builder of a new Brazil." The recruitment campaign was infused with the notion of Brasília as a catalyst for national identity. It conveyed this both by stressing the need for Brazilians from all regions and backgrounds to participate and by emphasizing the "frontier solidarity and democracy" of these "pioneers." This notion of solidarity, Holston suggests, may have been rooted in their perception of "direct access to elite persons and soon-to-be important places. Their sense of democracy had absolutely nothing to do with political rights or institutions, of which they were entirely deprived. Rather, it had to do with their being proximate to, in a visual, tactile, physical way, 'things' elite and charismatic." As it was being built, Brasília and the nation seemed more concretely theirs. This sort of attachment helps explain, perhaps, the evident collapse of any such camaraderie following the inauguration of the city. Denied a place in the city they had built, Brasília's builders found their solidarity undermined by divisions into various classes having different interests, privileges, and powers.[47] As Holston points out, the government did not create a "city *of* bureaucrats" but a "city *for* bureaucrats"; they were "a minority population with privileged access to a public domain of resources which excluded the vast majority." Thus, he concludes, "even before its inauguration, Brasília was a stratified city in which differential incorporation was the fundamental condition of social organization."[48]

In spite of this central, overriding incongruity, the planners believed they could avoid such issues of stratification within the residential areas reserved for government employees in the *Plano Piloto*. Here they spoke of the "principle of equality," yet here too this would prove to be an illusion. Unlike the planners of Canberra, New Delhi, and Chandigarh, whose initial plans assumed class segregation and reinforced it by the provision of a hierarchy of residential patterns descending from the privileged position of the capitol, the designers of Brasília sought to incorporate all levels of income into each residential sector. Moreover, with all of the government workplaces grouped on a distant and separate axis, the plan seemed to deny high-income officials the privilege of high-status and low-density residential locations near their workplaces, since *none* of the residential sectors were located conveniently for work in government offices. The intended social idealism (and design determinism) of this policy was clearly articulated in a 1963 edition of the official journal of NOVACAP, the state corporation that planned, built, and administered Brasília: "The apartment blocks of a *superquadra* [the city's basic residential unit] are all equal: same façade, same height, same facilities, all constructed on *pilotis* [columns], all provided with garages and constructed of the same material—which prevents the hateful differentiation of social classes; that is, all the families share the same life together, the upper-echelon public functionary, the middle and the lower."[49] By 1963, however, the egalitarian intentions implied by the standardization of residential organization, put forth under the design guidance of the Brazilian Communist architect Oscar Niemeyer, were already corrupted. The radical spatial politics of Brasília's architects and planners was not matched by the society that was to inhabit the plan. While it is generally held to be true that the residential system did initially achieve some of the intended intermixture of classes in the same superquadra and club, traditional polarizations quickly took over. As Holston puts it, "The mixture proved explosive, igniting class and status conflicts among the residents." In turn, these conflicts led both to the demise of the planned collective structure of the superquadras and to alliances between more privileged members of the government bureaucracy and their social counterparts among the nonbureaucrats originally denied residence in the government apartments. Meanwhile, Holston notes, interclass alliances developed among NOVACAP recruits around demands for rights to reside in the *Plano Piloto*, demands that "led, rebelliously, to political mobilization, to violent confrontation with the state, and eventually to the creation of the satellite cities." Brasília's Federal District (DF) population has now surpassed two million, but approximately 90 percent of these people live outside the boundaries of the *Plano Piloto*, either in satellite cities, illegal condominium developments, or low-end squatter settlements. An additional million people live beyond the DF in the larger urbanized city-region. In the words of one recent assessment, Brasília's "urbanization process has a dismal tale to tell. The exclusionary Pilot Plan design induced urban dispersion over the entire territory . . . The expectation that a planned core would induce an orderly occupation of the territory—an essential utopia of Modernism—did not come to pass." Instead, the DF reproduced the same sort of distinction between privileged center and impoverished periphery that is so characteristic of other cities, both in Brazil and elsewhere. From the perspective of the local population, James Scott wryly concludes: "it is almost as if the founders of Brasília, rather than having planned a city, have actually planned to prevent a city."[50]

As Brasília grew, the satellite cities soon came to house the lower-income members of the government bureaucracy as well as the other low-income groups who had always been denied a place in the city. Following the decision in 1965 to make most of the apartments in the superquadras available on the open market, prices increasingly forced the lowest ranks of the civil service out of the city. With the nearest satellite city separated from the *Plano Piloto* by a fourteen-kilometer greenbelt, the whole of Brasília's poor had been effectively (if artificially) eliminated from the city. As Holston observes, "The important point is that in separating the places of work and residence, and in concentrating the former while dispersing the latter, modernist planning leads to the stratified use of the city along class lines, especially for purposes other than work. . . . Since the poorest people live farthest from the *Plano Piloto*, it is obvious that commuter costs take a large portion of the working poor's family income. Thus, the burden falls heaviest on those who can least afford to travel to the principal source of employment."[51] As early as 1961, one Brazilian journalist (who chose to identify himself only by his initials) could comment that "contrary to Lucio Costa's intention, class distinctions are more marked in Brasília than anywhere else in Brazil."[52] Another early commentator noted that a clear spatial separation of classes was already in place in 1962, with "laboring classes" in satellite towns, "middle and junior ranks of government and business" in the superblocks of the *Plano Piloto*, and an "elite" decamped to lakeside residential subdivisions,[53] in direct countervention of Article 20 of the Master Plan, which stipulated that the lakeside area be left undeveloped.[54]

An abundance of rhetoric about the superquadras notwithstanding, Costa's plan is, like all of the designed capitals that preceded it, focused on its capitol complex, which is located not at the point of crossing but at the culmination of the major axis. This capitol complex, designated in Brasília as the Three Powers Plaza (Praça dos Três Poderes), contains the buildings for the three branches of national government—the Congress (legislative assembly halls and secretariat), the Planalto Palace (executive offices), and the Supreme Court—as well as a museum devoted to Brasília's history. The museum, a windowless building with a flat facade broken by an enormous head of Juscelino Kubitschek, houses the texts of his speeches, with highlights carved into the walls in enormous letters.[55] In 1987, a Pantheon of Liberty and Democracy was added on the plaza's far eastern edge. This white pantheon is said to resemble doves taking flight and is dedicated to Tancredo Neves, the Brazilian president who died only weeks after assuming office in 1985. All of these buildings on the plaza were designed by Niemeyer, who had been associated with Kubitschek since 1940 and who had served on the jury that selected Costa's plan. Niemeyer, like Costa, was a Brazilian disciple of Le Corbusier, and, though I have found no evidence of any direct inspiration from Chandigarh, the Brasília capitol design draws heavily upon the United Nations headquarters, a project which engaged the services of both Niemeyer and Le Corbusier.

As in the "world parliament" for New York, the dominant element of the Brasília capitol complex is its skyscraper Secretariat. In Brasília, the slender slab of the U.N. tower has been given a Siamese twin, joined by a walkway. The symbolic dominance of the bureaucracy over the legislature, so vehemently and repeatedly decried by Lewis Mumford with regard to the United Nations buildings,[56] is repeated on the Brazilian plateau. Yet in the Brasília capitol complex, the dome-and-bowl legislative Assembly chambers stand out, as they do not in the United Nations headquarters, as distinctive shapes; though the quirky twin towers dominate, the Assembly chambers remain part of this central and distinctly memorable image of Brasília (4.11, 4.12).[57]

4.11 Ramp approach to the capitol complex.

4.12 Plaza of the Three Powers, Brasília.

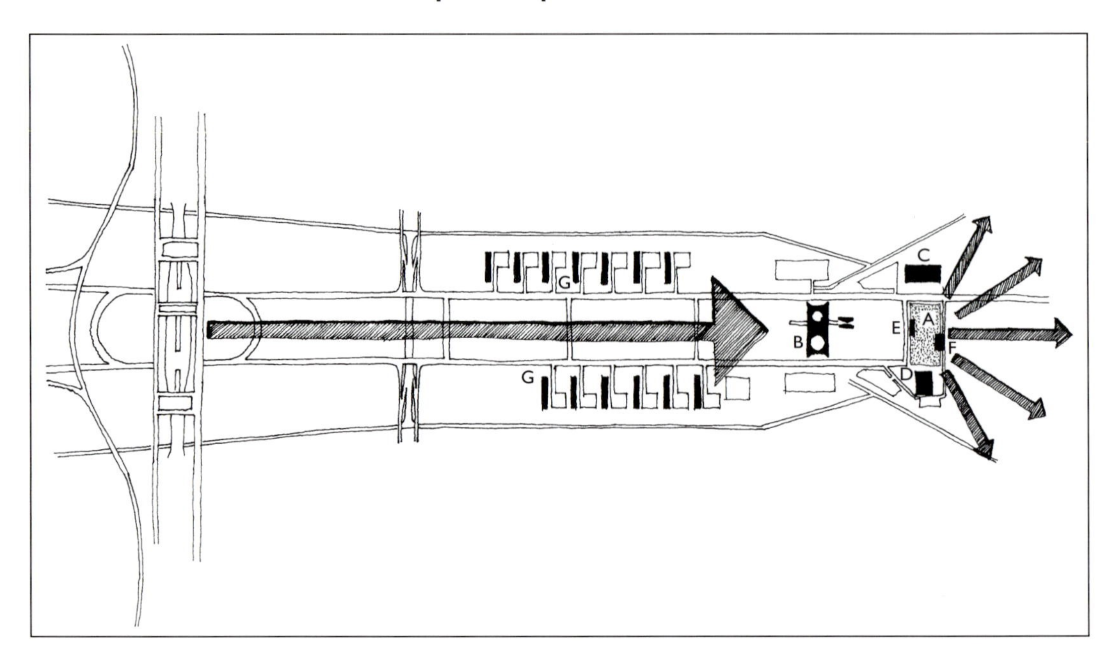

4.13 Monumental axis, but open to the landscape.

A Plaza of the Three Powers
B Congress Buildings with paired-tower Secretariat
C Presidential (Planalto) Palace
D Supreme Court
E Museum
F Tancredo Neves Pantheon
G Ministries

Niemeyer's capitol complex offers another new twist. Through elaborate regrading, the portion of the Monumental Axis that is flanked by ministry buildings was made flat, enabling the capitol complex, oriented transversely at the end of the axis, to rise abruptly above it. The pedestrian who wishes to reach the government buildings is confronted by a glass acropolis, surmountable by a concrete ramp. At the top of the ramp is the propylaeum of the paired Secretariat. Descending to yet another level, the hardy pedestrian reaches the Three Powers Plaza. In Brasília, the end of the axis is not the end of the capitol complex, as it is in Washington, Canberra, and New Delhi. Instead, as at Chandigarh, the ultimate destination is not a building but a plaza with a panoramic view of the landscape beyond. And, as at Le Corbusier's capitol complex, once one is presented with the plaza and the drama of the distant view into the landscape, much of the rest of the city of Brasília is blocked from sight. From the Three Powers Plaza, open wide to embrace the clouds and the view of Lake Paranoá, the presence of the city is treated as secondary. Kubitschek's head gazes not toward the city he inspired but toward the open landscape and his Presidential Palace on the lake (4.13, 4.14).[58]

Even in the name *Monumental Axis*, Costa made evident his desire for a clear architectural hierarchy, emphasizing the presence of government. The cross-axial *Plano Piloto* insured maximum visibility for the highest structures on the Monumental Axis: the twenty-eight-story Secretariat slabs and the television tower. Each in its own way was an appropriate symbol of government administration, though neither would satisfy a Lewis Mumford. Evenson suggests that the jury selecting Costa's plan for Brasília felt that Rio lacked "a ceremonial focus." Because "government buildings were more or less integrated with the commercial buildings of the city," she writes, there was no adequate consciousness of the city as a capital.[59] Costa's capital consciousness was undeniable. "The *monument*, in the case of a capital," he

4.14 Kubitschek surveying the countryside, not the city.

wrote in 1962, "is not an afterthought, that can be left for later, as in the modern little English cities, the *monument* here is intrinsic to the thing itself, and opposed to the . . . city which one wishes discreetly inscribed into the landscape, the capital city must be imposed and command [the landscape]."[60] And, as is the case in other designed capitals, it is politically revealing to note which buildings command the landscape most insistently.

It is not, of course, the whole of Brasília which commands the landscape but chiefly the buildings of the Monumental Axis, and especially the monuments of the capitol complex. In the capitol complex, however, the relationship of building to landscape is reversed. From the Plaza of the Three Powers, it is the landscape that commands the buildings. In the thousand-foot expanse that separates the Planalto Palace from the Supreme Court, there is a fourth power—the plaza itself. As Niemeyer describes it, the forms of the government "palaces" are inextricably tied to his goals for the plaza:

> When thinking out the forms for those Palaces, I also bore in mind the kind of mood they would impart to the Plaza of the Three Powers. It should not seem, as I saw it, cold and technical, ruled by the classical, hard and already obvious purity of straight lines. On the contrary, I visualized it with a richness of forms, dreams and poetry, like the mysterious paintings of Carzou, new forms, startling visitors by their lightness and creative liberty; forms that were not anchored to the earth rigidly and statically, but uplifted the Palaces as though to suspend them, white and ethereal, in the endless nights of the highlands.[61]

Costa, too, stressed the importance of the triangular plaza in his triangular plan and, like Niemeyer, emphasized the formal relationships among buildings more than the political relationships among branches of government:

> The highlights in the outline plan of the city are the public buildings which house the fundamental powers. These are three, and they are autonomous: therefore the equilateral triangle—associated with the very earliest architecture in the world—is the elementary frame best suited to express them. . . . At each angle of the triangular plaza—the Plaza of the Three Powers, as it might be called—stands one of the three buildings: the Government Palace and the Supreme Court at the base; the Congress Building at the tip.[62]

Equilateral triangles do not necessarily make for equilateral politics. In the political ideogram for Brasília, though little effort was made to diminish the appearance of the Secretariat in relation to the Assembly chambers (the Senate meets under the dome, the House of Representatives in the bowl), legislative functions do predominate.

There is surely some irony in this, given the all-powerful executive needed to make Brasília a reality during one man's five-year term. Israel Pinheiro, president of NOVACAP, made clear the relationship between executive and legislature. Asked to explain how he managed to obtain all necessary funds to move forward without getting bogged down by parliamentary committees, he responded, "We have fixed a D-Day—April 21, 1960. The town must be ready then. I have said to Parliament, 'If you criticize me, you do not get your town.'"[63] Costa put it even more succinctly: "We have to finish in five years or the forest will come back."[64]

Kubitschek's team met this deadline, and the city was inaugurated with ten months still remaining in the president's term. This accelerated timetable and abbreviated period of presidential tenure may well have greatly affected the symbolic juxtaposition of the buildings. Perhaps because he realized that he would not be president long enough to set up his office at the Three Powers Plaza, Kubitschek established his presence in other ways. Rather than leave an especially prominent building in the capitol complex for his presidential successors, Kubitschek's supporters marked the executive presence on the Brazilian *caput mundi* with his own head, suitably enlarged.

Equally indicative of the place of the executive within the three powers was Kubitschek's ability to build his own residence before anything else. What appears on Costa's *Plano Piloto* almost as an afterthought, a numbered notation located on the faded periphery of his drawing, was in fact designed first, independent of the plan, and became Brasília's most elaborate structure, the Dawn Palace. "I chose the name myself," Kubitschek explained. "What else will Brasília be . . . if not the dawn of a new day for Brazil?"[65] And, as in Ankara and elsewhere, the dawn of a presidential residence would signal many more new days of elite construction nearby, nearly ringing the rest of the lake.

This quality of being new and modern remains at the heart of Brasília's symbolism, more than the design of any particular building. It may be, as Evenson has observed, that few Brazilians will take much note of the symbolic juxtaposition of the structures, though surely they are made aware of the architectural presence of the Congress in an unprecedented way: "The government complex photographs effectively and is not without its own sense of poetic drama. The National Assembly, moreover, easily recognizable and frequently reproduced throughout the country, has provided Brazil with its first truly national architectural symbol."[66] It is a symbolism based entirely on future aspirations, a modern tableau set out for a society still enamored with the prospects of mechanization. Writing in the early 1970s, Evenson observed that "Brasília tends to reflect a somewhat dated glorification of the machine; yet because Brazil is an unmechanized, relatively unindustrialized country, the facade of modern technology retains an appeal it may have lost elsewhere. The automobile in Brazil is not a commonplace possession; the romance of the machine is still a thrilling thing, and to have built an entire city to the scale of the motorcar is a source of great pride."[67] Thirty-five years later, much of this romance has almost certainly diminished.

Niemeyer, born in 1907 and still in charge of designing all federal buildings in Brasília a century later, has proved to be remarkably resilient (and Costa, who died in 1998, also lived to the age of 96). To the extent that Niemeyer's work exemplifies a Brazilian contribution to the International Style, it is in the lightness with which he employs curvilinear forms. His work on the Three Powers Plaza makes no overt reference to anything specifically Brazilian, though Niemeyer himself claims to have forged "a link with the old architecture of colonial Brazil, not by the obvious use of the elements common to those days, but by expressing the same plastic intention, the same love of curves and richly refined forms that is so telling a characteristic of the colonial style."[68] Though Niemeyer's curvilinear geometries may be said to resonate with the curves of the Brazilian baroque and art nouveau architecture of Rio, these highly abstracted forms are much more immediately related to other developments in modern architecture than they are to memories of past capitals or ongoing vernacular traditions. The sleek curvilinear forms may arguably have entered modern architecture in great profusion first in Brazil, but soon this style proliferated elsewhere, in work such as Harrison and Abramovitz's egg-shaped Albany Performing Arts Center and in buildings by Minoru Yamasaki, not to mention a more recent revival of sorts in the less disciplined swoops of Koolhaas or Hadid. Brasília's modernity places the city at a specific moment in the history of architecture and urbanism, but it cultivates Brazilian-ness in only the most abstract of ways. Brasília is Brazilian because it is in Brazil, was designed and built by Brazilians, is named for Brazil and because its overall plan emphasizes the connection of the city to the larger landscape of its place. As Evenson puts it, the "essential purpose" of Brasília is "to exist where it is."[69] Here, as elsewhere, nationalism is in the act as well as in the forms.

As a frozen moment in the history of modern architecture duly marked by designation as a World Heritage Site, the monumental center of Brasília is unrivaled in its sheer totality of modernist built form; as a political ideogram for Brazil, it is equally forward-looking. Brasília was an executively directed project designed to demonstrate the power of the legislature, in symbol if not in fact. For people used to the rule of church and autocrat, a city that has as its centerpiece the mechanism for constitutional government (even if it is the administrative part that dominates) was a step forward. Yet, only four years after Brasília was inaugurated, Brazil suffered a military coup. More than twenty years would pass before a semblance of democracy returned. Until the election of Neves in 1985, the bold architectural presence of the Congress, front and center, was ironic at best. Since the return of an elected civilian presidency, however, there has been more temptation to revive André Malraux's phrase, the "Capital of Hope."

Taken as a whole, the modernist venture of Brasília's architecture, urban design, and planning invites diverse political interpretations. Both the architects and the politicians viewed modern architecture and urbanism as a symbolic break with the colonially inspired past, and a leap into the future. Within this broad consensus, however, there were differences in priorities. As Holston observes,

> For the architects, immersed in the political history of modernism in Europe, this symbolic rupture was interpreted as the opportunity to break with the capitalism of that past. For them, the anticolonialism of modern architecture signified anti-capitalism as well. For the government, modernist architecture also meant the effacement of the colonial past from public building projects. But for its leaders, this symbolic anticolonialism was associated with modernization and nationalism and not socialist revolution.[70]

This flexibility of symbolism, explains, perhaps, how a city "planned by a Left-center liberal, designed by a Communist, constructed by a developmentalist regime, and consolidated by a bureaucratic-authoritarian dictatorship"[71] could have been championed by such diverse constituencies. More than this, as an act of urban design which effectively discourages mass involvement with the "exemplary center," the central area of Brasília could surely hold much appeal for all forms of authority. At the same time, however, the burgeoning pattern of automobile and truck ownership has permitted the monumental axis of Brasília to become sometimes a locus for monumental drive-in protests.[72]

Costa has claimed that the Plaza of the Three Powers is "the Versailles of the People,"[73] yet many visitors find its majesty to be aloof at best. Reactions vary depending on what aspects of the plaza experience are being judged. Edmund Bacon, writing in *Design of Cities*, found the aesthetic experience especially moving: "This great plaza . . .," he wrote, "does not depend on crowds to produce an experience that is deeply satisfying."[74] Sibyl Moholy-Nagy, responding on more than aesthetic terms, reacted quite differently: "Like runners, unable to change their course, [Costa and Niemeyer] raced down their 1200-feet-wide avenue of triumph, shouting with winded voices that what they were after was the triumph of the people and not the rulers. On a high platform they planted sculptured symbols of the Three Powers of government over the people, just as palace, fortress, cathedral and court house had symbolized the power of one class over another since the beginning of urban history."[75] These two responses well illustrate the futility of any form of definitive commentary that fails to set out the basis of its own criteria for judgment. If one wishes to try to grapple not only with Brasília's design but also with the circumstances of its cultural production, Bacon's assessment seems rather limited. For me, whatever the political intentions of its promoters or potential aesthetic epiphanies, this capitol complex comes across as yet another privileged sanctuary for government. Isolated from any residential, commercial, or recreational purposes, Brasília's administrative head is in the clouds. However beautiful those clouds may be on some days, there is a more enduring message about the relationship between government and those who are governed. Given the intimidating distances involved and the need for private transport to get there, public use of the plaza is premised on prior privilege.[76] As at Chandigarh, the very openness of the shadeless plaza is a form of political closure. Whatever the egalitarian tenets of its architects and planners, the economic and political realities of this iconically modern capital serve only to recapitulate an ancient theme: distancing the masses from the seat of courtly power.

CHAPTER 5

Designed capitals since 1960

The urban experiments of Chandigarh and Brasília have spawned a series of successors. Pakistan's Islamabad was the earliest of these, and governments across Asia, Africa, and South America have periodically proposed capital-building ventures ever since. I focus here on the plans for Nigeria's Abuja and Tanzania's Dodoma. Planned in the 1970s, these are two ambitious examples (one now substantially built, the other slowly moving forward) of somewhat more current thinking about designed postcolonial capitals. Both raise issues about pluralism—and the difficulty of symbolizing it—that will become central to the discussion of capitol complex architecture in Part 2. In these places, and in many that have drawn inspiration from them, the application of modern architecture and urbanism to the design of capital cities has not diminished the privileged position of the capitol.

ISLAMABAD: BUILDING "DYNAPOLIS" FOR THE STATUS QUO

Planned between 1959 and 1963 in accordance with a master plan prepared by Doxiadis Associates of Athens, Islamabad provided the first occasion for capital planners to reconsider the city designs put forth for Chandigarh and Brasília. Though designed capitals share certain features, each is produced by a unique set of physical, social, economic, cultural, and political forces, centered on the wishes of powerful designers and politicians. Constantinos Doxiadis was not exactly lacking in confidence about his abilities to meet this challenge: "My subject is the problem of the creation of a new capital city and its solution."[1]

Karachi served as Pakistan's first capital following the independence and partition of British India in 1947, but many forces soon led the leadership to advocate a move inland from this colonially developed port city. A large number of those forces wore military uniforms. Pakistan's capital transfer was an outcome less of independence than of the military takeover by

General Ayub Khan in 1958. Thus, the conception and most of the planning of Islamabad took place during a period of martial law and of ongoing disagreements about the meaning of Pakistan's position as an Islamic republic. Some of the reasons for leaving the first capital sound familiar. "President Ayub had found that civil servants in Karachi were too exposed to political agitators, corrupting influences, and control by the strong business community. By taking it north to a physically and morally healthier climate, he meant to give his administration a new clean outlook." In Pakistan, however, the situation was made more complicated by the advocacy of ties between the notion of purity and the promotion of Islam. As Imran Ahmed puts it, "Islamabad attempts to naturalize the new nation-state of Pakistan; though the rhetoric attached to the choice of site, through the reference to a supposed Islamic geometry in its grid layout; through the Islamic references of its architectural styles, and through the network of Sector mosques." The struggle to envision, emplace, and implement Islamabad is no less than the Pakistani national struggle itself. Ahmed observes that "In Islamabad, the ideological agenda and its vitalizing narrative in architecture and urbanism has two roots: the urge to Westernization, where nationhood with its ostensibly colonial origins is taken as a sign of modernity and progress; and a will to fundamentalism, where the religious community of Islam is the originary and omniscient source of the Pakistani identity."[2] The promise of a modern and pure white city to the north had spiritual as well as political overtones. Yet not all motives for movement were so pure.

The move of the capital into West Pakistan's interior was, in sharp contrast to the situation in Brazil, a move toward the country's most developed region rather than away from it. One of the elements that was most developed in the interior was the army, whose headquarters were in Rawalpindi. The move to this high plain was a move to a more bracing climate, in more than one sense. In addition to the advantage gained by the consolidation of civil and military powers in a single place, the siting was more conveniently central for travel to and from East Pakistan, the other piece of an implausibly configured country which had one thousand miles of India between its two "wings." More to the point in terms of transportation links, both real and imagined, its place on the historic trade route linking the great capitals of west Asia to the Arab world had much to commend it to the new Islamic leadership. Adding to the geopolitical and geostrategic appeal of Islamabad's site was its proximity to the sensitive and disputed border areas of Kashmir, combined with its safe distance from the border with the Indian Punjab.[3] Considering all perspectives, Islamabad's site seemed well suited as a kind of national citadel.

General Ayub Khan's public justifications for Islamabad centered not on these sorts of reasons, however seductive they must have been to a military mind, but on the city's symbolic role in the consolidation of a post-independence national identity. "Islamabad has been my dream always," he asserted:

> The capital of a country is the focus and the centre of the people's ambitions and desires, and it is wrong to put them in an existing city. It

> must have a colour of its own and character of its own. And that character is the sum total of the aspirations, the life and the ambitions of the people of the whole of Pakistan. With the two provinces of Pakistan, separated as they are from each other, you want to bring the people on a common platform. The thing to do was to take them to a new place altogether.[4]

How the geographic, ethnic, and linguistic barriers that divided West Pakistanis from the Bengalis in the East could be improved by a "common platform" that had been located to reaffirm the political and economic dominance of Pakistan's West wing was far from clear. Erected on the high plains of West Pakistan, Ayub Khan's own platform rested on a much narrower base than his optimistic words would suggest.

The siting of Islamabad on a fan-shaped area wedged between a wall of steep hills and the existing city of Rawalpindi was intended to allow the two cities to grow in tandem. This was an implied critique of nearly all of the designed capitals that had come before. Unlike Washington, Canberra, New Delhi, Chandigarh, and Brasília, each of which was designed as a bounded area and presented as a static entity which would eventually be filled out, Islamabad was promoted by Doxiadis as a "dynapolis," beginning with one

5.1 Doxiadis's "dynapolis" plan for Islamabad.

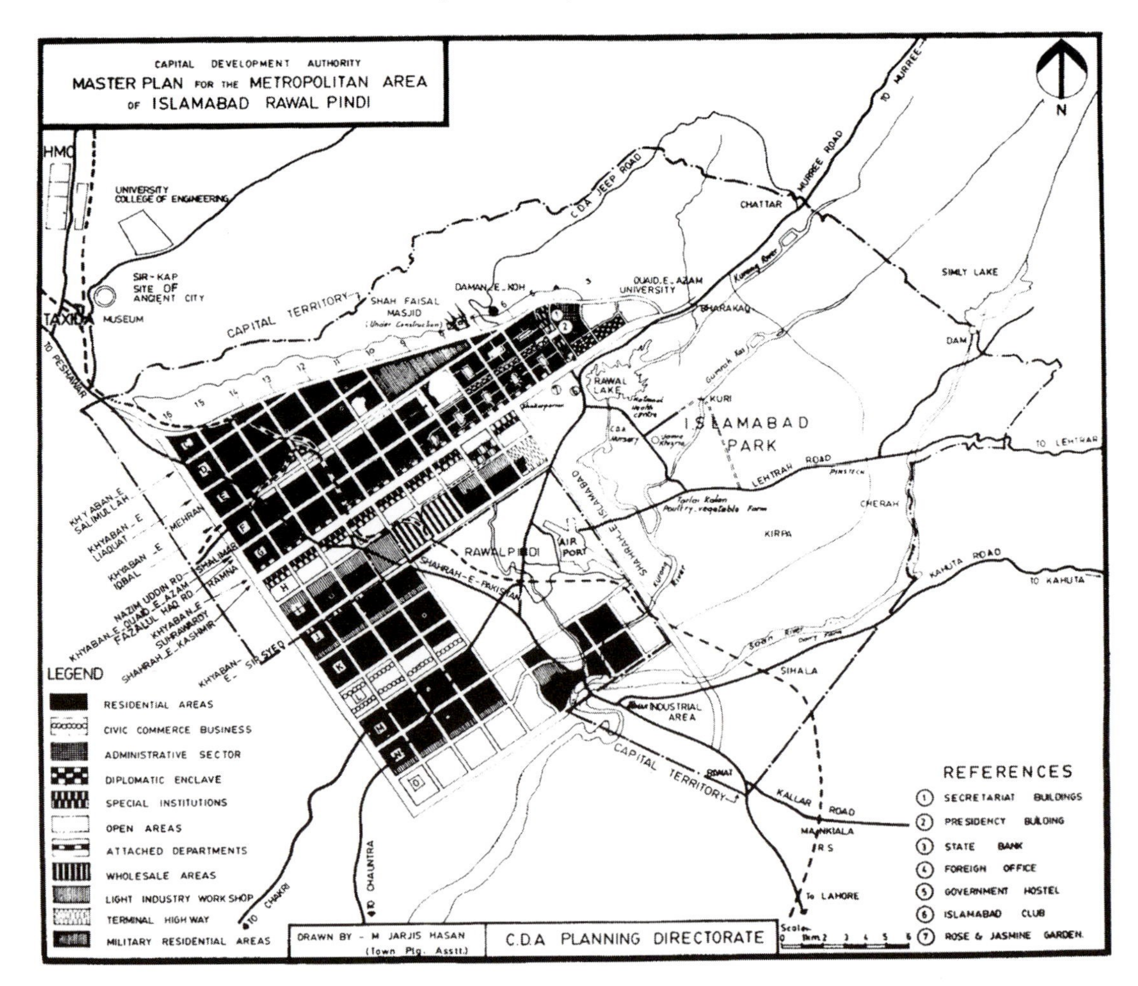

node in the top corner of the fan and, over time, spreading unidirectionally to the southwest (5.1).[5] In all this planning for dynamism, however, one thing remained static: the capitol complex. Doxiadis's dynapolis was premised on the exalted placement of government buildings and institutions of national culture. Though arguably less distinctly separated than either Chandigarh's head or Brasília's Plaza of the Three Powers, Islamabad's capitol complex was nonetheless located as the culmination of a long axial way, which Doxiadis referred to as Capitol Avenue (now known as Jinnah Avenue) (5.2, 5.3).[6] In this sense, the chief buildings of government occupy a position more akin to the spatial politics of New Delhi, especially since, until a parliament building was completed in 1986, the capitol complex was identifiable chiefly by the presence of the modernist wedding cake of its Presidential Palace and a series of secretariat buildings. Information provided by the Pakistani government in 1986 confirms this perception and its intended significance: "The central axis of the city which traverses its entire length and terminates in front of the Presidency (Aiwan-i-Saddar) is flanked on either side by important civic and commercial buildings . . . [and] is expected to assume the role of a ceremonial route."[7] In this way, the institutional power of the Pakistani presidency was given appropriate (if anachronistic) urban preeminence in Islamabad. Although the president and the parliament have been neighbors in Islamabad's exalted and isolated zone of government buildings for more than twenty years, the meaning of this juxtaposition depends on the perpetually stormy status of Pakistani politics.[8]

Oddly enough, Doxiadis had criticized planners of past designed capitals for starting with "the governmental buildings, the monumental areas and the high income dwellings." "This process," he insisted, "cannot lead to success for it is imperative that the lower income groups—those which can *build* a city are settled first. If this is overlooked, the result is a composite settlement consisting of a central monumental part and several other non co-ordinated areas, including several with slums." Instead, he claimed, "we must start by covering needs, and not by building monuments."[9] In carrying out his own prescriptions, however, Doxiadis initiated a certain rethinking of the *sequencing* of building priorities, but his design did nothing to challenge previous attitudes toward the privileged position and the isolation of the capitol complex. The process was adjusted, but this part of the product remained cast in the same old mold.

Because other urban functions (such as the housing for construction workers—the bane of Brasília's planners) were directed toward Rawalpindi, Islamabad itself became, at least initially, a city dominated by the institutions of government administration. As of 1968, the new capital could be described as "a little administrative island, neatly separated from the crowds of the big cities" and affording "the feeling of complete isolation from life in the rest of the country."[10] Although the city was planned to include at least a narrow range of income groups in each of its residential sectors (using a system of eight house types correlated with civil service rank), Doxiadis also made provision for exclusively elite residential areas in the privileged positions closest to the capitol complex.[11] Planner Richard Meier, reflecting on the first twenty-five years of Islamabad's growth, saw much of the genesis of

5.2 Presidential Palace, Islamabad.

5.3 Capitol Avenue, as envisaged in the model of Islamabad.

Islamabad's structure resulting from the confluence of civil/military systems of rank with the need to exalt the position of government. The rectilinearity of the plan, in this view, was conditioned by "the need of a capital city for a formal processional way leading to the seat of power" and "the long view lines imposed a hierarchy based upon squares." "After that," Meier continues,

> the rank of a person could determine the section of the city in which he should live. In the military hierarchy ordinary soldiers were assigned places in the barracks on the periphery, but each level above merited increasing levels of privileges. Non-commissioned officers deserved a bit more space, according to rank, and junior officers needed an extra room for a servant, but those at the top of the pyramid were allotted quarters for four servants. Civil ranking could exactly parallel the military, except that the unskilled workers were granted 1½ room flatroofed raw brick hutments instead of the barracks![12]

Islamabad's socioeconomic segregation was not carried out in quite such rigid terms, but its inhabitation was initiated on the expectation that all comers to the city would be assigned a residence according to their salary and that, with the exception of high government officials and diplomats already provided with special housing, all others would be expected upon promotion to "change houses and settle into a higher class of community."[13] "Public order in a capital city," Meier comments, "was easier to understand if like lived next to like."[14] What was true for residential districts was even more blatantly apparent in the privileged treatment given to the capitol complex. In Islamabad, as in designed capitals built before it and since, a new regime's need to promote public order was reinforced in no uncertain terms through the means of urban design.

AFTER 1960: THE GLOBAL SPREAD OF DESIGNED CAPITALS

Few governments have devoted the money and resources that went into the seminal projects in India, Brazil, and Pakistan; fewer still have employed well-known architects and planners. Yet, from Belmopan in Belize (designed after Hurricane Hattie decimated the coastal capital in 1961) to the abortive Argentinian proposal to build its own version of Brasília in Patagonia,[15] ambitious plans for new capitals continue to be put forth all over the world. Mauritania and Botswana had to build new capitals because, after independence, the cities from which they had previously been administered ceased to be within their boundaries. Chile decentralized its legislative functions away from its capital in Santiago by constructing a lavish congress building in Valparaiso (the hometown of General Augusto Pinochet, who championed the move during what turned out to be the waning years of his rule).[16]

Many Asian, African, and South American leaders of all political persuasions have invested much time and great energy in the task of symbolizing the power of their regimes to their citizens and to the rest of the world. In most places where new capitals have been envisaged, they have been planned, designed, and constructed by Western consultants, and then evaluated by them as well. Financing these ventures has been quite another story—most remain long-dormant proposals or have emerged slowly.

Malawi announced the transfer of its capital from Zomba to Lilongwe (close to the heartland of President Hastings Kamuzu Banda's ethnic group) in 1965, though the capital—replete with its "capital hill"—was still without a purpose-built parliament building forty years later. Instead, in 1975, Banda began construction of an ornate 300-room $100-million presidential palace dominating the city, but then rarely used it. Apparently, Malawian leaders shunned the palace as haunted, though the *New York Times* described it as "notorious not as the locale of evil spirits, but as a monument to the wretched excess of mortals." According a Canadian newspaper, "locals claimed if all its lights and appliances were turned on at once, they would blow the grid, plunging Lilongwe into darkness." Eventually, after the end of Banda's thirty-year rule, the country's parliament took up residence in the palace. In 2004, however, newly elected President Bingu wa Mutharika claimed this "New State House" for himself, and suggested that the parliament should move to a bombed-out sports stadium that needed major repairs. Finally, in July 2005, wa Mutharika laid the foundation stone for a new parliament building, calling for every MP to bring ten medium-sized stones from his or her constituency. "That way," he concluded, "all Members of Parliament can feel proud that in the Parliament Building in Lilongwe, there are stones from their home area."[17]

Other new capitals, in pursuit of varying agendas, continue to be built or proposed elsewhere. In 1983, Côte d'Ivoire shifted its official capital from the port city of Abidjan to Yamoussoukro, the home village of its president and founding father, Felix Houphouët-Boigny. The Ivorian leader willfully outfitted it with "six-lane boulevards, luxury hotels, a presidential palace with a crocodile-filled moat—and the world's largest church, even bigger than St. Peter's in Rome, with 7,000 seats equipped with individual air-conditioning ducts." After Houphouët-Boigny's death in 1993, however, his immediate successors showed little interest in Yamoussoukro and it became "a ghost town, a capital in name only." Even so, in 2000, the national assembly met for the first time in Yamoussoukro; to the surprise of many, the village capital may yet have some political future.[18]

At the time of this writing, the world's newest new national capital is the northern Pacific settlement of Melekeok, which replaced Koror as the seat of government for Palau in October 2006. Remote Palau, independent since 1994, can boast a population of little more than 20,000 but now has a $45 million capitol complex replete with a neo-Washingtonian domed parliament building, as well as separate structures for executive and judicial branches. Honolulu architect Joe Farrell, who previously designed the capitol for the Federated States of Micronesia, stressed the need to promote national identity: "They wanted something that would give their nation instant recognition as a new nation in the world, and that's what they got." Although some questioned the appropriateness of a "huge white dome sticking up" out of the forest, the manager of the Palau Capital Improvements Projects Office defends its imported imagery: "We're proud of the democracy that the United States helped establish here and wanted a building that shows that, just as the U.S. Capitol harkens back to the Western world's Greek traditions."[19]

At the opposite extreme, in 2007 the military rulers of Myanmar (formerly Burma) unveiled Naypyidaw, a lavish new capital constructed in near secrecy. Naypyidaw translates as "Abode of Kings" and its sponsors offered none of the usual pretense about promoting democracy. Located about 300 miles north of Yangon (formerly Rangoon), the partially completed city features a fortress-like complex for General Than Shwe, along with apartment buildings for the government workers required to move there.[20]

Other new capitals continue to be necessitated by either natural disaster or by political change. Montserrat, a British overseas territory in the eastern Caribbean, suffered severe destruction during Hurricane Hugo in 1989 followed by even more total devastation after a major volcanic eruption in 1997. The island's capital, Plymouth, buried under as much as twenty feet of ash and rock, had to be abandoned. Approximately two-thirds of the population evacuated the island, some never to return. The entire southern side of the island still remains uninhabitable due to ongoing volcanic activity. This has forced the government to relocate the capital facilities to buildings at Brades Estate, located near Carr's Bay/Little Bay in the far northwest of the island.[21]

Political realignments also continue either to foster the development of new capital cities or at least to lead to proposals for new parliamentary districts. To date, the most dramatic recent capital city development has been in Kazakhstan, occasioned by the break-up of the Soviet Union. In 1997, the newly independent republic shifted its capital from Almaty to Astana (meaning 'capital'), and embarked upon an extensive project of de-Sovietization through design. As a *New York Times* correspondent put it, "the ambition [is] to create not only a national capital but also a national identity shaped almost exclusively by a single man: the country's president since its inception, Nursultan A. Nazarbayev."[22] Nazarbayev explicitly compared his decision to move the capital to Atatürk's Ankara and Peter the Great's St. Petersburg adventure. Not only a move to claim the heart of the national territory (though it is well north of the true center), the move also marked a move away from the more vulnerable border with China and a parallel effort to manage relations with Russia. By moving the capital closer to Russia at a time when many thought that the Russian-majority population of northern Kazakhstan might seek separation, Astana could serve as a bulwark against such aspirations.

As with all capital moves, the motives for this one have been multiple and mixed: the sheer personal vanity of a leader gets artfully combined with rational and technical arguments about economic decentralization and territorial development, complaints about the inadequacies of the former capital, geopolitical machinations, international image building, and a variety of efforts to symbolize and consolidate state power while emphasizing the centrality of a single dominant ethnic group. In contrast to all other post-Soviet new states whose titular ethnic group constituted a numerical majority as of 1991, in Kazakhstan Russians initially outnumbered Kazakhs. In this context, Nazarbayev faced a unique double challenge: to construct a distinctly different post-Soviet state and to engage in the sort of nation building needed to consolidate Kazakhstani identity. As Edward Schatz makes clear, Kazakhstani identity also has its internal complexities since sub-ethnic units of the formerly nomadic "hordes" still dominate particular territories. Astana signaled a "tacit alliance" between the Greater Horde (Nazarbayev's own people) and the Middle Horde (inhabitants of the Astana area). In turn, insertion of the national capital into their territory encouraged Middle Horde Kazakhs to identify more centrally with Kazakhstan and to resist movements by ethnic Russians and Cossacks. Moreover, the shift of power toward these two groups of Kazakhs limited the influence of the Lesser Horde Kazakh elite, whose territory contained important oil, natural gas, and mineral resources. Astana also served nation-building aims by embodying Nazarbayev's strategic use of "Eurasianism" (*evraziistvo*) as a means to appeal to the nation-state's diverse component peoples. As Schatz puts it, the city is intended to provide "symbols that would broadly resonate across the Kazakhstan multi-cultural landscape." By invoking the seemingly more inclusive notion of Eurasianism, Kazakhstani leaders could achieve a dual purpose: present "an appealing discourse to the non-Kazakh population" and retain a "diffuse set of privileges" for Kazakhs. In these ways, Astana—like so many other new capitals that may otherwise seem rather inexplicable creations—firmly supports the agenda of the ruling elite.[23]

Astana, whose initial plan was drafted by prominent Japanese architect Kisho Kurokawa, continues to become even more ambitious. Chief architect Shokhan Mataibekov cites plans to transform the barren steppes with 185,000 acres' worth of trees and a variety of signature towers, with all projects to be approved by the president. Financed by a booming oil industry, there are already facilities for the parliament, supreme court, an elaborate presidential palace, a 62-meter-high "Pyramid of Peace" designed by Sir Norman Foster, and a steel observation tower called Baiterek ("high poplar") "which symbolizes a mythical tree of Kazakh legend where a bird named Samruk laid its [golden] eggs." Astana's version of Washington's National Mall culminates not in the parliament building but in the presidential palace, with the two houses of parliament located along one side (5.4).[24]

The entire developing city received an extreme symbolic makeover starting in the late 1990s. Nazarbayev replaced all Soviet-era street names and monuments, and renamed, repurposed, and remodeled various Soviet institutions using a variety of abstractly historicized postmodern facade treatments (in a manner reminiscent of the 1980s work of Michael Graves). As one commentator notes, "Irreverent locals have given many of the new buildings nicknames based on their shape, such as Grain Silo, Cigarette Lighter, and Seven Kegs. The observation tower is sometimes called Big Chupa Chups, after a well-known brand of lollipop." Suitably de-Leninized and de-Marxified, Kazakh leaders anticipate that Astana will reach a population of one million by 2030.[25]

Other new capitals have been prominently carried out—or at least seriously proposed—in Malaysia, South Korea, and Japan, as part of efforts

5.4 Astana's rapidly growing new administrative center.

to decentralize national administration.[26] To date, Malaysia has proceeded furthest along this path. Prime Minister Dr. Mahathir Mohamad, in power from 1981 until 2003, not only directed the rapid modernization of the country but gave it spatial form. He championed construction of the Multimedia Super Corridor (MSC), intended as a Malaysian version of California's Silicon Valley, as a north–south link between the national capital, Kuala Lumpur (KL), and a new international airport (designed by the ubiquitous Kisho Kurokawa). At the midpoint of the MSC, he proposed Putrajaya as a new seat of government and administration for the country. Putrajaya (with a target population of 300,000) is paired with Cyberjaya, intended to house 240,000 people and contain a vast array of IT and multimedia companies.[27]

The winning competition entry for Putrajaya, selected in 1994, envisioned a long axial city culminating in a hilltop parliament complex, but this is not the symbolic message of the city that has been built. Instead, the island-like axis leads not to the seat of the legislature but to a massive domed office block for the prime minister (PM), completed in 1999 (5.5). In part, this change of plan resulted from the realization that the terms of the federal government's agreement with the state of Selangor would allow the Federal Territory (including KL) to revert to Selangor if ever the parliament and the king moved out of KL. As Ross King explains, "The threat of KL being returned to Selangor certainly legitimized the decision to keep both King and Parliament out of Putrajaya and instead to place the PM at the pinnacle. But then the Sultan of Selangor became the King in Malaysia's system of rotating monarchy, and expressed a clear wish to have a presence in the new city." The new king's home received an off-axis hilltop site overlooking the prime minister's office, with a second palace added for the sultan of Selangor in his own right, thereby allowing the host state to visibly remind the prime

5.5 Axial plan focused on the Prime Minister, Putrajaya.

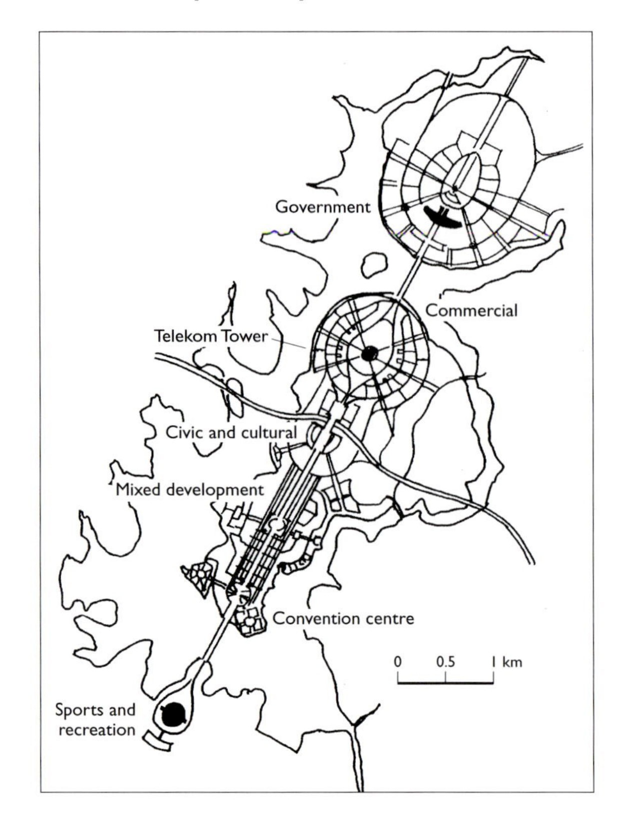

minister of its significant status at all times. With parliament left behind in KL, Mahathir's priorities stood fully realized. As King puts it, "The distancing of the executive and the bureaucracy from the legislature, and then the celebration of the former, is a profoundly political act."[28]

Of the most recent generation of designed capitals, two seem particularly relevant to the present discussion, each adding a different dimension. The most extensive and monumental of the new postcolonial designed capitals has been carried out over the last three decades in Abuja, Nigeria. Also ambitious, but in very different ways, is Tanzania's Dodoma, an intriguing attempt to design a nonmonumental capital city according to socialist principles, a proposition that would seem to be at odds with city-making ideas nearly everywhere else. Like Dodoma, some of the world's newest capital cities remain largely unrealized, yet it is possible to examine the urban design envisioned in their master plans to see how thinking about the place of a capitol complex in a postcolonial capital has developed, or, more precisely, to see how much has remained the same.

ABUJA: NIGERIA'S WASHINGTON, D.C.?

When the Nigerian government proposed, in 1975, to shift its capital from Lagos to Abuja, this relatively unheralded decision portended the largest building venture of the twentieth century—a city of 1.6 million people to be constructed in only twenty years, with a ultimate projected size of 3.1

million. The Nigerian government formally inaugurated Abuja in 1991, and the city and its region have continued to experience rapid expansion. By the first years of the twenty-first century, in fact, the population of the Federal Capital Territory already surpassed 5 million, though much of this growth has occurred well outside the boundaries of the planned city (5.6).[29]

The international team of consultants who prepared the master plan for Abuja (published in 1979), headlined by the prominent Philadelphia-based firm of Wallace, McHarg, Roberts, and Todd, were clearly conscious of the first generation of postcolonial capital city planning. They looked at the planning and development of such capitals as Brasília and Chandigarh and also at other new towns, especially those in England. Continuity with past efforts at city planning also operated even more directly, since the larger team of planners for Abuja included both Doxiadis Associates (entrusted with developing a regional-scale master plan for the entire Federal Capital Territory) and Milton Keynes Development Corporation (charged with developing an "Accelerated District" for initial upper- and middle-class residential settlement along Euro-American suburban lines).[30] For the city as a whole, the master planners pondered the examples of earlier Western capital cities such as Washington, D.C., Paris, and London as possible sources of form (5.7). Unlike the two European precursors, however, the

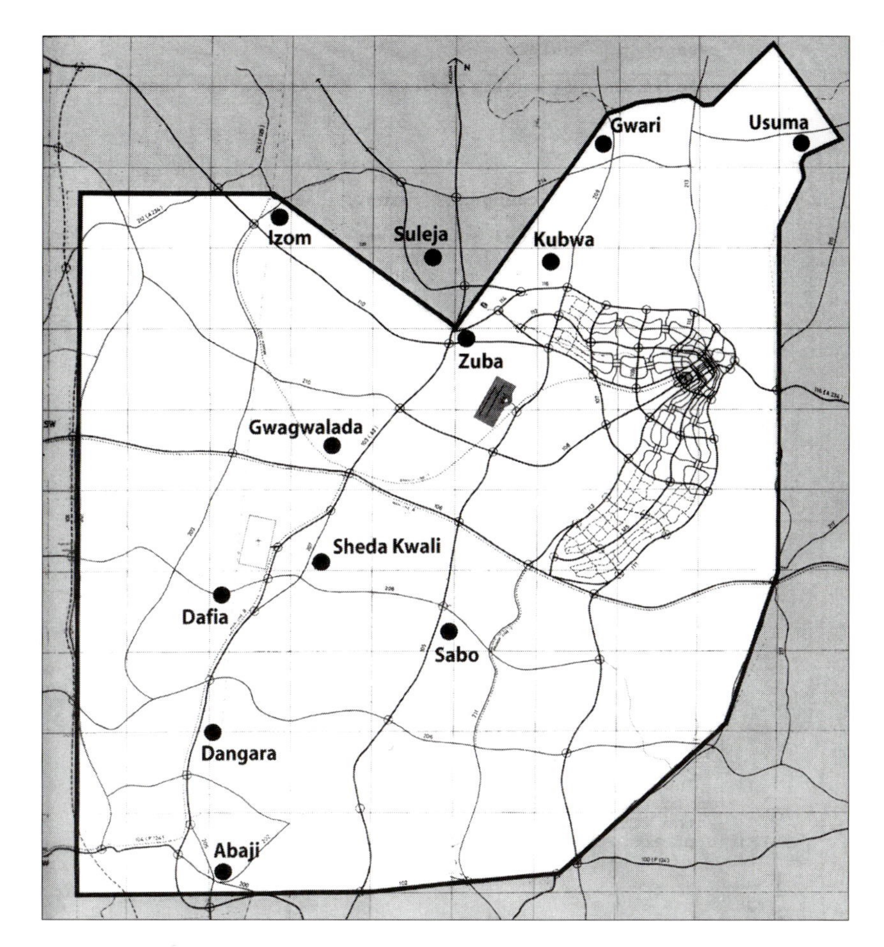

5.6 Nigeria's Federal Capital Territory (FCT): Abuja and its satellites. The two-winged planned city of Abuja itself takes up but a small portion of the overall FCT (outlined in black).

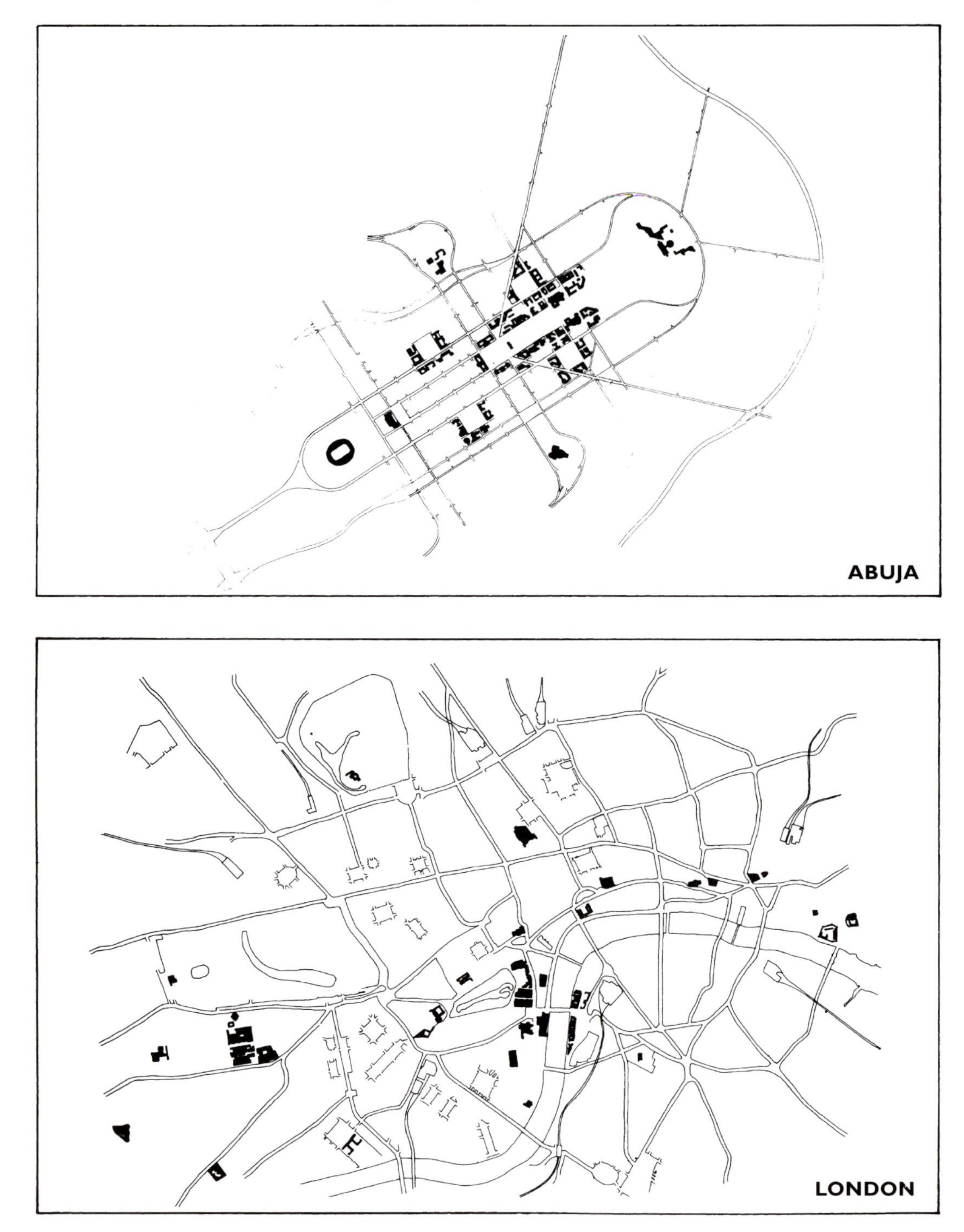

5.7 Centers compared: scale and distribution of major government and civic institutions and monuments in two evolved capitals and two designed ones.

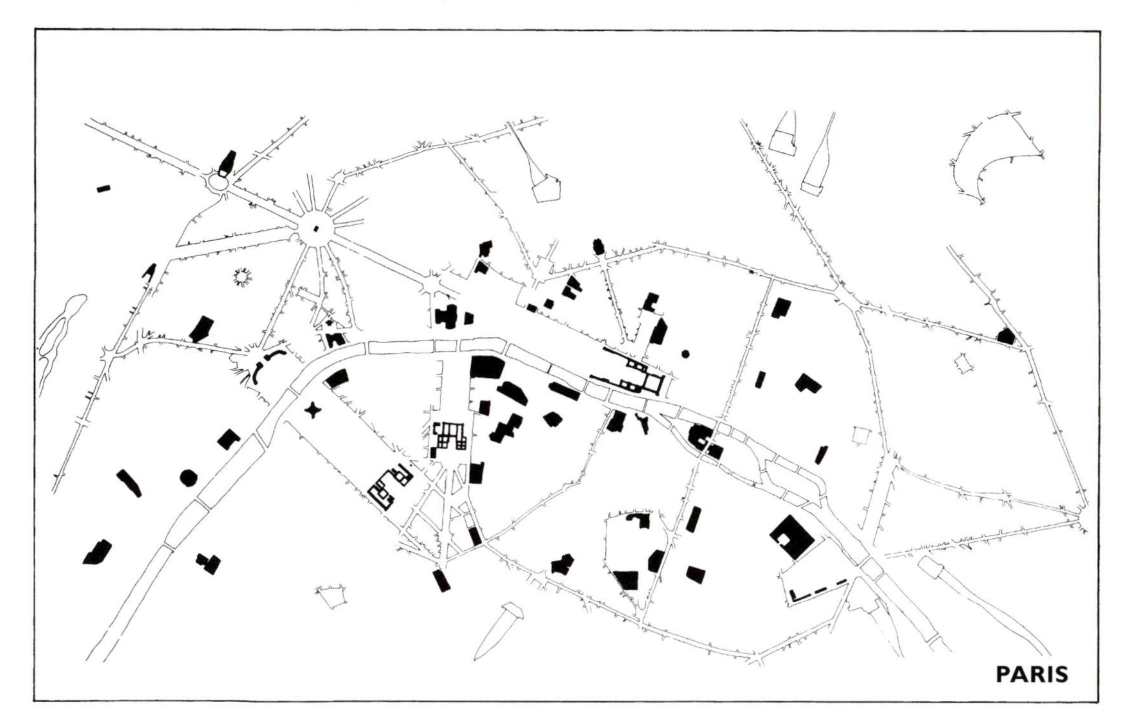
PARIS

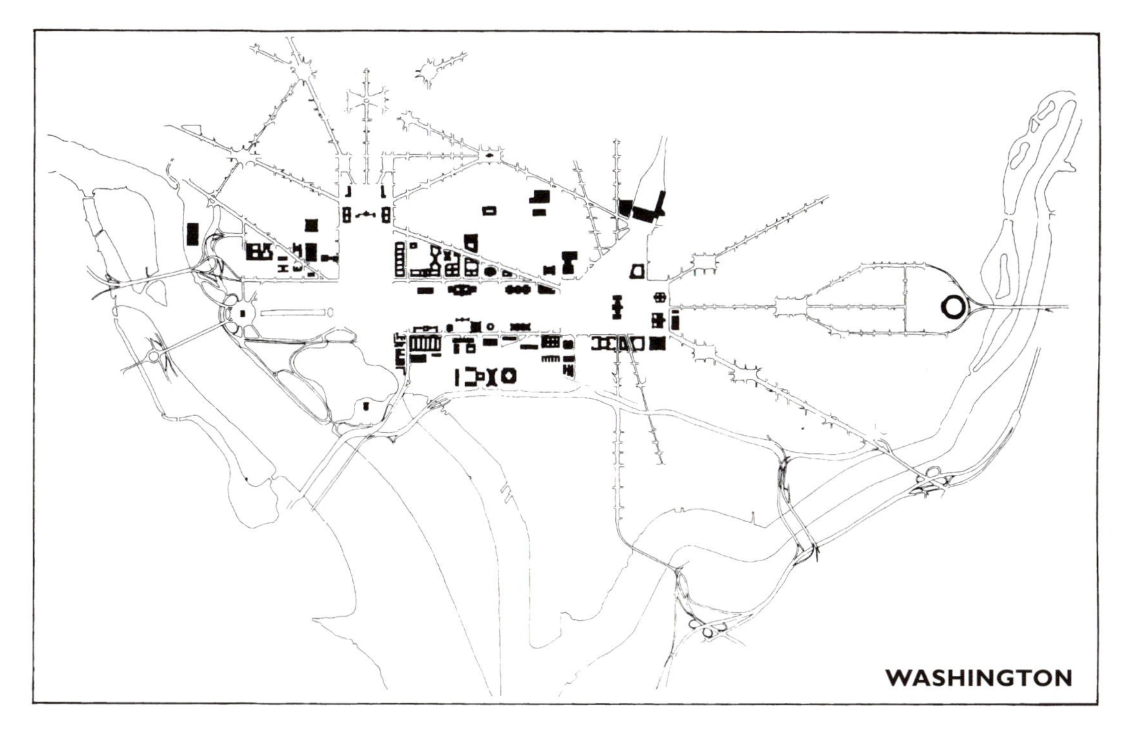
WASHINGTON

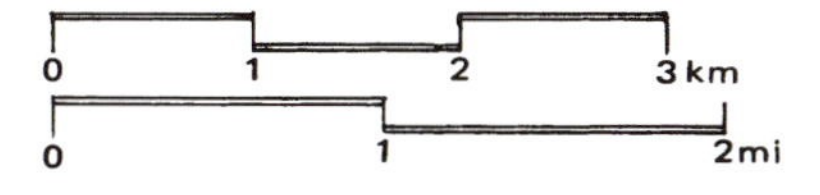
0 1 2 3 km
0 1 2 mi

new African capitals such as Abuja were intended to be both products and expressions of the advent of postcolonial independence.

Promoters of Abuja as a designed capital placed great emphasis on the production of national identity, at least in the rhetoric that accompanied the plans. While Abuja shares with Chandigarh and Brasília a commitment to rapid modernization, in Abuja this task has been compounded by the persistence of deep ethnic schisms within the country. Whereas Chandigarh's designers encountered the problem of the divided and subdivided Punjab, Abuja's planners had to contend with the multiple divisions of an entire country. With perhaps 250 different ethnic groups sharing territory, and the searing memories of the Civil War over secessionist Biafra that cost more than a million lives between 1967–1970, the idea of building an entirely new city to realize an intended "federal character" carried an understandable appeal. If the touchstone for the earlier capitals was progress, the challenge for Abuja was not only progress but unity, closely tied to that slippery concept, national identity. At the same time, as Abuja's leading scholar Nnamdi Elleh argues, the new capital also marked a continuation of efforts by the Nigerian elite to consolidate power and profits.[31]

The Abuja plan not only signaled a decision to move the national capital to a new city but also implied a rejection of the existing capital of Lagos. In 1976, a panel appointed to recommend a new site for the Nigerian capital described Lagos as "one of the dirtiest capitals in the world"; an assessment from 1982 concluded that "the perennial traffic jams, the intolerable congestion, the chaotic sanitary situation, inadequate social amenities, and the lack of available land for expansion were rendering the city ineffective as the seat of government of the Federation." The government-appointed panel concluded that Lagos's problems were so severe as to make the expense of building an entirely new capital a "cost advantage." As Elleh makes clear, moreover, this "cost advantage" had clear beneficiaries—those who would get to build the new city.[32]

Whatever the deficiencies of Lagos (and these had been documented repeatedly since the days of British colonial rule), the Nigerian government's decision to move the capital is yet another example of a postcolonial desire to leave a colonial port city in favor of a centrally located plateau. Abuja is located close to the geographical heart of Nigeria, a matter of some significance. At one level, the move can be explained in terms of climate, for surely the upland plateau offered a welcome respite from the tropical heat of the coast. Yet the move to claim the center goes more deeply than this: it implies a recognition of national boundaries (5.8).

The radials drawn on the map depicted in the master plan are vectors of political control, gestures of inclusiveness, and spatial promises of unity. The decision to move the Nigerian capital into the interior is nearly as dramatic as the imposition of Brasília onto an isolated frontier plateau. In both cases the capital's willful centrality had much to do with the desire to develop the interior of the country and create the nexus for a modern transportation network. The centrality of the new capital is an affirmation by the government that Nigeria, however artificial its existence in terms of

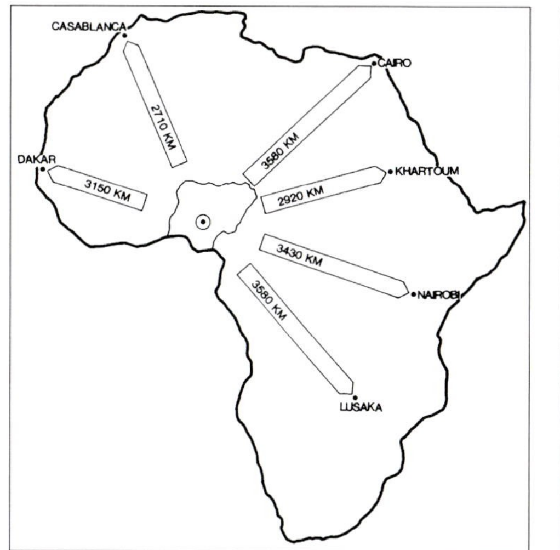

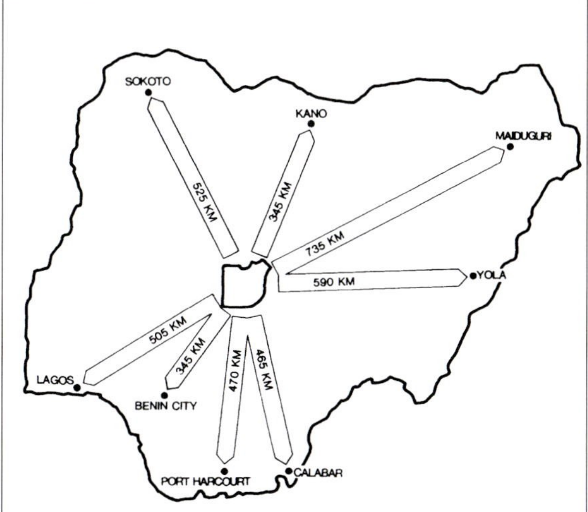

5.8 Idealized centrality of Abuja, Nigeria's Federal Capital Territory.

internal or transnational group loyalties, should act as a unified, independent state. Topological centralism signals more than a retreat from the overgrown coastal metropolis; it is a spatial declaration of political equality among disparate and distant parts. It is an affirmation that the national government exists to serve (or to rule) all of its component states. Sited for metaphorical as well as actual elevation—as in Brasília—the central highland capital becomes a kind of political watershed. It is the point from which central political power flows in all directions, and conversely it becomes a point of pilgrimage.

Yet topological centralism, like many other political maneuvers, can be deceptive. The shift of the colonial capital of British India from Calcutta to New Delhi confirms that such movement can often be in the service of existing hegemonies. Even when the capital shift occurs after decolonization, spatial choices are determined by political as well as geographical calculations. It is one thing to move out of an overcrowded and tainted colonial city; it is quite another to choose to move to the center of the country.

The centrality of Abuja may well be viewed less as a watershed than as the eye of a hurricane. Nigeria's heterogeneous and fractious population has lived through eight military rulers and a thirty-month civil war during its first thirty-five years of independence. Abuja itself was designed as a mediator—or at least was intended to *appear* as such. The diagrammatic radials that extend from Abuja toward the other cities of Nigeria, symbolizing a transportation network that did not yet exist, connect not just points or cities but perennially antagonistic groups of people. The schisms operate in various ways: there are tribal divisions among the Yoruba in the southwest, the Ibo in the southeast, and the Hausa/Fulani in the north; there are religious differences between the predominantly Muslim north and the largely Christian and animist south (and tensions among Muslims as well). There are socioeconomic differences between the south, influenced by Western-style development, and the less-developed north; and there are further tensions between the three largest tribal groups, known collectively as the Wazobians, and the 29 percent of Nigerians from minority groups.[33] The move to Abuja must therefore be understood in the context of these polarities: Abuja is closer to the northern Islamic power base of the military regimes of the 1970s, 1980s and 1990s; and, conversely, acceptance of Abuja as the national capital has had to overcome the Yoruba southerner's resistance to relinquishing Lagos.[34]Thus, the polarities that are hinted at by the southwest skew of Lagos's placement do not disappear with the centripetal adjustment signaled by Abuja.

At least in theory, Abuja's central location mediates between north and south and sites the capital in an area that is, to use the language of the site selection committee, "ethnically neutral."[35] The existence of Abuja cannot be understood apart from the long history of European colonial presence and efforts to govern the diversity of the region. Just as the port city capital of Lagos (whose very name is derived from the Portuguese word for lakes) is an explicit legacy of colonialism, so too the very concept of "Nigeria" is an early twentieth-century invention of the British, implemented by Governor-General Frederick Lugard in 1914. As early as 1898, the British colonial rulers had struggled over the governability of the territory, and chose to divide it into two zones, one north and one south, while treating the "Middle Belt" of the country—the future site of the Federal Capital Territory—as a buffer zone. Tensions persisted even after amalgamation into a single Nigeria in 1914, and the British debated the possibility of a more northerly alternative capital.[36] Six decades later, the report of the Committee for the Relocation of the Federal Capital noted that while "Lagos is identified with predominantly one ethnic group," Abuja's "more central location would provide equal access to Nigeria's great diversity of cultural groups."[37] In service to this end, the committee chose Abuja because its area was sparsely populated by a variety of Nigerian ethnic groups and it was not a place associated with control by any of the three major groups. As Elleh points out, this attitude led Nigerian officials to treat the capital site as "virgin land" enabling them to ignore its 2,000-year history of inhabitation, its sacred ancestor-worship sites such as Aso Rock, and its complex litany of conquests by fifteenth-century Islamic forces and nineteenth-century British colonialists. The "virgin land" viewpoint also downplayed the original town of Abuja itself, founded in 1828 by its namesake, Emir Abu Ja. Now seen as an obstacle to the new Federal capital, the capital authorities demolished the old town and rebuilt it elsewhere under a different name. Duly stripped of all inconvenient associations, the new Abuja could be built "as a symbol of Nigeria's aspirations of unity and greatness."[38] Consequently, Abuja's designers were charged with the exceedingly difficult double task of planning to meet the needs of divergent cultural groups while also creating the image of Nigerian unity.

For a short while in the 1970s, as national revenues skyrocketed due to the oil boom, Nigeria's fortunes looked especially promising. In 1979, the Abuja Plan was published in auspicious conjunction with the return to civilian government after more than a decade of military rule. At the same time, a new Draft Constitution, based on that of the United States (as an alternative to the British parliamentary model initially adopted by the Nigerians), was promulgated as a signal of renewed democratic commitment.[39] Proposed under the military rule of General Murtala Muhammed (a Hausa Muslim northerner) and formalized under the rule of General Olusegun Obasanjo (a Yoruba Christian from the southwest), the move to Abuja was immediately championed by the new civilian president Alhaji Shehu Shagari (a Fulani Muslim northerner) to whom Obasanjo voluntarily relinquished power. Like Brasília's Kubitschek before him, Shagari wished to make the transfer of the capital politically and financially irreversible during his own term of office. Yet the heady days of the late 1970s, epitomized by the grandiosity of the Abuja venture, were not to last. Within four years, Shagari was ousted by a military coup, a widely supported effort to restore order and regenerate a devastated economy.[40]

The price of oil had tumbled and, with it, much of the revenue (if little of the hubris) that had inspired Abuja. At the time of the 1983 coup, Abuja was described—with some justification—as "synonymous with patronage and waste."[41] Major-General Muhammadu Buhari's military government regarded the Abuja project as a patronage machine for the deposed Shagari regime and remained content to rule from the Dodan Barracks in Lagos, but Major General Ibrahim Babangida overthrew Buhari in 1985 and affirmed support for Abuja. Even though the city still remained largely unbuilt, he viewed it as a potential safe haven for his regime and continued to provide it with one of Nigeria's largest ministerial budgets.[42] Babangida promised a return to civilian rule by 1992, but annulled the eventual elections, paving the way for the exceptionally corrupt dictatorial rule of General Sani Abacha between 1993 and 1998. In 1999, not long after the death of Abacha, Obasanjo returned to power, this time as an elected civilian leader, and remained president until 2007. Despite Obasanjo's two terms of democratically elected rule, however, the geo-ethnic tensions that have plagued Nigeria both before and after independence have continued to dominate national politics. Even the election of Obasanjo's successor, Umaru Yar'Adua—marking Nigeria's first-ever peaceful transfer of power between civilian governments—was marred by significant corruption that received widespread international dismay.[43]

In the context of such fraught politics, Abuja's urban design and planning have played an important role in the ongoing pursuit of national identity and national unity. As the city has developed, it has revealed much about the potential of city planning to reorient the balance of power of a country by shifting the political center of gravity, but it has also exposed the limitations of planning and design to affect such change. Abuja began as an attempt by the various ruling regimes to consolidate power where it could be most useful for nationwide control, while also supporting and allocating lucrative new investment opportunities. In moving to this new place, the leadership simultaneously reinforced the power of the existing political and economic hierarchies. As Nnamdi Elleh puts it, "The Nigerian elite exploited architectural nationalism and national unity in order to spend the nation's petroleum wealth." The Nigerian military rulers of the 1970s, he argues, deliberately increased the problems of Lagos in order to marginalize the city and make inevitable the decision to move the capital. Then, by controlling the Federal Capital Development Authority the rulers were able to misappropriate land parcels in the nascent city for themselves and their associates, with scant regard for the intent of the overall plan.[44]

In terms of Abuja's effect on ethnic cleavages, the record seems mixed. According to an early analysis made in 1984, Abuja initially contributed more to divisiveness than to unity: "Abuja is widely perceived today as a Northern, not a Nigerian capital. Instead of healing the country, Abuja threatens to become a symbol of North–South discord, and this may well become perilous to the stability and growth of a united Nigeria." More recent assessments seem to bear this out. When U.S. President Bill Clinton visited the Nigerian capital in 2000, the *New York Times* reporter commented that "telltale signs of the dominance by Nigeria's Muslim northerners dot Abuja. The new National Assembly building looks like a mosque. A gold-domed mosque sits in the middle of the city, not far from an unfinished church" (5.9). Although the four minarets of the Saudi-financed mosque seem to be identical in height to the campanile of the officially nondenominational (and nonexternally funded) church, the two parallel institutions located on the capital's east–west "Cultural" corridor bespeak separation rather than mere symmetry. Perhaps intentionally, the mosque is located to the north of the church, paralleling the divide of the country. Fortunately, one informal study shows, the North–South division signaled by mosque versus church does not seem to have been accompanied by any larger urban segregation along religious lines within the city. Even so, it remains difficult to tell: for the 2006 national census (the first one held in fifteen years), questions about religious and ethnic affiliations remained too politically sensitive to include.[45]

The master plan for Abuja is a document of political idealism rather than of uncertainty, though in its seeming confidence may be read something of the problems that were soon to come. Abuja was planned and designed not in a time of national search for a political system, but in a time of confidence

5.9 Abuja's massive mosque and unfinished church, 2005.

that one—based on the U.S. Constitution—had already been found. To a large degree, the new Nigerian capital's plan was meant to provide a form and a forum for American-style democracy. The master plan for Abuja proposed a single-centered city in which all elements combine to focus attention upon the most important federal government buildings. In discussing "the plan for the seat of government," its authors note that "the new Constitution indicates that the major elements to be housed in the New Federal Capital include the National Assembly, Legislative Offices, Executive Offices, the Judiciary and residences of the President and Vice President. Other national government facilities would be the Ministries and various commissions and parastatals. Any combination of these elements can be used—through urban design—to create the physical image of the National Government."[46] The urban designers of the Central Area chose to combine these elements into a broad mall lined with high-rise ministries and axially focused upon the National Assembly building at its apex (5.10, 5.11). The mall, adapted in both

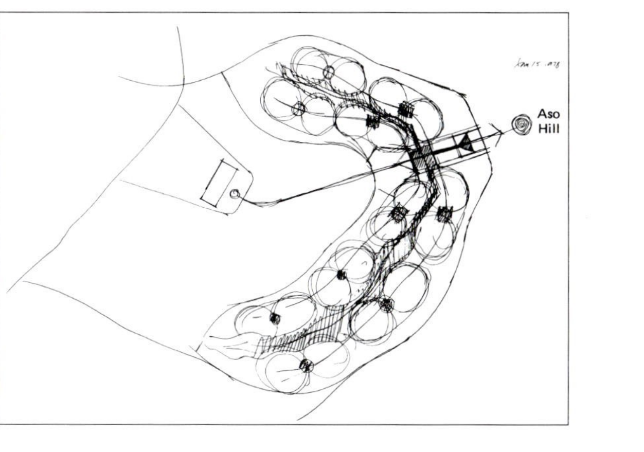

5.10 Abuja: another "bird" plan that may not fly.

5.11 Abuja Mall, looking toward parliament and Aso Hill.

5.12 ***(far right)*** **Monumental core, Abuja master plan.**

form and scale from that of Washington, D.C. (presumably to go along with the anticipated adoption of the American Constitution), reaches toward the dramatic rock outcrop of Aso Hill. Even the First Concept Plan from 1978 shows a Brasília-like separation of residential and monumental axes, the latter aligned with this hill. The placement of the government buildings on axis with the Aso massif seeks to gain strength by association, not unlike the Griffins' axial alignment of Canberra with the site's surrounding mountains. At the same time, by siting the new capital in relation to the older sacred shrines of Aso Rock (and nearby Zuma Rock), the designers also hoped to root Abuja in the indigenous landscape. Since the abrupt 1300-foot rise of Nigeria's hill is far too craggy and steep to locate buildings atop it (in the manner of capitol hills in Washington, Canberra, and New Delhi), the major government buildings are to be located on its lower slopes. Here they are grouped as the Three Arms Zone, a slightly more militaristic sounding update on Costa's Plaza of the Three Powers in Brasília.

The difference between a plaza and a zone goes much further, however. Unlike the plaza in Brasília, Abuja's Three Arms Zone is not intended as a place of public gathering from which the larger landscape may be viewed. Rather, as the drawing of the Monumental Core in the master plan makes clear, it is to be a separate zone for government, divided from the rest of the city by distance and by topography (5.12, 5.13). Though a sketch of this central area shows a continuous arrow leading down the center of the mall and through the Three Arms Zone to the Arboretum and Aso Hill beyond, this is not an axis that the public can traverse. In this respect, Abuja's plan is more reminiscent of Lutyens than of Mayer or Costa. Abuja's capitol complex is the terminus of an axis, like Lutyens's Viceroy's Palace, with extensive gardens behind.

In Abuja, according to architect Omar Take, a principal in the firm of Kenzo Tange & URTEC, which was entrusted with refining the design of the Central Area, this prominent architectural trinity is a spatial translation of the American concept of federal government institutions: "Concerning the location of the three-powers complex, the constitution of Nigeria is a replica

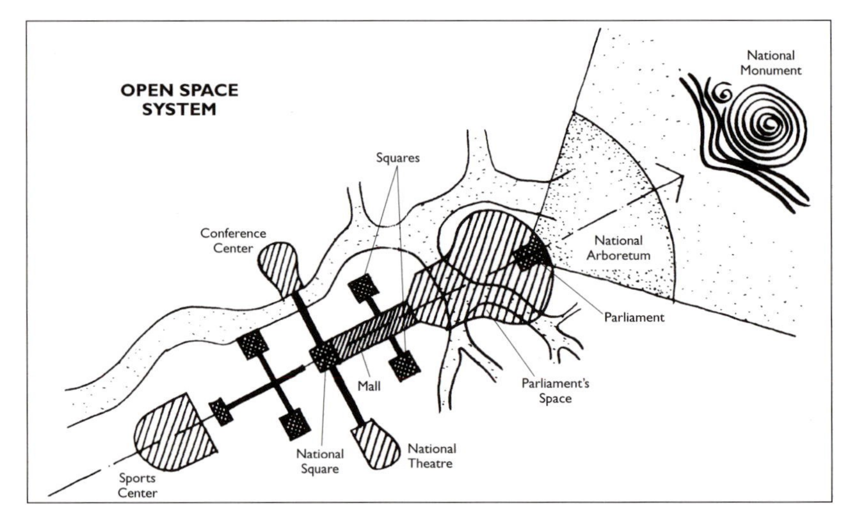

5.13 The arrow and the error, Abuja master plan.

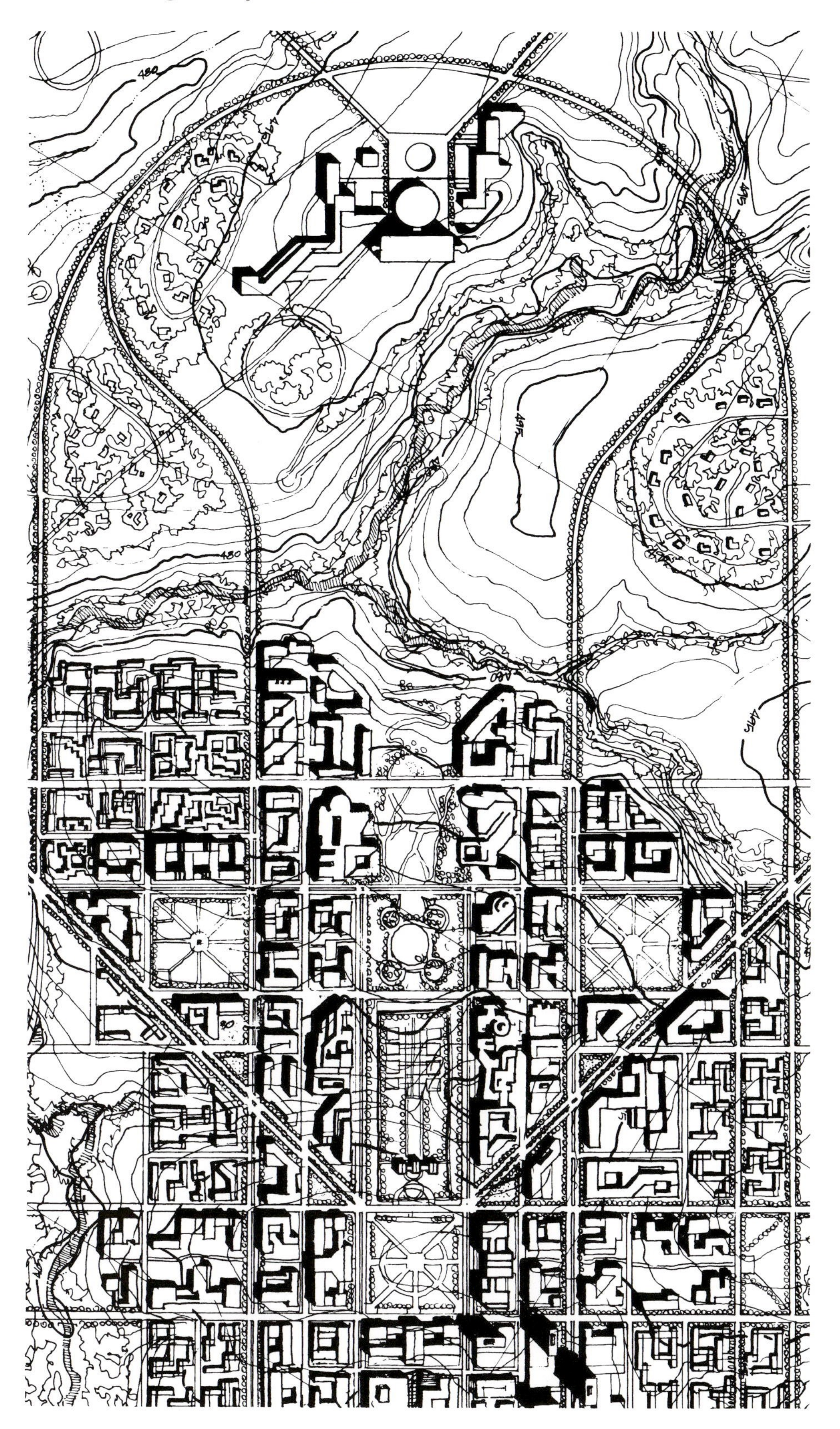
480
480

5.14 Model of the proposed central area of Abuja. Unlike the master plan, in which the parliament building alone was given privileged placement at the detached end of the central axis, subsequent development of the urban design plans envisioned a Three Arms Zone which isolated all three of the major branches of government from the rest of the city.

of the constitution of the United States, adopted by President Chagari [*sic*] when he established the democracy. This means that the three arms of government—executive, legislative, and judiciary—have the same symbolic significance that they have in the United States and should be shown together" (5.14).[47] Take disregards the fact that the relationship among these three branches of government under the American Constitution is defined precisely by the desirability of their *separation* rather than their togetherness. Of course, it was just this sense of the separation of powers that was lost on Nigeria's politicians as well. The result, in urban design as well as in political terms, is a separation of power instead of separation of powers: the isolation of the government from the governed.

The original Abuja master plan located two of these three powers—the executive and the judicial—on considerably less Olympian heights. They were to form two sides of the National Square, to be situated in the very heart of the Central Area, near the lower end of the mall axis, at the place where it joins a cross-axis lined with cultural facilities. The presidential residence is described as facing the National Assembly, though in fact it was to face it across more than a mile of mall and hillside.[48] Undaunted, the authors of the plan stressed that the president's residence on the National Square and the National Assembly on the hillside were "connected . . . visually."[49] This kind of connection was not quite good enough, however. As Take explains, "In the Master Plan, the presidential palace was located at the central square, but nowadays for security reasons it is folly to expose any president to a national square."[50] Good advice, perhaps, but even this mid-course correction could not save civilian rule in Nigeria. Four months after Take spoke, President Shagari was ousted—while staying in the Tange-designed presidential palace then being enlarged to represent the executive fist among the Three Arms on Abuja's hillside.

Eventually, General Babangida constructed a new presidential palace closer to Aso Hill to replace "Shagari's Villa," seen as having been stigmatized by the coup. The building for Abuja's third arm of government, the Supreme Court, also came into being under a military regime, joining the other powers beneath the Aso Massif in 1998. The completion of this building, designed nearly twenty years earlier by Tange with three Nigerian colleagues, was certainly an ironic counterpoint to the lawlessness of the Abacha era. Nnamdi Elleh condemns the resultant militarization of the country's key symbolic government precinct in the strongest possible terms: "Under Babangida and Abacha, architecture, power, and ambiguous concepts of national security treacherously converged into inseparable military decrees which raped the democratic consciousness of the Nigerian people, the psyche of the nation, mother Nature, and mother Africa, by planting numerous military barracks around the nation's citadel of democracy, in the heart of a national park." The intended three powers had been firmly joined by a fourth—a fortified archipelago of villas and bungalows for the military officers most loyal to the regimes. As a result, Elleh concluded (writing in 2000, a year after the restoration of civilian rule): "from the foot of Aso Rock, the military breathes down the throats of Nigeria's Lawmakers, Presidency, and Supreme Court."[51]

In setting out the "Determinants of Form," the Abuja master plan emphasized three issues: imageability, efficiency, and flexibility.[52] Given the extreme vicissitudes of Nigerian politics, it has indeed been very efficient for the city to have a flexible image. Abuja's designers defined *imageability* as "the perception by the observer of a city's purpose, organization and symbolism."[53] In seeking an imageable Abuja, these planners sought a clear differentiation of its role as the seat of the federal government from all its other purposes. The goal, according to the master plan, was "to organize the principal elements of both the natural and the built environments to emphasize the symbolic aspects of the Government of Nigeria."[54] Since the strife-torn Nigerian government has had many "symbolic aspects" that the designers were not encouraged to convey, the plan understandably needed to be an idealization of what the polity might become. The planners pursued this goal by designing a single-centered city in which the government buildings were related to the dominant feature of the natural landscape. More generally, they aimed to create "identifiable units of organization" and "distinctive sectors with a character all their own" instead of the "endless superblocks of Brasília and Chandigarh."[55]

The authors of the master plan expended a good deal of effort to elucidate how the plan for Abuja had drawn upon the form of traditional Nigerian cities. Noting that "a major shortcoming in past planning for Nigerian cities has been the failure to recognize and accommodate the indigenous patterns of urban organization and adaptation already present in the country," the planners undertook a study of twenty-seven Nigerian cities, including all of the existing state capitals, to determine precedents for overall urban form, the role of central public spaces, and the organization of residential areas. In designing the federal capital, they were faced with the formidable challenge of designing a city that "must simultaneously permit the different segments of the Nigerian population to maintain an important continuity with their social and cultural traditions while encouraging, where appropriate, amalgamation of the various streams of urban tradition and lifestyle into a new and common modern Nigerian context."[56]

Yet, while they found legitimate evidence of a "strong tradition of single center cities,"[57] it is hard to reconcile the design proposed for the Central Area with anything resembling Nigerian "tradition." Nonetheless, they tried to do just this. The National Square, surrounded (in the original plan) by the Presidential Residence, the Supreme Court, the National Museum, and the Municipal Administrative Center, was envisaged as an updated version of traditional Nigerian cities, which "were often characterized by defensive walls pierced by gates and radial roads leading to high density cores dominated by the residence of the Chief, Oba or Emir." In Abuja's plan, however, there are no defensive walls—unless one counts the semi-impenetrable barrier of its multilane boulevards. And the only Abuja City Gate is a massive neo-medieval concrete archway that greets visitors on the road from the airport.[58] Moreover, the "high density core" is transmuted into the void of the square and the mall, and the emir has justifiably fled up the hill.

Undaunted by such discrepancies, the planners insisted that Abuja was related to Nigerian tradition. They set out three possibilities for the location of the "Major Symbolic elements with respect to the Central Area": within it, on the edge of it, and outside of it. Defending their treatment of the Abuja Central Area, they note that "traditional Nigerian capital cities exhibit characteristics of both options one and two" but conclude that "location of the major symbolic core in a downhill location would obstruct its visual connection to Aso Hill and could be construed as suggesting that buildings closer to the major vista and uphill are more prominent."[59] More to the point, perhaps, it could be construed as making downhill buildings more vulnerable. Defending the choice of the mall as an organizing principle, the planners conclude that "the use of formal open spaces and the relationship of major activities reflects a mixture of historic Nigerian practice blended with contemporary functionalism."[60] Yet, only a few pages later in the master plan, the authors note that "in traditional Nigerian town planning, parks and gardens are in the private sector rather than the public sector."[61] In claiming to have represented the "essence" of Nigerian tradition in the chosen option, however, the authors neglected to explain how the tradition of the dominant axial vista fits in to the history of what they mysteriously term "traditional Nigerian urban design."[62]

In defending the images of Washington and Brasília with the rhetoric of Nigeria, the authors of the master plan consistently reveal a powerful ambivalence. It is, perhaps, an unresolvable one for the design of a modern urban capital that is to be a symbol of a largely rural country. The urban–rural schism, combined with the tribal rivalries and the Muslim–Christian split, make national identity so easy to claim and so difficult to implement, especially when the regime in power is not necessarily committed equally to all groups in the nation. The professed goal of designing an "ethnically neutral" capital can easily be diffused and diluted into cultural irrelevance.

Modernity itself becomes the symbol, and Kenzo Tange's firm was well equipped to deliver it. Tange seems to have viewed the Abuja commission as his chance to revisit and exhibit the totality of his oeuvre, much in the way that Le Corbusier treated Chandigarh and Niemeyer used Brasília. Not surprisingly, when I wrote to him to request permission to use photos of his designs for Abuja, he graciously responded with a long letter and a multivolume set of his complete works. In Abuja as elsewhere, the rhetoric of national identity strains against the personal identity of the designer's quest and embraces the international identity that such designs are thought to deliver. Nigerian leaders coveted not only the grand mall, but also Tange's neo-metabolist office high rises that were to flank it and sprout even higher in the Central Business District, on the other side of the National Square. It is this that is at the heart of the drive for Abuja's imageability. The other two categories set out in the master plan—efficiency and flexibility—are in service of the modern image. As long as the price of oil was high, Abuja's sponsors wanted the biggest and best of everything and wanted it fast. The grade separations at all major highway junctions were to be the most technically sophisticated in the world, illustrative of a burgeoning romance with the private automobile.

Abuja's plan, like many others, is heavily influenced by the projections of traffic engineers. For Abuja, however, the designers from Tange's firm took the unusual step of planning not for 70 percent reliance on public transportation and 30 percent on private autos, as set out in the master plan, but for 70 percent of both. According to Take, "Opinions differ, but we think that human nature is such that people working in this capital will want the social status of a car. It might not happen, but in the event that it does, it is already taken care of."[63]

Much of Abuja, in fact, is designed to accommodate the desires for such "social status." In the master plan, the National Assembly was allotted 20,000 square meters, but the prospective tenants subsequently upped their space requirements tenfold, with enormous cost consequences.[64] The Master Plan's urban design sketches envisioned a National Assembly building with a monumental hut-like dome, though Tange's more detailed architectural development, completed in 1981, soon proposed alternatives. Initially, he conceived of the mass of the capitol as a kind of split triangle (see 5.11 and 5.14). According to Elleh, however, this was "rejected by the Nigerian authorities who feared that it symbolized the two houses fighting between themselves (the Senate and the House of Representatives)." Tange countered with a lozenge-like dome that closely mimicked its Aso Hill backdrop. The Federal Capital Development Authority accepted this design, but eventually ended up constructing a much more contentious building in its stead. Rejecting the high modernism of Tange, the military rulers of the 1990s sought refuge instead in a much more traditional form, while also taking full advantage of the vast construction budget of more than $1 billion to allocate contracts and profits in a thoroughly corrupt manner. Egregious behavior extended to the realm of symbolism, as well: the architects (S.M.I. International) that designed the Assembly topped it with a green dome that looks remarkably similar to that of the Great Mosque in the northern Nigerian city of Kano (5.15, 5.16). Not surprisingly, Elleh comments, "Christian communities see the new edifice as an imposition of Islamic values" foisted upon them by the dictatorial rule of Abacha.[65]

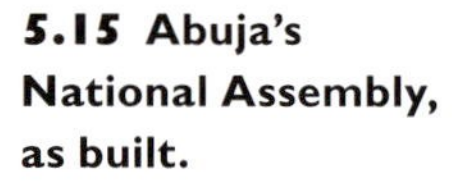

5.15 Abuja's National Assembly, as built.

5.16 Kano's Great Mosque: inspiration for a Capitol Dome.

Also typical of new capitals premised on the urgent need to attract a high-end workforce from an older city, the city is deliberately designed to marginalize the poor and cater to the wealthy. On the master plan, some of the villas for the elite were labeled Official Residences and others left untitled, but all were shown to be located between the National Assembly building and the eighteen-hole golf course. As Elleh comments, the resulting city embraced these priorities: "The higher up on the hill one's villa or bungalow is located, the more powerful and higher up the person is in Nigeria's social hierarchy. The sad truth is: the middle class cannot afford any property at all in any part of the city, not to mention people in the lower classes."[66] The "Ministers Hill" area, reminiscent of that which developed on the shores of Brasília's Lake Paranoá, is but the most extreme example of the master plan's advocacy of residential segregation by income. Whether inspired by Paranoá or paranoia, Abuja was planned without much regard for Nigeria's poor.

Though the language of the master plan emphasizes that "the New Capital City is for all the people," evidently "all" will not be equally welcome everywhere. True, four pages in the 286-page master plan are devoted to discussing the problem of affordable housing, but the resultant designs for residential sectors bear little relation to the income distribution of the population. According to one person who assisted in the design of one of the residential sectors, the brief called for housing people of "upper, middle and lower incomes," yet in reality the houses could be afforded by only two categories: "quite upper and relatively upper."[67] For the residential sectors nearest the Central Area, the planners envisaged large plots—single-family houses for first-generation technocrats. These plots were arranged to accommodate the possibility that an extended family might occupy several adjacent plots, yet the designers recognized that this traditional African extended family was expected to be deliberately left behind in the move to Abuja. Within the low-rise sections of some of the residential sectors there is a conscious effort to make the layout flexible enough to incorporate the traditional housing configurations of the major tribal groups. Yet, here too there is recognition that the desire to include traditional elements may be more closely correlated with the Western consultant's romantic notions about African village life than with the agenda of the Federal Capital Development Authority.

The largest disconnect of all, however, occurs between those who can and those who cannot afford to live in Abuja. Nonetheless, in an interview published in February 1987, Air Commodore Hamza Abdullahi, then minister for the Federal Capital Territory, chose to ignore the burgeoning slums that housed Abuja's construction workers and lower-level civil servants:

> It is impossible for slums to develop here in Abuja. Every inch of the city has been predetermined. The way and manner of the structure does not allow anybody to go out of this original plan. If we give you a plot, you have a boundary for the plot and you cannot exceed that. There is what is called our land-use plan and this is our bible. We follow it carefully. There is absolutely no room for anybody to just start building substandard structures. It is impossible.[68]

What the air commodore fails to point out, of course, is that Abuja was to have no slums because its founders intended to export them to points beyond the boundaries of its land-use plan.

Before construction on Abuja could commence, its planners discovered that there were already more than 300,000 people living within the boundaries of the Federal Capital Territory. Initially, due to the expense and political wrangling associated with resettling so many inhabitants, the Federal Capital Development Authority decided upon a more limited relocation plan focused on the area that needed to be cleared to build the city itself. In 1992, the government decided to permit some people to remain even in certain areas being readied for the expansion of Abuja, but in 1999 the policy changed again to favor a more complete resettlement, a policy made even more extreme in 2003. A 2004 report identified twenty-eight squatter settlements (totaling 2,412 hectares) located within the Federal Capital Territory, many within the boundaries of Abuja city itself. Moreover, especially during the excesses of the military government of the 1990s, even the carefully planned areas of the city center faced additional forms of rampant illegal development. As the *New York Times* reported in 1998, "The military officers who have ruled Africa's most populous nation for two decades, and siphoned off a good deal of its oil revenue, are busy building vast mansions on their Abuja real estate." Following the return of civilian rule after 1999, efforts to raze illegal settlements and to reimpose the tenets of the Plan led to controversial mass displacement, much of it interpreted as religious or ethnic discrimination.[69] As in Brasília and other capital cities before it, the contrast here between the opulence of the center and the squalor of the fringe is as great an inequality as any known to man. And this, too, is part of the Abuja master plan.

DODOMA: A SOCIALIST CAPITAL ALTERNATIVE?

The master plan for the new Tanzanian capital at Dodoma, published in 1976 and prepared for the Capital Development Authority by the Toronto-based Project Planning Associates, posited a city of 400,000 persons by the year 2000, with 1.3 million expected by 2020. Though a lack of funds has slowed the pace of development, and political change has shifted the underlying ideology of the plan and its realization, the project still progresses: Tanzania's 2002 census counted more than 300,000 urban residents in the Dodoma region, though presumably not all of these were in Dodoma itself.[70]
As in Nigeria, the move of the capital represents a departure from an overcrowded colonial port and an attempt to site the national government in the less-developed center of the country (5.17).

Dar es Salaam's deficiencies are not as egregious as those of Lagos, but the Dodoma master plan nonetheless detailed "growing problems," noting the city's "limited area for economical expansion, congested transportation facilities, substantial industrial growth and a surge of new population," all exacerbated by an "uncomfortable climate."[71] For the authors of the Dodoma plan, however, perhaps the most significant drawback of Dar es Salaam—or at least the most *ideologically* significant one—was its association with the "German Colonizers." The master plan, hardly a politically neutral document, notes that Dodoma and other inland sites were considered for a

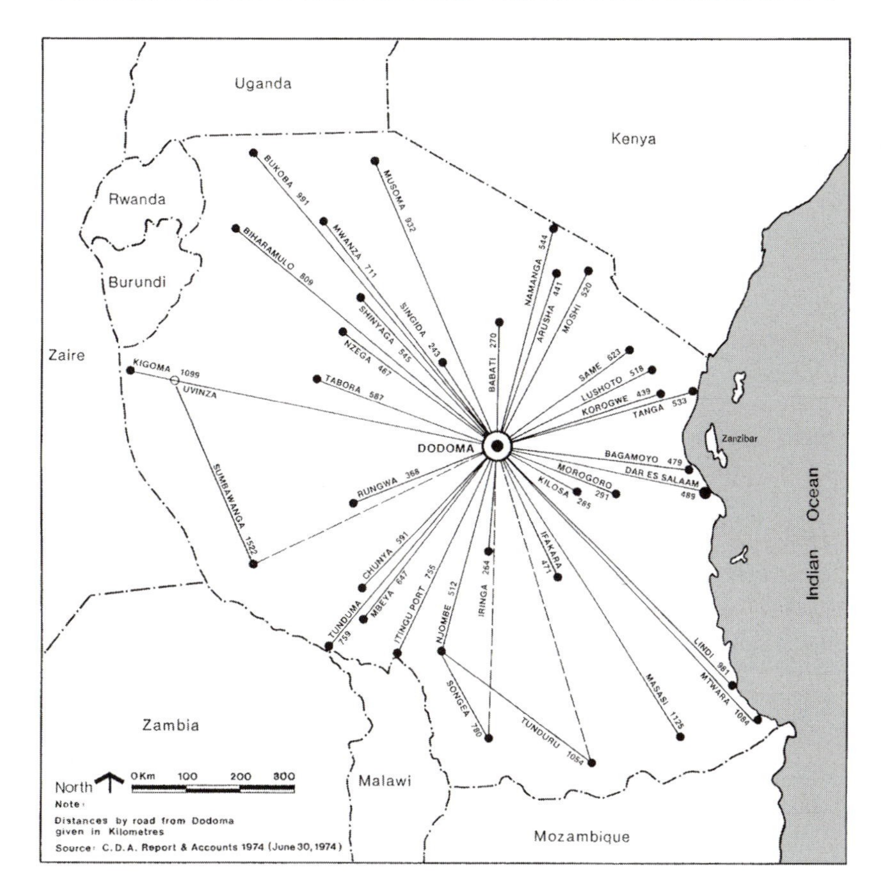

5.17 All roads lead to Dodoma?

new capital as early as 1915, but "imperial strategy was thought to be more important than healthy and attractive living conditions, and Dar es Salaam remained the Capital."[72]

In creating a new capital at Dodoma, the designers were charged with creating a symbol of Tanzanian unity, an aspect of the capital-building task that is less daunting here than in Abuja. As a *New York Times* reporter put it in 1995, "Despite 120 ethnic groups and many different languages, Tanzania has enjoyed three decades of domestic peace and is one of the few countries in East Africa whose people have a strong sense of national identity." Although Tanzania has significant divisions along ethnic, racial, and (especially) religious lines, according to a recent study of "religion, identity and politics," "no identity has become an all-encompassing category that takes precedence over other forms. In short, the concept of nation remains intact, despite the diversity of identity groups." Tanzanian tribal affiliations are even more fragmented than in Nigeria (none is politically dominant), and unification is aided by the fact that Kiswahili, now the national language, has been widely used for more than a century.[73] Equally important, political control is more centralized than in places like Nigeria and has been dominated by one political party, the Tanganyika African National Union (TANU). This party, known as Chama cha Mapinduzi (CCM) following merger with Zanzibar's party in 1977, has been in power since independence. Even after a multiparty political system was introduced in 1992, and followed by national elections held in 1995, 2000, and 2005, CCM has continued to control national political life. In the 2005 elections, the party won 89 percent of the contested seats, continuing a trend established in 1995 and 2000. With opposition parties demonstrating such a perennially weak track record, the Tanzanian National Assembly still lacks the ability to serve as much of a check on the power of either CCM or the president (who is also tied to CCM). Given this continuity of leadership, the decision to move the capital to Dodoma must be seen in relation to the agenda of this party, which championed a form of village-based socialism throughout the 1960s and 1970s. A national party-sponsored referendum (with 70 percent in favor) confirmed the resolution to relocate.[74]

The decision to move the capital to Tanzania's rural heartland was intimately tied to the government's version of an ideal socialist state. The move out of the congested, rapidly industrializing city of Dar es Salaam and into the sparsely populated central plateau was perfectly in keeping with the stated aims of the ruling party, as articulated by President Julius Nyerere in the Arusha Declaration of 1967. It is no coincidence that the declaration is reprinted in full as Appendix A of the Dodoma master plan.

The declaration stresses the importance of self-reliance and hard work by the local population, rather than the passive receipt of international aid. It underscores rural and agricultural development as the first priority, with industrial development only in support of these ends. For a government professing such aims, Dar es Salaam conveyed the wrong image. As the master plan puts it, the old capital, as "a dominant focus of development," is "the antithesis of what Tanzania is aiming for, and is growing at a pace, which, if not checked, will damage the city as a humanist habitat and Tanzania as an egalitarian socialist state."[75] Dodoma, by contrast, would send the right political message, even if the global infusion of consultants would, at least in the short run, do little to exemplify the goal of self-reliance. In any case, Dodoma's position at the junction of six major surface routes fit nicely with the "high priority . . . placed on widespread village and rural development where it is Government policy to maintain close and direct links with the rural population."[76] For the government of Tanzania and the planners of Dodoma, the new capital was to be an example of the ideal socialist city, one that "should demonstrate how city residents can maintain a close relationship to the land."[77] Thus, if Abuja's location was promoted as an endeavor to mediate between ethnic groups, the selection of Dodoma undertook to mediate between urban and rural populations.

In Tanzania during the early 1970s, Nyerere's plans for *ujamaa* villages, cooperative compounds based upon the traditional extended family, were met with considerable enthusiasm and participation. Such hopefulness was not to last, however. As James C. Scott scathingly observes, "The failure of ujamaa villages was almost guaranteed by the high-modernist hubris of planners and specialists who believed that they alone knew how to organize a more satisfactory, rational, and productive life for their citizens." Still, even Scott concedes that "the practice of villagization [was] far less destructive than the theory," and other commentators give the program a more commendable record of partial success. Meanwhile, however, the larger economy faltered. According to an analysis made in 1985, "Up to 1977, when the rapid decline set in, the country's growth rate was a steady 5% per annum, external reserves were equal to a healthy five months of imports; there was an overall budget surplus and, no less important, a food surplus."[78] This account attributes much of the decline to external factors, including the effects of the break-up of the East Africa Community, the massive increased costs of imported oil, machinery, and fertilizer after 1973, the impact of serious drought after 1979, the 50 percent deterioration in trade between 1977 and 1982, and the huge cost of the military operation to help oust Uganda's Idi Amin. Internally, the difficulties mounted as well, with serious miscalculations in fiscal and monetary policy decisions. Faced with such crises, and dependent on the international financial community for development assistance, Tanzania embarked on a program of economic liberalization starting in 1986, followed by further privatization and political liberalization during the 1990s. Instead of socialism and self-reliance, Tanzania's leaders increasingly emphasized "a model of accumulation hinging on increased foreign investment and exports." As Tim Kelsall puts it, "Arguably the government has been more responsive to the demands of external agents—the IMF, the World Bank, and other members of the Consultative Group of major donors—than it has been to its own MPs, especially when it comes to the broad contours of economic policy." The plan for Dodoma, in this context, now seems a lingering relic of a very different political moment, one that did not last long enough to see the imagined city actually get built. Even so, as an ideological document, the Dodoma plan remains quite compelling.[79]

In the broadest sense, whereas the designers of the master plan for Abuja

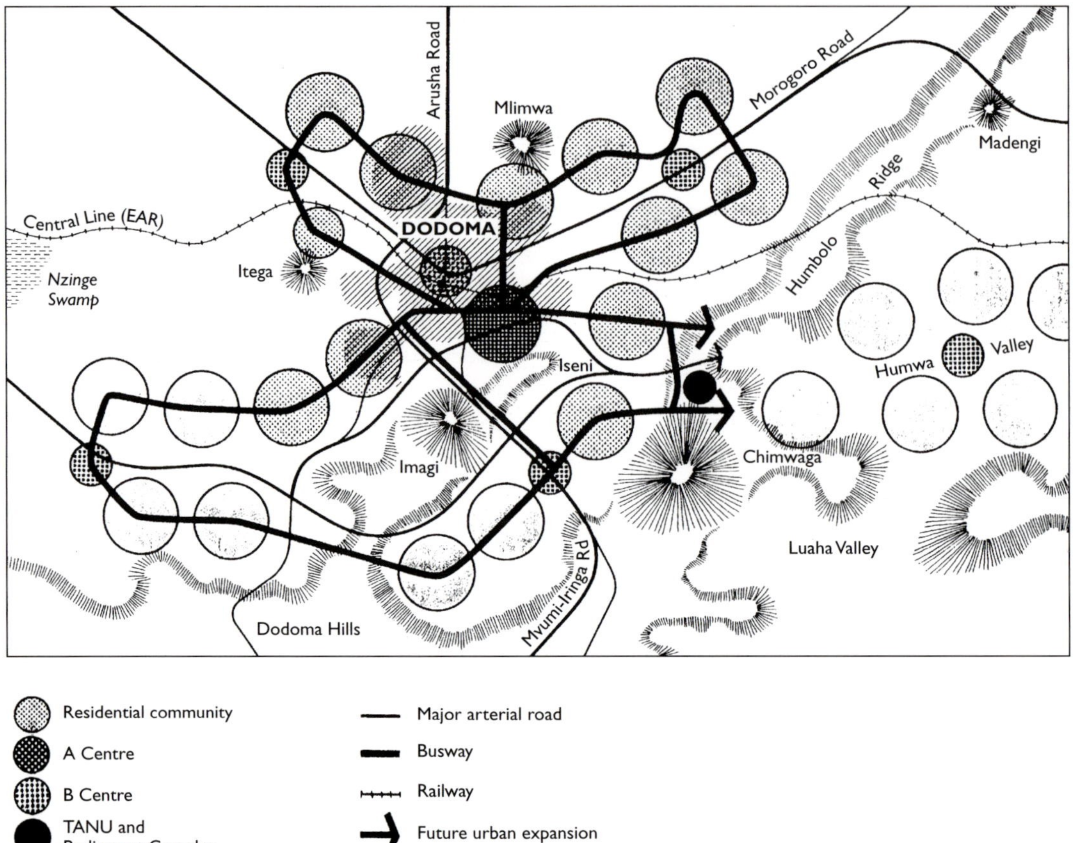

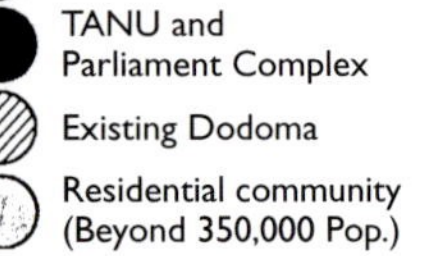

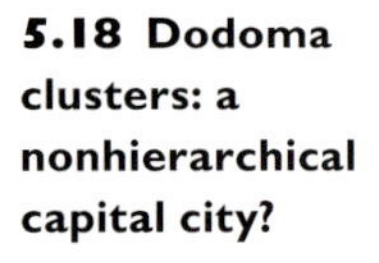
5.18 Dodoma clusters: a nonhierarchical capital city?

sought to improve upon existing models of capital city planning, the planners of Dodoma undertook a more radical critique of capital city form. At the most diagrammatic level, this basic difference may be seen by comparing Abuja's plan, which closely resembles Costa's cross-axial Brasília, with that of Dodoma, which appears as a polycentric cluster (5.18).[80] The texts of the two master plans emphasize the seemingly divergent priorities of the two notions: the Abuja text focuses on the design of the Central Area—the location of government and commerce—while the Dodoma text stresses the residential communities. The rhetoric of both plans implies that the new capitals are expected to contribute to national identity, yet very different identities are sought: Abuja was promoted as a response to subnational schisms (which it may well augment rather than ease), and Dodoma was seen as tying the village-based principles of *ujamaa* to national aspirations.

If my discussion of the Abuja plan ended with a reference to the ways the city's staggering inequalities are exacerbated by the city design, an analysis of the Dodoma master plan may begin at the opposite extreme: the commitment of its planners to create an egalitarian capital. This plan, too, contains lengthy discussions about "capital image" and "urban centres," but its tone is gentler, its scale is understated, and its priorities emphasize issues of human habitation. In short, the Dodoma plan is ambitious in its very modesty. It proposed nothing less than the first nonmonumental capital city. Monumentality and hierarchy do not truly disappear, but even so the plan is a telling critique of capitalist capital city form.

The text of the master plan for Dodoma is prefaced by a statement by Julius Nyerere, Tanzania's leader from independence to 1985. His remarks set the unpretentious style of the whole document: "We are a poor country, building a new capital city in a nation committed to the principle of *Ujamaa*. We have to build in a manner which is within our means and which reflects our principles of human dignity and equality as well as our aspirations for our development. . . . The town must be integrated into society as a whole; it must be neither an ivory tower nor a new version of our existing towns."[81] Nyerere went on to emphasize the need to use local materials and local building techniques, to build both inexpensively and solidly, and to be certain that all facilities are accessible to the handicapped. Before concluding by commending the master plan "to the people of Tanzania," he articulated what he perceived to be its relationship to the principles of Tanzanian socialism outlined in the Arusha Declaration:

> I believe this Plan, as it stands, is consistent with the ideology of Tanzania. Two very important examples can be given to show the way it reflects our philosophy. First, the Plan shows that Dodoma will be built as a series of connected communities, each having a population of about 28,000 people. . . . The second fundamental point about this Master Plan is the way it gives priority to the building up of an efficient public transport service and to the physical movement of people on foot and by bicycle.[82]

As Nyerere intimated, part of what is distinctive about the Dodoma plan is the extent to which it proposed a kind of compromise between city and country.

Most plans for new capital cities in developing countries have either failed to address the problem of rapid urbanization of a predominantly rural population or struggled to cope with it; for Dodoma's planners, this was a fundamental point of departure. The master plan recognized that most Tanzanians, 95 percent rural in 1975, were not accustomed to living in cities: "Traditionally, the Tanzanian people relate to small communities and wide rural areas; a dense urban environment is in many ways alien to national lifestyles and philosophies. The principle of self-reliance, as expressed in the Arusha Declaration, suggests that all families should live close to arable lands to enable them to grow at least part of their food requirements and, moreover, sociological considerations militate against cities of closely packed buildings and large paved areas."[83] Housing areas were therefore envisioned as being much closer to their village prototypes than those envisioned, for example, in Abuja.

In maintaining that "the Arusha Declaration is . . . essential to understand the framework within which the National Capital should be designed and built,"[84] the authors of the master plan related their designs to four aspects of national development policy cited in the declaration: (1) land and agriculture, (2) the people, (3) the policy of socialism and self-reliance, and (4) good leadership.

In recognition of the first criterion, the planners cited the Arusha Declaration's charge to use land collectively and productively: "Land is the basis of human life and all Tanzanians should use it as a valuable investment for future development. It is to be used for the benefit of the Nation and not for the benefit of one individual or just a few people." Out of respect for the land, the planners rejected "man-made geometrical forms" such as "grid iron and radial plans" as "inappropriate." Although Dodoma, like Abuja, was to have an axial downtown mall with some streets that meet at right angles, such orthogonality is the exception rather than the rule. Nearly all of the city was intended to undulate and curve with the forms of the existing topography, in an attempt to minimize the willfulness of the intervention. Related to this is a commitment to locate Dodoma's built areas on the land least suitable for agricultural purposes or water storage, part of a larger policy to maximize the availability of arable land and minimize any deleterious impact of the new city upon the larger region. "On a larger scale and at a more symbolic level," the authors of the master plan noted, "the city was laid out so as to enable the open space of the landscape to flow through it. In this way, every community would be close to major parkland, hills or green space."[85]

As Dodoma has grown from its existing town of 50,000[86] into a much larger city-region, its planners have struggled to preserve its rural feel. Seen most optimistically, the planners implemented a massive afforestation effort in an arid place, yet such laudable efforts at introducing a hierarchy of open spaces appeared to many locals as a "western design model . . . imposed in a cultural context which demanded a more comprehending and appropriate response" to the needs of those whose lives depended on livestock grazing, street vending, and petty trading, rather than on access to opportunities for "recreation." As an article in the *Journal of Political Ecology* put it, the "translation of these [ecological] aims into actual designs and development proposals led to conflicts with the livelihood activities of poor residents whose lifestyles and economic priorities were not taken into consideration." The government sought to maintain its strict land-use controls, and to channel initial "cluster" development in a linear way, toward the east, but could not contain the spread of informal settlements. Still, at its best moments, the plan did try to accommodate local practices. The authors of the plan stressed the close ties between family, land, and community and promised not only the ready accessibility of shared garden plots for partial subsistence farming within the city, but also "private outdoor space on the ground" for "every family with children."[87]

As to the second National Development Policy objective, the people, the authors of the plan were vague and prone to jargon. Nonetheless, the plan clearly came down on the side of a kind of urban intimacy. Recalling the warning in the Arusha Declaration that "we must not forget that people who live in towns can possibly become the exploiters of those who live in the rural areas," the planners stressed "the nature of the city as a forum" for all Tanzanians. While they acknowledged that the Capital Center will have a

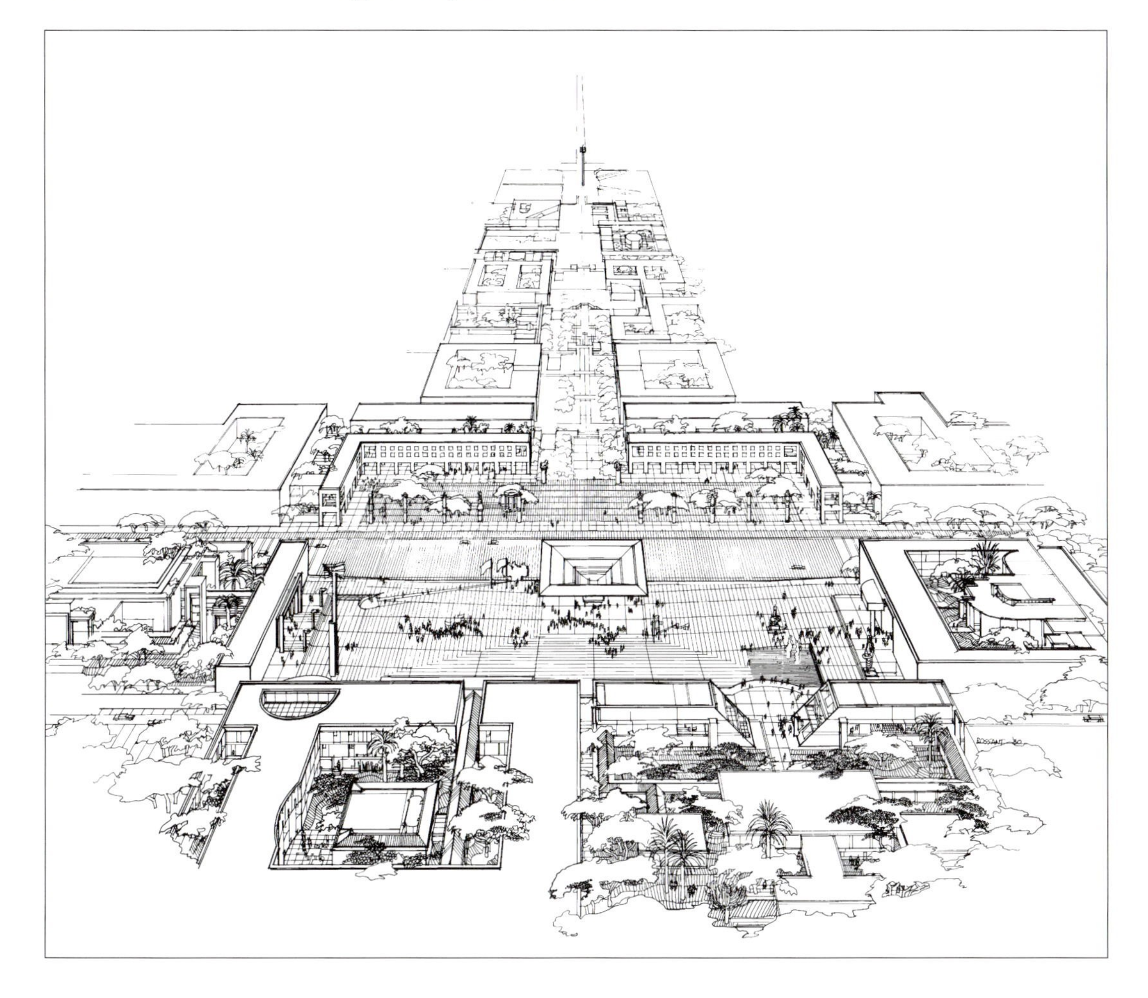

5.19 Perspective of Dodoma National Capital Centre, looking north.

Grand Mall as its "main focus,"[88] this place was to have an utterly different character from its Nigerian counterpart in Abuja.

Whereas in Abuja the width of the mall seems to have been chosen to match the grand proportions of the buildings that flank it and to mimic its predecessors in Washington and Brasília, the width of the Dodoma Grand Mall could easily fit within the width of many of Abuja's grand secondary streets. In the Dodoma master plan and in the drawings for the Capital Center made by consultants Conklin Rossant,[89] the inevitability of such a megascale central area is challenged (5.19). As conceived in the master plan, the Capital Center is to be "a major mall, an avenue for walking and meeting, with its important buildings carefully modulated and articulated to human scale."[90] The Conklin Rossant drawings for the Capital Center show an elaborate pedestrian path that traverses seven ascending terraces from the Uhuru ("freedom") plaza flanked by the Museum of Social and Political History, the National Library, and the Museum of Science and Industry to the city's major gathering place, *Ujamaa* Square (5.20, 5.21). This square, to be marked by a large monument in the form of an abstracted acacia tree (such shade trees remain the traditional village place of gathering), was to be faced by the High Court building and the offices for economic planning.

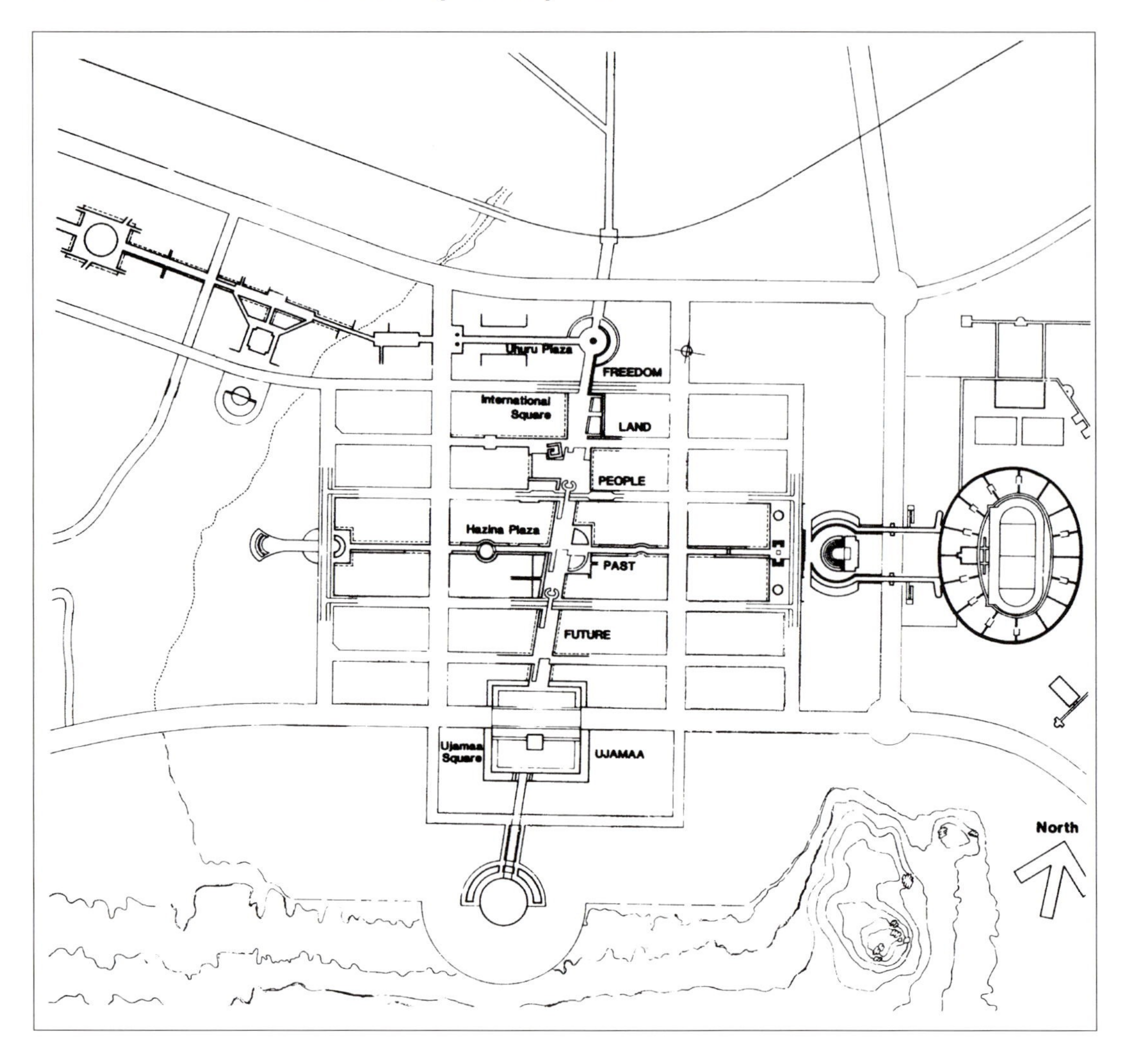

5.20 *(above)* **Schematic plan of Dodoma stepped terrace "mall."**

5.21 *(below)* **Looking south, toward Ujamaa tree.**

5.22 Pedestrian pathways, Dodoma.

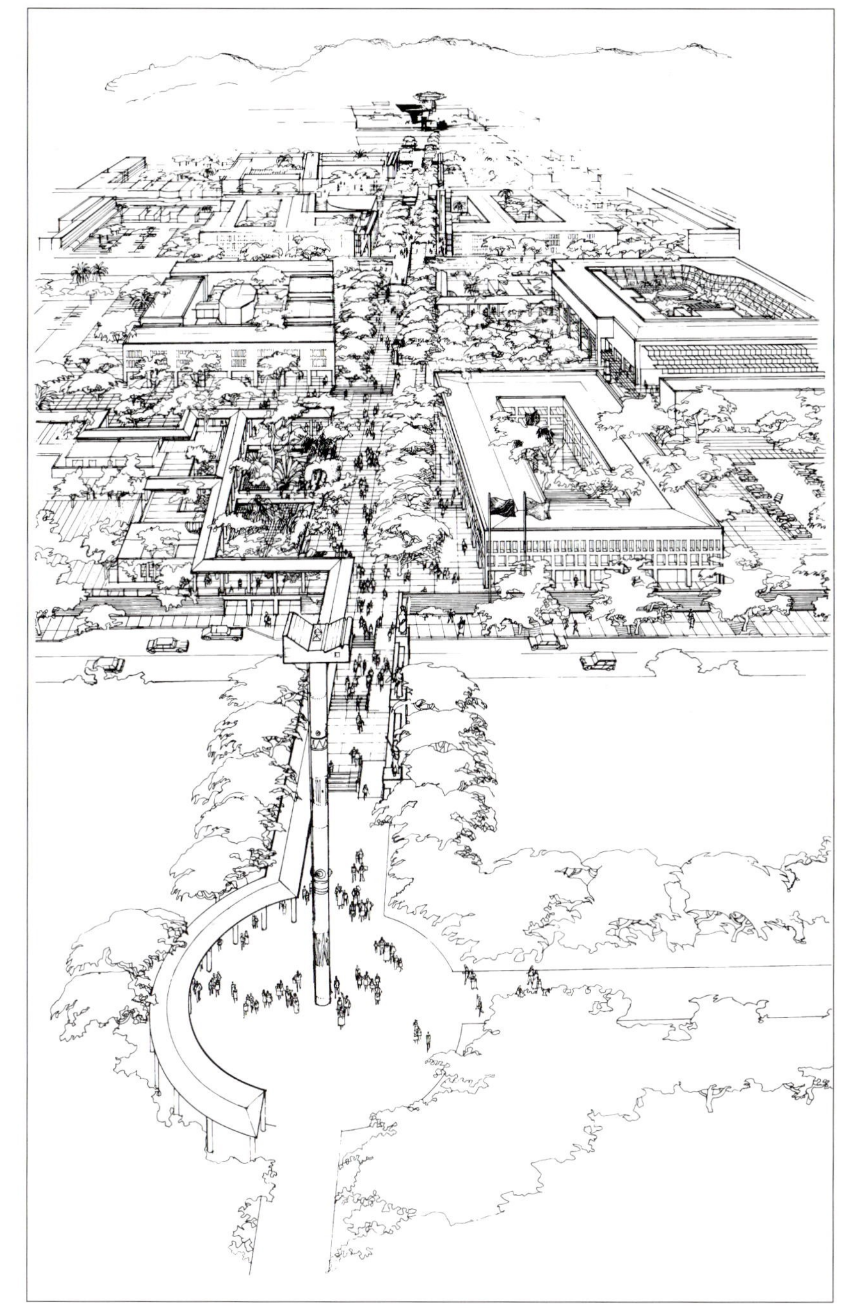

A bit farther on, but connected to this main pedestrian spine, would be the site for presidential offices (5.22). Throughout this capital center, instead of a mall flanked by high-rise megastructures, the plan proposes two- and three-story structures sized and oriented to require neither elevators nor air conditioning. In the drawings at least, careful planting and terracing make the scale of the Capital Center almost unrecognizably different from the drawings submitted by the Tange firm for Abuja. Moreover, in contrast to other designed capitals, the planners of Dodoma proposed a thorough

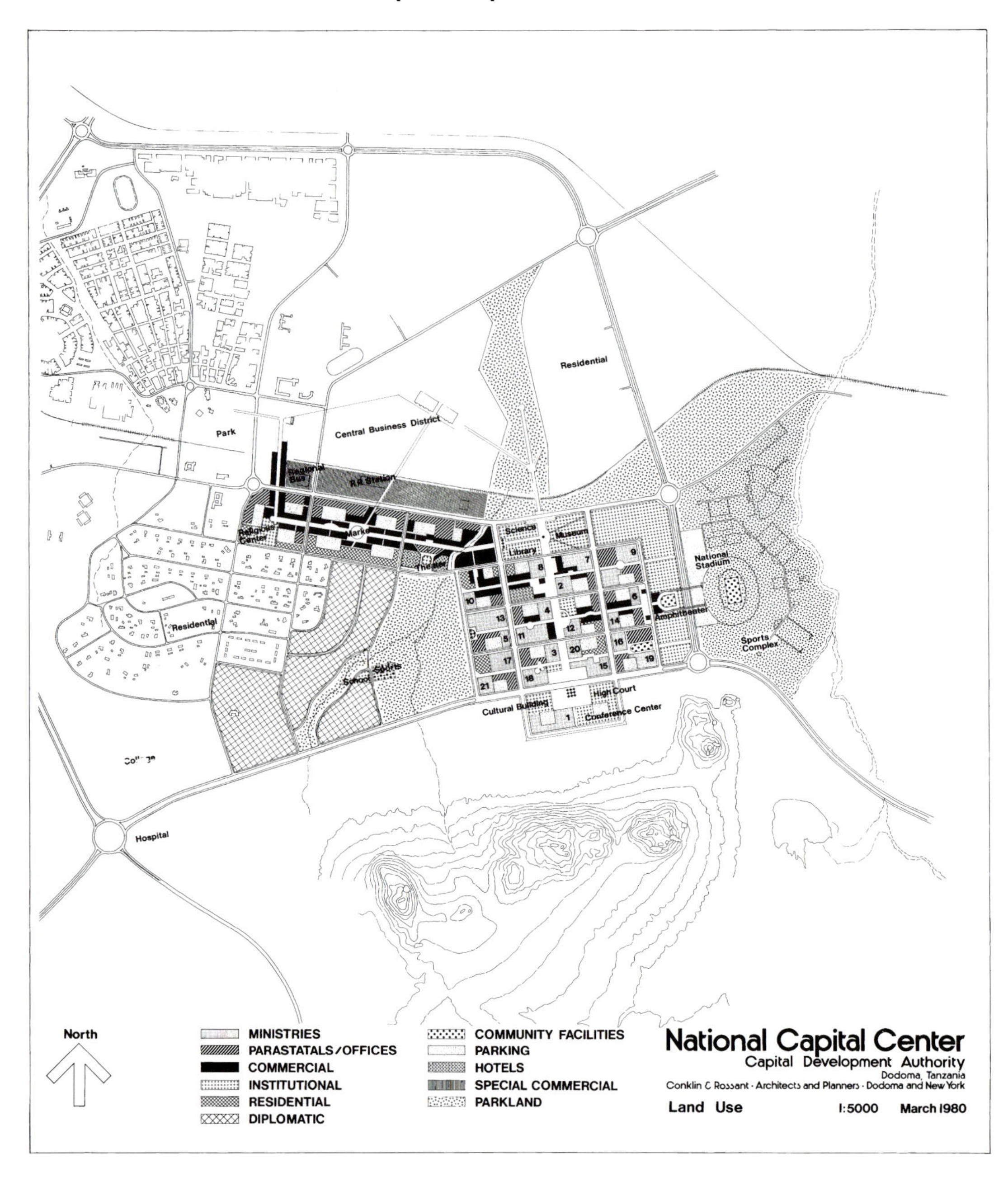

5.23 Diagram of mixed-use capital center, Dodoma.

intermixture of shopping, restaurants, apartments, and cultural facilities with the various government ministries (5.23). The Conklin Rossant plan describes the center of Dodoma as "an immense stairway symbolising Tanzania's progress upward and forward."[91]

As for the third National Development Policy from the Arusha Declaration that the Dodoma planners wanted to incorporate into their design—the policy of socialism and self-reliance—one may find evidence of this in the plan as well. The basic housing community is to be the "TANU ten unit cell," a group of houses closely related around a shared outdoor meeting

5.24 TANU/CCM "ten-unit cell."

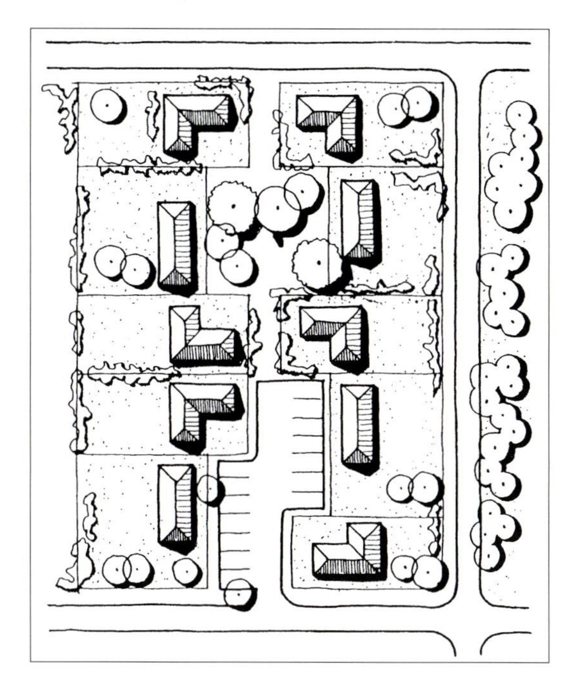

place (5.24). This cell was thought of not only as a fifty-person social unit but also as an economic and political one; it was expected to be the source of grassroots development in Tanzania.

The authors of the master plan, undoubtedly well coached by their Tanzanian client/partners, emphasized that "Tanzania is a socialist state and as such it has an inherent responsibility to provide housing for all who need it." The TANU ten-unit cell, according to the master plan at least, was intended to be available regardless of "normal market forces" or the "ability to pay." At another point, the plan's authors note that all communities "should include people of all income brackets and employment backgrounds. Land forms, rather than the size or type of housing will establish the character of all communities, and all will have equally pleasant open space patterns, though perhaps different in character. In this manner, it is expected that the avoidance of elitism, stressed in the Arusha Declaration, will be achieved."[92] The master plan is not detailed enough to reveal how many were to receive a place in these clusters of socialist suburbia, though it implied that they would include "all families with children."

A 1981 analysis of the planning and building of Dodoma suggested, however, that "initial signs are not encouraging" since Dar es Salaam's "colonial, residential, and institutional development patterns are being repeated" and "the chance of integrating people of different incomes and ethnic backgrounds may be missed."[93] Another early critic complained that "low-cost houses based on self-help (sites-and-services schemes) and squatter upgrading [favored elsewhere in Tanzania] will have no place in the new capital, where representation and image are the first consideration," and that Dodoma "will become exactly what Dar-es-Salaam has been hitherto: the concrete manifestation of the seat of a 'new African elite.'"[94]

Doubts and questions emerge in this regard when one turns to the master planners' translation of the final National Development Policy, good leadership, into urban design terms. To begin with, though the plan follows each of the first three development policies with separate sections on land, people, and socialism, when it comes to good leadership there is no such section. Perhaps they assumed that, given the merits of the plan thus far, the merits of the leadership were abundant and therefore best left implicit. More likely, they realized that the spatial juxtapositions articulated in the plan between the people and their good leaders were not entirely in keeping with the socialist spirit.

In both the master plan by Project Planning Associates and the subsequent development of the Capital Center by Conklin Rossant, the major buildings for the party and parliamentary leadership were shown to be located well outside of the pedestrian Capital Center (5.25). Indeed, a separate set of Chinese consultants was employed to design the buildings on Parliament Hill. In the master plan, the High Court was to be located a mile away from the main square of the Capital Center, along a sinuous and tree-lined Processional Way, and the Parliament and Party National Headquarters located at the terminus of this Processional Way, another mile farther on, atop a hill overlooking the rest of the city. In short, the Dodoma master plan made no provision in the Capital Center for any of the government buildings usually considered most vital to a national government. Certainly, it removed those institutions that were most central to the governance of Tanzania's CCM-dominated state. It showed the People's Square surrounded by the National Theater, the National Library, and, indicative of the need to draw national and international visitors, a hotel. As Donald Appleyard, one of Dodoma's urban design consultants, pointed out, "The issue is, which will be the principal landmarks of the future capital city?" George Kahama, director-general of the Capital Development Authority and a close ally of the president, told Appleyard in 1979 that these should be "Parliament and CCM [Party] National Headquarters, the Prime Minister's Office, the President's Office, the High Court and the Interdenominational Religious Center." Given this, Appleyard concluded, "The location and form of these buildings in the future urban context should ensure that they become the key landmarks in the image of Dodoma, and that other less important buildings do not dominate and distract attention away from them."[95]

In the Conklin Rossant development of the Capital Center portion of the master plan, the unusual institutional juxtaposition of the master plan scheme seems to have been reconsidered, but only to a very limited extent: the High Court and certain executive offices were brought within the realm of this central sector and placed on *Ujamaa* Square, but party and Parliament remained isolated on the hill, subject to the designs of a different consultant. As in Abuja, the leadership would be provided with hilltop refuge, in spite of the availability of the egalitarian plane of the *Ujamaa* Square. Even for socialist leaders, this sort of leveling seems not to have been desired. The result might yield appropriate "principal landmarks" but at the cost of appropriate principles of citizen–leadership relations. As A. M. Hayuma has charged, "The claim of bringing the Government and leaders close to the people rings hollow. In fact, poor people visiting the new capital will

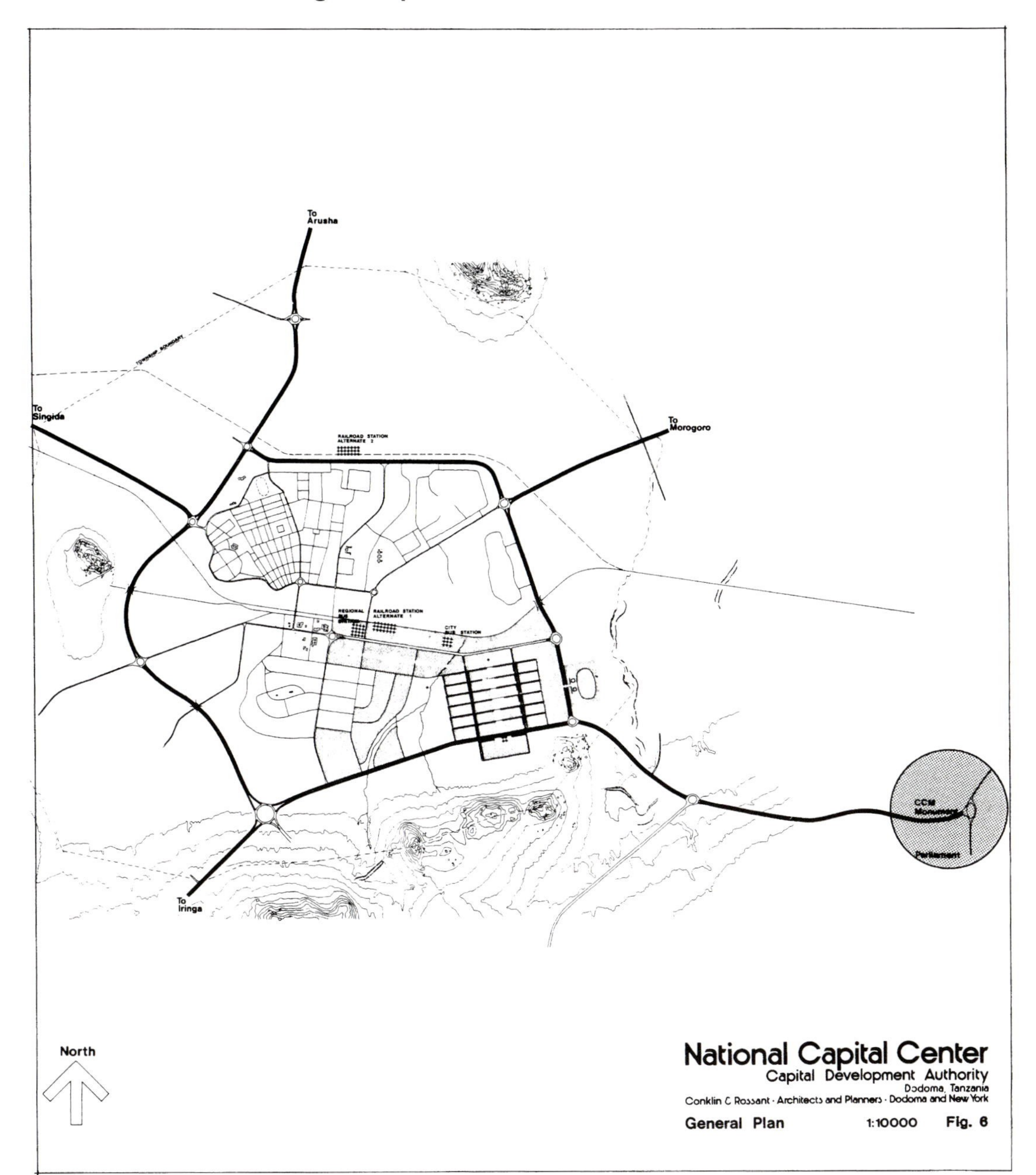

5.25 Parliament/ party and capital center: two separate realms.

have difficulties of access to government and Party officials to present their problems and receive services." In sum, he concluded from judging the plans, "What actually seems to be happening is the shift of the seat of Government from the Indian Ocean beach onto the summits and slopes of Dodoma. . . . Government offices and élite residences will be as aloof and isolated from the concerns of the people as they have been in Dar."[96]

While the rhetoric of the Dodoma master plan insists that "the major building complexes" were to be located to "emphasize the unity of the leaders, their buildings, the land forms and the people,"[97] such unity is hardly what first comes to mind when one looks at the larger plan. Though there is no equivalent to the Abuja plan's ministerial golf course, Dodoma's plan suggests that the Tanzanian leadership has, at least in urban design terms, repudiated its links with the people. In Dodoma as in other cities designed to showcase governments, the capitol is detached from the capital. In pondering this apparent contradiction to the otherwise remarkable proposal for integrating leaders and people, one is left with two unacceptable alternatives: either the Tanzanians who advocated this plan did not believe that the Parliament and party headquarters constituted "major building complexes" or they did recognize their importance but wished to hide the true sources of political power. Given that the Chinese drawings for the hilltop party and Parliament buildings depicted a large complex of decidedly monumental character, there would seem to be a modicum of calculated deception underlying the city planning for even this most understated of capitals. While Dodoma's plan lacked the axiality (and the historical associations with axiality) present in Washington, Canberra, New Delhi, Chandigarh, Brasília, and Abuja, its planned parliamentary complex reaffirmed timeworn associations of natural forms with political power.

If Abuja's Three Arms Zone is intended to be the culmination and focus of that city's urban design, Dodoma's parliamentary complex would seem intended to dominate somewhat more surreptitiously. Perched at the top of a curving Processional Way, the hierarchical separation between government and governed could be maintained, with big brother well placed to watch. Just as the capital cities themselves were moved to claim the central highlands of the country, so too the ruling politicians appeared destined to claim the central highlands of the city.

According to more recent assessments, however, much of both the promise and the critique of the Dodoma project is rather moot since so little of the city has been built in accordance with the plans. "The vast scheme for Dodoma—the residential communities, industrial sites, government offices, public utilities, ornamental vistas, and recreational facilities; the hospital, university, technical college, military academy, botanical garden, and international hotels; and the public streets and squares, fountains and pools, restaurants and cafes, national museum and library, and amphitheater—were never realized." The Tanzanian parliament officially relocated to Dodoma in the 1990s, but its grand, purpose-built new home was inaugurated only in 2006.[98] Moreover, the new parliament did not use the hilltop site specified in the original master plan, but instead sits prominently along a major diagonal road in the northeast part of the city center. The parliament is the dominant building in the city, clearly visible in a satellite view, but it does not dominate the city in urban design terms (5.26, 5.27). In short, it is not the spatially isolated building proposed in the master plan. Instead, its isolation is felt primarily in institutional terms: with most of Tanzania's capital functions still in Dar, Dodoma remains a rather lonely legislative outpost. Some of the intended infrastructure and road networks exist with sufficient clarity to reveal the capital's planned origins, but the anti-monumental socialist capital stands largely unrealized. The conceptual basis for Dodoma has withered away just like socialist state that was meant to inspire it.

5.26 Parliament as built, a more central location.

5.27 Satellite view of Dodoma, showing parliament location.

Even so, both the Dodoma plan and its limited realization show that it is possible to critique the common assumptions about capital city monumentality. Dodoma's planners (and their client) made the bold suggestion that the central portion of a capital city could be a series of mixed-use pedestrian enclaves integrating many activities rather than a mall of vast vistas or a plaza of heroic dimensions. There is little to show for this thus far, but the eventual nonaxial siting of the new parliament building seems a return to this initial well-cultivated humility. Dodoma so far lacks the urbanistically separate and privileged zone for the most important institutions of government that is so characteristic of other designed capitals. Certainly it is a far cry from the bombast of Astana or Putrajaya.

It may simply be too soon to judge, however. If Tanzania should proceed further with the transfer of government functions to Dodoma, it may well be that these institutions will cluster together in secured isolation just as they do in Abuja, Islamabad, and elsewhere. Tanzania, too, may resist intermixing the primary abodes of government power with other institutions or with residential areas. Capitol and capital may once again become separate realms.

CAPITOL VERSUS CAPITAL

The discussion of Abuja and Dodoma brings the account of the relationship between capital and capitol full circle. From ancient citadel to modern capital, cities have focused on the place of rule. Increasingly, politicians have moved to claim the privileged urban heights reserved in an earlier age for the gods. Promoted as a means to advance national unity and consolidate national identity, these capital cities have more obviously served to demonstrate the power of their sponsoring regimes. They convey, through urban design, the desired image of political impregnability, even as the regimes themselves face the challenges of military coups and civil unrest. The planning and building of a new capital city often revives the same hierarchies and problems that were present in the old capital. While the premise of a so-called administrative city implies an unusually high percentage of wealthy white-collar workers, the promise of this new city as a source of construction employment draws in poorer segments of the population as well. One solution, for many governments, has been to build not a new capital city but simply a new capitol complex.

Whereas in Nigeria and Tanzania, the leaders found it desirable to create new capitals distant from the colonial capitals of the past, the leadership of many other countries has preferred to stake out new enclaves in or near the existing capital. The decision to move a capital is not the only kind of significant decision; there are decisions *not* to move as well. A decision to stay put may derive from an inability to pay for a new capital, but often those in power also find it to their advantage to remain where they are. The projection of national identity is hardly limited to large-scale issues of urban planning and new city site selection; it is intimately tied to architecture as well.

Though I have mentioned several capitol complexes, discussion of them has thus far been directed more to their urban design than to their architecture. In the first part of this book, I have wanted to demonstrate the development of patterns in the relationship between capital and capitol. I have emphasized the placement of government buildings in relation to the plan of their city, while saying relatively little about the design of the buildings themselves. Where a whole new capital city has been designed, it is these macrosymbolic design issues that seem most important. In such places, buildings are inseparable from the vistas that frame them. The capitol complex, as the major focal point of a large and complex design, often has the visual support structure of an entire city to undergird its spatial importance. In cases in which a government commissions a new capitol without also commissioning a new capital to frame it, however, the situation differs substantially.

If the macrosymbolism of a new capital is lacking, government leaders and the designers they employ use other techniques to assert the importance of the capitol. Denied the opportunity to be the centerpiece of a new city, the newly designed seat of government is located either on the outskirts of the existing city, where a large parcel of land may be obtained, or else more centrally on a smaller site. In either case the old idea of the *caput mundi* suffers considerable distortion. The postcolonial capitol complex is either a head without a body or it is micro-cephalic. In the latter instance, in which a small capitol is inserted into the existing city fabric as part of a scheme of urban renewal, the siting still lacks some of the contrived prominence that is possible only in a designed capital. The long history of conquerors building upon the most prominent ruins of the conquered has as yet no exact parallel in the design of postcolonial capitols, since reuse of the quarters of the ancient regime has retained a certain appeal. Wherever possible, new governments have moved to claim as their own privileged places associated with past forms of rule.

Governments that are unable to build a new city as a national symbol of postcolonial identity can manifest their views for the nation in other ways. From Washington, D.C., to Abuja, the designed capital has been a diagram of political power, a physical expression of control and continuity. The architecture of capitols, like the planning of capitals, represents a continuation of political policies by other means. At one level, this physical articulation of the political tenets and social priorities of the government is indicated by the juxtaposition of government buildings, in relation to the capital and in relation to each other. At another level, however, urban design and architecture may themselves help carry political messages. In Nelson Goodman's terms, capitol complexes may denote a regime's propaganda through explicit use of text and iconography, may exemplify certain architectonic properties which invite or repel, may express through metaphor a regime's desired association with some other kind of favored environment, and may, through the process of mediated reference, encourage connection to certain broader concepts (such as democracy or nationalism) which may well stray far afield from strictly architectural units of meaning.

Many national parliament buildings clearly attempt to apply indigenous architectural forms to the task of housing a postcolonial government. No longer content to rely on the deliberate cultural anonymity or, alternatively, the deliberate Western hegemony of high modernism epitomized by the term *international style*, government leaders and their architects have produced design solutions that evoke local traditions. There are, however, many local traditions. The decisions as to which aspects of indigenous architectural form to elevate into a building that is meant to serve as the symbol of a modern nation-state are never arbitrary. Intended as a kind of compensation for the absence of a spatially supportive new capital city, parliament-building architecture can play an important role in the construction of national identity.

PARLIAMENT AS ARCHITECTURE AND AS INSTITUTION

Discussion of the capitol complex as a vehicle for the symbolic expression of national identity must recognize that these buildings are, in theory at least, expected to be functioning institutions. The iconographic discrepancy between the political proclamations of unity and the architectural evocations of factional preference is significant, but it is not the most fundamental incongruity. It is not enough to underscore the disjuncture between monumental architecture and feeble institutions; one must remember that it is often the institutions of parliamentary government—and not merely their monumental architectural treatment—that constitute the truly alien presence. Architecture is a symptom of a larger cultural condition caused by the rapid introduction of modern institutions into traditional societies.

In most countries that have gained independence since the Second World War, not only modern Western architecture has been imported, but also the forms and formalities of modern Western democratic institutions. In traditional societies, Edward Shils points out, conflicts are settled by an emergent consensus rather than by voting:

> The traditional image of "public life," moreover, has no room for *legislation* and for the public discussion preparatory to a compromise among conflicting contentions. Laws are not *made* in traditional societies. They are *found* in judgments made in the resolution of particular disputes. Debates in parliament and decisions by majorities, frequently composed of very heterogeneous interests, although having certain parallels in tribal discussions about succession, have no parallels in the major functions of policy formation and lawmaking. The rudimentary governmental apparatus of traditional societies is not oriented toward the making of laws or their implementation. It is oriented toward the maintenance of order by the enunciation of what is right. It does not seek to do new things, things which have never been done before. It does not promulgate new laws. Above all, it does not promulgate new laws to establish new social and economic arrangements. It is a mode of affirming established rules.[99]

To a greater or lesser extent depending on the nature of the independence movement and the practice of the colonizing power, this enormous procedural and conceptual gap between traditional and constitutional governments was bridged by the training of an indigenous elite during the waning years of colonial rule. Yet the schooling of this native elite to accept the institutional trappings of Western constitutional democracy usually did less to educate the majority of the population or even to guide the elected participants. The chief concern, according to Shils, is not only that constitutional democracy is "different in much of its particular content and in some of its fundamental values from the indigenous tradition," but also that "it is experienced as alien by its practitioners." This, he points out, "places it at a disadvantage where indigenous things are at a premium":

> The elites of the new states are, of course, different from the mass of the population, as they are, indeed, in any state. They are different, however, in a significant way by virtue of the cultural disjunction between themselves and their people. This makes . . . for impatience, but it also makes for a desire to make oneself more indigenous. Awareness of the decayed or rudimentary condition of their indigenous cultural inheritance has made men feel the need to revive it; it has made them feel the need to affirm its value and to deny derogations whether explicit or implicit. In an atmosphere of sensitive nationalism where the dangers to the institutions which have arisen from this still fragile and scantily diffused sense of nationality are real, symbolic affronts to the need to be "of the people," to be authentically indigenous, are tangibly felt. . . . The proponents of "alien" institutions feel themselves vulnerable to accusations that they are defenders of "alien" practices.[100]

Though some of these schisms may have healed as new states have become older and have invented hybrid traditions, the symbols of constitutional democracy have often proved more resilient than the constitutions themselves.[101] In such a situation, capitol buildings become especially powerful repositories of associations that the regime and its designers hope, often in vain, to control. The instability of capitol institutions and the infusion of symbolic vernacular references into much of capitol architecture are thus ultimately and intimately connected.

Part 2

Four postcolonial capitol complexes in search of national identity

CHAPTER 6

Papua New Guinea's concrete haus tambaran

The National Parliament building in Papua New Guinea (PNG), formally opened in 1984, raises a number of intriguing questions about the architectural representation of political power and the role played by government buildings in the development and consolidation of a viable national identity for a new state, independent only since 1975. The design by the architect Cecil Hogan marks a clear attempt to move beyond the bland internationalism of much of the postcolonial urban built environment (6.1, 6.2). While seeking an architectural expression that was somehow modern and thus in keeping with the overall development of the country, he tried to use vernacular building traditions to mold an identity for the state. At a time when most less-developed countries relied on eminent foreign-based architects to fly in and bestow a design conception upon the country, the leaders in PNG insisted upon at least a quasi-indigenous solution: Hogan, an Australian expatriate, was director of the architecture division of the Department of Works and Supply in the PNG capital city of Port Moresby.

Hogan's work did not proceed unimpeded, and his insider's role was controversial. The design competition, originally open only to architects in

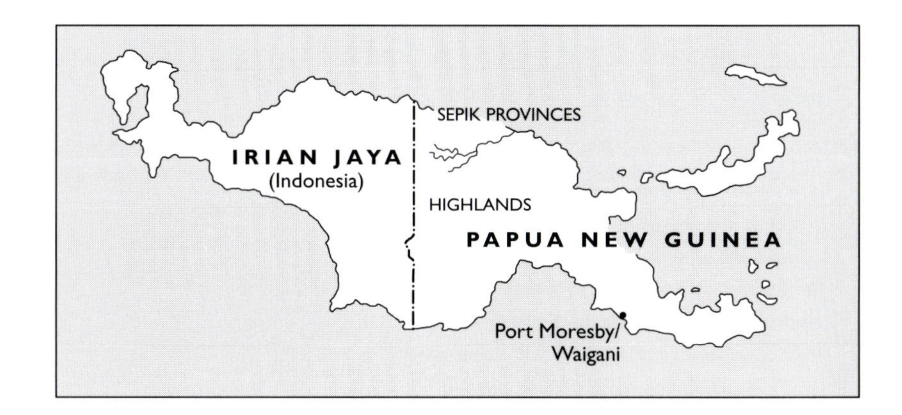

6.1 Papua New Guinea (PNG).

6.2 Architect's rendering of the PNG Parliament House.

Hogan's department (now part of the National Works Authority), yielded Hogan's design as the concept thought most worthy of further development. Following objections, however, an officially adjudicated national competition was held in 1977, this time open to private architects as well. Hogan was forbidden to enter since he and his design were so well known. In 1978, Bill Phillips, a less senior member of the Works Department staff, was declared the winner of the second go-round. His design, which drew less directly upon indigenous forms and emphasized the lushness of the landscape, was published prominently in the Port Moresby newspaper, and the matter appeared settled. Shortly afterward, however, owing to circumstances still unclear to me, the Phillips design was rejected, and it was decided to revert to Hogan's original scheme.

The National Parliament Commemoration booklet, issued to mark the opening of the building, is ambiguous about the situation: by the time the Phillips design was chosen "the original design brief had become outdated and the designs submitted to the competition were accordingly in many ways unsuitable. Whereas Mr Hogan's design had always been undertaken in conjunction with advice from persons who had a great deal of knowledge and experience of the running of a Parliament and the design had, in several instances, been modified accordingly."[1] Perhaps this cryptic passage is suggesting that Hogan was well connected politically, having from the beginning discussed his design with Prime Minister Michael Somare and other members of the government. Somare, one of the three judges of the official competition, may well have preferred this first design to that of the declared winner. In any case, Phillips sued the government and subsequently received a much-publicized 25,000 kina (approximately $30,000) out-of-court settlement. Hogan's design was carried out, and newspaper headlines charted every turn in the whole tortuous process. Strangely, the fiasco of the design competitions received no write-up in any architectural journal, and even the Hogan design has never received more than cursory mention.[2]

In settling on a local architect, PNG's leaders acted to keep their building out of the mainstream of international architectural culture, even as their country sought international recognition and needed international assistance to get the building built.

The PNG parliament building—like those in Sri Lanka, Kuwait, and Bangladesh—seems to be representative of a second generation of attempts to reconcile modern architecture and postcolonial national identity. As such, it may be viewed in the context of the earlier essays at Chandigarh and Brasília. Not surprisingly, the "Papua New Guinea Parliament House Design Brief," of December 1975, refers to the Indian and Brazilian capitals.[3] Though Papua New Guinea was then a small archipelagic nation of three million people, the ambitious design brief included a chart and sketches comparing parliamentary facilities in Canberra, London, Ottawa, Washington, Kuala Lumpur, Lagos, New Delhi, Brasília, and Chandigarh. In setting general parameters for the PNG parliament design, the authors singled out the capitol buildings at Brasília for special disdain: "The new capital of Brazil is a city of vast dimensions and formal architecture. The design of the parliament group is deliberately monumental and sited well clear of other buildings." The solution for PNG, they countered, "need not be monumental. It may be more appropriate to have a group of buildings of a deliberately human scale, which invite public involvement and participation."[4] Whatever the rhetoric about avoiding the "monumental," few commentators are able to avoid using the term when describing the resultant building.

The first indication of deviation from the Brasília approach was made clear in the choice of site for the building. Although the Select Committee on Constitutional Development chose the remote town of Arona in the East Highlands province as the preferred site for a new capital, the design brief favored development on the outskirts of the existing capital.[5] Arona, located at the geographical center of the new nation, was considered an appropriate symbolic choice, but it was certainly not convenient. Inaccessible by road from Port Moresby because of high mountains and dense jungle, it epitomized the problems of a country in which most provinces are connected only by air travel. Given that it took a century-and-a-half of discussion before Brazilians moved to urbanize the Amazonian frontier, it is not unexpected that caution prevailed in Melanesia. As explained in the commemoration booklet, "Arona was considerably isolated in terms of communications and it would have put an extremely heavy financial burden on Papua New Guinea to change this and introduce such facilities as are necessary in a modern Parliament."[6] A report issued by Peddle Thorp & Harvey, the Australian firm hired as consulting architects for the project, was even more blunt in its assessment of Arona, rejecting it as "totally unrealistic" because of the "logistic problems in erecting such a complex structure in a remote area."[7]

Choosing the alternative to a frontier capital, the government decided on a capitol complex on the frontiers of Port Moresby, PNG's only large city. Sited in the administrative district known as Waigani, the parliament became part of a master plan for civic and office development. At the ceremony marking PNG's formal independence in 1975, Prince Charles unveiled a plaque and "officially pronounced" Waigani the site of the parliament building. From that moment forward, the progress of the building became symbolically identified with the progress of independent constitutional democratic government. In the design brief, the chairman of the Parliamentary Design Committee called for it to be "a key building and an example" within the "Waigani City Centre."[8]

WAIGANI CITY CENTER

Emblematic of a trend in new countries that have chosen to build a new capitol rather than a new capital, Waigani is a city center without a surrounding city. It is a Three Powers Plaza, a Raisina Hill, or a Mall bereft of its city. The function of the capital city is distilled into its administrative and touristic essences. The new parliament takes its place among the other buildings intended to promote the existence of national culture. Approaching Waigani from Port Moresby, one comes upon the cultural monuments on one side of the road and office buildings on the other (6.3). The parliament building stands in the receiving line of symbolic institutions. Here, it enjoys distinguished company, including the National Library, the Supreme Court, Independence Hill, the National Museum and Art Gallery, and the State Reception Center. Nearby, too, are a National Theater complex and Mirigini House, the prime minister's official residence. Unlike many other designed

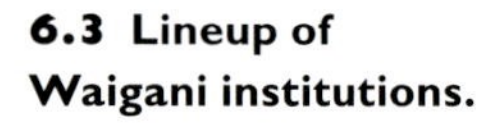
6.3 Lineup of Waigani institutions.

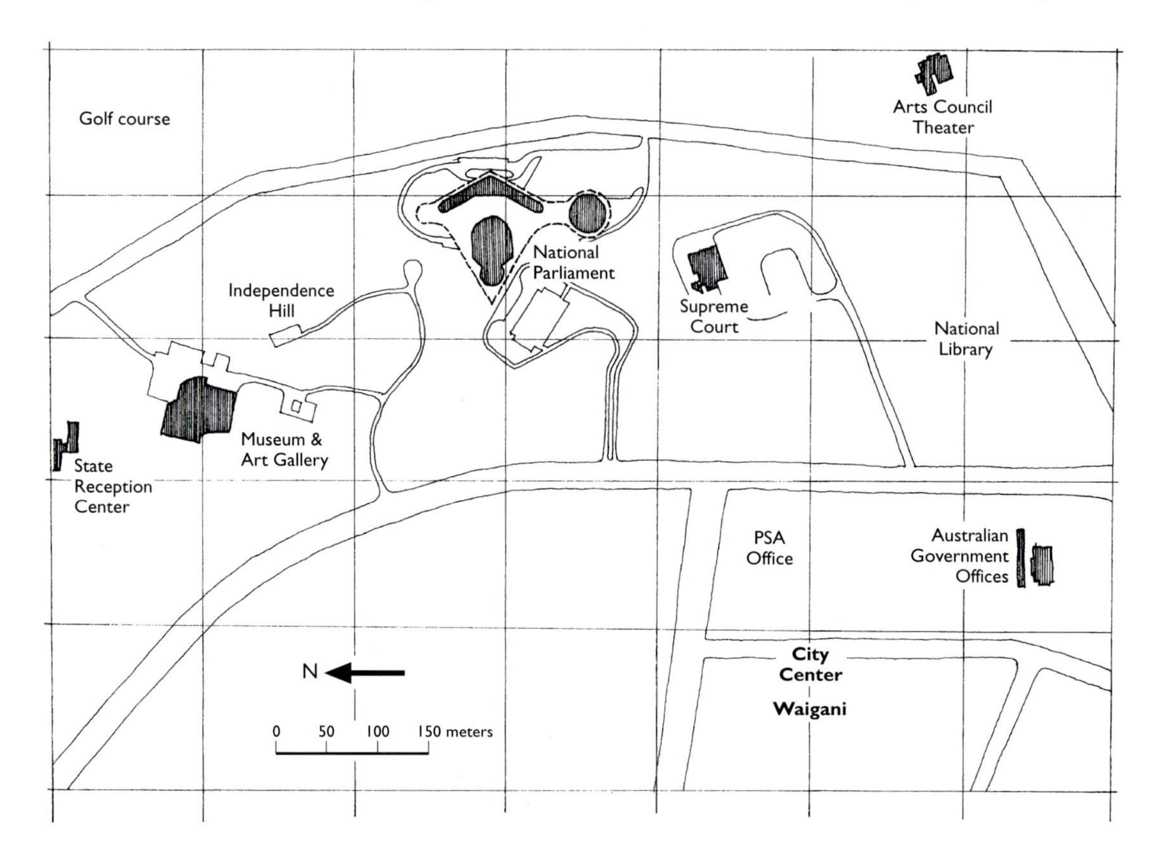

6.4 Satellite view of Waigani, 2007.

capitol complexes, however, the buildings are not choreographed along some rigid axis of constructed vistas or carefully arranged around a plaza. Neither Independence Hill nor the Parliament House is a focus of any large urban design (6.4). Like the structures of many PNG towns that grew up along an airstrip, the monuments of the PNG government are strung out along the side of a road, at intervals of approximately three hundred feet. Still, it is too soon to pass definitive judgment on the site qualities of Waigani since much of the intended parklike environment has not, at this writing, been fully planted, maintained, and developed. A quarter-century after the 1982 Master Plan for the Waigani area was first promulgated, PNG officials continue to debate measures to improve the appearance of the district at a time when many important buildings have deteriorated significantly. Most prominent is a revived proposal for Constitution Park, to be located in front of Parliament House in a way that would frame the building as the terminus of a boulevard. It would also provide additional office space for both government and commercial purposes.[9]

As built, however, nothing in the urban design treatment of the National Parliament reinforced its preeminence in relation to either Port Moresby or the other monuments of Waigani, so its designers had to rely on architecture alone to convey the necessary symbolism. For a country so newly independent and for a population so overwhelmingly unaccustomed to the theories and practices of constitutional democratic rule, an enormous amount of highly explicit symbolism was thought necessary. And, for sheer density of such symbolism, the resultant building has few equals anywhere.

BUILDING NATIONAL SYMBOLISM

Since it must accommodate a system of parliamentary democracy that is still largely alien, Papua New Guinea's Parliament House cannot possibly blend in easily, as architecture or as politics. Not only does the resultant building reveal these sorts of strains, but its designers appear to revel in them. The Parliament House is intended as a monumental announcement of PNG's arrival on the international scene. In its architecture, art, and furniture it purports to create a representative collage of designs from many of the country's diverse component cultures. Designed and built during a period of backlash against any monumentalism that was thought culturally irrelevant, the building seeks to promote an image of Papua New Guinean identity.

At first glance, the parliament building design exemplifies the enormous dislocation caused by rapid development. Though a parliamentary framework of sorts had existed for more than a decade before independence, many of PNG's influential politicians felt that it could benefit from architectural structure as well. A new parliament building was also thought necessary for practical reasons: to replace a centrally located but undersized, makeshift structure that once served as the city's first hospital (6.5).[10] Whatever the pressing programmatic needs, the desire for symbols steered the design thinking behind the building. The superimposition of Westminster-inspired parliamentary democracy upon a rural archipelago inhabited by a thousand

6.5 Old assembly building, Port Moresby.

tribes speaking more than seven hundred languages and dialects was thought to require the authority of an imposing edifice. Timothy Bonga, speaker of the National Parliament, described the building as "a symbol of political independence" and emphasized its importance as visible evidence of political progress: "We have adopted many ideas from overseas and have integrated them with our traditional consensus systems. Democracy comes naturally to Papua New Guineans. The particular form we have adopted—the Westminster system—less so. To reinforce this system, a suitably impressive and monumental building was needed. In this parliament we have it."[11]

The design brief, composed in 1975 during the heady days of newly gained independence, is a document brimming with references to Papua New Guinean identity. The first steps to consolidate such an identity were undertaken with a directness as unequivocal as it was disingenuous. The National Identity Bill of 1 July 1971 ratified the designs for the national emblem and flag and, looking toward independence, named the country Papua New Guinea.[12] Yet even the name of the country, chosen to encompass two once separate political entities, is indicative of barriers to a single identity. The chairman of the Parliamentary Design Committee called for a building "suitable to the lifestyle, climate, geography, cultural and social aspirations and traditions and economy of the people"[13] but did not say how a designer should proceed to accomplish this aim, given that "the people" were not one but one thousand. Similarly, the chairman concluded that the building should demonstrate "Papua New Guinea's worthy traditions of art, architecture and settlement planning (of which there is little proper documentation and almost no public knowledge)" and should assist in the "development of industries, crafts and materials of a Papua New Guinean nature so that the substance of the Parliament will also be of the country."[14]

The problem here is that to assume some "Papua New Guinean nature" begs the question. To define *Papua New Guinean* in terms of products available within the territorial bounds of the new nation is far easier than to define it in terms of cultural practices. One task asks only for a list of indigenous—that is, symbolically acceptable—materials, while the other demands that one ask *who* uses *what* for *which purposes*. When the design brief discusses the structure of the proposed new parliament and asserts that it "should be functional and yet express an acceptable, traditional design and art form," one may ask what it means to be acceptable and to whom.[15] Juries and authors of competition programs may commonly believe it possible to arrive at either a consensus or a compromise on such issues, but knowing which of the multiplicity of culturally differentiated artistic traditions could be thought acceptable and on what criteria is difficult.[16] That the brief served as a guideline for a design competition and that Cecil Hogan, the man ultimately chosen as architect, was a member of the Parliamentary Design Committee that prepared it are definite grounds for suspicion. Yet the issue of deciding which traditional designs and art forms are acceptable is fundamental and transcends the ethics of architectural competitions.

The limits of acceptability were, however, remarkably clear and well defined in the design brief. In both words and illustrations, it was reiterated throughout that an acceptable design would rely heavily on "traditional" architecture. A final chapter containing comments on the proposed building by five "well-known citizens" seems calculated to ensure that the report would not be dismissed as a product of Australian expatriates. One reads that Mrs. Tamo Diro, who was the wife of the chief of defense forces, "opts for the Highlands *'raun haus'* [round house] style" and that Mr. Bernard Narokobi (described in one newspaper account as a "writer, barrister, law reformer, former judge, constitutional expert, visionary, family man and villager")[17] insists that the design "take full account not merely of the building styles of our people, but also the very essence of our people's architecture."[18] Both Mr. Pokwari Kale and Father Ignatius Kilage, the Chief Ombudsman, stressed the need to use local materials and to keep "any steel and concrete well concealed," and Mr. Pious Kerepia, commissioner of police, emphasized the need for adequate security, suggesting that public access be maximized but that the means of access be limited in number.[19] "In summary," the brief concludes, "there is a solid consensus" in the views put to the chairman of the Parliamentary Design Committee: "The building should be of solid local materials, embody traditional architectural values and, while not being over ostentatious, should reflect the strength of the nation. Father Kilage suggests that all this can be obtained by ensuring that the appearance of the building is decided upon by national graduate architects."[20] The citizen commentators are consistent in their belief that the parliament's architecture should reflect indigenous architectural traditions, though only one offers a particular preference for a "style." The Narokobi suggestion for a "full account" of many styles and a demonstration of some architectural "essence" is both the most comprehensive and the most vague.

The authors of the design brief attempt to steer the architectural decision making toward some specific acceptable examples, providing a six-page compilation of photos and sketches titled "Art and Architecture." These examples, which include samples of both Highlands round houses and coastal haus tambarans (spirit houses), are presented as a catalogue of styles, none of them national but all found within the nation-state. The design brief concludes by noting that "a truly Papua New Guinean National Parliament" would appear as "a prime symbol and example in the manner of the *'Haus Man'* [men's house] in a village society. As with designing a '*Haus Man'* it is very important to Melanesian attitudes to involve everyone concerned and reach a consensus."[21] This idea of parliament building by "consensus" seems to have been very directly played out in the nine years between design brief and finished structure, and the result is an amazingly literal carrying out of the initial charge to design "in the manner of" a village men's house. Significantly, some of the very same photos used in 1975 to illustrate the design brief were reused in 1984 to explain the finished design.

The building that ensued appears, at least from its ceremonial entrance, as a gargantuan version of a village haus tambaran (see 6.2). While no one would dispute the imposing size of the parliament building, the choice of this kind of haus tambaran is less of a dimensional shock than might first be thought. Some village haus tambarans are immense, one of the few instances in the world in which truly monumental architecture is found at the level of the smallest settlement. Still, though some village spirit houses

6.6 **A Sepik haus tambaran in its village context.**

are almost as tall as Hogan's Parliament House, these traditional buildings have nowhere near the bulk of the new building complex. In Hogan's design, a single two-acre roof covers six stories of government offices [Block B] arranged in the form of a boomerang behind the council chamber [Block A] and a smaller circular building [Block C] (a raun haus containing amenities such as conference rooms, a billiards room, bars, and sporting facilities). The allusion to the haus tambaran, however, inevitably remains the building's most striking feature, and press reports often identify the building as being in the haus tambaran style. Though it is true in some sense that the haus tambaran, like a parliament building, served as a center of village decision making, the new building is dedicated to an entirely novel deity: the spirit of nationalism.[22] In the transition from village sacred space to national symbol, the haus tambaran is transformed into concrete and mosaic, transported out of the jungle and into suburban Port Moresby, and transmigrated into the largest and most costly structure ever built on the island (6.6).[23]

Undeniably and even avowedly glib, the transformation is nonetheless dramatic and provocative. The decision to capitalize on the essence of an autochthonous architectural form, rather than construct yet another internationalist box, has everything to do with promoting nationalism. This need for national symbols, it would seem, is the central justification for a new Parliament House, even one which, more than two decades ago, cost an estimated $30 million.[24]

National identity cannot come easily to several million citizens whose primary loyalty has been to family, clan, and tribe rather than party, province, and country. And nationalism is not an easy thing to promote where national boundaries have little to do with traditional clan boundaries and small village-based groupings, with their complex social and political links forged by land inheritance, gift-giving, marriage, kinship ties, and various defensive and offensive alliances. Though formally independent from Australia since 1975,

PNG remained economically dependent for decades, and bitter reminders of other aspects of the colonial legacy are not easily overcome. More than anything, perhaps, the harsh artifice of the straight line border separating Papua New Guinea from West Papua (a place that is Papuan-populated but Indonesian-controlled) indicates the extent to which both colonial and postcolonial administrations can be indifferent to the affiliations of indigenous peoples. Even the name *Papua New Guinea* bespeaks its legacy as a forced merger among different peoples and contending colonial presences, harkening back to German "New Guinea" (annexed by the German state in 1884) and British and Australian claims to the Territory of "Papua." Australians administered much of the territory after 1914, supported first by a League of Nations mandate during the 1920s and, after World War Two, by a United Nations Trusteeship. After 1949, the Australians consolidated the separate administrations of the territory and launched policies intended to prepare PNG for nation building and state creation, although some parts of the Highlands did not come under government influence until the 1960s or even 1970s. The Australians gradually introduced representative democracy, starting with local councils in the 1950s, and proceeding to an elected House of Assembly in 1964 in which Papua New Guineans held the majority of seats. Subsequent elections in 1968 and 1972 paved the way for self-government in 1973 and independence two years later.[25]

Due largely to the circumstances of this late decolonization and the overwhelming complexities of ethnic micro-allegiances, the PNG government's efforts to forge a national identity for the new country have been supported by a relatively low level of nationalist sentiment among the general population. In contrast to many newly independent countries that could boast of a weighty precolonial past as a functioning state, the very notion of a "state" had been recently introduced to PNG. Colonizers neither inherited a centralized government bureaucracy nor fully succeeded in creating one before independence.[26] Similarly, PNG's stateless indigenous political traditions did not permit resort to any single basis for marshalling nationalist sentiment around the lingering symbols or evocative ruins of some deeply rooted single precolonial civilization.

As political scientist Charles Hawksley puts it, "independence was thrust upon PNG rather than achieved as the result of the efforts of an organized nationalist movement." Australian Prime Minister Gough Whitlam regarded PNG's independence as a moral issue, arguing that Australia was "no longer willing to be the ruler of a colony." At the same time, spearheaded by Michael Somare and others, PNG also gained leaders eager to take on self-government. This quest for self-determination, however, faced additional obstacles even before independence as secessionist movements arose in Papua, New Britain, Bougainville, and other regions. As Laura Zimmer-Tamakoshi puts it, "many places with different colonial histories and patterns of economic development feared for their particular interests under a centralized government dominated by Papua New Guineans from other regions."[27]

Even after more than thirty years of independence, Hawksley comments, "nation-building and state-building should be viewed as works in progress."

On the one hand, democratic governance in PNG has been continuous and has thus far avoided the military interventions characteristic of many other fledgling states; on the other hand, democracy has been so volatile that no government in the first three decades managed to last until the end of its full parliamentary term. Of PNG's first six prime ministers, three have held office twice or more; independence leader Somare was himself chosen again as prime minister in 2002. Such political volatility, marked by weak parties and high electoral turnover, has made long-term economic planning difficult. The country has also endured a variety of crises, most prominently a protracted and bloody conflict over possible secession of the resource-rich eastern island of Bougainville (which eventually led to autonomy in 2005). The Bougainville struggle (which caused the deaths of at least 5,000 people, perhaps even 20,000) fractured the illusion of unity, and has been coupled with other calamities including destructive tsunamis and a volcanic eruption, all against a backdrop of rampant crime and government corruption. Given the enormous obstacles PNG has had to overcome to remain a viable nation-state, it is not surprising that the government has used architecture and other manifestations of national symbolism as a form of cultural engineering.[28]

Out of necessity, then, the national identity of Papua New Guinea is pursued selectively. The soaring, upswept front facade of the Parliament House is far more than a gesture of form. It is a gesture rooted in social, political, and cultural choices, with both national and international implications. From the air, according to the interpretation of Prime Minister Somare, the building's shape is "modelled on a spear head flying towards the future" and "symbolises the . . . astonishing rate" of progress since independence" (6.7).[29]

6.7 Aerial view of PNG Parliament House, Waigani: spear head flying toward the future?

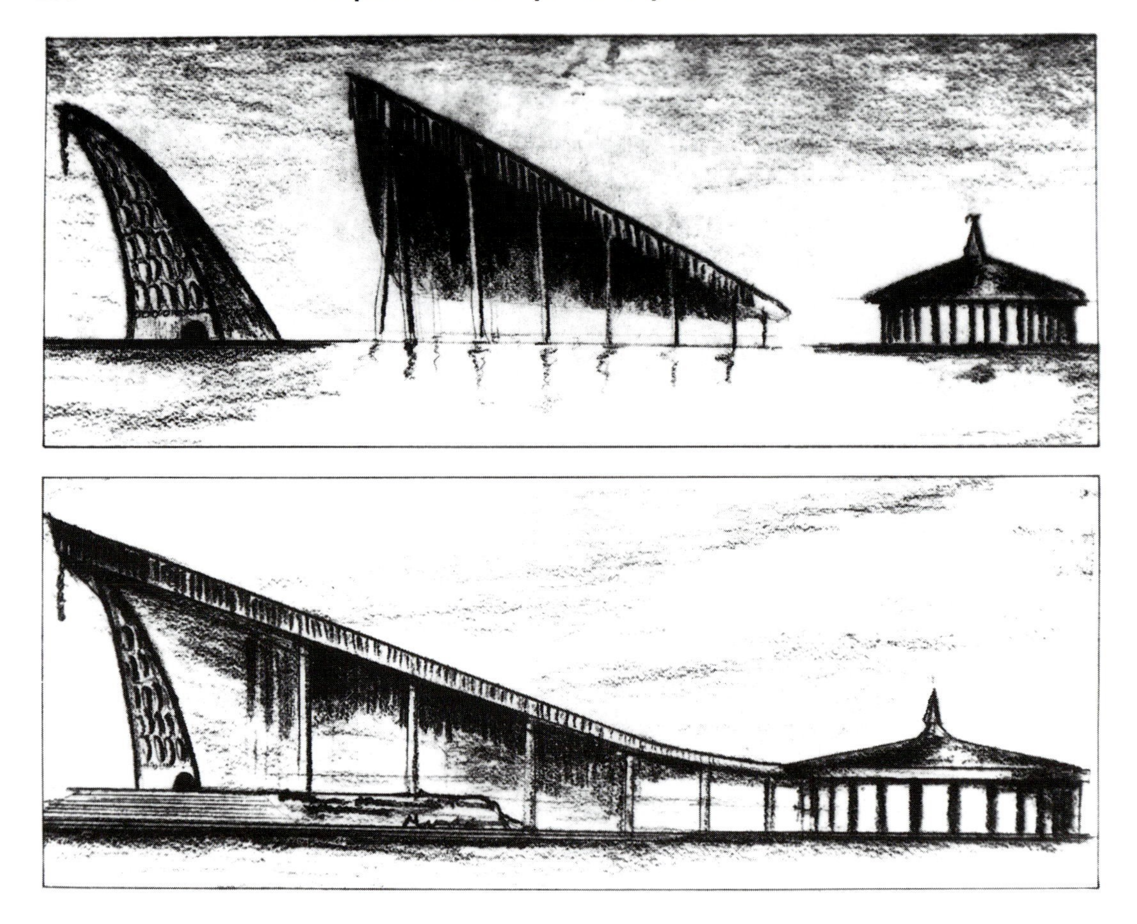

6.8 Hogan sketches: fusing a parliament.

While the commemoration booklet states that the building's form was inspired by the village haus tambaran, not all haus tambarans are created equal.[30] Sketches by Cecil Hogan explain the building's formal genesis as a fusion of two kinds of East Sepik province haus tambaran, with a Highlands raun haus appended to one end (6.8).

The forward-sloping thrust of the haus tambaran type adapted for use as the parliament building's ceremonial entrance may be among the most memorable for the Western observer, but it is by no means a representative piece of architecture for Papua New Guinea as a whole. Although conceivably it can be regarded as a generalized spirit house, this building resonates with the village architecture of a small part of one province, differing from others in the area that have either twin peaks or no leaning upsweep at all (6.9). A closer look at Hogan's haus tambaran precedents reveals that Papua New Guinea's democratic spirit is expected to reside within haus tambaran forms found only in that part of the East Sepik province near the town of Maprik.[31] Not surprisingly, PNG's Somare, who championed this design for the new parliament, was a member of parliament from this same Sepik province.[32] Moreover, this choice of source material for the parliament building is almost completely alien to the village architecture of the Highland provinces, where many tribes did not develop even the institution of the haus tambaran. While there is an explicit reference to

6.9 Haus tambaran from the Maprik area *(below right)* and four kinds of Sepik haus tambarans which do not resemble the kinds found around Maprik.

6.10 Raun haus, Highlands.

6.11 "Raun haus," Waigani.

one type of Highlands raun haus, this is relegated to the recreation block, a secondary aspect of the total composition (even though it does house important state dinners and other festivities) (6.10, 6.11).

The lack of relevance to the building traditions of the Highlands may be seen in the context of a long rivalry between the Highland areas and coastal zones to the north and south. As an exhaustive study of the development of PNG political parties notes, "Highlands members . . . saw themselves as a distinct and neglected section of the country, for which they blamed the [Australian-controlled] administration. Whether the immediate issue was a hospital, a transmitter or a secondary school it seemed to them that some other Districts, especially coastal Districts, were more favoured and found it easier to get what they wanted."[33] Many Highland leaders actually resisted independence, fearing it would provide unfair advantages to the more educated coastal peoples.[34] Osmar White's *Parliament of a Thousand Tribes*, a detailed history of the PNG independence process, emphasizes that the people from the various provinces suffered from "antagonisms" which are "deep rooted in ethnic, cultural and environmental differences."[35] Writing shortly before independence, he concluded: "For many years the prime task of central government in Papua New Guinea will be to prevent destructive fragmentation of the country by secessionist movements or by reversion to inter-tribal warfare. Its methods of keeping cohesion must encourage the growth of 'national' sentiment to the point at which it supersedes the primitive rivalries and jealousies of groups and provides an emotional base for national solidarity."[36] I have found no evidence of special resentment of the building's design on the part of Highland MPs, some of whom held important posts in the Independence coalition government and who would have been in a position to voice objection over the choice of design; yet the dominant Sepik image can still be seen as potentially provocative. Alternatively, however, the metaphor of haus tambaran and raun haus conjoined under a single roof may well convey in architectural terms precisely the desired coalition of opposing forces—lowlands and Highlands, coastal and interior—that is advocated as central to nation building.[37]

SUBNATIONAL AND SUPRANATIONAL SYMBOLISM

The Maprik-area haus tambaran form of the parliament building entrance is not merely a distinctive and memorable shape or the personal favorite of a Sepik-based minister; it is also the indigenous architectural form most widely known to foreigners. Despite the genuine complexities of the building's hybrid architectural lineage, it is clear that the power of its Sepik-derived upswept front remains the dominant shorthand image. Websites for PNG embassies abroad describe the Parliament House building as "constructed in the style of a traditional Sepik River Haus Tambaran," and the official PNG tourism site markets the building as "built in the style of a Maprik Haus Tambaran." For the outsider contemplating the investment of either tourist dollars or development capital, it is an instantly recognizable image derived from the most widely visited and publicized area of the country, an architectural iconography also used for the contemporaneous PNG High Commission in Canberra[38] (6.12). In the international competition for development funding, it is a striking visual image without a hint of factional discord, exactly what a government would wish its national parliament building to convey. The building, thoroughly modernized yet rooted in a traditional village culture, rises as a veritable advertisement for political stability. To an international audience, it will not matter that the designer has iconographically tied the national heritage to the sacred forms of one village culture in particular. This audience will not be told about the multiplicity of cultures that are scrupulously represented in the facade details and full artistic program; it will see only the powerful and marketable massing of the haus tambaran metaphor, the building's main iconic view. In this sense, it is not the use of a particular Sepik form that is at issue, but the more general question of why any *one* highly parochial vernacular form should be charged with the task of representing the multiple cultures of the country as a whole. Although the raun haus appendage and the extensive system of nationally diversified art in all parts of the building mitigate the dominant haus tambaran presence, the appeal of a single central image for the building would seem to be more international than national.

The international nature of the Parliament House audience is made manifest in other ways as well. While the proceedings inside the chamber

6.12 PNG High Commission, Canberra, Australia.

are trilingually transmitted to members (some of whom can neither read nor write) through earphones, the constitutional quotations on the facade are in English (6.13): the facade asserts, in white tile lettering just below a mosaic interpretation of a mighty river, "ALL POWER BELONGS TO THE PEOPLE—ACTING THROUGH THEIR ELECTED REPRESENTATIVES." This credo no doubt attracts the attention of the Australo-Western visitor, but it belies the multilingual discussions within. In the effort to demonstrate the existence of a constitutionally backed national identity, the English facade reveals the international nature of the audience that the designers and promoters of the parliament building wish to reach and convince. Equally important, it is a reminder of the nonorthographic nature of many of PNG's languages and of the fact that English, the language of the most recent colonials, is the government's preferred national language, even if it is not the one most widely spoken in the country. The English language itself is an attempt to mediate among factions and impose a kind of linguistic common denominator.

If the overall massing of the building is intended to be a composite of two Sepik province haus tambarans and a raun haus, the facade treatments and interiors carry the analogy of democratic representation in architecture to a much greater extreme. Throughout the building, there is an attempt to depict the enormous diversity of PNG's component peoples through the symbolic evocation of their art and architecture. Yet, despite the evident sincerity of the effort to make certain that all component peoples will feel duly represented in the design of the National Parliament—the artistic practices of many of PNG's component cultures are indeed alluded to at the level of fine detail—the dominant imagery of the Sepik region seems inescapable.

Archie Brennan, a Scottish designer associated with the National Arts School, was brought in to coordinate the art and architectural embellishment of the building. Brennan's design for the sixty-three-foot-high mosaic on the front facade is adapted from an amalgam of drawings by various "national artists."[39] In its position on the facade, this mosaic replaces the traditional (but far less durable) painted bark totemic and ancestral figures of a Maprik-area haus tambaran with a collection of symbols of wealth taken from everyday PNG village life. Hogan's competition drawings show this facade

6.13 Haus tambaran facade of PNG Parliament House.

as a much more literal evocation of haus tambaran designs than does the Brennan-coordinated eclectic imagery of the finished mosaic, which includes adaptations from drawings made by Highland village artists.[40] In this way, the facade-as-built appears—at least in some of its details—less unequivocally Sepik-based than it did in the architect's original proposal.

If Brennan's interventions permitted a more multivalent set of images within the Sepik framework of the facade, the result is nonetheless an imagery firmly tied to village-based practices, rather than to rapid-paced development. With the exception of a single small image of a helicopter, so stylized as to be almost unrecognizable, the imagery is entirely an evocation of the rural interior, its land, water, and sky. Dress is traditional, not Western, and residences are shown as huts. Wildlife abounds; birds of paradise are depicted as larger than humans (and, indeed, the building as a whole is arguably bird-shaped).[41] Together with symbols of aspiration toward ideals not yet achieved—signified by the constitutional quotations and the equal iconographical treatment given to women—there are symbols of danger: a snake and a crocodile. In spite of the attempts of the facade details to render the Sepik haus tambaran association of the whole more multivalent, this lingering provincialism seems to hold a potential danger of its own.

At the base of the entrance facade mosaic there is a ten-meter lintel of *kwila* wood spanning the entrance, an important feature of some Sepik haus tambarans. On it are nineteen ancestral masks, representing the nineteen provinces, each carved by an artist from a different province (6.14).[42] The carvings differ from one another, but as a representative democracy of artwork they yield a rather bland and studied result, perhaps because the carvers were asked to design masks of exactly the same size and were not permitted to use color.[43] To a Western eye, the result may suggest a lamentable loss of both diversity and vitality, not to mention the wholesale transformation of ritual context, yet the regularity of representation may have been intended to convey egalitarianism among provinces. Perhaps the tension between the dual attractions of equality and individual liberty will always be a part of attempts to forge democracy; here this tension seems to be expressed aesthetically, another instance of national messages being conveyed through a Sepik formal framework.

To enter the building, one pushes door handles carved in the shape of *kundu* drums, another instance of a ritual object being lifted from context and transformed into simply a secular shape that looks indigenous. Inside the building, mixed messages abound (6.15, 6.16). The building retains one unique feature of the traditional haus tambaran in that it has two exits but only one entrance: yet the rest of the interior is the very antithesis of a traditional one, which René Gardi has described as a labyrinth of dark anterooms "where one can make progress only by stooping."[44] In an artificially lit and thoroughly air-conditioned series of large chambers in which the closest thing to spirit figures are periwigged clerks, the sudden shocks still present are very different from those of the village. At no point does the building complex convey the experience of being in one of the traditional structures. All is surface imagery that seems aimed at diluting and uniting diverse traditions into an aesthetically and politically palatable whole.

6.14 Detail of mosaic on haus tambaran facade, with carved lintel below.

6.15 Fish-eye view of PNG Parliament's two-exited entry hall, showing assemblage of carved poles.

6.16 Ground-floor plan of Block A of Parliament House.

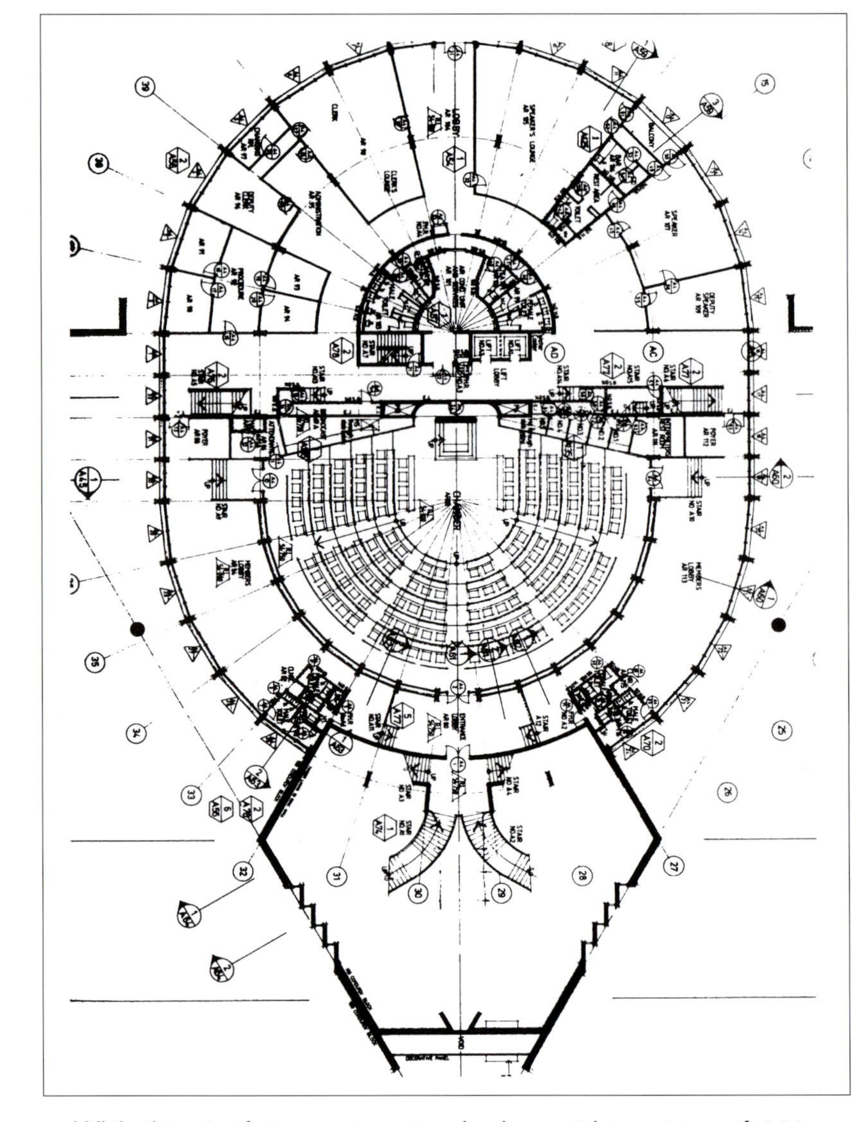

While there is of course no reason why the spatial experience of visiting a modern, functioning Parliament House *should* recreate the spatial experience of the village spirit house, the degree of disconnection here calls into question the nature of the designers' commitments to vernacular precedent. The designers appear to seek useful new roles for old motifs, recognizing that even if these must be dislocated from their village contexts they may retain some value in the consolidation of national identity. By choosing new, collaborative works rather than museum-quality examples of older ritual objects, the designers affirmed that the new building strives to forge a contemporary identity, not a merely nostalgic one, nor one premised on the curatorial judgments of outsiders. Similarly, by insisting on the use of modern, permanent artistic media while eschewing the bush materials traditionally used (and often then discarded) in the course of village cultural practices, the designers and political leadership emphasized the desired durability of the new formal and institutional practices they were trying to invent.

In trying to give equal treatment to the artistic traditions of all the provinces and to exemplify a process of artistic cooperation, the designers encouraged carvers from different tribes and even different regions to work together, a metaphor and ideally a precursor for the integration that politicians sought. According to the official iconography set out in the building's promotional booklet, the speaker's chair, for example, is intended to be a cross between the "basic form" of the one used in the British House of Commons and the traditional "orator's stool" used in ceremonies in the Sepik region; it is analogous to the kind of hybrid political system being molded as well (6.17). Though the idea of the orator's stool comes from the Sepik, the intricate carving surrounding it draws upon motifs from the Trobriand Islands and Milne Bay areas, where the orator's stool is not employed. Moreover, these particular motifs in those places are used not for purposes of ritual gathering but to "decorate . . . ceremonial canoes." As the explanatory booklet concludes, "The whole stylistic range of these motifs has been adapted to the needs of this striking setting." To meet the very

6.17 PNG Parliament interior, showing multicultural speaker's chair.

real need to make the Westminster parliamentary system seem indigenous, the hybrid motifs of PNG's component cultures are admixed with the older invented traditions of the British, producing a new and compound whole.

Such artistic democracy continues: carved into the front of the speaker's desk is a "garamut—a long cylindrical drum carved from one log—[which] has long been used to call people together" in ceremonies on "Manus Island, along the coastal and island communities and in many regions of the mainland"; and the wall surrounding the speaker's chair is "screen printed with paintings of carved masks from the Gulf and Western Provinces." Only the carved wooden panels that surround the chamber and decorate the fronts of the members' desks are provincially neutral: "The motif . . . cannot be identified with any specific region of Papua New Guinea but," we are reassured, "it is closely linked to traditional design."[45]

Inside the Entrance Hall leading to the Parliamentary Chamber there is a fifteen-meter-high assemblage of carved poles which literally bolts together the carving traditions of a dozen regions. Here, the Sepik area work seems dominant, in medium if not necessarily in motif, since the great lengths of *kwila* wood needed for the poles had to be brought from the northern coastal forests. This sculpture, known as *Bung Wantaim* (Coming together), a term frequently used by politicians, refers not only to the finished composite product but also to the composition process itself, the kind of collaboration among artistic traditions that seems intended to project a model for cooperation among partisan factions in parliament as well.[46] In other significant places in the building, however, the coming together is of a different kind. The chairs in the prime minister's lounge, for example, were carved out of one thousand sticks of timber distributed to craftsmen from various Sepik villages, each with a distinctive style of carving, then assembled and padded in Australia.[47]

In all this, there is a certain irony in the artists' efforts to depict a rural and preindustrial life-style in an urban parliament building. In the adapting of traditional forms for this purpose, an enormous dislocation has inevitably occurred. Even if the various permutations of artistic collaboration do undercut some of the dominant Sepik presence of the building itself, collaboration with the demands of a modern institution and building type unknown to any of the earlier village contexts is even more difficult and entails important changes in meaning. What once were intrinsic parts of ritual are now rendered as sculpture. Once-sacred items have been lifted from intricate systems of meanings at the level of family and village and been ascribed new roles having to do with PNG as a nation-state. Thus objectified, under guidance from Western consultants, they are now set to be viewed in Western terms, as art. To begin to fathom how such objects are interpreted by villagers in PNG (or by PNG's more Western-oriented elite), however, would require much further research. Do the sculptures, carvings, and other artwork of the parliament building play a different role from that of the older objects displayed just down the road in the National Museum? Even if these too are displayed in Western terms as art, does it matter that the museum's objects did once play an actual role in rituals? Or are these questions only of concern to Western critics?

In the Parliament House, it may be that this sequence is reversed; the creation of art may precede the creation of its ritual context, and both may become transformed. The process of constructing new rituals for the state, what Hobsbawm calls "the invention of tradition," may over time succeed in infusing the motley objects in the Parliament House with a revived and altered significance for national culture.

To be sure, Brennan claims that the work selected was meant to represent PNG as a whole: "We worked very hard to design something which we felt belonged to this country yet of which one could not immediately say: yes that is Sepik, that is West Highlands, that is Trobriand."[48] In spite of his efforts, a certain Sepik-centrism seems to remain. Much of this was made inevitable by the choice of the dramatic haus tambaran form as the building's ceremonial entry point, a large and structural gesture which sets a frame within which the smaller design gestures operate. Though there are architectural and artistic counterweights to the Sepik presence, other design gestures reinforce it. A commendable cross-cultural fusion can be found in the details of the building, but many of its most prominent gestures advance somewhat less inclusivist messages, while also necessitating dependence upon foreign expertise for their implementation.

Brennan's design for the enormously complex and vibrant ceiling design topping the grand entrance hall and part of the council chamber, for instance, is adapted from that of the painted sago bark "courthouse" ceiling found in the Sepik village of Ambunti. His designs were then flown to Sydney, transferred onto panels with the aid of a photoscanning technique and rendered in a synthetic material that, it is said, resembles a "coarse velvet" when viewed from sixty feet below.[49] If it is true that there were few qualms about making the Ambunti designs shelter an entire country's lawmakers, this suggests a certain loosening of tribal copyright (whether through time-honored processes of asking for permission or through more indiscriminate borrowing) that is at the heart of the nation-building process.

As I have indicated, however, such collaborations occur not only among villages and provinces, but also internationally. The combination of native workmanship and Australian technology appears repeatedly in the stories of how "the big meeting house"[50] was realized. The PNG Department of Works and Supply hired Peddle Thorp & Harvey to manage the project, with the stipulation that the Australians maximize and diversify the national involvement in the effort. The need for outside assistance was acute since, as of 1984, the building industry in PNG was dominated by expatriate-owned firms, with indigenous builders accounting for only 5 percent of the output.[51] The realization of the parliament building represents a logistical and managerial triumph, one endowed with harrowing tales of moving large objects (such as ten-meter logs) from Sepik swampland to the building site. In an effort to use local material resources, the desgners employed as little steel as possible, and all concrete bricks were made nearby. A high percentage of the work force were PNG nationals, and local subcontractors were used whenever possible.[52]

One benefit of the Parliament House of potentially lasting significance for the building industry was the initiation of a glulaminate factory, formed to manufacture the ceiling beams. This factory was expected not only to continue to function, but also to use new milling techniques developed during the parliament project which would allow white oak (found in abundance on the island) to be used for furniture and other wood products.[53] Nonetheless, there are grounds for skepticism about the effects of the parliament building on the PNG building industry. Much of the technology developed may well have been irrelevant to at least the immediate postparliament building needs. As John Nankervis of Peddle Thorp & Harvey noted, evidently without grasping the full irony of his words, "This project has been of immense value to this country. The expertise which has been developed among the nationals involved in the building is considerable. Unfortunately, a lot of their expertise will be lost as most of them will be unable to find a similar job again, which is really a shame now that they have gained the skills."[54] Despite having learned a great deal "in terms of structural problems and material problems," Nankervis adds, most of those employed on the project "will either go back to their villages or just hang around Port Moresby with nothing to do."[55]

Yet, on many levels, the building is very appropriate for its purpose. As an advertisement for independence and as an idealization of the hopes for representative democracy, the building inspires confidence. Both the process and the product show evidence of a nationalist assertiveness, despite the inevitable reliance upon Australian and expatriate expertise. Nonetheless, if this ten-year process of decision making and construction indicates anything, it is the supreme importance attached to the design of this building and the overarching concern that it contribute to national identity, whatever the cost.

That cost was judged far too high by the building's many detractors. They protested against the expenditure for the building when its $10-million-dollar estimated cost was first announced, and they continued to complain as actual costs tripled during the next eight years. One 1984 editorial in the Papua New Guinea *Post-Courier* condemned the "craze on building national monuments," and suggested that the new Parliament House was good only for the "flattery all those visiting VIPs will heap on us."[56] Another suggested that not only the building but the parliamentary members themselves were "a waste of the taxpayers' money."[57] Such disparagement did not go uncountered, and, a month before the building was formally opened on 7 August 1984, Prime Minister Somare railed against the "persistent and narrow-minded criticism" of some newspaper writers who, he claimed, resisted "our continued efforts to make our new Parliament a place of national significance."[58]

Even as an estimated 20,000 people gathered outside to hear the amplified words of Prince Charles, complaints continued. More than two hundred University of PNG students marched to protest the "unnecessary expenditure" of a building described as "a useless monument only for the privileged few"; they were offered ten minutes to air their views at the opening ceremony.[59] The student protests were backed by members of the Public Employees Association, a union of 50,000 government workers whose president, Napolean Liosi, complained that "there were signs of financial difficulties in PNG and in the midst of all these, we have a K24 million monument."[60] Adding to the dissent, a local MP charged that the Parliament House was built on "stolen land" and insisted upon restitution in full to the Motu-Koita people.[61] Others had yet a different gripe. Following the opening ceremony, the government of the North Solomons Province demanded an apology from Prime Minister Somare, whose parliamentary dedication speech had failed to acknowledge "the contributions by the North Solomons people and their elected leaders."[62] It is unclear whether these people felt any sense of iconographic under-representation as well or, more generally, whether any specific architectural aspects of the building had much effect on its initial reception. In a special edition of the *Post-Courier* on 10 September 1985 marking the tenth anniversary of PNG's independence, complaints went public again, and one politician charged that the Parliament House was "a monument to our blind dependence on outside know-how."[63]

Whatever the view of its architectural merits or the nature of the collaborations involved in producing it, the completion of the Parliament House evidently prompted much reflection not only on the building but also on the institution to be housed within it. In fact, it is rare to find an instance of the two issues being differentiated. The opening-day speeches of PNG government officials and Prince Charles (who was about to begin his self-appointed reign as the world's most prominent critic of architecture) consistently emphasized the connections between architectural symbolism and political practice. House Speaker Bonga spoke of the need to integrate the Westminster system of parliament and the Melanesian consensus system of decision making and described the new building as "our monument to that development and our pledge to its continuance."[64] Prime Minister Somare, oscillating with seeming ease between talk of architecture and talk of political institutions, described the "new Parliament" as "inspiring and beautiful" and concluded that "its construction will be recorded in history as the major achievement of the post independence decade."[65] Somare implied that the construction of a "magnificent building" was not only a symbol of governmental progress, but a necessary precursor to the construction of a magnificent parliamentary institution. Even more wishful in his comments was the Prince of Wales, who noted that a building in the "haus tambaran style" would have "real meaning for the people of PNG" and stated that "such a building will help to reinforce the importance Papua New Guineans attach to such things as parliamentary institutions, membership of the Commonwealth, concern for the peace, stability and prosperity of South-East Asia and the South Pacific, [and] the links of the churches—things that form some of the principal values of this nation."[66] Though the prince's articulation of a far-flung realm of mediated references for the building attests to its potential for instilling pride and confidence, a more balanced *Post-Courier* editorial summed up the mixed feelings engendered by the completion of this building:

> For Mr Somare, and others, the new House is a fitting monument to Papua New Guinea's status and its perpetuation of parliamentary democracy. . . . Those far removed from Parliament's heady influence are not impressed. They argue, many of them cogently, that symbols

> and monuments are worthless unless the ideals those symbols and monuments represent are transformed into living, tangible assets.
>
> Where, they ask, are life's fundamentals: health services for all; education for all; employment.
>
> Amid the pageantry, the praise and the pride of this morning's official opening, MPs should remember that out there in the real world, away from the rosewood and Stuart crystal and carpet, all is not well.
>
> That in their electorates there are people whose bellies crave for real sustenance and who expect, indeed demand, that their elected leaders strive to get it for them.
>
> Only when MPs demonstrate that they are deserving of their peoples' trust will their people concede that MPs are deserving of this magnificent House of Parliament.[67]

Any expensive building sponsored by a government that has pressing responsibilities will be criticized not only in terms of its architecture but in terms of opportunities lost, funds misdirected. Papua New Guinea's Parliament House is no exception. Also typical of government efforts to use architecture in the production of national identity is that some aspects of this identity are pursued more obviously than others.

The costs of this building seem very high, and not just in terms of money. For all the attempts at introducing and highlighting the artistic traditions of the multitude of cultures that compose the new state, there is a danger that this exercise in national identity-making will act to trivialize the roots of the culture it professes to promote. Just as self-conscious as the building itself, many of the sculptural details appear compromised and enervated, if they are to be judged by Western criteria for art. Can it be that art-by-committee is more commendable for its process than for its product? And, if the process is the most important part of the product, who besides the artists themselves and the leadership of the National Arts School will be able to convey the value of these collaborative processes to visitors? Is the process of collaboration among PNG tribal groups to be valued differently from the process of collaboration among village artists, Western art consultants, and Australian technology?

In the synthetically reproduced Ambunti "courthouse" canopy, for instance, the designs are stripped of their traditional associations with a legend or an event and are valued only for color and texture: "The mural consists of more than 300 panels, each approximately 2m × 1m. A close study will reveal that only 14 different design units are used but, by careful juxtaposition and rotation and by the nature of the design of the panels, an ever-changing imagery is achieved."[68] While there is a facile appeal to the analogy between "the power and guidance gained from ancestors overlooking" important decisions in the haus tambaran and the "fitting canopy" hung over the National Parliament, the manipulation of "design units" to achieve "ever-changing imagery" is a total reversal of the traditional role. Yet, perhaps such judgment misses the point.

The distortion that takes place between the traditional canopy and the modern one is probably not only functionally necessary but also symbolically appropriate. Surely it would have been no less disconcerting if the deteriorating Ambunti bark cloth ceiling had been inserted in its original form. And, over time, the new ceiling may also come to be associated with legends and events tied to parliamentary rule. The mediation of high technology in the transformation of art is thoroughly in keeping with the arrival of modern parliamentary institutions and the recognition that the village cultures are, themselves, rapidly losing their insularity. Does this kind of pseudo-literal transformation mark a change of meaning that will hasten the decline of the village original? Or can this art continue to exist simultaneously in two different contexts, playing two different roles? The original bark paintings were never intended as direct representations of ancestors, legends, and events. Their interpretation always depended on prodigious powers of abstraction by the villagers, even when specific iconographical references were widely known. In the Suau language there is a word, *gigibori*—translated literally as *heat*—which describes this nonformal property of objects having a special power, authority, or prestige. According to the editors of a now-defunct journal bearing this name, *gigibori* refers to "the inner strength of the carving, to its magical potency, its soul or expression."[69] In the Parliament House, however, the abstraction is of a different order and seems far more limited. For better or worse, the transformed and transposed ceiling is related to the phenomenon known as tourist art and is completely in keeping with the tourist architecture that frames it.[70]

TOURIST ARCHITECTURE?

Tourist art, a phenomenon of increasing prevalence in recent decades, is defined as "a process of communication involving image creators who attempt to represent aspects of their own cultures to meet the expectations of image consumers who treat art as an aspect of the exotic."[71] In that the parliament building is not available for purchase and is more than a tourist attraction, it cannot be considered tourist art, but there is a sense in which the building is consumed. What is consumed is its image—the image that the leadership of the new state wishes to convey to its own people and to the world. While such consumption occurs in the case of any public building with a strong image, whether in Waigani or in Washington, there may be special consequences when its presence acts to consume a vernacular tradition as well. The production of tourist art and, by extension, tourist architecture inevitably involves the negation of the original culture-bound meanings and ritual associations of a given artifact and its transmutation into a marketable work of art. As Nelson Graburn has observed, this transaction "involves an increasing tendency among the artists to speak *only* to the consumer and to remove those elements of style or content that might prove contradictory, puzzling, or offensive to the unknown buyer. . . . In the headlong rush to please the tourists and the taste-makers the artisan finds himself in danger of surrendering control of his product."[72] In Papua New Guinea, the emerging class of indigenous "taste-makers" cultivates a kind of sophisticated primitivism that projects both a domestically advantageous demonstration of political order and an internationally palatable, and stylistically recognizable, artistic identity. Only in the context of a Western notion of art (a notion long since understood even in remote villages where carvers now cater to the tourist urge for some tribal decorations) could the Westerner's preference for Sepik products be understood by those who designed the parliament building.

Sometimes, though, Westerners prefer the "real thing." This phenomenon reached a controversial peak in 2004 when an Australian gallery owner, aided by the PNG National Museum, purchased an actual Maprik haus tambaran, replete with all of its "wood carvings, totem poles, storyboard, and other historical traditional artifacts," ostensibly for reassembly and "preservation" in Melbourne.[73]

Gellner argues that those who are actively concerned with the process of nation-building in a rapidly evolving society often try to eliminate many aspects of "the alien high culture" but do not replace this with "the old local low culture." Instead, he claims, nationalist ideology "revives, or invents, a local high (literate, specialist-transmitted) culture of its own," which retains certain connections to the "earlier folk styles and dialects." We see such invention in the hybrid links between village tradition and Westminster practice that pervade both the parliament and the Parliament House of PNG. What, though, is the attitude of designers and more cosmopolitan national politicians toward the village cultures that are the subject of such formal allusions? "Generally speaking," Gellner contends, "nationalist ideology suffers from pervasive false consciousness. Its myths invert reality: it claims to defend folk culture while in fact it is forging a high culture."[74] Is this what motivates the art and architecture of the PNG Parliament House? On what basis can the forging of a national high culture be judged? It is easy to chart discontinuities and the often crude attempts to bridge them, but hard to know how new meanings are being created and received by various constituencies.

If the Waigani parliament building is termed tourist architecture, for instance, it must be pointed out that not all tourists are foreigners. Still caught up in the intrigue of independence, the general populace is quite taken with the building; those who can afford to do so seek to visit it, and protests against the wisdom of this great expenditure have dissipated.[75] To point out that the building's artists and architects were concerned with fashioning the international identity of their country is not at all to dismiss their creation or to demean the personal rewards that participation in this venture may well have brought.

As PNG approached its twenty-fifth anniversary of independence during the millennial year of 2000, the Parliament House gained new controversy when parliamentary speaker Bernard Narokobi arranged for a large illuminated cross to be affixed to the top of the edifice. To Narokobi, a devout Catholic in a country where the 2000 census found that 96.2 percent of the population self-identified as Christians, the cross represented "the light of Calvary." He called it "a memory of our hope in the future as Christians." Other members of parliament strongly criticized

Narokobi's actions. Rather than argue that the cross might give offense to the country's many non-Christian minority groups, however, the counter arguments centered on "the inappropriateness of putting a cross on a 'profane' building like the House of Assembly." The debate occurred not only in the parliamentary chamber but also in the pages of daily newspapers. As one commentator put it, the juxtaposition of forms was an insult to the symbolism of the cross, since "the National Parliament has become a place where Members of Parliament argue, swear and plot ways to destroy each other. The National Parliament is not a holy place. You can never put darkness and daylight together." Another citizen preferred to leave the cross intact and to instead disassemble the "immoral naked carvings" of the mosaic haus tambaran facade beneath it, since "these images represent and manifest the activities of unseen ungodly evil spirits that have been the force behind all these wrong doings." Speaker Narokobi defended the cross as a reminder of PNG's Christian values and argued that parliamentary decisions were also sacred since they were for the common good of the people. Eventually, however, other politicians overturned support for the rooftop cross on a day when Narokobi was absent from the Speaker's chair, so it was removed. As one scholar of Melanesian politics and religion observes, Narokobi's failed campaign illustrates a tension in contemporary Papua New Guinea between a theology that sees "an unavoidable conflict between the kingdom of God and the realm of Satan" and a theology that could view parliamentary action as a sacred extension of the public good. Given such tension, religion and politics are necessarily commingled.[76]

As the building settles into its various cultural roles, it may take on wholly unforeseen meanings. Some of these may have only tangential relation to its architectural form, some may be intrinsically tied. Perhaps it will become a rallying point for representative democracy, a symbol of its institutional strengths and shortcomings. Perhaps it will become a hated symbol of the dominance of one part of the country over another. Possibly a future generation of feminists will object to a National Assembly inspired by a village "men's house," where the presence of women was forbidden.[77] Or perhaps most visitors will be reassured by the literal references to village life and the multicultural richness of the metaphors, and the building will, through its art and architecture, carry proudly the integrative nationalist ideology championed in the rhetoric of its sponsors. Ideally, future Papua New Guinean architects will be encouraged to explore the rich, diverse architectural heritage of their country in ways which transcend the reliance upon the Maprik-area haus tambaran as a type and which do so in transformative ways that are less prone to oversimplification. Though it now seems a product of a unique combination of social, political, technological, artistic, and architectural conditions, over time the building itself may well become a factor in subsequent change. The spirit of collaboration and cross-fertilization, however forced and awkward, already plays a part in the invention and evolution of new national traditions. The concrete haus tambaran of the Papua New Guinea Parliament House may someday even develop a *gigibori* of its own.

CHAPTER 7

Sri Lanka's island parliament

Sri Lanka, known as Ceylon until 1972, gained independence from its British colonial administration in 1948, but its new parliament building was not commissioned until thirty years later (7.1–7.3). The parliament complex, built on the outskirts of Colombo in a place called Sri Jayawardhanapura Kotte (meaning "the blessed fortress city of growing victory"), was more the result of internal party politics since independence than of national liberation from the British. Although the need to expand the facilities of the Sri Lankan government had been acknowledged for many years, the inspiration for the project came only with the election in 1977 of members of Junius R. Jayewardene's United National Party to five-sixths of the seats in

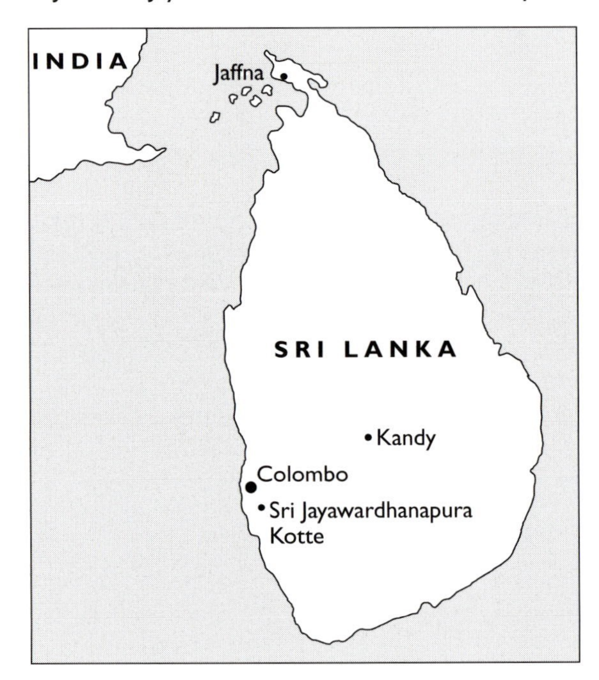

7.1 Sri Lanka.

7.2 Sri Lanka's island parliament.

7.3 Interior of Sri Lanka's parliament building.

the national assembly, an abrupt electoral turnaround that ended the control of the United Front government led by Sirimavo Bandaranaike's Sri Lanka Freedom Party.

Inspiration for the new building coincided not only with a new regime, but also with two other crucial political developments, each of which weakened the National Parliament institutionally. The first was a new constitution in 1978, which brought in a Gaullist presidential model and entailed a sizable increase in executive power that enabled Prime Minister Jayewardene to take on the title of president as well.[1] In 1982, he gained further control over the machinery of constitutional government. Having been reelected for another six years, he proceeded to freeze the electoral cycle with a referendum delaying general elections until 1989.[2] The second incursion into the potential authority of the National Parliament was the revival of fighting

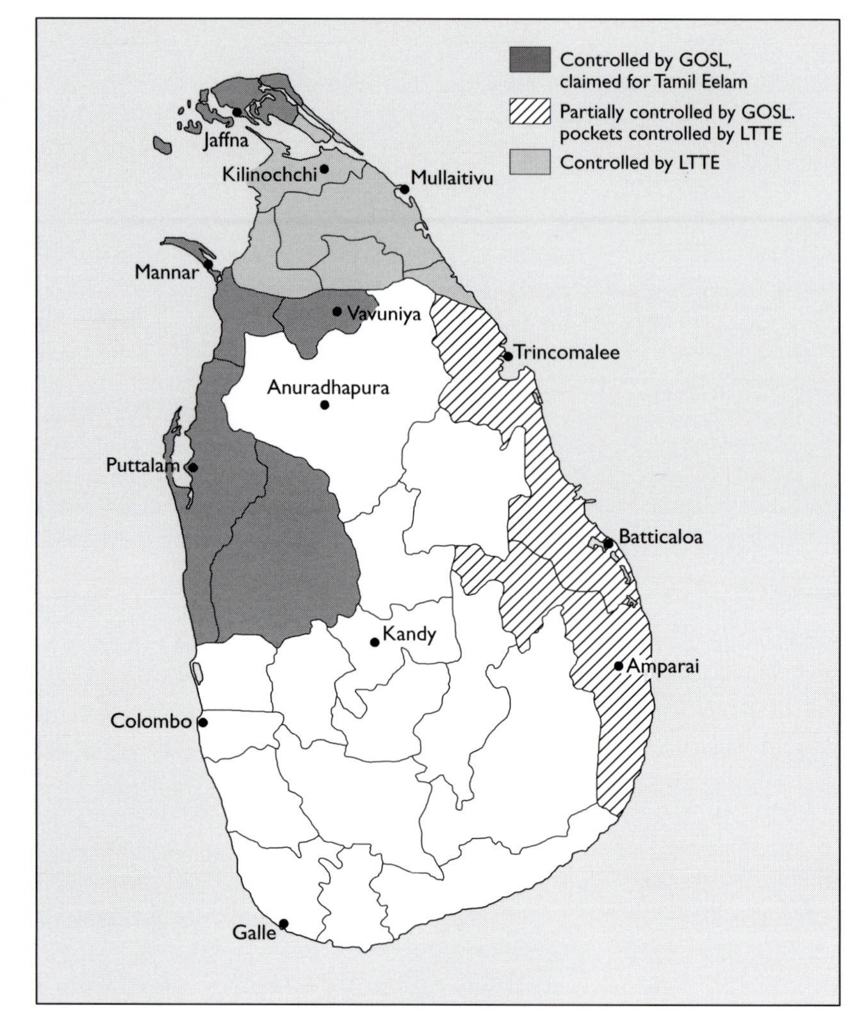

7.4 Sri Lanka, showing areas claimed by/for Tamil Eelam as of 2006.

LTTE = Liberation Tigers of Tamil Eelam

GOSL = Government of Sri Lanka

between the two major ethnic groups on the island, the Sinhalese majority, who controlled the government, and the Tamil minority, who were pressing for a separate state of Tamil Eelam (7.4).

The patterns of ethnic, religious, linguistic, and political affiliations in Sri Lanka are extremely complex and have been the subject of numerous books and articles. This chapter, focusing on issues of architecture and urban design, cannot do justice to the intricacies of these strains, yet, because the issues of capitol complex design are inextricable from these more basic conflicts, some background is necessary. According to the census of 1981 (the last census that was able to survey all areas of the country), of a population of about 15 million, Sinhalese Sri Lankans constitute approximately 74 percent of the total and are predominantly Buddhist. The predominantly Hindu Tamil minority constitutes about 18 percent of the population; two-thirds of them are known as Sri Lankan, or Jaffna, Tamils. The other one-third, the Indian Tamils, number about one million and live primarily in the Central Highlands and south. They are descendants of low-caste bonded laborers brought by the British in the nineteenth century to work the tea plantations. By contrast, the heterogeneous and predominantly high-caste Jaffna Tamils, whose roots on the island date back two thousand years, are proud heirs of the ancient Tamil kingdoms; it is they who have been leading the fight for an independent homeland. In addition, there are some one million Muslims, constituting 7 percent of the population, and also a sizable and transethnic Christian minority, primarily Roman Catholic.[3] In recent decades, which have seen the Indian Tamils, Sri Lankan Tamils, and Muslims each forming movements and identities, the Sri Lankan political scene has been both diverse and divisive.

Tensions between the Sinhalese and the Sri Lankan Tamils have existed for two millennia; following independence and Sinhalese pushes for Sinhala as the single national language, passions once again exploded, exhibiting an unprecedented degree of ethnic mobilization and polarization. As Stanley Tambiah has argued, "It is in the postindependence, nationalistic, allegedly 'modernizing' epoch of democratic politics that the Sri Lankan ethnic conflicts have worsened."[4] Before independence, British imperial policy dictated a single English-speaking administration, and there was less evidence of sectarian strife: "The Sinhalese and the Tamils ruled jointly, the rulers being the élite of Ceylon's colonial 'old boys' club. They had grown up playing cricket and rugby together, had shared membership in the fashionable clubs, had gone through university together. They appeared to regard themselves as Ceylonese, not Tamils or Sinhalese."[5] The British "divide and rule" policy that had favored the professional advancement of the Tamil minority did not last long in a postcolonial environment. Indian Tamils were denied citizenship and thus could no longer vote,[6] and beginning in 1956 all Tamils, whether immigrant or not, suffered from the government's decision to make Sinhala the sole official language in place of English. Moreover, Tambiah notes, "the revival and sponsorship of Buddhism as an integral feature of Sinhalese 'national' identity and cultural pride resulted in adding religion to language as an emotionally charged factor in Sri Lankan politics." In 1972, the country's first postindependence constitution not only entrenched Sinhala as the official language, but also established Buddhism as the only religion meriting state support.[7] Between 1956 and 1980, the Tamils' share of government jobs dropped from 50 percent to 11 percent.[8]

In 1983, following a week of anti-Tamil riots that killed 3,000, destroyed at least 18,000 Tamil homes, damaged 5,000 Tamil places of business, and drove 150,000 into refugee camps,[9] the government asked Tamil parliamentarians to take an oath of allegiance to the "unitary state" of Sri Lanka. Asked to swear that they opposed even peaceful efforts to gain separatism in the north, the sixteen Tamil members of the parliamentary opposition refused, resigning their seats.[10] Riots and other disturbances related to the aims of Tamil separatists plagued the Jayewardene government throughout the 1980s and continued to preoccupy the governments of his successors.[11] Tamil/Sinhalese tensions were exacerbated by the violence of the radical Sinhalese of the People's Liberation Front, who resisted any concessions to the Liberation Tigers of Tamil Eelam.[12] Caught between the claims of many diverse factions—the separatist demands of the Tamils, the political clout of Buddhist monks, internal party schisms, unstable governing coalitions, and the attacks of the radical ultranationalists, all of which has led to violence and electoral boycotts—parliamentary democracy has struggled in Sri Lanka, however elegant the new building meant to house it. Jayewardene had swept to victory in 1977 on a platform of "righteous" conduct, but it had not been clear whether this meant evenhandedness or signaled a continued rise in the importance of Buddhism in national government. Some Tamil separatists may have expected him to be less of a Sinhalese chauvinist than his predecessors, but for the next thirty years the country faced extended civil unrest punctuated by tenuous ceasefires.

Civil wars are not resolved through architecture, though the new parliamentary complex for Sri Lanka, designed by Sri Lankan architect Geoffrey Bawa, provides far greater evidence of consolidation in the realm of architecture than has been possible thus far in the arena of politics. Yet Sri Lanka's parliament building cannot be understood separately from the government it is meant to house and serve. And in this, in spite of the architect's efforts, the Bawa parliament would seem not to serve all segments of Sri Lanka equally. While the design for the complex is praiseworthy in its acceptance and transformation of the architectural languages of many epochs, the building—when seen in relation to the mythohistorical manipulations of its highly charged site—seems an exercise in recalling and advancing an idealized golden age of unchallenged Sinhalese supremacy over the whole island.

This Sinhalese-centrism is not, however, primarily a matter of architecture but of attempts to manipulate urban design to serve political ends. To understand more about the realm of meanings in which this capitol complex may operate, it is important to discuss the political conditions surrounding the commission and the historical associations embedded in the choice of site. Thus, I differentiate among the following factors:

Geoffrey Bawa's architectural pluralism
The politics of a parliamentary island
The Sinhalese master plan.

GEOFFREY BAWA'S ARCHITECTURAL PLURALISM

Geoffrey Bawa's capitol complex stands squarely between the abstract universalism of high modernism and the literal localism of PNG's concrete haus tambaran. Occupying this middle ground, Bawa sought to capitalize upon indigenous formal traditions without either trivializing them or rendering them incomprehensibly abstruse. The monumentality of the Sri Lankan complex is mitigated by a recognizable iconography, one obviously rooted in Sri Lankan traditions. The success of the building is that it does not attempt to capture or represent all Sri Lankan culture with a single image or with a series of images in which each image represents a component culture. Its strength is the multivalence of its references, the willingness and the ability of its architect to draw upon many parts of Sri Lanka's eclectic architectural history. Bawa's parliament building design is inclusive in its approach to history without descending into caricature or pastiche. Although such a result could conceivably have been achieved without the design skills of an indigenous architect, Bawa's leadership is a milestone for postcolonial parliament building design.

However much one might wish to romanticize Bawa's indigenousness, he is far more than a locally produced phenomenon. Educated in English literature and law in Cambridge and London, he became a barrister, a world traveler, and the owner of a rubber plantation before returning to England in his late thirties to complete a degree in architecture at London's Architectural Association. His work, though attentive to the long tradition of Sri Lankan religio-royal architecture as well as to its vernacular roots, shows a thorough consciousness of modern Western architecture. After executing a flurry of commissions in the 1970s and 1980s, Bawa gained the international reputation that comes from glossy guest appearances on the pages of *Architectural Review* and *MIMAR*, leading to a full-length monograph published in 1986 and culminating in the publication of *Geoffrey Bawa: The Complete Works* in 2002, a year before the architect's death at the age of 83. After decades during which architecturally ambitious developing nations relied on foreign designers for reasons of prestige as well as expertise, the rise of Geoffrey Bawa heralded a heartening change in the balance of trade. Bawa's work exhibits a willingness to confront both the national and the international identities that new states as well as established ones seek to forge.[13] In any state, especially one in which subnational ethnic tensions run high, such identity is cultivated selectively.

Before I attempt to relate the capitol complex to Sinhalese–Tamil conflicts, it is important to recognize Bawa's success in transcending political cleavages. If it were possible to divorce the architecture from the politics, the building might well occupy a less potentially contentious symbolic place. Yet, precisely because parliament buildings are so directly engendered by politics and are commissioned with political as well as aesthetic intent, they cannot be separated from politics for very long. If one wishes to probe the relation between a capitol complex and its cultural context, a purely formalist analysis will not suffice.

Bawa himself resisted the need to infuse nonaesthetic perspectives into the evaluation of his work. In the cultural diversity he was willing and able to champion, he was more eclectic than most politicians would dare to be. As he put it, in a rare public statement by a highly private man, "I like to regard all past and present good architecture in Sri Lanka as just that—good Sri Lankan architecture—for this is what it is, not narrowly classified as Indian, Portuguese or Dutch, early Sinhalese or Kandyan or British Colonial, for all the good examples of these periods have taken the country itself into first account." And in his execution of the commission for a new parliament building, Bawa's "good Sri Lankan architecture" confronts an impressively panhistoric array of influences. Appropriately, too, his office's design and management team contained architect Vasantha Jacobsen (a Sinhalese Buddhist), engineer K. Poologasundram (a Jaffna Tamil), as well as Bawa himself—an agnostic Christian Burgher-Moor who, in his later years, preferred the self-appellation "Ceylonese."[14]

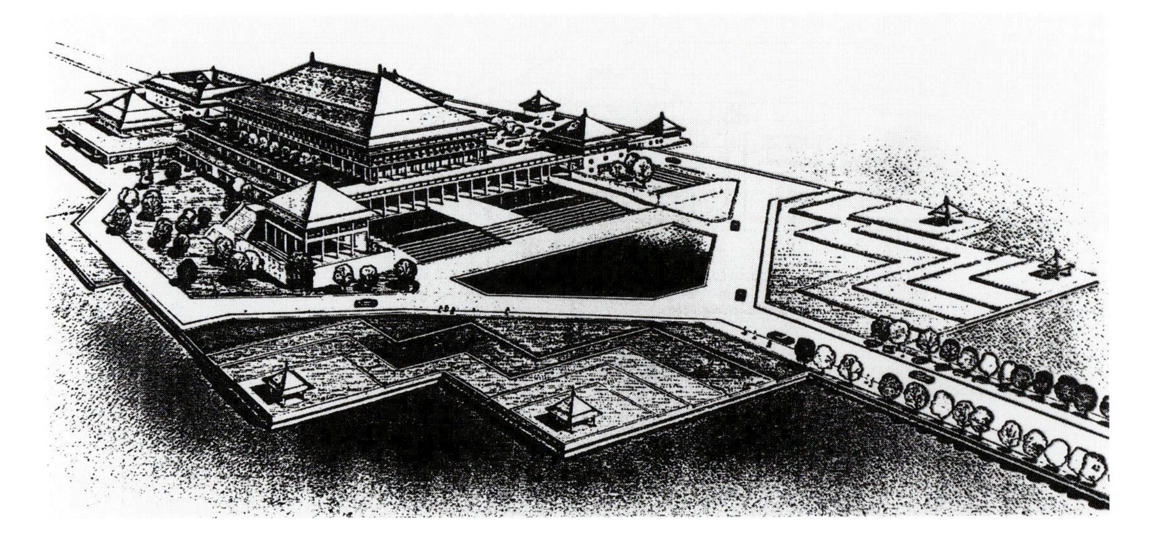

7.5 Perspective of parliament island.

The parliamentary compound is—like Sri Lanka itself—an island and rises from the water like some sacred fortress (7.5). As such, the new capitol complex may be seen as a direct evocation of waterfront temple complexes of the Sri Lankan past. It recalls the ancient habit of linking palaces with large, man-made lakes known as tanks, which are used for agricultural irrigation and are still a prominent feature of the Sri Lankan landscape.[15] Yet Bawa's work recalls not only classical Sri Lanka's waterfront temples, but also the blocky impregnability of the Portuguese, Dutch, and British colonial forts which guarded nearby Colombo in subsequent eras.

If it has aspects of a fortress, however, it is no monolith. Rather, it is a complex of buildings with a clear hierarchy. Like temple precincts of the past, it has one dominant structure in the center and smaller, subservient ones arrayed around it. Here, appropriately, the parliamentary chamber is granted visual supremacy, while other functions, such as an MPs' dining facility, a reception hall, a service block, and security offices, are distributed into smaller pavilions which radiate from the central portion in pinwheel fashion (7.6). The spaces are interconnected by open colonnades and arcades which are suggestive of streets in colonial Colombo, though the colonnades are even more reminiscent of precolonial examples, such as the Audience Hall in the Dalada Maligawa (Temple of the Sacred Tooth Relic) complex at Kandy. While also European in derivation, perhaps, the colonnades appear at the capitol complex in their indigenous adaptation, having been made with traditional craft techniques and intricate timberwork. The building provides visual evidence that the influence of the West upon Sri Lankan architecture began long before the import of twentieth-century modernism and materials; it bespeaks a willingness to accept cultural exchange as the operative rule throughout the island's turbulent history. This architecture appears to deny that Sri Lanka can be captured or represented through the invocation of any single architectural essence. To integrate indigenous forms from many cultures and many ages is to adopt a broad definition of what qualifies as Sri Lankan and to avoid the pitfalls of reductionism.

The Sri Lankan parliament building avoids the opposite pitfall, that of

7.6 **Plan of parliament island and section through parliament complex.**

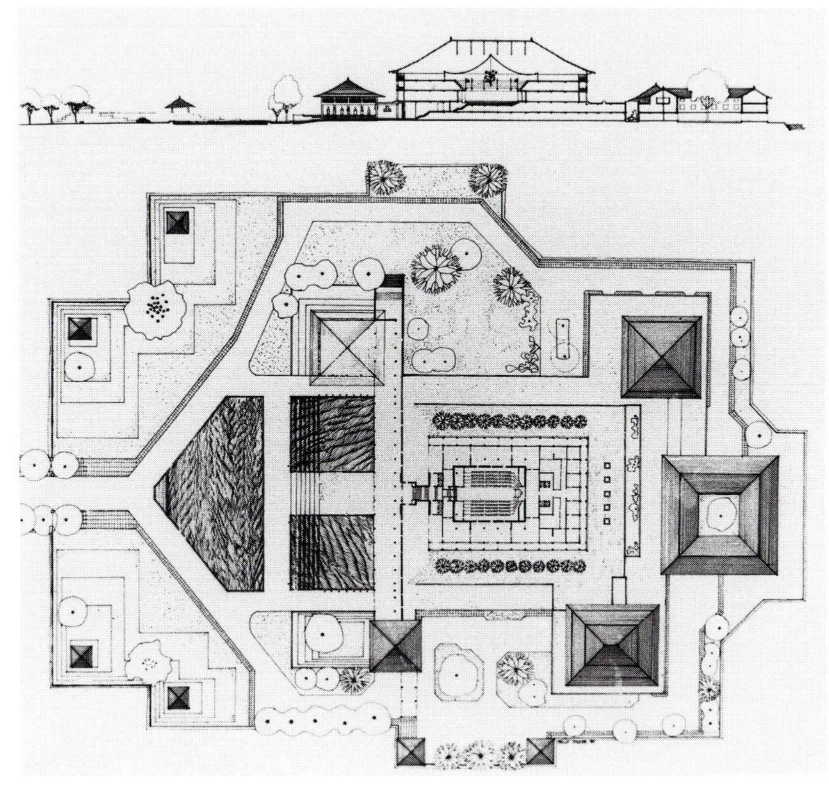

pastiche, largely because there is one dominant formal element in the design. More than anything, the parliamentary complex is identifiable as Sri Lankan because of its roofs. Whereas Hogan was confronted with a multiplicity of indigenous roof forms in Papua New Guinea, each associated with a particular group, Bawa worked within an integrated architectural tradition of roofmanship. Certainly there are important identifiably parochial exceptions to this, such as the Buddhist stupa, but the long history of intercultural exchange and architectural miscegenation has made most forms much less univocal in their references. In other words, Bawa could begin by working with roofs without necessarily choosing sides in so doing. As Bawa puts it, "One unchanging element of all buildings is the roof—protective, emphatic, and all important—governing the aesthetic whatever the period, wherever the place. Often a building is only a roof, columns and floors—the roof dominant, shielding, giving the contentment of shelter. . . . The roof, its shape, texture and proportion is the strongest visual factor."[16] Here, the roofs of the capitol complex adopt the characteristic double pitch of the monastic and royal buildings of precolonial Kandy, a roof form familiar from earlier architecture as well (7.7–7.9). This allusion to some of Sri Lanka's most revered monuments is a reminder, too, of the need for unity between the Kandyan highlands and the lowlands of Colombo. In contemporary Sri Lanka, though, the rift between highland and lowland peoples has paled beside that of the Tamil–Sinhalese schism. Bawa takes advantage of a tradition of roof design that does not connote Sinhala or Tamil, so even his reference to the roofscape of Kandy is not necessarily partisan. For several

7.7 Nineteenth-century view of Kandy's Temple of the Sacred Tooth Relic.

7.8 Lankatilaka Vihara, outside Kandy.

hundred years Kandy's queens and their entourages had come from mainland India: it is definitely not a purely Sinhalese city.

Though the graceful, evocative rooflines of the building may be the complex's dominant formal aspect, many who have visited it prefer to emphasize its careful, thorough integration with the landscape and climate of Sri Lanka, so characteristic of Bawa's smaller built projects. Yet the development of the Sri Jayawardhanapura Kotte site to some extent entailed working against the forces of nature. Though Bawa did site his buildings in relation to existing mangosteen trees, the island itself is largely an artificial creation of landfill and swamp draining and initially seemed somewhat at

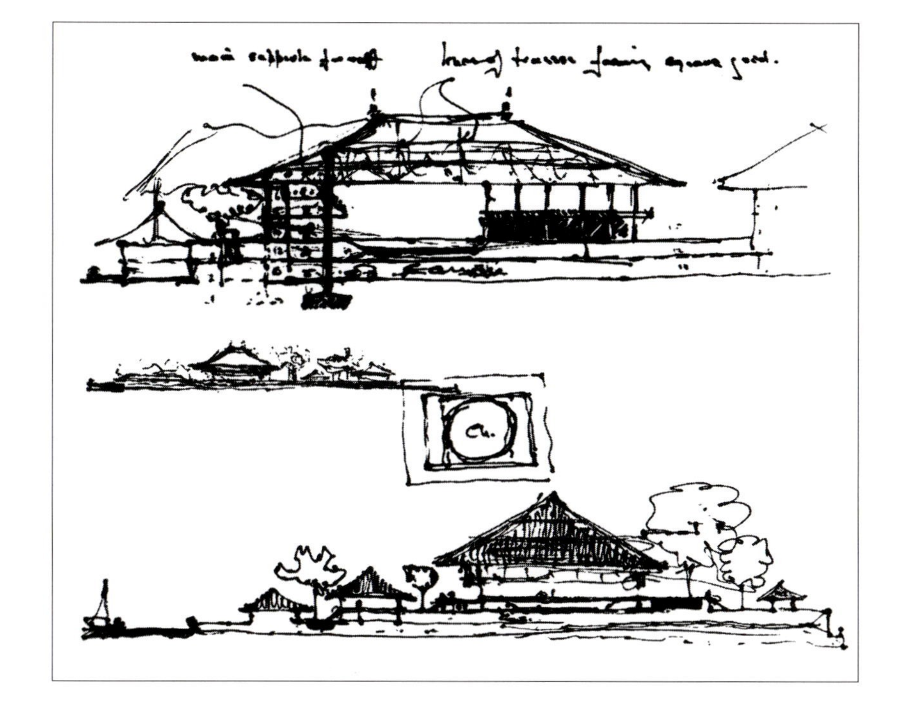

7.9 Preliminary sketches by Bawa, emphasizing the roofs.

odds with the lushness found nearly everywhere else in the Sri Lankan landscape. With the growth of the trees and the oxidation of the grand copper roofs, however, the buildings eventually approached the organic continuity with the landscape that is characteristic of Bawa's best work.

Part of the reason this building lacks some of the intimacy of Bawa's other work may be attributable to the construction process. Bawa, who preferred to work in the style of the traditional master builder, making numerous, often significant alterations in his designs in midconstruction based on on-site observations, was not permitted to do so in this case.[17] Instead, according to Brian Brace Taylor, he was held to an extremely tight timetable and found it "the trauma of [his] life,"[18] though this would seem to be something of an overstatement. Bawa and Poologassundrum had selected Mitsui, the Japanese construction company with whom they had worked on the Ceylon Pavilion at Expo '70 in Osaka, because they believed that no Sri Lankan or Indian firm could meet the desired schedule. Still, familiarity with the firm did little to compensate for the speed with which the design had to be devised or the elimination of opportunities for on-site adjustments. Such a disjuncture between project management and artistic practice is especially crucial not only to the construction process but also to the nature and detailing of the designs that Bawa proposed. Although when seen from a distance the structure seems to exude much of the Sri Lankan timelessness to which Bawa alludes when he writes of buildings composed only of "roofs, columns and floors," several critics have noted that more alien influences become pervasive when the building is viewed from close up. How environmentally suitable is reinforced concrete (mixed with crushed stone and epoxy for the outer surfaces) as the structural basis for a building in a tropical climate? The inappropriateness is only confirmed by the necessity of importing the services of Mitsui to implement it. Still, this use of reinforced concrete arguably is better adapted than the reinforced concrete used for modernist buildings elsewhere on the island. Combined with handcrafted timberwork, brasswork, murals, and banners—multiple reminders of indigenous artistic traditions and motifs—the alien presence of concrete is hardly the first thing which comes to mind when one sees this building.

What does seem apparent is the politically desirable haste with which the complex was realized. The building took only three years from conception to inauguration, a remarkably short time considering the size, complexity, and location of the commission,[19] and this may well have compromised the quality of many of its details. After the distant glimpse of the grand roofs above the trees, the midrange drama of the buildings growing out of the water, and the grand processional of drawing near, arrival at the building is, according to many commentators in the architectural journals, disappointing.[20] Even $43 million was insufficient to outfit the interiors with the same evocative grandeur that is present in the massing. With this commission even Geoffrey Bawa, Sri Lanka's first contribution to the international architectural scene, may have met his match.

THE POLITICS OF A PARLIAMENTARY ISLAND

Bawa's architecture seems relatively open to eclectic influences, yet the siting of the building reveals political purposes that are far more parochial. Though the symbolic references to past traditions of relating architecture to man-made bodies of water may have remained at the heart of Bawa's conception for the building, the choice of site, reachable only by a causeway from the surrounding land, likely had at least as much to do with security as it did with meditations on the purely formal aspects of historical precedent. To point this out, however, is not to diminish the importance of either concern but rather to recognize that form and social context are inseparable, and that architectural form responds simultaneously to many different considerations. In any case, the commission of an island parliament hints at a desire by the Sinhalese-dominated government to operate at a safe distance from public protest. As one former Sri Lankan prime minister puts it, one good thing about an island parliament is that "no one can surround it and demonstrate." Despite such seeming impregnability, in August 1987 radical Sinhalese nationalists succeeded in carrying out an armed attack during a United National Party meeting in the new parliament building, an apparent attempt to assassinate Jayewardene. One person was killed and fourteen were wounded, but the president was unhurt, and remarkably the perpetrator avoided capture.[21]

Other concerns prompted the construction of the new parliamentary complex, though none of these fully account for why the parliament was designed as an island. There was good reason to want a new building. The Old Parliament house in Colombo was originally designed for about fifty members but by the 1970s it had been forced to squeeze in 168 representatives. Only after a new constitution and the name change from

Ceylon to Sri Lanka in 1972 did Colombo accelerate the transformation of its colonial architectural legacy. The issue of a new capitol had been raised since the 1960s, and the government in 1970 had plans to construct it in Colombo at Galle Face, near the Old Parliament, but financial constraints at the time, combined with other architectural priorities (especially the construction of the massive Chinese-subsidized Bandaranaike Memorial International Conference Hall), delayed the project. As the government moved to develop the central business district of Colombo on a purely commercial basis during the 1970s, often using the work of imported foreign architects and turnkey developers, thoughts turned to the relocation of noncommercial functions, including the parliament—though, in fact, the Old Parliament was subsequently converted by Geoffrey Bawa to serve as the Presidential Secretariat and Archives.[22] Denying the wishes of those who liked the idea of an administrative capital located in one of the major historic centers of the country, such as Kandy or Anuradhapura, the government decided against such a dramatic move away from Colombo. Instead of a move to claim the historic Sinhalese heartland of the country as the seat of the government, the government chose to create both the appearance and the mythohistory of an important Sinhalese heartland closer to Colombo.

THE SINHALESE MASTER PLAN

In many ways, the capitol complex may be seen as a temple to Sinhalese nationalism and to the rule of President Jayewardene, whose government commissioned it. Most overtly, it is constructed in a district whose very name, Sri Jayawardhanapura Kotte, reminds citizens of the name of its patron. This conjunction of names is neither direct nor completely fortuitous: the place was named nearly five hundred years before a modern president moved to reclaim it. Moreover, the choice of Sri Jayawardhanapura Kotte as the site for the new parliament building could have, beyond the familiarity of the name, tremendous political appeal to many Sinhalese.

Though the selection of site had much to do with the availability of inexpensive land near the capital, its significance far transcends matters of economics. Four miles outside of Colombo, Sri Jayawardhanapura Kotte is no mere suburb: it was once a fortified island redoubt and a city of major stature in precolonial Sri Lanka (7.10). As a resplendent royal capital of the fifteenth century, it was the power base for Sinhalese control over the whole island, the last time such total control would be exercised until independence, five hundred years later. With this symbolic return to Kotte completed just as Tamil unrest renewed in 1983, no doubt Jayewardene wished he could regain a similar national control.

Though critics have noted general resemblances between Bawa's parliamentary island layout and that of Hindu temple complexes in south India, it seems to bear closer resemblance to Sri Lankan Buddhist complexes. Continuity of religio-royal architecture has been a hallmark of Sri Lankan history. As James Duncan points out, the ancient capital of Anuradhapura

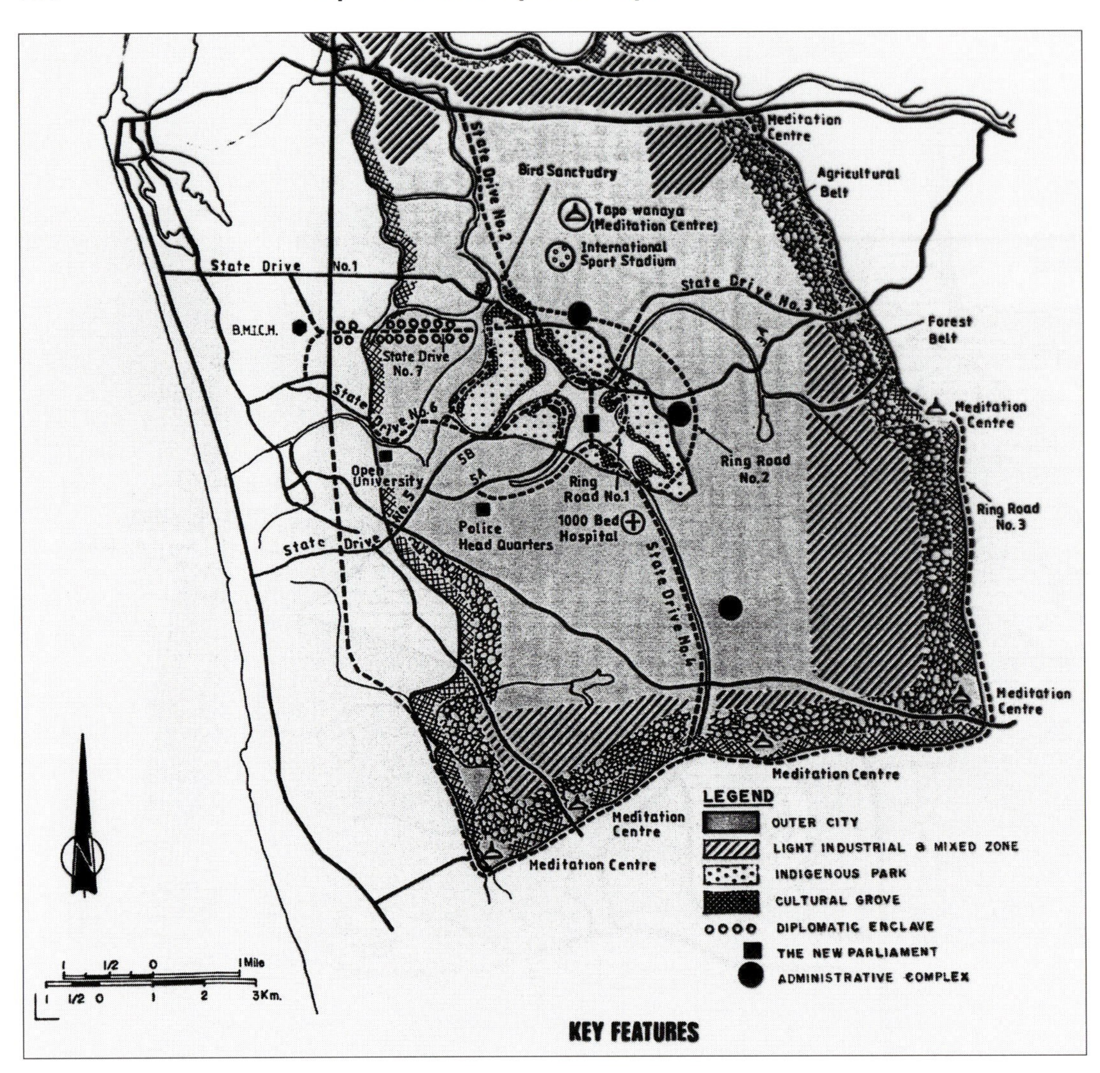

7.10 Overall diagram of Sri Jayawardhanapura Kotte, ringed by Buddhist meditation centers, with ancient capital and Parliament as central area.

has "inspired reverence and awe" and "furnished a powerful model" for later kings eager to emulate their glorious predecessors. Duncan demonstrates, drawing upon such precedents, the ways the landscape of Kandy was produced to "foster a certain hegemonic reading that spoke of the power, benevolence and legitimacy of the kings in their capital."[23]

This association between landscape and royal power has had some further continuity even in modern democratic Sri Lanka. Steven Kemper observes that Junius Jayewardene was the first elected Sri Lankan leader to address the nation from the octagonal pavilion (*pattirippuwa*) of Kandy's Dalada Maligawa: "Looking up at Jayewardene, the crowd saw a leader assuming an exalted, traditional position, for the last Kandyan king, Sri Vikrama Rajasimha, had the *pattirippuwa* built in order to watch spectacles from an elevated height." Perhaps Jayewardene (or his architect) imagined something similar for another royally associated place that in its heyday had previously housed the sacred tooth relic. As Nihal Perera argues, "Within the royal discourse he was constructing, Jayewardene also talked about moving the Dalada Maligawa to Jayawardhanapura. This connects back to the Sinhalese-Buddhist history in which the possession of the Tooth Relic of Buddha was a major sign of legitimate kingship . . .. This would inform the people that their government was safely in the hands of a Bodhisattva who is in the process of becoming a Buddha." Although the Tooth remained in Kandy, more subtle Buddhist aspirations could still travel. A description of the Sri Jayawardhanapura Kotte capitol complex written by one of Bawa's assistants also suggests some identification between the new capitol and older centers of Buddhist power: "In following the ambience of ancient arrangements of buildings, particularly those of over 2,000 year old monastic complexes of Anuradhapura, [the new parliamentary complex] also reflects the strong Buddhist influence that has moulded the character of the Sri Lankan Nation."[24] In this less-than-inclusive account of the makeup of the "Nation," the island parliament, in its institutional associations as well as its forms, would appear to aim for a specific kind of historical continuity.

As in most cases in which elements of the past have been recalled in ways that serve the needs of the present, Sri Jayawardhanapura Kotte is remembered with an artful interweaving of history and myth. Just as Sinhalese and Tamils have each sought to justify contemporary political causes through contending claims of greatest primeval presence on the island and traditional homelands, so too claim to the site of the island parliament has become charged with wishful meanings. And, as Tambiah has argued about the situation in Sri Lanka more generally, "the resurrection of long dormant politico-religious myths—as if they were memories continuously alive, energizing the actions of present day actors—opens up a number of problems for scholars concerning the uses of the past for present purposes, the role of ideology in interested action, and the contemporary functions of historical symbols." As Kemper puts it, the "Sri Lankan past is not so much imagined as contested and negotiated."[25]

Sri Jayawardhanapura Kotte was the seat of the most powerful of the three sovereign kingdoms found by the Portuguese when they arrived in 1505 (the others were based in Kandy and Jaffna), but its position in the grand scope of Sri Lankan history is far from preeminent. Within fifty years of the arrival of the Portuguese colonists, "Kotte sought Portuguese aid and devolved into a Portuguese client state," and its king even converted to Christianity in 1557, outraging many Sinhalese.[26] Though undoubtedly the most national of the historic sites near Colombo and a telling example of the changes brought to the island by European colonialism, Kotte's relatively brief period of power pales before either that of Kandy or those of the earlier ancient kingdoms of Anuradhapura and Polonnaruwa (c. 500 B.C.–A.D.1200), regarded at least by Sinhalese as emblematic of the island's golden age. Because these other sites were located too far from the power base of contemporary Sinhalese control to be plausible bases for national administration, the historical case of Kotte needed a certain amount of exaggeration to fit the political needs of the moment.

Through words and through design juxtapositions, it is this association between the glories of the old and the renaissance of the new that the promoters of the new capitol complex sought to portray. As the building neared completion in 1982, Colombo's *Sunday Observer* ran a series of articles which stressed this connection. Though most of the articles emphasized the historical value of the site, the intended relevance to contemporary politics was thinly veiled. The press reports about the new building and its site highlighted its importance as a symbol of Sinhalese hegemony, a viewpoint that permeates the text and drawings of the master plan as well.

As conveyed in *The Sunday Observer*, the story of Sri Jayawardhanapura Kotte reads as a kind of cautionary tale for present-day relations between Tamils and Sinhalese. Only the tenses are different; the tensions are the same. In the second half of the fourteenth century, when the southern parts of the island, including Colombo and Kandy provinces, were "under the usurped control of the rebel Prince Arya Cakravarti of Jaffna," the Sinhalese king's viceroy, Nissanka Alakesvara, "a zealous Buddhist," realized that "the Buddhist Church as well as the Sinhala race were in great danger." As a "precautionary step," he built "a formidable kotuva [from which Kotte, or "fortress"] at Daarugama to prepare for a great war." Going forth from Kotte, Alakesvara's forces handed the Tamil enemy a "crushing defeat." And, since Alakesvara's "famous victory (-Jaya) over the enemy" was carried out from Kotte, this fortress "became famous as the New JAYAVARDHANAPURA."[27]

While the account of this victory presented in the *Sunday Observer* is clearly told from a Sinhalese point of view, the description of Jayawardhanapura Kotte given in the master plan is even more overtly a product of Sinhalese nationalist aspirations. According to the text provided along with a drawing of the "Plan of Ancient Sri Jayawardhanapura," "The fortress city earned the name of Sri Jayawardhanapura on successfully conquering the North, in 1391."[28] This simple statement distorts the circumstances of the story in two intriguing ways. First, it is phrased to read as if the fortress itself had captured the North. Possibly the result of a grammatical error, such wording nevertheless lends support to anyone believing that the act of constructing a new parliament could actively assist in putting down Tamil insurrection. Second, there is a factual mistake that might lead an uninformed reader to overstate the historical parallel between the victory in 1391 and the political situation six hundred years later. The forces that set out from Kotte in 1391 went into battle with Tamil invaders from the south, not the north. Other Sinhalese troops forestalled that part of the Tamil enemy coming from the north. Many years would pass before a Kotte-based army defeated the Jaffna Tamils.

The high point in Kotte's history came a few decades after Alakesvara's triumph, during the fifty-five-year reign of King Parakramabahu VI. When the new king acceded to the throne in 1412, the island—then as now—"was torn by different rival political units, particularly Jaffna, which was [still] controlled by the [Tamil] rebel Arya Cakravarti." In consequence, a Colombo journalist continues, "from the moment of his ascendancy," Parakramabahu "felt uneasy and realised his sacred duty by the land of his birth to restore it to unity." He launched an "important national campaign against Jaffna, which was the greatest challenge to the sovereign identity of Sri Lanka as a single United Kingdom." Finally, in 1449, he captured the northern Tamil stronghold and "proudly set Sri Lanka on the map of the world once more as a supremely independent sovereign nation."[29]

Lest only Sri Lanka's Tamils find cause for alarm in the renewed Sinhalese rule from the famous fort, the article points out that, "after the subjugation of Jaffna, King Parakramabahu also found it expedient to send an army to attack the Chola Port of Adriampet in South India." More than anything, however, the king sought to advance the prestige of Buddhism: "During his glorious reign Buddhism received undiminished royal patronage to emerge from gradual neglect to pre-eminent glory; a magnificent Temple of the Tooth was built in the City which constituted the chief attraction of the Buddhist World." Guided by Buddhism, "art and architecture . . . blossomed and gradually a war-torn and depressed country steered towards peace and economic prosperity under one national banner." Five hundred years later, the one national banner flies again, from an island opposite the ruins. The journalist makes certain the analogy is not missed: "Along with the establishment of the magnificent new parliamentary complex in the historic Royal City of Sri Jayawardhanapura Kotte," he writes, "a quota of flesh and blood is given to the dry bones of this ancient city to resurrect with renewed prestige the splendour she last enjoyed under King Parakramabahu VI." The parliament building itself makes the connection obvious, as the official website of the Sri Lankan government makes clear: "Today, the glory and the beauty of Parakramabahu VI's Sri Jayewardenapura Kotte are lovingly shown on the Lobby walls of the Parliament by that legendary painter, Dr. L. T. P. Manjusri."[30]

Other journalists writing in the Colombo press were equally adept at forging connections between fifteenth-century Sinhalese kings and a twentieth-century Sri Lankan president. In a piece suggestively titled "The Glory that Was—and Is—Sri Jayawardhanapura," Wilfred M. Gunasekera began by noting, "It augurs well to have the Parliament of the Democratic Socialist Republic of Sri Lanka during the tenure of President J. R. Jayewardene installed in Jayawardhanapura Kotte." "This city," he continued, "which was founded by Alakeswara and adorned by Sri Parakrama Bahu VI is now enriched by the government of our elected President who will sustain good government in a unified Lanka and foster its culture and learning and inspire his countrymen over generations to come." This new Sinhalese dynasty in Kotte, he implied, may also need defensive protection: "The Kings of Ceylon made it their capital for one hundred and fifty years, but it was built originally only to serve as a base for military operations."[31] The parliament, too, seemed well equipped for military operations. According to the master plan for "The Nucleus" of the capitol complex,

> Security Units of all the Armed forces will stand sentinel to the North, East, South and the West of the New Parliament guarding this most important House of Assembly and the state residences. The Police will take position at the head of the ceremonial way, the Air Force adjacent to the state residences, the Army at the foot of the security access and the

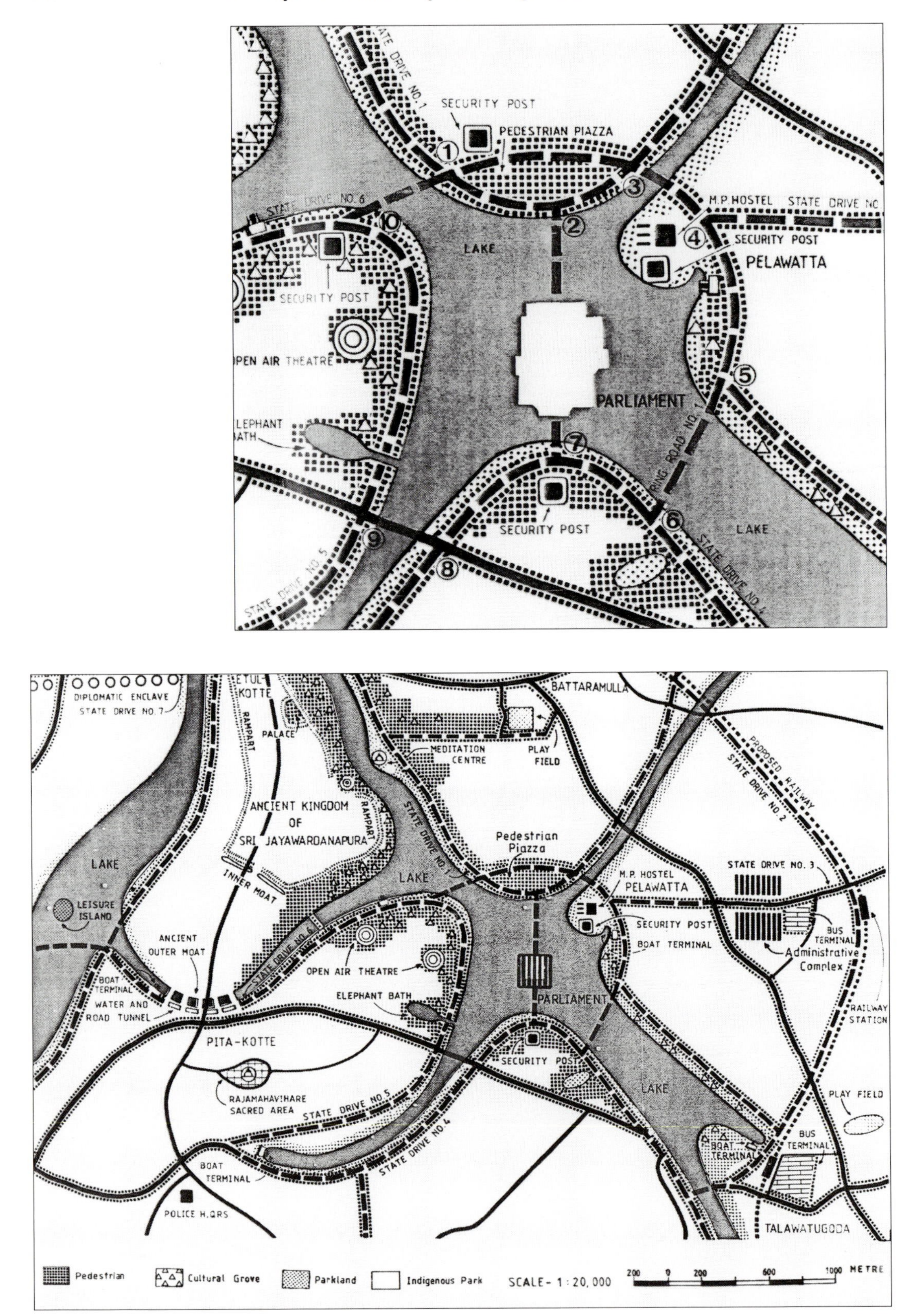
STATE DRIVE NO.1
SECURITY POST
PEDESTRIAN PIAZZA
STATE DRIVE NO.6
1
2
3
4
5
6
7
8
9
10
LAKE
M.P.HOSTEL
STATE DRIVE NO
SECURITY POST
PELAWATTA
SECURITY POST
PEN AIR THEATRE
PARLIAMENT
LEPHANT
ATH
RING ROAD NO.1
SECURITY POST
LAKE
STATE DRIVE NO.4
STATE DRIVE NO.5
DIPLOMATIC ENCLAVE
STATE DRIVE NO.7
ETUL-
KOTTE
RAMPART
PALACE
BATTARAMULLA
MEDITATION CENTRE
PLAY FIELD
ANCIENT KINGDOM OF SRI JAYAWARDANAPURA
RAMPART
STATE DRIVE NO.1
PROPOSED RAILWAY
STATE DRIVE NO.2
Pedestrian Piazza
LAKE
INNER MOAT
LAKE
LEISURE ISLAND
M.P. HOSTEL
PELAWATTA
STATE DRIVE NO. 3
SECURITY POST
BOAT TERMINAL
BUS TERMINAL
Administrative Complex
ANCIENT OUTER MOAT
STATE DRIVE NO.6
OPEN AIR THEATRE
BOAT TERMINAL
WATER AND ROAD TUNNEL
ELEPHANT BATH
PARLIAMENT
RAILWAY STATION
PITA-KOTTE
SECURITY POST
RAJAMAHAVIHARE SACRED AREA
STATE DRIVE NO.5
LAKE
PLAY FIELD
STATE DRIVE NO.4
BOAT TERMINAL
BUS TERMINAL
BOAT TERMINAL
POLICE H.QRS
TALAWATUGODA
Pedestrian
Cultural Grove
Parkland
Indigenous Park
SCALE- 1 : 20,000
200 0 200 600 1000 METRE

7.11 The plan to keep the island secure.

Navy across the waters at Baddegana. The Air Force will have a helipad and the Navy the blue waters for its patrol boats.[32]

While such a statement may keep all branches of the military appeased, this overwhelming need to provide for security—thoroughly justified by current political instability—inevitably detracts from the sense of openness and pedestrian freedom that was so consistently touted as a feature of the plan (7.11).

Though the new parliament building was intended to house the principal democratic institution of the country, both its design and its siting would seem to recall far-less-inclusivist forms of government. A two-part series in the *Sunday Observer* by Karel Roberts describes the effort to "turn this ordinary middle class sprawling township, once the home of the Kotte kings, into a new showpiece of the nation with Parliament as the central gem in the diadem." Indeed, few would doubt that the Sri Lankan *caput mundi* wears a royal crown. Noting that the old colonial parliament building in Colombo was felt to be "no longer in tune with the new national aspirations and image," Roberts observes that the new building "would reflect all the features of traditional Sinhala architecture."[33] Yet, since Sinhala is not necessarily equivalent to Sri Lanka, and ancient Kotte is far from uniformly touted as the golden age of the island's history, the design of the capitol complex (and not just the politics conducted within it) could easily become yet another symbol of alienation for disaffected Tamils. Under guidance from Jayewardene's successor, President Ranasinghe Premadasa, the parliamentary complex became linked to the *gam-udawa* (or "village reawakening") movement, and annual pageants held in various villages feature, among other cultural buildings, scaled-down replicas of the capitol.[34]

7.12 Two Sinhalese islands: one past, one present.

The intended Sinhalese character of the Sri Lankan capitol complex is made abundantly clear in the master plan, which shows the overt intentions behind the juxtaposition of modern parliament and ancient citadel. In the ambitious and multifaceted attempt to convey the Buddhist heritage of the country, ancient Jayawardhanapura operates by analogy as well as by proximity. Both the fifteenth-century fortress city and the twentieth-century parliament are on islands; both evidence an obsession with security; both are dominated by places for ceremony—an architecture of walls and temples. One island protects the embattled Sinhalese politicians, the other gives sanctuary to exalted Sinhalese traditions (7.12). Taken together, the parts of this cultural archipelago are described as an Indigenous Park: "This will form a zone designed to highlight and promote the growth of indigenous arts and crafts and indigenous planting and landscaping techniques to result in a truly national environment. It will form the Nation's identity and the City's pride. It will be her head and bosom."[35]

This "truly national environment" envisions the placement of most of its indigenous cultural features within the "inner moat" and ramparts of the Ancient Buddhist Kingdom (7.13). Interspersed with architectural remains that include a five-story "monastery where sixty Buddhist monks lived under the high priest" and a three-story "temple for the Sacred Tooth Relic of Lord Buddha," it is a landscape that defies any acknowledgment of cultural

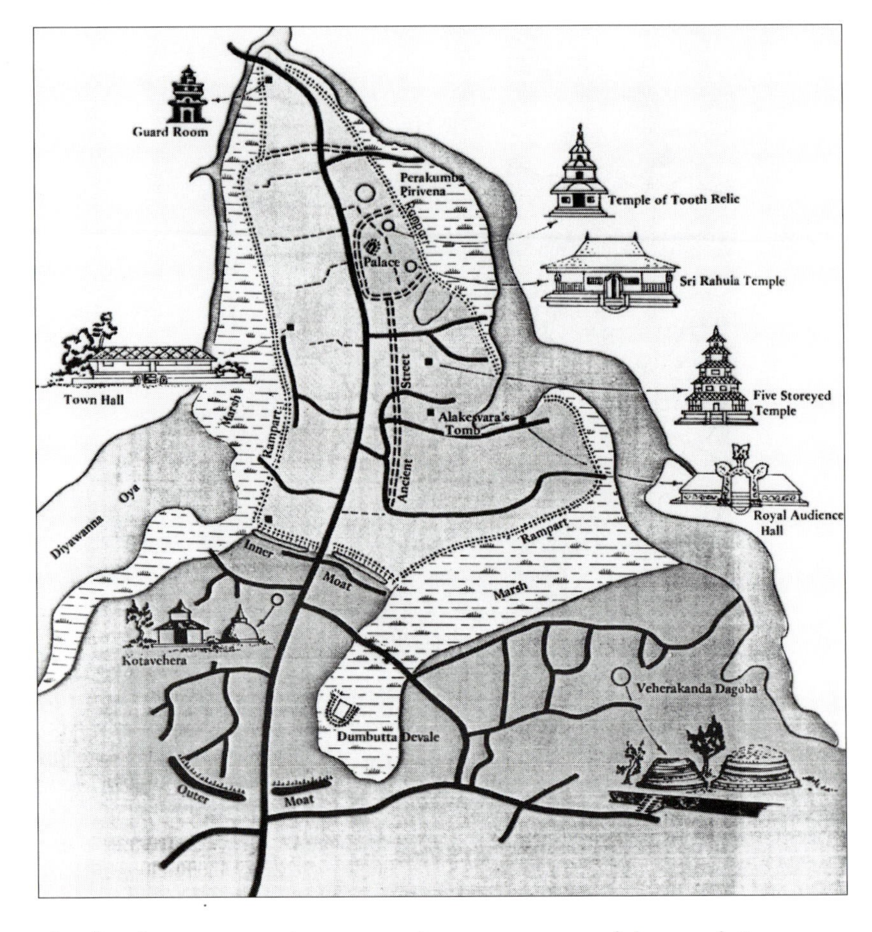

7.13 Architectural and archaeological remains of Sri Jayawardhanapura Kotte.

pluralism in a country where more than one-quarter of the population are not Buddhists.[36] While the indigenous plantings may be "truly national," the only culture that seems to be considered indigenous in the iconography of this master plan is that of the Buddhist Sinhalese. As the master plan reiterates, describing Kotte as Parakramabahu's "National Capital of Sri Lanka": "This King brought the country under one rule during his time. Buddhism, Sinhala culture and the country developed rapidly and attained its zenith of glory during his period."[37] For those who would reflect on this, the plan provides for a ring of Buddhist meditation centers (marked by stupas) that define the boundaries of the Outer City. Another Meditation Center is more centrally located along State Drive No. 1, where it approaches the ceremonial causeway to the parliament, and, within the bounds of the Indigenous Park itself, there is the Rajamahavihare Sacred Area. Although to his credit Geoffrey Bawa did not design the parliament to resemble a Buddhist stupa, the capitol environment as a whole was proposed to be far from ethnically and religiously neutral. Even Bawa's Kandyan pitched roofs, though arguably a reminder of a place that had been ruled by both Tamils and Sinhalese, have a nearby source that is unambiguously Buddhist: at the center of the Kotte King's Palace is the Sri Rahula Temple, replete with a Kandyan double pitch.

Though it is less easy to assume a Sinhalese bias in the more secular

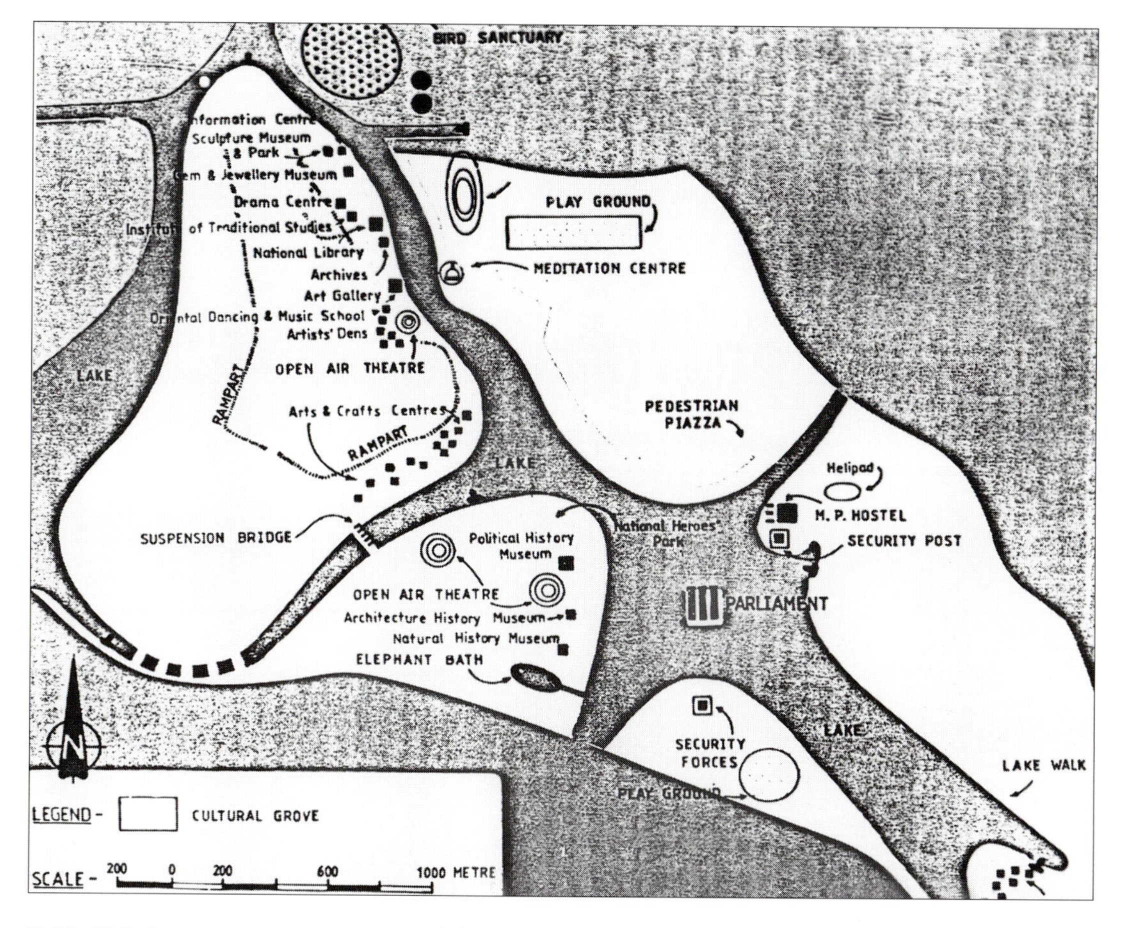

7.14 Sinhalese Cultural Grove.

attempts to exhibit "indigenous" culture, the Kotte master plan provides ample opportunity for this to occur. Between the ancient citadel (to be devoted primarily to the arts and to something known as the Institute of Traditional Studies) and the parliament island is a peninsula called Pita-Kotte, which contains other components of the proposed Cultural Grove (7.14). Here there was to be, in appropriate proximity, both an Architecture History Museum and a Political History Museum. According to the master plan, the Cultural Grove, with its "lowrise traditional style elegant buildings merging with natural landscape, . . . will provide an opportunity for enjoying a rich variety of indigenous cultural activities at a leisurely walk."[38]

Based on the assumptions and ideals of the master plan for the surroundings of the parliament island, surely this "leisurely walk" would be more reassuring to a Sinhalese. That said, those of a more inclusivist bent could point to Kotte as a key site of Sri Lankan unity before the intrusion of colonialism, and could even take solace in the mixed ethnic heritage of the Kotte kings. Such readings of the place and its history were simply made more difficult because the Sinhalese media and political leadership worked hard to filter history in service of a narrower nationalism. The government's choice of this site—so redolent with manipulable historical memories of Sinhalese hegemony—as the place for a national parliament is a reminder that architectural context has temporal as well as spatial dimensions.

However inclusivist the architectural references of Bawa's building, the national identity conveyed by the master plan for the Sri Lankan capitol complex extended national membership only to a carefully chosen group.

IMPLEMENTING NATIONALISM: THE LIMITS OF A MASTER PLAN

Fortunately for ethnic politics, however, very little of the master plan for Sri Jayawardhanapura Kotte was ever implemented. A quarter-century after Bawa's complex rose on a reclaimed island, it bears an ambiguous relationship to its surroundings. As Perera observes, when parliament is in session, the island is a fort and "the security system uses the water system to keep all unauthorized users out." By contrast, however, people "use the esplanade right in front of the parliament house for sports, particularly playing cricket, and for partying and picnicking." Further complicating the scene, "many people (some of them well dressed) also use the no-man's-land around the parliamentary island as an area for garbage disposal." Kotte, Perera concludes, "is growing into a national place with particular national functions mixed with daily practices of Kotte residents." The surrounding area included under the jurisdiction of the Sri Jayawardhanapura Kotte Municipal Council now houses well over 100,000 people, an overwhelming majority of whom are both Buddhist and Sinhalese—a demographic that is especially striking since Buddhists are now a minority in Colombo itself.[39] Despite this seemingly fertile ground for a Sinhalese nationalist planning effort, however, Kotte appears far less provocative on the ground than it did in the master plan of 1982.

Following completion of the parliament building itself, government spending priorities quickly turned toward the civil war and toward efforts to reduce poverty. The government of President Premadasa and his successors largely abandoned the master plan. The district gained the offices of cabinet-level Ministries of Education, Housing and Construction, Social Services and Social Welfare, Highways, Urban Development, and Environment but, as of 2006, thirty other major ministries remained based in Colombo.

Since the master plan for the Cultural Grove has been largely unrealized, Sri Lanka's new capitol complex has been stripped of its ideological content. As built so far, the capital territory of Kotte exhibits little of its Sinhalese nationalist aura. After twenty-five years, successive Sinhalese-led governments have left the once-glorified archaeological remains "in a state of neglect and disrepair." As Perera puts it, "The connection to history is more about the present than the past; [Kotte] provides a post-colonial political base for the Low-Country elite," a base that is conveniently accessible from the colonial and capitalist center of Colombo. Most of the area around the parliamentary lake has become residential, interspersed with a considerable amount of commercial uses, including IT businesses and a call center. The Urban Development Authority viewed its larger plan for the capital territory (encompassing the towns of Battaramulla, Ethulkotte, Pitakotte, and Thalawatugoda) as providing a kind of national zone for administrative activities. Yet since the ministerial complexes are scattered and have no visual relationship with the parliamentary complex, there is little sense of a unified district. In Perera's words, "For most users, the area is a continuation of Colombo made up of highly congested roads, evoking the image of a 'Third World' city with some visually interesting places around the capitol. For a professional observer, the city is coagulating near the capitol and gradually building outward, with little respect for the master plan." Moving the parliament to Kotte surely encouraged the eastward growth of Colombo, but most of that growth resulted from what David Robson calls "unbridled private investment and land speculation, neither subject to planning controls nor supported by infrastructure. Even the first tantalizing glimpse of the Parliament building that Bawa orchestrated at the turning of the road at Rajagiriya is now obscured by unauthorized developments on the edge of the lake in which it stands."[40]

The meanings of Sri Jayawardhanapura Kotte and its island parliament continue to evolve, always caught beneath the looming shadow of separatist politics. Since the district's most nationalistic urban design impulses were suppressed, however, the future symbolism of the capitol complex is far from settled. One may hope that Geoffrey Bawa's complex reconciliation in the realm of architecture may yet play a supportive national role in a more peaceful Sri Lanka.

CHAPTER 8

Precast Arabism for Kuwait

Kuwait's National Assembly building, like the contemporaneous parliament houses in Papua New Guinea and Sri Lanka, is a product of personal, subnational, national, and international concerns. Whereas the PNG building has played a part in what has been to date a gradual consolidation of that country's postcolonial parliamentary rule, and the Sri Lankan example may be related to violent ethnic clashes, the Kuwaiti counterpart has been produced in an increasingly turbulent context of a different kind. Even before it was invaded in August 1990 by Iraq, Kuwait was known to the world for three things: its oil, its wealth, and its precarious position in the war-torn Persian/Arabian Gulf (8.1).[1] Nestled between Iraq and Saudi Arabia and across the gulf from Iran, Kuwait struggled to remain officially neutral in the Iran–Iraq

8.1 Kuwait.

war during the 1980s, though it gave an estimated $1 billion a year in financial assistance to its Iraqi neighbors.[2] Such aid did not ease perennial border disputes and other tensions with Iraq, however, as the Iraqi invasion of Kuwait soon made clear. Because of the Gulf War of 1990–1991, the ideals and realities of democracy in Kuwait came under great international scrutiny. In the aftermath of the Iraqi ouster, Kuwaitis rebuilt their country and repaired their monumental parliament building with American assistance, even as Kuwait has become a distinctly different place, both physically and politically.

The external aggression directed at Kuwait in 1990 carried clear antecedents in the preexisting internal schisms that had threatened social and political stability. Though the framers of Kuwait's Constitution of 1962 mandated the creation of a National Assembly, a highly progressive step in a region known for autocracy and oligarchy, subsequent domestic rifts caused the ruling emir to order two lengthy dissolutions of this parliament. The first occurred between 1976 and 1981 while design and construction of the imposing new National Assembly building were under way, and the second began in 1986, only months after the building was completed, and lasted until 1992.

In early 1990, following numerous prodemocracy protests, the Kuwaiti leadership began to move toward reestablishment of a legislative voice for its citizens.[3] In late April the emir issued a decree establishing a seventy-five-member National Council—but this was a consultative body that would have even fewer powers than the old parliament. Prodemocracy activists urged a boycott of the elections and were arrested, forcing the opposition movement underground after elections were held. On 9 July, the Kuwait National Council held its inaugural meeting in the main chamber of the National Assembly building. This group, composed of fifty elected members and twenty-five appointed by the emir, was set up, according to the emir, to "pave the way for the anticipated Kuwaiti parliamentary life."[4] Only three weeks later, however, the Iraqi invasion put a stop to this new stage of experimentation with democracy. However brief and ill-fated this abortive attempt at reintroducing a precursor to "parliamentary life," it did serve to set an institution in motion and did once again identify the National Assembly building as the physical locus for future democratic prospects.

PRESTRESSED CONCRETE IN A PRESTRESSED SOCIETY

While no national assembly building can avoid being a political statement as well as an architectural exercise, the institutional instability of the Kuwaiti parliament raises compelling questions about the decision to give it monumental architectural treatment. In interpreting the form and purpose of a cultural artifact such as this (8.2), architectural analysis can benefit greatly from an examination of Kuwaiti sociopolitical tensions. Though national assembly buildings are presumably designed and built to transcend or avoid such tensions in a way that favors those in power, it is important to identify these schisms and judge what resonances they may have for the resultant building.

8.2 Kuwait National Assembly, viewed from Arabian Gulf Street.

Kuwait's great wealth has not come about without consequences. More than a half-century of oil-sponsored riches has led a tribally oriented sheikhdom to confront issues of global scope. But such wealth and the extensive welfare state that it subsidized did not provide equal comfort and privilege for all. And increasingly through the 1970s and 1980s, the attendant westernization, at one point more happily seen as synonymous with modernization, itself came into question. The very rapidity of change left an important residue, a concern for traditions and values of the past. Kuwait's National Assembly building, designed by the celebrated Danish architect Jørn Utzon in collaboration with his son Jan, is an attempt to confront some of these traditions; it is an architectural essay which endeavors to assemble national identity out of sections of concrete.

This consolidation of national identity in Kuwait has at least two unusual dimensions, one historical, one contemporary. First, Kuwait has never really been fully colonized, and second, with the massive influx of foreign workers, Kuwaiti citizens have become a minority group in their own country. The first factor, a long history of de facto independence that preceded legal independence in 1961, meant that Kuwait was able to escape much of the political turmoil that accompanied the accession to statehood in many other small countries. Though it struggled to avoid Ottoman hegemony and Wahabi incursions in the nineteenth century and was under British "protection" between 1899 and 1961, Kuwait City has been ruled by the same family (the al-Sabah) since the eighteenth-century settlement of the area.[5] Since British (and other colonial) interest in Kuwait long preceded the discovery of oil and was initially motivated by the strategic importance of access to a Gulf port, Kuwait lacks much of the history of economic exploitation by colonial powers that is so evident elsewhere. Though the vast petroleum resources of Kuwait have surely been exploited ever since the first export of oil in 1946, much of the profit from drilling concessions has gone to Kuwaitis. Because the terms of the oil exploration agreement signed in 1934 with the British "treated Kuwait as if it were the private property of its emir, and provided that all the income from the concession would go directly to him," the control and distribution of power in Kuwait became, at least in part, a function of al-Sabah largesse.[6] The al-Sabah dynasty, dating back more than two-and-a-half centuries, provides the backdrop for any consideration of the development of national identity in Kuwait.

The production of oil, however, brought an enormous introduction of foreigners intent on remaining in the country. Their very presence challenged the traditional social and political structure of Kuwait. Ironically, perhaps, foreign presence and influence may have been more strongly felt *after* formal independence than before it. By the mid-1960s, Kuwaitis had ceased to form a majority in Kuwait. After years of government efforts to suppress the true extent of this demographic imbalance, in early 1990 the Kuwait Planning Board revealed that Kuwaitis numbered only 27.3 percent of the total population; the board cited plans to improve their ratio to one-in-three by the end of the 1990s. Ironically, the seven-month Iraqi occupation of Kuwait in 1990–1991 may have accelerated the push for a Kuwaiti majority in Kuwait, since the wartime mass exodus provided a chance for Kuwaiti leaders to reassess policies regarding the number of foreigners in their country. Even so, by the end of the 1990s, Kuwaiti citizens still constituted only about 35 percent of the population, just about what had been forecast a decade earlier in advance of the war.[7] This ongoing minority rule by Kuwaitis not only militated against attempts at forging anything resembling a national perspective, but also prompted calls for more inclusive citizenship laws.

In a place where power was closely held by extended networks of a few Kuwaiti families, national integration could seem something of an irrelevancy, further hampered, at least initially, by the lack of a clear colonial enemy against whom sentiments could be roused at the time of independence. As others came to contest Kuwaiti hegemony, the search for a unified postprotectorate Kuwait became encumbered by factional discord, fueled by a divisive citizenship policy. The 1985 edition of the leading English language guidebook to Kuwait, addressed in large part to foreigners going there on business, sought to minimize these concerns: "The numbers of foreigners assisting in the country's development have served to compound the Kuwaiti sense of identity rather than diminish it. The effects of this potentially disruptive demographic imbalance, with Kuwaitis numbering less than half of the total population, have been greatly mitigated by Islam and the cohesive force it represents: the overwhelming majority of expatriate residents in Kuwait are Arab and Asian Muslims."[8] Yet the rosy tones of this guidebook, written with government cooperation, masked deepening tensions over the denial of citizenship—with its attendant privileges—as well as the strains that exist between and among different Muslim groups.

Conditions for naturalization being very strict and numbers tightly limited, citizenship remained "an almost impossible goal for expatriates."[9] Thus, well before an invasion attempted to turn Kuwaitis into Iraqis, claiming residence in Kuwait was not at all equivalent to holding Kuwaiti citizenship. Yet, without citizenship a resident was automatically condemned to a second-class existence. And in political matters, even citizenship did not guarantee the right to vote, unless one was a "first-class Kuwaiti"—a literate male over the age of 21 who could prove that he or his parents or grandparents was resident in Kuwait in 1920. Denial of citizenship affected far more than voting rights, however; it pervaded many aspects of daily life. While the government supplied an enviably wide range of social benefits to its population of more than 2 million (both natives and foreigners), the non-Kuwaitis were discriminated against in housing, employment, and other economic regulations. Only Kuwaiti citizens were allowed to own real estate,[10] and all Kuwaitis were guaranteed jobs. The 90 percent of them on the government payroll were also guaranteed higher salaries than their non-Kuwaiti counterparts, even when the work was the same.[11]

Moreover, Kuwait's law required the participation of a Kuwaiti citizen in almost every type of business activity: a Kuwaiti or Kuwaiti entity had to hold at least 51 percent ownership in any foreign business venture; Kuwaiti agents were required on most purchasing contracts; only Kuwaitis could speculate in the local stock market; imports had to be in the name of registered Kuwaiti importers; and the government made a strenuous effort to see that Kuwaiti contractors were involved in government projects.[12] Because of the restrictions on property ownership, the government provided all expatriate workers with a housing allowance, and all non-Kuwaitis seeking housing were subject to the decisions of Kuwaiti landlords. In this context, government-sponsored Kuwaiti-only housing districts were "a highly visible and easily understood symbol of the difference" between the privileged Kuwaitis and the majority of the population,[13] though in practice many wealthy non-Kuwaitis were able to rent homes in the so-called Kuwaiti-only districts.

It is not surprising, then, that one assessment of Kuwait's political and economic situation concluded that, of all the problems associated with rapid social and economic change just prior to the Gulf War, the most serious was the "ill-will built up by resident aliens."[14] While many of the alien majority living in Kuwait may well have been satisfied transients, present in Kuwait under relatively short-term lucrative contracts, this was not the case for most of the Palestinians, who numbered nearly 400,000 at the time of the Iraqi invasion.[15] Arguably Kuwait's most disaffected group, the vast majority of Palestinians lacked Kuwaiti citizenship but were otherwise bound to Kuwait, even if this did not necessarily imply loyalty to the Kuwaiti state. Many immigrated to Kuwait following the creation of Israel in 1948 or after the territorial occupations of 1967 and thus, in the absence of a separate Palestinian homeland, considered themselves stateless. Long residence in Kuwait and status as "the predominant force in Kuwait's civil service and professions" did not protect most Palestinians from being denied naturalization into the country: the Palestinian or other foreigner who had lived in Kuwait for twenty years without citizenship had "no more right to stay in Kuwait and enjoy its benefits than the most recently arrived Korean construction worker." Even though many Palestinians did not covet Kuwaiti citizenship because they longed to return to an independent Palestine, the presence of a large and economically secure yet disenfranchised group led during the 1980s to "growing bitterness" and "increased the possibilities for internal disruption." According to a report written in 1985, "even the most liberal western-educated Kuwaitis" supported a policy of Kuwait for Kuwaitis and believed that justice and rights of citizenship for Palestinians must be accomplished in Palestine rather than Kuwait, a sentiment "underscored by Kuwait's very vocal pro-Palestinian foreign policy."[16] The Iraqi occupation brought matters to a head: even though many of Kuwait's Palestinians actively resisted Saddam's incursion (countering his claims that the invasion was conducted on their behalf), Kuwaiti leaders treated them harshly in the aftermath of the Iraqi ouster. Accused of sympathizing or actively collaborating with the Iraqis, many who had remained were subjected to "ruthless police harassment, enforced unemployment, and the withdrawal of social services," and by the early 1990s only about 20,000 Palestinians remained—one-twentieth of the prewar population.[17]

Kuwait's Palestinians were not alone in feeling that they had been mistreated. Intra-Muslim religious tensions had substantially increased in the wake of the Iranian revolution and the surge of Shi'i fundamentalism that followed it. The Kuwaiti government struggled with Iranian-fomented subversion, fearing its spread. This struggle focused on Kuwait's own large Shi'i population, variously estimated to have included between 18 and 25 percent of its residents before the Iraqi occupation and approximately 30 percent thereafter.[18] Sunni–Shi'i tensions, in their domestic as well as international manifestations, led to increasing security problems, even as the growth of Islamist political agendas also attracted Sunni adherents.

In addition to day-to-day strife and institutionalized discrimination during the 1980s, there were terrorist attacks on public officials and commercial facilities. A coordinated bombing spree on 12 December 1983 targeted the U.S. and French embassies, Kuwaiti government installations, and American commercial concerns. Six persons were killed and eighty-six were wounded in the ninety-minute spate of explosions, attributed to Iraqi Shi'i financed by and operating from Iran.[19] Another incident that had direct impact upon the security precautions in Kuwaiti public buildings such as the National Assembly was the plot in May 1985 to assassinate the emir.[20] Though he was not seriously injured in the attempt, in which a suicide bomber drove a car into his motorcade, the incident seems to have made the previously "very unassuming" leader much more security conscious: a new armored Mercedes limousine soon replaced his Chevrolet, and, now escorted by an armored convoy, he began to vary his once predictably timed movements between residence, office, and palace.[21] The timing of this assassination attempt nearly coincided with the completion of the National Assembly building, in which the emir was to have had an extensive office and reception hall complex, and surely prompted even greater concern for his security within it.[22]

Added to all of the factional and regional tensions was some degree of financial constraints, present even in a state as economically sound as Kuwait in the 1980s. The most telling fissure, one that had social as well as financial repercussions, was the crash in 1982 of the informal Suq al-Manakh stock market, involving some $90 billion in unpaid commitments. Following the crash, the government is thought to have spent more than $7 billion to support share prices on the official stock market, compensate small investors, and shore up the financial community.[23] Beyond the monetary losses, the crash laid open class and generational conflicts within Kuwaiti society by undermining "the essential trust and confidence which formerly underlay transactions in Kuwait"; it also unveiled "latent hostilities" between the favored old ruling families and the nouveau riche.[24]

Though Kuwait's per capita GNP remained among the highest in the world, the 1980s brought a distinct letdown from the skyrocketing oil prices of the 1970s. Commissioned and designed at this peak of wealth and financial optimism, plans for the National Assembly apparently did not suffer from the subsequent budgetary squeeze. This is not surprising, since Kuwait's immense foreign investments assured the financial well-being of the country regardless of the price of oil and since the construction of buildings thought to be of national importance has rarely succumbed to budgetary problems even in far less wealthy places. Though construction costs for the building did come in higher than estimated[25] and Utzon's firm was asked to eliminate its intended conference center facilities, a separate $400-million conference center was subsequently commissioned and inaugurated in 1987 on the outskirts of the city. Thus, it seems probable that chiefly nonfinancial reasons prompted the elimination of the convention hall from the National Assembly building. One thing is certain: much changed during the twelve years between initial design and first occupancy.

Given all the changes in the social and political environment that have taken place in Kuwait since 1973, the building has occupied many different symbolic places and been subjected to increasing overlays of mediated references as well as other nonarchitectural associations. Taken together, these changes have altered the cultural role of the building and subverted or rendered less relevant the stated original intentions of its designers. In the course of grappling with all of the problems described above, government leaders and their evolving attitude toward democracy came under question, and, with the invasion and its aftermath, the legitimacy of the Kuwaiti government as a whole was challenged. One can view the completed building in the context both of the Iraqi invasion and the design brief that preceded it. On the one hand, this building can be seen as evidence of the ruling family's ambivalent and superficial commitment to the democratic sharing of power; on the other, if the advent of the new Kuwait National Assembly building is seen in the context of the gulf region as a whole, where even a halfhearted gesture to democratic power sharing is notable, the gesture might represent a significant, if stumbling, step forward. In the country's more liberal moments before 1990, twice undercut by the dissolution of the assembly and restrictions on the press, Kuwaitis enjoyed a far greater measure of freedom of expression than most other Arabs in the Middle East.[26]

When the National Assembly was established, following the declaration of Kuwait as an independent sovereign state in 1961, the creation of such a legislative body must have seemed a remarkable development. Even so, however, the al-Sabah placed strict limitations on its power. In devising these limitations, the ruling family probably recalled an ill-fated attempt by Kuwaiti merchant groups in 1921 to establish an "advisory council" and an attempt in 1938 to institute a "legislative assembly," which ended six months later by emirial dismissal after two assembly members were shot, one fatally, in a palace chamber by the ruling family's tribal militia.[27] With the resumption of formal efforts to institute democratic reforms in 1962, the al-Sabah moved cautiously. Most indicative of this was the provision for a minuscule electorate, designed to help ensure that the same large families who dominated Kuwait's economic life would retain their political influence.[28] In a country where, in the late 1980s, the eligible electorate numbered only about 70,000 out of a population of 2 million, the National Assembly could hardly be said to assemble the representatives of a nation-state. At the same time, simply having a parliament at all helped consolidate the legitimacy of Kuwait as an independent entity. As one comparative analysis of Arab legislative politics puts it, "An assembly made up of representatives of the people was as critical to the making of Kuwait and to the legitimacy of the al-Sabah as it had been to the making of England and the consolidation of its monarchy in an earlier era."[29]

As for the National Assembly institution itself, restrictions on voting rights constituted only part of the checks upon democracy. Most of the power in pre-invasion Kuwait remained with a group of sixteen ministers appointed by the emir, rather than with the fifty elected representatives. As a consequence, an oligarchy ruled the country whether or not the assembly was functioning. The power of these ministers is spatially illustrated in the assembly chamber, where the seating was initially designed so that in front of the rostrum focal point is a wide dais capable of accommodating a wall of ministers sixteen men wide. Though this dais literally outflanks the front-row parliamentarians, an official at the building commented that, when the assembly was in session, it was the ministers themselves who usually claimed the front-row seats (see 8.9). Following the second dissolution of parliament in 1986, the building was described in a Ministry of Information publication as the Council of Ministers' Building,[30] though it served this function only on a temporary basis. These ministers, some of whom came from old Kuwaiti merchant families who had been trusted supporters of the al-Sabah for two centuries, held full voting rights in the assembly, the most important portfolios being retained by members of the ruling family. Thus, with sixteen of sixty-six votes essentially guaranteed to support the emir's position, it required the support of only seven of the fifty elected parliamentarians to prevent the necessary two-thirds majority from passing legislation that would be against the wishes of the emir. Moreover, he had the right to initiate, sanction, and promulgate laws and to rule by decree when the assembly was not in session.[31] The ultimate limitation upon the assembly's power was, of course, the emir's constitutional right to dissolve it by decree.

The parliament was dissolved, however, not because of its weakness or its irrelevance, but rather because of its unanticipated strength and its challenges to the power of the emir and the Council of Ministers. Citizenship, while greatly curtailed in numbers, nonetheless cut across many of the other factional discords in the country. As a result, the parliament that was intended in large part as "a rubber stamp for policies set forth by the ruling class as embodied in the executive"[32] proved to be far more contentious than its creators had envisioned. In 1976, when the parliament was dissolved for the first time, the emir charged that the representatives had "exploited democracy and frozen most legislation in order to achieve private gain"[33] and expressed concern about the "Lebanization of Kuwait," referring to increased discord between rival religious groups seen to have been fostered by excessive openness. More directly, perhaps, the ruling family simply resented receiving direct criticism from the leftist and Arab nationalist opposition in the assembly, and resisted its intrusions into foreign policy, inter-Arab politics, and national security—considered the prerogatives of the al-Sabah.[34] Jassim Khalaf's dissertation on the institutional structure and function of the Kuwait National Assembly notes that the government contended that the drastic measure of dissolution was taken in order for the country "to deliberate upon the democratic experience in Kuwait."[35] Yet, in the very act of dissolution, the context for such deliberation was undermined.

By 1980, however, the ruling family had concluded that the benefits of a national assembly as a means of political participation outweighed the risks that opposition could become too virulent, and elections were held again in 1981 and in 1985. The first round of elections yielded substantial parliamentary support for the al-Sabah, but opposition candidates fared better in 1985 elections, so the feistiness of the National Assembly resumed. In 1986, the emir dissolved parliament, for complex reasons that resembled those of a decade earlier. In a speech to his countrymen, he declared: "I have seen democracy shaken and its practices decline . . .. This has been accompanied by a loosening of the inherited cohesiveness of Kuwaiti society."[36] According to a press report,

> No one is quite sure what triggered the government's decision to dissolve the Assembly. In his speech to the nation announcing the decision, Emir Sabah said the parliamentarians had fanned secular divisions. This was seen as a reference to questions raised by parliament members about the loyalty of Kuwait's Shiite Muslims. . . . But Kuwaitis interviewed for this story unanimously said that they thought the government's chief reason for dissolving the Assembly was the parliamentarians persistent, increasingly aggressive questioning of government policies.[37]

Whether for reasons of factional discord rooted in foreign policy or owing to power politics tied to more purely domestic concerns apparent in the aftermath of the Suq al-Manakh crash, it was clear that the ruling family and its associates were coming under unaccustomed criticism. What was surprising, at least to Western embassy officials quoted in the Western press, was that many Kuwaitis did not seem to be especially disturbed by the sudden loss of what democratic freedoms they had gained. "We were frankly surprised when the Assembly was dissolved," noted one Western diplomat. "But the big-business families weren't as upset as you might think. The bottom line here is that everyone is rich and the basis for political dissent doesn't really exist. So a lot of Kuwaitis just sort of shrugged." According to the *Christian Science Monitor*'s reporter, the "most consistent theme in conversation with Kuwaitis" after the dissolution was that these were "regrettable but necessary steps." One wealthy Kuwaiti commented, "The members of parliament were not acting responsibly . . .. It was good that the government sent them home."[38] The *Wall Street Journal* reported that Kuwait's financial community was so encouraged by the demise of the quarrelsome parliament that Kuwait's local stock market rallied. As one banker put it, "The new government, when it's formed, will have more direct impact, without going through the National Assembly . . . without any delay."[39] In spite of this cautious optimism on the part of some, others presciently warned that the dissolution of parliament and the censorship of a press that had once offered "some of the liveliest reporting in the Arab world"[40] could well increase tensions: "In the long run, the Amir of Kuwait's rescinding of parliament elections and press freedom shuts what has always been considered an important safety valve that allowed Kuwaitis to vent political grievances. The danger is that these grievances now will be pent up and even driven underground, adding another potential source of political instability."[41] With a war going on off its north coast during the 1980s and increasing division within its borders, Kuwait faced ever-greater threats, pressures that were dwarfed in turn by the Iraqi invasion. What follows is an attempt to demonstrate how Utzon's building fits into this troubled picture.

UTZON'S ARABISM

Prior to the Iraqi takeover, the Kuwait National Assembly building existed symbolically in at least two very different ways. Most explicitly, it was a symbol to the world of Kuwait's commitment to democratic institutions in a region known only for monarchical and oligarchical control. This is the kind of symbol that Utzon's firm sought to create. In proposing the building for an Aga Khan Award in 1986 (which it did not win), the designers proclaimed, "It stands as an impressive symbol of Kuwait's representative form of government, an imposing public monument which lends dignity and strength to its urban setting, and a soaring architectural tribute to Kuwait's faith in its future."[42] But there is also a second symbolic interpretation, likely of equal importance to the government as the first: to Kuwait's residents the building could be a symbol of the government's commitment to perpetuating the special privileges of Kuwaiti citizens, underscored by efforts to reduce the foreign segment of the population.[43] In the absence of a functioning parliament, however, the two symbolic purposes of the building were each reduced to cruel ironies, at least until the 1990s. Not only was the experiment in democracy summarily cut short twice by emirial fiat and once by invading tanks, so too both forms of crackdown called into question the predominance of the ruling family and the rest of the elected Kuwaiti elite.

8.3 Diagram of Kuwait city center. The siting of Utzon's National Assembly building may be seen as part of a larger trend in the 1970s and 1980s to site certain major buildings in Kuwait City along the waterfront (or near it). This siting did not, however, challenge the pride of place given to the emir's ever-expanding Sief Palace complex.

While it may be no great task to challenge the quality of Kuwait's fledgling democracy of the 1970s and 1980s (and even unfair to do so given the autocratic tendencies of the region), these limitations had spatial implications that affected the design and the interpretation of the building.

In hindsight, the building appears to be designed for a physically—as well as politically—much more open society than existed when it was designed and built. This is a building which, from its grand entrance portico to its overscaled central street, demands a certain public involvement. But such a public presence was at odds with the political situation during the time of its design and construction, given the understandable emphasis upon the need for security, and one wonders if the government client ever intended anything resembling free public access to the building. Whether he realized it or not (and his words suggest that he did not), Utzon designed a public building for an exclusive club.

According to its architects, the Kuwait National Assembly building is "an excellent synthesis of traditional Arabic architectural principles and contemporary design expression."[44] It is this synthesis and these principles I wish to probe here. The attempt by Utzon to define and promote a national identity for Kuwait has two aspects. First, there was a perceived need to assert a Kuwaiti identity, based in a culture with deep historical roots, which went beyond relatively recent matters of petroleum and riches. And, second, closely tied to this wish to emphasize historical depth was the recognized urgency to stress and maintain the privileged claims of Kuwaiti citizens within the plural society in which they remained a minority. The initial decision to commission a prominent building to house the National Assembly and the particular forms of the building itself are each manifestations of this dual search for identity.

With the founding of the first National Assembly in 1962, following full independence, Kuwait's leaders took the notion of democracy well beyond the idea of a consultative body operating within the inner sanctum of the emir's waterfront Sief Palace: they gave it its own building, a vital first step toward a separation of executive and legislative powers. During the 1960s and 1970s, the National Assembly was housed in a bland, international modernist building located well inland from the seat of emirial power (8.3–8.5). The decision in 1972 to commission a new home for the assembly was also a directive to bequeath this institution a far more prominent site and a commitment to give it a more indigenous looking architectural presence. The siting of the new National Assembly along Arabian Gulf Street may be seen as part of a larger strategy for redevelopment of this part of the center of Kuwait City, intended to yield a district of buildings of national importance. The presence of the Sief Palace and other historical associations with the early days of Kuwait had long since established this stretch of coastline as the most prestigious zone of the city, and the National Assembly was to join not only the emir's palace, which was itself expanding along the waterfront in both directions during the 1970s and 1980s, but also the Ministry of Foreign Affairs and National Museum and, just inland from these, the State Mosque, Palace of Justice, Central Bank of Kuwait, and the Kuwait Stock Exchange. Most of these buildings being treated as isolated islands in

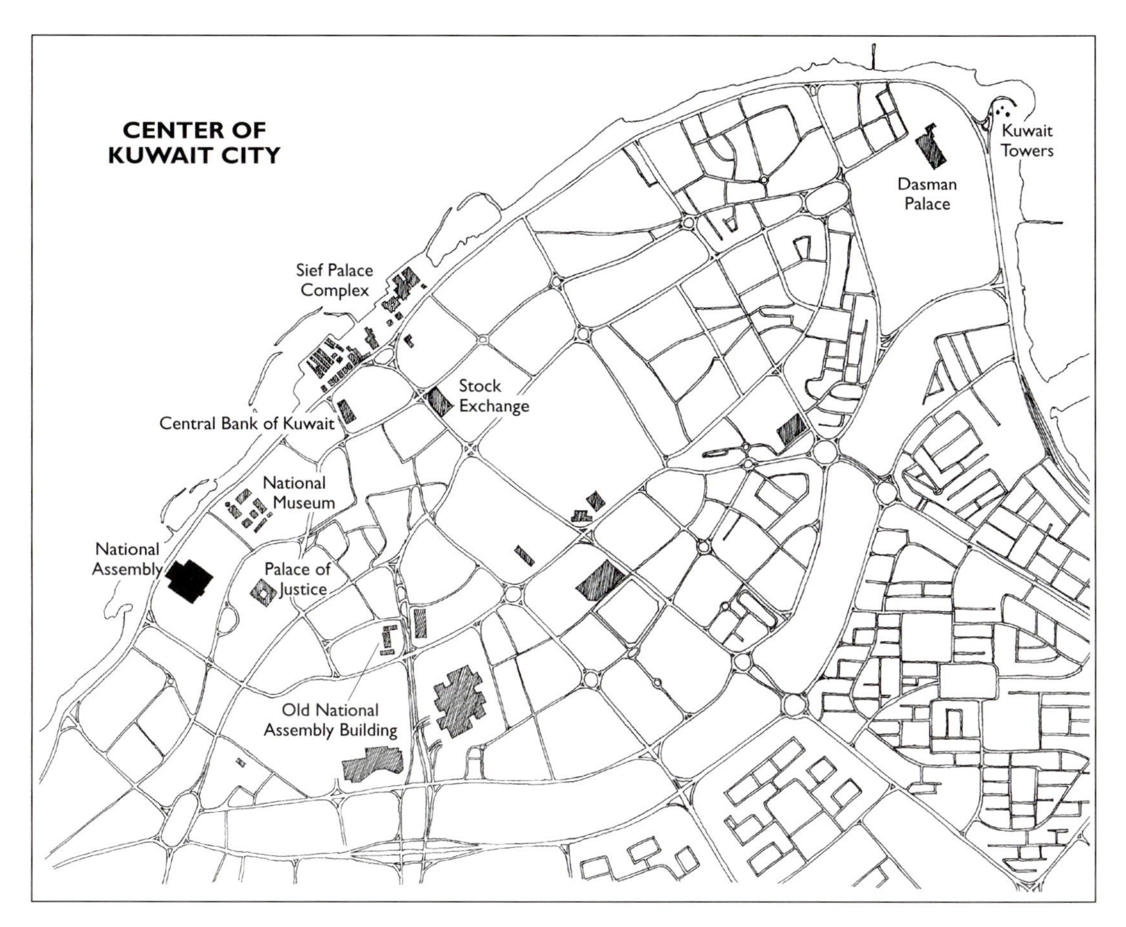

8.4 Old Assembly Building, Kuwait City.

a sea of parking lots, the area is reminiscent of the lineup of institutions in PNG's Waigani. In Kuwait, however, these national institutions have not been given a new capitol complex setting in the suburbs. Instead, a substantial part of the center of the city has been gradually razed to accommodate them.

As a global reconsideration of the urban losses sustained through such so-called renewal schemes set in during the 1970s and 1980s, Kuwaitis, too, looked for architectural solutions that could recapture elements of past indigenous environments, sometimes rather literally. On the water side of Arabian Gulf Street, almost directly opposite the National Assembly

8.5 Utzon's Kuwait National Assembly: an island on the edge of the sea.

building, they constructed a replica of a traditional Kuwaiti village. And just inland from the parliamentary complex, the Ministry of Public Works began work during the 1980s to revitalize certain of the old marketplaces in order to "preserve the place of the souk in Kuwait's society, its connection with the country's tradition and its compatibility with modern requirements."[45] As for residential architecture, according to Ibrahim al-Shaheen, head of the National Housing Authority, "in the nineteen-sixties, everyone wanted to build a Western-style villa. In the seventies, people began to ask for old-fashioned Islamic arches and traditional Arab lines. Now [in the late 1980s] the trend is to return to Kuwaiti-style buildings—simple houses, with the rooms giving on a courtyard, and with small openings to keep out the sun . . .. People here are leaning more and more toward Kuwaiti architecture, talking more and more about their traditions, trying to get closer to their cultural origins."[46]

Though much of Kuwait's commercial architecture continued to make use of internationalist modernism, the buildings for state institutions were, by the late 1970s, tending to be more self-consciously Islamic in character. Still, given the country's enormous construction industry directed and staffed largely by non-Kuwaiti consultants and workers, no national building could be entirely autochthonous. In this regard, Islamic appearance was only one small part of the need for a design—and its designer—to be perceived by sponsoring Kuwaiti officials as politically correct. Especially at a time of ongoing border disputes with Iraq, fears of pan-Arab nationalism, and a perceived need to increase the role of Kuwaiti consultants, design commissions were often awarded for reasons that had little to do with architectural merits. The design for Kuwait's National Assembly building was the product of an architectural competition limited to six invited entries, sponsored by a parliamentary committee, and juried by an international team chaired by Britain's Sir Leslie Martin. After early elimination of four of the entries, the decision came down to a choice between the Utzon scheme and one proposed by the firm of the noted Iraqi architect Rifat Chadirji. Chadirji, in a long, detailed memo which has not been made public, convincingly argues that he was denied victory in the competition, after intense lobbying efforts on both sides, largely because he was an Iraqi at a time when this could be considered a political liability in Kuwait and because he was seen to have committed his firm to work with a British consultant, Ove Arup, thereby constraining the possibility of contracting out to a Kuwaiti firm. A Danish team, however less likely to be versed in the cultural complexities of Islamic design, was apparently thought more appropriate in the cultural complexities of Kuwaiti politics.[47]

Despite the decision to build an imposing home for the National Assembly along the waterfront near the emir's Sief Palace, there was little indication that this architectural power sharing would have political ramifications of equal magnitude. The process of obtaining the design commission (at least as convoluted as the one in PNG, if one is to believe Chadirji's account) is indicative of the ways democratic procedures are often undercut by acts of executive political will.

Intended to replace a rootless international style edifice, Utzon's new building draws upon a wide range of building types and urban forms from throughout the Gulf region, but in the process of their abstraction and admixture these are dislocated and trivialized. As elegant as this building is in some of its manipulation of precast concrete elements, it is clumsy in its attempts to modernize Islamic symbols and typologies. In discussing the building, Utzon refers to three aspects of "traditional Arabic" architecture—the nomad's tent, the bazaar, and the covered square (as a place for political gathering).

The nomad's tent

Though the story of the region is a dual history of fishermen and desert nomads, the history of the al-Sabah is tied firmly to the latter. The early history of Kuwait, subject to the usual semimythology that surrounds any discussion of founding fathers, is especially potent since the direct descendants of these founders continued to rule the country without interruption for centuries. By the eighteenth century, after other family groups had moved on or focused their energies on seafaring trades, the al-Sabah family gained administrative control over Kuwait. As the American diplomat Barbara Bodine describes it, the al-Sabah were never called a "royal" family, and Kuwaitis do not consider their rule to be a hereditary divine right. Rather, their role as part of the "national story" is that they traditionally had the role of "the city managers." The al-Sabah were a kind of "civil servant caste." "They internalized the idea that 'it's not ours, we just run it.'" The al-Sabah and many other prominent Kuwaitis regard themselves as descendants of the Bani Utub (People Who Wandered), a branch of one of the largest tribal confederations in the Arabian Peninsula, the Anaza, who migrated to Kuwait early in the seventeenth century from central Arabia. By 1716, the People Who Wandered had ceased to do so, and in 1756 the first al-Sabah sheikh had commenced management of an important port of call, connecting maritime traffic from India with desert caravans headed inland. Though settled in the place that would become Kuwait City, the al-Sabah retained close ties with the Bedouin of the interior.[48] In contrast to many

8.6 Springtime commuter's encampment, outside Kuwait City, 1990.

tribally oriented families whose interests turned toward the sea (and whose ties with the Bedouin consequently diminished), the al-Sabah remained oriented toward the desert, based on their interest in international trade. They continued an active relationship with the Bedouin tribes, camping out with them regularly and marrying into them.[49] In the early days, "Sabah power was based upon the family's relationship to the desert."[50] Sabah power today is fueled by oil rather than desert trade, yet the Bedouin remain an example of the overweening importance of family, clan, and tribal ties even in an age of diminishing pastoralism. According to one assessment, "The self-identity of most native Kuwaitis is based on the extended family and larger kinship groups. These loyalties are important not only in a social sense but also in a political sense in that blood ties are the predominant determinant of Kuwaiti citizenship and membership in the political elite." The political structure of Kuwait—in which the emir, the crown prince/prime minister, and sixteen appointed ministers run the government—is still largely dependent upon the memory of these eighteenth-century family ties forged in the desert. More than two hundred and fifty years later, wealthy Kuwaiti families in springtime commonly decamp into tents in the outlying desert, commuting to their jobs by car (8.6). Even so, left to choose between desert and shore, these days they will more frequently prefer a weekend sojourn at a beachfront chalet. As Bodine puts it, Kuwaitis hold "a romanticism but not an affection for the desert." The basic Kuwaiti view is "'We are descended from Bedouin but we are not Bedouin.'"[51]

In these ways, the connection of the ruling family and its associates to the Bedouin is largely based on what Geertz terms "assumed blood ties," an untraceable kinship thought to be real.[52] Yet Bedouin political power became actual as well as metaphysical, especially before the Iraqi takeover. The role of the Bedouin as traditional supporters of the ruling family to some extent carried over into the various attempts at legislative government since 1962, with the parliament of the mid-1980s having "a significant proportion of Bedouin, or at least deputies with tribal links and support—more than

50 per cent according to some estimates."[53] National redistricting in 1981 had increased the number of voting constituencies from ten to twenty-five, a controversial tactic designed to increase the representation of outlying areas, usually more tribally oriented, while cutting across ethnic and confessional enclaves in the metropolitan area.[54] According to one report, twenty-four of the elected members were "Bedouin with a background of loyalty to the ruling family" and "charges of bribery and gerrymandering to increase the strength of the Bedouin were rife."[55] In this context, it is not difficult to perceive the symbolic appropriateness of the Bedouin tent as an influence on the architecture of the National Assembly building. These Sunni Bedouin, in light of their overrepresentation in parliament,[56] and of their primordial connection to the ancestors of the ruling families, were certainly to be iconographically preferred.

The most striking aspect of the Kuwait National Assembly building is its two tent-like roof forms (see 8.2). According to the architects, "The shape of the roof of the Assembly Hall and the covered Public Square in front of the main entrance conveys the lightness of a billowing Arabian tent. This concave shape is also an ideal acoustical element which excludes disturbing echoes."[57] All matters of acoustical soundness aside, it is a decidedly remarkable feat to make six-hundred-ton concrete beams billow, though disturbing echoes remain.

At first glance, and even upon reflection about Kuwaiti society, the decision to evoke the Bedouin tent seems an inspired move. If ever there were a symbol that fit with the al-Sabah view of Kuwait's deeper history, it is the Bedouin. Kuwait City is built where the desert meets the sea, and the National Assembly, located on Arabian Gulf Street, is sited and designed to emphasize this duality. Its billows arguably evoking sails as well as tents, the building's dominant imagery could not only satisfy Kuwaitis who traced their past to the desert but also seem relevant to the imagined past of Kuwait's sea-oriented merchant families. By abstracting billows, which evoke both maritime and desert traditions, Utzon's design appears to attempt a synthesis of two conceptions of the past, though Utzon's published descriptions of the building mention only tents.

If the building is regarded metaphorically as a seaside concrete tent (rather than as a beached *dhow*), it is an apt commentary on the urbanization of the Bedouin. Use of the tent form is presumably intended to evoke the memory of this selectively imagined collective past. In his attempt to abstract a visual image from a disappearing way of life, however, one may question Utzon's use of a technology that makes that past feel yet more distant and alien. The billows may seem an adequate allusion on the drawing boards of imported Danes—and even in the minds of the international jury called upon to select the architect—but do they really invite serious contemplation of a desert past, a heritage that so many Kuwaiti leaders claim to cherish? Does this use of the imagery deliver more than the Western stereotype of Arab = tent?

Intentionally or not, Utzon seems to have grasped the importance of the tent's symbolism for modern Kuwaitis. In the way he has abstracted it, however, he has delivered little of its imagery and even less of its principles.

8.7 Bedouin tent in the courtyard of House Museum, Kuwait City (1990).

Utzon's portico tent not only is of a scale far exceeding any precedent but also fails to address the traditional tent's central purposes: portability and protection from the elements. Not unlike the disjunctions inherent in Hogan's transformation of aspects of a village haus tambaran into concrete and mosaic, Utzon's concrete tent works against the impermanence that is essential to a tent's usual function. Moreover, a traditional tent must not only provide shade from an intense desert sun, but also afford refuge from wind and sandstorms (both of which are often a problem in Kuwait City). Of Utzon's two tentlike, white concrete roofs, one covers an open plaza that lacks an adequate protective enclosure, while the other shields the totally enclosed environment of an air-conditioned assembly hall—neither space has much to do with a tent. Moreover, traditional Bedouin tents of this area—examples were displayed prominently in the courtyard of a house museum nearby—are brown or black, not white (8.7). Like Hogan's haus tambaran facade, Utzon's tented roof provides a quick image of a vernacular typology with deep roots in the assumed blood ties of some of the citizens but does little to recall the complex ways the earlier use of such forms was tied to social and cultural patterns. What results is an image without a purpose. That the traditional Bedouin shelter and Utzon's tentesque abstraction of it are poles apart does not negate the appeal of Bedouin imagery, however superficial and distorted, to the Kuwaiti government authorities who approved the design.

Underlying all this is a contradiction that the architect seeks to address: the functional requirements of a modern urban government institution do not call to mind the necessity of a nomad's tent, yet there remains a certain powerful collective wish to remember the desert past and to identify it with the founding of the nation. In the case of a National Assembly building this impulse may be especially strong, because it is the Bedouin tradition of consultation with their elected sheikh in his tent that could be seen as the earliest manifestation of democracy in Kuwait. Utzon recognizes both the relevancy and the irrelevancy of the Bedouin tent for modern Kuwait, and his basic impulse is to transform the traditional form. As an impulse, this seems unassailable. What is questioned here is the nature and value of the allusion in the new artifact. How does one modernize a tent so that the new version can also play a productive cultural role?

The use of concrete to translate the sense of a desert nomad's billowing tent into a seaside politicians' immovable hall seems rather perverse, but it does convey the sense that the People Who Wandered have conclusively decided to settle down. In his best moments here, Utzon succeeds brilliantly in "making concrete breathe, or perhaps sigh,"[58] though one may still wonder why he begged such trouble. Presumably he might have employed a fabric structure—as was done for Skidmore Owings & Merrill's Aga Khan Award-winning Hajj terminal at the Jeddah airport. In choosing to avoid such tensile structures, Utzon likely was encouraged by his earlier success at using concrete to evoke cloth, most notably at the Sydney Opera House. In any case, he showed both little inclination to learn from a nomadic people who had managed to create structures out of minimal materials and much determination to learn from the formal and structural preoccupations of his own earlier work. In this way, the Kuwait National Assembly building is another example of the ways an architect's personal identity is a central part of any effort to help consolidate the identity of others. What is memorable about Utzon's building is less the Bedouin precedent or even the idea of a tent than the structural tour de force of the portico.

Utzon's design language is more specific in its architectural references to a tribal group that has no direct ties to Kuwait, the Marsh Arabs. This group, although they lived a short distance away in southern Iraq, had adapted their architecture to a very different topography (an adaptability that tragically reached its limits when Saddam Hussein ordered the marshes drained). Utzon's design of the Assembly Chamber interior unmistakably shows inspiration from Marsh Arab *mudhifs*, which are used as places of consultation with the sheikh (8.8, 8.9). What is transferred, however, has little to do with the spirit or function of these extraordinary buildings: Utzon extracts only the imagery, without the principles, the scale, or the need to have a close fit between form and social purpose. The Marsh Arab

8.8 Interior of a Marsh Arab *mudhif*, Iraq.

8.9 Marsh Arab-esque interplay between column and infill.

references are presumably included not only because of their beauty, but also because of some supposed relevance. *Mudhifs* are well published[59] and an acknowledged part of the canon of vernacular building types, yet they bear no resemblance to any buildings found in Kuwait. Thus, while it is understandable that an architect might want to make reference to them in the effort to make his building seem rooted in the region, what results is a regionalism that does little justice to the cultural and climatic place of these forms.

What is visually similar in the National Assembly hall and the Marsh Arab *mudhif*—for example, the alternation of thick pole and delicate infill—is tectonically completely unrelated. Similarly, though Utzon makes elegant reference to the Marsh Arab use of reed lattice in the mullion pattern of his assembly hall windows, his abstracted palmfronds are stripped of their organic resonance when he applies them *upside down* above the entranceway. This inversion of the frond not only kills the plant, it kills the metaphor as well. The superficiality of his distorting abstractions is nowhere more evident than in his insistence that the National Assembly building is architecturally related to the form of the traditional Arabian bazaar.

The bazaar

According to Utzon, the National Assembly building is "organized . . . in a fashion close to traditional Arabian bazaars."[60] "The system of the bazaar is so simple and clear," he continues, "that it results in an administration building that functions superbly."[61] Yet the similarity Utzon asserts is only a surface resemblance; the differences between the assembly complex and the traditional bazaar are far more telling.

Utzon claims to utilize an organizational principle from the bazaar but does so in such a reductive way as to negate the value of the analogy. In planning the building so that the entrances to all departments are accessed from a "central street" that is "similar to the central street in an Arab bazaar,"[62] Utzon isolates the clarity of a bazaar plan at the expense of its richness. Even a glance at the plan of a traditional bazaar, for example those in Aleppo or Istanbul, reveals that it is far more than a "simple and clear" organizational diagram (8.10, 8.11). In the treatment of the bazaar as merely an organizational diagram, Utzon's central street is detached from the Islamic roots he wants to claim for it. He could just as plausibly have claimed ancient Roman town plans as his inspiration, though such a comparison does little justice to those towns. The central street of the assembly complex is far closer to the organization of a Western shopping mall or an airport wing than it is to a traditional bazaar.

The plausible resemblances to the bazaar and its warren of souks are few. There is a halfhearted attempt to use "traditional Arabic light wells"[63] to provide some of the secondary "side streets" with "daylight and ventilation,"[64] but this bears little relation to the ever-changing filtered light of the marketplace or to the usual practices for its ventilation (8.12). In a like manner, though the architects claim adherence to Islamic principles in their design of courtyards within the various office modules, these openings serve none of the functions of the traditional court. Since they are unenterable, they play no role in circulation, either human or atmospheric. While they provide welcome opportunities for landscaping and natural light, they linger as half-remembered formal gestures that have lost their social role.

In the end, the most convincing aspect of the bazaar metaphor is in its capacity for growth. According to Utzon, "The departments consist of modules of various sizes built around small patios or courtyards—connected to the central street by side streets. Each department can be extended at any time by adding modules. The building can grow sideways, away from the central street, and its outer boundaries will change as time goes by. These free-flexing outer boundaries of the system are very much related to traditional Islamic bazaar architecture."[65] Yet even here the analogy falters: the modular office building and the traditional bazaar expand in different ways. Whereas the traditional bazaar could break free of the rectilinear bounds of its central street and accommodate itself to the peculiarities of

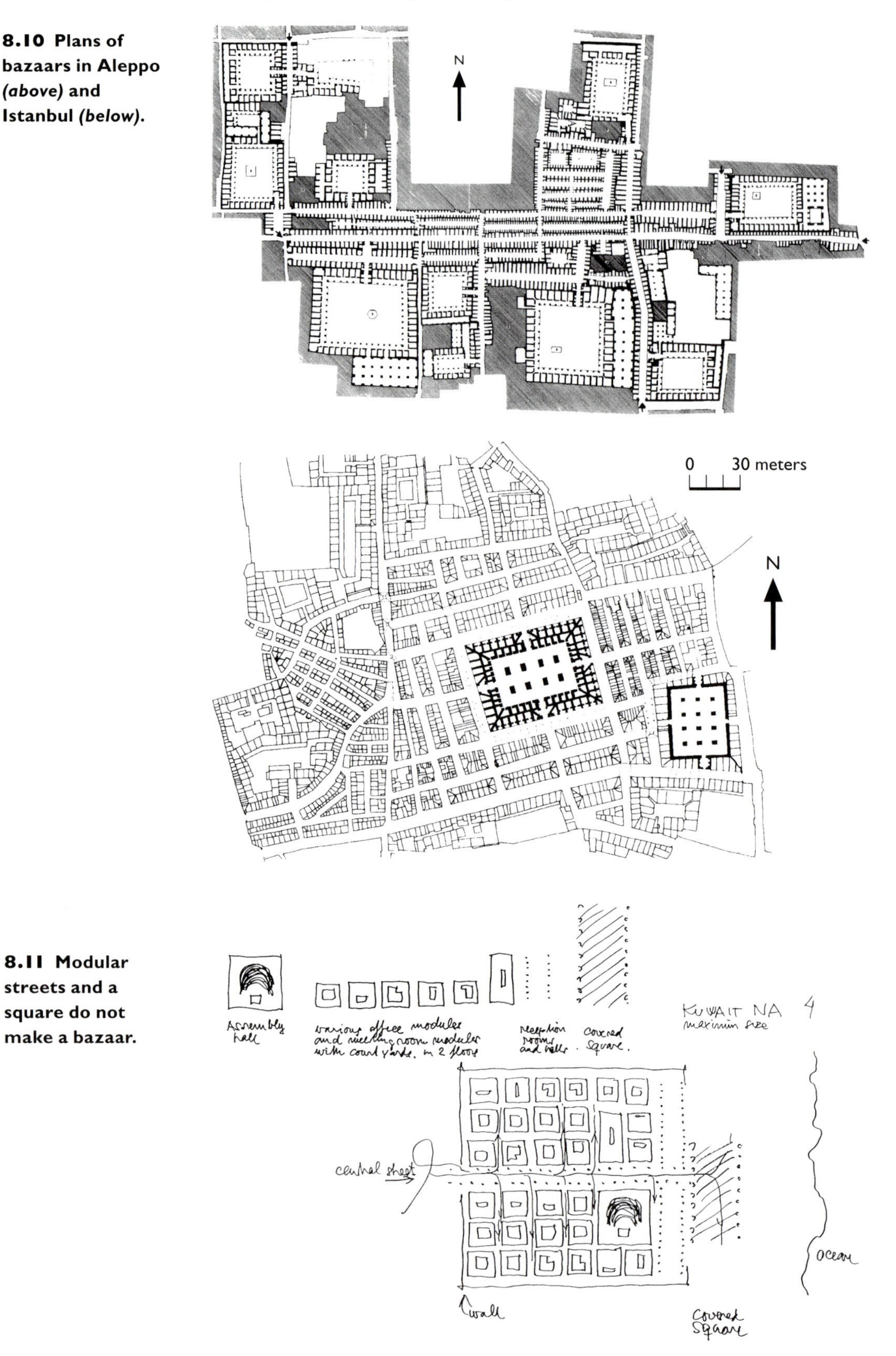

8.10 Plans of bazaars in Aleppo *(above)* and Istanbul *(below)*.

8.11 Modular streets and a square do not make a bazaar.

8.12 View of souk, Kuwait, 1939.

the surrounding urban fabric, Utzon's National Assembly complex is a walled island, imprisoned in its own grid.

The interest for Utzon is the flexibility of the module rather than the composition of the facades, the spatial dynamism of the overall form, or the relation of that form to the surrounding city. For decades Utzon has extolled the merits of "additive architecture":[66] "When working with the additive principle, one is able, without difficulty, to respect and honour all the demands made on design and layout as well as all the requirements for extensions and modifications. This is just because the architecture—or perhaps rather the character—of the building is that of the sum total of the components, and not that of a composition or that dictated by the facades."[67] A strength of this approach is that it allows the building to remain relatively low to the ground, respecting the two-story height of the old city, though almost nothing of that old city was extant.[68] Only the rooflines of the ceremonial spaces break this plane. On the other hand, however, the flexibility to add modules on the edges correctly presupposes that there is room on the site to do so. It is one thing to provide this room on a rural site and quite another to do so in the center of a city. What may be appropriate in Utzon's design for a Danish educational center ("to be developed in stages or continuously as a growing organism") (8.13, 8.14) seems self-contradictory in a security-conscious urban setting, though the correspondence of formal elements is striking. While there is room on the site for the National Assembly "organism" to expand—especially to the south—security considerations have turned these open spaces into a cordon sanitaire around the building (see 8.5). While Utzon invokes the analogy of the bazaar—perhaps the most quintessentially urban form known to man—his building is designed to deny any relationship with the real city that exists beyond the bounds of the precast souk. In the plan of a Roman military camp, the main

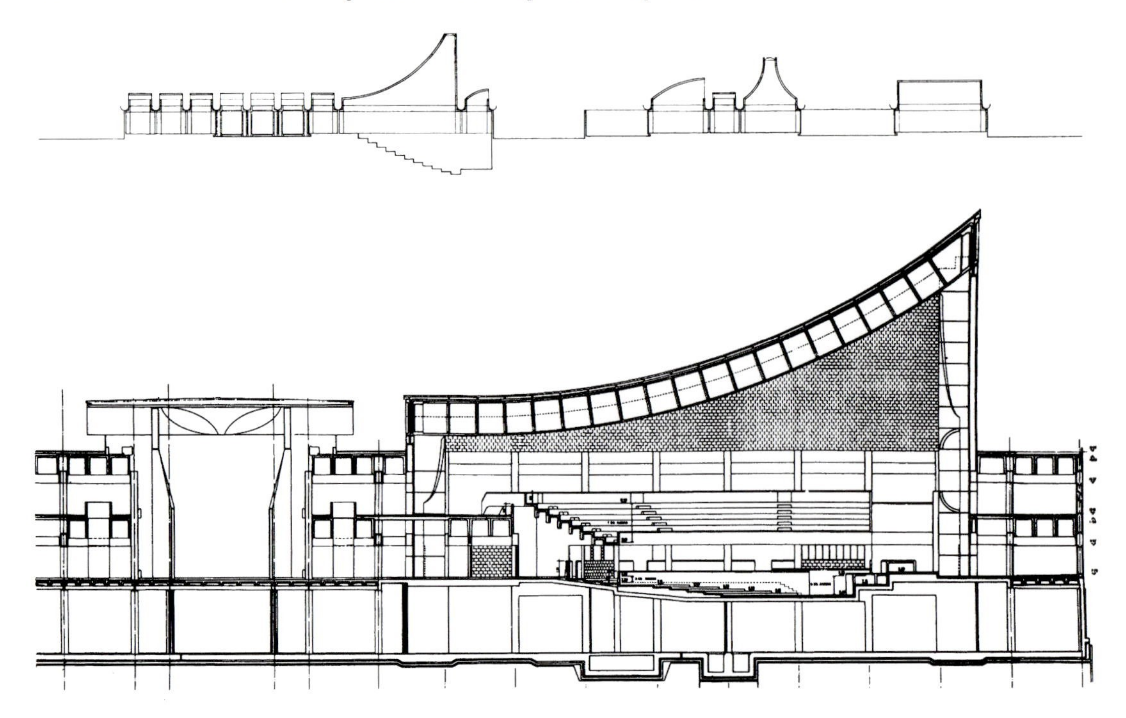

8.13 ***(above)*** **Partial section through Utzon's Herning School project: expanding across a rural site.**

8.14 ***(below)*** **Partial section through Utzon's parliament building: additive forms in the city.**

street, known as the *decumanus*, originates at the primary gateway to the complex and is sited to face away from the enemy. In Utzon's government encampment, the enemy would seem to be the rest of Kuwait City. The so-called central street, Utzon's indoor *decumanus*, leads nowhere, joins nothing. What begins on Arabian Gulf Street in overblown grandeur peters out into what appears to be an Islamicized bus shelter.

Yet the designing of an urbanistically connective building may have been impossible as well as undesirable to the political leadership. At the time Utzon received the assembly commission, much of the traditional mud-brick domestic architecture in the center part of Kuwait City had been destroyed, in accordance with the ideas of a British town planning firm brought in as consultants in the 1950s. Applying New Town planning principles, Kuwait's development officials had set aside the old town as a center for commercial development and government buildings, removed the old town wall, imposed a pattern of radial and concentric roads, and replaced a great number of courtyard houses with shoddily built alternatives.[69] Only isolated pockets of the vernacular fabric survived. It could be argued, then, that there was no urban context for Utzon's intervention, at least no traditional one. Still, if Utzon's analogous city is an attempted evocation of what was lost, the analogy remains a poor one.

A bazaar and its souks are more than clever pieces of well-engineered infrastructure: they are a distinctive social and economic environment. Even if Utzon had managed to evoke a spatial experience reminiscent of the bazaar, the new institutional presence could not help but alter the meaning of the spaces: a bureaucrat's bazaar shares little with a merchant's souk.

In its descriptions of the building, Utzon's firm represents it as a familiar, even neighborly place—an atmosphere that the formality of the design does not convey. "The arrangement of major uses around the Central Street makes it a general meeting place for government officials, politicians, visitors and the public. It is designed as a lively 'street' in which exhibitions of interest to politicians and the public may be displayed, and at times of festivities or crowded meetings it can be used as a grand foyer."[70] Yet this chilly corridor, with its deadening rhythm of awkwardly arranged couches, hardly calls to mind a lively street. However it is described, the National Assembly complex is an office building designed for a fixed and regulated community of bureaucrats rather than a bazaar planned to accommodate an ever-changing variety of visitors of all ages and incomes. This is a public building in silhouette only.

Admittedly, Utzon did not choose the site of the building—it is located close to the commercial center of the city—but he did choose to deemphasize almost all connections to its urban surroundings. Despite being adjacent to the National Museum (like so many other parliament buildings), in Kuwait the two remain deliberately separated, divided by an oblong parking block (see 8.3). Utzon designed an object building that unconvincingly pretends to be part of some larger system. Like the Sief Palace and many other large residences, it faces the Gulf. Yet in contrast to the palace, which has undergone a long and evolving series of extensions and additions, the National Assembly building stands alone. In time, it too may become a source of some larger piece of coordinated urban design. For now, however, this capitol remains detached from its capital.

The covered square

The "covered square" at the Gulf-side entrance is the place where the designers' notions of public participation seem farthest from the social and political realities of Kuwait. According to Utzon, the "Central Street leads toward the ocean and out into a great open 'hall,' a big open covered square, in the shade of which the people can meet their leaders."[71] Such billowy rhetoric aside, the result looks more like a monumental carport, in the shade of which the leaders can meet their chauffeurs.

Utzon is hard-pressed to explain the "open covered square" in terms of Kuwaiti precedent, but, ever the intrepid iconographer, he forges onward: "Arab countries have a tradition of very direct and close contact between leaders and people. The dangerously strong sunshine in Kuwait makes it necessary to protect oneself by seeking refuge in the shade. The shade is vital for existence, and this hall, this Covered Square, which provides shade for public gatherings, could perhaps be considered symbolic of the protection extended by a leader to his people. There is an Arab saying: 'When a leader dies, his shadow is lost.'"[72] Another Arab saying, less poetic, might be: "When an amir has been attacked, his shadow is kept inside a very secure building." Even the name *Kuwait* is derived from the Arabic words for "little fort."[73] Security considerations, which dictated that this building must protect Kuwaiti leaders from far more than the sun, have multiple spatial implications.

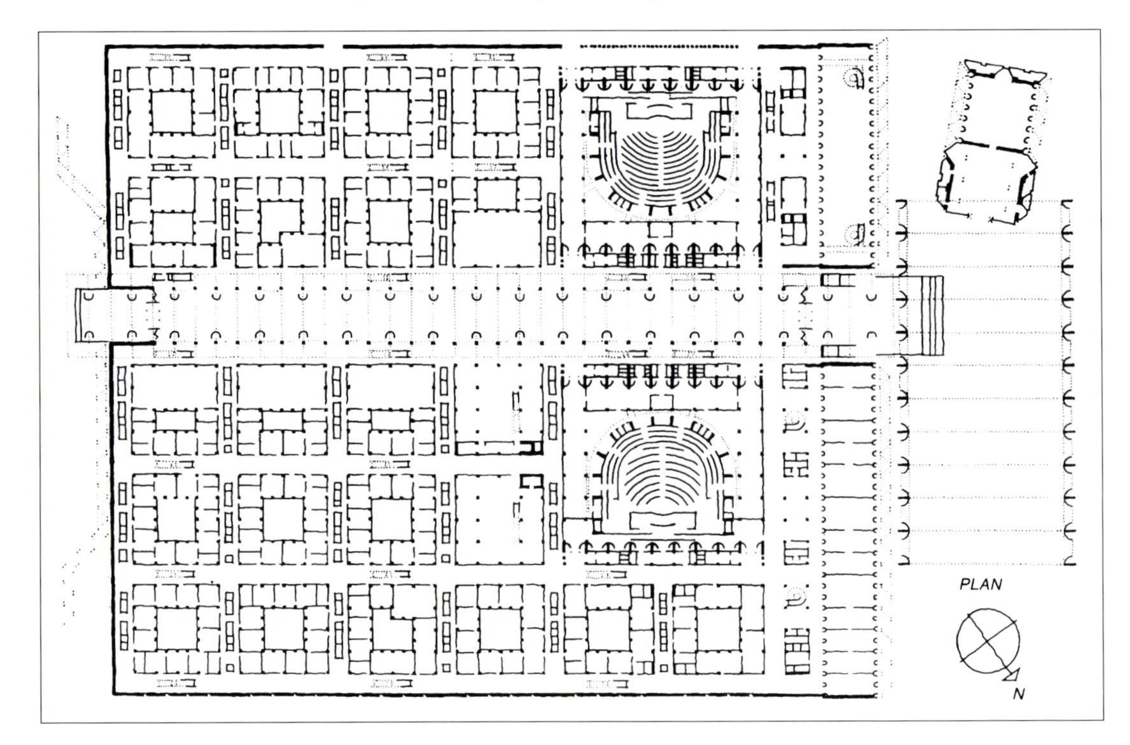

8.15 Early version of Kuwait National Assembly Building, with mosque and conference hall still included.

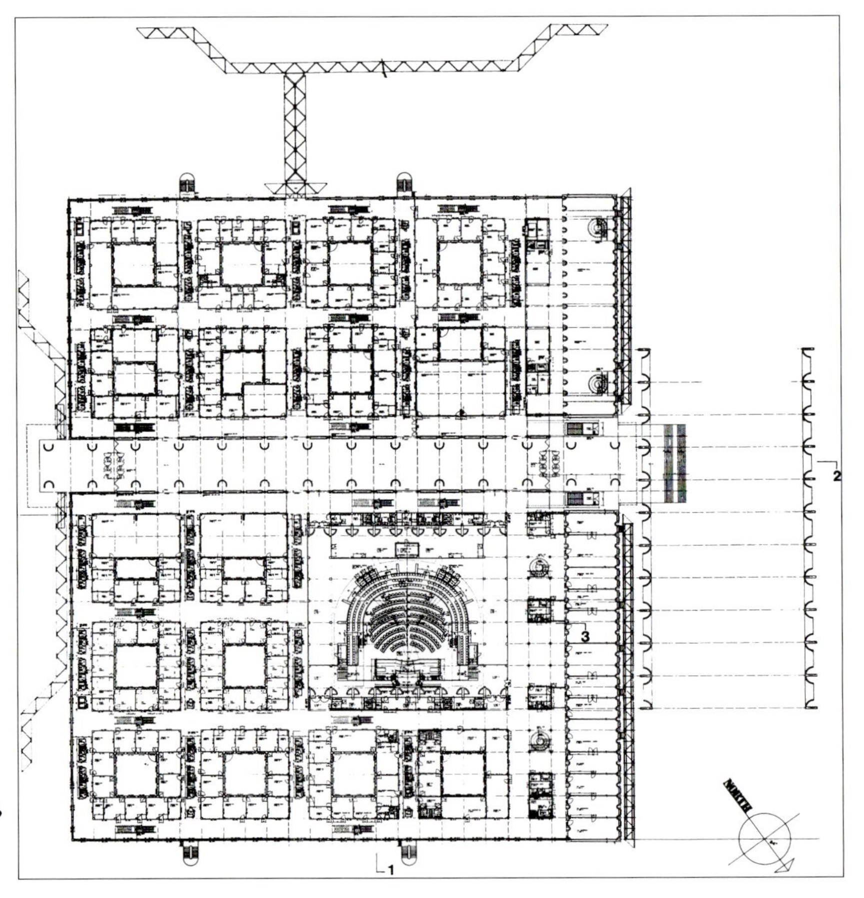

8.16 Later version of assembly building, without second hall or mosque.

To understand the origins of the portico/porte-cochère, one may look to Utzon's early drawings. These show the open covered square not as the highest status parking area that it became, but as the shaded forecourt to a mosque (8.15, 8.16). As later drawings reveal, this mosque was soon eliminated. If the planners had proceeded with the mosque, it would have been difficult to maintain fully controlled access to the site, since Islamic tradition insists on freedom of access to a mosque for those wishing to pray. The elimination of the mosque may have had another political component. Though Kuwait had always been an officially Islamic state, the rising tide of fundamentalism had made the degree of government involvement with Islam an increasingly volatile subject.[74] After the decision to move the mosque inside the building, presumably owing to considerations of security, the outside square lost its spatial definition as well as its most palpable function. At the same time, the National Assembly complex lost its most outwardly visible indication of human presence, leaving only the ubiquitous security guards.

Utzon is right to emphasize the long tradition of informal political discussion and the equally old custom of face-to-face audience with the emir, but his covered square bears no resemblance to such traditional places of meeting. Nightly gatherings known as *diwaniyas* have been referred to as "the true heart of Kuwaiti society" and are a tradition dating back many centuries to the time "when only tribes roamed Arabia and chieftains gathered their men to drink coffee and consult on everything from politics to gossip." In the years following the establishment of constitutional government, these meetings continued to serve as the place for electoral maneuvering; candidates made rounds of these gatherings and even the emir's own *diwaniya* was open to all comers.[75] Much of Kuwait's internal political turmoil in late 1989 and early 1990 took place in nightly *diwaniya* activity, flourishing primarily in private homes and courtyards rather than in coffee stalls. The word *diwaniya* connotes both the gathering and the place in which it is held. The physical nature of such places, then, would seem to be a matter of some significance. These places, the most widely shared loci of Kuwaiti face-to-face political dealings, take many forms. Sometimes they are held in air-conditioned rooms, sometimes outdoors. Though in some cases the *diwaniya* actually is a front-yard tent, it bears little formal, spatial, or social relation to the faulty metaphor of Utzon's open portico. And, since the gatherings are usually held after dark, there is no need for sun-shading (and, shade or no shade, during much of the year Kuwait's intense heat makes any kind of outdoor gathering uncomfortable). Thus, while Utzon is correct to point to the value of shade and to the need for "very direct and close" political contact in countries having a strong heritage of such consultation, his architectural solution bears no relationship to existing social practice.

PRECAST ARABISM

Utzon's often elegant form-making is as superficial in its evocation of the nomad's tent and the merchants' bazaar as it is irrelevant in its social accommodations. With its so-called Islamic references treated as purely formal devices, the building is Arabist rather than Arabic. Though Utzon alludes to many vital aspects of traditional Kuwaiti architecture and urbanism, elements that do retain an ongoing relevance in the culture, the abstraction seems aloof or even meretricious. It is architecture that advertises the past with the casual gloss of a tourist promotion brochure, thriving on image without principle. It simplifies and romanticizes and seems unlikely to reward introspection. In short, it seeks only to confirm and extend a stereotype. Whitewashed and packaged, it gives the outside world more of what it already knows: it is not only the concrete that has been precast. In providing only surface symbols, so overblown in scale as to contort their meaning, it does not even try to probe deeper questions of identity. This kind of architecture increases, rather than decreases, the perceptual distance between modernism and traditional forms of building because it fails to convey any spatial or experiential principles which can alert and stimulate the collective memory. Only in the reference to the Marsh Arab structures does Utzon come close to abstracting an evocative principle—one having to do with the relationship between solid and void. But that architectural quotation, ironically, is one that has no bearing on *Kuwaiti* identity, since it is a building type from a minority group in Iraq. It is no surprise, therefore, that Utzon does not acknowledge it as an influence. Moreover, even if this spatial principle were relevant, the purely formal nature of Utzon's reference divorces the Marsh Arab *mudhif* image from the highly evolved specificity of its social use.

Though the building is unsuccessful in conveying principles from traditional architectural and urban forms, it may provide a useful iconographic perspective on group relations in Kuwait. It is, thus, significant even in its superficiality. Though the reference to Bedouin tents has little phenomenological richness, it does underscore what would seem to be a deeply felt need to remember a nomadic past. Moreover, it simultaneously reminds Kuwaitis of the political influence of the rapidly urbanizing Bedouin. Both aspects of Bedouin iconography serve the interests of the ruling family and its associates, for it is these families, clinging to the benefits of limited citizenship rights, who often shared with the Bedouin both presumed kinship and definitive political alliance (at least during the prewar period). What is disappointing about the building is not that it recognizes the importance of these formative nomadic ties, but that these ties—if they are indeed so crucial—are conveyed architecturally in such a disengaged manner.

Ultimately, the building stands as a symbol of Kuwait's attempt to institute a measure of democracy in a region never known for power sharing. Designed during a period of hope, constructed during a period of renewed anticipation of democratic freedoms, the building instead became a principal victim of the Iraqi occupation of 1990–1991. Iraqi soldiers gutted the building's interiors as part of a systematic campaign to destroy all symbols of Kuwaiti sovereignty and culture. Barbara Bodine, who was the U.S. deputy chief of mission in Kuwait at the time of the invasion, describes it as nothing short of "ethnic cleansing." The Kuwait Emergency Recovery Office and its contractors faced daunting challenges: more than 700 public and state buildings (including the Sief Palace, the Bayan Conference Center,

8.17 View of damaged executive office waiting area in the Parliament building, as of August 1991. The repaired building reopened in 1992, to coincide with the restoration of parliamentary elections.

the National Museum, and the airport) had been thoroughly looted and vandalized, some with fire damage (8.17). Restoring the National Assembly building proved to be the largest task. With repairs initially budgeted at $24 million, the U.S. Army Corps of Engineers expected to use one of its existing contractors for the job. However, Kuwait's Council of Ministers regarded the building as "a symbol of Kuwaiti sovereignty," and insisted that a Kuwaiti contractor be hired for the structural work. At the same time, though, the Kuwaitis directed the Corps to appoint the U.S.-based firm Hellmuth, Obata, and Kassabaum (HOK) to handle interior design, with a budget of $2.5 million. The project took on special urgency once the emir decreed in June 1991 that parliamentary elections would be held in October 1992. The rush to complete the building in advance of the voting did not stop Kuwaiti officials from giving additional directions to HOK, which caused the design proposals to come in "tens of millions of dollars greater than the funds available." Still, given the importance of the project to the Kuwaitis—especially to Sheikha Fatima al-Sabah, an architect from the ruling family who worked with the design team—progress accelerated (8.18). The Corps chartered 747 and DC-10 aircraft to fly in materials and supplies, including

8.18 Sheikha Fatima al-Sabah *(right)* strolls the restored parliamentary "Main Street" with David Leach, U.S. Army Corps of Engineers Parliament reconstruction manager.

8.19 Once restored, the assembly chamber lost its elegant proportions (compare with 8.9).

$500,000 worth of Italian marble for the floors. Other international vendors supplied 5,600 sofas, tables, chairs, and mirrors. $67 million dollars later, the building was ready on time.[76]

The restoration of the National Assembly building entailed far more than mere restitution of the earlier structure. In particular, the assembly chamber reemerged in a markedly altered manner. The interior design team from HOK entirely reconfigured the back wall of the chamber (perhaps necessitated by structural changes). This destroyed the elegant proportions of the original, losing the evocative pillars and billows of Utzon's central concept for the room. Gone is the allusion to the Marsh Arab *mudhif*; evocations of plant forms have been replaced by a panoply of more intricate and conventional Islamic design motifs. Other design changes may have been taken in response to new parliamentary demands. In functional terms, the front dais is now no longer longer furnished to seat an imposing wall of ministers, and the parliamentarians' desks on the assembly floor are now divided into three ranks rather than two. Both changes convey a less oppositional appearing geometry, which may or may not reflect political reality (compare 8.19 with 8.9).[77]

Of course, restoration of the physical building meant little without restitution of its institutional purpose. Prior to the Iraqi invasion and occupation, parliamentary democracy in Kuwait had been intermittently proffered in limited forms, and could easily be perceived by the disenfranchised majority as part of the continuing attempt to consolidate Kuwaiti hegemony over noncitizens. At the same time, many Kuwaiti citizens had clamored for more meaningful political participation. Despite such concerns, Kuwaiti solidarity in the face of the Iraqi takeover revealed widespread support for the al-Sabah government even among those who had been most vocally opposed in the months just before the invasion. As Abdulkarim Al-Dekhayel puts it, "Since the institutional source of legitimation is very weak in Kuwait . . . the legitimacy of the Al Sabah regime is based on the state's functional role. The great achievements of the state in public policies—such as education, public employment, housing, health services, the private sector, and the provision of public assistance and social welfare services which materially benefited Kuwaitis—came to be positively reflected in the citizens' attitudes towards the al Sabah regime during the Iraqi invasion." Political economist Mary Ann Tétreault observes that the Kuwaiti prodemocracy movement also gained strength during the time of the occupation: "The invasion deepened most Kuwaitis' democratic values and taught them new techniques for expressing those values in their daily lives. During the occupation, Kuwaitis inside Kuwait mobilized in protected spaces to maintain their society as best they could, aided by resources from outside smuggled to them by their fellow citizens, Kuwaitis inside and outside turned the occupation itself into a protected political space, one from which they continued, publicly and privately, to press their leader for the restoration of the constitution after liberation." Barbara Bodine adds that "because of the *diwaniya* system, when the parliament was shut down the Kuwaitis still had other outlets for gathering and discourse. It was inevitable that the parliament would be reestablished" once the Iraqis were pushed out.[78]

Following the restoration of Kuwaiti sovereignty in 1991, much has changed. For a brief period, Kuwaitis became the largest ethnic group in the country, but already by 1992, they resumed their minority role. As Anh Nga Longva puts it, "The initial relief which the Kuwaitis felt at being the majority in their own country was quickly swept away by the realization that the enormous tasks of tidying up and rebuilding Kuwait after the looting and wanton destruction by the occupying forces could simply not be carried out without the expatriates. The gates to labor migration were consequently flung wide open again." Following the ouster of most of the Palestinians, however, the new labor force came to be dominated by Asian migrants; Kuwait's traditional preference for Arab manpower was abandoned. The net result, Longva concludes, is that "the Kuwaitis' perception of their own vulnerability, which lies at the root of their politics of dominance and exclusion, has been heightened."[79]

At the same time, however, the trauma of the Iraqi occupation and defeat certainly seems to have accelerated the forces of democratic change among the Kuwaitis themselves. As Tétreault drily comments, "The takeover of a country by a foreign power is hardly recommended as a recipe for expanding freedom and human rights. Yet one outcome of the Iraqi invasion and occupation of Kuwait was to increase the political capital of Kuwait opponents of domestic autocracy."[80] The restored National Assembly building has housed an increasingly feisty National Assembly, with elections held successfully in 1992, 1996, 2003, and 2006. Moreover, the National Assembly extended voting rights and the right to hold elective office to the sons of naturalized citizens in 1994. And, on 16 May 2005, the National Assembly extended suffrage to those adult women who had been citizens for at least twenty years, thereby making females the majority of eligible voters. Despite this, in 2006, none of the twenty-eight women on the ballot won election to the National Assembly, and Islamist bloc candidates garnered an increasing number of seats. Contradictions and complexities abound, but it is clear that the expanding Kuwaiti electorate has continued to use the parliament to oppose the government, and to call for further electoral reforms.[81]

Even so, the Kuwaiti political system continues to place significant checks on the power of the parliament. By tradition, the crown prince serves as the prime minister and, together with the emir and close advisors, "chooses the cabinet, leads the government, and exerts continual psychological and political pressure on the parliament as an institution and its members as individuals to surrender their limited autonomy to the demands of the ruling family."[82] Increasingly, however, the ruling family and its government have needed to find new ways to work with the people that the Kuwaiti citizens elect. In fits and starts, Kuwait's National Assembly as an institution slowly seems to be attaining a more significant role in the governance of the country, one more in keeping with the grandiosity of its architectural setting.

CHAPTER 9

The acropolis of Bangladesh

Bangladesh's capitol complex in Dhaka is both an important facility for an emerging nation-state and a stage in the evolution of an architect's work; as such, like the cases discussed in Chapters 6–8, it can be seen in relation to both a society and an individual's career. While this is not the place to review the whole of Louis Kahn's architectural oeuvre, it would certainly seem that the massive concrete National Assembly building and its brick outbuildings, completed in 1983, are more easily located in relation to Kahn's other works than in relation to the rest of Dhaka. That the building complex is in fact perceived by some as an *alternative* to Dhaka rather than a part of it may be judged from the persistence of references to it in Western architectural shorthand as "Dhaka" or "the Dhaka building," as if this city-region of well over 10 million people had no other (9.1–9.3).[1]

To assess a capitol complex, one must examine it both in terms of the intentions of its architect and in terms of the society it is expected to serve. Kahn, to a far greater extent than Hogan, Utzon, or Bawa, is an enigmatic figure of international renown, a source and a subject for an ever-growing

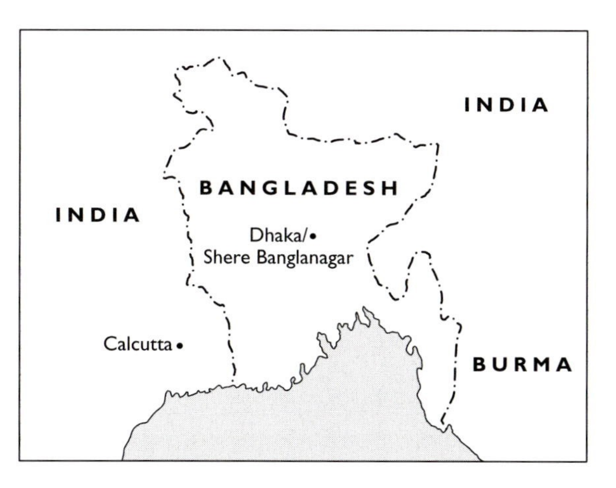

9.1 Bangladesh.

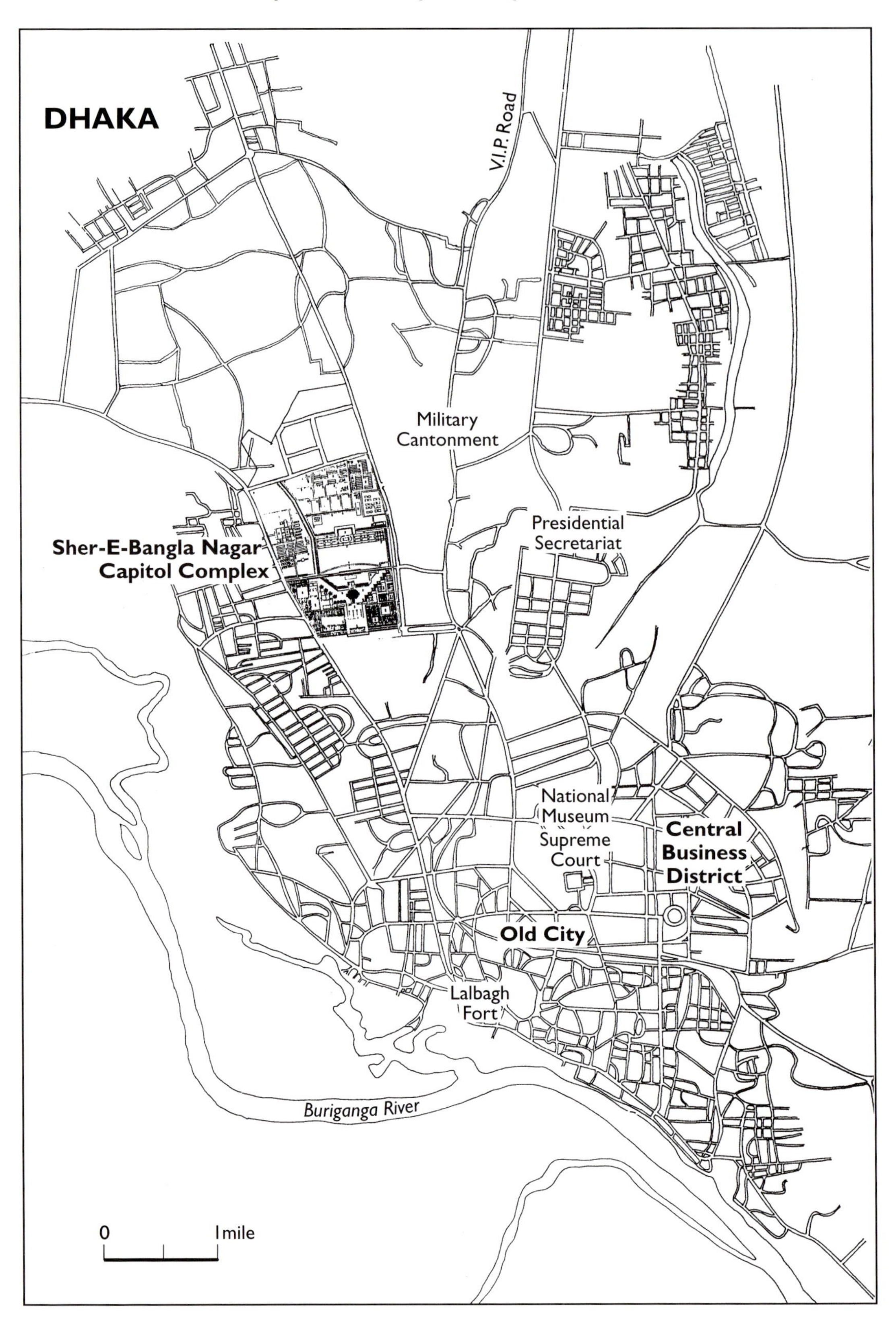
DHAKA
V.I.P. Road
Military Cantonment
Presidential Secretariat
Sher-E-Bangla Nagar Capitol Complex
National Museum
Supreme Court
Central Business District
Old City
Lalbagh Fort
Buriganga River
0
1 mile

9.2 ***(left)*** **Location of capitol complex in Dhaka.**

9.3 ***(above)*** **The Citadel of Assembly, Sher-e-Bangla Nagar.**

amount of critical inquiry, and there is a correspondingly larger archive of drawings and commentary available to consult. Notwithstanding the extensive discussion it has received, Kahn's work has all too rarely been seen in the light of the political history of this part of Bengal.

Dhaka as a city has undergone an extraordinary history of glory and decline. In the late seventeenth century, under Mughal rule, the city was among the largest in the world, with a population estimated at 900,000. Subsequently, however, came Mughal imperial decline, floods, famines, and British colonization, which transformed a thriving cosmopolitan center of trade and commerce into a market dependent on Britain. By 1867, most laborers in the countryside were working to satisfy European demand for raw materials, and Dhaka's population numbered only about 50,000.[2] Though the city briefly regained provincial capital status in 1906, when the British decided to partition Bengal, only five years later the British reunified Bengal and made Calcutta its administrative capital in an attempt to pacify Bengali opposition to the transfer of the British Raj capital to Imperial Delhi. Following the partition of British India and the creation of two-part Pakistan in 1947, Dhaka once again regained a provincial administrative role. West Pakistan, where the new state's government, military, and economic strength was concentrated, contained an extraordinarily large mixture of cultural groups, unified by an adherence to the beliefs of Islam. East Bengal (later renamed East Pakistan) also had an overwhelming Muslim majority, but the Bengalis, sharing a common language written in a different script from the official Urdu of the West Pakistanis, were both culturally more homogeneous and, significantly, somewhat more numerous. Ultimately, the detached and culturally distinct wings of Pakistan would fly in the face of any attempt to keep East and West as one nation-state. In 1971, after a civil war in which 300,000 were killed, East Pakistan became Bangladesh.[3]

Though the national government of Bangladesh makes use of the buildings designed by Louis Kahn, the buildings were not designed for the capital of Bangladesh; they were intended for the capital of East Pakistan. This is far more than a semantic distinction or historical curiosity, given that a civil war was fought against the original client. Moreover, since the place was premised on the need to provide temporary accommodation for visiting officials and MPs from West Pakistan (and on the assumption that the bulk of the national bureaucracy would be housed in Islamabad), Bangladeshi independence altered several central aspects of the architectural requirements for the complex and transformed the meaning of the urban design logic undergirding Kahn's initial conceptions.

There are, of course, many instances in which a new government, following a revolution, appropriates the edifices of the ancien regime. Architecture and its symbolism are never so closely wed as to prohibit divorce and eventual remarriage. The difficulties in Bangladesh were made more reconcilable by the fact that the National Assembly building, while groomed for Pakistan, was not completed until after the war. Thus, its union with Islamabad remained unconsummated.

Nevertheless, certain questions remain: What happens when a building designed to refer to the unity of East and West Pakistan is instead asked to be a symbol of Bangladesh? Who will remember the moment when the cornerstone was laid and thousands shouted, "Long live Ayub Khan!"?[4] When a building has been sponsored by a government against whom a civil war is fought, is there a stigma attached to it and, if so, how long does the stigma remain?

To posit a partial answer, it seems likely that the abstraction of Kahn's architectural language reduced the time needed for the building to begin to function as a positive symbol in a new political context. The lack of specific visual references to the sponsoring Ayub Khan regime or to West Pakistan's former domination has made the transition easier. Following the independence of Bangladesh, the name of the complex was changed from Ayub Nagar to Sher-e-Bangla Nagar (City of the Bengal Tiger), a reference to the nom de guerre of Bengali nationalist leader Fazlul Huq;[5] the renaming was intended to give this place a role in the annals of freedom fighters that it would not otherwise have had. This change, together with many more gradual and subtle shifts of association facilitated by the passage of time, serves to confirm and intensify the Bangladeshi symbolism of the complex. Given that the idea of a Bangladeshi identity (as opposed to a Pakistani or Bengali one) is itself a product of independence, the need to develop such symbols is understandably acute.[6] In the end, it may be that the difficulties associated with this capitol complex are tied more closely to Louis Kahn than to Ayub Khan.

In designing the parliamentary complex for East Pakistan, Kahn viewed his task as that of finding a spatial representation for a philosophical ideal, and, as was his practice, the philosophical premises were of his own design as well. Insisting that the client's program is "only an approximation of a need,"[7]

Kahn sought to demonstrate that "they need things they never knew they needed."[8] That such needs may be expensive he did not deny. His Dhaka edifices, he modestly noted, "cost more because I reveal the truth in those buildings."[9]

More than most architects, Kahn felt he understood his client's needs better than the client did. He viewed each commission as an opportunity to further his inquiry into the nature of institutions. In the case of the capitol for Dhaka, Kahn had the opportunity to design the chamber for the legislature, the institution that he believed was empowered to create other institutions. Kahn's compositional process was highly personalized and began with a notion of an appropriate "Form," what the building "wants to be." "Design" itself commenced only after Kahn felt he had sensed the essence of a building's Form. He viewed the building as having a will of its own, which pressed it into being in a particular way. It is this Form rather than the program itself which was the point of departure.

However much Kahn might wish to claim a certain inevitability about his choice of Form, such a design methodology leaves a great deal of latitude for idiosyncrasy and intuition. Kahn operated best when the client seemed willing, even eager, to acquiesce in deviations from the stated program, as in Dhaka. "What I'm trying to do," he noted, "is establish a belief out of a philosophy I can turn over to Pakistan, so that whatever they do is always answerable to it. I feel as though this plan which was made weeks after I saw the program has strength. Does it have all the ingredients? If only one is lacking it will disintegrate."[10] The "philosophy" he sought to bestow was, at base, centered on the idea of architecture's transcendence of politics, but this was not consistently acknowledged. "I kept thinking how these buildings could be grouped and take their place on the land," he recalled. "On the night of the third day, I fell out of bed with the prevailing idea of the plan, the realization that assembly is of a transcendent nature."[11] Kahn wanted many things—he wanted the "nature" of assembly to be transcendent and he wanted to create an architecture that confirms and enhances this. He assumed a social ideal, one that is extremely tenuous in any fledgling state, and claimed to design in accordance with it. Kahn, whose clarity with words rarely approached his facility with forms, obscured his intentions by confusing three kinds of possible transcendences: the transcendence of architectural form over temporal and social circumstances, the transcendent nature of "Assembly" as an abstract—almost primeval—ideal, and the transcendent power of the National Assembly as an institution. This confusion among architectural methodology, metaphysical ideals, and social realities appeared frequently when Kahn spoke or wrote about his work. By passing beyond the level of metaphor to that of reification, Kahn's poetics obscure the difference between what *he* wants his buildings to be and what the building itself "wants to be." However appealing, such verbal trickery can be used to cloak very personal design decisions in the mantle of universal law. As a design conceit it may be an acceptable manner of working, but it is a method with profound social consequences, particularly when Kahn was designing for a society and a culture radically different from his own.

For Kahn, this transcendence was to be embodied not merely in the creation of an overpowering presence in space, but also in the creation of a building capable of overcoming time, an edifice rooted in the past and hardened against the future. As Kahn put it, "What I try to insert is that quality which touches the desires of people beyond needs and that which would motivate similar desires on the part of those who may use the building after the client who orders it. . . . It must have qualities beyond the dictates of the moment."[12] In his assembly building, Kahn said that he wanted to design walls "that look as though they were there a thousand years" and that "have a virility that is like the memory of a giant."[13] In an essay from 1944 which seems to anticipate his concerns for the Dhaka capitol, Kahn defined monumentality as "a spiritual quality inherent in a structure which conveys the feeling of its eternity, that it cannot be added to or changed. We feel that quality in the Parthenon, the recognized symbol of Greek civilization. . . . We dare not discard the lessons these buildings teach for they have the common characteristic of greatness upon which the buildings of our future must, in one sense or another, rely."[14] His preoccupations can hardly be construed in terms as narrow as a search for national identity or a union of East and West Pakistan; Kahn sought a "recognized symbol" that would bestow membership in a timeless and universal civilization. According to his daughter, Kahn's "triumph" with the Dhaka commission was his success in communicating his "belief that the language of form transcended cultural differences."[15] Not all "cultural differences" can be so easily or thoroughly "transcended," however: architecture is produced not only by brilliant formgivers but also by the culture that gives it meaning and by the heterogeneous society in which it must stand. Especially when the architect comes from a different social and cultural background from those who sponsor or use the architecture, it is hard to avoid the temptation to elevate unacknowledged bias to the status of universal truth.

Kahn's design decisions in Dhaka were colored not only by his own personal agenda, but also by larger currents in architectural culture and international relations. In this regard, as one architectural historian points out, Kahn's work attempts to reconcile a postwar revival of interest in both humanism and regional identity, since each could be seen as an antidote to the stultifying uniformity of "mass culture." Kahn's insistence on the power of individual identity expressed the American side of Cold War politics of the late 1950s. This helps explain his central focus on the possibilities for participatory "assembly" in public space and his emphasis on the importance of institutions as a source of civic culture. At the time Kahn received his commission, the United States badly needed to embrace Pakistan as its ally in a region surrounded by Communist influence.[16] Both Ayub Khan and Louis Kahn seemed intent on finding parallels between the two countries, however disparate their early paths to democracy. To the extent that the United States government worried about the militarism of the Pakistani leader, the transcendent idealism of the American architect offered an appealing hope for the future.

While Kahn's complex is a product of a highly personal design methodology and a U.S. national geopolitics, it is also explicitly intended to generate international recognition. As much as the capitol complex is and was put forward in the name of national identity (whether Pakistani or Bangladeshi), it is a cry for *international* identity. As Mehmet Doruk Pamir points out,

> One can regard Sher-E-Banglanagar as an investment in establishing an international medium of communication. I regard "development" as a metonym for global interaction because it demands increasing contact with other parts of the world at different modes and levels. Until very recently about all the rest of the world knew about Bangladesh was that it was a country of human misery and social instability: floods, famines, and occasional coups. Then all of a sudden this building put Bangladesh on the roster of nations boasting the most sophisticated examples of contemporary architecture.[17]

As with Le Corbusier and the design of Chandigarh, the arrival of modern architecture as practiced by an internationally acknowledged Western master could be championed as a positive sign of development. Kahn's commission was for more than a group of important buildings; it was a mandate to develop the indigenous construction industry and infrastructure necessary to support the project and future ventures.

Yet the importation of Kahn brought more than Western modern architecture: the capitol complex is part of Kahn's attempt to restore meaning to monumentality in architecture. Asked to design a capitol complex to link East and West Pakistan, Kahn searched for forms to link East and West more generally. In an essay written in 1984, William Curtis provides a thorough overview of the architectural sources that Kahn digested and assimilated into his own designs. From Western tradition and his Beaux Arts educational training, Kahn nurtured an admiration for centralized buildings and clear hierarchy, as exemplified in the villas of Palladio or Jefferson's University of Virginia campus. He combined a predilection for simple, restrained exterior geometries not unlike those found in the work of Ledoux or Boullée with an almost Piranesian delight in interior geometrical complexity. As a designer in the Beaux Arts tradition, he distinguished between what he calls "servant" and "served" spaces, made ample use of ceremonial axes, and exhibited an almost baroque emphasis on the diagonal.

If Western classical inspirations were at the heart of Kahn's architectural ideas, he also learned from his visits to the Indian subcontinent. Kahn made thorough studies of Mughal garden designs and tombs, including Humayun's Tomb in Delhi, Agra's Taj Mahal, and, closer to his site, Dhaka's Lalbagh Fort (9.4). As Curtis puts it,

> Kahn's grasp of buildings he admired went far deeper than particular elements or surface effects. The Mogul tradition held out numerous brilliant examples in the handling of primary and secondary axes, level changes, diagonal perceptions of structure, and the linking of one formal theme to another. . . . In any of the monumental complexes of India,

9.4 Part of Lalbagh Fort, Dhaka.

> Kahn could have sensed an animating character, a material expression of the world of the spirit, in accord with his own search for fundamentals. Whether the particular inspirations for his centralized form belonged more to Eastern or Western traditions is not clear. The fact is that he found common denominators between the two.[18]

Above all, perhaps, Kahn's love was for Western classical antiquity, an affection that embraced such buildings across time, as intact designs and as ruins. Kahn described his inspiration for the Dhaka capitol complex as "the Baths of Caracalla, but much extended."[19] And surely the top-lighting he used in the assembly chamber and its prayer hall was intended to evoke the perceptual experience of the Roman Pantheon. Again and again in his writings and sketches, Kahn referred to the expressive possibilities of light, as exemplified in classical ruins. It is in the mastery of such patterns of light and shade that Kahn located his concept of the eternal; it is this, for Kahn, that makes the Parthenon "the recognized symbol of Greek civilization." In other projects, Kahn stated explicitly that he was concerned with creating "ruins wrapped around buildings."

Though he was less direct in making such references to the Dhaka capitol, the idea of a light-controlling wrap of ruins seems undeniably present. One story told to Kahn, perhaps apocryphal, has it that the National Assembly building escaped damage during the war because of its already-ruined appearance: "The pilots making the runs over Dacca saw this building and they thought that it had already been bombed, because there were so many holes in it, so they wouldn't waste another bomb on it!"[20] At the base of his urge to design thousand-year-old walls that evoke "the memory of a giant" was a near-obsession with the interconnectedness of architectural beginnings and architectural ruin. For Kahn, a ruin conveys neither decay nor decline but "reveals again the spirit out of which it once stood as a proud structure. Now it is free of its bonds."[21] At another point, he rhapsodized further: "The quiet ruin now freed from use welcomes wild growth to play joyously around it and is like a father who delights in the little one tugging at his clothes."[22]

One cannot know how much emphasis to place upon the content of Kahn's often mystical utterances, though surely his words must be taken seriously. Henry Wilcots, Kahn's assistant (and successor) on the Dhaka project describes Kahn's visit to the site in January 1974: "The top walls had started to go up so you could see the air circulating shafts coming down and the light wells and to him[self] he said: 'I think it's finished.'"[23] In short, Kahn was equally, if not disproportionally, concerned that the assembly chamber be occupied by light as by legislators. While Kahn was not the first architect to delight in envisioning his buildings as ruins (Sir John Soane, one hundred fifty years earlier, actually designed such engravings and showed them to his client), the thought that Kahn-the-father may prefer his buildings "freed from use" is surely a disturbing extension of poetic license.

Whether or not the assembly building was designed to be a ruin—a fate which nearly befell it during the twenty years it took to complete it—it was definitely designed in accordance with Kahn's own rather limited preoccupations with certain forms and materials. Kahn's vocabulary of Forms seems very limited; what the building "wants to be" always seems somehow to fit with recognizable elements of Kahn's other work. This consistency is in most ways a strength, but it is also a reminder of the willfulness that undergirds Kahn's choice of a generating idea.

Not surprisingly, the generating form behind the National Assembly building is similar to many of Kahn's designs for religious institutions. Kahn sought to convey a religious feeling in this building as well. Even the language he chose to describe his design process ("On the night of the third day . . .") has a biblical resonance. Yet, similarity to the National Assembly design extends not only to Kahn's Rochester Unitarian Church but even to his most secular works, such as Erdman Hall, a dormitory for Bryn Mawr College in Pennsylvania.

Even more striking is the similarity between the Dhaka assembly building and the library Kahn designed for Philips Exeter Academy in New Hampshire, a project begun slightly later (9.5–9.8). Both appear fortresslike and are internally focused on a full height central space; both are organized, in plan, as a kind of double doughnut, where the perimeter doughnut is visually and structurally independent from the inner one. At Exeter, however, the center of the building is a great void, and Kahn stresses the importance of the perimeter, the need to "bring a book to the light." In Kahn's Dhaka building, perhaps partially conditioned by the need to shield the chamber from the harsh sun and by the need to shield the legislators from harsh opposition, the center of the building is supposed to be the focal point of activity. While this is a major difference between the two buildings, I am struck by the ease with which the Bangladeshi legislators could be made

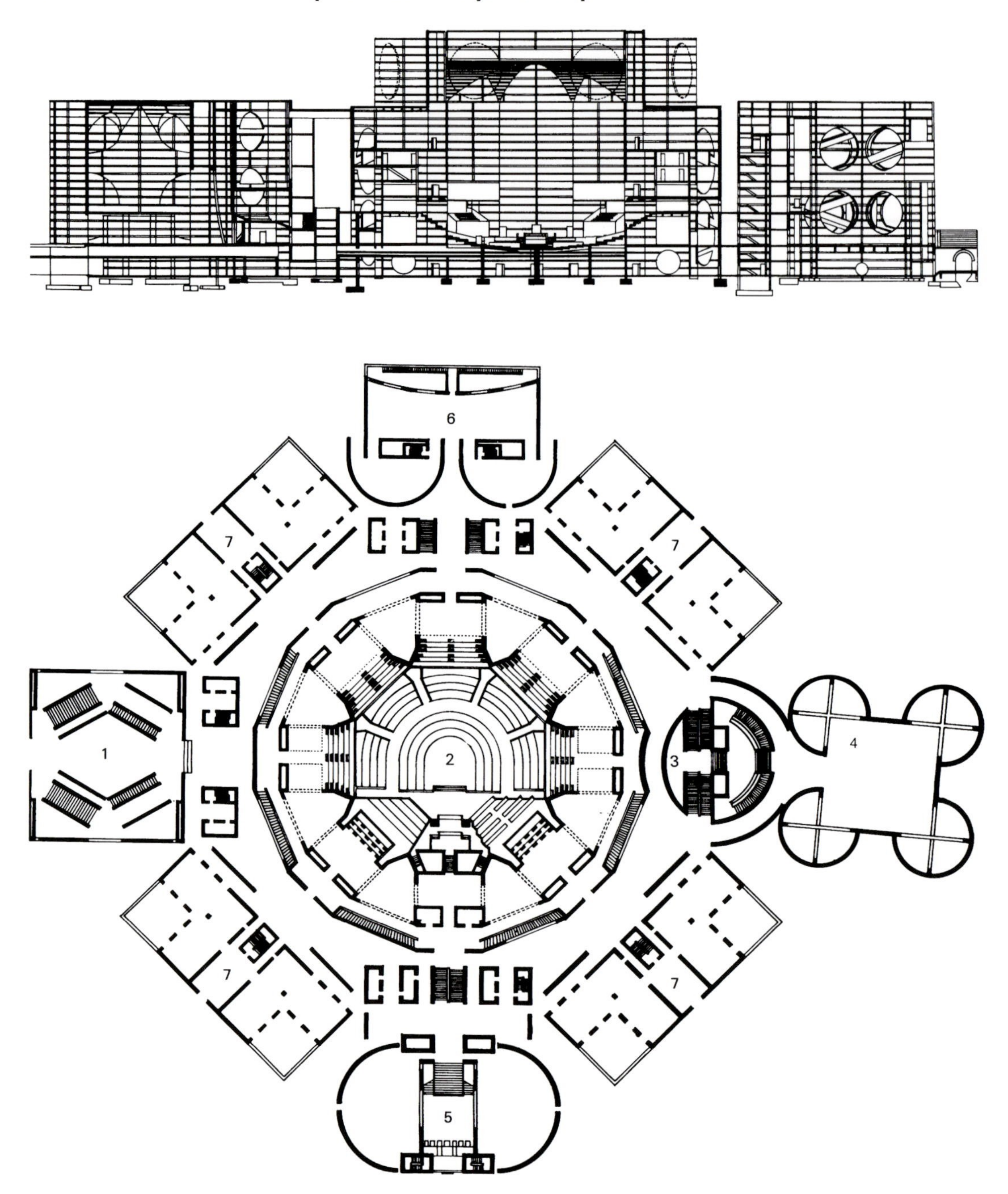

9.5 ***(above)*** **Section through National Assembly Building, Dhaka.**

9.6 ***(below)*** **Plan of National Assembly Building, Dhaka.**

to occupy the voided center of the Exeter Library. For an architect so concerned with discovering the essence of each institution, the resultant designs of these two places are curiously similar. For Kahn, there seem to be too many transcendent human activities and too few Forms with which to express them.

If Kahn's Forms for expressing the nature of institutions were caught up in his private vocabulary, a silent sign language of preferred constructs, his choice of materials too was circumscribed by personal preference,

9.7 *(above)* **Section through Exeter Library, Exeter, New Hampshire.**

9.8 *(below)* **Plan of Exeter Library.**

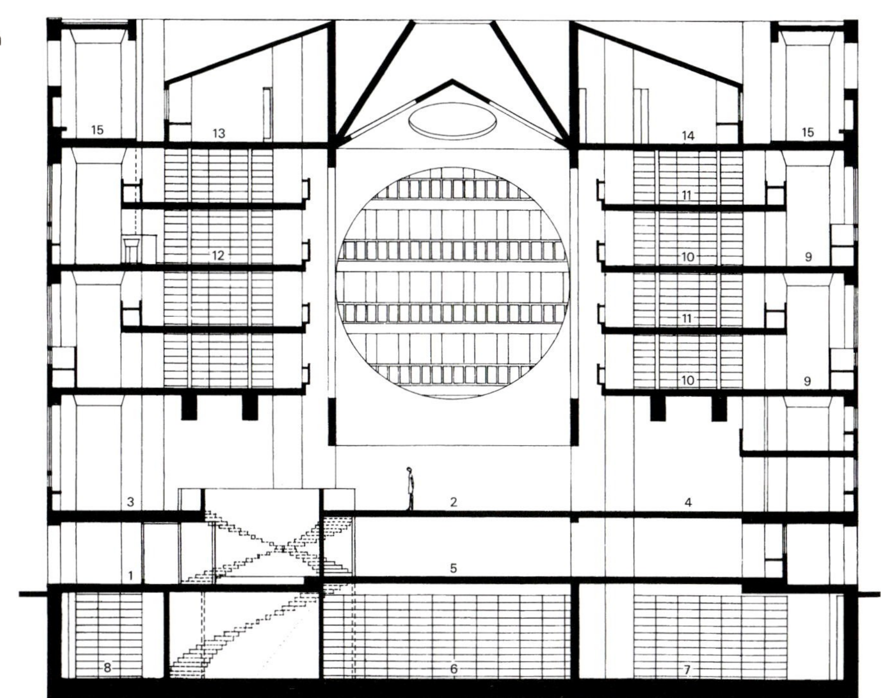

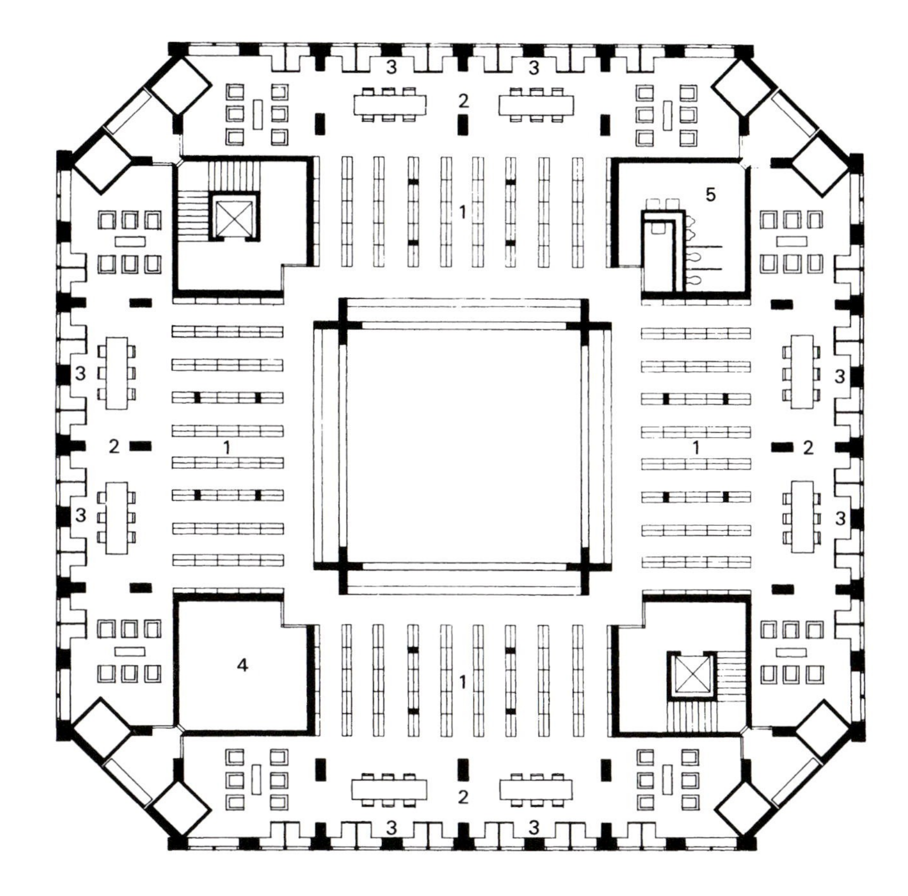

regardless of ease or availability. When design work began, Kahn naively planned to use reinforced concrete for all of the buildings, not just the National Assembly. As Kahn acknowledged, "I got into doing brick because I could not use any other material. So I had to use it. It was self-protection to use brick in Dacca. I knew concrete would be a complete failure. But still my love for concrete couldn't be denied, so I tried to make these people a purse, let's say, out of a sow's ear."[24] In the end, Kahn noted, the decision to use concrete for the assembly building rested on his greater familiarity with the use of concrete for large spans and the fact that brick "didn't satisfy something in me."[25] Still, if Kahn's love for concrete "couldn't be denied," the problems thus engendered are no less undeniable.

Kahn's goal for the Dhaka capitol complex was a profound synthesis, what he termed an "architecture of connection."[26] Discussing the arrangement of buildings for the capitol, he contended that "the architect should work to bring out a relationship, the architecture of connection, of the realm of spaces, where a rapport of buildings and spaces can be felt."[27] Yet this is only one kind of connection—connection at the level of form, connection between solid and void. One would expect that an architect who professed to be so concerned about the meaning of institutions would consider more than formal relationships. Spatial distance and juxtapositions have social implications and, perhaps even more important, existing social relationships may imply the need for certain design constraints. In his overarching desire to design his own idealizations of the Pakistani institutions, these reciprocal social-spatial implications were rarely acknowledged.

Though Kahn professed no interest in politics, he nonetheless made designs with strong political assumptions and implications.[28] While he claimed to be designing an "architecture of connection" he actually contributed to a radical spatial-social disjuncture. All architectural commissions are fraught with political problems; in this case, the epic struggle to get the capitol complex built closely paralleled the political fortunes of Pakistan and Bangladesh. Since Kahn was commissioned to design an explicitly and avowedly political group of structures, his design can, and should, be judged in relation to the political conditions that prompted the commission. That these political conditions have changed since the commission was given makes the building especially difficult to place in its proper range of contexts. Kahn cannot, of course, be blamed for having failed to anticipate that his buildings would eventually be used by the government of an independent Bangladesh. It is, however, important to examine how the shifting needs of a changing government client prompted alterations in Kahn's design, alterations that profoundly affect the symbolic readings of the complex as a whole.

The 1962 Constitution of Pakistan mandated the creation of a "second capital" at Dhaka; Kahn's commission was an outcome of this need and should be seen in relation to the broader purposes of the constitution as well. Islamabad, discussed in Chapter 5, was designated as the first capital, and this entirely new city—located conveniently close to the headquarters of the armed forces—was to become the future home of the Pakistani Central Government. Though the 1962 constitution signaled a return to civilian rule after several years of military control, the role of the military was still vital, and the political and economic hegemony of West Pakistan over East was still secure. Nonetheless, there were growing signs of Bengali agitation, and the creation of the second capital in the East must be seen as a gesture of appeasement. According to August Komendant, Kahn's engineer during the early stages of the Dhaka work, the political urgency of the commission was made very clear during Kahn's initial visit to Pakistan in March 1963: "[President Ayub] told us that there was unrest in East Pakistan and he wanted to start with construction of the citadel before the elections in the fall."[29]

If appeasement indeed laid the political groundwork for Kahn's commission, it was of a very unconvincing sort. First of all, this second capital was not to be a new capital at all; whereas Islamabad was to be an entirely new creation, the second capital was to be no more than a new capitol district, a few hundred acres on the fringe of an existing provincial capital. Kahn's magisterial designs may have managed to mitigate this discrepancy, but it seems clear that the gesture of a second capital did little to alter the balance of power between the two Pakistans. The second capital was to be only the "legislative capital" of the country, the seat of the National Assembly, whereas the "principal seat of Central Government," Ayub Khan's presidential throne, was to be in Islamabad, designated in the constitution as the "Capital of the Republic."[30] Though President Ayub, in his "Speech Announcing the Constitution of 1962," proclaimed "The National Assembly is the source of law,"[31] the political system ushered in by the new constitution was, in essence, an attack on the power of the assembly and a legal justification for the consolidation of political power by the president.

On 24 June, nine Bengali leaders jointly issued a statement condemning the intent of the new constitution:

> The present document is framed on a distrust of popular will, whatever be the justification put forward for that. A body of 80,000 electors have been provided for as the base of the system in a population of more than 80 million.
>
> The Assemblies created on the vote of these electors have practically been given no power to decide anything. Nothing can be done by these bodies unless the President agrees. Whereas the President after the initial start can rule without agreement of the Assembly both in the legislative and in the executive fields.[32]

In addition to complaining about the inefficacy of the National Assembly's powers, Bengali politicians alleged that they were underrepresented, since the 150 seats were allocated to the two provinces on the basis of parity rather than population and, in 1961, East Pakistanis outnumbered West Pakistanis 50.8 million to 42.9 million.[33] According to a report from 1964, sixty of the seventy-five East Pakistan members of the National Assembly were opposed to the constitution of 1962.[34] Underrepresented in the only institution which, through majority rule, could theoretically have helped to effect a legal redress against West Pakistani power, East Pakistan members found little solace in the fact that the National Assembly was located in their province.

While claiming to be replacing a parliamentary system with one based on the American presidential model, Ayub in fact appropriated those elements of each system which best served the consolidation of executive power.[35] Even the constitution's preamble shows this bias: "I, Field Marshall Mohammad Ayub Khan," not "We, the People of Pakistan," "do hereby declare and promulgate the Constitution"—popular sanction mattered little.[36] In his autobiography, *Friends Not Masters* (1967), Ayub cites his views from 1954 as evidence of his long-held conviction about the need for a strong executive: "The President should be made the final custodian of power on the country's behalf and should be able to put things right both in the provinces and the centre should they go wrong."[37] As one commentator put it, reflecting a broad consensus, the constitution of 1962 "reduced parliamentary bodies to debating forums."[38] In lieu of power being vested in the National Assembly, "The Presidency was constructed on the theory that in the legislative as well as the executive sphere, the President was able to maintain his supremacy."[39] If, as another commentator put it, "Ayub's main aim was to provide a constitutional facade for a dictatorial design,"[40] can Louis Kahn be accused of providing its architectural equivalent? Tempting as it may be to castigate Kahn for complicity in this charade of representative democracy, Kahn's design methodology provides him with a built-in way out. While another architect in his place might have seen through the weakness of the institution and refused to give it monumental treatment, resigning the commission if necessary, Kahn (to the extent that he thought about such political considerations at all)[41] maintained that his job was not to create a home for the institution that *is*, but to build the shrine for the institution that *could be*. As he has remarked, "Reality is the dream. Reality is the fairy tale. . . . The unattainable, the yet not made, yet not said, is what motivates man."[42] It is ironic that Kahn used one architectural device after another to monumentalize the importance of the National Assembly at precisely the point in its history when its authority was being most directly undermined.

In a design that went through many stages having significantly dissimilar configurations, one element remained constant: the visual dominance of the National Assembly building. In the words of Kahn's associate David Wisdom, "The building is centered on the site on a north–south axis and is made the focal point of interest and attention not only by its size but also by the placement of the smaller hostel buildings on diagonals to east and west, facing a man-made lake that separates them from the capitol."[43] Moreover, its position atop a plinth, the large scale of its wall openings, and the gray of its concrete in a capitol complex that is otherwise built of brick also serve to increase its dominant appearance (9.9).

Designed in an atmosphere of political unrest and skepticism about the new constitution, this central core of the project alone has, at the time of this writing, endured not just Kahn's death in 1974 but also forty years of famine, flood, military coups, electoral boycotts and violent general strikes. It has survived all this plus a civil war during which it was occupied at

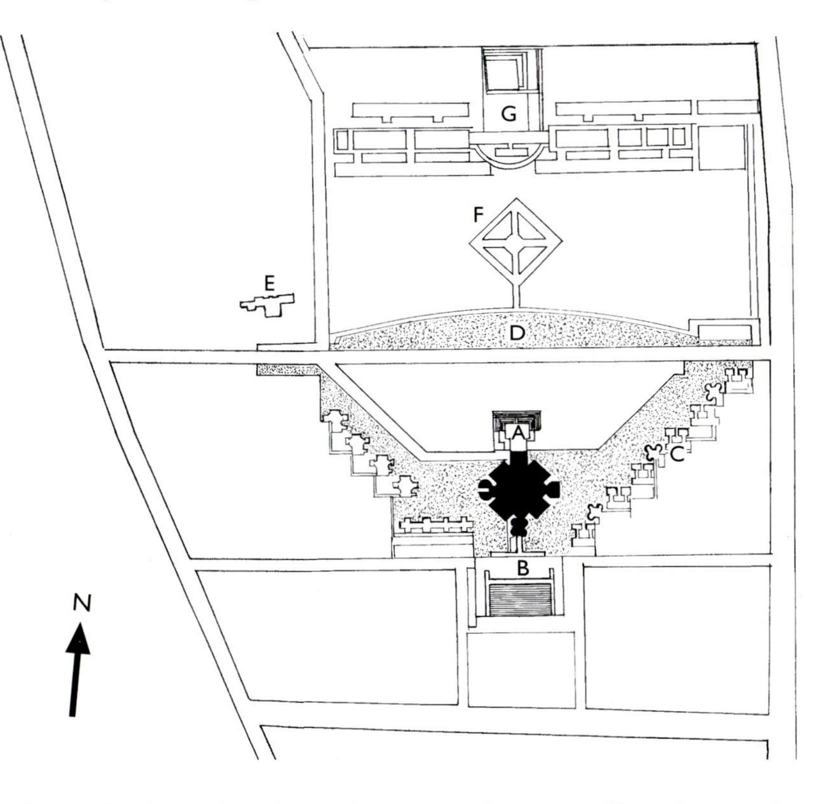

9.9 Site plan highlights National Assembly Building.

A Presidential Plaza
B South Plaza
C MP Hostels
D Crescent Lake
E State Guest House
F Mausoleum
G Proposed Secretariat

various points by armies who used it as a warehouse, munitions depot, and headquarters.[44] Over this period it has become a finished building more or less in accord with Kahn's original intentions for its design.

And yet, especially because the complex as a whole did not come into being as Kahn had wished, its central structure carries altered meanings. I have mentioned the symbolic shift from a building associated with West Pakistani domination and a distrusted constitution to a building associated with the independence of Bangladesh. Such a change was not lost on Kahn: "I toured the land and saw what happened during time of war. They are very different people. They hold the state first, religion second. What held East and West together was supposedly the religious agreement, but when the East was freed from the West, they considered the country first."[45] This new nationalism was perhaps the most important shift, but the political restructuring had other repercussions for Kahn's grand design. First, with the independence of Bangladesh the whole purpose of the second capital was eliminated; Dhaka was previously the provincial capital and already had an assembly hall sufficient to serve for the national capital, once a separate provincial assembly was no longer needed. According to one Bangladeshi architect, "The new nation's National Assembly could easily fit into the old provincial assembly building. For the structures already completed, other uses had to be found. Available funds were diverted to more pressing needs, and no significant construction was attempted for some time. The symbol of unity became an embarrassment to the new nation, the unfinished project constantly reminding them both of their incapacity to finish it and of its redundancy."[46] Although resources remained scarce, commitment to the project was revived after 1975 by a series of military regimes whose leaders viewed the task of its completion as indicative of the new country's accomplishments. Yet the war and the extended period of construction delay had considerable financial implications and, hence, design implications:

> Costs had skyrocketed. Materials were not available. Since almost 80 percent of the materials required to finish the buildings had once come from West Pakistan, it now had to be bought in foreign exchange. Corners were cut: aluminum window frames—which Kahn had always resisted—were used; the upper parts of the building constructed later were visibly less refined. In the assembly chamber terrazzo was substituted for marble. Other major problems were delays and the accompanying cost overruns.[47]

The most far-reaching design change necessitated by the emergence of Bangladesh concerned the provision of facilities to house the executive branch of government. When it was designed as the second capital most of the executive functions were to be based in Islamabad. When Dhaka became the capital of an undivided government, there was a large and continually growing need for new construction of office space for the various executive departments. There was, however, little or no role for the concept or the institutions of bureaucracy in Kahn's original designs.

Kahn's ideogram for the transcendent polity was based on the relationship of two "citadels"—the "Citadel of Assembly" and the "Citadel of the Institutions of Man"; this relationship is problematic not only for what it symbolizes but also for what it leaves out (see 9.10). According to Kahn, "The assembly establishes or modifies the institutions of man. So I could see the thing right from the start as the citadel of assembly and the citadel of the institutions of man, which were opposite, and I symbolized the institutions of man."[48] "Does it have all the ingredients?" Kahn had asked about his plan. "If only one is lacking it will disintegrate. This is my problem."[49] And, indeed, the need to insert the missing Secretariat would become Kahn's central problem. In the Citadel of Assembly, he initially included the National Assembly with its Mosque, the Supreme Court, and the hostels for legislators and high officials. In the Citadel of the Institutions, he initially grouped a "center for athletics and physical culture," a school of arts and a school of sciences, a performing arts center, a public library, a hospital, a market, a bazaar, a small mosque, various government offices, and housing for officials. Through ten years of designing, Kahn seems always to have felt a need to justify his juxtapositions. Since the juxtapositions kept changing with each successive version of the master plan, he had a great deal of explaining to do. Through it all, according to almost everyone who worked with him, he was solicitous of a wide range of opinions and willing to adapt to the latest change in the client's demand. Kahn's willingness to change his mind, however, did not prevent him from remaining equally dogmatic at every turn. Contradictions were thus inevitable.

KAHN'S MISCONNECTIONS

There are four chief discontinuities embodied in Kahn's "architecture of connection":

The misleading emphasis on the National Assembly building as the locus of political transcendence.

The inappropriateness of a capitol design that, paradoxically, overcompensates for and underestimates the demands of climate.

The excessively strong reliance on the connection between the mosque and the National Assembly, in a changing society in which the role of Islam remains contentious.

The extreme disjunction between the citadels and the city.

The National Assembly and government hierarchy

The visual dominance of the National Assembly building in Kahn's master plan would seem to arise in part from the wish to symbolize Dhaka's originally intended role as a legislative capital and in part because of Kahn's belief in the transcendence of assembly. In the several decades that have passed since Kahn began to think about this project, Dhaka has become the seat of government for an independent country, but the institutional power of the National Assembly has grown only slowly and intermittently, during the lapses between coups and crackdowns. Political control by a strong executive, with or without a military uniform, has been the rule for Bangladesh, as it was for Pakistan. Although the institutional legitimacy of the National Assembly has finally seemed to stabilize in the years since 1991, "the task of making parliament the focal point of politics and policy making in Bangladesh has remained elusive."[50]

As a result, the discontinuity between Kahn's architectural ideogram and Bangladesh's political reality is acute. Kahn premised his separation of the two citadels on the belief that "the assembly establishes or modifies the institutions of man."[51] As Kahn phrased it, "The place of assembly was really the maker of the institutions. . . . It gave the right for the school to exist, for the place of health to exist, and even for the house of legislation to exist—all the institutions of man." In taking poetic refuge in an idealized view of the primal origins of democracy, however, Kahn did little to adapt to the contingencies of a rapidly changing and decidedly undemocratic place.

The discontinuity between Kahn's words and his ideogram is evident in his justification for the placement of the Supreme Court. Kahn was faced with the decision about what to do with an institution that really might have the potential for the more detached, contemplative spiritual nature that Kahn wished to assign to the National Assembly. Given that the constitution of 1962 was no kinder to the idea of a powerful Supreme Court than it was to the notion of a strong National Assembly, Kahn faced two difficulties: the Supreme Court was of secondary importance to the client's program and it had no distinct relationship to Kahn's notion of transcendent Assembly. In other words, while Kahn could imagine the justices "miles away just thinking of law and its relation to man in a general way,"[52] this picture seems at odds with his overarching commitment to the concept of assembly, the coming together and joining of forces. This is symptomatic of a curious dichotomy underlying the whole of Kahn's impulse for this project: he would seem to have sought simultaneously a centralized assembly and a detached place for contemplation, a paradoxical coming together to stand apart.

Kahn first resolved the position of the Supreme Court by concluding that "its position had to be on axis with the assembly."[53] Early on in the design process, in the site plan of 12 March 1963, the Court–Assembly axis is used to give special emphasis to the position of the Supreme Court—the Court building stands between the Assembly/Mosque and the Citadel of Institutions and is given an unobstructed axial view from both parts (shown as no. 3 in 9.10). It is at this point that Kahn had his celebrated conference with the chief justice:

> I explained I wanted to put the Supreme Court near the Assembly, and he said "Oh, no, don't. I can't bear to be near those rogues." I made a sketch of the whole complex. He looked at the mosque entrance, he looked at the Assembly, the gardens and everything else. "Well," he said, taking the pencil out of my hand, "I'd agree to put the Supreme Court here," and he put it exactly where I wanted him to put it. He said, "The Mosque is sufficient insulation for me."[54]

In his delight at their spatial concordance, Kahn failed to see that he and the justice were not necessarily favoring the placement for the same reasons.

Kahn, at least in part, placed the court where he did in order to define an edge of a courtyard; the justice was interested in maintaining a social as well as spatial distance yet did not apparently wish to sacrifice the prestige of a spot on the assembly citadel's plinth. These two kinds of reasons for the juxtaposition are potentially complementary, yet they do suggest very different priorities, and it is the justice's priorities which seem to lose out as the architect's design passed through multiple transformations. Though Kahn did maintain the axial relationship between the assembly building and the court in his site plan dated 10 May 1964, the "insulation" of the large mosque is now gone (see 9.13). By February 1965, the axis is still there and the edges of the south courtyard are still defined, but the Supreme Court building has been shifted to one side (see 9.15). On the spot opposite the Assembly Building where Kahn had once dogmatically insisted on placing the Supreme Court, he now substituted a museum. If this building, too, "had to be" on axis with the assembly, he offered no new theory of paired transcendences to justify the shift. Kahn claimed that "the architect should work to bring about a relationship, the architecture of connection, of the realm of spaces, where a rapport of buildings and spaces can be felt."[55] Yet, as his willingness to shift the placement of major institutions reveals, the need to improve spatial order takes precedence over the need to maintain social and political hierarchies. Not surprisingly, in the site plan of January 1973, Kahn's final published version, the Supreme Court building is tucked in behind one end of the massive Secretariat complex, with neither axis nor sight line to connect it with the assembly functions (see 9.16). Progressively shunted aside in the drawings, it has remained unbuilt, a reminder that the Supreme Court of independent Bangladesh could be housed in a previously existing building nearer to the center of the city.

It is the Secretariat complex, taking the position in the master plan long reserved for Kahn's Citadel of the Institutions of Man, that provides the greatest social/spatial irony of all. The high drama of Kahn's division of the capitol complex into two citadels is subverted. Across from the Citadel of Assembly stands only the potential for a Citadel of Bureaucracy.

Though Kahn did not initially plan for the large bureaucracy that would come about following Dhaka's promotion to full-fledged national capital, he did make provision to house the president. Given that the capitol complex was originally intended as the seat of legislative government only, and given that Ayub Khan wished to stress publicly the importance of the National Assembly, the placement of the chief executive within the plan must have been a matter calling for great sensitivity (especially since Kahn at that same time was busy designing a "President's Estate" for Ayub in Islamabad, a project that was ultimately unrealized).[56] What to do with the president, a political force who had nothing to do with Kahn's notion of assembly but who controlled both the government and Kahn's commission, was an issue of special importance.

The answer seems to have been to go ahead with planning for an elaborate presidential residence but not always to label it in the drawings! While the "President's house" and "President's grounds and gardens" are included in a prominent position on the initial site plan (12 March 1963) (9.10), all documentation of the presidential presence soon ceases. In this

9.10 Two citadels: Citadel of Institutions *(left)* and Citadel of Assembly in early site plan (12 March 1963).

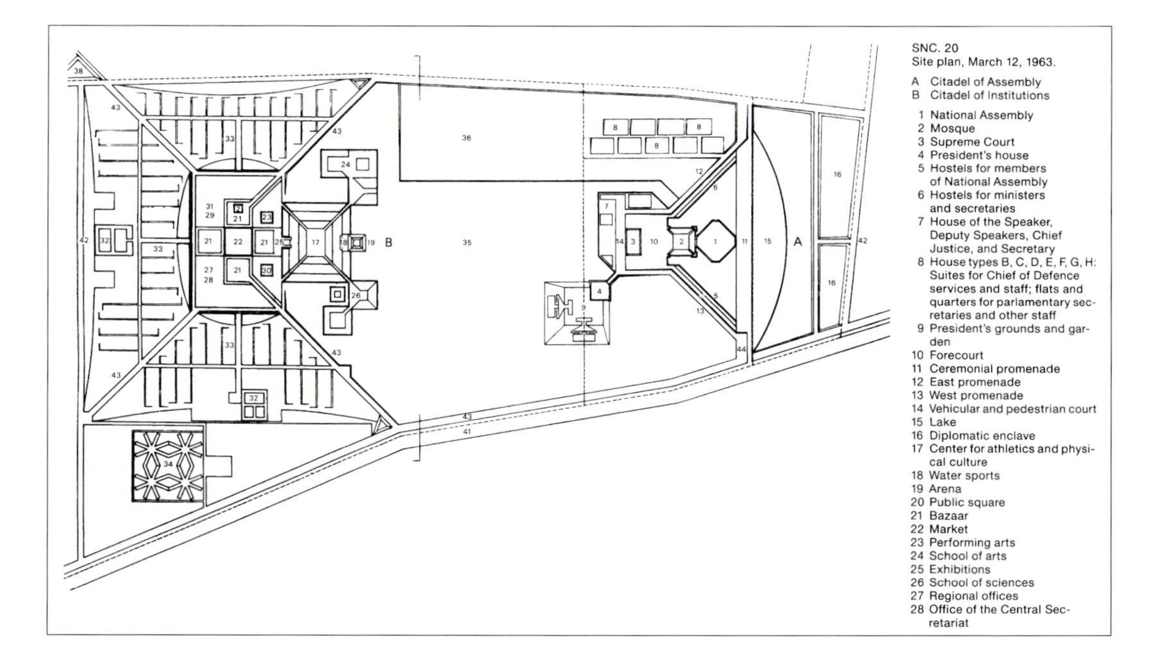

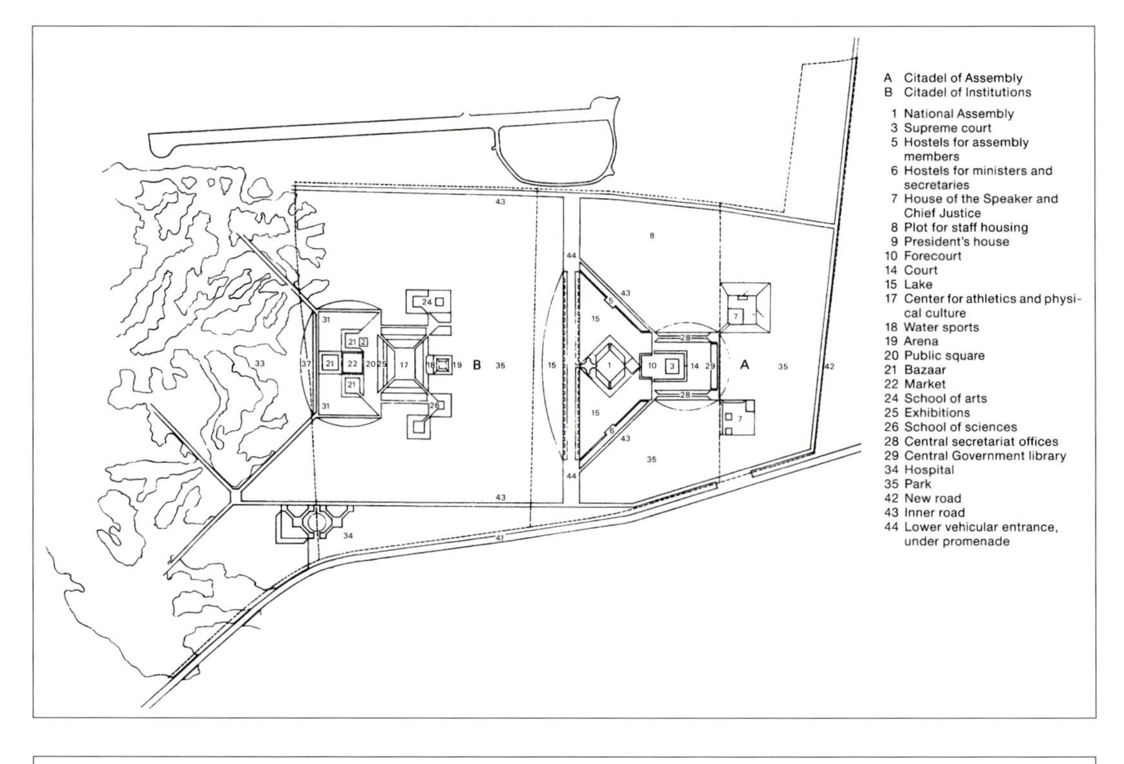

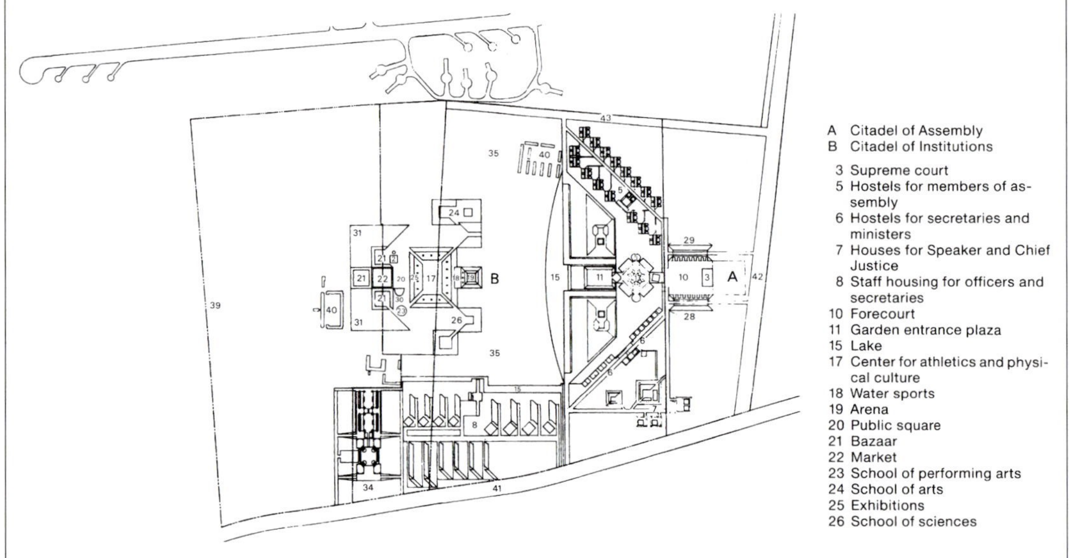

9.11 ***(above)*** **Site plan 3 May 1963: the president is missing.**

9.12 ***(below)*** **Site plan 21 December 1963: the president is still missing.**

first printed version, the palace complex appears on its own island with a roadway bridge to the rest of the assembly plinth, like a citadel's corner battlement/watchtower. In the plans of 3 May and 21 December 1963, however, it is nowhere to be found (9.11, 9.12). Yet, in the 10 May 1964 version (9.13), the presidential presence returns with a vengeance, in exactly the same position it occupied initially, though now no longer joined by bridge to the assembly plinth. Severed from the rest of the Citadel of Assembly, it rises from an island as large in area as the National Assembly building itself

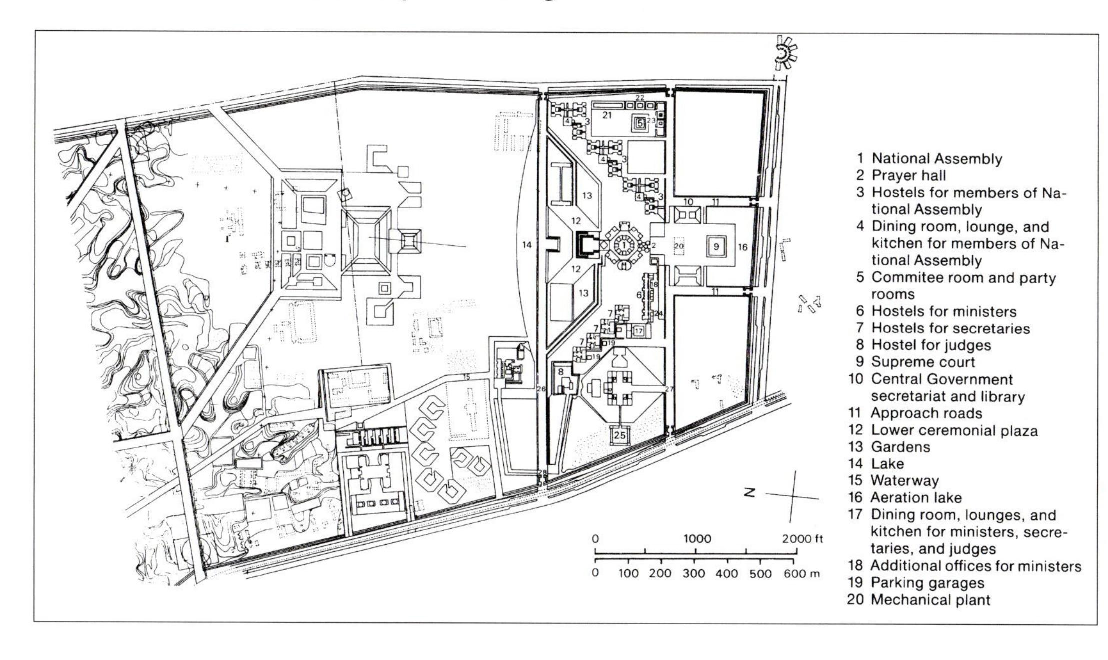

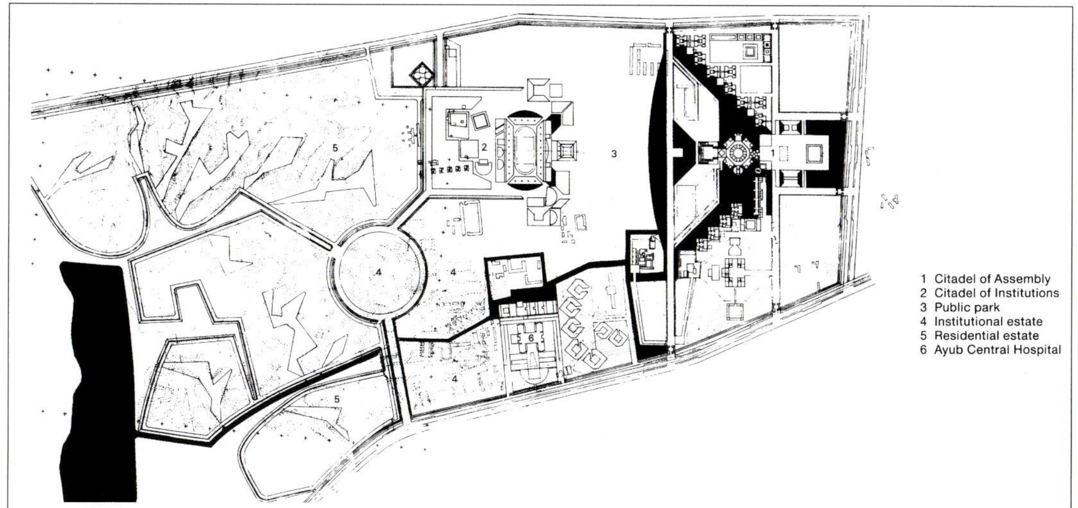

9.13 ***(above)*** **Site plan 10 May 1964 (revised 6 July 1964), revealing reduction of Prayer Hall and loss of Supreme Court's "insulation."**

9.14 ***(below)*** **Site plan August 1964: presidential island between the citadels.**

and is surrounded by a kind of moat crossable by a single bridge at the end of a private roadway leading from the "control gate house." And yet, in this meticulously labeled drawing, the presidential island receives no mark of explanation. In the August 1964 site plan "showing lake and waterways" it is again unlabeled but stands out sharply as an island between the two citadels (9.14). Only in the February 1965 site plan is the president's house labeled again, though the key makes no mention of "presidential grounds and garden" (9.15). Apparently, Pakistan's political uncertainties made site programming a sensitive matter. In Kahn's final site plan of January 1973, drawn after the overthrow of Ayub and the subsequent independence of Bangladesh, all evidence of a presidential palace island disappears once again; the only visible presence of a chief executive is the vast Presidential Plaza to the north of the National Assembly building (9.16). In the end, the President's

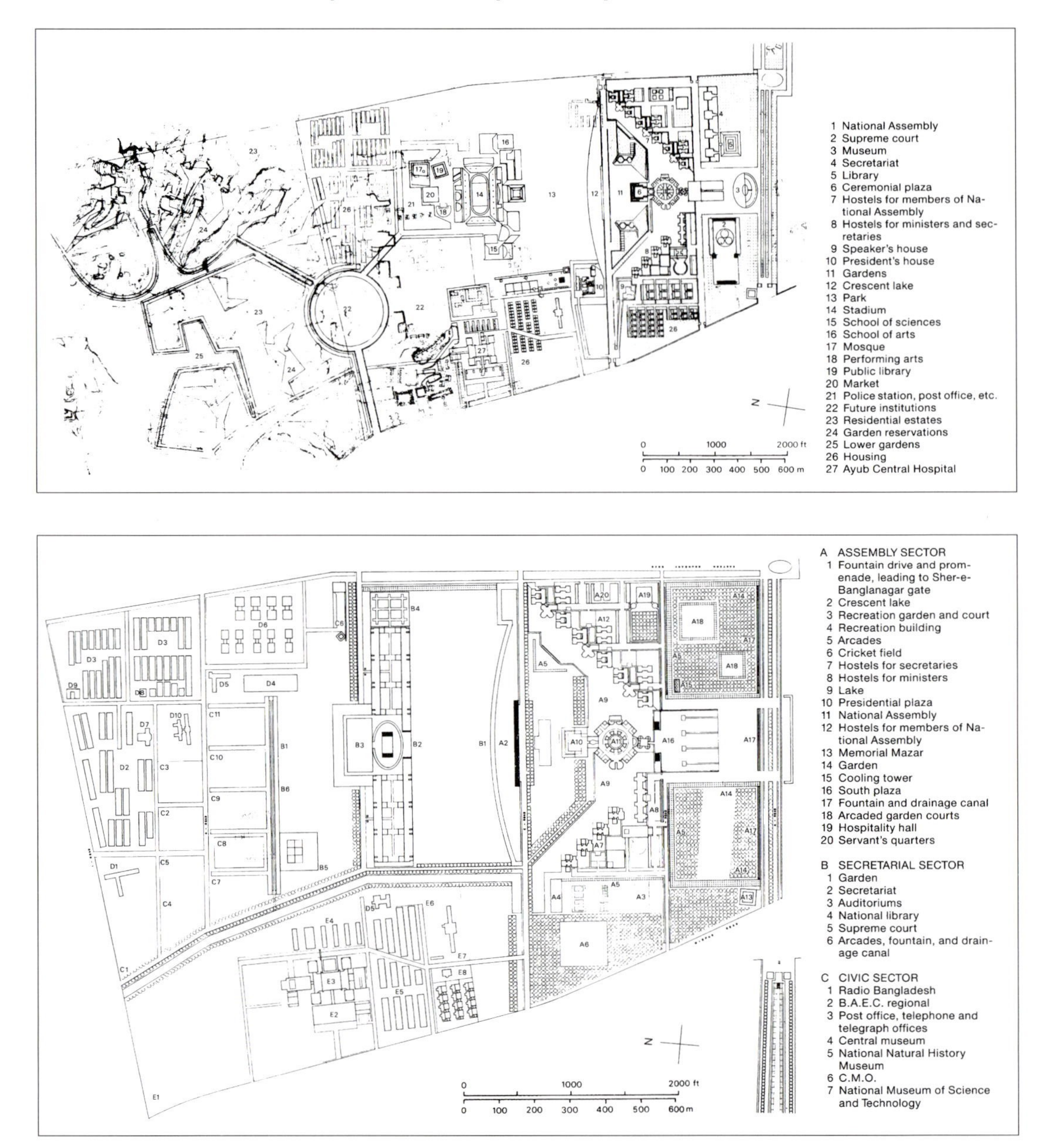

9.15 ***(above)*** **Site plan February 1965: Supreme Court (2) is now off-axis from National Assembly.**

9.16 ***(below)*** **Site plan January 1973: Supreme Court (B5) is no longer very supreme.**

House was built on its intended site but was reconceptualized to serve as the State Guest House instead (see 9.9).

It is difficult to know how much to make of this inconsistency in the provisions made for the president and the curious absence of labels on some of the drawings. The nonlabeling is probably not a serious attempt to hide the facilities for the president, and it may be simply an office or archival oversight. In the context of the periodic disappearance of the *building* as well as its label, however, it is worth noting, if only as an example of the ways Kahn was forced to accommodate his design to his client's changing needs. It is impossible to reconstruct the reasons for each change and omission—how much was due to Kahn's indecision and how much was due to the changing whims of the client—but plainly Kahn had difficulty resolving what to do with an element that simply would not fit with his vision of transcendent assembly.

The problem of symbolizing the presidential presence persisted after the independence of Bangladesh. For more than thirty-five years, some Bangladeshi political parties and commentators have advocated a parliamentary system based on British or Indian models, while others have argued for a presidential system with a strong executive. In practice, however, the first two postindependence decades were characterized by authoritarian forms of military rule led by president-generals.[57] The large Presidential Plaza on the north side of the National Assembly advertises the role of the chief executive—it is not, one notes, named Speaker's Plaza, to reflect parliamentary control. Even more important, the military government of President-General Hussain Mohammad Ershad, who ruled the country between March 1982 and December 1990, appropriated this entire side of the complex for its own purposes, occupying some of the parliamentary hostels and sealing off the whole area south of the Crescent Lake Road from all public access. Thus, the north approach to the assembly complex was privatized, available only for staged ceremonies. In December 1987, with many leaders of opposition parties under house arrest, Ershad dissolved the Bangladeshi parliament, and major opposition parties boycotted subsequent elections, charging that Ershad's supporters would rig them. Inside the assembly building, according to an architect in Dhaka, Ershad during the late 1980s claimed certain parts for himself, marking his executive presence by retrofitting portions of the building with all-marble offices and revamping and marbleizing the presidential gallery that overlooks the assembly chamber.

The urban and architectural treatment given the president elsewhere in Dhaka was even more revealing of the balance of Bangladesh's political forces during this era. Using the site of the earlier parliament building, Ershad established a vast alternative compound adjacent to military facilities, set well back from the "Islamic arch"-lined "V.I.P." road leading to the international airport (see 9.2). Though this Presidential Secretariat long served as the true seat of power for the country, official maps of Dhaka treated this whole presidential/military district as an unlabeled blank, and all photography of the place (even of the exterior) was prohibited—a practice rendered moot by all-seeing satellites (see 9.20). In this sense, the ambivalence about symbolizing the president, a problem when Dhaka was slated to be Ayub Khan's legislative second capital, persisted at least through 1990. After 1991, however, Bangladeshi leaders restored the parliamentary system under which the prime minister becomes the head of government, and the president holds a merely ceremonial role (with enhanced presidential leadership powers granted only when a caretaker government assumes power temporarily to oversee general elections after dissolution of the parliament).

From Kahn's own iconographical perspective, what was even more curious than his seeming indecision about what to do with the president was his treatment of the interior of the building he put forth as his preferred source of transcendence. Even though the National Assembly building dominates the site (and is visible from much of the north part of Dhaka),

9.17 Dhaka assembly chamber: an anticlimax.

the core of the building—the assembly chamber—is something of an anticlimax. Despite all of his efforts to give primacy to the building in plan and in massing, the actual chamber impresses one as small and unremarkable, except for its monumental acoustical problems caused by reverberation off bare concrete (9.17). The acoustical problems may some day be minimized, but the potential lack of sufficient seating area is more troublesome. There was little provision made for expansion despite the likelihood of persistent rapid population growth and demands by some political parties for a greater total number of representatives; in this sense, Kahn's approach is the very opposite of Utzon's additive premise. The politically active Bengali architect Mazhrul Islam suggested to an interviewer that this lack of foresight might someday pose a serious problem:

> Let me whisper something to you now. This building, the National Assembly, will be unsuitable for Bangladesh. Going to be unsuitable. It is designed for only 350 members. Today Bangladesh has 100 million people. Very soon there will be need for 1,000 representations at the Assembly. The current Assembly space is unable to accommodate that. So, paradoxically, because of the limited capacity of this National Assembly we have got to keep the number of its members at 350![58]

Though his interviewer, in turn, wryly exclaimed, "Good news! At last architecture is controlling politics!" it may be that the decision to limit the size of the chamber was a political one.

Quite apart from its size, the assembly chamber pales in comparison to the drama of the island setting and the mysterious simplicity of the

9.18 High drama of the ambulatories, Dhaka assembly building.

building's deep facades. More immediately, the assembly appears as a static disappointment after the Piranesian flourishes of the one-hundred-foot-high ambulatory that surrounds it, expanding and contracting as one moves around (9.18).[59] Kahn readily admitted to a long struggle over the design of this room, especially its roof system.[60] The roof as built seems of an entirely different architectural vocabulary from the rest of the building and fails to make possible the "columns of light" that Kahn wished to introduce into the chamber. Part of the problem stemmed from the fact that the foundations for the building were put in before what was to go on top of them was fully designed; as is often the case with important state buildings, the political expediency needed to demonstrate that construction was well under way had unfortunate consequences for the building's design. Other problematic aspects of the building, however, seem to have been the deliberate result of considerable study.

Response to climate

Kahn's insistence upon new lakes for a flood-prone capital is emblematic of a larger design attitude that sought to romanticize the extravagant climate in this part of Bengal rather than to design in accordance with its demands. While Kahn is certainly to be praised for being in the vanguard of modern architects who sought to alter design to accommodate local climatic conditions and who sought to learn from traditional methods of environmental control, much of this effort was seemingly misguided in the designs for the Dhaka capitol. It is not only that Kahn tried to design in accordance with the Dhaka climate and failed; it is that he tried so extravagantly and failed with such enormous social and financial consequences. This paradoxical overcompensation for and underestimation of climate takes many forms, all of them both expressive and expensive. Not content simply to elevate the structures above the floodplain, Kahn elaborated a system of waterways that provided a means for preventing the actuality of floods while preserving and domesticating their memory. At a basic site engineering level, the desire to build a plinth for buildings led to the excavation of adjacent areas. As Kahn put it, "It's necessary to make lakes in Dacca because the land is so flat and the floods are high. One must have a raised area, so these are all raised buildings, and the way to make ground for, even for grading, is to make lakes there. Everybody does it, so I did it, too. But at first I saw the Assembly as a transcendent place."[61] While for much of the rest of the country the monsoon would remain an annual peril, for the capitol rising out of its placid reflecting pools, water was an extension of sculpture and its plinth gave a boost to transcendence.

In a similar way, Kahn's deep facades became a sculptural barrier against the joint forces of sun and rain. As he put it, "In the capital I recognized the fact that a deep porch was the answer to the serious sun problem. One deals with the coolness of a shadow before you get to a window."[62] While this is a poetic reminder of the ill effects of excessive heat gain, one may also note that the facades of the National Assembly building are not differentiated according to orientation; no "serious sun problem" could explain the need for porches on the north. Instead of a serious sun problem much of the interior of the building suffers from just the opposite difficulty—it is too dark and is in need of considerable amounts of artificial illumination. Here, as elsewhere, Kahn's overall concept for the building seems to have taken precedence over the consideration of its functional requirements.

Moreover, in his battle to control the adverse effects of sun and rain, Kahn neglected to account for the frontal assault of wind and humidity. With their exposed brick streaked white by uncontrollable efflorescence, their reinforced concrete blackened by tropical fungi and needing yearly hand cleaning with brushes, their dripstone courses overwhelmed by the volume of wall-staining water, their walls behind even the deepest porches drenched by windblown rain, Kahn's buildings were ill-clothed for battle with the tropics. The provision of air conditioning throughout the assembly building was a preadmission of defeat, revealing the deep, uninhabited porches to be a formal device, a mere gesture to the exigencies of climate.[63] While it may be true, as Kahn's collaborator Anne Tyng claims, that "the double walls of Dacca provide 'air conditioning' in the extreme heat of Bangladesh,"[64] they provide little cooling in comparison to the real air conditioning inside. Not only is the building air conditioned throughout, it is air conditioned year-round, even though it is largely unoccupied when the National Assembly is not in session. Why give a pretense of passive environmental control in a building which costs millions of dollars a year to operate and maintain and whose energy consumption shortly after it was finished was estimated to be equal to that of half the rest of Dhaka?[65] Perhaps the stark outer walls are less an attempt to shield from sun and rain than they are a means to mask the high-tech high energy consumption of the modern building within.

However one may assess the climatic impact of Kahn's deep porch double facades, they did have an impact on the amount of usable space in the building. Seen this way, the spatial extravagance of Kahn's response to climate had a substantial effect on the cost of the building. Kahn defended his decision in warriors' terms: "It costs money to fight the sun."[66] True, but it is especially costly to fight the sun by trading off precious square footage. Kahn staunchly defended his unusually high percentage of unusable space as necessary to what he called "full expression":

> I offered the Pakistani a way of building a house. I did it much beyond the objections of everyone there. They gave me particulars, like the plinth, the platform of a building, can have fifty percent usable and fifty percent unusable. They would add corridors and porches on the plinth. In my buildings, there is a hundred and twenty-five percent unusable space, not fifty percent, because the only way I could express it was with deep porches. . . .
>
> The idea was very attractive to them because they don't have to answer to the people politically. I think those who have representation and control over budgetary conditions would have objected to it very strongly, and I probably would have failed to have full expression made. But where opportunity is, let's just be done.[67]

For the assembly building, Wisdom notes, Kahn successfully persuaded the Building Committee "to raise the proportion of gross area of building to net programmed area" out of a recognition that the "meager allowance" was "too restrictive for a good plan."[68] The spectacular—if thoroughly disorienting—ambulatories of the assembly building attest to Kahn's ability to make grand use of such extra floor space, though the undersized chamber is a reminder of yet another form of his overcompensation. Though Kahn fell short of creating the modern pantheon by means of dramatic top-lighting in this chamber, he never ceased trying to infuse his design with a grand spiritual mission, nowhere more than in the mosque entrance.

The National Assembly and national religion

Kahn's initial inspiration for the separation of the program into two citadels—one sacred, the other profane—was apparently some notion of the need to symbolize the duality of man's spiritual and physical nature. Seen somewhat more parochially, one Kahn scholar argues, the separation of the site into two zones, also reflected "American concerns about the erosion of civic responsibility in the face of mass culture. Kahn insisted upon articulating a difference between that collective forum in which private needs are served—the citadel of institutions—and that collective forum which demands and defines civic duty." Given his belief in the transcendence of assembly, whatever weakness it might have had in the constitution of 1962, Kahn insisted that "the institution of assembly would lose its strength if its sympathetic parts were dispersed. So this Citadel of Assembly came about to express the psychological interplay of parts which leads to inspiration."[69] As Sarah Williams Goldhagen puts it,

> Kahn sequestered the government buildings to make them extraordinary, different from the places where the pedestrian activities of everyday life are housed. He believed that anyone who crossed into the special arena of his Capitol Complex, whether government official or common voter, would be transported from the self-interested, small-minded preoccupations of daily life—not to mention the filth and squalor of downtown Dhaka—to be reminded of her elevated status as a citizen of a polity.[70]

Kahn's search for capitol design that would inspire the legislators carried an explicitly religious impulse: "A house of legislation is a religious place. No matter how much of a rogue you are as a legislator, when you enter the assembly, there is something transcendent about your view." This first idea, according to Abul Bashar, chief architect of the Public Works Department from 1965 to 1982, was that an MP approaching the National Assembly would be discouraged from telling lies by passing the twin houses of judgment—the Supreme Court ("judgment in this world") and the Mosque ("judgment by Allah thereafter").[71]

Kahn's association of religious inspiration and legislative inspiration as joint creators of man's secular institutions and physical well-being seemed unyielding. In Kahn's confluence of sacred and secular, the East Pakistani capitol would conjoin Jupiter's Temple with Michelangelo's Campidoglio in a way the Romans never managed. Not surprisingly, trouble arose when he tried to translate this into an architectural plan.

In Kahn's first design, the focus of the Citadel of Assembly was an enormous mosque with four minarets rather than the National Assembly itself; Kahn called this mosque "the pivotal center of the plan, the center of life."[72] "Observing the way of religion in the life of the Pakistani, I thought that a mosque woven into the space fabric of the assembly would express this feeling. It was presumptuous to assume this right. How did I know that it would fit their way of life? But this assumption took possession."[73] In this initial scheme, Kahn stressed the primacy of Islam in a way that went far beyond anything that his client would have dared to request. Whereas the initial program contained "a note which said that there should be a prayer room of three thousand square feet, and a closet to hold rugs,"[74] Kahn proposed a dramatic alternative: "I made them a mosque with thirty thousand square feet, and the prayer rugs were always on the floor. And that became the entrance, that is to say, the mosque became the entrance. When I presented this to the authorities, they accepted it right away."[75] Kahn neglects to point out the second thoughts that were soon to follow.

The role of Islam in relation to the state of Pakistan (or of Bangladesh, where it was not the official religion until Ershad ordered a constitutional amendment in 1988) has never been a matter where consensus is clear, and it would seem that Kahn underestimated the magnitude of this controversy. Though raised in a country that prides itself on its separation of church and state, and though himself a member of a religious minority, Kahn was forced to confront these issues when asked to design for East Pakistan. To be sure, Kahn was not free to ignore his client's expectation that the assembly building must have a place for prayer, but this did not prevent a protracted struggle over how to translate his own ingrained sense of the "separation between church and state" into a vastly different socioreligious context. Kahn's first instinct was to keep the mosque separate from the parliament, and, once this was rejected, he chose to express the separateness of the religious function in the massing of the building. To this extent, he can be seen as resisting the spatial confluence between religion and state, yet by consistently making the mosque's presence more dominant than his client had asked, Kahn paradoxically made the presence of Islam in this government building much more visible than it needed to be.

Explaining this genesis of the mosque entrance, Kahn comments that he was "inspired by the devotion of the Moslems to their prayers five times a day" and that "the mosque was a citadel of the assembly around which the members would gather."[76] Kahn was doubtless correct to note the devotion to Islam of many of the Pakistani leaders, yet the mosque entrance idea was shortsighted in view of the cultural and religious diversity of a place that is, at present, about 9 percent Hindu. Moreover, the Hindu share of the population was notably even higher at the time of Kahn's initial commission.[77]

Komendant is more forthright than Kahn on this matter of representing Islam in the capitol. "The Pakistani authorities," he notes, ". . . were fascinated about Kahn's work and his ideas," but "their main concern seemed to be the Islamic features of the building and of the mosque, its location and orientation."[78] Far from being immediately acceptable, Kahn's mosque entrance inspired great controversy. "They argued among themselves; there was no agreement. Back in our hotel we considered the question. Even though most government officials were Moslems, they had no right to ignore the other religions. Finally we agreed that the only solution possible will be to provide a meditation place for everyone, regardless of religion, where even an atheist could enter. It could be oriented toward Mecca but should not look like a typical mosque."[79] Just as his artificial lakes and deep porches overcompensate for the demands of climate, his initial "devil of an idea" to

9.19 The Prayer Hall/Mosque: light from above.

provide a 30,000-square-foot mosque entrance overreacts to the role of Islam. And, just as he underestimated the forces of the monsoon, so too he misjudged the resistance to the monumental mosque.

In the solution, as built, the entrance to the National Assembly building is a passage *under* a much-scaled-down prayer hall; by putting it one level above the plaza entrance, it became directly accessible only from the interior of the building (see 9.5, 9.6). As such, it is but a vestige of Kahn's initial epiphany, although the revised mosque entrance remains strongly articulated. With its curvilinear corner light shafts and its inflection toward Mecca, it constitutes a highly visible break from the prevailing rectilinearity of the massing and the symmetry of the plan. Though the angle of inflection of the prayer hall portion toward Mecca is a relatively minor departure from the orthogonals of the rest of the assembly building plan, Kahn took care to emphasize the shift by setting up a strong axial symmetry in the adjacent ablution block that reveals a skewed view into the prayer hall beyond.

Several knowledgeable architects in Dhaka and elsewhere told me that the mosque was misoriented in relation to Mecca. Some even spoke of considerable local embarrassment about this and alleged that there was a long cover-up of this supposed violation of the first principle of mosque design. One senior architect who was with the project from its inception suggested that "no one caught [the error] until it was built"; it was revealed in 1980, when one of the contractors spoke up. Yet, though the misperception is an understandable one, none of these charges bears up under scrutiny. Mecca is located slightly south of due west from Dhaka, so it does seem plausible that the orientation of the *qibla* wall of the protruding mosque entrance would look to the visitor to be pointing to the *north*west. This perception may even withstand a cursory glance at the plans. Upon examination, however, it seems clear that it looks this way only because the orthogonal South Plaza outside the mosque entrance is itself not cardinally oriented but instead faces slightly southeast. Since there is nothing in the Koran to stipulate that a south plaza must face due south, the architect has made no error; in his orientation of the mosque at least, Kahn stayed in line with prevailing local sentiment. That some in Dhaka have raised misorientation as an issue, however, may be symptomatic of other concerns about the building and about its imported designer's interpretation of the role of Islam.

In the labels on drawings and in some correspondence between Kahn's Philadelphia office and its Dhaka representatives, references to "the Mosque" rather than "the prayer hall" persisted well after it had been scaled down and incorporated into the massing of the assembly building.[80] Whether, as Komendant and others have suggested, this redesign truly did transform the mosque entrance into a prayer hall capable of functioning as a spiritual place for persons of all faiths, or whether the changes merely rendered it a mosque with a neutral-sounding name, is a matter best left to the individual worshiper. To the extent that Kahn succeeded in creating a space that overcomes religious divisiveness, perhaps this hall, with its complex play of light from above, is a greater evocation of the transcendent spirit of assembly than is the legislative chamber itself (9.19).

The scaling-down of the mosque/prayer hall had another important implication, less often considered. Kahn's initial design of the immense mosque entrance with its four corner minarets (see 9.10) was indicative of his early commitment to the public character of the capitol complex, a commitment that would soon come under challenge. The minaret, as an element in Islamic design, has usually served two purposes—it is a sign of an Islamic presence that can be seen from afar and a platform from which the muezzin can best call the surrounding public to prayer. The first was no doubt at the heart of Kahn's early attempt to convey the power and importance of Islam, but the element of prayer-call could have little function in a mosque connected to a National Assembly building on an island. The four minarets and the 30,000 square feet of space suggest that a large crowd was to be called to prayer, one far exceeding the number of high government officials for whom the capitol was designed. Just as Utzon removed the publicly visible mosque from the design for the National Assembly building in Kuwait, so Kahn seems to have initially envisioned a much more public place than local politics would permit. Such architectural invitations to public participation were further undercut by his moat-and-castle approach to urban design (a tendency that would reach its apotheosis in Bawa's island parliament for Sri Lanka).

Bringing together this larger community was, perhaps, central to what Kahn most wanted, yet this impulse was contradicted both by the need for high security in the assembly building and by the variety of ways Kahn's master plan emphasized the detachment of the capitol complex from the rest of the city. The move, in subsequent designs, to a less public articulation of the mosque component was thus a recognition by Kahn that this most central precinct of the capitol was intended to be used by a more limited and controllable clientele. Kahn's notes from 20 May 1964 confirm this recognition: "Mosque now interrupts entrance. It should not be for general public. Therefore, it can be raised to connect with Assembly on a higher level."[81]

Given the highly public and political nature of his commission, Kahn's search for higher-level architectural connections cannot be considered in isolation from the changing cultural circumstances of the capitol's larger setting. Just as Islam played markedly different roles in East Pakistan and Bangladesh as a source and marker of identity-formation, so too the role of Islam has remained heavily contested even among Bangladeshi Muslims. It is not simply a question of elevating one religion over another in the iconography of a building, it is an issue of whether the government as a whole should retain an essentially secular base. In recent years, attacks on both non-Muslims and on secular Muslims have increased, and an Islamist nationalism has gradually but consistently gained greater influence in Bangladesh since the mid-1970s. By the late 1990s, Ali Riaz argues, "Islamists had emerged as a formidable political force, 'Islam' had become a prominent political ideology, and religious rhetoric occupied a central position in political discourse."[82] In this context, the National Assembly's 'Mosque entrance' meant one thing when it was first designed in the early 1960s for East Pakistan, quite another thing when the designs were finished in the early

1970s in constitutionally secular Bangladesh, and something quite different when the building opened in the mid-1980s under the increasingly Islamic banner of military regimes. And today it means something else still.

The citadels and the city

Though many aspects of the unbuilt Citadel of the Institutions might have helped to tie the capitol complex to the rest of Dhaka, Kahn seems to have regarded the whole of Sher-e-Bangla Nagar as a separate entity. He viewed the commission for the capitol complex as a chance to build a "world within a world."[83] If the outer world was Dhaka, however, Kahn's inner world was to grow not within it but beside it, more than three miles from the city center (see 9.2). According to his longtime assistant, Henry Wilcots, Kahn wanted a site even farther to the north, where there was more vegetation and less traffic.[84] In any case, this shift outward to form a new center was in keeping with the history of new sector formation in Dhaka and was probably inevitable if a large parcel of land that did not involve enormous relocation of population were to be found. As in other capitals, the prospective prestige of having government neighbors encouraged investment nearby. Though Kahn did not choose the site, a largely undeveloped area used by an agricultural college, he did insist on enlarging it; from an initial 210 acres, the government eventually agreed to a fourfold increase. Whatever its size and placement, however, he had contradictory ideas about the degree to which he wanted his citadels to relate to the rest of the city.

On the one hand he described the capitol complex as "a thousand acre reservation" and said that he sought to "give self-containment to an inspired way of life."[85] Yet, on the other hand, Kahn felt strongly that there should be a close connection between the general public and these government buildings. As the architect phrased it, with no shortage of mystifying abstractions,

> I felt that there was in the village a lack of the nation's sense of the institutions of man. The seat of the institutions of man is the measure of a city. . . . The institutions that are there; the availability of these institutions; the exchange of them; the architecture of connection which connects them in which the garden being the private place, the court being the place of entrance, the plaza being the place of meeting, the court being the boy's place, the place of meeting being man's place; city hall is an exchange of the desire for the extension of the talents of the individuals.[86]

Through the multiplicity of evocative images one detects Kahn's desire for both a "reservation" and "available institutions"; he sought both "self-containment" and "connection." And, in the end, it may be that he failed to sense the full contradiction in these impulses.

Though the city of Dhaka has long since grown northward far enough to encompass Sher-e-Bangla Nagar, its embrace is a cautious one (9.20). Access to the Citadel of Assembly varies according to the winds of a perpetually

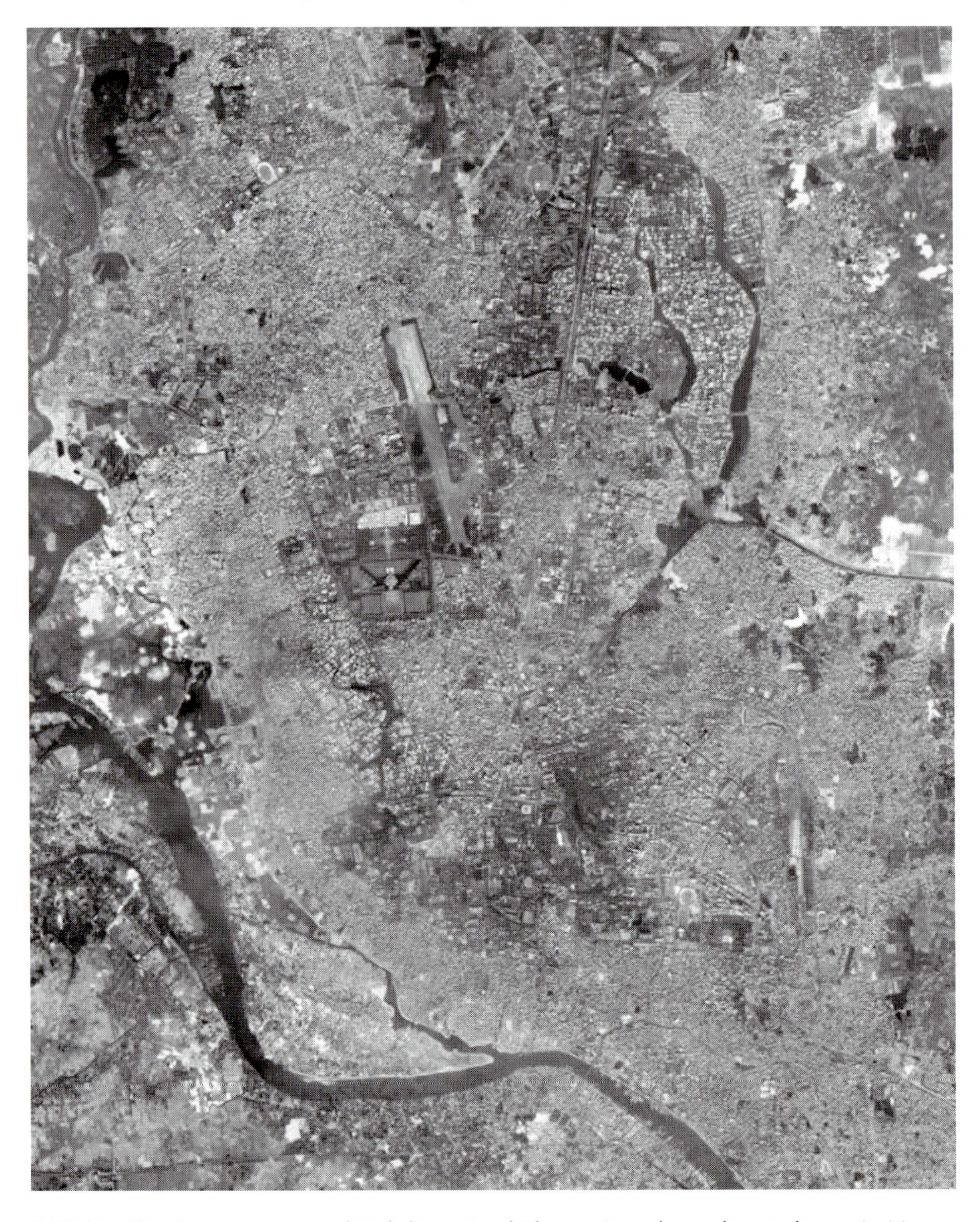

9.20 Satellite view of Dhaka, showing how Sher-e-Bangla Nagar stands out from the dense urban city that has grown to surround it.

stormy political climate in which security and crowd control are priorities. Under Ershad's rule, at least, the capitol complex was perhaps most integrated with the area around the airstrip to its east, a zone containing the military cantonment. Though the day-to-day relations of the capitol with the capital are a product of political decisions, Kahn's design choices contribute mightily to this perception as well.

Exactly why Kahn chose the rather provocative term *citadel* to characterize his architectural ensembles is far from clear. Surely *citadel* has never had connotations of assembly. To the contrary, it has most often been associated with decidedly undemocratic forms of military control and with structures intended to protect the rulers from the unruly.[87] Why would Kahn go out of his way to build-in such an association, especially when his commission came at a time of growing political unrest? Was he, perhaps, seeking to capitalize on the uneasiness of his Pakistani clients by providing a preview of greater security soon to come? Maybe Kahn interpreted the word *citadel* literally—as the Italian diminutive of *città*—and saw his citadels as this, a little city, a "world within a world."[88] In any case, Kahn's National Assembly building undeniably stands as a citadel, even without its architect's appropriate annotation.

Other than the castlelike massing, what is most central to the perception of the building as a citadel is Kahn's treatment of water, which, in combination with large open areas of grass and stone, heightens the perception of distance, both among the parts of the complex and between the capitol complex and its city. Such accentuation of distance is deliberate, though Kahn fails to make it clear how this may be reconciled with notions of assembly or connection. Defending his initial grouping of the assembly, hostels, and supreme court into the Citadel of Assembly, Kahn said that together they "suggest[ed] a completeness causing other buildings to take their distance."[89] To intensify this "suggestion" to the point of insistence, Kahn reinforced the separation by the creation of artificial lakes.

The deliberate creation of artificial lakes on a flood plain in a country with a history of devastating floods was a controversial decision. Cost was not the only issue. According to Wisdom, "In a country where people sometimes see too much water in the form of rain and floods, retaining it in any form seemed too insensitive to the Building Committee." But Kahn overcame such objections "by showing that the control of water is what is important, especially where there is much of it. His walled lakes are interconnected with drains and canals in a complete system that collects and leads rainwater away from the site and into the Brahmaputra River."[90] According to office notes from May 1964, however, Kahn himself was not entirely convinced of his response: "Lou justified the lakes to the committee. In the end he said he had the lakes because he wanted them. They were satisfied. But Lou isn't. We need our experts to help us justify lakes."[91] Such a glimpse into design negotiations is further evidence of Kahn's frustration over his inability to explain his design impulses; he did give another partial explanation for the lakes: "Because this is delta country, buildings are placed on mounds to protect them from flood. The lake was meant to encompass the hostels and the assembly and to act as a dimensional control."[92] Exactly how Kahn wanted the lakes to control "dimensions" as well as water, he does not make clear, though it would seem to have the contradictory effect of making the buildings appear both more inaccessible and, because of reflections, less distant.

Setting off buildings by the use of lakes, moats, and bridges, however much Kahn's "experts" justified them in terms of Mughal tradition, contributes to the overall perception of the capitol complex as a series of

9.21 View of Zia Mausoleum, looking north across Crescent Lake Bridge (2006).

9.22 View from Zia Mausoleum, looking south toward the National Assembly (2006).

vast, empty spaces. In part, this unpeopled purity looks intentional, as if Kahn wanted to extend his play with form and light to include not only his buildings but the whole of their site. When asked, in an interview published not long before his death, about the spareness of his landscaping, Kahn replied that he wanted "nothing but grass as a setting, a great carpet in front of a strong geometry." "But," his interviewer countered, "the people who live there might want some trees." To which Kahn replied, "If they want trees, then that's their concern, *I* must make it so strong that they *don't* want them."[93] In this rather sharp exchange, Kahn's ambivalence surfaces; here it is posed as the tension between "form" and habitation, but lurking beneath is the struggle between the desire to promote assembly and the need to control it. Without its market, stadium, or other truly public institutions, Kahn's capitol complex could all too easily become a reservation rather than a place of assembly; instead of a district within the city it could form an inland island above it. As Sarah Williams Goldhagen notes, the two enormous plazas that flank the capitol total "more than 800,000 square feet of unprogrammed, unrequested, and—in functional terms—unnecessary public space, all abutting the limited-access National Assembly. The South Plaza is said to be still the largest paved area in Bangladesh."[94]

At the time of this writing, some of the forbidding nature of the place has undergone a positive transformation, while in other ways the capitol complex has become more isolated than ever. Most positively, those parts of Sher-e-Bangla Nagar where the public is permitted to venture provide some of the few open areas available for safe family recreation in Dhaka. The public is allowed access to the pathways north of the Crescent Lake, an area Kahn intended to be a public park between the citadels. The addition of Chandrima Park in the 1980s gave citizens a reason to go there. Despite the absence of either Kahn's Citadel of the Institutions or even a more prosaic Secretariat, two more recent construction projects have helped to draw activity to this area of the complex (see 9.9 and 9.20). First is a large aluminum-clad convention center, funded by a Chinese grant and built by Chinese workers. The second major structure marking this northern area is a mausoleum for Ziaur Rahman, military ruler of Bangladesh from 1975 until his assassination in 1981. This addition—a formal, symbolic alteration to the capitol complex that dominates the axis north of the Crescent Lake—is not apt to encourage citizens to view Sher-e-Bangla Nagar as a forum for the contemplation of a more democratic future. That said, since General Zia's widow led his Bangladesh Nationalist Party to electoral victory under more democratic terms, his mausoleum received considerable architectural embellishment after her election in 2001. With a massive pedestrian bridge and canopy added, the 74-acre mausoleum attracts great crowds, especially during the evenings and on holidays (9.21, 9.22).[95] Unfortunately, the attraction of Zia's mausoleum is a kind of default option for Bangladeshis, since many of the other desirable areas of Sher-e-Bangla Nagar are off limits.

On the south side of the complex, opportunities for public engagement were initially plentiful, but at the time of this writing are now carefully

delimited. From the rear base of the South Plaza there are ghat-like steps leading to the water of the V-shaped lakes that flank the assembly, but no bathing, boating, fishing, or swimming is allowed. Signs are posted to prohibit vendors and forbid game-playing or even walking on the grass, and security personnel are there to remind the illiterate or intransigent. The signs further warn (in Bengali) that "it is a duty for every citizen to keep the Assembly Building area beautiful," a worthy aim that is pursued chiefly by forcing people to assemble elsewhere. It used to be possible to ascend all the way to the top of the brick plaza, traverse the bridge over the moat, and step right up to the door of the assembly building (even though that door was always locked). People could gather on the South Plaza, especially around sunset as the weather cools, and the sum total of such visitors was even more impressive numerically than their scattered presence on the vast site would indicate. Such public assembly on this plaza is featured prominently near the end of *My Architect*, Nathaniel Kahn's brilliant and elegiac film about his enigmatic father. The Oscar-nominated motion picture, released in 2003, underscores the capitol's place in the popular embrace of democracy (even though one maintenance worker amusingly identifies the architect as Louis Farrakhan rather than Louis Kahn). More recently, however, security concerns have led Bangladeshi authorities to prohibit public access to the plaza entirely. Instead, the area near the South Plaza now houses residences for the speaker and deputy speaker, built amidst great controversy, and vehicular and pedestrian access to the south area of the site is sharply curtailed. Ironically, it was possible to get closer to the (locked) entrance door of the Assembly Building during Ershad's military rule than it is under more democratic conditions.

Kahn's idea in setting up this grand axial ascent to the entrance apparently was to enable the public to approach and proceed into the building at the level of the Assembly Chamber's public gallery. As this book goes to press, public access to the South Plaza remains eliminated, and it is impossible to enter the Assembly Building in this manner. Parliamentarians gain access through a tunnel on a lower level, as do any others who have obtained permission to attend the sessions.[96] Yet, security concerns aside, the plaza level public entrance would surely have made for poor crowd control anyway. If the locked-shut National Assembly building fronted by a deliberately emptied plaza is a telling aspect of the limitations of Bangladeshi democracy, the axial approach to those elaborate unopened doors seems a vestige of Kahn's own ideal of Assembly and the ambiguous messages that these looming facades project.

MISCONNECTIONS: THE COSTS AND BENEFITS

If Kahn's claims for an "architecture of connection" are undercut by political, climatic, religious, and urban discontinuities, so too the capitol complex both produces and perpetuates socioeconomic disjunctures. While there are always disjunctures in a developing country when new institutions (and new forms for housing them) are introduced, the problems seem exacerbated in

Dhaka by Kahn's rhetoric and designs. It is too simple to dismiss or discredit this building venture purely on the grounds of its extraordinarily high cost. Though one may surely question the size of this expenditure [97] in one of the most impoverished nations on earth, the high costs were as much a result of construction delays as of the architect's extravagance. Moreover, the epic tale of the Dhaka capitol is about far more than the provision of expensive buildings to house government officials.

To judge the true costs and benefits of this project one must view it in its larger context—as an attempt to bring international recognition to Dhaka and to develop a modern building industry in the city. Komendant points out that, because of this larger agenda, Kahn was to receive a 7 percent commission instead of the customary 5. In his memoirs, Kahn's engineer recalls his early justification of this to the finance minister:

> First, we will use local architects and engineers and teach and train them from the design phase to the finished structures. Second, we will use construction methods and equipment which could be used after our work is finished. We have studied your situation, the materials and labor available. The first thing we will do is to establish a precasting and prestressing plant to produce the carrying elements required so badly in your country and train your engineers and workers to run it. In connection with this plant there will be a batching plant and ready-mix trucks for delivery of concrete to any place in Dacca. If you like, we could even design and build you a cement factory which is badly needed and also deliver some cranes and excavation equipment to stretch sand from riverbeds. You can be sure that after the capital buildings are finished East Pakistan would be, in construction matters, the most advanced country in this part of the world.[98]

A full evaluation of either the desirability or the success of this ambitious technology transfer goes well beyond the scope of this chapter, though a few observations may be set out.

The construction of the capitol has indeed provided the Dhaka building industry with an education in modern techniques for using concrete and exposed brick. Of the two materials, only the latter has come into widespread use as yet. Brick flourished following its use for the capitol complex hostels and other buildings and by 1990 it was "so extensively used that it has become a kind of official building material."[99] The use of exposed brickwork (challenging local practice, which plastered all wall faces) was a revival of the use of this material for public buildings and a visible departure from the stucco facades associated with many buildings constructed by the colonial British.

The story of concrete, however, is quite different. An assessment of the capital's impact on local design concludes that exposed reinforced concrete was both inappropriate to the humid climate and "too expensive" for the local economy, since "all its ingredients, including the forms, had to be imported."[100] Not imported was the labor force, 80 percent of which was unskilled. Still, many of the workers trained to build with the concrete of the

9.23 Building the National Assembly with concrete, Dhaka.

assembly building have had to leave Bangladesh in order to find employment in the industry. Darab Diba, in his "Technical Review" of the assembly complex (1989), which was commissioned as part of the process that led to its receiving an Aga Khan Award for Architecture, concluded, "This is the first major work [in Bangladesh] which uses this material, and may well be the last."[101] Perhaps the "love for concrete [that] couldn't be denied" was as much the infatuation of a government desiring a modern building industry as it was the romantic urge of Kahn (9.23).

In any case, Kahn's use of concrete leaves a mixed legacy. While the future use of poured concrete as both a structural frame and an enclosure material for major projects is in doubt, the herculean effort to employ it remains a stunning gesture in form and technique. The white marble bands on the assembly walls are not arbitrary lines: they represent the maximum height of a concrete pour in a single day, celebrated by a multifunctional strip of marble. With marble and concrete conjoined, the five-foot human scale may be read both literally and metaphorically. As Kahn phrased it, "The concrete is made like rotten stone. The marble inset mixes the fine with the rough, and the fine takes over."[102] Unfortunately, even before the building had housed its first National Assembly session, pieces of the marble started falling off, to be replaced by plastic inserts. Despite Kahn's efforts at making fine joints, his design has not yet fit easily in Bangladesh.

RESISTING A CONCLUSION

If the various misconnections explored thus far tell us anything, it is that this is a building complex that cannot properly be judged for a long time. Kahn has claimed that his buildings were expensive because they "reveal the truth," but his eternal verities seem distant from the various forms of authoritarian rule and political corruption that have frequently characterized both East Pakistan and Bangladesh in the forty-five years since the architect first rhapsodized about the transcendent nature of assembly. The disconnect reached its nadir in December 1987, when General Ershad placed many leaders of opposition parties under house arrest and dissolved the Bangladeshi parliament. The ongoing threat of military manipulation made electoral participation seem futile.[103] Twenty years later, the situation looks quite different, yet clear limitations to democracy and good government remain. Multiparty parliamentary democracy in Bangladesh has been restored for more than fifteen years under civilian rule, but opposition parties have continued frequent electoral boycotts. Moreover, the legacy of dictatorial presidents and military interventions casts long shadows over the parliament's ability to manage this impoverished and flood-ravaged country. Bangladesh's two major parties, the Awami League and the Bangladesh Nationalist Party (BNP) have supplied the prime ministers and opposition leaders since 1991. Both parties have been led since the 1980s by women who share a deeply personal connection to the country's history of political violence—and a legendary disdain for one another. The BNP, championed by Khaleda Zia (Ziaur Rahman's widow) has fought protracted battles with Awami League's Sheikh Hasina, the daughter of Sheikh Mujibur Rahman, Bangladesh's founder-president who was assassinated in 1975. By 2005, intra-Muslim political strife coupled with anti-Hindu actions led one *New York Times* writer to refer to "Louis Kahn's ethereal Parliament" as "a relic of a more hopeful period in Bangladesh's democracy." In lieu of scheduled national elections in 2007, the army-backed caretaker government declared emergency rule, "banned political activity, and suspended fundamental rights." As this book goes to press, then, the future of Bangladeshi democracy again seems uncertain at best.[104]

Can one yet form a judgment about the quality of a building complex that grants such an intimidating monumentality to such a timid institution? What sense does it make to try to single out qualities that are exclusively architectural when the architect himself professed to be so concerned with the meaning of institutions? Is the challenge posed by Kahn's idealistic formalism too great for any government? As James Dunnett has asked, "Could any delegates be good enough, heroic enough, for the building. Will the architecture belie the mundane business of the Assembly?"[105] How can there *not* be discontinuities when a Western architect brings a Western system of construction to house a Western form of government in a non-Western land?

Kahn wished to communicate a spirit of assembly to everyone, but surely not everyone will see it in the same way. What to the privileged legislator is a penetrable volume may be seen by the average citizen as a forbidding citadel rising from the water. The image, whether rooted in the East or in the West, is a familiar one—magisterial authority, distant yet full of intrigue. Kahn is famous among architects for his ability to instill in his buildings a clear hierarchy through structural, formal, and functional differentiation of their "served" and "servant" parts, yet notions of servant and served have far more than an architectural resonance. Seen against a backdrop of its social and political standing, most parts of Sher-e-Bangla Nagar (except the mausoleum area) may be viewed as a kind of served space, with servants invited in only when needed. How the building will ultimately serve Bangladesh is uncertain. Kahn's geometric cutouts screen more than the sun: they deny the proximity and the scale of the city. How can a building that denies access both literally and figuratively be construed

9.24 The Acropolis of Bangladesh.

as an image of democracy (9.24)? And yet, if one looks at other such capitol complexes, perhaps this denial is not really so extreme. Even though it may seem an imperious edifice set off by water, at some times and in some places there has been far greater possibility for public presence near this National Assembly building than there is, for example, in Sri Lanka or Kuwait.

It is too easy to see the Dhaka capitol as some oddly appropriate military citadel. The complex, having taken on a complicated series of meanings and associations, is much more than this. The connotations of *citadel* for Kahn may be less that of army stronghold or little *città* than of a kind of acropolis. Surely, his incantations in light and space and his arrangement of forms on plinths owes much to his love for the Parthenon and its neighbors. And yet, if this is the Acropolis of Bangladesh, where is the agora? If these capitol buildings are temples, who are the gods?

As Kahn's words fade, the disturbing resonances of his almost Speerian evocation of "ruin-value" begin to recede. Though verbal annotations and political connotations never fully give way, the buildings persist, waiting patiently in "the coolness of a shadow." Over time, the manifold shortcomings and misconnections may dissipate. Some greater semblance of democracy may come to the chamber; religious harmony may make a mosque more truly a prayer hall; a city may grow up to and among the island edifices; humans may occupy the empty porches of climatic overcompensation. And the Acropolis of Bangladesh may truly become a place of Assembly.

CHAPTER 10

Designing power and identity

Taken together and seen in relation to the history of designed capitals, the capitol complexes in Papua New Guinea, Kuwait, Sri Lanka, and Bangladesh constitute a broad array of attempts to symbolize political power and design national identity. If the range of conceivable design approaches is envisioned as a spectrum encompassing everything from the most willfully international to the most obstinately local, then all four capitol designs fall somewhere in the middle. Yet they do not group easily together.

The ultrainternationalist position may be an invisible part of this spectrum. A work that is in every respect international is a logical impossibility to design because no building actually constructed can avoid being a product of its place and its producers. Even the most positive interpretation of an internationalist stance—one that views *international* as being synonymous with universal applicability rather than as equivalent to some active denial of local influences—does not negate the power of local construction labor, local climate, and local culture to transform both the appearance and the meanings of a building even in a single, globally interconnected economy.

The opposite extreme—call it the infra-local—may also be considered as outside of the visible spectrum, though in a different way. Here, the modern architect's intervention is, in theory, indistinguishable from some part of the existing vernacular built environment. This, too, would seem to be a logical impossibility. Even the existence of the term *vernacular* implies a supralocal influence capable of defining it. Moreover, vernacular architecture is itself in continuous evolution, especially in heterogeneous societies subject to ever-increasing architectural cross-pollination, globalized markets, and rapid urbanization. As new technologies, new functions, and new forms are introduced, new meanings evolve. In the modern world of global communication, the local is inevitably influenced by the supralocal, while any movement toward the international is tempered by the narrowly provincial.

In the four late twentieth-century postcolonial capitols discussed in

Chapters 6–9, the architects seem—in varying degrees—to have adapted their designs to the challenges of cultural pluralism. In each case, the architects have made clearly visible assumptions about the social and cultural preferences of their clients. Each, for example, attempted to grapple with the issue of indigenous roof traditions, and this is one way that their architectural attitudes can be differentiated. Hogan adapted a kind of compendium of roof typologies from PNG and fused them through the use of new materials; Bawa designed a Parliament House as a series of Kandyan-roofed pavilions, turning a domestic form into an institutional one. Utzon, finding no obvious roof tradition that was uniquely Kuwaiti, borrowed from desert tents and Marsh Arab structures from elsewhere in the region; while Kahn, ignoring the traditional Bangala roof form, struggled mightily (if rather unsuccessfully) to develop a distinctive roof tradition of his own. Whatever the particular solution each architect devised for the nation-state's big roof, each was caught in Ricoeur's paradox of "universal civilization" and "national cultures," trying to deliver both but at least partially aware that either extreme is an impossibility. Which forms, if any, are universal ones? Which culture is the national one when there are many contenders? These are questions that remain unstated but ever-present, necessarily implied by a building type that is asked to symbolize a country both to the world and to itself. In confronting the twin pulls of the international and the local, each architect looks first at one and then back to the other.

The very diversity of these recent capitol complexes suggests that any notion of a style for government buildings—whether international neoclassicism or its mid-twentieth-century bland equivalent—has been rejected, even transcended. There are, however, many different kinds of transcendence, and many nonstylistic ways parliament buildings remain supreme articulations of nationalist political power.

The problem of representation in a capitol complex is at least twofold. First, decisions must be made about how to represent the diversity of cultural groups that may coexist within a state, a heterogeneity that, especially in newly independent countries, is prone to factional infighting. Second, there are decisions about how to represent spatially the political system of the country, judgments about how to depict the legislature in relation to the city and in juxtaposition to other institutions, both civic and governmental.

Given the weakness of most parliaments as institutions, architects can respond in three general ways to the double problem of symbolizing an unstable political system and depicting a pluralist state. First, the architect may claim to be disinterested in the political role of the building, now and forever. Second, the designer can accept the insignificance of the legislature and minimize the monumentality of its architectural treatment, both in its siting and its massing. This concern for presenting the capitol complex as a microcosm of the nation-state places a premium on accuracy of representation. Such a concern for microcosmic accuracy, taken to the level of iconography, would tend to deny pluralism and stress the presence of some dominant group. Third, architects may wish to look toward a more sanguine future, free of factional discord. They may think they can anticipate or even encourage the potential centrality of representative democracy by allowing the visual importance of the building to prefigure its future institutional weight. Similarly, by declining to provide obvious preferential treatment to the architectural and urban design traditions of the most influential groups, the architect may hope to anticipate or encourage a more equal sharing of political power. The three approaches may be categorized as follows:

Capitol complex as beyond politics
Capitol complex as microcosm
Capitol complex as idealization.

APPROACHING CAPITOL DESIGN

Capitol complex as beyond politics?

When an architect is designing a building to serve the needs and symbolize the aims of political leaders, his or her protestations of political disinterest sound either hollow or insincere. This does not mean, however, that architects must promote some unequivocal political message through their buildings or play an active role in ongoing political conflicts. It means that although an architect must decide whether to accept or refuse a commission on the basis of a large variety of factors, he or she should make a concerted effort to study the politics and the cultures of the country to be symbolized. Unless the architect becomes aware of the group-based biases of the client and the degree of honesty with which this client pursues the aims of parliamentary democracy, he or she may end up with a building that is, at best, elegant but irrelevant and, at worst, overbearing and inflammatory. Moreover, an architect should also look inward to identify and confront the assumptions and biases brought to any new project by virtue of personal background and preferences.

The architecture of government buildings is political architecture. For the clients, it is often a matter of putting the best possible face on whatever exists, a wide means to serve narrow ends. Capitol complex design is inexorably a product of the political conditions prevailing at the time of the commission and during construction (though this hardly need be the only force affecting design). All buildings are politically engendered, but some buildings are arguably more political than others. Buildings that seem to be an important part of the public realm, such as capitols, should perhaps be judged by broader criteria than those which attend to narrowly private interests. Unlike a hotel, for example, parliament buildings are brought into being by forces closely related to the institution housed within. Capitol complexes are produced by ascendant groups who wish to give evidence of ascendant political institutions.

Another dimension linking architectural and political design is the close identification between politicians and public works. The architect is not the only person whose reputation rides upon the outcome of a new capitol or new capital. Hitler's Thousand Year Reich, in spite of its well-developed plans and models for a vast capitol complex with buildings of unprecedented scale, did not last long enough for most of its monuments to be built. Rulers in other places have tried to get an earlier start. They have worked hard to get their architectural visions of government built during their own political lifetimes. In the decades of postfascist backlash, the dreams of Hitler and Speer for a monumental new Berlin have been supplanted by equally audacious plans for modern capitals under political systems as diverse as those of Brazil, Nigeria, and Kazakhstan.

Hitler claimed to be rebuilding Berlin not to bolster his own rule, which he knew to be limited in time, but as an imposing backdrop for the führers of the future who might need this most solid form of support. While this future-orientation might well inspire any government leader contemplating the wholesale creation of a new capital (or even, as in Berlin, what amounted to a very large-scale capitol complex), there remains a remarkable degree of identification between the new capital and its government sponsor. Kubitschek and Brasília, Nehru and Chandigarh, Banda and Lilongwe, Nyerere and Dodoma, Mahathir and Putrajaya, Nazarbayev and Astana—the power pairings continue.

In the case of capitols that do not involve the abandonment of an old capital and the creation of a new one, the identification between the regime and the complex also seems close. Both new capitals and new capitols involve visions of inordinately rapid development; the slow growth that characterized the early decades of Washington and Canberra is anathema to those who commission capitals and stake their political reputation to do so. Some architects, notably Kahn, have managed to resist the pressures to design and build rapidly, but in other instances—Bawa's case is an extreme—the quality of the architecture has been compromised by the political demands of expedience. In this way, too, no architect of a parliament building can fail to be deeply connected to the demands of politicians.

In insisting that capitol complexes must be judged together with the institutions they house, I am not asking that these buildings be judged only—or even primarily—in terms of the political freedom of their sponsoring regimes. It is enough to stress that they are a product of these conditions and that their political pedigree is made manifest in the choice of site, in the relationship between capitol and capital, and in the often-partisan iconography of the architectural forms. If architecture is to retain or regain a position as an integrated and integral part of culture rather than a detached club for aestheticians, both architects and architecture critics must probe the dynamics of the relationship between a building and its society. To judge a public building one must understand something about the public as well as the building. Whether or not the architect claims to care about politics, many politicians use architecture and urban design as political instruments.

Capitol complex as microcosm?

To the extent that an accurate microcosm reflects poorly on the status of the parliamentary institution or gives symbolic credence to groups who are opposed to the government, the approach that treats the capitol complex as a microcosm is likely to be unacceptable to the government leaders who sponsor architects and urban designers. Most government clients have vested interests in promoting the idea of a national assembly and wish to see their own biases enshrined. Regimes that commission new capitols and capitals almost inevitably seek to maximize the presence of the branch of government most belonging to the people. Whether they support the monumentality of a new parliament building as a genuine move toward democracy or as a form of appeasement, masking the consolidation of executive power, remains open to question and, I believe, is a question that architects and urban designers should ask.

Perhaps it is a deeply rooted condition of contemporary professionalism that architects and urban designers—like advertising executives and lawyers—need not believe in the aims of their client to serve and serve well. Yet, if true, this sad fact should not linger unexamined. The mention of law and advertising may act as a reminder that, at least from the client's point of view, the design of capitols and capitals is fundamentally about promoting and defending the corporate power of a government.

Is it possible to develop a capitol complex that is an accurate microcosm of extant political relations, both among institutions and among cultural groups, a juxtaposition that reveals the true hierarchy of rule (and misrule)? Who would be the judge of its accuracy? How would the system accommodate change?

It is conceivable to envisage a capitol complex as a series of interlocked but moving parts, with the institutions housing executive, legislative, and judicial government able to change relative positions according to the political developments of the day, month, or year. Such a sensitively calibrated capitol complex could project not only institutional relationships but also cultural pluralism. It is possible to imagine a parliament building whose changing facade communicated whatever balance of images the leadership desired, a kind of travelogue and cultural inventory that emphasized the dominant presence of certain privileged groups. What if the form of the whole city changed immediately upon the advent of a major political change such as a coup or a dramatic election victory? This, of course, is not the way things happen. Most cities change slowly, in response to countless factors only indirectly tied to political leadership. To increase the number and speed of physical reconfigurations, even in an age of digital media and programmable facades, would be prohibitive in terms of cost and logistics.

But it could happen on the drawing-board. What if the designers of Abuja, for example, had adjusted the scheme for the Central Area to respond to every coup and countercoup? To some extent, as I have indicated, they actually did this in an anticipatory sort of way—by moving the presidential palace away from the National Square. Yet what if the idea had been carried further? What if the building at the terminus of the grand axis had been changed from the National Assembly to the offices of the military leader and the National Assembly building had been shunted off to one side? Surely this would be the most accurate representation of the country's political realities in the 1980s. Since the buildings were not yet constructed, it would have been a relatively simple matter to reconfigure their hierarchy in the drawings to reflect changed conditions. The point is that there are no guarantees that any given regime will choose to care about the accuracy of its symbolic urban representation of the balance of national political power. Architecture and urban design can have much political value as a mask, or even as a deliberate form of lie.

Once built, major government buildings tend to remain in place; it is the meanings associated with such buildings that never remain static. Lutyens's viceregal palace can be reused in an independent Indian democracy. Batista's palace can be adopted to serve Castro's Cuba. A parliament house designed for East Pakistan can later come to symbolize independent Bangladesh. Throughout history, buildings have taken on new functions and been judged in new ways under changed contexts. When the institutions of government are in flux, as they are in most new or impoverished countries, the symbolic role of a parliament building may alter even more rapidly than it does under stable conditions, changing with the reputation of the institution it houses. It is impossible to measure the relative influences of the various factors that bring about a change in the symbolic role of a building. While I do not claim that a parliament building's partisan iconography or its location within a city or capitol complex is the decisive factor in how it is perceived, these acts of deliberate symbolism cannot be discounted. Especially since there is no way to build a microcosm—of either political institutions or cultural groups—that is both politically feasible and accurate, the symbolism of capitols is a matter of some significance. Architects must be made conscious of the gulf between the hegemony of their client's preferences and the more inclusive promises implied by a building that is called a "national" assembly.

Capitol complex as idealization?

If the changing and often unflattering nature of existing power politics makes the task of designing a microcosm either impossible or undesirable, should the designer attempt instead an idealization of political institutions and intergroup relations? Every design solution is to some extent an idealization of the political realm. The more basic and pressing issues are which ideals are pursued and who gets to decide. One must analyze both ideals and their architectural depiction carefully. A capitol complex is always a kind of crude diagram of power relations, but there is no direct correlation between a particular diagram and a particular form of political organization. The danger here is that idealization will be used not to anticipate some more perfect future order but to mask the severe abuses of power in the present. The inclusion of a sizable assembly building for the Supreme Soviet in the heart of Moscow's Kremlin in 1960 did not mean that a democratically elected legislature would immediately begin to control the major decisions of the USSR. Conversely, the symbolic presence of this large legislative building in the historic heart of authoritarian rule did not tempt post-Soviet Russia to install its Duma within the Kremlin walls. Protodemocratic symbolic shifts give little hint of the timetable or commitment to the corresponding political change. The conception of government organization and balance implied in the design of a Three Powers Plaza or a Three Arms Zone initially did little more than cloak the reality of a strong executive in a seemingly more democratic mantle. This ideal, exemplified by Chandigarh, Brasília, and Abuja, comes across as a mixed message at best. The professed desirability of separating executive, legislative, and judicial functions as the spatial representation of some constitutionally assumed separation of powers is contradicted, at least in part, by the actuality of the plans, which group the three powers and separate them from the rest of the city.

Thus, even if the idea of the Three Powers separation is justified as a future ideal rather than an achieved reality, the physical form of the triple grouping ensures that the ideal can never be met. Yet even if it is placed within a walled fortress or isolated atop a governmental island, the very act of including a legislature in such a prime urban site may play some role in the eventual emergence of democratic forms of power sharing. It may be that urban design placement of the capitol is of greater symbolic importance than its embryonic architectural form. There is something important to be learned from the slow growth of Washington's Capitol, which began as a relatively modest structure on the city's prime site and, over a period of seventy years of national development, sprouted its wings and a series of ever-more-soaring domes.

Questions about the formal depiction of political ideals raise issues relating to ideals of cultural pluralism as well. While Kahn thought it a great inspiration to expand both the size and the importance of the mosque and ablution block well beyond what the client had expected, how does one justify this presence to Bangladesh's 11 million Hindus? If a village men's house is thought to be an appropriate ideal on which to base a modern parliament, how is this choice to be justified to women?

To ask how a designer chooses certain spatial forms as appropriate to accompany a given political ideal or preferred model of cultural pluralism raises an even more fundamental question: who decides which ideals are to be pursued? In many of the cases that I have analyzed, new capitols and new capitals were commissioned in close relationship with new constitutions. The architects and urban designers were implicitly charged with designing buildings and complexes that fit with such texts. In Papua New Guinea, portions of the text appear literally on the facade. The issue becomes more complex when the architect has political ideals of his or her own.

In the case of capitol complexes, such expression of personal ideals has occurred most overtly and with greatest documentation in the work of Le Corbusier and Kahn; both designers had strong ideas about the cosmic role of government that bore little relation to the words of any constitution. In Kahn's case, this resulted in a work of high drama for an institution of low priority. Ignoring the clearly stated executive bias of the Pakistani constitution that mandated the Dhaka project and made clear the parliament's institutional subservience, Kahn designed a building complex for his own ideal polity. Because he asserted his own agenda beyond those of his Pakistani and Bangladeshi clients, he cannot fully escape complicity in the persistent disjunctions of the result. His complicity is, however, of a different nature from that of architects who use architecture to champion the iniquities within cultural pluralism more literally. In his otherwise admirable insistence on transcending the timebound parochialism of political conflict, Kahn may well have gone too far. Surely the denial of all conflict in the name of transcendent assembly is no less a distortion than the invocation of partisan symbolism in the name of national identity. The chief difference is that, should parliamentary democracy become more robust in Bangladesh, Kahn may yet be proven wise.

CAPITOL COMPLEX AS CRITICAL SYNTHESIS?

Ultimately, architects have a power that politicians lack. While the notion of the political promise may have as long and checkered a history as anything known to man, the promise of architecture need never be so literal. In democratic societies, politicians are always being asked to clarify their positions on the issues. Clarity is also a virtue in architecture, but it is not the only virtue. A great building is not only the result of its architect's critical imagination; it must also reward the critical imagination of those who come to see it and question it. As Whitman put it in *Democratic Vistas*, "Not the book but the reader need be the complete thing."

The building need not provide all or even any of the answers, but it must, to be effective, pose questions and frame them in a new way. Yet for rulers of fledgling countries, in which questions are too many and answers are at a premium, the prospect of a building that fails to contribute unambiguously to the consolidation of rule may be unsettling. In consequence, architects in government employ are not likely to work against the aims of their clients, but they may—through their buildings—raise important objections.

If architects and urban designers are well informed about the institutional and group relations that exist at the time a capitol complex is commissioned, they may be encouraged to design more flexibly. Only if the building is able to change along with the rapidly changing society around it can it avoid being the projection of some frozen moment in political and cultural history, associated with a single stage in an institution's growth and a single regime's iconographical preferences. The capitol complexes of Kahn, Bawa, and Hogan are designed to appear as self-contained and completed objects in the landscape, appearing utterly resistant to the possibilities for further accretion and expansion. And, in this regard, even Utzon's additive approach has been compromised by the political necessity of a cordon sanitaire.

Similarly, such buildings need not literally be able to move or to have interchangeable facades like some grand opera set, but their designers must be conscious of the gap between the present and some more hopeful future. If the architect is too literal in adapting the iconographic preferences of some politically ascendant elite, the building may enshrine for generations an image that does not retain the iconographical associations that inspired it. These alterations of meaning are beyond the control of architects and urban designers, especially when complex buildings outlast the society and culture that produced them. No palace architect in imperial Beijing could have predicted the advent of massive portraits of Chairman Mao, let alone more recent events. Few persons know how to interpret a classical frieze or a medieval cathedral's stained glass, yet once these served as far more than mere decoration. The issue of changing meanings embraces a central question for the designer of a parliament building to consider. The alternatives need not be a bombastic representation of the status quo in all of its inequity versus a pristine, abstracted vision of some distant ideal. There are other options.

The central problem with a concrete haus tambaran is not that it is concrete or that the haus tambaran upswept facade was reused in a parliament building. The problem is that the form is presented so literally that, when it reappears, it does so merely as a sign. There is no rethinking of the haus tambaran (or of the Highlands round house); the village structures are treated merely as decorative shells in which to house a modern program that is totally unrelated to the original purposes. The bark-cloth designs of the villages are (or at least were) the outcome of prodigious powers of abstraction and the dynamic absorption of outside influences; no similar imaginative leap is made or called for in the design of the PNG parliament building. Deprived of its integration with a system of meaning and a way of life, much of its iconography is reduced to mere illustration. While the PNG parliament building may well be a place of learning for the visitor, it would seem to provide an enervated and limited version of the cultures it depicts and to do so in a way that is as expensive as it is cheapened. Though its recombinant new forms may eventually help to invent new national traditions of art and architecture in which the whole is greater than the sum of its parts, there would seem to be a long way to go.

It seems too simplistic to convey the cultural strains caused by rapid development through the easy formula of traditional designs executed in modern materials with the aid of modern technology. Such a tactic shows strains but not development. More difficult questions challenge designers. There is value in using architecture to help component peoples see themselves in the new state. But what do they see when they see the ceiling mural of the Ambunti courthouse refabricated to resemble "coarse velvet?" What does it mean that the nomad's tent now shelters automobiles? What does it mean that the Sinhalese are seeking refuge in the shadows of an ancient kingdom while the present one is being gradually but inexorably peeled back? If the art and architectural traditions of the vernacular and of the golden ages of the past are valued enough to be included in the design of a parliament building, what is it about them that is valued? Are they measures of distance already traveled? Or evidence of some psychosocial need to remember roots? If roots are to be valuable, they must nourish new plants and new growth.

The trick to forging a national identity is, as Geertz puts it, "to make the nation-state seem indigenous."[1] Analysis of the four capitol complexes in the last four chapters suggests a more specific manifestation of this: the need to make selected aspects of the indigenous seem more like the nation-state. In Papua New Guinea, Sri Lanka, Kuwait, and Bangladesh, this can lead to discriminatory symbolism and architectural perjury. While no one, including me, may wish to prosecute these capitol crimes, there is clearly room for improvement.

The search for architectural forms that symbolize incipient democracy and pluralist nation-states yields many solutions and even more questions. On the question of portraying pluralism, Hogan's Parliament House in PNG seems almost obsessively concerned with a near-literal representative documentation of the art and architecture of the country's multitudinous component cultures, brought together under one roof (like a food arcade in an American shopping mall). At the other extreme, Kahn's Citadel of Assembly for Dhaka pursues a national identity only at the highest levels of abstraction. Hogan treats architectural representation as analogous to the process of political representation, though, as I have argued, it can be seen as a representation gerrymandered to favor the claims of Sepik-based ministers and a Sepik-aware international constituency. His building is a collage without the necessary overlap of pieces. The building as an entirety, like its most prominent decoration, reads as a cultural mosaic: forced to fit, the parts form a whole, but the juxtaposition is flat and without critical interpenetration.

By contrast, Kahn's complex is much less literal in its acceptance of pluralism. Though he does make a mosque a feature of the design, thereby explicitly favoring the Muslim majority (a gesture necessitated by the need to accommodate prayer by those working in the building), his complex is otherwise remarkably neutral with respect to component cultures. It is a neutrality achieved not by attempting to represent everyone side by side but by trying to integrate many assimilated references taken from two thousand years of Western and Eastern architectural history into some new product. Kahn's pluralism is so vast that it goes beyond the narrow group divisions of the present, perhaps even to the point of ignoring them. Precisely because the iconography of the Citadel of Assembly does not choose sides in some ongoing group dispute, its symbolic interpretation is flexible. To allow for this, however, is not to transcend politics but rather to make a political statement of a different kind. Kahn's political concerns in designing a national capitol have less to do with a present-day cultural pluralism than with a timeless institutional absolutism.

While Hogan's building is a pavilion along the side of a road, sited in a series of buildings so as to appear to be one important institution among many, Kahn's parliament, by contrast, is the focal point of a complex inspired by his own dream of idealized government. Kahn's approach, filtered through American eyes and Western notions of government, claims to focus on the institution itself—the act of Assembly—yet this architect deliberately paid little attention to the way that the institution functioned in the political context of his design commission. The building complex as a whole, not a particular iconographical piece of it, is the symbol. As such, it is capable of being accepted by many different political systems. This raises issues which go beyond the apparent capacity of a single building complex, over time, to be associated with Bangladesh rather than Pakistan.

Kahn's formal vocabulary has often been praised for its evocation of Mughal monuments from the region, yet this richness is not without its drawbacks. Sheer masonry walls rising above water—even with quirky geometrical cutouts—evoke aspects of earlier fortress and tomb typologies that seem distant from Kahn's professed ideal haven for near-sacred democratic discourse. To put it in Goodman's terms, Sher-e-Bangla Nagar exemplifies its fortress properties much more than other aspects of the design, and these may evoke unintended metaphorical associations and mediated references. This second kind of symbolic flexibility—in the realm of political institutions as distinct from the realm of cultural groups—is exactly what Kahn wished to deny. His purity of forms is more politically ambiguous than his rhetoric allows.

As for the urban design of the legislative institutions in Kuwait and Sri Lanka, Utzon's capitol seems closer to the urbanistic isolation of Hogan's building within the loosely linear Waigani plan, while Bawa's siting of his parliament on an island imitates Kahn's citadel as the central focus of a larger complex. Though Bawa's island parliament commands its site without recourse to principles of Western baroque urban design, it shares with the Dhaka citadel a certain institutional ambiguity. It, too, can easily read as a kind of exemplified, metaphorical fortress in which intended symbolic associations with representative democracy are not readily apparent. Utzon's capitol, though located near the heart of its capital, is a detached building offering only feigned urban connections. Like Hogan's parliament house, it is near other civic and governmental institutions but is not visually tied to them through any larger urban design.

In their architectural treatment of cultural pluralism the complexes in Kuwait and Sri Lanka stand more centrally between the poles of literal representation and universalist abstraction than do those in PNG and Bangladesh. Bawa's evocation of an indigenous Sri Lankan roof tradition places his building seemingly closer to Hogan's, and Utzon's abstractions of regional typologies are closer to Kahn's. The parliament buildings for Kuwait and Sri Lanka are characterized by clear references to vernacular and historical forms, with architectural allusions that are probably recognizable by the general populace in each country, even though they are abstracted from any specific existing buildings. Utzon, designing in the romantic expressionist tradition of Eero Saarinen, deliberately tries to make his Kuwait capitol complex resemble a known object. Yet, in Kuwait, his billowed tent is a less ideologically neutral gesture than the sails of the Sydney Opera House or Saarinen's avian terminal for TWA in New York.

Bawa's island temple, though undeniably associated with Sinhalese nationalism by virtue of its pairing with a revived ancient Sinhalese capital, nonetheless is more architecturally inclusive. The building is less partisan than its site. Bawa's capitol, since it alludes to many influences and phases in Sri Lanka's long, cosmopolitan past while still managing to evoke an architectural coherence and an empathy for the landscape, contains the germ of an encouraging approach toward addressing Ricoeur's paradox of universal civilization and cultural pluralism. Bawa observed the residues of past civilizations, absorbed them, and tried to bring forth a new generation of forms that recalled the past without mimicking or trivializing it. In this, his work is but the most recent example of an architectural dialectic that in Sri

Lanka has been producing new syntheses for more than a thousand years, as each initially alien influence became incorporated into indigenous traditions. In working within this dialectic, Bawa was aided by the availability of a Sri Lankan tradition in roof design that is ethnically neutral in its associations. For countries that have a shorter and more fragmented tradition of architectural synthesis, like Papua New Guinea, the architectural generation of a modern parliament building that responds to indigenous civilizations of the past as well as to modern architectural attitudes of the present is even more difficult to achieve.

Whatever the degree of inclusion and synthesis of past and present architectural forms, the thing that is least easily assimilated is the institution of parliament itself. However familiar and integrated the architecture, the institution remains alien; even when the chairs of Westminster are embroidered with the motifs of PNG, the parliamentary system does not yet sit comfortably. While the parliament buildings in PNG, Sri Lanka, Kuwait, and Bangladesh were all intended to be monuments to national democracy, each of these countries has seen parliamentary rule undermined by civil unrest or outright war. Moreover, as I have emphasized, the existence of a functioning parliament does not guarantee that the legislature is the supreme decision-making power in the country. In new countries, the executive often reigns supreme—with or without military stripes. In short, the parliament building is usually far more prominently placed in the landscape than the parliament institution is placed within the culture.

It may be an acceptable position for an architect like Kahn to take the moral high ground by looking only toward some future ideal, but such an attitude cannot mask the many ways parliament buildings are inextricably tied to the shifting political fortunes of the present. For different reasons, Kahn's Platonic citadel is just as jarring as Hogan's concrete spirit house. Both are powerful reminders of the gulf separating fledgling national governments inspired by the tenets of Western parliamentary democracy and the often impoverished and factionalized countries this system is asked to manage.

In the design of a capitol complex, there would seem to be two very different objectives at work. On the one hand, the complex is intended to advance the consolidation of political rule; on the other, it is expected to advance the cause of national unity. In many places, this implies a contradiction: the leaders want the capitol complex to symbolize the person or group holding power and, simultaneously, to represent the nation-state as a whole. It must symbolize both faction and state, both part and whole. If one rejects the idea of attempting to design a literal microcosm, then one must resort to some form of abstraction. Yet, if a building is too far abstracted from any known reference points, it may be resisted, resented, or, worse still, ignored. As Vikram Prakash usefully warns,

> Abstraction is a concept, an epistemic claim, which has its own history and specificity. It is an aesthetic concept claiming that the higher truths of the world immediately visible to us lie "behind" or "beyond" that world, in another more fundamental and unitary place of being. As such,

> it is also a moral assertion, since it entails the claim that the abstracted representation of the world is better, purer, and closer to some ultimate underlying truth that unifies all differences . . . It is no doubt a powerful concept. Yet, one can hardly doubt that it is nothing more than that—a concept, another representation of the world. The important point is that abstraction is a historical aesthetic device, a technique, a claim to seeing the world in a particular way, which has been privileged only in a particular cultural history and whose coherence stems only from its own particular genealogy. Abstraction has been valued, especially in the West, because of its claim to represent the world neutrally, above and beyond the particularities of history and culture. But other cultures and other aesthetics make other claims. There are no aesthetic claims that are in fact universal and transhistorical. To present one's claims as such is always ideologically motivated.[2]

Given this, the challenge is to abstract in a way that contributes to the existing nation-state, that builds upon what is there without exacerbating interethnic tensions. The task is to develop a rich ambiguity, one that can be interpreted according to many different kinds of aesthetic preferences and schemas, so that the building neither seems to serve one faction nor seems so neutral that it could exist anywhere.

Of all the capitol complexes I have discussed, Bawa's work at Sri Jayawardhanapura Kotte and Kahn's at Sher-e-Bangla Nagar best embody this kind of progressive ambiguity, though each has its limitations. Bawa's remains a highly conservative work dramatically sited in a supremely reactionary setting. Though few countries have experienced as long-standing and complex a history of architectural miscegenation as Sri Lanka, Bawa's work on the capitol complex may be seen more as a summary than a critical synthesis that advances the state of Sri Lankan architecture. The design interweaves many precedents, but it does not stray far from any of them, especially those most redolent of predemocratic institutions. If it feels Sri Lankan as opposed to Sinhalese/Buddhist or Tamil/Hindu it does so with caution rather than conviction. It may be that this caution is part of its appeal, yet it is also a mark of its limitations. There is no innovative jump comparable to the great leaps of faith, sponsorship, and architectural skill that characterized the first designs of the once-startling, now-timeworn, precedents upon which Bawa draws so lovingly. At base, the most important symbolic aspect of this new capitol may well be its site, rather than any component of its architectural form. Above all, it is a building on an island in a sea of Sinhalese nationalism. If more of the highly contentious master plan had been implemented around it, the ethnic neutrality of Bawa's design would surely have been subverted. Even so, in the context of a lingering civil war, the architecture of the parliament building matters far less than the politics that swirls around it. Every citizen's view of the building is filtered through his or her view of the legitimacy of the institution housed within.

Kahn's parliamentary edifice also serves as a monumental backdrop for the shifting political winds in Bangladesh. Gradually, however, it is becoming a symbol *of* Bangladesh even if much of its inspiration was not derived *from*

Bangladesh. At what point, one may ask, did the pyramid become an Egyptian form? At first those sentinels at Giza must have seemed far more alien intrusions than anything Louis Kahn has conjured for Bangladesh. Yet today they remain the unchallenged architectural symbols of Egypt. And, like the Pyramids of Egypt or the Eiffel Tower, the Citadel of Assembly may someday be seen as being quintessentially *of* its country as well.

This of/from distinction is fundamental to the concept of national identity and to distinguishing among the various methods by which this elusive goal is pursued. An excess of concern with making a building seem from its country can easily lead to a design that looks like a National Tourist Office pastiche. There are other ways of promoting a collective identity that are both more subtle and less retrograde. Only if the traditional architecture of a given country's component cultures (cultures that have always been open to outside influence) is abstracted and combined into new and inventive hybrids can that architecture, often wonderful in itself, also play an active and progressive role in the modern world. It is possible to attract both an international audience and a sincere local empathy for a building without making instantly recognizable architectural allusions, which, once noted, may be quickly dismissed in favor of the so-called real thing, whether desert tent or village house. Even advertisers sell by evoking a mood rather than by explicitly plugging a product.

Over the last twenty years, coinciding with the completion of the parliamentary complexes discussed here, the term *critical regionalism*, initially coined by Alexander Tzonis and Liane Lefaivre, has come into vogue as a way of categorizing and praising certain buildings that, in Kenneth Frampton's words, attempt to "mediate the impact of universal civilization with elements derived *indirectly* from the peculiarities of a particular place."[3] Frampton draws a sharp distinction between the "resistant" capacity of "Critical Regionalism" and the "demagogic tendencies" of "Populism," viewed as "simple-minded attempts to revive the hypothetical forms of a lost vernacular." "In contradistinction to Critical Regionalism," he continues, "the primary vehicle of Populism is the *communicative* or *instrumental* sign. Such a sign seeks to evoke not a critical perception of reality, but rather the sublimation of a desire for direct experience through the provision of information."[4] The distinction between populism and critical regionalism may be of use for understanding the difference between buildings such as Hogan's and Bawa's; the issues of national identity raised in my discussion of new capitols, however, suggest that regionalism as a mode of architectural analysis has limitations.

A region is at best a hazy notion. Regions may be subnational or supranational and are rarely coterminous with a nation-state. My informal survey of the use of this term suggests that the largest of such alleged regions are often those that are farthest from the home base of the critic who purports to identify them. Only through ignorance of the importance of political conflict can Switzerland's Ticino and the Indian subcontinent be equivalently classified as "regions." In a politically charged environment, all forms are not available equally to the designer, and all sites within a region are not ideologically equal: any regionalism that is to be truly critical must embrace this realization. If the goal is to foster *national* identity, should any regional influence that is nonnational be discouraged? What, for instance, would be the significance of the Ticino as a region in the design of a new capitol complex for Switzerland? Would a new parliament designed in the spirit of a Ticinese farmhouse be perceived as provocatively parochial or would it be seen as sensibly representative of Swiss-ness? The nature and degree of national identification vary a great deal, and even if one could derive an answer that would hold for a time-tested confederation such as Switzerland (where subnational identification remains strong), this would not necessarily reveal much about national identity in newer multiethnic or multilingual states. Here, nonnational and pseudonational alternatives to an all-inclusive concept of nation abound, and such subnational and supranational affiliations often coincide with the group preferences of a government client/ruler. Given this history of abuse, the chief value of national identity as a concept may be as a tool for diagnosing the societal ills that work against it.

At a time when architects and their clients are seeking buildings that are more overtly tied to their place and culture than was the case under high modernism, Frampton's cautionary insistence that references from the region must be drawn "indirectly" is another way of stressing the need for abstraction. In the case of national parliament buildings and other politically charged institutional environments, this need seems of special import. In these buildings, it matters not only which references are made; it matters that they are well integrated. Skillful architects may be able to fuse many layers in a novel, evocative way, but contentious issues are raised by those layers that stick out. An institution that is supposed to be the seat of a representative democracy is not well served by a building that too obviously symbolizes the preferences of any single elite, be it a regime, a province, or a rising class of Western-influenced tastemakers. Such a building, however, reveals an immense amount about the power structure of the nation it is asked to symbolize.

At the same time, efforts to revitalize and reframe modernist architecture through the lens of "critical regionalism" have another important limitation. As Prakash cautions, this strategy can be seen as a form of "palliative ethno-aestheticism" that fails to see that the shortcoming of high modernism in developing countries was not fundamentally a matter of aesthetics. Rather, he maintains, "it failed because it relied on the ideological conviction that an enlightened elite could lead the rest of the populace simply by relying on the strength of symbolic demonstration . . . [T]he problem was not that of a lack of *translation* of idiom—people accept the foreign quite easily as their own if it is useful and beneficial to them. Rather the problem was the lack of *transfer* of idiom. Modernism came top-down." As Prakash concludes, the challenge is to "rethink modernism, its successes and failures, as fundamentally interwoven with the larger political and ethical textile of the nation-state and its peoples."[5]

FOUR TEMPTATIONS OF NATIONALISM

Ultimately, designers of capitols and capitals usually succumb to one or more of what may be termed the four temptations of nationalism. The politicized design histories of capitol complexes in Sri Lanka and PNG illustrate the first of these: the temptation of subnationalism. In these pluralist nation-states, the built environment becomes a symbolic battleground for contending conceptions of "the national." Or, more precisely, buildings and their urban design settings become mechanisms for asserting the supremacy of the dominant culture in tenuous nation-states where this dominance is challenged. Nationalism, in this sense, is no more (and no less) than the search for legitimacy by the largest subnational group.

This search for nationalist legitimacy is often carried backwards into the past, in what could be called the temptation of invented history. Historian Eric Hobsbawm's notion of the "the invention of tradition" has frequent resonance in the nervous cultural landscapes of national capitals. In such places, governments frequently use bombastic evocations of the past to mask the uncertainties of the present. If there is a politically expedient historical practice or referent to claim, many regimes seem willing to leap back across any chasm of time, politics, and development to invoke it.

In addition to the temptations of subnationalism and invented history, nationalism asserts itself through the built environment even more commonly through the mechanisms of display. Capital cities are particularly prone to the use of long axial vistas leading to privileged points, and these vistas are often used as ritual stages to demonstrate the power and achievements of the regime. Capitals always do more than house the institutions of sovereignty: they must also *display* them. This has happened most blatantly in Soviet-era Moscow, Maoist Beijing, and Communist Pyongyang, but more democratic governments are hardly immune from the temptation of display. The rulers of modern India, for instance, artfully appropriated the central display zone of the British Raj in New Delhi. India's government invented its own traditions for a space that was too tempting to relinquish, yielding a Republic Day display that remains a bizarre hybrid of lingering colonialist imagery and nationalist fervor.

Urbanistic and architectural expressions of nationalism also give in to a fourth mode of representation—the temptation of isolation. In contrast to the gregarious ideological presence of parades and other displays, nationalist impulses can also appear in a more inward looking guise. Especially for nation-states where the hold on power remains uncertain and contested, part of the regime's challenge is to maintain and enhance its own security, typified by the literal and figurative parliamentary islands in Sri Lanka and Bangladesh. This temptation of isolation is not limited to capitol complex precincts; it is nearly ubiquitous in postcolonial capital city urbanism. Like many other instances of single-use zoning that have infected the planet since 1945, designed capital cities have assumed the need for a separate zone for government. All of the most famous designed capitals—from Chandigarh to Brasília to Islamabad to Abuja—have treated the seat of government as an object to be isolated in space.

These four temptations of nationalism—the temptations of subnationalism, invented history, display, and isolation—are not the only spatial manifestations of political machinations, but they do seem to appear with particular frequency in the constructed landscapes of postcolonial governance.

NATIONAL IDENTITY: CAN IT BE DESIGNED?

Buffeted by temptations, the designer of new capitol complexes must confront a series of contradictions, none of which allows for a full resolution. There are contradictions implied by the program and its distribution: the capitol complex must house a large, modern series of functional and ceremonial spaces and must accommodate a vast and expanding bureaucracy without letting this symbolically overwhelm the legislative chambers, whose membership grows more slowly. There are contradictions of security: the capitol must be defendable yet appear to be open to the public. There are contradictions of visual communication: the capitol must have a memorable and easily reproducible silhouette yet must not be openly derived from any one architectural source, unless it is a source that the sponsoring government wishes unabashedly to represent. The architect's ethical dilemma is itself a contradiction: the capitol commission is an opportunity to design not only a building but an ideal, yet the ideal may be incomprehensibly far from the present political realities or the political desires of the client. The difficulties, and the contradictions within them, go on and on. Somewhere within the barrage of conflicting demands is the persistent question of national identity.

What can the architecture and urban design of capitol complexes accomplish? Which of these accomplishments can the designer hope to control? These are two very different questions. The problem of national identity, while it may be addressed by the siting and symbolism of a capitol complex, is not, in the end, something an architect or urban designer can firmly mold. Architects and urban designers must recognize that, even when a building exemplifies certain of its properties more than others, all symbolism depends on interpretation. Because they often fail to apprehend that the associations between architectural objects and cultural ideals are fundamentally unpredictable, many architects, when describing their work, emphasize control of precisely the part or aspect of the built environment over which their influence is least assured.

Architects and urban designers cannot determine symbolism over time, least of all a symbolism as amorphous as a national one. They can, however, accept their complicity with the regimes that commission them and try to act responsibly. Responsible capitol architecture would work against the hegemony of any one group by the careful crossbreeding of architectural parentage. Almost by definition, hybrids are both hardier and more beautiful. Yet, however carefully they are planted into the landscape, there is no guarantee of a perennial bloom.

Architects are unable to control the propagation of symbols for many reasons, but one looms large. Though an architect may be responsible for only a single building or a capitol complex, the symbolism of these places is not bounded by the limits of the architect's commission or even by the edges of some master plan. What are the boundaries of a capitol symbol? The issue is crucial to discussions of new capitals, places that are designed not only for the functions of government, but also for the functions of a total city housing a diverse population. In what sense are the capitol buildings, rather than the city-building venture, the central symbol? Where does one draw the boundary of a Brasília or an Abuja? Is it at the limits of the monumental axis, the limits of the postcard views? Is it at the limits of the "pilot plan" and "master plan," with their housing neatly organized into delineated communities strung out and curved to converge on the monumental center? Or is the boundary the satellite cities and the squatter shacks so illegally and so undeniably present? Though not shown on the plan, these too are part of the meaning of a new capital city or a new capitol complex as well.

In emphasizing the central plaza as much as the individual buildings, Le Corbusier's Chandigarh and Costa/Niemeyer's Brasília provided for a public place at the apex of their compositions, framing a vast landscape. For better or worse, such spaces seem to have been abandoned in the more recent generation of capitol complexes. Here, the buildings are the focal point, and the public may observe them from a distance, greater or lesser depending on the level of government security. In Abuja, despite the decided resemblance of its Central Area to the monumental axis of Brasília, the design for its capitol complex is in the tradition of Imperial Delhi. Rather than a public viewing platform for the countryside, the Three Arms Zone has become the privatized termination of a Mall axis. The green-domed National Assembly building, with Aso Hill as visual reinforcement, is the ultimate focus of an enclosed, inward-directed scheme in which politics combines with urban design to delimit public access.

Similarly, the four capitol complexes discussed in Chapters 6–9 are premised upon the parliament building as an object in defendable space, rather than one dominated by a space formed by the careful placement of architectural forms, each subservient to the whole. Kahn's neobaroque site plan focuses its diagonals in upon the central structure and sets it off by water, Bawa's building is a shrine isolated on an island, Hogan's haus tambaran (though much more accessible than the others) rises out of park and parking lot, and Utzon's complex is completely closed off from the rest of its city, an object to be viewed from the sea or from some inland high-rise. None of these capital complexes features a composed public space that ties the new government buildings into their surroundings. Though the Kahn complex does contain the potential for a series of such complexly carved public spaces, the public is currently discouraged from approaching all but the Zia mausoleum across the crescent lake. With vast empty spaces between the buildings of the capitol complex and anything else, it will take both time and a more peaceful politics for this place to loosen its sense of overexposed isolation.

In places where the programmatic requirements of a capitol complex are distributed into a silhouette that has a single focus, great symbolic weight is placed upon this most central place. When a single form is charged with becoming a major symbol of the state, one may assume that the choice of that form is a matter of significance. Whether it be a Bedouin billow, a haus tambaran, or a Kandyan palace, the chosen parliamentary icon—since it is a design ratified by a government client—seems likely to be closely related to the government's vision of, and for, the state. Only when the central form is abstracted to the point where it takes on multiple meanings, as at Sher-e-Bangla Nagar, is the limited and time-bound nature of partisan iconography partially transcended. Sometimes, as with Kahn, the personal quest strains the bounds of appropriateness to the place. Yet it is surely possible for a building to take part in the search for both a personal identity and an international identity, before finally settling down to be accepted as a national symbol.

TOWARD A GOOD CAPITOL

It is my hope that the mood of future capitol complexes will be less callously and prematurely monumental. This can occur if architects and their government sponsors resist the temptation to symbol-monger and if, over time, the legitimate power of the parliamentary institutions that are symbolized is increased. In the meantime, however, it is useless to deny the many ways new capitols and new capitals are manipulated to serve ends that have little connection to democratic government. The monumentality of the buildings—from Brasília to Dhaka, from Abuja to Waigani—is a response to a multitude of pressures, pressures which ensure that parliament buildings are far more than exercises in architectural form. These pressures have most often yielded capitol complexes that have denied cultural pluralism by emphasizing the iconography of the sponsoring elite and too often disfigured the legitimate promise of democratic government by giving premature prominence to fledgling institutions. That said, in those cases where democratic elections do take place, it is surely a great gift to the hopes of a nation-state to have a prominent building ready and available to house and symbolize the growing power of a legislature. In the years since 1991, the grand buildings for Kuwait and Bangladesh have—both literally and figuratively—played a role in making democracy concrete.

There is, in all probability, no building or building complex that can be considered public in as many different senses as a capitol. They are publicly owned, constructed with public funds, and house publicly funded institutions; they are places to gather with the public and to make public statements; and they are expected to represent the public interest. They are even, in theory much more than in practice, supposed to be open to the public.[6]

Ironically, many capitols may well fail to be public in the most important way of all, that is, by being under public *control*. The denial of free public access to so-called public places is a central fact of political life that most designers of parliament buildings seem to ignore. While Washington's capitol rotunda and the summit of Canberra's capital hill may be places for relatively unsupervised public perambulation, such freedom is not common and does not develop quickly. Moreover, even Washington and Canberra have markedly curtailed their accessibility during fearful post-9/11 times.

In most places, notably where democratic government is not established and political conditions are unstable, so-called democratic institutions are to be looked at but not entered. Capitols are designed with a cordon sanitaire around them. There are limits, defined by some combination of landscaping, guardposts, bollards, gates, surveillance systems, moats, and fencing, beyond which special permission is required to proceed. Completely legitimate reasons exist for such security precautions, and these need not be challenged. There are, however, design implications that follow from this paradoxical nature of the capitol's public character: architects, urban designers, and planners must recognize the limitations of public participation and not be deluded into thinking that these buildings are a place of assembly for any more than a select elite.

Two further implications follow. First, it may be that the focus of a capitol complex in a democracy should be not a building but some other realm for public gathering, and, second, it may be that the functional center of the capitol complex, the legislative chambers, should not also be the ceremonial and symbolic centerpiece. These two ideas partly inspired the plazas for Chandigarh and Brasília. Yet, as the designs for the capital center of Dodoma suggest, public participation need not take place in a monumental plaza. Instead, public participation can be organized to occur in a series of smaller spaces in which government institutions are intermixed with other civic and commercial activities that provide the public with some reason to gather in the capitol complex. And, unlike the initial proposal for Dodoma, which incongruously isolated parliament and party into a precinct separate from the rest of the "capital center," the capitol buildings themselves should be integrated into this more normalized urban environment.

While this ideal of the hybrid capitol in the integrated city may be taken as a challenge to the practicing designer and urban planner, there are other challenges for those pursuing architecture and urban design as fields for research. I have stressed that the quest to design national identity raises many issues that fall outside the scope of the designer's control; these questions also warrant further investigation. The designers and their clients interpret the meaning of a building *before* it is built. As it gets built and after it is finished, it is viewed by a much broader public and is subject to a far greater range of interpretations, assessments that will change and multiply over time. Gestures of symbolism that seemed significant at the time the building was designed may fade from importance, while new readings never considered by the architect or client may gain currency.

How many people know that there is a statue of Freedom atop the U.S. Capitol dome, or care what is conveyed by its rotunda frieze? How carefully do most people look at architecture? Do average urban Papua New Guineans recognize a Sepik Province haus tambaran when they see one transmuted into a parliament house? Or do they just have a vague notion that some traditional design was employed? How are these buildings brimming with symbolism interpreted by those who do not know the history of architecture, who do not apprehend the social and political circumstances under which the building was commissioned, who do not hear the architect's explanation or read the critic's book? How quickly do the original symbols become dated? In this book, I have provided partial and highly speculative answers to such questions. What may be needed is some attempt to measure, in a sustained and detailed way, the nature of the public response to public places such as capitol complexes and to analyze the ways individuals from different backgrounds interpret buildings differently. If national identity is to be a valuable concept, it has to be an idea that percolates throughout the general populace, a populace that may have little understanding of the intricacies of either architectural design or parliamentary institutions.

It would seem significant that the jury that conferred an Aga Khan Award for Architecture on Kahn's Sher-e-Bangla Nagar in 1989 justified its selection, in part, on the basis of the complex's supposed popular reception in Dhaka as a symbol of democracy. The method used to gauge the public's acceptance was several hundred interviews carried out under the direction of the award's "technical reviewer." Establishing popular support as a criterion in a technical review seems a major step forward, albeit one that is at odds with almost every other process of juried architectural judgment. Yet, assessing popular reaction to any controversial public building is an immensely problematic task. In addition to the usual difficulties associated with developing unbiased surveys, there is the widespread reluctance of government civil servants in many countries to criticize their workplace. According to the report of the technical reviewer, the majority of Sher-e-Bangla Nagar's employees *refused to answer* his survey questions, partly out of fear of conflicting with government views and partly out of a perceived lack of specialized competence to judge architectural matters. Their confusion—wholly legitimate—was about how to separate the space of architecture from the space of politics, and this is a problem for anyone who seeks to set clear criteria for evaluating success in public building design. Another common problem pointed out in the Sher-e-Bangla Nagar technical review is the fact that much local response can be "strongly influenced" by the opinions of foreign or official visitors who have inspected the site; such influence limits the capacity of the local population to respond "spontaneously and intuitively."[7] In this sense, the cultural production of identity through design is neither wholly local nor even confined by the limits of the nation.

This investigation of capitol complexes began by considering the ways they can, being politically charged, convey meaning, and it is to these initial concerns that I now return. Capitol complexes—whether separate parliamentary districts or zones created within new capital cities—raise troubling questions about the criteria used for judging them. If one truly cares about the popular reception of such public buildings, why is it that abstraction should be considered an issue of overwhelming value in interpreting this type of architecture? In nascent democracies, such as Papua New Guinea, is it possibly preferable for citizens visiting Waigani from distant provinces to see in their capitol complex something familiar, to feel some connection to their own village roots being embraced in the design of this otherwise alien institution? How does one deal with the contradiction between the refusal of many seasoned Western designers to take this building seriously as a work of good architecture (or even to publish it in an architectural journal) and the acceptance that it seems to have had in PNG? It is ironic that the building that probably would have least appeal to architects is the one which—unique among the four case studies—has, immediately following its completion, housed a regularly functioning parliament that has included the participation of all major political parties. While no inevitable connection exists between heavy-handed symbolism and perennially legitimate democratic institutions (most historical experience suggests the opposite), the PNG case does seem to make it even more difficult to set out multidimensional criteria for evaluating success in parliamentary design.

If a designer chooses to make blatant use of vernacular precedent in architecture or urban design, I have argued, he or she must try to use it in iconographically nonpartisan ways. Since government leaders often seem to favor particular design alternatives precisely because of their partisan qualities, the architect who makes obvious use of politically charged precedents may be asking for trouble. If the designer is committed to the kind of political pluralism that is a corollary of any genuine democracy, he or she would be prudent to convey it through high levels of abstraction. Moreover, my own advocacy of abstraction is based on the sense that, in the hands of a talented architect who is able to meld and assimilate many factors, it can encompass a deeper and more multifarious engagement with the cultural issues involved in the creation of new institutions than can easily recognizable, more literal transformations.

Abstraction, however, can also be advocated as a form of political disengagement, valued because it offers the designer the illusion of an apolitical response. Does this reflect a lingering wish by many design professionals to judge these places as autonomous sculptural artifacts, independent of their conditions of production? Generations of architectural historians have demonstrated that it is possible to separate the response to a building's architectural qualities from the response to its institutional presence in a society, but can this distinction ever be more than a moderately useful intellectual construct? How does it help us to cope with the likelihood that most Kuwaitis in the late 1980s probably saw Utzon's building as symbolic not of tents or dhows but of evanescent democratic institutions? Similarly, as places such as Kuwait or Bangladesh moved toward more active parliamentary life in the 1990s and thereafter, presumably citizens and noncitizens alike continued to read their capitols as expressions of the current state of national politics, not just as works of architecture.

In our assessments of the ways these buildings are used by governments to keep citizens at a respectful distance, narrow sets of formal criteria can help us understand some of the how but little of the why. If a designer's incorporation of architectural precedents is viewed as no more than a subtle (or crude) cross-reference to formally similar typologies from the region, such as forts and temples, this fails to engage the ways that use of such typologies may carry forward not only formal properties but also cultural, social, and political associations. A capitol complex can also carry meaning through its embedded metaphors. Purely formal concerns cannot account for the potential of these places to become appropriated as populist symbols and to play a more positive cultural role in present and future prodemocracy movements. The political use (and misuse) of a capitol complex may provoke shifting, diverse, and often contradictory responses in those who experience it, whether as employees or as visitors. At least as long as these buildings are relatively new and controversial, it would seem likely that such views cannot often be wholly separated from views about the building's physical presence, its process of construction, and its costs, including opportunity costs. In the production of political legitimacy, the architecture and urban design of capitol complexes are far from epiphenomenal.

Figure 10.1 shows two views of the Washington Capitol from the first half of the nineteenth century, fifty years before Thomas Ustick Walter's towering central portion of the building was completed. The top view is architect Latrobe's idealized watercolor of a Capitol set off by a gentleman's carriage and by perspectivally converging rows of perfect poplars. The bottom view shows the same building at almost exactly the same moment in time, sketched from nearly the same spot. Here, however, the focus is not on the Capitol but on a procession of slaves in chains passing in front of it, under threat of a brandished whip. The poplars fade into the background, while the gentleman and his parasol-carrying companion stand to one side. In the top picture the building seems a symbol of stability and harmony, even in the absence of its central portion. In the bottom view, the presence of the Capitol sends very different symbolic messages: it stands in ironic counterpoint to the systematic violence and inequity of its larger social setting. These two views of the Capitol are not, I would argue, views of the same building. So, too, it is a different building on the day of Lincoln's inauguration when it symbolizes "a house divided," a different building with its dome complete and the Union healed, a different building with its Mall laid out, a different building during the protest marches of the 1960s, and a different building when approached through a security-conscious underground visitor's center rather than a flight of stairs. As a changing symbol of a changing country, its meanings also vary significantly not only over time but also among demographic groups. In the end, I would argue, a good capitol complex is one which maximizes the number of constituencies that will judge it successful using their own sets of criteria. Whose view of the Capitol do we care about?

Perhaps there are lessons to be learned from Washington. This capital and its capitol complex may have begun to achieve, after almost two centuries of growth and development, the kind of normalized relations I have advocated. Centuries from now, Washington may even seem as natural and polycentric a capital as London or Paris. Surely, though, there is some better alternative than to build the isolated monuments before the city. Washington's lingering success is rooted in the ability of the American democratic system to keep its monuments so readily and accessibly a part of the public realm, even though this has necessitated costly retrofits in the face of twenty-first-century concerns about terrorism. This openness is politically very difficult to achieve and sustain, and has little to do with the particulars

10.1 Two capitols.

of architectural form, and much more to do with seemingly prosaic aspects of urban design.

Especially in contemporary capital cities, planners and designers are being defeated by the temptation to construct what may be called the *securescape*—the uneasy confluence of security, landscape, and escape from public contact.[8] At a time when urban designers across the globe are seeking ways to retrofit massive modernist superblocks, often by reintroducing the finer-grained networks of premodern streets, the tenets of the securescape work in precisely the opposite direction. Urban designers extol mixed-use developments with street-level retail and enhanced pedestrian connectivity, but the pressures of the securescape push toward street closures, enhanced setbacks, and strict design guidelines for those types of buildings that are considered most vulnerable. More and more, noncapital cities are taking on the security-conscious demeanor already so prevalent in capitals.

A security-driven urban aesthetic of 'stand-off' setbacks changes the boundary between public and private space, alters the relationships among streets, sidewalks, and facades. It changes the way buildings are seen and the way they are entered. It can change the sequence with which they are experienced. The setback may affect the sense of welcome that the institution conveys, and result in subtle changes of attitude on the part of the visitor. A building with multiple entrances conveys a different hierarchy than a complex that must be accessed through a single secure portal, let alone one that is first entered below ground. On the positive side, buildings designed to have a single securable entrance will need also to make such an entrance accessible to visitors with disabilities, thereby eliminating the two-class system of access that currently remains prevalent.

Making sense of a landscape of risks entails an ethics of urban intervention, asking designers and planners to reflect on their practice and the value systems that drive it. Every decision about bollard intervals, hardened benches, strategic plinths, stand-off dimensions, community gates, CCTV cameras, rerouted traffic, private police forces, racial profiling, and privacy policy is taken in relation to judgments about terrorist risk, impact on the global capitalist economy, media coverage, and political will. Those who care about quality places and sustained civic participation in public life must recognize the imperative to address the urban fear that comes from perceived threats to security, but they must also set boundaries on the technologies of control and regulation. Ultimately, the challenge for designers, planners, and those who commission them is to strike a balance between the risks of insecurity and the risks of a diminished public life.

In the meantime, we need to look more critically at how the urban design of our capital cities and the architectural trappings of our governments sometimes mislead us. All too often, capitol districts provide clear symbolic centers that both bear little relation to true hierarchies of power and actively discourage public visitation. Places designated for public gathering are frequently either separated off from the actual places of governance or are so huge as to be intimidating to all but the largest assemblages. Among designers and sponsors of capitol complexes, there seems to be great resistance to the idea of imbedding the central symbolic buildings of a government into the fabric of the capital city. Instead, it is almost as if these places were intended to form a separate category of land-use classification labeled *elite*. Places designed as capitol complexes rarely include anything that remotely resembles the multiuse, pedestrian-scaled streets and squares that mark civic centers in many older capitals and in other less self-consciously "national" cities. And when separate government precincts are designed to be visitable chiefly by those possessing automobiles, more general public participation is denied by a combination of physical and socioeconomic means.

The haughty reliance on hillside ascents, the calculated drama of long, broad axes, the fearful arrogance of protected cantonments, the coveted security of massive structures set off by water, and the hierarchical distribution of residence according to courtly rank are all familiar features of a premodern Western urbanism that seems to linger in the designed capitals and capitols of the twentieth century and beyond. The privileged zones once reserved for the gods and for kings claiming divine sanction are still opportunistically commissioned by intermittently powerful secular regimes. Even as the rhetoric and the reality of democratic political institutions have burgeoned, the support systems of authoritarian rule have been encouraged to reemerge when these new institutions are given architectural form and urban status. Wolfgang Braunfels concludes his sweeping survey of a thousand years of urban design in Europe with a triple epigram: "One cannot build for strangers; history cannot be planned in advance; what is necessary needs aesthetic exaggeration."[9] These thoughts, written to reflect on the designs of the tenth through the nineteenth centuries, have continued relevance for more recently built capitol complexes. Regimes build capitol complexes chiefly to serve personal, subnational, and supranational interests rather than to advance national identity; designers cannot mold political change; and governments still find it necessary to demonstrate their power through aesthetic exaggeration.

Notes

CHAPTER 1 CAPITAL AND CAPITOL

1 Clifford Geertz, *The Interpretation of Cultures* (New York: Basic Books, 1973), 245.
2 Nelson Goodman, "How Buildings Mean," in Goodman and Catherine Elgin, *Reconceptions in Philosophy* (Indianapolis: Hackett, 1988), 33.
3 Ibid., 43–44. For an extended discussion of the history of the Lincoln Memorial and the evolution of its constructed meanings, see Christopher Thomas, *The Lincoln Memorial and American Life* (Princeton: Princeton University Press, 2002). For a sophisticated analysis of the changing nature of constructed meanings of many other American "icons," see Albert Boime, *The Unveiling of the National Icons: A Plea for Patriotic Iconoclasm in a Nationalist Era* (Cambridge: Cambridge University Press, 1997).
4 More than a mere stand-in, such buildings can serve as metonyms. For a discussion of the architectural aspects of metonymy, in which "a word or an icon stands for something else, to which it is related by contiguity," see James S. Duncan, *The City as Text: The Politics of Landscape Interpretation in the Kandyan Kingdom* (Cambridge: Cambridge University Press, 1990), 21. Duncan cites examples of metonymy given by Umberto Eco in *Semiotics and the Philosophy of Language* (Bloomington: Indiana University Press, 1986). These include cases in which a place of origin is used to stand for the original object, cause is used to stand for effect, container for content, instrument for operation, and emblem for object emblematicized.
5 Murray Edelman, "Architecture, Spaces, and Social Order," in Edelman, *From Art to Politics: How Artistic Creations Shape Political Conceptions* (Chicago: University of Chicago Press, 1995), 75. See also Murray Edelman, *The Symbolic Uses of Politics*, rev. ed. (Urbana: University of Illinois Press, 1985).
6 Edelman, "Architecture, Spaces, and Social Order," 76.
7 Ibid., 77.
8 Charles T. Goodsell, *The Social Meaning of Civic Space: Studying Political Authority through Architecture* (Lawrence: University Press of Kansas, 1988), 198–199. Goodsell subsequently extended his analysis to include state capitols in the United States; see *The American Statehouse: Interpreting Democracy's Temples* (Lawrence: University Press of Kansas, 2000).
9 It is possible also to distinguish between two different types of citadels—"crag-citadels" built on isolated outcrops of rock (such as the acropolis of Athens or certain Rajput fortresses), and "swamp citadels" (such as Ravenna or the Aztec capital of Tenochtitlan), built on a cluster of islands. See Arnold Toynbee, *Cities on the Move* (London: Oxford University Press, 1970), 26–30.
10 Lewis Mumford, *The City in History* (New York: Harcourt, Brace, and World, 1961), 10. Mumford here seems to draw heavily from the writing of the archaeologist Henri Frankfort and from

V. Gordon Childe, whose scholarly work and more popularized accounts address many factors affecting the origins of cities, especially *Man Makes Himself* (New York: New American Library, 1951), 117–119. Mumford's work also seems colored by the pioneering work of Numa Denis Fustel de Coulanges, *The Ancient City* (Baltimore: Johns Hopkins University Press, 1980 [1859 original]), especially book 3. For an illuminating discussion of Mumford's evolving ideas, together with an appreciative response to them by a variety of academic specialists, see Carl H. Kraeling and Robert M. Adams, eds., *City Invincible*, A Symposium on Urbanization and Cultural Development in the Ancient Near East Held at the Oriental Institute of Chicago, 4–7 December 1958 (Chicago: University of Chicago Press, 1960), esp. 224–248.

11 Clifford Geertz, *Local Knowledge: Further Essays in Interpretative Anthropology* (New York: Basic Books, 1983), 125.

12 Ibid.

13 Peter Murray, *The Architecture of the Italian Renaissance* (London: Thames and Hudson, 1969), 178–179. One story has it that the Roman capitolium got its name from the word caput after workmen digging the foundations for the Temple of Jupiter (consecrated 509 B.C.) found "a skull of immense size which was regarded as prophetic of the future greatness of the city": Paul Norton, *Latrobe, Jefferson and the National Capitol* (New York: Garland, 1977), 264, n. 4.

14 Kevin Lynch, *Good City Form* (Cambridge: MIT Press, 1984), 73–77.

15 Mumford, *The City in History*, 64.

16 Ibid., 65.

17 Ibid., 9.

18 Ralph Merrifield, *London: City of the Romans* (London: Batsford, 1983), 71–72.

19 Wolfgang Braunfels, *Urban Design in Western Europe: Regime and Architecture, 900–1900*, trans. Kenneth J. Northcott (Chicago: University of Chicago Press, 1988), 328.

20 Peter Hall, "Seven Types of Capital City," in David L. A. Gordon, ed., *Planning Twentieth Century Capital Cities* (New York: Routledge, 2006), 8–14. For an alternative framework, see Amos Rappaport, "On the Nature of Capitals and Their Physical Expression," in John Taylor, Jean G. Lengellé, and Caroline Andrew, eds., *Capital Cities/Les Capitales* (Ottawa: Carleton University Press, 1993).

21 See Carola Hein, *The Capital of Europe: Architecture and Planning for the European Union* (New York: Praeger, 2004).

22 Toynbee, *Cities on the Move*, 80.

23 Ibid., 70.

24 Even in the United States, where democratic institutions have long been in place, a dramatic increase in the size of the bureaucracy is evident. When Franklin Roosevelt took office in 1932, the White House staff numbered about a dozen—it now includes more than 300 persons; the Capitol Hill staff serving senators and representatives, according to a recent count, numbers 18,659, as compared with only 2,030 in 1947, and executive departments have experienced similar increases (cited in James Reston, "Speakes: Product of the System," *New York Times*, 17 April 1988, E27).

25 Braunfels, *Urban Design in Western Europe*, 328.

26 David Cannadine, "The Context, Performance and Meaning of Ritual: The British Monarchy and the 'Invention of Tradition', *c.* 1820–1977," in Eric Hobsbawm and Terence Ranger, eds., *The Invention of Tradition* (Cambridge: Cambridge University Press, 1983), 127–128.

27 Martin Pawley, "A Precedent for the Prince," *Architectural Review* 187 (January 1990): 80–82. See also H.R.H. The Prince of Wales, *A Vision of Britain: A Personal View of Architecture* (New York: Doubleday, 1989); Peter Davey, "Fairy-Tale Prince," *Journal of Architectural Education* 42 (Summer 1989): 34–38; and Peter Davey, "Prince's Political Manifesto," *Architectural Review* 186 (August 1989): 4 and 8. On the Parliament Building for Scotland, see Charles Jencks, *The Scottish Parliament* (London: Scala, 2005) and EMBT: Enric Miralles, Benedetta Tagliabue: *Work in Progress* (Barcelona: Actar, 2004). On the National Assembly for Wales, designed by the Richard Rogers Partnership, see Catherine Slessor, "National Assembly for Wales," *Architectural Record* (August 2006), 100–105.

28 Braunfels, *Urban Design in Western Europe*, 318.

29 Norma Evenson, *Paris: A Century of Change, 1878–1978* (New Haven: Yale University Press, 1979), 279. See also, Anthony Sutcliffe, *Paris: An Architectural History* (New Haven: Yale University Press, 1993); and Paul White, "Paris: From the Legacy of Haussmann to the Pursuit of Cultural Supremacy," in Gordon, ed., *Planning Twentieth Century Capital Cities*, 38–57.

30 Carl Schorske, *Fin-de-Siècle Vienna: Politics and Culture* (New York: Vintage, 1981), 31.

31 Braunfels, *Urban Design in Western Europe*, 213–214.
32 Ibid., 220.
33 Gordon A. Craig, *Germany 1866–1945* (Oxford: Oxford University Press, 1981), 39.
34 Albert Speer, *Inside the Third Reich* (New York: Macmillan, 1970), 77, 70, 152–153, 103, 156, 151.
35 Stephen Helmer, *Hitler's Berlin: The Speer Plans for Reshaping the Central City* (Ann Arbor, Mich.: UMI Research Press, 1985), 70.
36 Ibid., 8. See also Barbara Miller Lane, *Architecture and Politics in Germany, 1918–1945*, 2nd ed. (Cambridge: Harvard University Press, 1985); Mathias Schmidt, *Albert Speer: The End of a Myth*, trans. Joachim Neugroschel (New York: St. Martin's Press, 1984); and Robert Taylor, *The Word in Stone: The Role of Architecture in National Socialist Ideology* (Berkeley: University of California Press, 1974).
37 See T. H. Elkins and B. Hofmeister, *Berlin: The Spatial Structure of a Divided City* (London: Methuen, 1988), 156–214; Brian Ladd, *The Ghosts of Berlin: Confronting German History in the Urban Landscape* (Chicago: University of Chicago Press, 1997).
38 Elkins and Hofmeister, *Berlin*, 201, 205; Wolfgang Sonne, "Berlin: Capital under Changing Political Systems," in Gordon, ed., *Planning Twentieth Century Capital Cities*, 206; Michael Z. Wise, *Capital Dilemma: Germany's Search for a New Architecture of Democracy* (New York: Princeton Architectural Press, 1998).
39 Wu Hung, *Remaking Beijing: Tiananmen Square and the Creation of a Political Space* (Chicago: University of Chicago Press, 2005).
40 Toynbee, *Cities on the Move*, 84–85. Other historians have suggested different preferable alternatives to Rome, most prominently Milan and Bologna. Several cities—including Milan, Genoa, Palermo, and Naples—had larger populations than Rome in 1870.
41 Spiro Kostof, *The Third Rome, 1870–1950: Traffic and Glory* (Berkeley, Calif.: University Art Museum, 1973), 9.
42 Braunfels, *Urban Design in Western Europe*, 365.
43 Cited in Spiro Kostof, "The Emperor and the Duce: The Planning of Piazzale Augusto Imperatore in Rome," in Henry Millon and Linda Nochlin, eds., *Art and Architecture in the Service of Politics* (Cambridge: MIT Press, 1978), 284.
44 Kostof, *The Third Rome*, 37.
45 An official Marxist-Leninist history of Moscow contends that the site of Moscow has been "inhabited from time immemorial," with settlements in the area known to date back five thousand years. The USSR Academy of Sciences and The Institute of History of the USSR, S. S. Khromov, ed., *History of Moscow: An Outline* (Moscow: Progress, 1981, Eng. trans.), 13.
46 Moscow's historic centrality between major river systems, facilitating both commerce and tax collection, helps explain its initial growth as a Russian capital. See Kathleen Berton, *Moscow: An Architectural History* (New York: St. Martin's Press, 1977), 13–16. In the official explanation, "The emergence of the united Russian state was the result of the growing social division of labour, the development of productive forces, in the towns first and foremost. Moscow was the heart of an economically advanced area": Khromov, ed., *History of Moscow*, 21.
47 While this is the etymology suggested in the *Oxford English Dictionary* and elsewhere, others have suggested that the term is derived from the Russian word *krem*, meaning "conifer," used as a building material.
48 James H. Bater, *The Soviet City* (London: Edward Arnold, 1980), 15–16. The Nevsky Prospect now terminates not with the monastery but, appropriately enough, with the Moscow Railway Station.
49 Cited in Steve Crawshaw, "Again, Power Shifts in the Kremlin," *The Independent*, 7 July 1990, 26.
50 Berton, *Moscow*, 197, 202, 239.
51 Ibid., 36, 146, 159, 164.
52 Ibid., 43.
53 Ibid., 222–225. See also Anatole Kopp, *Town and Revolution: Soviet Architecture and City Planning, 1917–1935* (New York: Braziller, 1970), and *L'Architecture de la Période Stalinienne* (Grenoble: Presses Universitaires de Grenoble, 1978), as well as Peter Lizon, "The Palace of the Soviets: Change in Direction of Soviet Architecture" (Ph.D. diss., University of Pennsylvania, 1971).
54 See Lawrence J. Vale, *The Limits of Civil Defence in the USA, Switzerland, Britain and the Soviet Union: The Evolution of Policies since 1945* (London: Macmillan Press, 1987), 164, 174.
55 L. Maurer, *Das Griechisce Volk* (1835), cited in Dimitris Loukopoulos and Polyxeni Kosmaki-Loukopoulos, "Athens 1833–1979: The Dynamics of Urban Growth" (Master of Architecture in Advanced Studies thesis, Massachusetts Institute of Technology, 1980), 23.

56 Loukopoulos and Kosmaki-Loukopoulos, "Athens: 1833–1979," 23–25.
57 Eleni Bastéa, *The Creation of Modern Athens: Planning the Myth* (Cambridge: Cambridge University Press, 2000), 29; E. J. Hobsbawm, *Nations and Nationalism since 1780* (Cambridge: Cambridge University Press, 1990), 84.
58 Cited in Loukopoulos and Kosmaki-Loukopoulos, "Athens: 1833–1979," 26.
59 Stamatios Kleanthes and Eduard Schaubert, *Explanation of the Plan for the City of New Athens* (1832), reprinted in full as an Appendix in Bastéa, *The Creation of Modern Athens*, 217.
60 Cited in Bastéa, *The Creation of Modern Athens*, 71.
61 Loukopoulos and Kosmaki-Loukopoulos, "Athens: 1833–1979," 30–37.
62 Bastéa, *The Creation of Modern Athens*, 83. See also Alexander Papageorgiou-Venetas, "Green Spaces, Archaeological Excavation Areas and the Historic Site in the Town Planning Schemes for the City of Athens: German Plans and Other Concepts during the Foundation Decade (1833–1843)," *Planning Perspectives* 6 (1991): 69–94.
63 For more detailed discussions of the various plans for Athens, see Bastéa, *The Creation of Modern Athens*, 69–92, 151–156.
64 Ibid., 106, 108, 121, 137.
65 V. Vassilikos, cited in Loukopoulos and Kosmaki-Loukopoulos, "Athens: 1833–1979," 219–220.
66 Bastéa, *The Creation of Modern Athens*, xix.
67 Mumford, *The City in History*, 375.

CHAPTER 2 NATIONAL IDENTITY AND THE CAPITOL COMPLEX

1 See Anthony D. King, "Actually Existing Postcolonialisms: Colonial Urbanism and Architecture after the Postcolonial Turn," in Ryan Bishop, John Phillips, and Wei-Wei Yeo, eds., *Postcolonial Urbanism: Southeast Asian Cities and Global Processes* (New York: Routledge, 2003), 167–183; Clifford Geertz, *The Interpretation of Cultures* (New York: Basic Books, 1973), 238.
2 Crawford Young, *The Politics of Cultural Pluralism* (Madison: University of Wisconsin Press, 1976), 71.
3 Geertz, *Interpretation of Cultures*, 239.
4 Ibid., 240.
5 Ernest Gellner, *Nations and Nationalism* (Ithaca, N.Y.: Cornell University Press, 1983), 1.
6 Massimo d'Azeglio, cited in E. J. Hobsbawm, *Nations and Nationalism since 1780* (Cambridge: Cambridge University Press, 1990), 44; see also 60.
7 Ibid., 121. Although Hobsbawm suggests that the term *nationalism* is of late nineteenth-century origins, Peter Alter attributes its first use to the German philosopher Johann Gottfried Herder, in 1774. The term "did not begin to enter into general linguistic usage until the mid-nineteenth century"; Peter Alter, *Nationalism* (London: Hodder Arnold, 2nd ed., 1994), 3.
8 Hobsbawm, *Nations and Nationalism since 1780*, 42; Benedict Anderson, *Imagined Communities: Reflections on the Origins and Spread of Nationalism* (London: Verso, rev. ed., 2006), 36.
9 Hobsbawm, *Nations and Nationalism since 1780*, 83.
10 Ibid., 77.
11 Ibid., 31–38.
12 Ibid., 136–137.
13 Ibid., 153.
14 Geertz, *Interpretation of Cultures*, 252.
15 Neil Brenner, *New State Spaces: Urban Governance and the Rescaling of Statehood* (Oxford: Oxford University Press, 2004), 3, 16.
16 Geertz, *Interpretation of Cultures*, 237, 245.
17 Young, *Politics of Cultural Pluralism*, 65.
18 Ibid., 38.
19 Ibid., 261–263. Young challenges Geertz's use of the term *primordial* and argues convincingly that the consciousness of these ties to larger groups is of relatively recent origin. Nonetheless, Geertz's categories seem a useful analytical tool for assessing the present situation (see Young, *Politics of Cultural Pluralism*, 65).
20 Gellner, *Nations and Nationalism*, 57, 112.
21 Arjun Appadurai and Carol Breckenridge, "Public Modernity in India," in Breckenridge, ed., *Consuming Modernity: Public Culture in a South Asian World* (Minneapolis: University of Minnesota Press, 1995), 2; Arjun Appadurai, *Modernity at Large: Cultural Dimensions of Globalization* (Minneapolis: University of Minnesota Press, 1996), 41; Anderson, *Imagined Communities*, 6.
22 Geertz, *Interpretation of Cultures*, 258. Geertz here is drawing upon the writings of Isaiah Berlin and Edward Shils.
23 Edward Shils, "The Military in the Political Development of the New States," in *Center and Periphery: Essays in Macrosociology* (Chicago: University of Chicago Press, 1975), 486.

24 James C. Scott, *Seeing Like a State: How Certain Schemes to Improve the Human Condition Have Failed* (New Haven: Yale University Press, 1998), 4–6, 82.

25 Paul Ricoeur, "Universal Civilization and National Cultures," in *History and Truth*, trans. Charles A. Kelbley (Evanston, Ill.: Northwestern University Press, 1965), 277.

26 Gellner, *Nations and Nationalism*, 48.

27 Eric Hobsbawm, "Introduction: Inventing Traditions," in Eric Hobsbawm and Terrence Ranger, eds., *The Invention of Tradition* (Cambridge: Cambridge University Press, 1983), 13–14; Anderson, *Imagined Communities*; Appadurai, *Modernity at Large*, 8; Steven Kemper, *The Presence of the Past* (Ithaca, N.Y.: Cornell University Press, 1991), 6.

28 See Anthony D. King, *Urbanism, Colonialism and the World-Economy: Cultural and Spatial Foundations of the World Urban System* (London: Routledge, 1990), 79.

CHAPTER 3 EARLY DESIGNED CAPITALS

1 E. J. Hobsbawm, *Nations and Nationalism since 1780: Programme, Myth, Reality* (Cambridge: Cambridge University Press, 1990), 78.

2 Lewis Mumford, *The City in History* (New York: Harcourt, Brace, and World, 1961), 403–404.

3 L'Enfant's father spent eight years there, beginning in 1758, when his son was four. See John W. Reps, *Monumental Washington: The Planning and Development of the Capital Center* (Princeton: Princeton University Press, 1967), 5; Scott W. Berg, *Grand Avenues: The Story of the French Visionary Who Designed Washington, D.C.* (New York: Pantheon, 2007), 25–26; 113. As Berg puts it, at Versailles, L'Enfant "would have seen for the first time in his life a true man-made vista, a place where the eye could run all the way to the horizon without interruption, a world seemingly without end" (26). Berg also notes that, while an art student at the Royal Academy in Paris, L'Enfant would have "watched the Champs-Élysées punch its way westward . . . ruler straight and 160 feet broad—a figure that L'Enfant would later duplicate down to the foot in the grandest of his avenues in America's capital" (29).

4 See Robert Fortenbaugh, *Nine Capitals of the U.S.* (York, Penn.: Maple Press, 1948). The others were New York, Philadelphia, Baltimore, York (Pennsylvania), Lancaster, Princeton, Annapolis, and Trenton.

5 *New York Advertiser*, 27 January 1791, cited in Lois Craig, ed., *The Federal Presence* (Cambridge: MIT Press, 1984), 16.

6 In this regard, it may be recalled that four out of the first five U.S. presidents came from Virginia. For a more extended discussion of L'Enfant's complicated relationships with many key political figures of the era, see Berg, *Grand Avenues*.

7 Elbert Peets, "Famous Town Planners III—L'Enfant," 1928 essay included in Peets, *On the Art of Designing Cities: Selected Essays of Elbert Peets*, ed. Paul Spreiregen (Cambridge: MIT Press, 1968), 4.

8 Reps, *Monumental Washington*, 2; Berg, *Grand Avenues*, 70–71; Carl Abbott, *Political Terrain: Washington, D.C., from Tidewater Town to Global Metropolis* (Chapel Hill: University of North Carolina Press, 1999), 29. Some of the power of northern and eastern states is made apparent in the hierarchy of street names provided for L'Enfant's plan: Pennsylvania and Massachusetts gained some limited appeasement through the toponymy of significant roadways.

9 Abbott, *Political Terrain*, 29, 31, 34–35, 37, 62–63.

10 Cited in Reps, *Monumental Washington*, 9. See also Berg, *Grand Avenues*, 35–65, 78–79, 84.

11 Reps, *Monumental Washington*, 16.

12 The comparison is noted in Peets's essay of 1928, included in Peets, *On the Art of Designing Cities*, 17.

13 Author's conversation with Reginald Griffith, executive director of the National Capital Planning Commission (NCPC), 1990. In the late 1990s, under Griffith's leadership, the NCPC produced the *Extending the Legacy* plan, which included a proposal to move the Supreme Court: "If the Supreme Court decides to move, it should be located at the tip of South Capitol, on the river. Such a move would follow the Architect of the Capitol's suggestion that a special site for the Court be found within the Core that underscores the importance of three separate branches of government"; NCPC, *Extending the Legacy: Planning America's Capital for the 21st Century* (Washington, D.C.: NCPC, 1997), 20.

14 This group, also known as the Senate Park Commission, was sponsored by Senator James McMillan and consisted of landscape architect Frederick Law Olmsted Jr. and architects Daniel

Burnham and Charles McKim, working together with McMillan's assistant Charles Moore. Their full report is reprinted in Reps, *Monumental Washington*, 112–133. See also Wolfgang Sonne, *Representing the State: Capital City Planning in the Early Twentieth Century* (Munich: Prestel, 2003), 50–89.

15 Dickens, *in American Notes* (1842), cited in Reps., *Monumental Washington*, 41. For a vivid account of the attack on Washington in 1814, see Anthony Pitch, *The Burning of Washington: The British Invasion of 1814* (Annapolis, Md.: United States Naval Institute Press, 2000).

16 Cited in Paul Norton, *Latrobe, Jefferson and the National Capitol* (New York: Garland, 1977), 263, n. 1.

17 Jefferson, letter to Latrobe, 12 July 1812, cited in Craig, *The Federal Presence*, 38. For a full account of the role of Latrobe and Jefferson in the design and promotion of the Capitol, see Norton, *Latrobe, Jefferson and the National Capitol.*

18 Henry Adams, *The Education of Henry Adams* (Boston: Houghton Mifflin, 1918), 99.

19 Craig, *The Federal Presence*, 136.

20 Ibid., 137.

21 Mumford, *The City in History*, 199.

22 Latrobe, letter to Jefferson, 21 May 1807, cited in Craig, *The Federal Presence*, 37.

23 Cited in ibid., 24.

24 Reps, *Monumental Washington*, 21.

25 NCPC, *Extending the Legacy*, 19. For overviews of planning in Washington during the twentieth century, see Howard Gillette Jr., *Between Justice and Beauty: Race, Planning, and the Failure of Urban Policy in Washington, D.C.* (Baltimore: Johns Hopkins University Press, 1995) and Isabelle Gournay, "Washington: The DC's History of Unresolved Planning Conflicts," in David L. A. Gordon, ed., *Planning Twentieth Century Capital Cities* (New York: Routledge, 2006), 115–129; for a discussion of public space in Washington, see Michael Bednar, *L'Enfant's Legacy: Public Open Spaces in Washington, D.C.* (Baltimore: Johns Hopkins University Press, 2006).

26 Anthony D. King, *Urbanism, Colonialism and the World-Economy* (London: Routledge, 1990), 20–22. For an account of French colonial urbanism and architecture, see Gwendolyn Wright, *The Politics of Design in French Colonial Urbanism* (Chicago: University of Chicago Press, 1991).

27 Rachel Swarns, "Bidding Farewell to the Names that Evoke Apartheid," *New York Times*, 5 November 2000; Michael Wines, "Pretoria Renames Itself Tshwane," *New York Times*, 9 March 2005.

28 Thomas R. Metcalf, "Imperial Building in South Africa: The Work of Herbert Baker" and "The Union Buildings, Pretoria," in *An Imperial Vision: Indian Architecture and Britain's* Raj (Berkeley: University of California Press, 1989), 180–199. See also Christopher Vernon, "Projecting Power on Conquered Landscapes: Constructing National Capitals at Pretoria and Canberra," in Norman Etherington, ed., *Mapping Colonial Conquest: Australia and Southern Africa* (Perth: University of Western Australia Press, 2007), 227–293.

29 Memo (1909) from Baker to the secretary of the Public Works Department, cited in Metcalf, "Imperial Building in South Africa," 194.

30 See Nigel Mandy, "Class, Race and the Group Areas Act," in *A City Divided: Johannesburg and Soweto* (New York: St. Martin's Press, 1984). For a politically disingenuous discussion of the urban design for one of the homeland capitals, see "Mmabatho," *Architecture SA* (Autumn 1981): 39–49, and "Government Square, Mmabatho," *Architecture SA* (May/June 1984): 34–41.

31 National Capital Commission, *A Capital in the Making: Reflections of the Past, Visions of the Future* (Ottawa: Planning Branch of the National Capital Commission, 1987), 10, and National Capital Commission, *Compendium: International Survey of Capital Cities and Urban Centres* (Ottawa: National Capital Commission, 1986), 59–68. For an overview of Ottawa's planning history which casts doubt on the motives and the efficacy of attempts to use capitals for the invention of tradition, see John H. Taylor, "City Form and Capital Culture: Remaking Ottawa," *Planning Perspectives* 4 (1989): 79–105. See also John H. Taylor, *Ottawa: An Illustrated History* (Toronto: Lorimer, 1986).

32 Jaap Schouten, "Ottawa: Evolution of a Capital," *Urban Design International* 4 (Winter 1983): 23–24; Taylor, *Ottawa: An Illustrated History*, 146–150.

33 The provincial divide in the national capital region is accompanied by rather divergent patterns of linguistic affiliation: see National Capital Commission, *Compendium*, 62. For an overview of twentieth-century capital city planning in Ottawa, see David L. A. Gordon, "Ottawa-Hull:

Lumber Town to National Capital," in Gordon, ed., *Planning Twentieth Century Capital Cities*, 150–163; David L. A. Gordon, "A City Beautiful Plan for Canada's Capital: Edward Bennett and the 1915 Plan for Ottawa and Hull," *Planning Perspectives* 13 (1998): 275–300; David Gordon, "Weaving a Modern Plan for Canada's Capital: Jacques Gréber and the 1950 plan for the National Capital Region," *Urban History Review* 29, 2 (2001): 43–61.

34 Taylor, "City Form and Capital Culture," 96.

35 For a full account, see Roger Pegrum, *The Bush Capital: How Australia Chose Canberra as Its Federal City* (Sydney: Hale and Iremonger, 1983). On the further evolution of Canberra's growth and development, see Paul Reid, *Canberra Following Griffin: A Design History of Australia's National Capital* (Canberra: National Archives of Australia, 2002). Reid, chief architect of the National Capital Development Commission from 1968 to 1982, devoted his efforts to reviving and realizing Griffin's sidetracked visions. See also David Headon, *The Symbolic Role of the National Capital: From Colonial Argument to 21st Century Ideals* (Canberra: National Capital Authority, 2003); Christopher Vernon, "An 'Accidental' Australian: Walter Burley Griffin," in Jeff Turnbull and Peter Y. Navaretti, eds., *The Griffins in Australia and India* (Melbourne: Melbourne University Press, 1998), 2–15; Paul Reid, "Walter Burley Griffin's Struggles to Implement His Canberra Plan, 1912–1921," in Turnbull and Navaretti, eds., *The Griffins in Australia and India*, 18–25; Peter Harrison, *Walter Burley Griffin, Landscape Architect* (Canberra: National Library of Australia, 1995); Anne Watson, ed., *Beyond Architecture: Marion Mahony and Walter Burley Griffin* (Sydney: Powerhouse, 1998); Debora Wood, ed., *Marion Mahony Griffin: Drawing the Form of Nature* (Evanston, Ill.: Northwestern University Press, 2005); and, for a controversial set of cosmological symbolic interpretations of the Canberra plan, Peter Proudfoot, *The Secret Plan of Canberra* (Kensington, NSW: University of New South Wales Press, 1994).

36 Pegrum, *The Bush Capital*, 37. Pre-Federation politician/journalist J. G. Drake called for an inland capital, using the sorts of economic development arguments later advanced as a rationale for siting Brasília; Headon, *Symbolic Role*, 18–19.

37 G. J. R. Linge, *Canberra: Site and City* (Canberra: Australian National University Press, 1975), 3.

38 Ibid., 154; Headon, *Symbolic Role*, 20–24.

39 Pegrum, *The Bush Capital*, 170–172.

40 Ibid., 170, 174. The "meeting place" alternative is cited, among other places, in Rory Spence, "The New Australian Parliament House," *Architectural Review* (October 1988): 48.

41 Quoted in Headon, *Symbolic Role*, 45.

42 The competition (held in 1911–1912) was limited by the nonparticipation of the Royal Institute of British Architects (as well as some of its imperial affiliates), which boycotted in protest over its adjudication by the minister for home affairs instead of by a town planner, as well as objection to a proviso that permitted the jury to combine aspects of several schemes rather than implement the design of the winner. None of the newly prominent British and American planners entered, nor did any Germans. Nonetheless, the competition yielded 137 entries, including 42 from Australia, 41 from the U.K., and 20 from the United States. See John W. Reps, *Canberra 1912: Plans and Planners of the Australian Capital Competition* (Melbourne: Melbourne University Press, 1997). Sonne's analysis of the competition entries divides them into five basic types of government district: Ring, Axis, Mall, Forum, and Castle; Sonne, *Representing the State*, 172–177.

Griffin struggled for seven years to implement his winning plan. Although he had the title of Federal Capital Director of Design and Construction, he faced innumerable obstacles to his authority, even before he arrived on the site. Griffin's struggles included battles over his contract, contending efforts to implement a different plan favored by the Departmental Board, and fights over where to build the "Initial City." As Reid points out, even the lake named in his honor was "built to the plan of his opponents." See Reid, *Canberra Following Griffin*, chapter 5; Reid, "Walter Burley Griffin's Struggles."

43 Christopher Vernon, "Canberra: Where Landscape is Pre-eminent," in Gordon, ed., *Planning Twentieth Century Capital Cities*, 134; Pegrum, *The Bush Capital*, 161.

44 K. F. Fischer, *Canberra: Myths and Models: Forces at Work in the Foundation of the Australian Capital* (Hamburg: Institute of Asian Affairs, 1984), 30.

45 Vernon, "Canberra: Where Landscape is Pre-eminent," 139; K. F. Fischer, "Canberra: Myths and Models," *Town Planning Review* 60 (1989): 169–170. This article is a revised and abbreviated version of Fischer's book.

46 Fischer, *Canberra: Myths and Models*, 159.
47 Griffin (1913), cited in ibid., 26; Sonne, *Representing the State*, 187.
48 Had Griffin been the designer of Washington, D.C., his proposed juxtaposition of the courts of justice above a "water gate" might have found a more appropriate home.
49 Pegrum, *The Bush Capital*, 161–162.
50 Linge, *Canberra*, 19.
51 For an account of the symbolism of the United Nations Headquarters, see Lawrence J. Vale, "Designing Global Harmony: Lewis Mumford and the United Nations Headquarters," in Thomas Hughes and Agatha Hughes, eds., *Lewis Mumford: Public Intellectual* (New York: Oxford University Press, 1990), 256–282.
52 A probing discussion of the political wrangling which transpired in parallel with the siting decisions and design efforts, together with an extended critique of the resultant building (as well as a compelling critical analysis of the critiques made by others) may be found in James Weirick, "Don't You Believe It: Critical Response to the New Parliament House," *Transition* (Summer/Autumn 1989): 7–66.
53 Cited in Fischer, *Canberra: Myths and Models*, 5.
54 Linge, *Canberra*, 83–84.
55 Though the firm included the Australian Richard Thorp, it was Romaldo Giurgola who exercised most of the control over the design. Giurgola himself subsequently moved permanently to Canberra.
56 Reid, *Canberra Following Griffin*, 309; NCDC cited in Weirick, "Don't You Believe It," 26.
57 Weirick, "Don't You Believe It," 26.
58 Joint House Department (Canberra), *Australia's Parliament House: The Meeting Place of Our Nation* (Canberra: Australian Government Publishing Service, 1989), 8.
59 Ibid., 28.
60 This is part of an elaborate interpretive description of the building's sequence of symbolic spaces contained in a celebratory volume sponsored by the Royal Institute of Australian Architects. Haig Beck, ed., *Parliament House Canberra: A Building for the Nation* (Sydney: Collins, 1988), 20–25.
61 It is certainly possible to interpret the Aboriginal Forecourt as a place of honor for the indigenous people, though this interpretation would be much enhanced if there were greater indications of Aboriginal presence beyond the forecourt. Although there are certainly Aboriginal artworks within the parliamentary building, the lingering Aboriginal protests, inscribed into the urban design of the larger Canberra capitol triangle, bespeak ongoing tensions.
62 The two legislative chambers are symmetrically placed and are articulated on the exterior by orange-tiled pitched roofs, in what seems to be a deliberate reference to the suburban houses that dominate so much of the rest of Canberra.
63 Weirick, "Don't You Believe It," 65.
64 To planning historian Wolfgang Sonne, however, Giurgola's building fails on all counts: "Neither completely hidden, nor frankly and confidentially displayed through architectural means, the result is a hybrid that bears an unfortunate resemblance to a nuclear bunker with a radio antenna. Fear of architectural monumentality thus resulted in a monument to alienation." Sonne, *Representing the State*, 188.
65 Fischer, *Canberra: Myths and Models*, 169.
66 Griffin's "casino" idea seems to have meant some sort of community center and open-air theatre-restaurant, not a place for gaming. It was removed from the drawings after 1915. Reid, *Canberra Following Griffin*, 65, 66; Sonne, *Representing the State*, 188.
67 Fischer, *Canberra: Myths and Models*, 169.
68 National Capital Authority, Commonwealth of Australia, *The Griffin Legacy: Canberra, The Nation's Capital in the 21st Century* (Canberra: NCA, 2004).
69 National Capital Authority, *Parliamentary Zone Review: Outcomes* (Canberra: NCA, March 2000), 4, 32. See also Headon, *Symbolic Role*. The Griffin Legacy book also contains a section on proposed improvements to the Parliamentary Zone.
70 Headon, *Symbolic Role*, 142–143.
71 Christopher Vernon, "Axial Occupation," *Architecture Australia* 91, 5 (September/October 2002): 84–90; Christopher Vernon, "Radar: Landscape: The Aboriginal Tent Embassy," *Architecture Australia* 91, 6 (November/December 2002): 36. See also Vernon, "Canberra: Where Landscape is Pre-eminent," 145–147.
72 Vernon, "Axial Occupation," 84–90.
73 Fischer, *Canberra: Myths and Models*, 166.
74 Robert Grant Irving, *Indian Summer: Lutyens, Baker and Imperial Delhi* (New Haven: Yale University Press, 1981), 27.
75 Ibid., 72–73.
76 Cited in ibid., 72.

77 Ibid., 73.

78 Ibid., 82, 68, 154–155, 73. Perhaps looking for excuses, Baker, whom Lutyens held responsible for the blunder, emphasized that the approaches to both the Athenian acropolis and the Roman capitol exhibit this same disappearance and reappearance of the major buildings. Others have suggested that Baker deliberately altered the gradient to enhance the prominence of his own buildings.

79 Griffin's selection as the planner of Canberra occurred just as the Town Planning Committee for Imperial Delhi were preparing their initial designs, and the viceroy requested plans for Canberra from the Australian governor-general. The Australian found it "interesting to note that those engaged in the building of the capital of one of the oldest of civilized countries are apparently not above accepting ideas from this, one of the youngest countries in the world" (cited in Irving, *Indian Summer*, 87). It is likely, however, that planning for New Delhi was well advanced before anyone in India saw the Canberra plans. According to Lutyens, the hexagonal basis for the Imperial Delhi plan arose because Lord Hardinge insisted that the plan relate to existing Indian monuments, resulting in a 30 degree angle between the main axis that pointed toward the Purana Kila and a second axis pointing from Raisina toward the Jama Masjid in Shahjahanabad. Although hexagonal planning was quite common in the era, it seems likely that the hexagons of New Delhi and those of Canberra came about independently; Sonne, *Representing the State*, 209. See also Eran Ben-Joseph and David L. A. Gordon, "Hexagonal Planning in Theory and Practice," *Journal of Urban Design* 5, 3 (2000): 237–265.

80 Sonne, *Representing the State*, 208.

81 Irving, *Indian Summer*, 89.

82 See Anthony D. King, *Colonial Urban Development: Culture, Social Power and Environment* (London: Routledge and Kegan Paul, 1976), 209–230, and Norma Evenson, *The Indian Metropolis: A View toward the West* (New Haven: Yale University Press, 1989), 99–102.

83 King, *Colonial Urban Development*, 244–246.

84 Ibid., 248.

85 Irving, *Indian Summer*, 125.

86 Ibid.

87 Cited in Metcalf, *An Imperial Vision*, 232, 234.

88 Irving, *Indian Summer*, 102.

89 Ibid., 306.

90 For an overview of twentieth-century planning efforts in Delhi, see Souro D. Joardar, "New Delhi: Imperial Capital to Capital of the World's Largest Democracy," in Gordon, ed., *Planning Twentieth Century Capital Cities*, 182–195.

91 For an overview and analysis of the intentions and accrued meanings of New Delhi, including an account of the city's reception in the press, see Sonne, *Representing the State*, 189–240.

92 Baykan Günay, "Our Generation of Planners: The Hopes, the Fears, the Facts: Case Study Ankara," Paper Submitted at the 20th Anniversary Salzburg Congress on Urban Planning and Development, 1988, 12–23; Lars Marcussen, *Settlement in Turkey* (Copenhagen: Kunstakademiets Trykkeri, 1982), part 5; Malcolm D. Rivkin, "Creation of Growth Regions: Some Experience from Turkey," *Ekistics* 18 (September 1964): 146–151; Tugrul Akçura, *Ankara: A Monographic Study* (Ankara: Middle East Technical University, 1971), and Gönül Tankut, "Building of Ankara as the New National Capital" (in Turkish with English abstract), *M.E.T.U. Journal of the Faculty of Architecture* (Middle East Technical University, Ankara) 8 (1988): 93–104.

93 Arnold Toynbee, *Cities on the Move* (New York: Oxford University Press, 1970), 97–98.

94 Sibel Bozdoğan, "The Predicament of Modernism in Turkish Architectural Culture: An Overview," in Sibel Bozdoğan and Resat Kasaba, eds., *Rethinking Modernity and National Identity in Turkey* (Seattle: University of Washington Press, 1997), 136–137; Sibel Bozdoğan, *Modernism and Nation Building: Turkish Architectural Culture in the Early Republic* (Seattle: University of Washington Press, 2001), 7. See also Zeynep Kezer, "Contesting Urban Space in Early Republic Ankara," *Journal of Architectural Education* 52, 1 (September 1998): 11–19; and Güven Arif Sargin, "Displaced Memories, or the Architecture of Forgetting and Remembrance," *Environment and Planning D: Society and Space* 22, 5 (October 2004): 659–680.

94 Günay, "Our Generation of Planners," 15.

95 Ibid., 2, 16.

96 Inci Aslanoglu, "Evaluation of Architectural Developments in Turkey within the Socio-Economic and Cultural Framework of the 1923–38 Period," *M.E.T.U. Journal of the Faculty of Architecture* (Middle East Technical University, Ankara) 7 (Spring 1986): 15–41.

97 Holzmeister's designs included not only the Presidential Palace and the Grand National Assembly, but also buildings for the Ministries of Defense, Internal Affairs, Construction, and Commerce; the General Staff Headquarters, Officers' Club, and Military War School as well as the High Court Palace and the Turkish Republic Central Bank. See Aslanoglu, "Architectural Developments in Turkey," 16–19.

98. For a brief discussion of the Grand National Assembly competition, see Bozdoğan, *Modernism and Nation Building*, 279–283. Jansen's plan, Bozdoğan observes, was plagued by "the overall absence of a land-use and planning policy in the government program," and "when his propositions against land speculation proved unpopular among influential people close to the government, his contract was terminated in 1939" (70).

99 Bozdoğan, *Modernism and Nation Building*, 286. A substantial proportion of Ankara's population of more than four million are squatters, and official planning documents did not take such persons into account until 1966. See Günay, "Our Generation of Planners," 37, 49–51; 2005 Census.

100 The bronze original is in Ankara's Museum of Anatolian Civilizations (generally referred to as the Hittite Museum), located adjacent to the citadel. As Bozdoğan puts it, "Prehistoric Hittite emblems became the official municipal symbols of republican Ankara, today a point of controversy between their Kemalist defenders and a growing Islamic movement that would prefer to replace these 'pagan symbols' with religious Muslim ones such as the crescent and the dome"; Bozdoğan, *Modernism and Nation Building*, 244.

CHAPTER 4 DESIGNED CAPITALS AFTER WORLD WAR TWO

1 Cited in William J. R. Curtis, *Le Corbusier: Ideas and Forms* (New York: Rizzoli, 1986), 189.

2 Ravi Kalia, *Chandigarh: In Search of an Identity* (Carbondale: University of Southern Illinois Press, 1987), 12.

3 Ibid., 13. Over time, Chandigarh has become a significant point of migration. The city surpassed its target population of 500,000 in 1991, and reached at least 750,000 by 2001, with several hundred thousand more people living in the surrounding periphery. Newer phases of growth have taken higher-density form, and the current plan expects the Union Territory of Chandigarh to reach a population of 1.3 million, with an additional 1.2 million in the nearby cities of SAS Nagar and Panchkula, and a further 1.3 million in the periphery. See Kiran Joshi, "Birth and Evolution of a Modern City in India," in Maristella Casciato, ed., *Le Corbusier & Chandigarh: Ritratto di una città moderna* (Rome: Edizioni Kappa, 2003), 62–64. For further population and displacement statistics, see Prakash, *Chandigarh's Le Corbusier: The Struggle for Modernity in Postcolonial India* (Seattle: University of Washington Press, 2002), 7–8, 15.

4 Prakash, *Chandigarh's Le Corbusier*, 10, 11, 18, 151. See also Jon Lang, Madhavi Desai, and Miki Desai, *Architecture and Independence: The Search for Identity—India 1880 to 1980* (Delhi: Oxford University Press, 1997), 187–243, and Sunil Khilnani, *The Idea of India* (New Delhi: Penguin, 1997).

5 Prakash, *Chandigarh's Le Corbusier*, 26; Nihal Perera, "Contesting Visions: Hybridity, Liminality and Authorship of the Chandigarh Plan," *Planning Perspectives* 19 (April 2004): 175, 179, 195. For other accounts of Chandigarh's origins, in addition to Curtis and Kalia, see esp. Stanislaus von Moos, *Le Corbusier: Elements of a Synthesis* (Cambridge: MIT Press, 1979), chap. 6, and Russell Walden, ed., *The Open Hand: Essays on Le Corbusier* (Cambridge: MIT Press, 1977), pt. 5.

6 Kalia, *Chandigarh*, 54.

7 Ibid., 23.

8 Ibid., 109.

9 Ibid., 59.

10 Prakash, *Chandigarh's Le Corbusier*, 149; Madhu Sarin, *Urban Planning in the Third World: The Chandigarh Experience* (London: Mansell, 1982), 70; Perera, "Contesting Visions," 187.

11 Mayer, letter to Maxwell Fry, 31 January 1951, cited in Kalia, *Chandigarh*, 59.

12 Kalia, *Chandigarh*, 60.

13 Mayer, letter to Nowicki's brother Jacek, 21 August 1959, cited in Kalia, *Chandigarh*, 66.

14 Maxwell Fry, "Le Corbusier at Chandigarh," in Walden, ed., *The Open Hand*, 353.

15 Ibid., 354.

16 Ibid., 110, 113.

17 Le Corbusier, *Le Corbusier Sketchbooks, Volume 2 (1950–1954)*, ed. Françoise de Franclieu (Cambridge: MIT Press, 1981), sketchbook F26, no. 826.

18 Le Corbusier, *Le Corbusier Sketchbooks, Volume 3 (1954–1957)*, ed. Françoise de Franclieu (Cambridge: MIT Press, 1982), sketchbook H31, no. 23, 14 February 1954.
19 *Le Corbusier Sketchbooks, Volume 2*, sketchbook G28, no. 951, 14 June 1953.
20 Françoise de Franclieu, in *Le Corbusier Sketchbooks, Volume 4 (1957–1965)* (Cambridge: MIT Press, 1982), introd. to sketchbook P59; Prakash, *Chandigarh's Le Corbusier*, 70.
21 Von Moos, *Le Corbusier*, 259.
22 Ibid., 260. For a photograph showing the temporary Governor's Palace, see Julian Beinart, "Chandigarh 1999: Diagrams and Realities," in Jaspreet Takhar, ed., *Celebrating Chandigarh* (Ahmedabad: Mapin, 2002), 159. This essay also contains interesting proposals by MIT urban design students for densifying the capitol complex, as well as other suggestions for improving the form and livability of Chandigarh.
23 Alexander Gorlin, "An Analysis of the Governor's Palace of Chandigarh," *Oppositions* 19/20 (1980): 161. The Corbusier comment may be found in his *Oeuvre Complète 1952–1957*, ed. W. Boesiger (Zurich: Girsberger, 1957), 102.
24 Gorlin, "Analysis of the Governor's Palace," 161, 166.
25 Prakash, *Chandigarh's Le Corbusier*, 83–85, 153–155.
26 Ibid., 68.
27 Though late-developing São Paulo is not an Atlantic port, it is nonetheless a primary source for the export of coffee. See Alex Shoumatoff, *The Capital of Hope: Brasília and Its People*, 2nd ed. (Albuquerque: University of New Mexico Press, 1987), 12. See also Glenn V. Stephenson, "Two Newly-Created Capitals: Islamabad and Brasília," *Town Planning Review* 41 (October 1970): 317–332.
28 Shoumatoff, *The Capital of Hope*, 13.
29 Furtado de Mendonça, cited in ibid., 60.
30 David G. Epstein, *Brasília: Plan and Reality* (Berkeley: University of California Press, 1973), 42–46.
31 Ricardo L. Farret, "The Justification of Brasília: A Political-Economic Approach," *Third World Planning Review* 5 (May 1983): 146.
32 James Holston, *The Modernist City: An Anthropological Critique of Brasília* (Chicago: University of Chicago Press, 1989), 201.
33 Shoumatoff, *The Capital of Hope*, 39.
34 Ibid., 22.
35 Ibid., 30.
36 Norma Evenson, "Brasília: 'Yesterday's City of Tomorrow,'" in H. Wentworth Eldredge, ed., *World Capitals: Toward Guided Urbanization* (Garden City, N.Y.: Anchor Press, 1975), 475.
37 Cited in Epstein, *Brasília*, 38.
38 Shoumatoff, *The Capital of Hope*, 38.
39 Evenson, "Brasília," 476.
40 Costa himself advocated an elaborate pedestrian system, but this aspect—to his great frustration—was not realized.
41 Cited in Evenson, "Brasília," 481.
42 Cited in ibid., 481.
43 See L. Arturo Espejo, *Rationalité et formes d'occupation de l'espace: Le projet de Brasília* (Paris: Éditions Anthropos, 1984).
44 Cited in Shoumatoff, *The Capital of Hope*, 19.
45 Of the six jurors it was the three non-Brazilians (Stamo Papadaki, André Sive, and William Holford) and Niemeyer who most strongly favored Costa's competition scheme. One Brazilian juror, Paulo Antunes Ribeiro, who represented the Institute of Brazilian Architects, refused to sign the verdict and submitted a separate report (see Norma Evenson, *Two Brazilian Capitals: Architecture and Urbanism in Rio de Janeiro and Brasília* [New Haven: Yale University Press, 1973], 121–122).
46 Holston, *The Modernist City*, 74.
47 Ibid., 206–215.
48 Ibid., 199 and 205.
49 Cited in ibid., 20. See also Geraldo Nogueira Batista, Sylvia Ficher, Francisco Leitão, and Dionísio Alves de França, "Brasília: A Capital in the Hinterland," in David L. A. Gordon, ed., *Planning Twentieth Century Capital Cities* (London: Routledge, 2006), 164–181.
50 Holston, *The Modernist City*, 206 and 28; Batista, Ficher, Leitão, and Alves de França, "Brasília," 175; James C. Scott, *Seeing Like a State: How Certain Schemes to Improve the Human Condition Have Failed* (New Haven: Yale University Press, 1998), 126. For discussion of the sprawl of contemporary Brasília, see also Claudio C. Acioly Jr., "Incremental Land Development in Brasília: Can the Urban Poor Escape from Suburbanization?" *Third World Planning Review* 16, 3 (August 1994): 243–261.
51 Holston, *The Modernist City*, 160.
52 F.G., "Crisis in Brasília," from *Jornol do Brasil*, 14–15 November 1961, revised version in *Ekistics* 14 (October 1962): 144.

53 David Snyder, "Alternative Perspectives on Brasília," *Ekistics* 18 (November 1964): 330.
54 Holston, *The Modernist City*, 281.
55 Epstein, *Brasília*, 55.
56 See Lawrence J. Vale, "Designing Global Harmony: Lewis Mumford and the United Nations Headquarters," in Thomas Hughes and Agatha Hughes, eds., *Lewis Mumford: Public Intellectual* (New York: Oxford University Press, 1990), 256–282.
57 In the placement of the legislative chambers on the roof of a long, low building containing offices and support facilities, Niemeyer's work may well have been influenced by Nowicki's unexecuted design for Chandigarh.
58 The inscription accompanying the sculpted head reads in translation: "To President Juscelino Kubitschek de Oliveira, who tamed the wilderness and raised Brasília with audacity, energy and confidence, the homage of the pioneers who helped in the great adventure." Cited in Evenson, *Two Brazilian Capitals*, 199, n. 21. Elsewhere, there is a larger Juscelino Kubitschek memorial, with a statue of the former president raised high to survey the city.
59 Evenson, "Brasília," 478.
60 Cited in Epstein, *Brasília*, 51. Epstein notes that the diminutive cidadezinhas, translated as "little cities," is employed "in quite a pejorative sense."
61 Cited in Evenson, *Two Brazilian Capitals*, 204.
62 Cited in Evenson, "Brasília," 483. As built, the rectilinearity of the central part of the plaza adds little to this sense of triangulation.
63 Cited in ibid., 488.
64 Ibid., 485.
65 Shoumatoff, *The Capital of Hope*, 54.
66 Evenson, "Brasília," 503.
67 Ibid., 485.
68 Cited in Evenson, *Two Brazilian Capitals*, 197. For an account of the later part of Niemeyer's career, see Michael Kimmelman, "The Last of the Moderns," *New York Times Magazine*, 15 May 2005, 60–69.
69 Evenson, "Brasília," 503.
70 Holston, *The Modernist City*, 96.
71 Ibid., 40.
72 For a photo of farmers protesting in a fleet of massive trucks in front of the Congress buildings, see Batista, Ficher, Leitão, and Alves de França, "Brasília," 176.
73 Holston, *The Modernist City*, 73.
74 Edmund Bacon, *Design of Cities*, rev. ed. (London: Thames and Hudson, 1975), 240.
75 Sibyl Moholy-Nagy, *Matrix of Man: An Illustrated History of Urban Environment* (New York: Praeger, 1968), 155.
76 The addition of the Tancredo Neves Pantheon at the plaza's rear does provide a legitimate public destination, and the contemplative darkness of its interior is a striking contrast to the blinding sunlight that bedazzles the capitol complex as a whole. See Oscar Niemeyer, "Pantheon Tancredo Neves," *L'Architecture d'Aujourd'hui* 251 (June 1987): 4–5.

CHAPTER 5 DESIGNED CAPITALS SINCE 1960

1 C. A. Doxiadis, "Islamabad: The Creation of a New Capital," *Town Planning Review* 36 (April 1965): 1.
2 Leo Jamoud, "Islamabad: The Visionary Capital," *Ekistics* 25 (May 1968): 333; Imran Ahmed, "The Journey for New Delhi to Islamabad: Dependence and Subversion in the Ambivalent Expression of Nationhood" (Unpublished master's thesis, Massachusetts Institute of Technology, 1992), 151, 152.
3 See Glenn V. Stephenson, "Two Newly-Created Capitals: Islamabad and Brasília," *Town Planning Review* 41 (October 1970): 317–332.
4 Cited in ibid., 323.
5 Though Islamabad itself had only one generating node, Rawalpindi's existing commercial area constituted a parallel second node. See Doxiadis, "Islamabad," 20 ff., and Nicholas Taylor, "Islamabad: Progress Report on Pakistan's New Capital City," *Architectural Review* 141 (March 1967): 211. For an account of the design of Islamabad from the perspective of the Doxiadis firm, see Orestes Yakas, *Islamabad: The Birth of a Capital* (Karachi: Oxford University Press, 2001).
6 Doxiadis, "Islamabad," 31.
7 "Islamabad," in National Capital Commission of Canada, *Compendium: International Survey of Capital Cities and Urban Centres* (Ottawa: National Capital Commission, 1986), 41.
8 While West Pakistan's Islamabad was under control of Ayub Khan and the army, legislative functions did eventually receive more prominent visual treatment (though not greater

constitutional significance) in a second capital begun in East Pakistan on the outskirts of Dhaka. In Dhaka, however, the pace of political change so outstripped the pace of construction that the major buildings of the capitol complex were completed only after East Pakistan had become independent Bangladesh. The Dhaka capitol complex is the subject of Chapter 9.

9 Doxiadis, "Islamabad," 17.

10 Jamoud, "The Visionary Capital," 333.

11 See Jamoud, "The Visionary Capital," 329–331, and Taylor, "Progress Report," 211.

12 Richard L. Meier, "Islamabad Is Already Twenty-Five," *Ekistics* 52 (May/June 1985): 213.

13 Jamoud, "The Visionary Capital," 329.

14 Meier, "Islamabad Is Already Twenty-Five," 213.

15 See Kevin C. Kearns, "Belmopan: Perspective on a New Capital," *The Geographical Review* 63 (April 1973): 147–169. Belmopan remains a remarkably small capital city, with a population estimated at about 12,000. Belize City, substantially rebuilt after the hurricane, remains much larger. On Argentina's proposal to move to Viedma, see Alan Gilbert, "Moving the Capital of Argentina: A Future Example of Utopian Planning?" *Cities* (August 1989): 234–242; Sigurd Grava, "Look South, Argentina," *Planning* (February 1988): 28–30; and Randall Hackley, "'A Lovely Madness'—Argentina Builds New Capital in Patagonia," *Jerusalem Post*, 7 July 1987. In fact, the idea prospered only during the presidency of Raúl Alfonsin, and was rejected by his successors. On other new capitals, see also Sten Ake Nilsson, *The New Capitals of India, Pakistan and Bangladesh*, trans. Elisabeth Andreasson (Lund, Sweden: Studentlitteratur, 1973).

16 Botswana's new capital, initiated in 1961, was Gaborone (replacing Mafeking in South Africa), while Mauritania initiated plans for Nouakchott in 1957 (with Saint Louis a part of Senegal). For a discussion of the Botswana case, see A. C. G. Best, "Gaborone: Problems and Prospects of a New Capital," *Geographical Review* 69 (1970): 1–14. On Nouakchott, see "Capital Replaces Mauritania Huts; Nouakchott, Made-to-Order City, Is Still Growing," *New York Times*, 26 March 1967, 7. On Valparaiso, see Malcolm Coad, "White Elephantine Congress that Pinochet Built," *The Guardian* (London), 9 March 1990; Tim Frasca, "A Controversial Congress for Chile," *Christian Science Monitor*, 13 February 1990; Shirley Christian, "Valparaiso Journal: Home Port for Lawmakers; Seafarers' Old Haunt," *New York Times*, 2 March 1990.

17 See Deborah Potts, "Capital Relocation in Africa: The Case of Lilongwe in Malawi," *Geographical Journal* 151 (July 1985): 182–196; "Banda Will Shift Malawi's Capital," *New York Times*, 24 January 1965, 22; "Banda Says Work Will Start on Shifting Malawi Capital," *New York Times*, 24 August 1966, 4; "Malawi Will Shift Her Capital City," *New York Times*, 27 January 1967, 54; Dennis Mzembe, "President Ejects MPs, Makes Palace Home: $100-million Edifice Built by One of the World's Poorest Nations," *National Post* (Ottawa), 23 December 2004, A14; "Malawi: President Wants Parliament for Himself," *New York Times*, 22 July 2004; Sharon LaFraniere, "Lilongwe Journal; A Ghost Story Turns Very Scary for Malawi Journalists," *New York Times*, 29 March 2005; Bingu wa Mutharika, "The House of Honour," speech delivered at the laying of the foundation stone at the site of the New Parliament Building, City Centre Lilongwe, 27 July 2005, http://www.malawi.gov.mw/presidential_speeches/SPEECH%20-%20GROUNDBREAKING%20CEREMONY%20OF%20PARLIAMENT%20BUILDING.pdf, accessed 18 January 2007.

18 See Allen Armstrong, "Ivory Coast: Another New Capital for Africa," *Geography* 70 (1985): 72–74; Kaye Whiteman, "Houphouët's Promise," *West Africa*, 26 December 1988–8 January 1989, 2418; Gerald Bourke, "Beauty or Beast?: Pope Paul Consecrates a Controversial $200m Basilica," *West Africa*, 17–23 September 1990; Norimitsu Onishi, "Yamoussoukro Journal: For a Great White Elephant, a New Lease on Life," *New York Times*, 25 May 2001; and Nnamdi Elleh, *Architecture and Power in Africa* (Westport, Conn.: Praeger, 2002).

19 Mike Leidermann, "Pride in Palau for New Capitol," *Honolulu Advertiser*, 12 November 2006.

20 Jonathan Head, "Burma's New Capital City Unveiled." BBC News, http://news.bbc.co.uk/2/hi/asia-pacific/6498029.stm, accessed 29 September 2007.

21 Larry Rohter, "Under Raging Volcano, Montserrat People Chafe," *New York Times*, 17 August, 1997; Larry Rohter, "In the Mirror, a Ghostly Replica of Pompeii," *New York Times*, 7 September 1997; Ryan Brandt, "Montserrat Rises from the Ashes," *New York Times*, 23 October 2005.

22 Steven Lee Myers, "Kazakhstan's Futuristic

Capital, Complete with Pyramid," *New York Times*, 13 October 2006.

23 Edward Schatz, "When Capital Cities Move: The Political Geography of Nation and State Building," Working Paper #30, February 2003, Kellogg Institute for International Studies, University of Notre Dame, http://kellogg.nd.edu/publications/workingpapers/WPS/303.pdf, accessed 24 January 2007, 16, 18. See also Philipp Meuser, "Building One's 'I': In Search of National Identity," *Project Russia* 30 (2003–2004), 26–33; Philipp Meuser, "Astana: Green City Between the Steppes and the Swamps," *Project Russia* 30 (2003–2004), 34–35.

24 Myers, "Kazakhstan's Futuristic Capital"; Website of the Prime Minister of the Republic of Kazakhstan, http://www.massimov.kz/?p97&version=en, accessed 12 January 2007; David Holley, "Building Kazakhstan's Bridge to the 21st Century," *Los Angeles Times*, 16 March 2005.

25 Tsubokura Takashi, "Astana as the New Capital: Reconstruction of Central Square in 1997," http://www.astanamp.kepter.kz/sub3.html, accessed 12 January 2007; Holley, "Building Kazakhstan's Bridge."

26 South Korea has come close to implementing a decision to decentralize national administration away from Seoul and Japan's leaders also continue to consider a move away from Tokyo. See T. John Kim and Yong Je Hwang, "A New Capital City for South Korea," and Richard L. Meier, "Socio-Technical Considerations in Planning a New Capital for South Korea," *Ekistics* 46 (July/August 1979): 258–267; John Larkin, "Capital Maneuver," *Time*, 11 January 2004; Jonathan Watts, "South Korea to Move Capital 100 Miles South," *The Guardian*, 12 August 2004; "South Korea: Capital Move Rejected," *New York Times*, 22 October 2004; and Yoav Cerralbo, "Is This a 'Capital' Move?: Nation Divided on Changing 'The Soul' of Korea," *The Seoul Times*, http://theseoultimes.com/ST/?url=/ST/db/read.php?idx=1047, accessed 12 January 2007. On Tokyo, see for example "So You Want to Live in a World Capital . . .: In Tokyo, Quantity Without Quality," *World Press Review* (October 1988): 34–35; Eric Talmadge, "Fearful of Earthquake Damage, Japan May Build New Capital Outside," *Milwaukee Journal Sentinel*, 12 September 1999.

27 Ross King, "Re-Writing the City: Putrajaya as Representation," *Journal of Urban Design* 12, 1 (February 2007): 117–138.

28 Ibid.

29 *The Master Plan for Abuja, the New Federal Capital of Nigeria* (Lagos: Federal Capital Development Authority, 15 February 1979), 4.

30 *Abuja Master Plan*. The master plan, by International Planning Associates, was produced as a joint venture between Archi-systems International, the Planning Research Corporation, and Wallace, McHarg, Roberts, and Todd. For detail on this team, and on the roles of Doxiadis Associates and the Milton Keynes Development Corporation, see Nnamdi Elleh, Abuja: *The Last Debate on Monumental Modernist Urban Design* (Pretoria: University of South Africa Press, forthcoming), Chapter 5.

31 See Elleh, *Abuja: The Last Debate*, and Nnamdi Elleh, *Abuja: The Single Most Ambitious Urban Design Project of the 20th Century* (Weimar: VDG, 2001).

32 See "Nigeria's Road to Abuja," *West Africa*, 18 September 1978, 1825; "The retreat from Lagos," *New African*, February 1979, 47–48; Jimoh Omo-Fadaka, "Abuja: Caravans Arrive at the New Capital," *New African*, October 1982, 3; Elleh, *Abuja: The Last Debate*, introduction.

33 For a brief historical overview of such tensions, see Kole Omotoso, "The Search for National Unity," *West Africa*, 30 September 1985, 2021–2022. See also Lee Lescaze, "Nigerian Stability Threatened by Schism among Moslems," *Wall Street Journal*, 13 August 1987, 14.

34 "Capital Folly of Nigeria," *Architect's Journal*, November 1985, 70. In addition, since the major access roads to Abuja come from Kaduna, this gave northern-based contractors an advantage in obtaining work. See also, Elleh, *Abuja: The Last Debate*, Chapter 3.

35 *Abuja Master Plan*, 27.

36 Ibid., 78; Elleh, *Abuja: The Last Debate*, Chapters 1 and 2.

37 *Abuja Master Plan*, 27.

38 Elleh, *Abuja: The Last Debate*, Chapter 5; *Abuja Master Plan*, 27. Elleh notes that some of the original inhabitants of the Abuja site who were not relocated have attempted to claim ownership over parts of the Federal Capital Territory.

39 For an analysis of Nigeria's American-style constitution, see James S. Read, "The New Constitution of Nigeria, 1979: 'The Washington Model'?" *Journal of African Law* 23 (1979): 131–174. Large parts of the constitution are reprinted here. See also Claude S. Phillips, "Nigeria's New

Political Institutions," *Journal of Modern African Studies* 18 (1980): 1–22.

40 See, for example, the editorial "Change and Accountability," *West Africa*, 2 September 1985, 1787.

41 Major General Mamman Vatsa, cited in Mohammed Haruna, "Abuja: A Capital in Waiting," *West Africa*, 7 October 1985, 2090. This same General Vatsa later became minister for the Federal Capital Territory, after having published a volume of poetry about Abuja (see "Who's Who in the SMC," *New African*, March 1985, 53). Vatsa's assessment of Abuja's negative symbolism seemed to be a common view in the mid-1980s. The political scientist Jonathan Moore, writing in 1984, describes the capital as "a symbol of waste, mismanagement and corruption": "The Political History of Nigeria's New Capital," *Journal of Modern African Studies* 22 (1984): 168.

42 Support for the new capital was not undisputed, however. In the election campaign of 1979 Chief Obafemi Awolowo, with a Yoruba power base that included Lagos, maintained that, if elected, he would hire the Walt Disney Corporation to convert the Abuja site into an amusement park (cited in Moore, "The Political History of Nigeria's New Capital," 173). On Buhari and Babangida, see Elleh, *Abuja: The Last Debate*, Chapter 3.

43 See, for example, "Nigeria: IBB Speaks on Coup Plot," *West Africa*, 9–15 July 1990, 2073; "Nigeria: Business as Usual," *West Africa*, 7–13 May 1990, 756; Paxton Idowu, "A Bloody Attempt: The Story of the Eighth Plot to Change the Government of Nigeria by Force," *West Africa*, 30 April–6 May 1990, 696; "Nigeria: Countdown to 1992," *West Africa*, 11 April 1988, 659; "Nigeria: Grassroots Elections Begin," *West Africa*, 4–10 June 1990, 949; Bola Olowo, "Painless Succession?: The Reality of Third Republic Politics Is Different from the Dream," *West Africa*, 6–12 August 1990, 2234; "Nigeria: Pondering the Future," *West Africa*, 1 April 1985, 603; Ad'Obe Obe, "Nigeria: The Political Debate," *West Africa*, 14 April 1986, 769; Ikenga Nuta, "Nigeria: The Diarchy Proposition," *West Africa*, 1 April 1985, 610; and Olugbenga Ayeni, "Who Succeeds IBB [Babangida]?: Dormant Themes Underline Search for Third Republic President," *West Africa*, 20–26 August 1990, 2316. For an account of early difficulties encountered by government officials in their move to Abuja, see Kolawole Ilori, "Trauma of Moving: External Affairs Officers Battle with Accommodation Problems in Abuja," *Newswatch*, 10 September 1990, 21–22. On the 2007 elections, see "A First in Nigeria: A Peaceful Succession of Power," *New York Times*, 30 May 2007.

44 Elleh, *Abuja: The Last Debate*, Chapter 4.

45 Moore, "The Political History of Nigeria's New Capital," 175; Norimitsu Onishi, "Abuja Journal; Nigeria's Showplace Awaits 'Big Man' from U.S.," *New York Times*, 25 August 2000. An informal spatial census of Abuja's churches and mosques in the central districts of the city, based on studies of aerial photographs, suggests that these structures are rather widely dispersed in the city; see Ifeoma N. Ebo, "City Design and Social Exclusion: Abuja, Nigeria in Review" (Unpublished master's thesis, Massachusetts Institute of Technology, June 2006), 47–48.

46 *Abuja Master Plan*, 102–103.

47 Omar Take, "Abuja, the New Capital of Nigeria, and the Urban Design of Its Central Area," in *Continuity and Change: Design Strategies for Large-Scale Urban Development* (Cambridge: Aga Khan Program for Islamic Architecture, 1984), 54.

48 *Abuja Master Plan*, 9.

49 Ibid., 6.

50 Take, "Abuja, the New Capital," 54. See also Clifford D. May, "Nigerian Ruler Tells Diplomats Why He Took Over," *New York Times*, 5 January 1984, A9.

51 Elleh, *Abuja: The Single Most Ambitious Urban Design*, 49–50.

52 *Abuja Master Plan*, chapter 4.

53 Ibid., 61.

54 Ibid., 82.

55 Ibid., 62.

56 Ibid., 65–66.

57 Ibid., 103–104.

58 Ibid., 67; Elleh, *Abuja: The Single Most Ambitious Urban Design Project*, 10–13.

59 *Abuja Master Plan*, 69.

60 Ibid., 100.

61 Ibid., 128.

62 Ibid., 104.

63 Take, "Abuja, the New Capital," 55.

64 Ibid., 54.

65 On the role of the Tange firm, see Elleh, *Abuja: The Last Debate*, chaper 6. See also Elleh, Abuja: *The Single Most Ambitious Urban Design*, 44–45. Tange's firm was chosen over Toronto-based Project Planning Associates, the firm that had

recently produced the Master Plan for Dodoma, Tanzania.

66 Elleh, *Abuja: The Single Most Ambitious Urban Design*, 75.

67 Roger Simmonds, interview with the author, 8 May 1987. See also Olu Sule, "The Nigerian New Capital City: From Lagos to Abuja," in E. Y. Galantay, A. K. Constandense, and T. Ohba, eds., *New Towns World-Wide* (The Hague: International Federation for Housing and Planning, 1985), 344.

68 "'Abuja Is Now a Reality,'" interview with Air Commodore Hamza Abdullahi, conducted by Okechukwu Ifionu, *African Concord*, 5 February 1987, 17.

69 Ibrahim Usman Jibril, "Resettlement Issues, Squatter Settlements and the Problems of Land Administration in Abuja, Nigeria's Federal Capital," Paper delivered at the 5th FIG Regional Conference, Accra, Ghana, 8–11 March 2006, http://www.fig.net/pub/accra/papers/ts18/ts18_01_jibril.pdf, accessed 10 January 2007; Roger Cohen, "Abuja Journal; Marble Mogul Caters to the Nigerian Capital's Elite," *New York Times*, 30 July 1998; Lydia Polgreen, "Abuja Journal; In a Dream City, a Nightmare for the Common Man," *New York Times*, 13 December 2006. For one account of the controversies over evictions, see: "Break the Silence on the Evictions: Defend Housing Rights in Nigeria!," International Alliance of Inhabitants website, http://www.habitants.org/article/articleview/1577/1/439/, accessed 10 January 2007. For an earlier description of the horrific conditions existing in Nyanya Camp, outside of Abuja, see Okechukwu Ifionu, "Nyanya: Just the Place for a Holiday!" *African Concord*, 5 February 1987, 17.

70 *National Capital Master Plan: Dodoma, Tanzania* [Dodoma Master Plan], prepared for the Capital Development Authority, United Republic of Tanzania Under the Agreement dated 1 August 1974, by Project Planning Associates, Toronto, Canada, May 1976. This team, led by Macklyn Hancock, was selected over bids from Doxiadis Associates and other groups of planning consultants from Japan and West Germany. Project Planning Associates had already worked in Tanzania on the 1968 master plan for Dar es Salaam, leading one critic in Tanzania to complain that their reemployment suggested that "the incompatibility of Western planning ideology and contradictions of the previous Master Plan had failed to be recognized" (cited in Peter Siebolds and Florian Steinberg, "Dodoma: A Future African Brasília?: Capitalist Town Planning and African Socialism," *Habitat International* 5 (1981): 683; United Republic of Tanzania, 2002 Population and Housing Census, http://www.tanzania.go.tz/census/districts/dodomaurban.htm, accessed 30 January 2007. See also Dirk Bolt, "Dodoma: The First Decade," in Galantay, Constandense, and Ohba, eds., *New Towns World-Wide*, 353–354.

71 *Dodoma Master Plan*, 11.

72 Ibid., 9, and Bolt, "Dodoma: The First Decade," 351–352. For a more detailed account of Dodoma's development, see A. M. Hayuma, "Dodoma: The Planning and Building of the New Capital City of Tanzania," *Habitat International* 5 (1981): 653–680.

73 Philip Marmo, "A One-Party State: The Role of Parliament in Tanzania," *The Parliamentarian* (April 1989); Donatella Lorch, "A Joyful but Anxious Vote in Tanzania," *New York Times*, 29 October 1995; Bruce E. Heilman and Paul J. Kaiser, "Religion, Identity and Politics in Tanzania," *Third World Quarterly* 23, 4 (2002): 694. For a less sanguine account of Tanzanian race relations, see Ronald Aminzade, "From Race to Citizenship: The Indigenization Debate in Post-Socialist Tanzania," *Studies in Comparative International Development* 38, 1 (Spring 2003): 43–63.

74 Ngila Mwase and Mary Raphael, "The 1995 Presidential Elections in Tanzania," *The Round Table* (2001): 245–269; Vibeke Wang, "The Accountability Function of Parliament in New Democracies: Tanzanian Perspectives" Working Paper 2005: 2 (Bergen Norway: Chr. Michelson Institute for Development Studies and Human Rights, 2005); "The Road to the New Capital," *Africa* 120 (August 1981): 89. This article points out that Dodoma is probably the world's first "elected" capital. 2005 election statistics are reported in Bilal Abdul-Aziz, "New Parliament Meets in Dodoma," *IPP Media*, 27 December 2005, http://www.ippmedia.com/ipp/guardian/2005/12/27/56634.html, accessed 12 January 2007.

75 *Dodoma Master Plan*, 11.

76 Ibid., 9.

77 Ibid., 86.

78 James C. Scott, *Seeing Like a State: How Certain Schemes to Improve the Human Condition Have Failed* (New Haven: Yale University Press,

1998), 247; "Tanzania: Did Socialism Fail?," *New African*, May 1985, 25; Tim Kelsall, "Governance, Democracy and Recent Political Struggles in Mainland Tanzania," *Commonwealth & Comparative Politics* 41, 2 (July 2003): 65, 66.

79 "Tanzania: Did Socialism Fail?," *New African*, May 1985, 25. See also Lorch, "A Joyful but Anxious Vote"; "A Father of Socialism Now Sires Shift to Capitalism," *New York Times*, 19 February 1992. Post-socialist Tanzania has faced increased conflict over race relations, as the "race-blind socialist experiment" has given way to tensions, both within CCM and internationally, over indigenization (especially the role of wealthy Asian-Tanzanians) during a period of economic and political liberalization; Aminzade, "From Race to Citizenship," 43–63.

80 In this regard, the Dodoma plan is not unrelated to the polynuclear proposal for Brasília by the Roberto Brothers, which was rejected in favor of the Costa submission.

81 *Dodoma Master Plan*, vii. Arguably, the first nonmonumental capital city plan could be Mayer's original plan for Chandigarh, though the intended modesty of Dodoma's plan is much more marked.

82 Ibid., viii.

83 Ibid., 15.

84 Ibid., 13.

85 Ibid., 69–70. As it turned out, however, Dodoma has suffered water shortages and been criticized as an unsustainable intervention into a rural landscape. See Nick Van Vliet, "Dodoma, the New Capital of Tanzania: A Case of Non-Sustainable Development," *Landscape Architectural Review* 11, 4 (October 1990): 13–18; Aldo Lupala and John Lupala, "The Conflict Between Attempts to Green Arid Cities and Urban Livelihoods: The Case of Dodoma, Tanzania," *Journal of Political Ecology* 10 (2003): 25–35.

86 As of 1990, the population had more than doubled from the base of 50,000 but still lagged behind the projected pace of increase. Author's conversation with James Rossant, June 1990. Growth has continued apace, but increasingly little of it has had much relationship to the broader Dodoma plan.

87 Lupala and Lupala, "The Conflict," 31–32; *Dodoma Master Plan*, 69.

88 Ibid., 70, 50.

89 Capital Development Authority, *Urban Design for the National Capital Centre*, prepared by the Tanzania Capital Development Authority and Conklin and Rossant, June 1980.

90 *Dodoma Master Plan*, 70–71.

91 *National Capital Centre Plan*, ix.

92 *Dodoma Master Plan*, 63, 71.

93 Hayuma, "Dodoma: The Planning and Building," 675.

94 Siebolds and Steinberg, "Dodoma: A Future African Brasília?," 686.

95 Donald Appleyard, *Urban Design and Architectural Policies for Dodoma, New Capital of Tanzania* (University of California, Berkeley: Institute of Urban and Regional Development, 1979), 22.

96 Hayuma, "Dodoma: The Planning and Building," 675.

97 Appleyard, *Urban Design for Dodoma*, 71.

98 Janet Berry Hess, "Envisioning *Ujamaa*: Architecture in Dodoma and Dar es Salaam," in *Art and Architecture of Postcolonial Africa* (Jefferson, N.C.: McFarland & Company, 2006), 125; Bilal Abdul-Aziz, "Kikiwete Inaugurates New Parliament Building," IPPMedia, 13 June 2006, http://216.69.164.44/ipp/guardian/2006/06/13/68263.html, accessed 12 January 2007.

99 Edward Shils, "The Fortunes of Constitutional Government in the Political Development of the New States," in *Center and Periphery: Essays in Macrosociology* (Chicago: University of Chicago Press, 1975), 469.

100 Ibid., 474–475.

101 For a discussion of some of the ways that "traditions" have been "invented," see Eric Hobsbawm and Terrence Ranger, eds., *The Invention of Tradition* (Cambridge: Cambridge University Press, 1983).

CHAPTER 6 PAPUA NEW GUINEA'S CONCRETE HAUS TAMBARAN

1 *The National Parliament Building*, booklet issued "In Commemoration of the Opening By His Royal Highness, The Prince of Wales," 7 August 1984, 13.

2 I am grateful to Professor Balwant Saini, who served as one of the judges of the official competition, for clarifying certain aspects of this complex situation (conversation of 28 April 1988). In addition to an article in the Air Niugini flight magazine and the commemoration booklet, the design appears to have been published only

once: a now-defunct British engineering journal shows a top view of the model and gives a few construction details. See "Papua [*sic*] Parliament Building Nears Completion," *Consulting Engineer (UK)* (November/December 1983): 29. The building receives much fuller coverage in Pamela C. Rosi, "Papua New Guinea's New Parliament House: A Contested National Symbol," *The Contemporary Pacific* 3, 2 (1991). See also Rosi, "Bung Wantaim: The Role of the National Arts School in Creating National Culture and Identity in Papua New Guinea" (Unpublished doctoral dissertation, Bryn Mawr College) (Ann Arbor, Mich: University Microfilms International, 1994), 501–542.

3 "Papua New Guinea Parliament House Design Brief," prepared by the Parliamentary Design Committee for the National Executive Council, December 1975.
4 Ibid., 36–37.
5 *The National Parliament Building*, 11.
6 Ibid.
7 Peddle Thorp & Harvey, "Final Report on the Papua New Guinea Parliament House," by Ron Burgess, Project Architect, 1984, section 2.
8 Brian Holloway, "Letter of Transmission to Prime Minister Michael Somare," in "Design Brief," 5.
9 "City Centre Plan Revival," *PNG Post-Courier*, 27 August 2003, 5; Jessie Lapou, "Bid to Speed Up Park Work," *PNG Post-Courier*, 31 January 2006, 7. Meanwhile, many of the Waigani structures other than the Parliament House itself have suffered serious neglect in the decades since independence. The "badly underfunded" National Museum and Art Gallery has faced repeated break-ins and thefts. One Waigani office building, Marea Haus (known because of its appearance as the "Pineapple Building") was "left to rundown and rot for several years after it was condemned as a fire death trap," and was described in 2001 as "completely vandalized and stinking" at the time of proposed renovations. Similarly, the Central Government Building in Waigani was abandoned for five years during the late 1990s after its "walls began to fall apart." Enterprising townspeople soon colonized it to grow taro and cassava before this building, too, was proposed for renovation. Even the National Library, an independence gift from Australia, fell into significant disrepair and required a major bailout from the Australians as a thirtieth anniversary present in 2005. "Museum Robbed," *PNG Post-Courier*, 25 January 2002, 7; Jessie Lapou, "Museum 'Badly Underfunded,'" *PNG Post-Courier*, 10 August 2005; "Facelift for the Pineapple," *PNG Post-Courier*, 13 November 2001, 3; Beverly Puton, "Govt House Now Garden," *PNG Post-Courier*, 8 August 2003, 4; Barnabas Orere, "National Library Needs Attention," *PNG Post-Courier*, 22 June 2004, 11; "News on Library Welcome Indeed," *PNG Post-Courier*, 2 September 2005, 10.
10 Judy Newman, "Parliament House," *Paradise: Air Niugini Magazine*, 1984, 9. Following construction of the new Parliament House, the old structure in downtown Port Moresby fell into disuse and disrepair, and eventually became inhabited by squatters. In 2005, the National Capital District Commission issued a demolition notice. "Sir Pita Moves to Fast Track Project," *PNG Post-Courier*, 4 June 2001; Oseah Philemon, "G-G 'Scandalized,'" *PNG Post-Courier*, 10 August 2005, 3; "Retired Staff Told to Move Out," *PNG Post-Courier*, 24 August 2005, 6; Jesse Lapou, "Museum Boss Mum on House Renovation Fund," *PNG Post-Courier*, 31 August 2005, 7.
11 "Speaker's Foreword," *The National Parliament Building*. As evidence of the magnitude of the educative task involved in introducing constitutional democracy, preparations for the elections of 1964 entailed five hundred patrols visiting 12,000 villages, distributing pamphlets in many languages, showing films, charts, and drawings, and giving talks on the processes of democratic elections (*The National Parliament Building*, 5).
12 Ibid., 5–6.
13 "Design Brief," 5.
14 Ibid.
15 Ibid., 11.
16 Bernard Narokobi's writings since independence constitute the most thorough attempt to think through and articulate a notion of Papua New Guinean cultural unity, what Narokobi calls "the Melanesian Way." See, especially, *The Melanesian Way: Total Cosmic Vision of Life* (Boroko: Institute of Papua New Guinea Studies, 1980), and *Life and Leadership in Melanesia* (Suva, Fiji: Institute of Pacific Studies, 1983).
17 "Narokobi: The Political Arena Beckons," Papua New Guinea *Post-Courier*, 29 May 1981, 5.
18 "Design Brief," 46.
19 Ibid., 47.
20 Ibid.
21 Ibid., 48.

22 For an account of the appearance and function of the haus tambaran in the villages of the Maprik area, see René Gardi, *Tambaran: An Encounter with Cultures in Decline in New Guinea*, trans. Eric Northcott (London: Constable, 1960), 135–147.

23 Originally estimated to cost about 7 million kina ($10 million), estimates had risen to K12.9 million by mid-1980 when Peddle Thorp & Harvey came to the job. Extra costs associated with a fire sprinkler system, furniture and fittings, consultants' fees, and changes to the design of the prime minister's offices necessitated by shifting priorities during two changes of government helped to push final costs to approximately K24 million ($30 million). See John Moses, "K7.4m Parliament House Needs Scrutiny by Cabinet" [letter], Papua New Guinea *Post-Courier*, 10 November 1976; "House of Park [sic] to Now Cost K11 Million," *Post-Courier*, 1 March 1979, 1; James Birrell, "Cost of New Parliament Could Be Kept Down" [letter], *Post-Courier*, 17 April 1979; "Parliament House Quotes In," *Post-Courier*, 23 January 1980, 1; "Govt Re-Thinks on Parliament House Tenders," *Post-Courier*, 26 May 1980; "House Takes Shape," *Post-Courier*, 30 March 1981, 1; "Signing for New House Today," *Post-Courier*, 18 February 1981, 1; "Long Row over Price," *Post-Courier*, 6 August 1984, 12; and "Major Rehash for 'Big Baby'," *Post-Courier*, 6 August 1984, 13.

24 "Long Row over Price," *Post-Courier*, 6 August 1984, 12.

25 Charles Hawksley, "Papua New Guinea at Thirty: Late Decolonisation and the Political Economy of Nation-Building," *Third World Quarterly* 27, 1 (2006): 161–164, 166; Laura Zimmer-Tamakoshi, ed., *Modern Papua New Guinea* (Kirksville, Mo.: Truman State University Press, 1998), 4–7.

26 Peter Larmour, "State and Society in Papua New Guinea," in Zimmer-Tamokoshi, ed., *Modern Papua New Guinea*, 21.

27 Hawksley, "Papua New Guinea at Thirty," 166; Zimmer-Tamokoshi, ed., *Modern Papua New Guinea*, 7.

28 Hawksley, "Papua New Guinea at Thirty," 162–163, 167–169; Sinclair Dinnen, "Law, Order, and State," in Zimmer-Tamokoshi, ed., *Modern Papua New Guinea*, 333–350; Sean Dorney, "Why Is Papua New Guinea so Hard to Govern?," Australian Institute of International Affairs, 1998, http://www.aiia.asn.au/news/dorney.html, accessed 20 November 2007.

29 *The National Parliament Building*, vii.

30 Ibid., 14.

31 While both of the haus tambarans depicted in Hogan's sketch are East Sepik Province types, the dominant upswept one which inspired the Parliament House main facade is similar to spirit houses found in and around Maprik itself, whereas the one with the exposed poles—which gets fused into the middle of the Parliament House—is similar to one found in Tongwinjamb village, located about forty miles southwest of Maprik. For a well-illustrated discussion of several Sepik-area haus tambaran forms, see *The Sepik-Ramu: An Introduction* (Boroko: PNG National Museum, 1988).

32 Osmar White, *Parliament of a Thousand Tribes: Papua New Guinea: The Story of an Emerging Nation* (Melbourne: Wren Books, 1972), 195. Somare's home village is Karau, located in the Murik Lakes area in the Sepik delta, relatively distant from Maprik.

33 P. Loveday and E. P. Wolters, *Parties and Parliament in Papua New Guinea 1964–1975: Two Studies* (Boroko, Papua New Guinea: Institute of Applied Social and Economic Research, 1976), 70.

34 Rosi, "PNG's New Parliament House," 319, n. 1.

35 White, *Parliament of a Thousand Tribes*, 205.

36 Ibid., 224.

37 See Rosi, "PNG's New Parliament House," 297.

38 "Special House," Papua New Guinea *Post-Courier*, 19 March 1981, 3. Lest one think that the question of architectural provenance is a matter only for specialists, it may be pointed out that this local newspaper's brief description of the new diplomatic edifice described it as "styled like a Sepik Haus Tambaran." See also http://www.pngembassy.org/culture.html and http://www.pngtourism.org.pg/png/export/sites/TPA/provinces/ncd/ncd.htm, accessed 29 June 2006.

39 The term *national artist* used in the National Parliament Building Commemoration booklet does little more than beg the question of what makes the artist "national." Presumably, it refers to the national composition of the participants at the National Arts School.

40 Rosi, "PNG's New Parliament House," 300.

41 Images of birds and the elaborate use of their feathers for adornment are central to the ritual activities of many tribes in PNG. For a more complete analysis of the iconography of this facade, see Rosi, "PNG's New Parliament House," 300–301.

42 Newman, "Parliament House," 5.

43 Some of the lintels of the traditional Maprik-area haus tambaran also feature a series of identically sized and deliberately repetitive carved wooden heads, though these often make magnificent use of vibrant colors.
44 Gardi, *Tambaran*, 142.
45 *The National Parliament Building*, 22–24.
46 Rosi, "PNG's New Parliament House," 302–303.
47 *The National Parliament Building*, 8.
48 Newman, "Parliament House," 5–6.
49 Ibid., 6.
50 According to Newman, and corroborated by the reports of other travelers, this is how the building is frequently referred to in rural areas distant from Port Moresby.
51 Alan Stretton, *The Building Industry in Papua New Guinea: The Industry Structure and Labour Market* (Boroko, PNG: Institute of Applied Social and Economic Research, 1984), 138.
52 Newman, "Parliament House," 8.
53 Ibid., 9. I have not been able to get an update on this factory's operations.
54 Cited in ibid., 8.
55 Ibid., 8–9.
56 Pama Anio, "For a National Monument, Add a Golden Gleam to 'Liberty Hill,'" *Post-Courier*, 27 July 1985, 5.
57 N. Leat, "House of Fools" [letter], *Post-Courier*, 20 July 1984, 4.
58 Michael Somare, "Viewpoint—Symbol of Our Nation," *Post-Courier*, 10 July 1984.
59 Angwi Hriehwazi, "Students Get 10 Minutes," *Post-Courier*, 7 August 1984.
60 Ibid.
61 "Parliament Built on 'Stolen Land,'" *Post-Courier*, 7 August 1984.
62 "'Somare Ignores North Solomons,'" *Post-Courier*, 13 August 1984, 17.
63 "The Truth," *Post-Courier*, 10 September 1985, 3.
64 "Tradition Is 'Our Guide,'" *Post-Courier*, 8 August 1984, 2.
65 Somare, "Viewpoint—Symbol of Our Nation."
66 "'A Fitting Symbol:' 20,000 Hear Charles Open New House," *Post-Courier*, 8 August 1984, 3.
67 "The Worth of that House" [Editorial], *Post-Courier*, 7 August 1984.
68 *The National Parliament Building*, 19–20.
69 See *Gigibori: A Magazine of Papua New Guinea Cultures* 1 (December 1974): iv, published by the Institute of Papua New Guinea Studies in association with Niugini Press, Boroko, PNG. For a more extended discussion of the role of gigibori in Suau culture, see Cecil Abel, "Suau Aesthetics," *Gigibori* 1 (December 1974): 34–35.
70 See, for example, Benetta Jules-Rossette, *The Messages of Tourist Art: An African Semiotic System in Comparative Perspective* (New York: Plenum, 1984).
71 Ibid., 1.
72 Nelson H. H. Graburn, ed., *Ethnic and Tourist Arts: Cultural Expressions from the Fourth World* (Berkeley: University of California Press, 1976), 32. For a similar critique that is grounded specifically in the Papua New Guinea context, see Peter Kros, "Tourism: Does It Help to Preserve Our Culture?" *Gigibori* 1 (December 1974): 28–29. There is also a gender dimension to this phenomenon. As one critic puts it, part of the subjugation of women in PNG is due to "the sentimental nationalism of urban elite males who idealize the lives of village women and fail to see that 'harking back to a utopian "traditionalism"' is unfair to both rural and urban females who, in common with one another, continue to suffer economic, social, cultural and political oppression" (Zimmer-Tamakoshi, ed., *Modern Papua New Guinea*, 11).
73 "Haus Tambaran Sold for K20,000," *PNG Post-Courier*, 16 July 2004, 7; Wanita Wakus, "Haus Tambaran Sale Concerns," *PNG Post-Courier*, 12 August 2004, 6.
74 Ernest Gellner, *Nations and Nationalism* (Ithaca, N.Y.: Cornell University Press, 1983), 123, 57.
75 This assessment of the building's popularity is based on anecdotal evidence from my own visit and from the reports of a few travelers with whom I have conferred. I have not, however, heard of any more systematic attempt to judge national feeling about the building, though it would seem that knowledge of its existence is quite widespread.
76 Philip Gibbs, "Political Discourse and Religious Narratives of Church and State in Papua New Guinea." State Society and Governance in Melanesia Working Papers, Australian National University, Canberra, SSGM Working Paper 2005/1. See also *PNG Post-Courier* "Viewpoints" (27 June 2000, 10; 3 July 2000, 10; 5 September 2000).
77 Despite strong rhetoric about the equality between men and women expressed at independence, few women have gained seats in parliament and there have been periods with no women parliamentarians at all.

See Martha Macintyre, "The Persistence of Inequality: Women in Papua New Guinea Since Independence," in Zimmer-Tamakoshi, ed., *Modern Papua New Guinea*, 211–230.

CHAPTER 7 SRI LANKA'S ISLAND PARLIAMENT

1 Mohan Ram, *Sri Lanka: The Fractured Island* (New Delhi: Penguin, 1989), 59; Stanley J. Tambiah, *Sri Lanka: Ethnic Fratricide and the Dismantling of Democracy* (Chicago: University of Chicago Press, 1986), 39–41; and K. M. de Silva, *Managing Ethnic Tensions in Multi-Ethnic Societies* (Lanham, Md.: University Press of America, 1986), 287–304.
2 Mary Anne Weaver, "The Gods and the Stars—A Reporter at Large," *The New Yorker* (21 March 1988), 46; and Tambiah, *Sri Lanka: Ethnic Fratricide*, 39.
3 Weaver, "The Gods and the Stars," 58; Tambiah, *Sri Lanka: Ethnic Fratricide*, 4–5. Other accounts of Sri Lankan social and political tensions include the books of K. M. de Silva as well as Chelvadurai Manogaran, *Ethnic Conflict and Reconciliation in Sri Lanka* (Honolulu: University of Hawaii Press, 1987), Stanley J. Tambiah, "Ethnic Fratricide in Sri Lanka: An Update," in Remo Guidieri et al., eds., *Ethnicities and Nations: Processes of Interethnic Relations in Latin America, Southeast Asia, and the Pacific* (Austin, Tex.: Rothko Chapel, 1988), K. M. de Silva "Independent Again: The Trials and Tribulations of Nationhood since 1948," and Mallika Wanigasundara, "Modern Sri Lanka: Economic and Political Success Stories of the 1980s," in *Sri Lanka* (Englewood Cliffs, N.J.: Prentice Hall/APA Productions, 1984), 55–65.
4 Tambiah, "Ethnic Fratricide Update," 294.
5 Weaver, "The Gods and the Stars," 40.
6 These Tamils were reenfranchised only in 1989 (Ram, *Sri Lanka*, 82).
7 Ram, *Sri Lanka*, 43.
8 Ibid., 38–41; Tambiah, "Ethnic Fratricide Update," 295; and Weaver, "The Gods and the Stars," 40. The constitution of 1978 maintained the status of Sinhala as *the* official language, but it also, for the first time since independence, recognized Tamil as a "national" language (de Silva, "Independent Again," 297).
9 Ram, *Sri Lanka*, 53.
10 Weaver, "The Gods and the Stars," 57. Following the elections of February 1989, Tamil parties won control of thirteen independent parliamentary seats in the Jaffna Peninsula, thereby regaining a small foothold in a parliament still dominated by Premadasa's United National Party. Barbara Crossette, "Amid the Killings, Sri Lanka Hopes for New Start," *New York Times*, 3 March 1989.
11 Barbara Crossette, "Blood, Alienation and Chauvinism Accompany Sri Lankans to Polls," *New York Times*, 17 December 1988.
12 Barbara Crossette, "For Sri Lanka, an Election with a Sense of Disintegration: Violence Confronts the New President," *New York Times*, 25 December 1988, E4. See also Ram, *Sri Lanka*, 104–105.
13 David Robson, *Geoffrey Bawa: The Complete Works* (London: Thames and Hudson, 2002). For a bibliography of work on Bawa's architecture, see http://www.geoffreybawa.com/bibliography.php. One Colombo journalist describes Bawa's appeal as follows: "It had become fashionable among the Western-educated social elite to have a house designed by Geoffrey Bawa because his houses were different from the hideous so-called American style dwellings of the new rich in the post independence period. Bawa brought back traditional Sinhala and Dutch colonial architectural styles into his buildings." Karel Roberts, "The New Parliament Complex, Sri Jayawardhanapura, Kotte," *The Sunday Observer* (Colombo), 21 March 1982.
14 Geoffrey Bawa, "Statement by the Architect," in Brian Brace Taylor, ed., *Geoffrey Bawa* (Singapore: MIMAR, 1986), 16; Robson, *Geoffrey Bawa*, 15. In its purest meaning, a Sri Lankan "Burgher" is someone who can claim an unbroken paternal lineage back to a European employee of the Dutch East India Company, and a "Moor" connotes a person of mixed Arab descent (see Robson, *Geoffrey Bawa*, 273).
15 For an overview of Sri Lankan architectural history see, for example, R. Raven-Hart, *Ceylon: History in Stone* (Colombo: Associated Newspapers of Ceylon, 1964), and Ronald Lewcock, Barbara Sansoni, and Laki Senanayake, *The Architecture of an Island* (Colombo: Barefoot, 1998).
16 Bawa, "Statement by the Architect," 16.
17 See J. M. Richards, "Geoffrey Bawa," *MIMAR* 19 (January–March 1986): 46.
18 Brian Brace Taylor, "A House is a Garden," in Taylor, *Geoffrey Bawa*, 15.
19 "Parliament, Kotte, Colombo," in *MIMAR* 19: 59.
20 Rupert Scott, "Parliament Building, Sri Lanka"

Architectural Review 157 (May 1983): 21–22, and William J. R. Curtis, "Towards an Authentic Regionalism," *MIMAR* 19: 30–31.

21 Interview with former prime minister Ranil Wickremesinghe, April 2006; "Sri Lanka Attack Misses President," *New York Times*, 19 August 1987, 1. According to Ronald Lewcock, the consensus (at least among architects in Colombo) is that the death toll and damage could easily have been much higher and that architect Geoffrey Bawa's "soft finishes saved the day." Ranil Wickremesinghe, who as an MP was present during the attack, adds that the intruder accessed the parliamentary chamber though a room used for bringing in soft drinks to the parliamentarians. The grenade bounced off a table with the president at the center, then exploded on the other side of the room (Wickremesinghe interview, 2006).

22 C. Anjalendran and Rajiv Wanasundara, "Trends and Transitions: A Review of Styles and Influences on the Built Form in Sri Lanka (1940–1990)," *Architecture + Design* 7 (March–April 1990): 32. For a larger history of Colombo and its complex and evolving identities, see Nihal Perera, *Society and Space: Colonialism, Nationalism, and Postcolonial Identity in Sri Lanka* (Boulder, Colo.: Westview Press, 1998).

23 James S. Duncan, *The City as Text: The Politics of Landscape Interpretation in the Kandyan Kingdom* (Cambridge: Cambridge University Press, 1990), 27, 182.

24 Steven Kemper, *The Presence of the Past: Chronicles, Politics, and Culture in Singhala Life* (Ithaca, N.Y.: Cornell University Press, 1991), 173; Jayewardene, quoted in Kemper, 173–174; Nihal Perera, "The Making of a National Capital: Conflicts, Contradictions, and Contestations in Sri Jayawardhanapura," in Michael E. Geisler, ed., *National Symbols, Fractured Identities: Contesting the National Narrative* (Middlebury, Vt.: Middlebury College Press, 2005), 248; C. Anjalendran, "Data on Parliament," 10 November 1983. For a view of Hindu temple complexes in South India that are based on different principles of organization see, for example, Susan Lewandowski, "The Hindu Temple in South India," in Anthony D. King, ed., *Buildings and Society: Essays on the Social Development of the Built Environment* (London: Routledge & Kegan Paul, 1980), 123–150.

25 Tambiah, "Ethnic Fratricide Update," 295, 306; Kemper, *The Presence of the Past*, 7.

26 Duncan, *The City as Text*, 31.

27 Senarath Panawatta, "A Glimpse into the History of Sri Jayawardhanapura," *The Sunday Observer* (Colombo) (March/April 1982).

28 New Capital Project Division, Urban Development Authority, "Master Plan for Sri Jayawardhanapura," 4.

29 Panawatta, "The History of Sri Jayawardhanapura."

30 Ibid.; http://www.priu.gov.lk/Parliament/ParliamentHistory.html, accessed 28 August 2006.

31 Wilfred M. Gunasekera, "The Glory that Was—and Is—Sri Jayawardhanapura," *The Sunday Observer* (Colombo), 25 April 1982.

32 "Master Plan," 46.

33 Roberts, "The New Parliament Complex."

34 Anjalendran and Wanasundara, "Trends and Transitions," 33.

35 "Master Plan," 44.

36 Department of Census and Statistics, Sri Lanka, *Census of Population and Housing, 2001*; http://www.statistics.gov.lk/census2001/index.html. The 2001 national census (the first one conducted in twenty years) counted 77 percent of Sri Lanka's residents as Buddhists, but was unable to collect data in certain Tamil-dominated areas, so the overall non-Buddhist population in the country is certainly higher than reported.

37 "Master Plan," 4.

38 Ibid., 45.

39 Perera, "The Making of a National Capital," 265; Department of Census and Statistics, Sri Lanka, *Census of Population and Housing, 2001*; http://www.statistics.gov.lk/census2001/population/district/t002b.htm. Residents of Sri Jayawardhanapura Kotte were found to be 81 percent Buddhist and 87 percent Sinhalese. By contrast, however, the urban population of the Colombo Muncipal District housed a Buddhist minority, with large populations of both Muslim and Hindu residents.

40 Perera, "The Making of a National Capital," 251–252, 257; Robson, *Geoffrey Bawa*, 146–153.

CHAPTER 8 PRECAST ARABISM FOR KUWAIT

1 The choice of the term *Persian Gulf* or *Arabian Gulf* is, of course, itself controversial, often indicative of perceptions about the preferred relative hegemony of Iran versus the Arab states.

2 This figure, a "tightly guarded secret," was reported in Milton Viorst, "Out of the Desert," *The New Yorker*, 16 May 1988, 44.

3 See Ahmed Al Jarallah, "Premier Vows Change; Focus on Dialogue, Form," *Arab Times*, 17 January 1990, 1; "Minister Rules Out Return of Parliament," *Middle East Economic Digest* 34, 2 (19 January 1990): 21–22; "Crown Prince Speaks Out on Constitution," *Middle East Economic Digest* 34, 3 (26 January 1990): 20; "Amir Calls for Dialogue on Democracy," *Middle East Economic Digest* 34, 4 (2 February 1990): 19–20; "Dialogue to Avoid Old Pitfalls: Premier" and "Optimism over Dialogue with Deputies," *Kuwait Times*, 10 February 1990, 1, 3; "In Affluent Kuwait, One-Party Rule Is Assailed by Mainstream and Militants," *New York Times*, 11 March 1990; Jonathan Crusoe, "Kuwait: Meeting the Challenge of Progress," *Middle East Economic Digest* 34 (27 April 1990): 11; and "Council Elections to Be Held in June," *Middle East Economic Digest* 34 (11 May 1990): 19.

4 Abdulkarim Al-Dekhayel, *Kuwait: Oil, State, and Political Legitimation* (Reading, UK: Ithaca Press, 2000), 217–218; "Amir Opens National Council," *Arab Times*, 10 July 1990, 1; and Ahmed Salman, "Amir Signals Quantum Leap: 75-Member National Council Inaugurated, Deputies Urged to Learn from the Past," *Kuwait Times*, 10 July 1990, 1. For an analysis of Kuwaiti democratic aspirations both before and after the Iraqi occupation, see Mary Ann Tétreault, *Stories of Democracy: Politics and Society in Contemporary Kuwait* (New York: Columbia University Press, 2000), 68–75.

5 For an authoritative account of the historical development of Kuwait, see Ahmad Mustafa Abu-Hakima, *The Modem History of Kuwait, 1750–1965* (London: Luzac, 1983). More recently, additional research touted prominently by the Centre for Research and Studies on Kuwait has identified earlier origins for both Kuwait and the al-Sabah dynasty, citing a variety of evidence to suggest settlement by 1613 and al-Sabah control by at least 1716: http://www.crsk.edu.kw/PageModule.asp?Module=10031, accessed 31 August 2006. Others have argued that the al-Sabah ascendancy is much more recent. Until the late nineteenth century the al-Sabah had been one among several prominent merchant families, and had simply been the one from among the Utub granted responsibility for managing administrative affairs: Anh Nga Longva, *Walls Built on Sand: Migration, Exclusion, and Society in Kuwait* (Boulder, Colo.: Westview Press, 1997), 22.

6 Viorst, "Out of the Desert," 58. A lengthy account of this agreement, and subsequent revisions to it, is provided in H. V. F. Winstone and Zahra Freeth, *Kuwait: Prospect and Reality* (London: Allen and Unwin, 1972), 122–163.

7 See "New Development Plan for the 90s," *Al-Qabas International*, 25 April 1990, and "Long Term Development Plan, 1990–2015," *Al-Suyasah*, 15 January 1990 (both articles in Arabic). Before this announcement, many official figures cited during the late 1980s suggested that Kuwaitis were already close to 40 percent of the population, noting that a Kuwaiti majority was expected by the year 2000. See, for example, Viorst, "Out of the Desert," 67. A 1999 Kuwait census estimate found a population of 2.273 million, including 792,000 Kuwaitis (35 percent): http://www.arabicnews.com/ansub/Daily/Day/991006/1999100633.html, accessed 31 August 2006. One reason that the estimates for the Kuwaiti portion of the population were higher in the mid-1980s is that these numbers initially included those classified as Bedoon—the so-called "stateless" people who held an ambiguous status in Kuwait. They served prominently in the army and police and enjoyed some of the same rights as Kuwaitis until 1985, when the government altered its policies. After the Iraqi occupation, many Bedoon who had fled were denied re-entry to Kuwait and those who remained in Kuwait faced serious discrimination: Human Rights Watch/Middle East, *The Bedoons of Kuwait: "Citizens Without Citizenship"* (New York: Human Rights Watch, 1995), 10–30; Longva, *Walls Built on Sand*, 50–52; Anthony H. Cordesman, *Kuwait: Recovery and Security After the Gulf War* (Boulder, Colo.: Westview Press, 1997), 60–61.

8 John Whelan, ed., *Kuwait: A MEED Practical Guide* (London: Middle East Economic Digest, 1985), 1.

9 Ibid., 109.

10 Ibid., 111.

11 *Kuwait: MERI Report* (Middle East Research Institute, University of Pennsylvania) (London: Croom Helm, 1985), 30. See also Viorst, "Out of the Desert," 65; Longva, *Walls Built on Sand*, 52–54. Many of the jobs allocated to Kuwaitis may actually be socially detrimental. In Anthony Cordesman's harsh assessment: "Roughly 80% of

all employed Kuwaitis have no economic function of any kind; their jobs are meaningless and a net liability to the nation" (Cordesman, *Kuwait*, 53).

12 *MERI Report*, 28.

13 Ibid., 30.

14 Ibid., 17.

15 Barbara Rosewicz, "Gulf Democracy Feeling Threatened, Kuwait Seeks to Keep Both Secure and Free, Amid Crackdown on Risks, Rights Are Still Exercised by Press and Parliament," *Wall Street Journal*, 20 December 1985, 19. See also Viorst, "Out of the Desert," 66–67.

16 *MERI Report*, 15, 25. Tensions in the 1980s continued to get worse. See, for example, Rosewicz, "Gulf Democracy," and Jonathan C. Randal, "Kuwaitis Tested: Growing Tension Seen after Attack on Leader," *Washington Post*, 14 June 1985.

17 Jerry M. Long, *Saddam's War of Words: Politics, Religion, and the Iraqi Invasion of Kuwait* (Austin: University of Texas Press, 2004), 31–34; John H. Cushman, Jr., "Under Harassment, Many Palestinians in Kuwait See No Choice But to Leave," *New York Times*, 9 June 1991, 3. The postwar Palestinian population estimate is given in Longva, *Walls Built on Sand*, 245. The Palestinian presence increased again modestly during the mid-1990s (Cordesman, *Kuwait*, 61).

18 *MERI Report*, 16, 23, 24, 36; Tétreault, *Stories of Democracy*, 120.

19 *MERI Report*, 36. In addition to the Iraqis, several Kuwaiti Shi'ites, two Lebanese Shi'ites, and one Lebanese Christian were also involved. In a measure to increase security, after Kuwait traced the identity of the U.S. embassy suicide bomber "by luckily finding his thumb in the rubble," the government introduced a fingerprinting requirement for everyone in the country over the age of 15 (reported in Rosewicz, "Gulf Democracy," 19). See also Viorst, "Out of the Desert," 44.

20 Christopher Dickey, "Kuwait Ruler Eludes Attack By Car Bomb," *Washington Post*, 26 May 1985, A1.

21 Randal, "Kuwaitis Tested."

22 With the completion of the Amiri Diwan extension of the Sief Palace complex, the emir was expected to receive visitors and have his main offices there. This joining of office and palace thereby reduced the need for his movement around the city (though it could do little to reduce his need for evacuation to Saudi Arabia when Kuwait was attacked).

23 Whelan, ed., *Kuwait*, 91, and Viorst, "Out of the Desert," 73.

24 *MERI Report*, 15, 34.

25 Although construction costs were high, it should be noted that few non-Western countries would have the indigenous resources to undertake a project as structurally complicated as this at all. Kuwait's capacity to do so is a direct result of the influx of immigrant workers.

26 Mary Curtis, "Few Kuwaitis Mourn for Democracy: Many See Need to Curb Dissent while Gulf War Rages," *Christian Science Monitor*, 11 February 1987, 9.

27 See Viorst, "Out of the Desert," 57–58.

28 Curtis, "Few Kuwaitis Mourn," 12.

29 Charles Wallace, "Kuwait Abrogates Much of Its Democracy—With Only Muted Reaction," *Los Angeles Times*, 15 February 1987, sect. 1, p. 6; Abdo Baaklini, Guilain Denoueux, and Robert Springborg, *Legislative Politics in the Arab World: The Resurgence of Democratic Institutions* (Boulder, Colo.: Lynne Rienner, 1999), 177–178.

30 *Kuwait: Facts and Figures—1988* (Kuwait: Ministry of Information, 1988), 77.

31 Jacqueline Ismael, *Kuwait: Social Change in Historical Perspective* (Syracuse, N.Y.: Syracuse University Press, 1982), 83.

32 Ibid., 86.

33 Whelan, ed., *Kuwait*, 16.

34 Wallace, "Kuwait Abrogates Much of Its Democracy," 6.

35 Baaklini, Denoueux, and Springborg, *Legislative Politics in the Arab World*, 180–181; Jassim Muhammad Khalaf, "The Kuwait National Assembly: A Study of Its Structure and Function" (Ph.D. dissertation, State University of New York at Albany, 1984) (Ann Arbor, Mich.: University Microfilms International, 1985), 208. Khalaf mentions that some Kuwaitis he interviewed contended that the dissolution was prompted by unspecified "external forces" (212 n.).

36 Baaklini, Denoueux, and Springborg, *Legislative Politics in the Arab World*, 181–184; Wallace, "Kuwait Abrogates Much of Its Democracy," 6.

37 Curtis, "Few Kuwaitis Mourn," 14.

38 Ibid., 9, 12, 14.

39 Barbara Rosewicz, "Kuwait's Dissolution of Parliament Risks Sparking Political Unrest in Long Term," *Wall Street Journal*, 7 July 1986, 16.

40 Curtis, "Few Kuwaitis Mourn," p. 9. The connection between parliament and the press was especially close in Kuwait since

the parliamentarians' printed speeches were protected by legislative immunity, thereby enabling newspapers to be more daring in their coverage (Curtis, p. 14).

41 Rosewicz, "Kuwait's Dissolution of Parliament," 16. The system of *diwaniyas*, discussed later on, would seem to assure that political passions would have many outlets, even without the presence of a functioning National Assembly.

42 Jørn Utzon and Associates, "Aga Khan Award Application: Client's Record, 12 January 1985," 6.

43 Rosewicz, "Gulf Democracy," A1.

44 Utzon, "Aga Khan Application," 6.

45 "Souk Al-Amir Inauguration," *Al-Qabas International*, 5 February 1990 (in Arabic).

46 Ibrahim al-Shaheen, cited in Viorst, "Out of the Desert," 61.

47 Rifat Chadirji, "Kuwait Parliament" [unpublished memorandum], and interviews with the author, October 1989. Regarding the use of Kuwaiti-based consultants, Utzon's firm notes that 15 percent of the workforce had to be imported (Utzon, "Aga Khan Application," 3). For an overview of contemporary architecture in Kuwait, see Udo Kultermann, *Contemporary Architecture in the Arab States: Renaissance of a Region* (New York: McGraw-Hill, 1999), 167–178.

48 Viorst., "Out of the Desert," 63, and Abu-Hakima, *Modern History of Kuwait*, 2–8, 12, 29; Barbara Bodine, interview with the author, September 2006. Abu-Hakima notes that the Bani Utub had, in fact, ceased their nomadic ways early in the seventeenth century, so, despite mythology about their "wandering," this may well have no direct connection to their settlement of Kuwait.

49 Ismael, *Kuwait: Social Change*, 27.

50 Ibid., 28.

51 *MERI Report*, 5 6; Bodine, 2006 interview. See also Jill Crystal, *Kuwait: The Transformation of an Oil State* (Boulder, Colo.: Westview Press, 1992), 65–89.

52 Clifford Geertz, "The Integrative Revolution," in *The Interpretation of Cultures* (New York: Basic Books, 1973), 261–262.

53 Whelan, ed., *Kuwait*, 64.

54 Ibid., 6.

55 *MERI Report*, 20.

56 Whelan, ed., *Kuwait*, 63.

57 Ibid., 6.

58 Roger Connah, "Kuwait National Assembly Complex," *Living Architecture*. 5 (1986): 123.

59 See esp. Wilfred Thesiger, *The Marsh Arabs* (London: Allen Lane, 1977).

60 Markku Komonen, "Elements in the Way of Life," interview with Jørn Utzon, *Arkkitehti* 80, 2 (1983), Eng. trans.: 81.

61 Ibid.

62 Ibid.

63 Utzon, "Aga Khan Application," 6.

64 Komonen, "Elements in the Way of Life," 81.

65 Jørn Utzon, "A House for Work and Decisions: Kuwait National Assembly Complex," in Denys Lasdun, ed., *Architecture in an Age of Scepticism* (New York: Oxford University Press, 1984), 222. This text differs only slightly from that included in the Komonen interview.

66 See, for example, Jørn Utzon, "Additive Architecture," *Arkitektur* 1 (1970): 1.

67 Ibid., 1.

68 It is also possible that this height limitation may have been imposed on Utzon by the Ministry of Public Works; they insisted that an adjacent car park be no more than two stories.

69 Whelan, ed., *Kuwait*, 147.

70 Utzon, "Aga Khan Application," 6.

71 Komonen, "Elements in the Way of Life," 81.

72 Ibid.

73 The word *Kut* (of which Kuwait is the diminutive) refers to a "house that is built in the shape of a fortress so as to be easily defended when attacked. . . . The name Kut is given to such a house only when it lies near water. . . . Then it was applied to the village built on such a site." Anistas al-Karmali, cited in Abu-Hakima, *Modern History of Kuwait*, 1, n. 4.

74 In 1983, for example, a law was passed to deny citizenship to non-Muslims (cited in *MERI Report*, 31).

75 Ibid., 20–21. After coffeehouses along Arabian Gulf Street were bombed during the mid-1980s, more of the still-flourishing *diwaniya* activity became concentrated in private homes.

76 Bodine, 2006 interview. For an account of the destruction, see Michael Kelly, "Kuwait City: Capital Damaged, But Not by Bombs," *Boston Globe*, 1 March 1991; Janet A. McDonnell, *After Desert Storm: The U.S. Army and the Reconstruction of Kuwait* (Washington, D.C.: Department of the Army, 1999), 71–73, 140, 180, 230–235.

77 Kristen Richards, "Back to Work: HOK Designs Modern Delegates' Desks for Kuwait's National Assembly Building With Just a Hint of Tradition," *Interiors* 152, 7 (January 1993): 18–28.

78 Youssef M. Ibrahim, "Kuwait Rulers See Democracy Moves: Prince Hints at the Revival of Parliament and Free Vote," *New York Times*, 14 October 1990, 1, 13; "Opposition Calls for Democratic Reform in Kuwait," *Boston Globe*, 15 October 1990, 12; Edward A. Gargan, "Kuwait Deeply Split on Vision of a Post-Occupation Order," *New York Times*, 19 May 1991, 1; Neil MacFarquar, "Kuwaiti Ruler Sets Elections for Fall of 1992," *Boston Globe*, 3 June 1991, 2; Al-Dekhayel, Kuwait, 219; Tétreault, *Stories of Democracy*, 75; interview with Barbara Bodine, 2006.

79 Longva, *Walls Built on Sand*, 243–244.

80 Tétreault, *Stories of Democracy*, 76.

81 Hassan Fattah, "Kuwaiti Women Join the Voting After a Long Battle for Suffrage," *New York Times*, 30 June 2006; Miriam Joyce, *Kuwait 1945–1996: An Anglo-American Perspective* (London: Frank Cass, 1998), 170; Baaklini, Denoueux, and Springborg, *Legislative Politics in the Arab World*, 187–199.

82 Tétreault, *Stories of Democracy*, 146–147. See also Helen Mary Rizzo, *Islam, Democracy, and the Status of Women: The Case of Kuwait* (New York: Routledge, 2005).

CHAPTER 9 THE ACROPOLIS OF BANGLADESH

1 My interest in this misuse of language was piqued in April 1987 when my letter to the editor of *Architectural Review* (expressing reservations about Kahn's National Assembly building) was printed under the title "Doubts about Dacca" [sic]. About Dhaka, I have no doubts. As the international architectural community begins to recognize other significant work in Dhaka, the tendency to think only in terms of Kahn should, fortunately, soon abate.

2 Sten Ake Nilsson, *The New Capitals of India, Pakistan and Bangladesh*, Scandinavian Institute of Asian Studies Monograph Series, no. 12 (Lund: Studentlitteratur, 1974), 185–187.

3 Charles Peter O'Donnell, *Bangladesh: Biography of a Muslim Nation* (Boulder, Colo.: Westview Press, 1984), 94; Richard Sisson and Leo E. Rose, *War and Secession: Pakistan, India, and the Creation of Bangladesh* (Berkeley: University of California Press, 1990); Muhammad Ghulam Kabir, *Changing Face of Nationalism: The Case of Bangladesh* (Denver, Colo.: iAcademic Books, 2000).

4 One who remembers is Abul Bashar, chief architect of the Public Works Department from 1965 to 1982 (conversation with the author, 27 March 1990).

5 James Dunnett, "City of the Tiger: Work of Louis Kahn at Dacca, Bangladesh," *Architect's Journal* 171 (February 1980): 231; Hasan Zaheer, *The Separation of East Pakistan: The Rise and Realization of Bengali Muslim Nationalism* (Karachi: Oxford University Press, 1994), 38–42.

6 The term *Bengali* includes West Bengalis in India and is therefore an identity which transcends the boundaries of either East Pakistan or Bangladesh. As of 2006, the most prominent national symbols of Bangladeshi national identity (other than the flag) also included the National Monument at Savar, north of Dhaka, and the Central Shahid Minar (honoring those who fought to preserve the Bangla language in 1952).

7 Richard Saul Wurman, *What Will Be Has Always Been: The Words of Louis I. Kahn* (New York: Rizzoli, 1986), 120. According to Abul Bashar, initially at least, Kahn was not given a written program at all (conversation with the author, 27 March 1990). The only written architectural program for the assembly building that I could find in the files of the Louis I. Kahn Collection at the University of Pennsylvania is apparently from January 1963 (Kahn Collection, Box 117).

8 Wurman, *What Will Be Has Always Been*, 117.

9 Ibid.

10 Cited in Alexandra Tyng, *Beginnings: Louis I. Kahn's Philosophy of Architecture* (New York: John Wiley and Sons, 1984), 119.

11 Wurman, *What Will Be Has Always Been*, 50.

12 Ibid., 120.

13 Ibid., 234.

14 Cited in Tyng, *Kahn's Philosophy of Architecture*, 59.

15 Ibid., 91.

16 Sarah Ksiazek, "Architectural Culture in the Fifties: Louis Kahn and the National Assembly Complex in Dhaka," *Journal of the Society of Architectural Historians* 52 (December 1993): 416–435. See also Sarah Williams Goldhagen, *Louis Kahn's Situated Modernism* (New Haven: Yale University Press, 2001), 162–198.

17 Mehmet Doruk Pamir, "Sher-E-Banglanagar, Dhaka: The Impact on Local Design," in *Continuity and Change: Design Strategies for Large-Scale Urban Development* (Design in Islamic Cultures 4) (Cambridge, Mass.: The Aga Khan Program for Islamic Architecture, 1984), 76.

18 William J. R. Curtis, "Authenticity, Abstraction and the Ancient Sense: Le Corbusier's and Kahn's Ideas of Parliament," *Perspecta* 20 (1983): 191–193. See also Apunam Banerji, *The Architecture of Corbusier and Kahn in the East* (Lewiston, N.Y.: Edwin Mellen Press, 2001), 41–63; Kazi Khaleed Ashraf and Saif Ul Haque, *Sherebanglanagar: Louis Kahn and the Making of a Capital Complex* (Dhaka, Bangladesh: LOKA, 2002).
19 Wurman, *What Will Be Has Always Been*, 106.
20 "Kahn for Dacca" (interview with Henry Wilcots by R. S. Wurman) *Domus* (July 1975), Eng. trans.: i.
21 Letter to Harriet Pattison, 15 September 1964, cited in Tyng, *Kahn's Philosophy of Architecture*, 166.
22 Cited in ibid., 166.
23 "Kahn for Dacca," i.
24 Wurman, *What Will Be Has Always Been*, 51.
25 Ibid.
26 Ibid., 25.
27 Ibid., 172.
28 According to the Bengali architect Mazhrul Islam, "Kahn had no time or interest for politics. I talked to him on this subject once, and found him totally uninterested." Cited in Anupam Banerji, "Conversation with Architect Mazhrul Islam in Dhaka, Bangladesh: January 1986" (mimeo), as adapted in Banerji, *The Architecture of Corbusier and Kahn in the East*, 105.
29 August E. Komendant, *18 Years with Architect Louis I. Kahn* (Englewood, N.J.: Aloray, 1975), 82.
30 G. W. Choudhury, ed., *Documents and Speeches on the Constitution of Pakistan* (Dacca: Green Book House, 1967), 727.
31 Ibid., 791.
32 Cited in ibid., 980.
33 Khalid B. Sayeed, *The Political System of Pakistan* (Boston: Houghton Mifflin, 1967), 191.
34 Cited in ibid., 194.
35 Mushtaq Ahmad, *Government and Politics in Pakistan*, 3rd ed. (Karachi: Space Publishers, 1970), 208–213.
36 Ibid., 222.
37 Mohammad Ayub Khan, *Friends Not Masters: A Political Autobiography* (New York: Oxford University Press, 1967), 190.
38 O'Donnell, *Bangladesh*, 61.
39 Ahmad, *Government and Politics*, 213.
40 Ibid., 208.
41 A file in the Kahn Archives at the University of Pennsylvania contains several Pakistani political documents from 1960–1962 that were presumably sent to Kahn to provide him with some background on such things as "Three Years of Progress under the Revolutionary Government of Pakistan" and Ayub Khan's "Analysis of Pakistan's Ideology, Problems and Their Solution." There are no notes or markings on any of these documents, all of which are in pristine condition; perhaps Kahn never even saw them.
42 Wurman, *What Will Be Has Always Been*, 251.
43 David Wisdom, "Kahn's Building at Dacca," *Rassegna* 7 (March 1985): 48.
44 "Kahn for Dacca," i; Raekha Prasad, "Cities Shaken by 350 Co-ordinated Attacks," *The Times* (London), 18 August 2005; Farid Hossain, "Bangladesh Police Fire Tear Gas at Anti-Government Protesters During General Strike," Associated Press Worldstream, 14 June 2006.
45 Wurman, *What Will Be Has Always Been*, 234.
46 Aminul Haq Khan, "Sher-E-Banglanagar, Dhaka: Design and Implementation," in *Continuity and Change*, 72.
47 Ibid. For images of the National Assembly Building under construction, see *Louis Kahn Dhaka Construction*, photographs compiled by Raymond Meier and Nathaniel Kahn, with William Whitaker, Curator and Collections Manager of the Architectural Archives, University of Pennsylvania (Zurich: Dino Simonett, 2004).
48 Wurman, *What Will Be Has Always Been*, 105.
49 Cited in Tyng, *Kahn's Philosophy of Architecture*, 119.
50 Nizam Ahmed, "From Monopoly to Competition: Party Politics in the Bangladesh Parliament (1973–2001)," *Pacific Affairs* 76, 1 (Spring 2003): 77.
51 Wurman, *What Will Be Has Always Been*, 24–25.
52 Ibid., 25.
53 Ibid.
54 Ibid., 172.
55 Ibid.
56 David B. Brownlee and David G. De Long, *Louis Kahn: In the Realm of Architecture* (condensed edition) (New York: Universe, 1997), 127–129.
57 See Kirsten Westergaard, *State and Rural Society in Bangladesh: A Study in Relationship* (Copenhagen: Scandinavian Institute of Asian Studies, 1985), 70–102, and Subir Bhaumik, "Bangladesh: League Offers Support to BNP," *India Abroad*, 15 March 1991, 4.

58 Banerji, "Conversation with Architect Mazhrul Islam in Dhaka, Bangladesh: January 1986" (mimeo), 12–13.
59 Dunnett, "City of the Tiger," 234.
60 See Florindo Fusaro, "The Dacca Assembly Building and New Capital," trans. Annabel Parkes, *Rassegna* 7 (March 1985): 37.
61 Wurman, *What Will Be Has Always Been*, 171.
62 Louis Kahn, "Louis I. Kahn: Berkeley Lecture, 1966." Transcribed in *Perspecta* 28 (Spring 1994): 22.
63 According to David Wisdom, Kahn did have hopes that the mosque could be naturally cooled by a system of ventilation and open-air screening. The system failed, however, and this part, too, had to be fully air conditioned (Wisdom, "Kahn's Building at Dacca," 48).
64 Anne Griswold Tyng, "Kahntext," *Architectural Forum* 138 (January/February 1973): 9.
65 Dunnett, "City of the Tiger," 233. Abul Bashar described the building as "substantially increasing the power needs for all Dhaka." He suggested that its electricity costs were comparable to those of the entire city of Comilla, which had a population of about 150,000 (conversation with the author, 27 March 1990). The annual maintenance figure of $2 million was supplied by the Public Works Department in 1990, and the actual amount is presumably higher now.
66 Wurman, *What Will Be Has Always Been*, 97.
67 Ibid., 171.
68 Wisdom, "Kahn's Building at Dacca," 48.
69 Ksiazek, "Architectural Culture in the Fifties," 430; Wurman, *What Will Be Has Always Been*, 50.
70 Goldhagen, *Louis Kahn's Situated Modernism*, 173.
71 Wurman, *What Will Be Has Always Been*, 24; Abul Bashar, interview with the author, 27 March 1990.
72 Wurman, *What Will Be Has Always Been*, 216.
73 Cited in Heinz Ronner, Sharad Jhaveri, and Alessandro Vasella, eds., *Louis I. Kahn: Complete Work 1935–1974* (Stuttgart: Birkhåuser Verlag, for the Institute for the History and Theory of Architecture, the Swiss Federal Institute of Technology, Zurich, 1977), 230.
74 Wurman, *What Will Be Has Always Been*, 106.
75 Ibid.
76 Ibid., 216.
77 President Ershad's constitutional amendment of 1988 making Islam the state religion was part of a more general campaign to advance the role of Islam in Bangladesh and was met by protests from many groups. In the 2001 parliamentary elections, Bangladeshis elected only five Hindu representatives to the Assembly.
78 Komendant, *18 Years with Kahn*, 79.
79 Ibid.
80 See, for example, "R[oy] V[ollmer] Report," sent from site to Kahn office in Philadelphia, dated 18 March 1965, Louis I. Kahn Collection, University of Pennsylvania.
81 "Lou's Notes," 20 May 1964, Box 122, Louis I. Kahn Collection, University of Pennsylvania.
82 Bertil Lintner, "Religious Extremism and Nationalism in Bangladesh." Paper delivered at "Religion and Security in South Asia—An International Workshop," Asia Pacific Center for Security Studies, Honolulu, Hawaii, 19–22 August 2002; Mushtaq Husain Khan, "The Political Economy of Secularism and Religion in Bangladesh," in S. Basu and S. Das., eds., *Electoral Politics in South Asia* (Calcutta: K. P. Bagchi, 2000); Ali Riaz, *God Willing: The Politics of Islamism in Bangladesh* (Lanham, Md.: Rowman and Littlefield, 2004), 5; Eliza Griswold, "The Next Islamist Revolution?," *New York Times*, 23 January 2005, Section 6, 35; "Explosions Add Further Instability to Bangladesh's Political Mix," *Financial Times* (London), 22 August 2005, 6; and Hiranmay Karlekar, *Bangladesh: The Next Afghanistan?* (New Delhi: Sage, 2005).
83 Cited in Tyng, *Kahn's Philosophy of Architecture*, 119.
84 Henry Wilcots, presentation at MIT, 3 November 1989.
85 Cited in Tyng, *Kahn's Philosophy of Architecture*, 119.
86 Wurman, *What Will Be Has Always Been*, 92.
87 At the time Kahn was designing the Dhaka capital, another connotation of the word *citadel* *was* gaining currency. In Britain's "Spies for Peace" controversy, in which several persons were punished for revealing the existence and location of underground nuclear shelters for government officials, the bunkers were decried as "citadels" affording an unfair and undemocratic kind of protection. Of course, Kahn may well have been unaware of this chiefly British usage of the word. Kahn's assistant Henry Wilcots, who was involved with the project from 1963, suggests that the term citadel for Kahn connoted the "place of citizenry, place of people." Wilcots, presentation at MIT, 3 November 1989.
88 As evidence in support of this "little city" notion,

one may note Kahn's response to a question about designing a city: "I didn't design a full city, but in the capital of Pakistan there's a reservation in the town which contains all the buildings that serve as a legislative capital." Wurman, *What Will Be Has Always Been*, 167.

89 Ibid., 127.

90 Wisdom, "Kahn's Building at Dacca," 48.

91 "Lou's Notes," 20 May 1964.

92 Wurman, *What Will Be Has Always Been*, 127.

93 John W. Cook and Heinrich Klotz, "Louis Kahn," in *Conversations with Architects* (New York: Praeger, 1973), 178. According to Wilcots, some trees which were planted near the South Plaza were subsequently bulldozed under direction from Bangladesh's General Zia. Henry Wilcots, presentation at MIT, 3 November 1989.

94 Goldhagen, *Louis Kahn's Situated Modernism*, 177.

95 During the early 1990s, the design of this secretariat was probably the major point of architectural controversy in the country. Owing to significant changes in programmatic requirements since Kahn's secretariat design was made, the architects of the Public Works Department proposed alternatives of their own. These were met with much hostility from other architects in Dhaka and elsewhere, and the secretariat was not built. "PM-Zia Mausoleum," *United News of Bangladesh*, 7 November 2004. Details on current use of the northern part of the site come from Professor Fuad Mallick, Chair of the Architecture Department at BRAC University. Personal communication with the author, October 2006.

96 The broad steps of the South Plaza are designed with a tread/riser ratio which effectively prohibits a direct approach to the building using anything resembling a normal stride. Is this another example of the way some aspects of the design seem to invite entry in defiance of political realities? Maybe, although—according to designers involved with the project—the odd width of the steps was more likely intended to accommodate chairs to be used for viewing pro-government rallies. Others who worked on the project have suggested that the plaza was thought of as a public extension of the mosque, though the need to permit direction of prayer to the west would make this seem a rather awkward proposition. Details on current access to the plaza come from Professor Fuad Mallick. Personal communication with the author, October 2006.

97 Assessing the cost of this building with any degree of accuracy is exceedingly difficult, given the long period of construction, extreme variability of exchange rates, and general secrecy about such matters. The $150 million figure is probably toward the high end of the numbers often cited, and the official Public Works Department figure of $53 million is probably quite low. Henry Wilcots, who remained with Kahn's office (and its successor firm) throughout the long gestation of the project, maintains that "they never told us what it cost" (Wilcots, MIT presentation, 3 November 1989).

98 Komendant, *18 Years with Kahn*, 78.

99 Pamir, "Sher-E-Banglanagar," 74.

100 Ibid.. Fred Langford's report on concrete technology (1966) contains a thorough overview of the availability of various materials and provides a detailed discussion of the many ways the whole process was adapted to meet the circumstances of Bengal (reprinted as "Concrete in Dacca," *MIMAR* 6 [1982]: 50–55). Some of the materials needed for concrete construction, such as stone and sand, could be brought in from the Sylhet area of Bangladesh, rather than purchased internationally.

As for other "local impacts" of Kahn's design, some manifestations (such as the Zia International Airport) have exhibited crude and superficial use of certain formal motifs, while other local architects have done some fine work with exposed brick. The major impact of Kahn's work in Dhaka thus far is probably more indirect, inspiring local architects and students to think more seriously and multidimensionally about architecture, while catalyzing the formal organization of the Bangladeshi architecture profession and the initiation of Departments of Architecture in the Ministry of Works and at Bangladesh University of Engineering and Technology.

101 Darab Diba, "Update of '1986 Technical Review Summary' by Kenneth Yeang," prepared for the Aga Khan Award, 9 May 1989, 16, 18. In fact, Dhaka does have many other large structures made of reinforced concrete, though certainly nothing as elaborate as the National Assembly Building. According to the Dhaka City Corporation, as of 2004, approximately 5 percent of the city's buildings were reinforced concrete structures; "Most Buildings in Dhaka Vulnerable to Earthquake," Xinhua News Agency, General News Service, 7 July 2004.

102 Wurman, *What Will Be Has Always Been*, 232.

103 "Bangladesh Parliament Dissolved," *Boston Globe*, 7 December 1987; "Democratic Opposition Destroyed: Opposition," *The Bangladesh Observer*, 25 March 1990, 1; and, for a pro-government view, A. Z. M. Haider, "Democratic Processes Forge Ahead," *The Bangladesh Times*, 26 March 1990, 3, 5.

104 See Barbara Crossette, "Revolution Brings Bangladesh Hope," *New York Times*, 9 December 1990, 4; Nicholas D. Kristof, "Cyclone in Bangladesh Tests the Fragile New Democracy," *New York Times*, 19 May 1991, 12; Griswold, "The Next Islamist Revolution?"; "Bangladesh: Elections to Be Delayed at Least 18 Months," *New York Times*, 6 April 2007; Julfikar Ali Manik, "Bangladesh: New Boss Delays Vote to 2008," *New York Times*, 13 April 2007.

105 Dunnett, "City of the Tiger," 234.

CHAPTER 10 DESIGNING POWER AND IDENTITY

1 Clifford Geertz, "The Politics of Meaning," in *The Interpretation of Cultures* (New York: Basic Books, 1973), 318.

2 Vikram Prakash, *Chandigarh's Le Corbusier: The Struggle for Modernity in Postcolonial India* (Seattle: University of Washington Press, 2002), 24.

3 Kenneth Frampton, "Towards a Critical Regionalism: Six Points for an Architecture of Resistance," in Hal Foster, ed., *The Anti-Aesthetic: Essays on Postmodern Culture* (Port Townsend, Wash.: Bay Press, 1983), 21. Frampton's argument is presented in a somewhat different form as "Prospects for a Critical Regionalism," *Perspecta* 20 (1983). Earlier discussions of the importance of a regional approach to architecture may be found in the Patrick Geddes-influenced writings of Lewis Mumford on the Regional Planning Association of America from the 1920s and 1940s. Sigfried Giedion's "The State of Contemporary Architecture: The Regional Approach" (*Architectural Record*, January 1954): 132–137, and the writings of Liane Lefaivre and Alexander Tzonis remain seminal contributions to this line of thinking. They introduced the term in 1981 and, more recently, have explored a variety of globally located exemplars in Liane Lefaivre and Alexander Tzonis, *Critical Regionalism: Architecture and Identity in a Globalised World* (New York: Prestel, 2003). See also William J. R. Curtis, "Towards an Authentic Regionalism," *MIMAR* 19 (January–March 1986): 24–31, Peter Buchanan, "With Due Respect: Regionalism," *Architectural Review* 157 (May 1983), and the November 1986 and November 1990 issues of the *Architectural Review* devoted to the "Anatomy of Regionalism" and "Regional Perspectives."

4 Frampton, "Towards a Critical Regionalism," 21.

5 Prakash, *Chandigarh's Le Corbusier*, 153.

6 See Donlyn Lyndon, "Public Buildings: Symbols Qualified by Experience," in Nathan Glazer and Mark Lilla, eds., *The Public Face of Architecture* (New York: Free Press, 1987), 158.

7 Darab Diba, "Sher-E-Bangla Nagar Capitol: 1989 Technical Review Summary," prepared for the Aga Khan Award for Architecture, May 1989, 4–5.

8 Lawrence J. Vale, "Securing Public Space," *Places: A Forum of Environmental Design* 17, 3 (Fall 2005), 38–42.

9 Wolfgang Braunfels, *Urban Design in Western Europe: Regime and Architecture, 900–1900*, trans. Kenneth J. Northcott (Chicago: University of Chicago Press, 1988), 371.

Illustration credits

Sources cited in shortened form here are given in full in the endnotes.

1.1 The Museum of Modern Art/Film Stills Archive. Courtesy of Columbia Pictures

1.2, 1.3, 1.7, 1.12, 1.13, 1.15, 1.16, 1.17, 1.18, 1.20, 1.25, 3.9, 3.17, 3.18, 3.19, 3.21, 3.26, 3.27, 3.29, 3.30, 3.31, 3.35, 3.40, 3.41, 3.42 , 4.3, 4.7, 6.12, 8.2, 8.4, 8.5, 8.6, 8.7, 9.3, 9.9, 9.17, 9.18, 9.19, 9.24 Photographs by Author

1.4 Wide World Photos

1.5, 1.6, 5.7, 5.8, 5.10, 5.12, 5.13 Wallace Roberts & Todd, PRC and Archisystems International, acting as International Planning Associates

1.8, 1.14, 1.19, 1.22 (after diagram in Bater, *The Soviet City*), 1.23, 1.26, 1.27, 1.28, 3.39 , 4.1, 4.13, 6.1, 6.3, 6.6, 6.9, 7.1, 7.8, 8.1, 8.8 (based on Thesiger), 9.1, 9.2 Kevin Low

1.9, 3.33, 3.36 (using data from King, *Colonial Urban Development*), 8.3 Saif-ul Haq

1.10 Copyright, 1969, Verlag Ulltein-Proplyäen, reprinted by permission

1.11, 1.21, 3.2, 3.3, 3.4, 3.5, 3.6, 10.1 Library of Congress

1.24 By permission of the British Library

3.1 Elbert Peets, *The Art of Designing Cities*, MIT Press, reprinted by permission

3.7 National Capital Planning Commission, Washington, D.C.

3.8 By permission of Henry Baker and by courtesy of the British Architectural Library, RIBA, London

3.10 National Capital Commission of Canada

3.12, 3.13 National Library of Australia

3.14, 3.15, 3.16, 3.22, 3.23, 3.24, 3.25, 3.28 National Capital Authority, Canberra

3.20 Joint House Department of Australia

3.32 John Murray (Publishers) Ltd., reprinted by permission

3.34, 3.37 Government of India

3.38 Department of City Planning, Middle East Technical University, Ankara

4.2, 4.4, 4.5, 4.6 Fondation Le Corbusier

4.8, 4.9, 4.10 Lúcio Costa

4.11 Stanford Anderson

4.12, 4.14 Peter Droege

5.1, 5.3 Doxiadis Associates. Consultants on Development and Ekistics, Athens, Greece

5.2 M. Hanif Raza, *Islamabad and Environs*, reproduced by permission

5.4 Nigel Young/Foster + Partners

5.5 Courtesy of Ross King

5.6, 5.15, 5.16 Courtesy of Nnamdi Elleh, from *Abuja: The Last Debate in Monumental Modernist Urban Design*, University of South Africa Press

5.9a, 5.9b Ifeoma Ebo

5.11, 5.14 Courtesy of Kenzo Tange, photograph by Osamu Murai

5.17, 5.18, 5.24 Project Planning Associates

5.19, 5.20, 5.21, 5.22, 5.23, 5.25 James Rossant, Conklin Rossant Architects

5.26 Government of Tanzania

5.27, 6.4, 9.20 copyright DigitalGlobe

6.2, 6.5, 6.8, 6.10, 6.11, 6.13, 6.14, 6.15, 6.17 Speaker of the House, Waigani, Papua New Guinea

6.7, 6.16 Peddle Thorp and Harvey

7.2, 7.3, 7.6, 7.9 Geoffrey Bawa

7.4 Courtesy of Kristian Stokke and reprinted by permission from *Third World Quarterly* 27, 6: 1023

7.5, 7.10, 7.11, 7.12, 7.13, 7.14 New Capital Project Division, Urban Development Authority, Sri Lanka

8.9 Kuwait Ministry of Planning

8.11, 8.13, 8.14, 8.15, 8.16 Jørn Utzon & Associates

8.12 Lewcock and Freeth, *Traditional Architecture of Kuwait*, Art and Archaelogy Research Papers, photograph by Alan Villers

8.17, 8.18, 8.19 U.S. Department of the Army, from *After Desert Storm: The U.S. Army and the Reconstruction of Kuwait*

9.4 Nurur-Rahman Khan

9.5, 9.6, 9.7, 9.8, 9.10, 9.11, 9.12, 9.13, 9.14, 9.15, 9.16, 9.23 (photo by Fred Langford) Louis I. Kahn Collection, University of Pennsylvania

9.21, 9.22 Fuad Mallick

Index